It Pays to Get Certified

In a digital world, digital literacy is an essential survival skill.

Certification proves you have the knowledge and skill to solve business problems in virtually any business environment. Certifications are highly-valued credentials that qualify you for jobs, increased compensation and promotion.

LEARN		CERTIFY	WORK	
IT is Everywhere	**IT Knowledge and Skills Get Jobs**	**Job Retention**	**New Opportunities**	**High Pay-High Growth Jobs**
IT is mission critical to almost all organizations and its importance is increasing.	Certifications verify your knowledge and skills that qualifies you for:	Competence is noticed and valued in organizations.	Certifications qualify you for new opportunities in your current job or when you want to change careers.	Hiring managers demand the strongest skill set.
• 79% of U.S. businesses report IT is either important or very important to the success of their company	• Jobs in the high growth IT career field • Increased compensation • Challenging assignments and promotions • 60% report that being certified is an employer or job requirement	• Increased knowledge of new or complex technologies • Enhanced productivity • More insightful problem solving • Better project management and communication skills • 47% report being certified helped improve their problem solving skills	• 31% report certification improved their career advancement opportunities	• There is a widening IT skills gap with over 300,000 jobs open • 88% report being certified enhanced their resume

Certification Helps Your Career

- **The CompTIA A+ credential** – provides foundation-level knowledge and skills necessary for a career in PC repair and support.

- **Starting Salary** – CompTIA A+ Certified individuals can earn as much as $65,000 per year.

- **Career Pathway** – CompTIA A+ is a building block for other CompTIA certifications such as Network+, Security+ and vendor specific technologies.

- **More than 850,000** – individuals worldwide are CompTIA A+ certified.

- **Mandated/Recommended by organizations worldwide** – such as Cisco and HP and Ricoh, the U.S. State Department, and U.S. government contractors such as EDS, General Dynamics, and Northrop Grumman.

Some of the primary benefits individuals report from becoming A+ certified are:
- **More efficient troubleshooting**
- **Improved career advancement**
- **More insightful problem solving**

4 Steps to Getting Certified and Staying Certified

1. Review Exam Objectives	Review the Certification objectives to make sure you know what is covered in the exam http://www.comptia.org/certifications/testprep/examobjectives.aspx
2. Practice for the Exam	After you have studied for the certification, take a free assessment and sample test to get an idea what type of questions might be on the exam. http://www.comptia.org/certifications/testprep/practicetests.aspx
3. Purchase an Exam Voucher	Purchase exam vouchers on the CompTIA Marketplace, which is located at: www.comptiastore.com
4. Take the Test!	Select a certification exam provider and schedule a time to take your exam. You can find exam providers at the following link: http://www.comptia.org/certifications/testprep/testingcenters.aspx
5. Stay Certified! **Continuing Education**	All new CompTIA A+ certifications will be valid for three years from the date the candidate is certified. After three years, those certifications must be renewed. For more information: http://certification.comptia.org/getCertified/steps_to_certification/stayCertified.aspx

How to obtain more information

- **Visit CompTIA online** - www.comptia.org to learn more about getting CompTIA certified.
- **Contact CompTIA** - call 866-835-8020 ext. 5 or email questions@comptia.org.
- **Join the IT Pro Community** – http://itpro.comptia.org to join the IT community to get relevant career information.
- **Connect with us :**

CompTIA® A+® Certification: A Comprehensive Approach (Exams 220-801 and 220-802)

CompTIA® A+® Certification: A Comprehensive Approach (Exams 220–801 and 220–802)

Part Number: 093001
Course Edition: 2.2

Acknowledgements

PROJECT TEAM

Content Developer	Media Designer	Content Editor
Kelly Popen	Alex Tong	Tricia Murphy
Pamela J. Taylor		Angie French

Notices

CompTIA® A+® Certification: A Comprehensive Approach (Exams 220-801 and 220-802)

About This Course

If you are getting ready for a career as an entry-level information technology (IT) professional or personal computer (PC) service technician, the CompTIA® A+® Certification course is the first step in your preparation. The course will build on your existing user-level knowledge and experience with personal computer software and hardware to present fundamental skills and concepts that you will use on the job. In this course, you will acquire the essential skills and information you will need to install, upgrade, repair, configure, troubleshoot, optimize, and perform preventative maintenance of basic personal computer hardware and operating systems.

The CompTIA A+ Certification course can benefit you in two ways. Whether you work or plan to work in a mobile or corporate environment where you have a high level of face-to-face customer interaction, where client communication and client training are important, or in an environment with limited customer interaction and an emphasis on hardware activities, this course provides the background knowledge and skills you will require to be a successful A+ technician. It can also assist you if you are preparing to take the CompTIA A + certification examinations, 2012 objectives (exam numbers 220-801, 220-802), in order to become a CompTIA A+ Certified Professional.

Course Description

Target Student

This course is intended for anyone with basic computer user skills who is interested in obtaining a job as an IT professional or PC technician. In addition, this course will help prepare students to achieve a CompTIA A+ Certification.

Course Prerequisites

Students taking this course should have the following skills: end-user skills with Windows®-based personal computers, including the ability to: browse and search for information on the Internet; start up, shut down, and log on to a computer and network; run programs; and move, copy, delete, and rename files in Windows Explorer. Students should also have basic knowledge of computing concepts, including the difference between hardware and software; the functions of software components, such as the operating system, applications, and file systems; and the function of a computer network.

An introductory course in a Windows operating system, or equivalent skills and knowledge, is required. Students can take any one of the following Logical Operations courses: *Introduction to Personal Computers: Using Windows® XP* or *Introduction to Personal Computers: Using Windows® 7.*

The following Logical Operations courses are also recommended: *Windows® XP: Introduction* or *Microsoft® Windows® 7: Level 1.*

Course Objectives

In this course, you will install, upgrade, repair, configure, optimize, troubleshoot, and perform preventative maintenance on basic personal computer hardware and operating systems.

You will:

- Identify the hardware components of a computer.
- Identify the basic components and functions of an operating system.
- Identify the operational procedures that should be followed by PC technicians.
- Identify and configure peripheral components.
- Manage system components.
- Identify and configure operating systems.
- Identify the hardware and software requirements for custom client environments.
- Identify network technologies.
- Identify, configure, and maintain SOHO networks.
- Support laptops.
- Configure mobile computing devices.
- Support printers.
- Implement concepts and techniques used to secure computing devices and environments.
- Troubleshoot hardware components.
- Troubleshoot system-wide issues.

The LogicalCHOICE Home Screen

The LogicalCHOICE Home screen is your entry point to the LogicalCHOICE learning experience, of which this course manual is only one part. Visit the LogicalCHOICE Course screen both during and after class to make use of the world of support and instructional resources that make up the LogicalCHOICE experience.

Log-on and access information for your LogicalCHOICE environment will be provided with your class experience. On the LogicalCHOICE Home screen, you can access the LogicalCHOICE Course screens for your specific courses.

Each LogicalCHOICE Course screen will give you access to the following resources:

- eBook: an interactive electronic version of the printed book for your course.
- LearnTOs: brief animated components that enhance and extend the classroom learning experience.

Depending on the nature of your course and the choices of your learning provider, the LogicalCHOICE Course screen may also include access to elements such as:

- The interactive eBook.
- Social media resources that enable you to collaborate with others in the learning community using professional communications sites such as LinkedIn or microblogging tools such as Twitter.
- Checklists with useful post-class reference information.
- Any course files you will download.
- The course assessment.
- Notices from the LogicalCHOICE administrator.
- Virtual labs, for remote access to the technical environment for your course.
- Your personal whiteboard for sketches and notes.
- Newsletters and other communications from your learning provider.
- Mentoring services.
- A link to the website of your training provider.
- The LogicalCHOICE store.

http://www.lo-choice.com

Visit your LogicalCHOICE Home screen often to connect, communicate, and extend your learning experience!

How to Use This Book

As You Learn

This book is divided into lessons and topics, covering a subject or a set of related subjects. In most cases, lessons are arranged in order of increasing proficiency.

The results-oriented topics include relevant and supporting information you need to master the content. Each topic has various types of activities designed to enable you to practice the guidelines and procedures as well as to solidify your understanding of the informational material presented in the course. Procedures and guidelines are presented in a concise fashion along with activities and discussions. Information is provided for reference and reflection in such a way as to facilitate understanding and practice.

Data files for various activities as well as other supporting files for the course are available by download from the LogicalCHOICE Course screen. In addition to sample data for the course exercises, the course files may contain media components to enhance your learning and additional reference materials for use both during and after the course.

At the back of the book, you will find a glossary of the definitions of the terms and concepts used throughout the course. You will also find an index to assist in locating information within the instructional components of the book.

As You Review

Any method of instruction is only as effective as the time and effort you, the student, are willing to invest in it. In addition, some of the information that you learn in class may not be important to you immediately, but it may become important later. For this reason, we encourage you to spend some time reviewing the content of the course after your time in the classroom.

As a Reference

The organization and layout of this book make it an easy-to-use resource for future reference. Taking advantage of the glossary, index, and table of contents, you can use this book as a first source of definitions, background information, and summaries.

Course Icons

Watch throughout the material for these visual cues:

Icon	Description
	A **Note** provides additional information, guidance, or hints about a topic or task.
	A **Caution** helps make you aware of places where you need to be particularly careful with your actions, settings, or decisions so that you can be sure to get the desired results of an activity or task.
	LearnTO notes show you where an associated LearnTO is particularly relevant to the content. Access LearnTOs from your LogicalCHOICE Course screen.
	Checklists provide job aids you can use after class as a reference to performing skills back on the job. Access checklists from your LogicalCHOICE Course screen.
	Social notes remind you to check your LogicalCHOICE Course screen for opportunities to interact with the LogicalCHOICE community using social media.
	Notes Pages are intentionally left blank for you to write on.

1 | Hardware Fundamentals

Lesson Time: 2 hours, 10 minutes

Lesson Objectives

In this lesson, you will identify the hardware components of a computer. You will:

- Identify computer system components.

- Identify storage devices.

- Identify personal computer device connection methods.

Lesson Introduction

A very large percentage of the work that most IT technicians do entails working with hardware, including installing, upgrading, repairing, configuring, maintaining, optimizing, and troubleshooting computer components. To install and configure computer hardware, you need to recognize the basic components that constitute most personal computers, along with the functionality that each component provides to the computing experience. In this lesson, you will identify hardware components and how they function.

Preparing for a career in computer support and maintenance can be a daunting task. A good place to start is with the basics: the essential hardware components that you find in most computers. Identifying hardware components and their roles give you a solid base on which to build the knowledge and skills you need to install, configure, and troubleshoot computer hardware.

This lesson covers all or part of the following CompTIA® A+® (2012) Exam 220-801 certification objectives:

- Topic A:
  - Objective 1.1
- Topic B:
  - Objectives 1.5, 1.7, 1.12
- Topic C:
  - Objectives 1.7, 1.11

TOPIC A

Computer System Components

In this lesson, you will identify the hardware components of a computer. The first step is to identify the hardware that you will find in virtually all computer systems. In this topic, you will identify computer system components.

If you are not familiar with the various components that a computer is made up of, it can seem like a jigsaw puzzle. Like most puzzles, each part of a computer connects to other parts in a specific place, but generally, you will find that the pieces fit together almost exactly the same way from one system to another. To help you put the puzzle together, you need to understand what these pieces look like and what they do.

This topic covers all or part of the following CompTIA® A+® (2012) Exam 220-801 certification objectives:

- Objective 1.1: Configure and apply BIOS settings.

Common Computer Components

Computing components are the physical devices that are required for a computer to operate properly. There are four main categories of components in a typical computer.

Component	Description
The *system unit*	The system unit, also commonly referred to as the CPU, or the tower, is the main component of a computer, which houses most of the other devices that are necessary for the computer to function. Traditionally, it is comprised of a chassis and internal components, such as the system board, the microprocessor, memory modules, disk drives, adapter cards, the power supply, fans and other cooling systems, and ports for connecting external components such as monitors, keyboards, mice, and other devices. System units are also often referred to as boxes, main units, or base units.

Component	Description
	In some newer computer models, the system unit is incorporated with the display screen and referred to as an all-in-one computer. Similar to laptops, the system unit is integrated into a smaller configuration, which may make it harder to manage or replace the system unit components.
Display devices	A display device is a personal computer component that enables users to view the text and graphical data output from a computer. Display devices commonly connect to the system unit via a cable, and they have controls to adjust the settings for the device. They vary in size and shape, as well as the technologies used.
	Common terms for various types of display devices include display, monitor, screen, cathode ray tube (CRT), *liquid crystal display (LCD)*, and flat-panel monitors.

Component	Description
Input devices	An input device is a personal computer component that enables users to enter data or instructions into a computer. Common input devices include keyboards and computer mice. An input device can connect to the system unit via a cable or a wireless connection.

Component	Description
External devices	You can enhance the functionality of practically any personal computer by connecting different types of external devices to the system unit. Also called peripheral devices, external devices can provide alternative input or output methods or additional data storage. You connect external devices to the system unit via cable or a wireless connection. Some devices have their own power source, while others draw power from the system. Common examples of external devices include microphones, cameras, scanners, printers, and external drives.

Component	Description

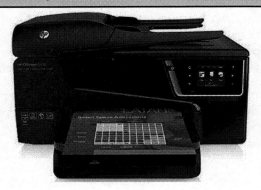

Computer Cases

The *computer case* is the enclosure that holds all of the components of your computer. Computer cases come in several sizes and arrangements. Some are designed to hold many internal components and have a lot of room to work around those components. These are usually tower or desktop cases and take up a good deal of room. Other cases are designed to use a minimum amount of space. The trade-off is that the interior of the case is often cramped, with little room for adding additional components. Because the tower proved to be popular, there are now several versions of the tower model. These include:

- Full tower, which is usually used for servers or when you will be installing many drives and other components.
- Mid tower, which is a slightly smaller version of the full-size tower.
- Micro, or mini tower, which is the size that replaces the original desktop case in most modern systems.
- Slim line, which is a tower case that can be turned on its side to save room

The Motherboard

The *motherboard* is the personal computer component that acts as the backbone for the entire computer system. Sometimes called the *system board*, it consists of a large, flat circuit board with chips and other electrical components on it, with various connectors. Some components are *soldered* directly to the board, and some components connect to the board by using slots or sockets.

Figure 1–1: A motherboard.

The CPU

The *central processing unit (CPU)* is a computer chip where most of the computing calculations take place. On most computers, the CPU is housed in a single microprocessor module that is installed on the system board in a slot or a socket.

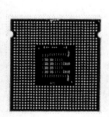   

Figure 1–2: CPUs.

Multicore Processors

Since mid-to-late 2000, the trend has been to build processors with two or more individual CPUs that work in parallel and that are contained in a single chip. Two or more individual processors can share a workload more efficiently than a single processor. Dual-core and quad-core processors are engineered to include two to four cores on a single chip, while hexa- and octa-core processors include six and eight cores, respectively.

Multi–CPU Motherboards

Prior to the development of multicore processors, some hardware manufacturers offered additional processing power by designing motherboards that could hold more than one CPU. With the advent of the multicore processors, these are less common in personal computers, but they are still widely used in server machines.

Memory

Memory is the computer system component that provides a temporary workspace for the processor. Memory refers to modules of computer chips that store data in a digital electronic format, which is faster to read from and write to than tape or hard drives. Memory chips each contain millions of transistors etched on one sliver of a semiconductor. *Transistors* are nothing more than switches that can be opened or closed. When a transistor is closed, it conducts electricity, representing the binary number 1. When it is opened, it does not, representing the binary number 0.

There are two types of memory used in computer systems: *Random Access Memory (RAM)* and *Read-Only Memory (ROM)*. RAM is a computer storage method that functions as a computer's main memory. This type requires a constant power source to access the data stored within the RAM. However, data stored on ROM is saved and stored without a constant power source. Once data is written to ROM, it cannot be modified easily.

Volatile and Non-volatile Memory

Memory is considered to be either volatile or non-volatile:

* Volatile memory stores data temporarily and requires a constant source of electricity to keep track of the data stored in it. When the power is no longer available, the data stored in volatile memory is lost. The computer's main RAM is an example of volatile memory. The computer can both read the data stored in RAM and write different data into the same RAM. Any byte of data can be accessed without disturbing other data, so the computer has random access to the data in RAM.
* Non-volatile memory retains the information stored on it whether or not electrical current is available. ROM is an example of non-volatile memory.

Figure 1–3: A sample memory module.

The System Bus

In computer communications, a *bus* is a group of wires or electronic pathways that connect components. The *system bus* is the wires, or *traces,* on the motherboard that provide the main communication path between the CPU and memory. The system bus enables data transfer between the CPU, memory, and the other buses in the computer, which connect other system components such as hard drives and adapter cards. It is sometimes referred to as the frontside bus or local bus.

Storage Devices

A *storage device* is a computer system component, such as a hard drive, that enables users to save data for reuse at a later time, even after the personal computer is shut down and restarted. Storage devices can save data magnetically, optically, or electronically, depending on their design.

Figure 1–4: Examples of storage devices.

Power Supplies

A *power supply* is a computer system component that converts line-voltage alternating current (AC) power from an electrical outlet to the low-voltage direct current (DC) power needed by other system components. The power supply is often referred to as the power supply unit (PSU). The power supply is typically a metal box in the rear of the system that is attached to the computer chassis and to the system board. While the power supply is not itself a component of the system board, it is required in order for system components to receive power. The power supply contains the power cord plug and a fan for cooling, because it generates a lot of heat. Some power supplies have a voltage selector switch that enables you to set them to the voltage configurations that are used in different countries. AC adapters are generally built in to the power supply for desktop systems and are external for laptops and other mobile systems.

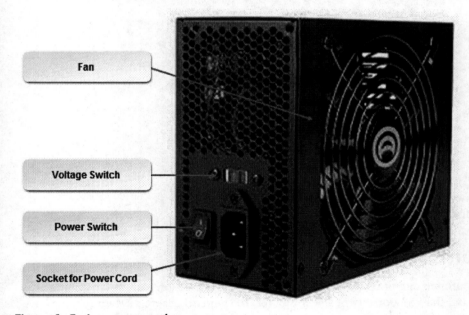

Figure 1–5: A power supply.

Fixed-Input Power Supply Voltage Selector Switch

Power supplies with voltage selector switches are called fixed-input power supplies. The voltage selector switches generally have two settings—for example, 220 and 110—depending on the manufacturer. If you set the switch to a higher voltage than supplied by the power source, the system will not receive enough power and will not function properly. However, if you set the switch to a lower setting than supplied by the power source—for example, if you set the switch to 110 volts (V) while connected to a 220 V outlet—you run the risk of burning out the power supply, damaging system components, or more seriously, creating a fire or electrocution hazard.

Auto-switching power supplies do not have a manual voltage switch, but detect the voltage level supplied by the outlet and set themselves to the correct voltage automatically. This can be convenient and safe for people who travel to various countries with portable computers.

Cooling Systems

A *cooling system* is a computer system component that prevents damage to other computer parts by dissipating the heat generated inside a computer chassis. The cooling system can consist of one or more fans and other components such as *heat sinks* or liquid cooling systems that service the entire computer as well as individual components, such as the power supply and CPU.

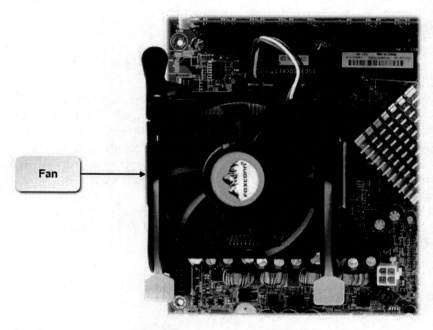

Figure 1-6: A typical cooling system for a CPU.

Components That Require Cooling

Computer systems contain several components that require cooling:

- The CPU.
- The power supply.
- Some adapter cards.
- Some hard disk drives.

Expansion Cards

An *expansion card* is a printed circuit board that you install into an expansion slot on the computer's system board to expand the functionality of the computer. In standard desktop systems, cards have connectors that fit into an expansion slot on a system board and circuitry to connect a specific device to the computer. Laptops, on the other hand, typically have slots located on the outside of the case for inserting expansion cards. These cards are often referred to as laptop expansion cards.

Figure 1–7: An expansion card.

 Note: An expansion card is also known as an adapter card, I/O card, add-in, add-on, or simply as a board.

Riser Cards

A *riser card* is a board that plugs into the system board and provides additional expansion slots for adapter cards. Because it rises above the system board, it enables you to connect additional adapters to the system in an orientation that is parallel to the system board and thus saves space within the system case. Riser cards are commonly found within rackmount server implementations to provide additional slots for expanding the features of a server and in low rise smaller cases to fit larger expansion cards.

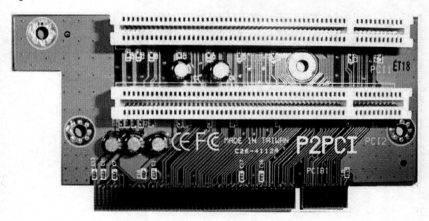

Figure 1–8: A riser card.

 Note: A riser card expands motherboard capabilities the way a power strip increases the capabilities of electrical outlets.

Daughter Boards

Daughter board is a general computing and electronics term for any circuit board that plugs into another circuit board. In personal computing, a daughter board can be used as a more general term for adapter cards. Sometimes, in casual usage, the term "daughter board" is used interchangeably with the term "riser card," but technically they are not the same.

Firmware

Firmware is specialized software stored in memory chips that stores OS-specific information whether or not power to the computer is on. It is most often written on an electronically reprogrammable chip so that it can be updated with a special program to fix any errors that might be discovered after a computer is purchased, or to support updated hardware components.

 Note: Updating firmware electronically is called *flashing*.

The System BIOS

A *Basic Input/Output System (BIOS)* is a set of instructions that is stored in ROM and that is used to start the most basic services of a computer system. Every computer has a *system BIOS*, which sets the computer's configuration and environment when the system is powered on. It is located in ROM chips on the system board. Computers may also include other devices that have their own BIOS to control their functions.

Figure 1–9: The system BIOS resides on ROM chips, and sets the computer's configuration and environment at startup.

The POST

The *Power-On Self Test (POST)* is a built-in diagnostic program that runs every time a personal computer starts up. The POST checks your hardware to ensure that everything is present and functioning properly, before the system BIOS begins the operating system boot process. If there is an error, then an audible beep will alert you that something is wrong.

The POST process contains several steps to ensure that the system meets the necessary requirements to operate properly.

 Note: The POST process can vary a great deal from manufacturer to manufacturer.

Hardware Component	POST Test Criteria
Power supply	Must be turned on, and must supply its "power good" signal.
CPU	Must exit Reset status mode, and must be able to execute instructions.
BIOS	Must be readable.
BIOS memory	Must be readable.
Memory	Must be able to be read by the CPU, and the first 64 KB of memory must be able to hold the POST code.
Input/output (I/O) bus or I/O controller	Must be accessible, and must be able to communicate with the video subsystem.

ACTIVITY 1-1
Identifying Personal Computer Components

Scenario
In this activity, you will identify personal computer components.

1. Your instructor might provide you with examples of computer components and ask you or other participants to identify them.

2. Identify the computer components in this graphic.

    A. System unit
    B. Display device
    C. Input device
    D. Peripheral device

3. Which computer components are part of the system unit?
   - ☐ Chassis
   - ☐ Internal hard drive
   - ☐ Monitor
   - ☐ Portable USB drive
   - ☐ Memory

4. What are the main categories of personal computer components?
   - ☐ System unit
   - ☐ Display
   - ☐ Input devices
   - ☐ Network devices
   - ☐ Peripheral devices

5. Identify the system unit and motherboard components in this graphic.

A. Motherboard

B. Power supply

C. Adapter card

D. Storage device

E. Memory

F. CPU

6. How many fans would you expect to find in a computer? How many do you think are in the computer you are using for this course?

7. Where is the system BIOS stored?
   - ○ On the primary hard drive
   - ○ In BIOS memory
   - ○ On ROM chips
   - ○ In RAM

8. Which hardware components are checked during the POST?
   - ☐ Power supply
   - ☐ CPU
   - ☐ Display
   - ☐ RAM

9. Which system unit components are connected by the system bus?
   - ☐ CPU
   - ☐ Memory
   - ☐ Power supply
   - ☐ System board
   - ☐ Cooling system

TOPIC B

Storage Devices

In the previous topic, you identified the main components of a personal computer. One of the primary reasons for using a computer is to electronically store data. In this topic, you will identify the types of storage devices used in personal computers.

As a computer technician, your responsibilities are likely to include installing and maintaining many different types of computer components, including storage devices. By identifying the various types of storage devices that can be found in most personal computers, you will be better prepared to select, install, and maintain storage devices in personal computers.

This topic covers all or part of the following CompTIA® A+® (2012) Exam 220-801 certification objectives:

- Objective 1.5: Install and configure storage devices and use appropriate media.
- Objective 1.7: Compare and contrast various connection interfaces and explain their purpose.
- Objective 1.12: Install and configure various peripheral devices.

Floppy Drives

A *floppy disk drive (FDD)* is a storage device that reads data from, and writes data to, floppy disks. Floppy disks are removable disks that are made of flexible Mylar plastic that is covered with magnetic coating and enclosed in stiff, protective plastic cases. The vast majority of floppy drives are internal devices that connect to the system board through a floppy disk *controller*, and they get their power from the personal computer's power supply. The *form factor* is usually 3.5 inches; 3.5-inch floppy disks can hold up to 1.44 MB of data. Floppy disk drives are not used much anymore and are considered a legacy technology, but you might still encounter them on older machines.

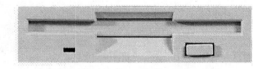

Front view of 3.5-inch floppy disk drive

Data Cable

Power Cable

Rear view of floppy disk drive

3.5-inch floppy disk

Figure 1-10: An FDD.

 Note: Although 3.5 inches is the most recent standard for floppy disks and drives, 5.25-inch floppy disks and drives were once the standard, and before that, 8-inch disks and drives were the standard. You will probably never encounter either of these, and even 3.5-inch models are essentially obsolete.

Hard Drives

A *hard disk drive (HDD)* is a storage device that reads data from, and writes data to, a hard disk. A hard disk consists of several metal or hard plastic platters with a magnetic surface coating. Data is stored magnetically and can be accessed directly. Although the HDD and the hard disk are not the same thing, they are packaged together and are often referred to interchangeably. HDDs are also referred to as hard drives, and they can be internal or external devices. Internal hard drives are mounted inside the chassis and connect directly to the system board through at least one cable for data and one for power, while external hard drives generally connect to the system by means of an expansion card or a port.

Figure 1–11: An HDD.

Disk Controllers

Both floppy drives and hard drives require circuitry to communicate with the CPU. This circuitry is known as the *disk controller*. Disk controllers can be built into the drive itself, or they can be contained on an expansion card. In most modern floppy drives and hard drives, the controller is built into the drive.

Jumpers

Jumpers are used to configure older hardware by shutting off an electrical circuit located on the component. Using jumpers, this is accomplished by sliding a jumper shunt over the jumper pins on the *jumper block* of the motherboard.

Hard Drive Speeds

The speed of a hard drive is based on how fast the disk is spun to retrieve the requested data. This is referred to as revolutions per minute (rpm). Common speeds include:

- 5,400 rpm
- 7,200 rpm
- 10,000 rpm
- 15,000 rpm

Types of Hard Drives

There are many types of hard disks that you might encounter as you work with personal computers, each of which has its own set of characteristics.

Hard Drive Type	Characteristics
Parallel Advanced Technology Attachment (PATA)	Also known as Integrated Drive Electronics (IDE), Enhanced IDE (EIDE), Ultra Direct Memory Access (UDMA), and *Advanced Technology Attachment (ATA)* drives, PATA drives have the following characteristics: • The controller is built into the drive. • PATA drives are limited to two channels, each with up to two devices.

Hard Drive Type	Characteristics
	• The earliest PATA drives came in "types," which corresponded to a particular internal geometry; the drive type needed to be set in the system BIOS. Modern drives are automatically detected. • If the drive type is not automatically detected, it must be set in the system BIOS. • Over the years, there have been several revisions to the standard, each supporting different data transfer rates. • To install PATA drives, you use jumpers to set the configuration.
Small Computer Systems Interface (SCSI)	SCSI drives have the following characteristics: • There is no controller built into the drive. A separate bus within the computer system enables SCSI drives to communicate with the CPU. • SCSI supports up to eight devices, but the host bus adapter (HBA) card installed in the computer counts as one of the devices, so you can actually connect only up to seven drives or other devices (15 devices in more recent versions). • You must configure separate SCSI ID settings for each device. • You might need to set the system BIOS to no drive, and then configure the SCSI firmware to recognize which drive to boot from. • There are several variations on the interface, each supporting different data transfer rates.
Serial Advanced Technology Attachment (SATA)	SATA drives have the following characteristics: • SATA supports one device per channel. • Data transfer rates are 150 MBps for SATA I and 300 MBps for SATA II. • SATA supports *hot swapping* of drives, which means that you can replace a SATA drive without powering down the system. • Recently, computers have started offering external SATA jacks.

PATA Configuration

.Each PATA interface can support up to two drives. Because the controller is integrated with the drive, there is no overall controller to decide which device is currently communicating with the CPU. This is not a problem as long as each device is on a separate interface, but to support two devices on the same channel, the master/slave configuration was developed. This configuration allows one drive's controller (the master) to tell the other drive's controller (the slave) when it can transfer data to or from the computer. Some drives feature an option called Cable Select (CS). With the correct type of connecting cable, these drives can be automatically configured as master or slave. Most drives today come preset for CS, which allows the BIOS to configure itself as needed

ATA and Related Specifications

Hard drive manufacturer Western Digital designed IDE technology as a replacement for even older drive technologies that did not include an integrated drive controller. American National Standards Institute's (ANSI) ATA standard was based on IDE and released in 1990. ATA referred to IBM®'s PC/AT. When SATA technology was introduced in 2003, ATA was retroactively renamed PATA.

The original IDE specification predated CD-ROM drives, and did not support hard drives larger than 504 MB. However, revisions of the specifications over the years have extended the capabilities to provide support for faster and larger hard drives and other devices. The following table describes PATA specifications.

Standard and Other Common Names for It	Description
IDE, ATA, ATA-1, or PATA	The original PATA specification supported one channel, with two drives configured in a master/slave arrangement. A second channel was added later.
EIDE, Fast ATA, ATA-2, or Fast ATA-2	Also known as ATA Interface with Extensions ATA-2, Western Digital called its implementation EIDE. Seagate's was called Fast ATA or Fast ATA-2. It could implement power-saving mode features, if desired.
ATA-3	A minor enhancement to ATA-2, this standard improved reliability for high-speed data transfer modes. Self Monitoring Analysis And Reporting Technology (SMART) was introduced. This is logic in the drives that warns of impending drive problems. Password protection was available as a security feature of the drives.
ATA/ATAPI-4, ATA-4, Ultra ATA/33, Ultra DMA, UDMA, or UDMA/33	This standard doubled data transfer rates. ATA Packet Interface (ATAPI) is an EIDE interface enhancement that includes commands used to control tape, CD-ROM, and other removable drives.
ATA/ATAPI-5, ATA-5, Ultra ATA/66, or UDMA/66	The ATA-5 specification introduced UDMA modes 3 and 4, as well as mandatory use of the 80-conductor (40-pin), high-performance IDE cable with UDMA modes higher than 2. Additional changes to the command set were also part of this specification. This standard supports drives up to 137 GB.
ATA/ATAPI-6, ATA-6, Ultra ATA/100, or UDMA/100	This standard supports data transfers at up to 100 MBps and supports drives as large as 144 petabytes (PB), which is approximately 144 million GB or 144 quadrillion bytes.
PIO	Programmed Input/Output (PIO) is a data transfer method that includes the CPU in the data path. It has been replaced by DMA and UDMA.
DMA	Direct Memory Access (DMA) is a data transfer method that moves data directly from the drive to main memory. UDMA transfers data in burst mode at a rate of 33.3 MB per second. The speed is two times faster than DMA.
SATA	This standard uses serial instead of parallel signaling technology for ATA and ATAPI devices. SATA employs serial connectors and serial cables, which are smaller, thinner, and more flexible than traditional PATA cables. Data transfer rates are 150 MB per second or greater.
SATA II, SATA2, or SATA 3 Gbps	This standard provides data transfer rates of 300 MBps.
SATA 6 Gbps	This standard doubled data transfer rates, and is designed to support the latest (and future) solid state drives (SSDs).

SCSI Standards

SCSI standards have been revised repeatedly over the years. The following table describes current SCSI standards.

SCSI Standard	Description
SCSI-1	Features an 8-bit parallel bus (with parity), running asynchronously at 3.5 MBps or 5 MBps in synchronous mode, and a maximum bus cable length of 6 meters, compared to the 0.45-meter limit of the PATA interface. A variation on the

SCSI Standard	Description
	original standard included a *high-voltage differential (HVD)* implementation with a maximum cable length of 25 meters.
SCSI-2	Introduced the Fast SCSI and Wide SCSI variants. Fast SCSI doubled the maximum transfer rate to 10 MBps, and Wide SCSI doubled the bus width to 16 bits to reach 20 MBps. The maximum cable length was reduced to 3 meters.
SCSI-3	The first parallel SCSI devices that exceeded the SCSI-2 capabilities were simply designated SCSI-3. These devices were also known as Ultra SCSI and Fast-20 SCSI. The bus speed doubled again to 20 MBps for narrow (8-bit) systems and 40 MBps for wide (16-bit). The maximum cable length stayed at 3 meters.
Ultra-2 SCSI	This standard featured a *low-voltage differential (LVD)* bus. For this reason, Ultra-2 SCSI is sometimes referred to as LVD SCSI. LVD's greater immunity to noise allowed a maximum bus cable length of 12 meters. At the same time, the data transfer rate was increased to 80 MBps.
Ultra-3 SCSI	Also known as Ultra-160 SCSI, this version was basically an improvement on the Ultra-2 SCSI standard, in that the transfer rate was doubled once more to 160 MBps. Ultra-160 SCSI offered new features such as cyclic redundancy check (CRC), an error correcting process, and domain validation.
Ultra-320 SCSI	This standard doubled the data transfer rate to 320 MBps.
Ultra-640 SCSI	Also known as Fast-320 SCSI, Ultra-640 doubles the interface speed yet again, this time to 640 MBps. Ultra-640 pushes the limits of LVD signaling; the speed limits cable lengths drastically, making it impractical for more than one or two devices.
Serial SCSI	Four versions of SCSI—*Serial Storage Architecture (SSA), Fibre Channel-Alternating Loop (FC-AL)*, IEEE 1394, and *Serial Attached SCSI (SAS)*—perform data transfer via serial communications. Serial SCSI supports faster data rates than traditional SCSI implementations, hot swapping, and improved fault isolation. *Serial SCSI* devices are generally more expensive than the equivalent parallel SCSI devices.
iSCSI	*Internet SCSI (iSCSI)* provides connectivity between SCSI storage networks over an IP-based network without the need for installing Fibre Channel.

Optical Disks

An *optical disk* is a storage device that stores data optically, rather than magnetically. The removable plastic disks have a reflective coating and require an optical drive to be read. In optical storage, data is written by either pressing or burning with a laser to create pits (recessed areas) and lands (raised areas) in the reflective surface of the disc. Common optical disks include compact discs (CDs) and digital versatile discs (DVDs).

Types of Optical Disks

There is a wide variety of optical discs available in the marketplace, each with its own requirements and specifications.

Optical Disk Type	Description
CD-ROM	Compact Disc-Read Only Memory. Data is permanently burned onto the disk during its manufacture.
CD-R	CD-Recordable. Data can be written to the disk only once.
CD-RW	CD-Rewritable. Data can be written to the disk multiple times.

Optical Disk Type	Description
DVD-ROM	Digital Versatile Disc-Read Only Memory. Data is permanently burned onto the disk during its manufacture.
DVD-R	DVD-Recordable. Data can be written to the disk only once.
DVD+R	Another format of DVD-Recordable. Data can be written to the disk only once.
DVD+R DL	DVD-Recordable Double Layer. A higher-capacity double-layer format. Data can be written to the disk only once.
DVD-RW	DVD-Rewritable. Data can be written to the disk multiple times.
Dual Layer DVD-RW	A DVD-RW disc that has two layer of writable space with a maximum capacity of 8.5 GB. These disks are not used widely due to the cost and the release of Blu-ray.
DVD+RW	Another format of DVD-Rewritable. Data can be written to the disk multiple times.
DVD-RAM	DVD-Random Access Memory. Data can be written to the disk multiple times.
BD-ROM	Blu-ray Disc-Read Only Memory. Blu-ray discs (BD) are intended for high-density storage of high-definition video as well as data storage. Current Blu-ray discs hold 50 GB total. However, companies such as Sony are testing experimental disks that have storage capacities of up to 200 GB and more.
BD-R	Blu-ray Disc-Recordable (BD-R). Data can be written to BD-R once.
BD-RE	Blu-ray Disc-Recordable Erasable. BD-RE is a disc that can be written to as well as erased. Data can be written to and erased from the disk many times without compromising the integrity of the disk or the data stored on it.

DVD Plus or DVD Dash?

There are several competing DVD formats. DVD-ROM, DVD-R, DVD-RW, and DVD-RAM are approved by the DVD Forum, while DVD+R, DVD+R DL, DVD+RW are not. Because some of the competing formats are incompatible, many hybrid DVD drives have been developed. These hybrid drives are often labeled DVD±RW.

Optical Drives

An *optical drive* is an internal or external disk drive that reads data to and writes data from an optical disc. Optical drives can be connected to the system by using IDE, SCSI, or other interfaces. Internal optical drives generally have a 5.25-inch form factor.

Types of Optical Drives and Burners

Optical drives include CD, DVD, and Blu-ray drives. Some optical drives provide only read capabilities, while others enable users to write, or burn, data to optical disks. CD, DVD, and Blu-ray drives have varying characteristics and specifications.

Optical Drive Type	Description
CD	Compact discs store data on one side of the disc, and most hold 700 to 860 MB of data, although older disks and drives may support only up to 650.4 MB of data. CDs are widely used to store music and data. To meet the audio CD standard, the CD drive on a computer must transfer data at a rate of at least 150 KBps. Most

Optical Drive Type	Description
	CD drives deliver higher speeds: at least eight times (8x) or sixteen times (16x) the audio transfer rate. There are also drives with much higher transfer rates, up to 52x. CD drives use one of two special file systems: Compact Disc File System (CDFS) or Universal Disc Format (UDF). CDs can be either CD-R (which can be written to once) or CD-RW (which can be written to multiple times).
DVD	Digital versatile discs can typically hold 4.7 GB on one side of the disk; it is possible to write to both surfaces of the disk, in which case the disk can hold up to 9.4 GB. There are also dual-layer disks, which store additional data on each side, and are capable of holding up to 17 GB. DVD drives access data at speeds from 600 KBps to 1.3 MBps. Because of the huge storage capacity and fast data access, DVDs are widely used to store full-length movies and other multimedia content. DVD drives use UDF as the file system. DVDs can be DVD-R (which can be written to once), or DVD-RW (which can be written to multiple times).
Blu-ray	Named for the blue laser it uses to read and write data, Blu-ray drives read and write data from Blu-ray discs. Blu-ray discs are primarily used for high-definition video, though they are also used for data storage. Blu-ray used to compete with high-definition (HD) DVD for market share, but has since emerged as the winner of that battle. The wavelength of the blue laser is shorter than that of the red laser used in previous optical drives, so data can be more tightly packed on a Blu-ray disc. A single-layer Blu-ray disc can hold up to 25 GB of information, and a dual-layer Blu-ray disc can hold up to 50 GB, dwarfing the capacity of a standard double-sided DVD. Blu-ray uses UDF v2.5.
Combination drives and burners	A combination drive, also referred to as a combo drive, can read and write to a number of different optical disc types. Older combo drives were equipped with the read/write function for CDs only, but could also read DVDs. However, most combo drives today are primarily DVD-RW burners that also have the ability to read/write CDs and Blu-ray discs. Depending on your needs, you may require a combo drive that can also support the use of dual-layer DVD-RW discs. Depending on the manufacturer, some combination Blu-ray drives and players can also read/write to CDs and DVDs. It is a best practice to check the specific manufacturer's drive capabilities to verify which media the device can support.

Tape Drives

A *tape drive* is a storage device that stores data magnetically on a tape that is enclosed in a removable tape cartridge. Data on the tape must be read sequentially. Sizes for external tape drives vary, but internal drives have a 5.25-inch form factor. Tape drives are most commonly used to store backup copies of archived, offline data in large data centers and are almost never used with desktop computers. Recent technological advances made by IBM have allowed for data on tapes to be accessed and read in a file format method similar to other storage media, such as optical disks and flash drives. The specification is called *Linear Tape File Systems (LTFS)*. LTFS is a tape format that determines how data is recorded on tape, and how specialized software will read that data.

Figure 1-12: A tape drive.

Solid State Storage

Solid state drives (SSDs), use flash technology to retain data in special types of memory instead of on disks or tape. Solid state storage uses non-volatile memory to emulate mechanical storage devices, but solid state storage is much faster and more reliable than mechanical storage because there are no moving parts.

Solid State vs. Magnetic Storage

Storage devices typically store data in either solid state or magnetic form. Solid state devices, such as *flash drives,* contain no moving parts and tend to be more reliable than magnetic drives. Magnetic drives, such as hard drives, store information on a magnetic coated media that is rotated underneath a read/write head.

Hot Swappable Devices

Hot swapping is a type of hardware replacement procedure where a component can be replaced while the main power is still on. Also called hot plug or hot insertion, hot swap is a feature of USB and FireWire devices, enabling you to install an external drive, network adapter, or other peripheral without having to power down the computer. It is good practice to use the safe removal option from the System Tray before removing a hot-swappable device or peripheral from the computer. Hot swapping can also refer to the system's ability to detect when hardware is added or removed. Non-hot-swappable devices require the system to be shut down and restarted before any device installation updates or removals are recognized by the system.

Types of Solid State Storage

Solid state storage comes in several formats, many of which are used in external devices such as digital cameras or mobile devices.

Solid State Storage Device	Specifications
USB flash drives	USB flash drives come in several form factors, including thumb drives and pen drives. Thumb drives can be small, from 50 to 70 mm long, 17 to 20 mm wide, and 10 to 12 mm thick. Data storage capacities vary, from 128 MB up to 128 GB. Data transfer rates also vary, from 700 KBps to 28 MBps for read operations, and from 350 KBps to 15 MBps for write operations.

Solid State Storage Device	Specifications

SSDs

Flash-memory-based disks do not need batteries, allowing makers to replicate standard disk-drive form factors (2.5-inch and 3.5-inch). Flash SSDs are extremely fast since these devices have no moving parts, eliminating seek time, latency, and other electromechanical delays inherent in conventional disk drives. The use of SSDs has been increasing over time due to their speed and quick data access times.

SSDs can be configured within systems to replace traditional computer hardware such as disk drives, optical drives, and network security appliances that include firewall and routing functions.

CF cards

CompactFlash (CF) cards are flash memory cards that are 43 mm long by 36 mm wide. Due to their compact size, they are typically used in portable devices. Type I is 3.3 mm thick and Type II is 5 mm thick. They hold 100 GB or more, and have a 50-pin contact. Transfer speeds of up to 66 MBps are possible.

Newer versions of the CF card offer speeds up to 1 Gbps and can store up to 1 terabyte (TB) of data.

CF cards are commonly used for additional storage in:

• Digital cameras
• Music players
• Personal computing devices
• Photo printers
• Digital camera recorders

Solid State Storage Device	Specifications

SM cards	SmartMedia (SM) cards are flash memory cards that are similar in size to the CF cards, and are 45 mm long by 37 mm wide by 0.76 mm thick. They can hold up to 128 MB and can transfer data at speeds of up to 8 MBps.

SM cards are commonly used for additional storage in:

• Digital cameras
• Digital camera recorders
• Older models of personal digital assistants (PDAs) |

xD	xD-Picture Cards (xD) are flash memory cards that are specifically designed for use in digital cameras. They are 20 mm long by 25 mm wide by 1.7 mm thick. They can hold up to 2 GB with plans for up to 8 GB. Data transfer rates range from 4 to 15 MBps for read operations and from 1.3 to 9 MBps for write operations.

Solid State Storage Device	Specifications

MSes

Memory sticks (MSes) are flash memory cards that are 50 mm long by 21.5 mm wide by 2.8 mm thick. They can hold up to 16 GB and are used extensively in Sony products such as VAIO® laptops. Data transfer rates are 2.5 MBps for read operations and 1.8 MBps for write operations.

SD cards

The original Secure Digital (SD) Memory Card is 32 mm long, 24 mm wide, and 2.1 mm thick. The miniSD Card measures 21.5 mm by 20 mm by 1.4 mm, and the microSD/TransFlash Card measures 15 mm by 11 mm by 1 mm. SD Memory Cards are currently available in several capacities, up to 2 TB. Data transfer rates range from 10 MBps to 20 MBps.

SD cards are used in many different devices, including:

- Laptops
- Digital cameras
- Smartphones
- Handheld gaming devices
- Audio players

Solid State Storage Device	Specifications

MMCs	MultiMediaCards (MMCs) are 32 mm long by 24 mm wide by 1.5 mm thick. Reduced Size MMCs (RS-MMCs) and MMCmobile cards are 16 mm by 24 mm by 1.5 mm. MMCmini cards are 21.5 mm by 20 mm by 1.4 mm, and MMCmicro cards are 12 mm by 14 mm by 1.1 mm. These cards can hold up to 8 GB, and data transfer rates can reach 52 MBps. MMC cards are generally also compatible with SD card readers and are used in many of the same devices.

ACTIVITY 1-2
Identifying Storage Devices

Scenario

In this activity, you will identify storage devices.

---

1. Your instructor might provide you with examples of storage devices and ask you or other participants to identify them.

2. Which storage device records data magnetically and is most often used for backups?
   - ○ FDD
   - ○ HDD
   - ○ Optical disk drive
   - ○ Tape drive
   - ○ SSD

3. What is the primary benefit of using solid state storage?

4. Which two optical drive media types enable you to write to an optical disk only once?
   - ☐ CD-ROM
   - ☐ CD-R
   - ☐ CD+RW
   - ☐ DVD+R
   - ☐ DVD-RW

5. True or False? No optical disk can hold more than 50 GB of data.
   - ☐ True
   - ☐ False

TOPIC C

Device Connections and Interfaces

You are already familiar with the common components that make up a personal computer. Next, you need to be able to identify how all the components are connected together to form a complete personal computer system. In this topic, you will identify device connection and interface methods.

A personal computer is made up of many different components. All of these components need to be able to communicate with each other in order for the computer to function properly. As personal computers have evolved over the years, a number of connection technologies have been implemented to provide communication among computer components. As a computer technician, identifying the different methods that are used to connect devices to a computer will enable you to install, upgrade, and replace personal computer components quickly and effectively.

This topic covers all or part of the following CompTIA® A+® (2012) Exam 220-801 certification objectives:

- Objective 1.7: Compare and contrast various connection interfaces and explain their purpose.
- Objective 1.11: Identify connector types and associated cables.

Ports

A *port* is a hardware interface that you can use to connect devices to a computer. The port transfers electronic signals between the device and the system unit. The port is either an electrically wired socket or plug, or it can be a wireless transmission device. Ports can vary by shape, by color according to the color coding standards, by the number and layout of the pins or connectors contained within the port, by the signals the port carries, and by the port's location. Ports exist for both internal and external devices. External ports often have a graphical representation of the type of device that should be connected to it, such as a small picture of a monitor adjacent to the video port.

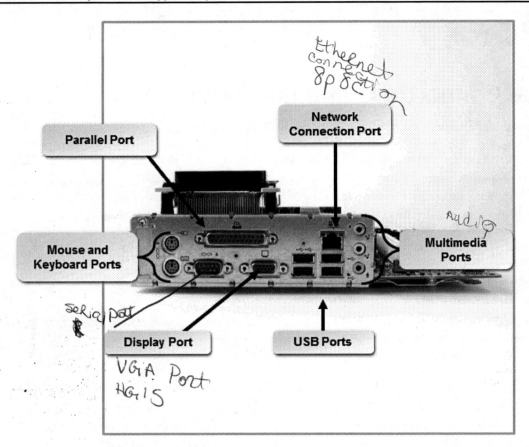

Figure 1-13: Ports on a personal computer.

Genders

Most ports and the cables that connect to them have genders. For example, most computer ports are jacks, into which you plug in the matching cable. The computer's jacks are most often the female connectors and the cable's plug is most often the male connector. You can always look directly at the innermost electrical connections on the connectors to determine the gender. The one with the protruding pins is the male and the one with the holes to accept the pins is the female.

Port Shapes

Ports can have different physical shapes such as round, rectangular, square, and oblong. There is some standardization of physical properties and functions, though. Most connectors are keyed in some way to restrict connecting devices into the wrong port.

PS/2 Ports

The round 6-pin port, also referred to as a mini-Din connector or PS/2 port, is an interface located on the motherboard. The Din-6 port is the larger 13.2 mm port. Many keyboards and mice use PS/2 ports to connect to the motherboard. To avoid confusion between the identical-looking keyboard and mouse ports, PS/2 ports are often color-coded to match the end of the cable on the device: purple for the keyboard and green for the mouse. Or, there may be a sticker with a picture of a mouse and keyboard near the connectors.

Computer Connections

Computer connections are the physical access points that enable a computer to communicate with internal or external devices. They include the ports on both the computer and the connected devices, plus a transmission medium, which is either a cable with connectors at each end or a wireless technology. Personal computer connections can be categorized by the technology or standard that was used to develop the device.

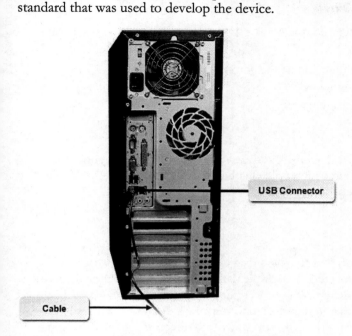

Figure 1-14: A personal computer connection.

Serial Connections

A *serial connection* is a personal computer connection that transfers data one bit at a time over a single wire. Serial connections support two-way communications and were typically used for devices such as fax cards or external modems. These legacy serial ports have either 9-pin (DB-9) or 25-pin (DB-25) male connectors. A legacy serial cable ends with a female connector to plug into the male connector on the system unit. On system units that have color-coded ports, the serial port is teal-colored. Serial connections that are seen today are used to attach printers, scientific devices such as telescopes, networking hardware such as routers and switches, and industrial products. In most cases, these devices will need to be connected using a USB adapter.

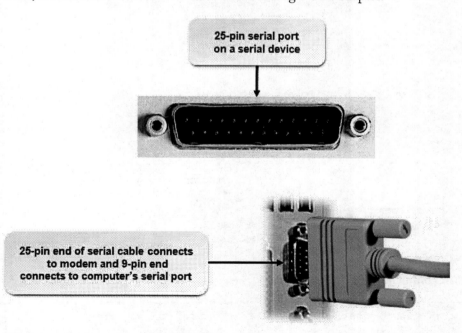

Figure 1-15: A serial connection.

Serial Transmissions

In a serial transmission, data is sent and received one bit at a time over a single wire. To accomplish this, the serial communication process:

1. Disassembles bytes into bits on the sending end of the communication.
2. Sends the bits across the communication wires.
3. Reassembles the bits into bytes at the receiving end.

Serial Port Naming

Serial ports are typically called COM1, COM2, COM3, and COM4, where "COM" is short for communications port. This port has been almost completely phased out in favor of USB. You'll probably find many systems with no serial ports at all.

Parallel Connections

A *parallel connection* is a computer connection that transfers data eight or more bits at a time over eight or more wires. Any components connected by multiple data pathways may be considered to have a parallel connection, but the term is generally used to refer to a standard legacy parallel port that uses eight data wires, and is typically used to connect a printer to a system unit. Parallel connections in older personal computers support only one-way or unidirectional communications. Newer computers have parallel ports that support bidirectional communications. Standard parallel ports have 25-pin female connectors. A parallel cable has a 25-pin male connector to plug into the system unit and a 36-pin male Centronics connector at the other end to attach to the external device. On system units that have color-coded ports, the parallel port is burgundy or dark pink.

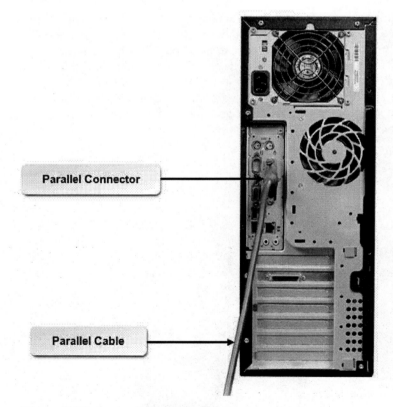

Figure 1–16: A parallel connection.

 Note: The standard parallel port has been phased out in favor of USB, so you may find many systems with no parallel ports at all.

FDD Connections

Internal FDDs have two primary connections: the power connection and the data connection. The data connection is a parallel connection. The FDD cable is a 34-pin flat ribbon cable with a twist, which is used to differentiate between multiple FDDs in a system.

USB Connections

A *universal serial bus (USB) connection* is a computer connection that enables you to connect multiple peripherals to a single port with high performance and minimal device configuration. USB connections support two-way communications. All modern PC systems today have multiple USB ports and can, with the use of USB hubs, support up to 127 devices per port. USB cables may have different connectors at each end. The computer end of the cable ends in a Type A connector. The device end of the cable commonly ends in a Type B connector, or may also end in a Mini-A, Mini-B, Micro-AB, or Micro-B connector. The mini connectors are typically used for portable devices such as smartphones. The size of the connector varies depending on the device. USB connections transfer data serially, but at a much faster throughput than legacy serial connections. USB devices also incorporate Plug-and-Play technology that allows devices to self-configure as soon as a connection is made.

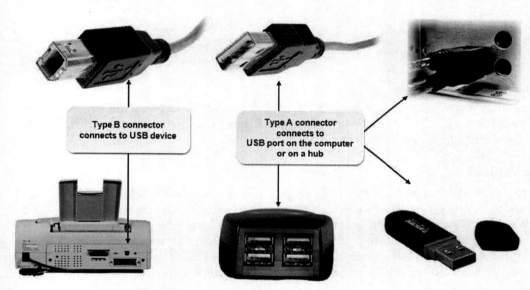

Type B connector connects to USB device

Type A connector connects to USB port on the computer or on a hub

Figure 1–17: USB connections.

USB Standards

USB 2.0, released in April 2000, is the most commonly implemented standard. It can communicate at up to 480 Mbps. The original USB 1.1 standard is still commonly found in devices and systems. It can communicate at up to 12 Mbps. A USB 2.0 device connected to a USB 1.1 hub or port will communicate at only USB 1.1 speeds, even though it might be capable of faster speeds. Generally, the operating system will inform you of this when you connect the device.

USB 3.0, also called SuperSpeed USB, is the latest USB standard released in November 2008. It features a maximum transfer rate of 5.0 Gbps. It is 10 times faster than the USB 2.0 standard, has enhanced power efficiency, and is backward compatible with USB-enabled devices currently in use.

USB cables have a maximum distance before performance suffers. To work around this, one or more hubs can be used to create a "chain" to reach the necessary cable length. USB 1.1 has a maximum cable length of 3 meters, while USB 2.0's maximum length is 5 meters. In each case, a maximum of five hubs can be used to extend the cable length. The maximum cable length is not specified in the USB 3.0 specification.

IEEE 1394 and FireWire Connections

A *FireWire connection* is a computer connection that provides a high-speed interface for peripheral devices that are designed to use the *Institute of Electrical and Electronic Engineers (IEEE)* 1394 standard. FireWire can support up to 63 devices on one FireWire port. FireWire 400 transmits at 400 Mbps and uses either a 6-pin, bullet-shaped, powered connector or a 4-pin square-shaped, unpowered, connector. FireWire 800 transmits at 800 Mbps and uses a 9-pin connector.

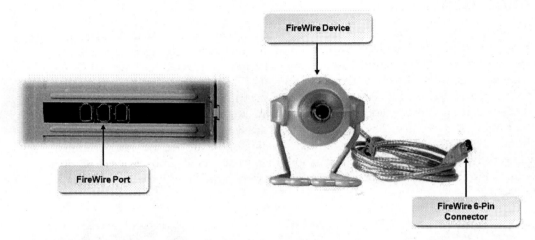

Figure 1–18: A FireWire connection.

FireWire Terminology

Apple® was the primary vendor to promote the IEEE 1394 Standard, and used the FireWire name as a trademark for the IEEE 1394 implementation included in its Macintosh® systems. FireWire has since become the common name for all IEEE 1394 devices.

FireWire vs. USB

FireWire predated USB and was faster than the original USB 1.1 standard. USB 2.0, with its increased speed, largely superseded FireWire. However, although USB 2.0 is faster by the numbers than FireWire, FireWire is actually faster on throughput, making it ideal for video/audio file transfers and external storage devices. A file transfer of 100 separate documents might be slightly faster on USB than FireWire, but a file transfer of a single 2 GB video file will be much faster in FireWire. Also, while USB provides a device up to 5 V power, FireWire provides up to 12 V power on the wire.

With the release of USB 3.0 and the latest FireWire S3200, the performance will still vary. USB 3.0 is 10 times faster than USB 2.0, and will remain the popular standard used for most devices. The FireWire S3200 standard, however, still has considerable advantages over USB. For example, FireWire uses much less CPU power, and provides more power over a single cable connection.

Similar to USB, FireWire has maximum distance restrictions. However, FireWire's distances are greater than USB's. A FireWire "chain," created with cables and repeaters, can reach up to 237 feet from device to host, while USB 2.0 can reach 30 meters (just under 100 feet).

SCSI Connections

SCSI, pronounced "scuzzy," is an older connection standard, typically used for storage devices such as tape and hard drives, that remains in use due to its reliability and high speed. A SCSI adapter has a port for external devices and a connection for internal devices. SCSI devices themselves can have multiple ports, enabling you to connect up to seven devices in a chain to one SCSI adapter. Each device in the chain requires a unique ID, which you configure by using switches or jumpers. SCSI cables have 25-pin, 50-pin, 68-pin, or 80-pin connectors, depending upon the type of SCSI in use.

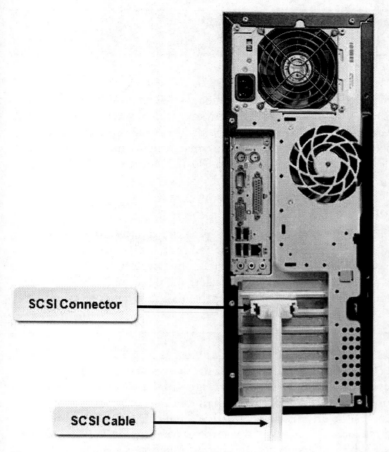

SCSI Connector

SCSI Cable

Figure 1-19: A SCSI connection.

PATA Connections

A PATA connection is a drive connection standard that provides a parallel data channel from the drive controller to the disk drives. Originally called ATA, IDE, EIDE, or UDMA, PATA connections are used to connect internal hard drives, optical drives, and tape drives to the system board. On the system board, two sockets provide connections for up to two drives per socket. PATA cables are ribbon cables with 40 or 80 wires and 40-pin connectors.

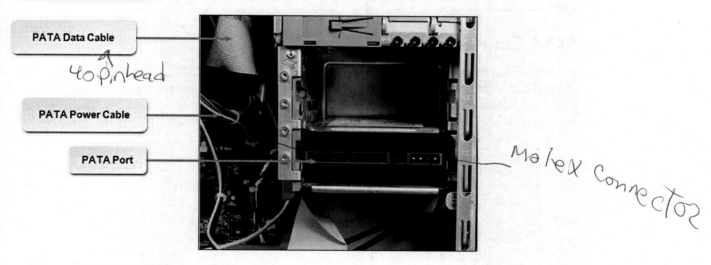

PATA Data Cable

40 pinhead

PATA Power Cable

PATA Port

Molex connector

Figure 1-20: A PATA connection.

Note: You might hear PATA pronounced "Parallel ay-tee-ay," "PEE-ay-tee-ay," "PAY-tuh," or "PAT-uh."

ATA, IDE, EIDE, and UDMA

IDE, EIDE, and UDMA are alternative names for the ATA standards that are now referred to as PATA. (After Serial ATA drives became popular, the PATA term was coined to refer to the parallel drives.) There have been several versions of the ATA standard, with successive versions providing support for different types of devices, or providing performance enhancements such as higher data rates. For example, ATAPI provides support for tape drives and CD-ROM drives, while ATA-7 supports data rates up to 133 Mbps.

Master and Slave Designations

PATA drives are configured in a master/slave hierarchy, usually by setting jumpers. Each PATA channel can support one or two devices. Because each PATA device contains its own integrated controller, you need to have some way of differentiating between the two devices. This is done by giving each device a designation as either master or slave, or by using the Cable Select (CS) feature to assign master and slave designations, and then having the controller address commands and data to either one or the other.

Scheme	Description
Master/slave	In the master/slave configuration scheme, the drive that is the target of the command responds to it, and the other one ignores the command, remaining silent. Each manufacturer uses a different combination of jumpers for specifying whether its drive is master or slave on the channel, though they are all similar. Some manufacturers put this information right on the top label of the drive itself, while others do not. Jumper information is available in the hard disk's documentation, or by checking the manufacturer's website and searching for the model number.
CS	With CS, you do not have to set jumpers to designate which device is master and which is slave. The connectors that are connected to the devices take care of the configuration. To set up CS, you need to use a jumper to set both devices on the channel to the CS setting, along with a special cable. This cable is similar in most respects to the regular PATA cable, except for the Cable SELect (CSEL) signal, which the devices use to determine which is the master and which is the slave.

SATA Connections

A SATA connection is a drive connection standard that enhances PATA by providing a serial data channel between the drive controller and the disk drives. SATA transfer speeds are much higher than PATA for the same drive technologies. SATA's physical installation is also easier because the SATA power and data cables are much smaller, thinner, and more flexible than traditional PATA ribbon cables. SATA connectors have seven pins.

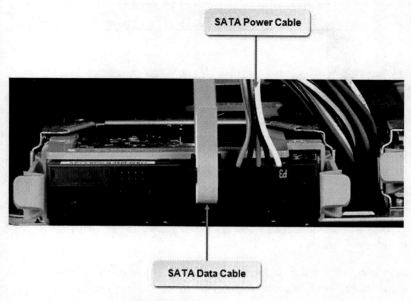

Figure 1-21: A SATA connection.

Note: You might hear SATA pronounced "Serial ay-tee-ay," "ESS-ay-tee-ay," "SAY-tuh," or "SAT-uh."

Note: Although current practice is to use the terms "IDE" and "PATA" interchangeably, you should be aware that SATA is also a type of IDE drive, but with a different interface.

eSATA

External SATA (eSATA) is an external interface for SATA connections. Like USB and FireWire, it provides a connection for external storage devices. eSATA connections provide fast data transfers without having to translate data between the device and the host computer. eSATA interfaces do require an additional power connector to function. You can provide eSATA functionality by installing eSATA cards in systems.

Display Cable and Connector Types

Display devices can use several different types of cables.

Cable Type	Description
Video Graphics Array (VGA)	The *DB-15* high-density VGA connector is the most common cable used for LCD monitors. It contains three rows of five pins. Pins 4, 11, 12, and 15 receive information from the device, while pins 1, 2, 3, 13, and 14 send information to the display.

Cable Type	Description

Mini-VGA is used on smaller devices, such as laptops, in place of the standard full-sized cables.

Digital Video Interface (DVI)

DVI cables keep data in digital form from the computer to the display. There is no need to convert data from digital information to analog information. LCD monitors work in a digital mode and support the DVI format.

- DVI-analog (DVI-A) is an analog-only format. It requires a DVI-A supported interface. The connector does not support dual link technology. It is commonly used to connect CRT or VGA devices to a computer using a DVI-A adapter.
- DVI-digital (DVI-D) is a digital-only format. It requires a video adapter with a DVI-D connection and a monitor with a DVI-D interface. The connector contains 24 pins/receptacles in three rows of eight above or below a flat blade, plus a grounding slot for dual-link support. For single-link support, the connector contains 18 pins/receptacles.
- DVI-integrated (DVI-I) supports both digital and analog transmissions. This gives you the option to connect a monitor that accepts digital input or analog input. In addition to the pins/receptacles found on the DVI-D connector for digital support, a DVI-I connector has four additional pins/receptacles to carry an analog signal. For single-link support, the connector contains 18 pins/receptacles, and four additional pins for analog transmissions.

High Definition Multimedia Interface (HDMI)

HDMI is the first industry-supported uncompressed, all-digital audio/video interface. HDMI uses a single cable composed of copper wires to provide an interface between any audio/video source, such as a set-top box, DVD player, or A/V receiver and an audio and/or video monitor, such as a digital television (DTV). The connector is made up of 19 pins and can support a number of modes such as High Definition TV (HDTV), Standard Definition TV (SDTV), and Enhanced Digital TV (EDTV) can run to 50 feet or more in length.

HDMI has largely superseded DVI and is compatible with the DVI standard. It can be used with PC systems that support DVI.

Cable Type	Description

Mini-High Definition Multimedia Interface (Mini-HDMI)

Mini-HDMI is similar to the full size HDMI connector, except that it is specified for use with portable devices. The connector is a smaller version of the full size with same number of pins. The difference between the full size and the mini is that some of pins have different transmission functions.

Separate Video (S-Video)

S-Video is an analog video signal that carries the video data as two separate signals (brightness and color). S-Video works in 480i or 576i resolution.

 Note: Video resolution is sometimes noted in the format shown here, particularly when television signals are being discussed. A resolution of 480i indicates a vertical frame resolution of 480 interlaced lines that contain picture information, while a resolution of 576i indicates a vertical frame resolution of 576 interlaced lines that contain picture information.

Component/RGB

Component video is a type of analog video information that is transmitted or stored as two or more separate signals. Analog video signals (also called components) must provide information about the amount of red, green, and blue to create an image. The simplest type, RGB, consists of three discrete red, green, and blue signals sent down three coaxial cables.

Cable Type	Description

Composite video

Composite video is the format of an analog (picture only) signal before it is combined with a sound signal and modulated onto a radio frequency (RF) carrier.

Coaxial

A coaxial cable, or coax, is a type of copper cable that features a central conducting copper core surrounded by an insulator and braided or foil shielding. An insulator separates the conductor and shield, and the entire package is wrapped in an insulating layer called a jacket. The data signal is transmitted over the central conductor. The outer shielding serves to reduce electromagnetic interference.

DisplayPort

DisplayPort is a digital display standard that aims to replace DVI and VGA standards. DisplayPort is not backward compatible with DVI and HDMI and is a royalty-free standard. However, by using special dual-mode ports and suitable adapters, it may be possible to use DVI and HDMI signals with DisplayPort. Similar to Peripheral Component Interconnect Express (PCIe), DisplayPort also supports high-quality gaming and other applications that use high-end graphics.

Cable Type	Description
Radio Corporation of America (RCA)	RCA cables and connectors are used to carry audio and video transmissions to and from a variety devices such as TVs, digital cameras, and gaming systems. In some cases, the RCA cable may also be used as a power cable, a loud speaker cable, and to carry digital audio. The female jacks on the devices are colored to provide a guide as to what type of connector can be attached. Common colors found are: <ul><li>Yellow for various composite connections.</li><li>Red for the right channel of the audio transmission.</li><li>White or black for the left channel of audio transmission.</li></ul> 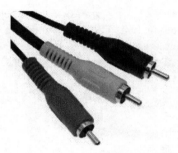
Bayonet Neill-Concelman (BNC)	The BNC connector is used with coaxial cable to carry radio frequencies to and from devices. The BNC cable can be used to connect radio equipment, aviation electronics, and to carry video signals. The actual BNC connectors come in two versions. The connector will be either 50 or 75 ohms, depending on the specific cable that is attached. 

Ethernet and Displays

Some display devices such as the Apple Thunderbolt display include an Ethernet port for connection directly to a network.

DVI Single Link vs. Dual Link

DVI cables use a technology called Transition Minimized Differential Signaling (TMDS) to transmit serial data over a high-speed connection. Single link cables use a single TMDS transmitter to carry data, while double-link uses two. Therefore, dual link cables can transmit larger images at higher speeds than single link.

Audio/Video Connections

There are a number of audio/video connectors that are used to connect a wide variety of devices, including PCs, DVD and Blu-ray players, surround sound systems, stereo equipment, projectors, and HDTVs. In addition to HDMI and DVI, common audio/video cable and connectors include those described in the following table.

Type	Description
Single-core/shielded cable	The single core wire is the positive, and the shield is the negative. This type of cable is used for unbalanced audio signals. Generally, unbalanced audio cables are short, because noise is less of an issue. 
One pair/shielded cable	Uses a pair (white and red) of cores with one wire being the positive, and the other wire being the negative. The shield acts as a ground. This type of cable is used for balanced audio signals. Balanced audio is a method for minimizing noise and interference in audio cables. 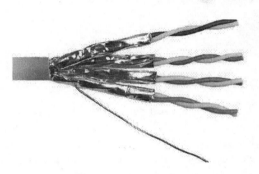
TS and TRS connectors	The most common connectors used in for unbalanced audio cables are the 1/4-inch tip-sleeve (TS) or tip-ring-sleeve (TRS) and RCA connectors, which are typically used with high-end audio equipment. The 1/8-inch tip-sleeve is typically used with smaller audio devices such as Apple® iPods®. TS and TRS connectors are also referred to as phone jacks, phone plugs, audio jacks, and jack plugs. Traditionally, TS connectors are used for mono, while TRS connectors are used for stereo. Some connectors can carry more signals; these are often used with camcorder, laptops, and other devices. Stereo connectors can also carry a single, balanced signal. Wiring configurations for TRS connectors include: • For unbalanced mono, the tip carries the signal, the ring is not connected, and the sleeve acts as ground. • For balanced mono, the tip is positive, the ring is negative, and the sleeve acts as ground. • For stereo, the tip carries the left channel, the ring carries the right channel, and the sleeve acts as ground. 

Type	Description
3-pin XLR connectors	The standard connector for balanced audio is the 3-pin XLR. The most common wiring configuration is: • Pin 1: Shield (ground) • Pin 2: Positive (hot) • Pin 3: Negative (cold)

Analog vs. Digital Video

Analog transmissions carry information in the form of a continuous wave. Analog signals are most often generated by electrical current, the intensity of which is measured in volts. An analog signal oscillates over time between maximum and minimum values and can take on any value between those limits. The size, shape, and other characteristics of that *waveform* describe the analog signal and the information it carries. *Digital transmissions*, unlike analog transmissions, which can have many possible values, hold just two values—ones and zeroes. These values represent an on and off state, respectively. Digital data, which is a sequence of ones and zeroes, can be translated into a digital waveform. In computer systems and other digital devices, a waveform switches between two voltage levels representing 0 and 1.

VGA vs. HDMI

VGA and HDMI are inherently different because one is analog (VGA) and the other is digital (HDMI). Many home theater environments will use one or the other, or in some cases both, if an adapter is applied. Traditional VGA has a maximum resolution of 800 by 600 pixels and Super VGA (SVGA) has a resolution up to 2,048 by 1,536 pixels or more, while the latest version of HDMI 4.1 has the capability of carrying a resolution up to 4,196 by 2,160 pixels.

Wireless Device Connections

Wireless is rapidly becoming the primary connection method for connecting a wide variety of computer components, as well as for connecting computing devices to each other. There are a number of connection methods you can use to accomplish this.

Connection Method	Description
Radio frequency (RF)	*Radio networking* is a form of wireless communication in which signals are sent via RF waves, in the 10 KHz to 1 GHz range, to wireless antennas. An antenna transmits by converting electrical energy into an RF wave. When an antenna receives a transmission, it converts the RF wave into electrical energy.

Connection Method	Description
	In wireless communication, low-frequency data or voice signals are transmitted through high-frequency radio waves by superimposing data on them.
Bluetooth	Bluetooth® is a wireless technology that facilitates short-range wireless communication between devices, such as personal computers and some of their components, laptops and some of their components, mobile phones, and gaming consoles and other gaming peripherals. Both voice and data information are exchanged among these devices at 2.4 GHz within a range of approximately 30 feet. A maximum of eight Bluetooth devices can be connected to each other at a time; this connection of two to eight Bluetooth-enabled devices is known as a *piconet*. Bluetooth devices operate at very low power levels of approximately 1 milliwatt (mW).
	Bluetooth is predominantly used in wireless personal area networks to transfer information between two computers or other devices. It is also used in mobile headsets for communicating with mobile phones. Computer peripherals such as the mouse, keyboard, and printer can also use Bluetooth for communication. Bluetooth-enabled devices such as gaming consoles and global positioning system (GPS) receivers are also popular.
Infrared (IR)	IR transmission is a form of wireless transmission in which signals are sent via pulses of infrared light. IR is generally used for short-range transmission, because receivers need an unobstructed view of the sender to successfully receive the signal, though the signal can reflect off hard surfaces to reach the recipient. Typically, IR communication takes place in the near-infrared frequency range that is in the visible region of the spectrum. Therefore, in some instances, wireless IR communication is also referred to as wireless optical communication.
	IR uses electromagnetic waves with frequencies ranging from 300 GHz to 400 THz. Their wavelengths range from approximately 1 mm to 750 nm. IR waves are classified into sub-bands called far-infrared, mid-infrared, and near-infrared. The near-infrared frequencies are visible to the human eye as red or violet light, while the far-I frequencies are not visible to the human eye but are radiated in the form of heat.
	IR technology is used in several ways in the computing and telecommunication fields. The primary application is to provide network connectivity in wireless personal area networks. IR devices facilitate short-term wireless connections between two computers or between a computer and a wireless handheld device such as a mobile phone. An IR-powered network can also be used as an extension network for a local area network where installing cable may be difficult. Wireless devices such as wireless mice, keyboards, television remote controls, and game controllers also use *IR waves* for their operation.

Allocation of the RF Spectrum

The RF spectrum is classified based on the frequency range.

Frequency Range	Name
3 Hz–30 Hz	Extremely Low Frequency (ELF)
30 Hz–300 Hz	Super Low Frequency (SLF)
300 HZ–3KHz	Ultra Low Frequency (ULF)

Frequency Range	Name
3 KHz–30 KHz	Very Low Frequency (VLF)
30 KHz–300 KHz	Low Frequency (LF)
300 KHz–3000 KHz	Medium Frequency (MF)
3 MHz–30 MHz	High Frequency (HF)
30 MHz–300 MHz	Very High Frequency (VHF)
300 MHz–3000 MHz	Ultra High Frequency (UHF)
3 GHz–30 GHz	Super High Frequency (SHF)
30 GHZ–300 GHz	Extremely High Frequency (EHF)

ACTIVITY 1–3
Identifying Device Connections and Interfaces

Scenario

In this activity, you will identify device connections and interfaces.

1. Your instructor might provide you with examples of device connections and interfaces and ask you or other participants to identify them.

2. Examine the following graphic and identify the ports.

   Identify the ports shown in the graphic. Use labels such as audio port, parallel port, PS/2 port, serial port, and USB port.

3. Which connection type supports up to 127 peripherals for a single connection?
   - ○ IEEE 1394
   - ○ SATA
   - ○ Parallel
   - ○ USB

4. Which type of connection features small, thin data and power cables?
   - ○ SCSI
   - ○ PATA
   - ○ SATA
   - ○ Parallel

5. Which connection type transfers data eight or more bits at a time over eight or more wires?
   - ○ Serial connection
   - ○ Parallel connection
   - ○ USB connection
   - ○ FireWire connection

6. Which connection type connects a series of internal hard drives in a master/slave configuration?
   - ○ Parallel connection
   - ○ USB connection
   - ○ SCSI
   - ○ PATA

7. Which connection type is associated with the IEEE 1394 Standard?
   - ○ USB connection
   - ○ FireWire connection
   - ○ SCSI connection
   - ○ Serial connection

Summary

In this lesson, you identified the components that make up most computers. The ability to identify the various parts of computers is essential foundational knowledge for every computer technician.

How many of the personal computer components described are familiar to you?

Which of the device connections discussed were familiar to you? Which were new?

 Note: Check your LogicalCHOICE Course screen for opportunities to interact with your classmates, peers, and the larger LogicalCHOICE online community about the topics covered in this course or other topics you are interested in. From the Course screen you can also access available resources for a more continuous learning experience.

2 Operating System Fundamentals

Lesson Time: 2 hours, 50 minutes

Lesson Objectives

In this lesson, you will identify the basic components and functions of an operating system. You will:

- Identify the most common personal computer operating systems.
- Identify the utilities that you can access via the Windows Control Panel.
- Identify command line tools and how they function.
- Identify Windows security settings.
- Identify Windows operating system tools.

Lesson Introduction

In the previous lesson, you identified the hardware components of standard desktop personal computers. The other major element of a personal computer is the operating system, which is the software that provides the user interface and enables you to access and use the hardware components. In this lesson, you will identify the basic components and functions of an operating system.

As a professional IT support representative or PC service technician, your job will include installing, configuring, maintaining, and troubleshooting personal computer operating systems. Before you can perform any of these tasks, you need to understand the basics of what an operating system is, including the various versions, features, components, and technical capabilities. With this knowledge, you can provide effective support for all types of system environments.

This lesson covers all or part of the following CompTIA® A+® (2012) certification objectives:

- Topic A:
  - Exam 220-802: Objective 1.1
- Topic B:
  - Exam 220-802: Objectives 1.1, 1.5

- Topic C:
  - Exam 220-802: Objectives 1.1, 1.3
- Topic D:
  - Exam 220-802: Objectives 1.2, 1.8, 2.3.
- Topic E:
  - Exam 220-802: Objectives 1.1, 1.4

TOPIC A

Personal Computer Operating Systems

In this lesson, you will identify the basic components and functions of personal computer operating systems. The first step is to learn about the various operating systems available today, and to identify those that are commonly used on personal computers. In this topic, you will identify the most common personal computer operating systems.

Aside from hardware, the operating system is the next most important piece of the personal computer system. Without a user-friendly operating system, most people would not be capable of using their computers to successfully perform the tasks required of them. As an IT professional, being familiar with the different types of operating systems that can be installed on personal computers can help you to support a variety of computer environments.

This topic covers all or part of the following CompTIA® A+® (2012) certification objectives:

*   Exam 220-802, Objective 1.1: Compare and contrast the features and requirements of various Microsoft Operating Systems.

Microsoft Windows

Microsoft® Windows® is the single most popular and widely deployed operating system on both desktop computers and server systems in the world today. The various versions of Windows all feature a graphical user interface (GUI), support for a wide range of applications and devices, a minimum of 32-bit processing, native networking support, and a large suite of built-in applications and accessories such as the Internet Explorer® browser. Windows currently comes pre-installed on many personal computers sold commercially.

There have been several versions of Windows since its inception. The three most current versions are often deployed on personal and professional computers.

*   Windows® 7, the latest in the Microsoft product line covered in the CompTIA® A+® objectives, was released in 2009. Windows 7 returned to the overall look and feel found in Windows® XP in response to the criticism of Windows Vista®'s interface. Rather than introduce a multitude of new features like Vista, 7 instead offered many critical upgrades to the system, including application and hardware compatibility, performance improvements, and a redesigned shell.
*   Windows Vista was released in 2007 and included many new features, the most noticeable change being to the user interface. While it offered many upgrades to the system, specifically to security features, many were critical of the redesigned interface.
*   Windows XP was released in 2001, and was available in both Home and Professional editions. It was highly praised as a consumer-friendly and highly usable operating system (OS) for personal use, not just for those in the professional environment. Windows XP is often still found on both home computers and in enterprise implementations; however, Microsoft no longer provides active product support for Windows XP.

 Note: Microsoft announced the latest version of Windows, Windows® 8, in 2012.

Older Windows Versions

There are other versions of Windows that are now unsupported and outdated. It is possible (but unlikely) that you will encounter some of these in a legacy implementation.

Version	Description
Windows 2000	Windows® 2000 was a prior version of Microsoft's enterprise operating system software. It was available in several Server editions as well as in a desktop version, Windows 2000 Professional. The Server version was the first to include Microsoft's standards-based directory service software, Active Directory®. Microsoft no longer provides active product support for Windows 2000 Server or Professional.
Windows 9x and Windows Me	Prior to Windows XP, the Windows® 9x group of operating systems were Microsoft's primary products for end-user and home PCs. They were complete operating systems with built-in networking, but they used a different code base and a different graphical interface design from the Windows Server® computers available at that time, as well as from the later Windows XP operating system family. This group of operating systems is no longer supported.

• Windows® 95 was Microsoft's first release of a complete graphical desktop operating system, as opposed to a system shell for lower-level system software. It was the first to provide a graphical interface based around the **Start** menu and taskbar.
• Windows® 98 was a popular and widely adopted version within the Windows 9x product line. An updated version was also released as Windows 98 SE (Second Edition).
• Windows® Me (Millennium Edition) was the final release in the Windows 9x code base family. It was released in 2000.

Windows NT	There were several prior versions of Windows Server software, all released under the Windows NT® brand. They employed the Windows 3.1 graphical interface (though NT 4.0 used the Windows 95 GUI) and implemented network domain configurations on a proprietary Microsoft model.

• Windows NT 3.1 Advanced Server and its client version, Windows NT 3.1, were the first 32-bit versions of Windows. They were released in 1993.
• Windows NT 3.5x and its client version, Windows NT Workstation 3.5x, were the first Windows versions considered to be robust enough for enterprise network support. They were released in 1995.
• Windows NT 4.0 and its client version, Windows NT Workstation 4.0, were the first versions to use Transmission Control Protocol/ Internet Protocol (TCP/IP) as the preferred protocol. They were released in 1996.

Older versions of Windows	The first Windows desktop operating systems released were shell programs that were designed to run on top of a DOS command-line-based operating system. They extended DOS by providing a graphical interface, extended memory support, mouse support, and the ability to have multiple programs open at once.

• Windows 1.0 (released in 1985) and Windows 2.0 (released in 1987) were earlier releases but were not very popular.
• Windows 3.0 was the first commercially successful version of Windows. It was released in 1990.
• Windows 3.1 was the primary end-user desktop version of Windows until the advent of Windows 95. It was released in 1992.

Version	Description
	• Windows for Workgroups was an extension of Windows 3.1 that incorporated workgroup networking support using the NetBEUI protocol. It was released in 1992.

Older Windows Server Editions

Windows is also available in various editions indexed specifically for user on server computers.

Version	Description
Windows Small Business Server 2011	Windows Small Business Server® 2011, Microsoft's network solution designed for small businesses, is available in two editions: • Small Business Server 2011 Standard, an all-in-one network solution that provides enterprise-level server features such as email, file and printer sharing, daily backups, remote access, and Internet connections, but for a small business with up to 75 employees. • Small Business Server 2011 Essentials, a network solution that uses the cloud to provide access and protection to business data, email, resources, and tools for very small businesses with up to 25 employees. Small Business Server 2011 Premium Add-on, an add-on for Small Business Server 2011 allows small businesses to deploy additional servers on the network.
Windows Server 2008	Windows Server 2008, Microsoft's current server-oriented operating system, is currently available as Release 2 (R2) and is available in several different editions: • Server 2008 Foundation, an affordable small-business platform for file and print sharing, remote access, security, and clean upgrade paths. • Server 2008 Datacenter, a highly scalable platform for large-scale virtualization. • Server 2008 Enterprise, optimized for applications, clustering, and identity management. • Server 2008 Standard, with enhanced security options, virtualization capabilities, and the ability to streamline management. • Web Server 2008, integrated with ASP.NET and the .NET Framework. • HPC Server 2008, which stands for High-Performance Computing, is able to scale to thousands of cores, and can be easily integrated with non-Microsoft HPC servers. • Server 2008 for Itanium®-based Systems, for large databases. Itanium is the name of a processor available from Intel®.
Windows Server 2003	Windows Server® 2003 was last updated with the R2 release in 2005. Windows Server 2003 R2 comes in several editions: • Windows Server 2003 R2 Standard Edition, for general purpose use as a file server or service host, or to support the needs of small and medium businesses. • Windows Server 2003 R2 Enterprise Edition, optimized to support enterprise network management for large numbers of users, computers, and services.

Version	Description
	• Windows Server 2003 R2 Datacenter Edition, for high-availability applications and databases.

Microsoft Retirement Schedules

To find out when Microsoft products will be retired or how long specific products will be supported, visit the Microsoft Product Lifecycle Search tool at **http://support.microsoft.com/lifecycle/search/**.

Microsoft Windows Features

Windows includes a number of features that distinguish it from other operating systems. Each version of Windows includes a unique combination of many of these features.

 Note: Other features of the Windows operating system will be covered in more detail throughout this course.

Feature	Description
Aero	Windows *Aero®* is a color scheme available in Windows Vista and Windows 7. Windows Aero provides a visually rich experience with its glossy and transparent interface. It also provides dynamic visual and animation effects such as Live Preview of taskbar buttons and a Flip 3D view of open windows. You can choose a color scheme from one of the predefined color schemes available in Windows Aero, or you can create a custom color scheme using the color mixer. Each color has a default transparency level that you can change for both predefined and custom color schemes.
Gadgets	The Desktop Gadget Gallery is a Windows 7 feature that displays different *gadgets,* which are mini applications that can perform many different information-display tasks, including displaying the date and time, central processing unit (CPU) usage, stock information, and user-selected news headlines. If a gadget for a particular need is not available from Microsoft or from a third-party developer, users can create their own. Available gadgets are stored in the Gadget Gallery, which provides a link to download additional gadgets.
BitLocker	Windows *BitLocker®* is a security feature of Windows 7 and Windows Server® 2008. This security feature provides full disk-encryption protection for your operating system, as well as all the data stored on the operating system volume. BitLocker encrypts all data stored on the operating system volume and is configured by default to use a Trusted Platform Module. This feature ensures the protection of early startup components and locks any BitLocker-secured volumes in order to prevent access or tampering when the operating system is not running.
Shadow Copy	The *Shadow Copy* technology is available on Windows XP and newer versions. It creates backup copies or "snapshots" of the system's data and stores them locally or to an external location of the user's choosing. You can perform Shadow Copy operations manually, or you can set up automatic backups at scheduled intervals.
System restore	The *System Restore* utility is available in Windows XP, Windows Vista, and Windows 7. It monitors the system for changes to core system files, drivers, and the Registry. It automatically creates a *system restore point,* which is a snapshot of the system configuration at a given moment in time that contains information about any changes to system components. Restore points are stored on the computer's hard disk, and you can use them to restore system settings to an earlier state without affecting changes in user data since that time.

Feature	Description
ReadyBoost	*ReadyBoost*® is a performance enhancer that is available on Windows Vista and Windows 7 and that enables the user to supplement the computer's memory with an external storage device such as a flash drive.
Sidebar	The *Sidebar* is a designated area of the Windows Vista desktop that is displayed vertically along the side of the desktop. Users can add gadgets of their choice to appear in the Sidebar, in order to provide information and access to frequently used tools or programs.
Compatibility mode	Compatibility mode enables older programs or applications to run on a newer version of Windows. You can configure compatibility for specific applications or programs by using the **Properties** options for the applications. Windows 7 can accommodate legacy applications dating back through Windows 95.
XP mode	Windows *XP mode* is a download that is available for Windows 7 versions and that is designed to enable users running Windows 7 to access and use Windows XP-compatible software and programs directly on their desktops.
Defender	Windows *Defender* is the antispyware software that is included with Windows XP, Vista, and 7 installations. You can configure Defender to scan for malicious materials at scheduled intervals, automatically remove any spyware detected during a scan, or even alert you in real time if spyware installs or runs on the computer.
Category view vs. classic view	In Windows XP and later versions, you can configure the **Start** menu, **Control Panel,** and other interface elements by using two options: • Category view, which is the default setting, displays the options available divided into high-level categories. For instance, in category view, the **Control Panel** displays categories of options such as **Appearance and Themes** or **Performance and Maintenance.** • Classic view displays a more traditional view from earlier versions of Windows, in which all of the available options are displayed, either in a list or icon form.

[handwritten note: Windows 8 does not have XP Mode]

[handwritten note: To 20 pieces of malware]

32-Bit vs. 64-Bit

A 32-bit operating system supports applications that use data units up to 32 bits wide, but no larger. A 64-bit operating system can support applications that use data units up to 64 bits wide, making 64-bit operating systems backwards-compatible (in other words, they are able to support 32-bit programs). A 64-bit operating system requires a 64-bit processor and 64-bit software. A 64-bit processor uses memory more efficiently; since it can use more memory, it can increase the use of RAM and decrease the amount of time spent using the hard disk. A 32-bit processor cannot use more than 4 GB of physical memory, while 64-bit registers (which store memory addresses) can address up to 16 terabytes (TB) of physical memory. Except Windows 7 Starter, all other versions come in both 32-bit and 64-bit versions.

x86 and x64

x86 is the most common and successful instruction set architecture, which supports 32-bit processors. If something is referred to as x86, it supports 32-bit software, and it *might* support 64-bit software. To clarify things, the term "x86-64" (also written as "x64") explicitly refers to a 64-bit x86 architecture.

Running Windows Compatibility Mode

You can either run the **Program Compatibility** wizard to automate the process of running programs in compatibility mode (by selecting **Start→Control Panel→Programs→Run programs made for previous versions of Windows**) or you can manually change the compatibility settings for a specific program. You can do this by right-clicking a program's executable (.exe) file, selecting **Properties,** and changing the appropriate settings on the **Compatibility** tab.

Microsoft Windows 7 Versions

Windows 7 is available in several different editions.

Edition	Features and Requirements
Windows 7 Starter *for Netbooks*	Windows 7 Starter is a simple, basic edition with very few features and limited customization. Windows Aero and the majority of the visual styles included on the higher versions are not included in Starter. Unlike the other versions of Windows 7, it is only available in a 32-bit version.
Windows 7 Home Premium	Windows 7 Home Premium is a low-cost edition for beginners and home users. This edition offers basic OS functions such as Windows Explorer and Internet Explorer 8, and support for other productivity software.
Windows 7 Professional	Windows 7 Professional enables users to run programs in Windows XP mode, connect to domains, and back up data to a network location.
Windows 7 Enterprise	Windows 7 Enterprise is available for enterprise organizations that need large volumes of Windows licenses for employee use. Enterprise features include support for multiple languages through the Multilingual User Interface (MUI), BitLocker, and compatibility with UNIX applications that may be present in the corporate environment.
Windows 7 Ultimate	Windows 7 Ultimate offers the same features as Windows 7 Enterprise, but is available for individual licensing for personal home use.

Microsoft Windows Vista Versions

Windows Vista is available in several different editions.

Edition	Features and Requirements
Windows Vista Home Basic	Windows Vista Home Basic is a lower-budget OS for beginners and home users who do not require advanced multimedia capabilities and who do not require networking more advanced than a workgroup.
Windows Vista Home Premium	Windows Vista Home Premium adds a media center, High Definition TV (HDTV) support, backup scheduling, and more support for alternate displays. It also includes the Windows Aero interface.
Windows Vista Business	Windows Vista Business offers the same features as Vista Home Basic, plus additional business-focused features such as Remote Desktop, an encrypting files system, and the ability to join a Windows Server domain.
Windows Vista Enterprise	Windows Vista Enterprise adds features to the Vista Business edition, including UNIX application support, BitLocker, drive encryption, and multilingual user interfaces.
Windows Vista Ultimate	Windows Vista Ultimate combines all of the features of the other editions, plus additional features, with support for up to 128 GB of Random Access Memory (RAM) but only in 64-bit.

Microsoft Windows XP Versions

Windows XP is one of Microsoft's most popular operating systems for desktop and laptop computers for both home and office use. It comes in several distinct editions.

Edition	Features and Requirements
Windows XP Professional	Windows XP Professional, the flagship Windows XP edition, is intended for office use in networked environments. It supports individual file-level security and encryption, policy-based configuration management, and domain and workgroup membership.
Windows XP Home Edition	Windows XP Home Edition is intended for home users. Windows XP Home is very similar in look and feel to Windows XP Professional, but does not support some of the Windows XP Professional networking, security, and management features.
Windows XP Media Center Edition	Windows XP Media Center Edition is optimized for media-based activities such as recording live TV, organizing and playing music, and managing digital photographs.
Windows XP Professional x64 Edition	Windows XP Professional x64 Edition has all the functionality of XP Professional, but is specifically designed for computers with 64-bit processors. *Server 2003 w text Taken out*

Other Operating Systems

There are a number of other operating systems available.

OS	Description
OS X	*OS X®* is the operating system developed by Apple® Computing, Inc. OS X is a Linux® derivative, and consists of UNIX-based operating systems and GUIs. This proprietary operating system is included on all Macintosh® computer systems. OS X features include: • Multiple user support. • Integrated Mac, Windows, and UNIX server, file, and printer browsing in the Finder. • The Safari® web browser. • Native TCP/IP networking. • Many file- and network-level security features. • Comprehensive hardware device support with a unique Macintosh computer system design.
UNIX	*UNIX®* is a trademark for a family of operating systems originally developed at Bell Laboratories beginning in the late 1960s. All UNIX systems share a kernel/shell architecture, with the kernel providing the core functionality and the interchangeable shells providing the user interface. Unlike many operating systems, UNIX is portable to different hardware platforms; versions of UNIX can run on everything from personal computers to mainframes and on many types of computer processors. UNIX also incorporates built-in multitasking, multiuser support, networking functions, and a robust platform for software development.
Linux	*Linux* is an open-standards UNIX derivative originally developed and released by a Finnish computer science student named Linus Torvalds. The Linux source code was posted publicly on a computing newsgroup, and the code was developed and tested cooperatively all over the world. Because the source code is open, it can be downloaded, modified, and installed freely. However, many organizations prefer to purchase and implement a *Linux distribution*. A Linux distribution is a complete Linux implementation, including kernel, shell, applications, utilities, and installation media, that is packaged, distributed, and supported by a software vendor.

(handwritten margin notes next to UNIX row: -Oracle, -Solaris, -BSD, -obsD)

Note: With the release of the latest version of OS X (Mountain Lion) in 2012 and with the increased use of iOS for mobile devices, Apple officially dropped "Mac" from its operating system's name. It is now known simply as OS X, pronounced "OS 10."

UNIX Versions

Many different companies and organizations have licensed the UNIX name and technology and marketed their own UNIX versions, leading to a proliferation of different UNIX families, system names, and interfaces. Different hardware manufacturers tend to favor particular versions, or "flavors," of UNIX. The following table lists some of the most important UNIX categories you will encounter.

UNIX Version	Description
Berkeley Software Distribution (BSD) UNIX	Any of a group of UNIX versions that followed the innovations incorporated into UNIX at the University of California at Berkeley. Darwin is a newer version of BSD.
System V Release 4 (SVR4) UNIX	The standard for UNIX systems that follow the AT&T development architecture. It was issued to unify standards and features in competing versions of UNIX, including BSD UNIX, and it is the foundation for most current UNIX-based systems.
Portable Operating System for Computer Environments (POSIX)	A set of Institute of Electrical and Electronic Engineers (IEEE) standards for portability of applications from one UNIX environment to another. A POSIX-compliant application should run identically on any POSIX-compliant platform.
Single UNIX Specification (SUS)	A set of specifications issued by The Open Group (**www.opengroup.org**), setting software standards for operating systems that qualify for the name UNIX.
Advanced Interactive eXecutive (AIX)	Launched by IBM® and used on their mainframe computers. AIX is closed-source, proprietary UNIX that uses the Common Desktop Environment (CDE) as its GUI. Based on UNIX System V.
Sun Solaris/Oracle Solaris	A scalable OS developed by Sun Microsystems with native support for Sun's own Java® Desktop Environment (though other desktop environments work as well), as well as their StarOffice™ productivity suite. Solaris™ has been closed source for much of its history, but moved more toward open source in recent years. When Sun Microsystems was acquired by Oracle® Corporation, the name was changed to Oracle Solaris and the open-source effort was discontinued.
HP-UX	A flavor of UNIX developed by Hewlett-Packard. Like AIX, HP-UX is also based on UNIX System V. HP-UX is distributed in Operating Environments (OEs), which are pre-packaged collections of software that ship with the OS.

Linux Release Versions

The first version of the Linux kernel that was publicly released was version .02, released in 1991. Linux kernel version 3.4.4 was available as of June 2012. For more information about Linux and its versions, see the Linux home page at **www.linux.org**.

Popular Linux Distributions

The following table lists some popular Linux distributions.

Vendor	Description
Red Hat® Linux®	A popular United States distribution designed to be easy for new users to install and use. Red Hat officially supports Red Hat Enterprise Linux, while the more user-oriented operating system (called Fedora) is community-supported.
SUSE®	A popular European distribution, now owned by Novell®, Inc. SUSE is properly pronounced "ZOO-zuh," but is often pronounced to rhyme with Suzie.
Mandriva Linux	Formerly known as Mandrake, Mandriva is a popular desktop Linux distribution. Its unique features include simplified administration and an easy-to-use package manager for software installation.
Debian®	An option-rich free distribution assembled by volunteers that contains many utilities and supports many hardware platforms.
Gentoo Linux™	A source-code distribution designed for professional developers and computer hobbyists.
Ubuntu®	A popular community-developed operating system derived from the Debian distribution. Ubuntu works on laptops, desktops, and servers, and has supported variants appropriate for educational, multimedia, or mobile uses.
Arch Linux®	A pared-down, binary-based distribution aimed at experienced Linux users and maintained by a volunteer community of users.

Mac OS Versions

There have been several versions of the Macintosh operating system.

Version	Description
OS X Mountain Lion	The latest version of OS X, released in 2012, will continue to add many of the features being developed and deployed in the updates to Apple's iOS, the operating system for its consumer devices such as the iPod® and iPhone®. New features will include Game Center, an online social gaming network; support for the iMessage messaging application; and the debut of Notification Center, a desktop version of the application alert center already used in iOS.
OS X Lion	OS X Lion incorporated many of the enhancements developed for Apple iOS and incorporated them into the operating system. New features included the Launchpad™ for easier navigation of applications, auto-hiding scrollbars, auto-save for documents, and same-state restarts for closed applications.
OS X Snow Leopard	The update to OS X Leopard was mostly an "under the hood" update that increased the performance and functionality of the operating system and other related programs. Changes included increased disk space after cleanups, faster Time Machine® backups, an updated version of the Preview application, and an improved Safari browser.
OS X Leopard	Leopard added many new features, including Time Machine, which is an incremental backup utility. Leopard also enhances dozens of Mac features, including the Dashboard, iChat®, Finder®, and Safari.
OS X Tiger	A version of OS X that could run on both Intel and PowerPC processors. It featured various enhancements to OS X, including Spotlight® search technology.
OS X	The first Mac operating system to be developed as a UNIX derivative. It is based on an open-source UNIX implementation called Darwin and features a user interface called Exposé®.

Version	Description
Prior Mac OS® versions	Older versions of the Macintosh operating system were based on a proprietary system architecture and utilized the proprietary AppleTalk® file and print services and LocalTalk™ network topology. Security was based on user roles, including administrative user accounts, normal user accounts, limited user accounts, and panel user accounts.

ACTIVITY 2-1
Discussing Operating Systems

Before You Begin

Every computer in the physical classroom is assigned a unique computer name. Some steps in the activities refer to computer names such as **Admin##**, where **##** refers to a student's number. A student whose number is 01 should enter **Admin01** as the user name on his or her computer, a student whose number is 02 should enter **Admin02** as the user name, and so on. The password is *! Pass1234* and is the same for each user.

Scenario

In this activity, you will discuss various personal computer operating systems.

---

1. Start your computer and log on to Windows.
   a) If necessary, power on your computer.
   b) On the **Welcome Screen,** verify that the user name **Admin##** is displayed, and then in the **Password** text box, enter *!Pass1234*
   c) Verify that you are logged on to the operating system and that the desktop is displayed.

2. Examine the desktop.

   Which screen element indicates that the Aero interface is active?

3. **True or False? Windows XP includes the Windows Aero interface.**
   ☐ True
   ☐ False

4. **What is the Windows Sidebar?**
   ○ A designated area of the desktop where users can add gadgets of their choice to provide information and access to frequently used tools or programs.
   ○ A performance enhancer, available in Windows Vista and Windows 7, that allows the user to supplement the computer's memory with an external storage device like a flash drive.
   ○ A security feature that provides full disk encryption protection for your operating system as well as all the data stored on the operating system volume.
   ○ An application that displays information such as local weather data.

5. Look for help on the Windows Sidebar.
   a) Select **Start→Help and Support.**
   b) In the **Search Help** text box, enter *sidebar*
   c) Select **1. What happened to Windows Sidebar?**
   d) Read the help information, and then select **Desktop gadgets: frequently asked questions.**
   e) Select **How do I add and remove gadgets from my desktop?**
   f) Read the help information.

6. Add gadgets to the desktop.
   a) Display the desktop's shortcut menu.

b) Select **Gadgets.**

c) Double-click **Calendar** and **Clock** to add the gadgets to the desktop.

d) Close the Gadget Gallery and the Windows Help and Support window.
The gadgets remain displayed on the desktop after you close the open windows.

7. **True or False? Gadgets must be downloaded from the Microsoft Windows website, or they will not work properly.**

☐ True

☐ False

8. Search for help on the ReadyBoost feature, and review the help articles titled **Using memory in your storage device to speed up your computer** and **Turn ReadyBoost on or off for a storage device.** Then, close the Help and Support window.

Do you think that you or your users might take advantage of this performance-enhancing feature? Why or why not?

9. Find out what edition of Windows your computer is running.

a) Select **Start**, display the shortcut menu for **Computer**, and select **Properties**.

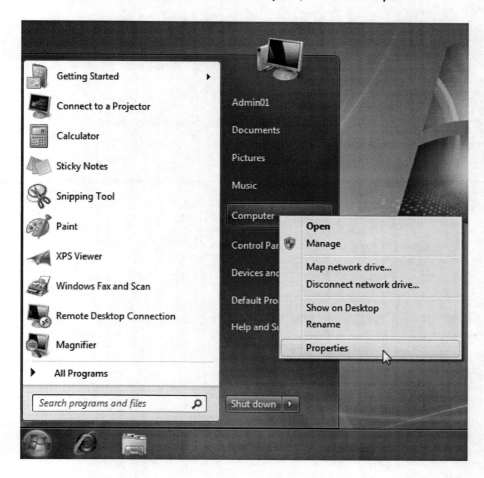

The **View basic information about your computer** window is displayed. The first section of this window provides information about the Windows edition running on your computer. This information can be helpful to IT professionals in determining whether a user issue is a true problem, or a misunderstanding of the capabilities of the operating system.

b) Close the window.

10. Which editions of Windows would be appropriate if you needed to add computers to a Windows domain?

☐ Windows Vista Home Basic

☐ Windows 7 Home Premium

☐ Windows 7 Professional

☐ Windows 7 Ultimate

11. Which statements about UNIX are true?

☐ There are many versions of UNIX from different developers and distributors.

☐ All versions of UNIX use the same shell, or user interface.

☐ UNIX versions are proprietary.

☐ UNIX is a multi-user, multi-tasking system.

☐ UNIX was developed using the open-source methodology.

12. Which statements about Linux are true?

☐ Linux was developed as open-source software.

☐ Developers must obtain permission to access and modify the source code.

☐ Development was initiated and managed by Linus Torvalds.

☐ Releases of Linux are unstable.

☐ Linux distributions can provide tools, utilities, and system support.

13. Which statements about Mac OS X are true?

☐ Mac OS X can be downloaded and modified freely.

☐ Mac OS X can integrate browsing for files created in other operating systems.

☐ Mac OS X provides many security features.

☐ Mac OS X can run the Windows XP user interface.

TOPIC B

Windows Control Panel Utilities

In the previous topic, you identified the major personal computer operating systems, including several versions of Microsoft Windows. To support these operating systems, you'll need to identify the elements of the system that make each Windows environment function, which are found in the **Control Panel**. In this topic, you will identify the utilities accessed via the **Control Panel**.

The Windows **Control Panel** provides centralized access to many of the elements of the Windows environment. As a professional support technician, knowing which utilities can be accessed through the **Control Panel** and what each utility does can help you to configure systems to meet users' needs, as well as assist users in configuring their systems.

This topic covers all or part of the following CompTIA® A+® (2012) certification objectives:

*   Exam 220-802, Objective 1.1: Compare and contrast the features and requirements of various Microsoft Operating Systems.
*   Exam 220-802, Objective 1.5: Given a scenario, use Control Panel utilities (the items are organized by "classic view/large icons" in Windows).

The Control Panel

The **Control Panel** is a graphical interface that provides access to a number of utilities that you can use to configure the Windows operating system or a computer's hardware. The specific **Control Panel** utilities that are available will vary depending on the version of Windows that you are using.

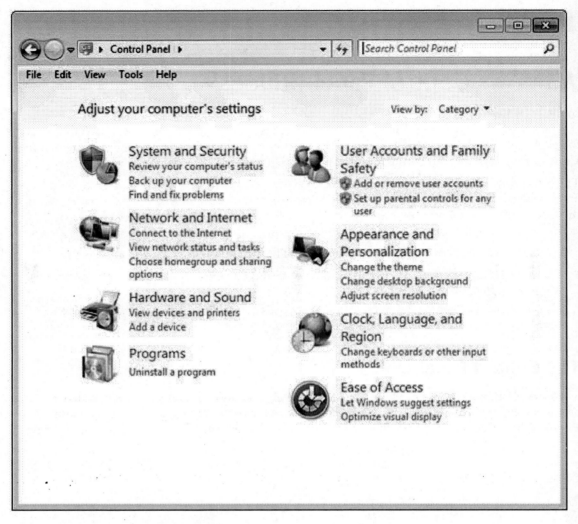

Figure 2-1: The Control Panel in Windows 7.

 Note: The **Control Panel** is available from the **Start** menu, and as a link in various **My Computer** views. In Windows 7, you can open the **Control Panel** by selecting the **Open Control Panel** button located below the address bar of the Computer window.

Internet Options

The **Internet Options Control Panel** utility has many settings that can be customized.

Setting	Description
General	• **Home** page: Defines which web page the browser opens to by default. • **History:** Defines how many days the browser will keep a record of visited pages. • **Colors:** Defines the user's preferred colors for text, page backgrounds, and hyperlinks. • **Fonts:** Defines the user's preferred fonts for viewing pages. • **Languages:** Defines the user's preferred default language for viewing pages. • **Accessibility:** Defines settings that enable visual- or hearing-impaired users to access web pages.

Setting	Description
Security	Defines levels of security for different groups of websites, known as zones. By placing sites in zones and then configuring zone settings, users can enable or disable features such as the blocking or acceptance of web pages, or whether web scripts or controls can run automatically, based upon user preference.
Privacy	Defines the level of access that third-party cookies have to the browser.
Content	Contains various content-related configuration settings, including settings that relate to using content ratings on websites, implementing Internet security certificates, and the AutoComplete function in web-based forms.
Connections	Determines how Internet Explorer will use the computer's network connections to access Internet content.
Programs	Determines which programs Internet Explorer will launch by default when the user clicks links that are associated with other types of Internet content, such as email or newsgroups.
Advanced	Defines a wide variety of settings including how the browser handles external scripts, whether or not hyperlinks are always underlined, and whether or not videos can be played within web pages.

Display

The **Display Control Panel** utility allows the user to configure the display properties for the system, including the physical appearance of the environment, such as the wallpaper, screen saver, color scheme, and font size used. The user can also configure the display settings for the monitor or monitors being used, including setting the primary monitor and the arrangement of additional monitors, extending the desktop onto another monitor, and determining the screen resolution and color quality for the monitors.

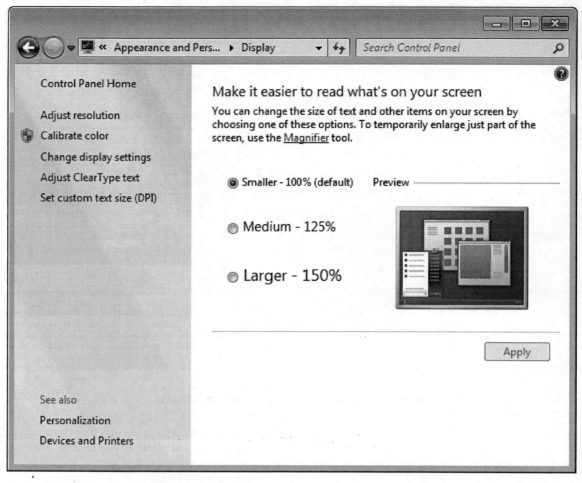

Figure 2-2: The Display utility in Windows 7.

Available Screen Resolutions

Common screen resolutions include 800 by 600, 1024 by 768, and 1280 by 1024, measured in pixels.

User Accounts

A *user account* is a collection of credentials and important information about a person who has access to the system. Most importantly, it defines the rights and privileges assigned to the user, determining what kinds of actions they can perform on the system. There can be more than one user account added to a specific system. There may be users with the same permissions or different permissions assigned to the same computer.

 Note: There will typically be at least two user accounts per system: the administrator and the user who owns or has been assigned the machine.

The **User Accounts Control Panel** utility lets you view and manage your own account, including changing your user name and password. If your account has been assigned administrator privileges, you may also be able to add, remove, or modify other user accounts to allow other users access to the system.

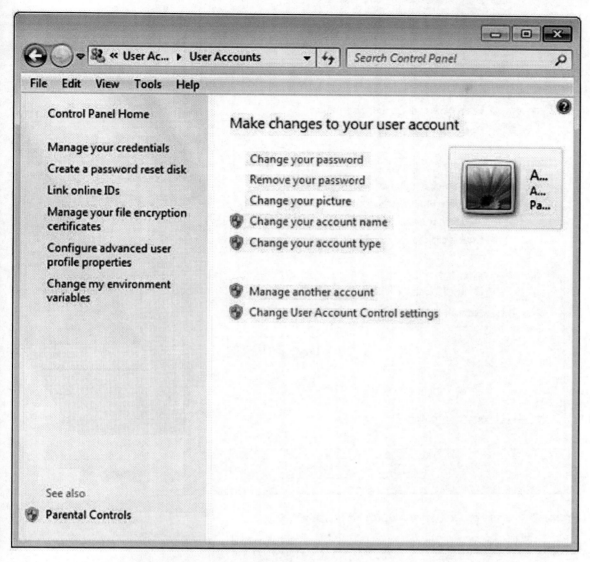

Figure 2-3: The User Accounts utility in Windows 7.

Folder Options

The **Folder Options Control Panel** utility lets you configure settings for how files and folders are displayed when they are accessed. **Folder Options** also lets you configure more general settings such as whether new folders will open in a new window or the existing window, what the layout of folders opened in the navigation pane will be, what action is used to open a file in a folder, and which program is the default for opening specific file types.

Using **Folder Options,** you can also configure the **Advanced Settings** for files and folders, including:

- Whether simple file sharing, the feature in Windows that allows users to share files and folders with other computers on the network without permissions, is enabled or disabled. The default for the system is that simple file sharing is enabled.
- If you can view hidden files and folders, including protected operating system files. The default is that hidden files and folders, including the protected operating system files, are not displayed when accessing a folder that contains the files to protect them from being accidentally deleted or modified.
- Whether to hide or display extensions for known file types within the folder structure. The default is to hide file extensions for known file types.

Figure 2–4: The Folder Options utility in Windows 7.

Simple File Sharing Over a Network on Windows 7

Simple file sharing is disabled by default in Windows 7. To enable it, log on as a user with administrative privileges, open the **Control Panel,** and select **Network and File Sharing Center.** From the left pane, select the **Change advanced sharing settings** link, and then select **Turn on file and printer sharing** and **Turn off password protected sharing** and select **Save changes.**

System

The **System Control Panel** utility lets you view and configure settings for the system.

System Property	Description
General	Provides information about the system, such as what operating system and version is running on the system, who the computer is registered to, and machine hardware information such as the central processing unit (CPU) type and speed and how much RAM is available.
Computer Name	Provides information about the computer's identification, including its description, name, and the domain it belongs to. Users can also add a description, change the name, or join a different domain.

System Property	Description
Hardware	• **Device Manager** displays all devices currently installed on the computer, and you can use it to modify the properties for these devices. • **Drivers** allows the user to configure driver signing options, such as what action to take if a driver being installed is not compatible, and determine how to connect to the Windows Update website when searching for matching drivers. • **Hardware Profiles** allows the user to configure and save hardware configurations, or profiles, and choose which profile to use at startup.
Advanced	• **Performance** allows the user to view and configure the performance options settings for visual effects, processor usage, memory usage, and virtual memory. You can also enable or disable **Data Execution Prevention,** which is a program that monitors security threats to essential Windows programs, through this utility. • **User Profiles** allows the user to configure settings for the user accounts registered to the machine. • **Startup and Recovery** allows the user to configure settings related to the system startup, system failure, and debugging.
System Restore	Allows the user to enable or disable **System Restore** and configure the amount of disk space allocated for **System Restore** to use.
Automatic Updates	Allows the user to enable or disable **Automatic Updates.** The default and recommended setting is that **Automatic Updates** are turned on, to protect the system from the most current threats.
Remote	Allows the user to configure settings for how the computer can be used from a remote location. • You can enable or disable **Remote Assistance** to allow the computer to be controlled remotely, typically from IT personnel troubleshooting a problem. • You can enable or disable **Remote Desktop,** and you can add remote users to define who will be able to remotely access the computer.

Action Center

The **Action Center Control Panel** utility provides information about any security software currently deployed on or missing from the system, and provides access to helpful resources about current security threats, including a check for the latest Windows Update. **Action Center** also provides links to the **Backup and Restore, Windows Update,** and **Windows Program Compatibility Troubleshooter** utilities, where you can manage specific settings regarding system security and troubleshooting.

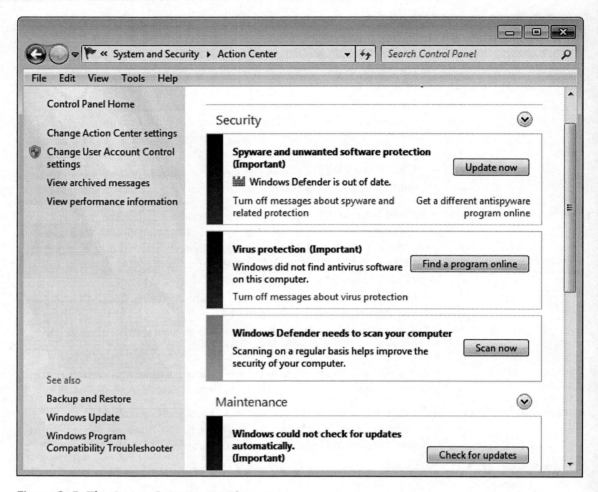

Figure 2–5: The Action Center in Windows 7.

Security Center

In Windows Vista and XP, the **Security Center Control Panel** included some of the same information as the **Action Center** does in Windows 7, but in the **Security Center,** links to the **Internet Options, Automatic Updates,** and **Windows Firewall Control Panels** are included.

Windows Firewall

A *firewall* is a device or program that blocks unauthorized data transmissions and protects the computer from unauthorized access. **Windows Firewall** is a software-based firewall, included with almost all Windows installations, that protects the computer against attacks through the Internet or the network. The **Windows Firewall** utility enables you to:

- Enable or disable **Windows Firewall.**
- View active networks.
- Configure notifications concerning blocked activity.
- Open blocked ports.
- Configure other firewall settings for both private (home or work) and public networks that the computer may access.

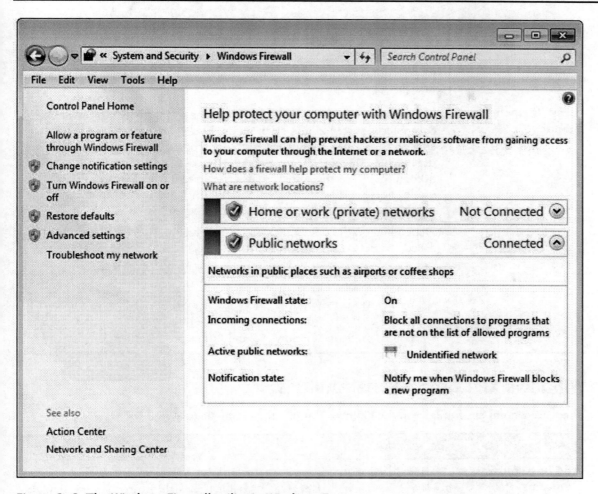

Figure 2-6: The Windows Firewall utility in Windows 7.

 Note: In the corporate environment, this utility is usually not accessible to individual users, as the **Windows Firewall** settings are configured and controlled by an administrator in the IT department, or **Windows Firewall** is superseded by a dedicated enterprise-level firewall system.

Power Options

Using the **Power Options Control Panel** utility, there are a number of power settings that can be configured for the computer.

Power Option	Description
Hibernate	In *Hibernate* mode, the computer will store whatever is currently in memory on the hard disk and shut down; when the computer comes out of hibernation, it will return to the state it was in upon hibernation.
	In the **Power Options** utility, you can enable or disable hibernation, and you can view how much disk space is needed and available for hibernation. Once hibernation is enabled, you can configure the settings for when hibernation occurs using the **Power Plans** settings.
Power Plans	**Power Plans** (called **Power Schemes** in Windows XP) are a set of built-in power configurations that a user can choose from to manage how the computer uses power. For each **Power Plan**, there are default settings for when to turn off the monitor, when to turn off hard disks, and when to enter system standby, depending on whether the computer is plugged

Power Option	Description
	in or, if it is a laptop, is running on batteries. You can modify and save these settings for the selected power plan, or you can create and save a new power plan.
Sleep/Suspend/ Standby	The user can determine the amount of time of inactivity after which the computer is switched into sleep mode. In sleep mode, the computer conserves as much energy as possible by cutting off power to the parts of the machine that are not necessary to function, excluding RAM, which is needed to restore the system to its state once it is woken from sleep mode. These settings can be configured for when the computer is plugged in or, if it is a laptop, if it is running on batteries.
	Depending on the operating system and version, sleep mode can be called a variety of things:
	• *Sleep* mode in Windows Vista, Windows 7, Windows Server 2008, and Apple OSs.
	• *Standby* mode in Windows 98, Windows Server 2003, and Windows XP.
	• *Suspend* mode in Windows 95 and Linux.

Windows XP Control Panel Utilities

There are a number of utilities in the **Control Panel** that are unique to Windows XP.

Windows XP Utility	Description
Add or Remove Programs	Used to install or remove applications and programs, view updates that have been installed, enable or disable optional features, and set default programs.
Network Connections	Used to view available connections, connect or disconnect from a connection, and manage all network and Internet connections.
Printers and Faxes	Used to add, remove, and manage any printers, scanners, or faxes installed on the computer.
Automatic Updates	Controls how Windows Updates are downloaded and installed.
Network Setup Wizard	Launches the setup wizard, which walks the user step-by-step through setting up an Internet connection and creating a network to share files, printers, and other resources.

Windows Vista Control Panel Utilities

There are a number of utilities in the **Control Panel** that are unique to Windows Vista.

Windows Vista Utility	Description
Tablet PC Settings	Under the Mobile PC utility, the user can configure settings for a tablet PC running Windows Vista through the *Tablet PC Settings* utility. Some of the settings that you can modify include:
	• Screen calibration.
	• Screen orientation.
	• Handedness.

Windows Vista Utility	Description
	• Handwriting recognition. • Button functions.
Pen and Input Devices	For a tablet PC running Windows Vista, you can use a pen or other input device such as a stylus to interact with the tablet. You can use the **Pen and Input Devices** utility to customize the settings for the pen and input devices that are used to interact with the tablet. Some of the settings that you can configure include: • **Pen Options:** You can configure the equivalent "mouse action" when an action is taken on screen with the pen (such as a double-tap) and customize settings for the pen buttons. • **Pointer Options:** You can enable or disable dynamic feedback for actions and select what the feedback method will be, and select whether or not the pen cursor is displayed. • **Flicks:** You can enable or disable the use of flicks as the pen gesture for navigating, and then customize settings for flicks including sensitivity.
Offline Files	You can use the *Offline Files* utility to enable or disable the use of offline files, which allows you to save and modify a local copy of a file from the network and then sync it back to the network. Some of the settings for offline files that you can configure include: • **Disk Usage.** • **Encryption.** • **Network settings.**
Problem Reports and Solutions	The **Problem Reports and Solutions** utility displays any recent problems that Windows has encountered. Depending on the issue, the user can find out more information about the issue or search online for a solution to resolve the issue.
Printers	The **Printers** utility is used to add, remove, and manage any printers installed on the computer.

 Note: The **Printers** utility in Vista replaced the **Printers and Faxes** utility in Windows XP and was replaced with the **Devices and Printers** utility in Windows 7. While the name changed in the various versions, the functionality of the utility has remained largely the same.

Windows 7 Control Panel Utilities

There are a number of utilities in the **Control Panel** that are unique to Windows 7.

Windows 7 Utility	Description
HomeGroup	With *HomeGroup,* the user can set up a home network of computers and printers, and then add users or computers to the **HomeGroup** to share libraries and resources.
Action Center	*Action Center* provides a single location where security actions are consolidated. When the system places an alert in the **Action Center,** you can view the solution to the problem and fix the issue immediately, if possible, through the **Action Center.** You can enable or disable

Windows 7 Utility	Description
	notifications for the **Action Center.** You can also configure settings such as how much information is sent or how often to check for solutions.
RemoteApp and Desktop Connections	With *RemoteApp and Desktop Connections,* users can access programs, remote computers, and virtual computers remotely that are made available by the network administrator. The **RemoteApp and Desktop Connections** utility displays all of the resources and connections available, and the user can select the resource or connection that they want to access.
Troubleshooting	The *Troubleshooting* utility provides troubleshooting resources for common Windows problems in five general areas: **Programs, Hardware and Sound, Network and Internet, Appearance and Personalization,** and **System and Security.** Users can also configure some basic settings for the **Troubleshooting** utility, including enabling or disabling scheduled computer maintenance checks, allowing search functionality through the Windows Online troubleshooting service, and allowing troubleshooting to begin on startup.

ACTIVITY 2-2
Exploring the Windows 7 Control Panel

Before You Begin
You are logged in to Windows as **Admin##**.

Scenario
In this activity, you will explore the components of the **Control Panel** in the Windows 7 operating system.

---

1. Examine the **Control Panel** utilities.
   a) Select **Start→Control Panel**. The **Control Panel** tools are grouped by function.
   b) Select **Appearance and Personalization**.
   c) Select **Taskbar and Start Menu**. The **Taskbar and Start Menu Properties** dialog box opens.
   d) Select **Cancel** to close the dialog box.
   e) Select the **Back** button.
   f) Examine the other categories in the **Control Panel.**

2. Change the **Control Panel** view.
   a) From the **View by** drop-down list, select **Large icons** to view the individual elements of the **Control Panel.**
   b) From the **View by** drop-down list, select **Small icons** to reduce the size of the icons.
   c) From the **View by** drop-down list, select **Category** to return to the original view.
   d) Close the **Control Panel.**

TOPIC C

Command Line Tools

In the previous topic, you identified the utilities in the Windows **Control Panel**. More experienced users should understand alternative ways to manipulate elements of the operating system, such as the command prompt. In this topic, you will identify command line tools and how they function.

The **Control Panel** provides a graphical interface to control many of the elements of the Windows environment. However, more advanced users, such as support personnel, often find that using command line tools can provide more granular control over the Windows environment.

This topic covers all or part of the following CompTIA® A+® (2012) certification objectives:

- Exam 220-802, Objective 1.1: Compare and contrast the features and requirements of various Microsoft Operating Systems.
- Exam 220-802, Objective 1.3: Given a scenario, use appropriate command line tools.

The Command Prompt

Windows provides the command prompt, which is an interface that enables you to enter text-based commands or run command line tools. Command line tools accept only text input, and they output information either in text format or by opening a graphic display window. You can use command line equivalents of graphical tools to create batch programs or scripts that automate administrative tasks. Some administrator and Power Users might also find command line management to be more streamlined and efficient than working through a graphical interface.

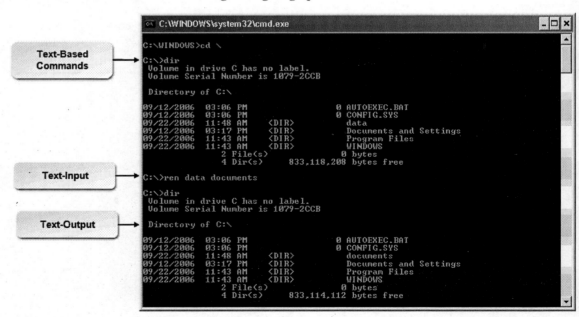

Figure 2-7: The command prompt interface.

 Note: The default path in Windows 7 for the prompt is the user profile folder for the current user (C:\Users\username). In Windows XP, the default path is C:\Documents and Settings \username.

 Note: Because you can run DOS-type commands at the command prompt, it is sometimes casually called the "DOS prompt."

Command Interpreters

Windows provides several different command interpreters. The typical command prompt interface is the standard Windows command interpreter, available in Windows XP and Windows 7. To access the command prompt interface, you can either run cmd.exe or select the **Command Prompt** shortcut from the **Accessories** menu.

Windows XP also includes the DOS command interpreter command.com to support running DOS-based applications with an MS-DOS subsystem. There are also the Windows PowerShell™ and Windows Recovery Console, which are used for more high-level administrative tasks.

Operating System Command Line Tools

There are a number of common command line tools that you can use to manage the operating system. For a list of all the available commands, type help at the command prompt.

Tool	Function
bootrec	Used to troubleshoot or repair startup issues with your operating system (via the command prompt in the Windows Recovery Environment in Windows Vista and Windows 7 only).
cd	Used to view the drive letter and folder for your current location, and to change to another directory or folder.
chkdsk	Used to identify hard drive errors and correct the error if possible. Often called "check disk."
[command name] /?	Used to view online help at the command prompt. Because the syntax for a tool might vary slightly between operating systems, you should check online help for the exact syntax.
copy	Used to copy a file or files.
del	Used to delete a file.
diskpart	Used to create, delete, or generally manage any hard drive partitions on the system.
fdisk	Used to partition or re-partition a hard drive.
format	Used to format a drive using the file system specified.
~~kill or taskkill~~ _Taskkill_	Used to stop or terminate a process or task that is running.
md _– Make di_	Used to create a directory.
rd _– Remove_	Used to delete a directory.
robocopy	Used to copy files and folders/directories from one location to another, but with more options than the simple copy command. Often called Robust File Copy.
sfc	Shorthand for System File Checker, it is used to verify system files and replace them, if needed. Sometimes referred to as the Windows Resource Checker. _Checks for Corrupt Files_
shutdown	Used to log off, restart, or shut down the system.
~~tlist or~~ tasklist	Used to display all processes currently running on the system.
xcopy	Used to copy files or directories from one location to another.

Networking Command Line Tools

Other command line tools can help you configure and manage network communications.

Tool	Function
ipconfig	Used to verify the configuration of TCP/IP and to release or renew Dynamic Host Configuration Protocol (DHCP) IP address leases. (Other operating systems use different commands rather than ipconfig. For example, Linux uses ifconfig.)
ping	Used to test TCP/IP communications. With the -t switch, you can ping the indicated host until the request gets interrupted; with the -l [number] switch, you can send a ping of a specified buffer size.
nbtstat	Used to display TCP/IP information and other important information regarding a remote computer. Also used to troubleshoot issues with NetBIOS. If there are issues with the NetBIOS resolution to TCP/IP addresses, then you can use the nbstat command to remove any preloaded resolution entries.
net	Used to manage Microsoft network resources from a command line. With the use option, you can connect or disconnect the computer from a shared resource. You can also retrieve information about current network connections. To see all of the available commands in this suite, type net /?
netstat	Used to show the status of each active network connection, netstat will display statistics for both TCP and User Datagram Protocol (UDP), including protocol, local address, foreign address, and the TCP connection state. Because UDP is connectionless, no connection information will be shown for UDP packets.
nslookup	Used to verify that the computer can connect to a Domain Name System (DNS) server and successfully find an IP address for a given computer name.
tracert	Used to determine and test all points along the route the computer uses to send a packet to a destination. If tracert is unsuccessful, you can use the results generated to determine at what point communications are failing.

The Recovery Console

Recovery Console is a minimal, non-graphical administrative version of Windows that is available in Windows XP and Windows 2000. You can boot to **Recovery Console** and use a command line interface (CLI) to manage the system even if Windows will not start normally.

In **Recovery Console,** you can:

- Enable and disable services.
- Manage files and disks.
- Correct boot problems.

You can use the following command line tools from the **Recovery Console** to address some common issues.

Tool	Description
fixboot	Used to create a new partition boot sector to a hard drive partition.
fixmbr	Used to repair the master boot recovery (MBR) record of the boot partition.

Note: You can install **Recovery Console** as a boot option or launch it from the Windows installation CD-ROM.

WinRE

In Windows Vista and Windows 7, the **Recovery Console** was replaced by the *Windows Recovery Environment (WinRE),* a set of tools used to diagnose and repair Windows errors at startup. WinRE includes several new recovery tools accessible via the **System Recovery Options** menu.

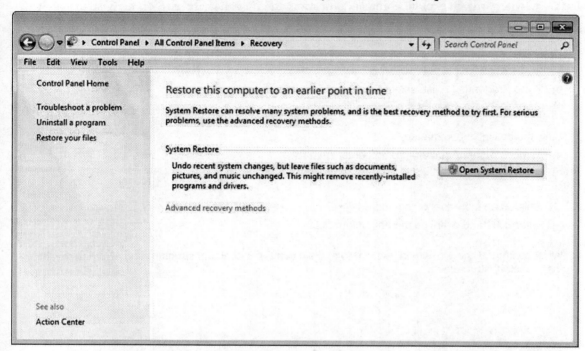

Figure 2–8: The System Recovery Options menu in Windows 7.

System Recovery Tool	Description
Startup Repair	Repairs system files that are missing or corrupted. Corrupt or missing system files can cause problems with starting Windows.
System Restore	Restores computer settings and system files to a user-defined time. However, **System Restore** does not affect the user's personal files and data.
System Image Recovery	Restores a system image created by the user. The system image is a backup of the partition in which Windows is installed.
Windows Memory Diagnostic	Checks the system's memory for errors. Usually, memory errors are caused due to faulty computer chips. So, with the results of the diagnostics, you should contact your computer manufacturer for possible fixes.
Command Prompt	Launches the command prompt where advanced users can perform recovery- and maintenance-related tasks.

 Note: In Windows Vista, **System Image Recovery** is called **CompletePC Restore,** and uses a CompletePC backup image to restore the computer.

ACTIVITY 2-3
Exploring Command Line Tools

Scenario

In this activity, you will explore command line tools and how they are used on the system.

---

1. Open the command prompt.
   a) Select **Start,** and in the **Search programs or files** text box, type *comm*
   b) In the **Programs (1)** list, select **Command Prompt.**
   c) Maximize the command prompt window.

2. View the available commands.
   a) At the **C:\Users\Admin##** prompt, enter *help*
   b) Scroll through the list of commands.

3. Get help on an individual command.
   a) Enter *cd /?* and examine the help information.

4. **What command line tool would you use to make a copy of a directory structure and all the files within that directory structure?**
   - ○ copy
   - ○ chkdsk
   - ○ robocopy
   - ○ md

5. **What is the best command line tool to use if you want to test TCP/IP communication to a specific IP address?**
   - ○ net
   - ○ ipconfig
   - ○ nbstat
   - ○ ping

6. **Which tool is used to create a new partition boot sector?**
   - ○ fdisk
   - ○ fixboot
   - ○ bootrec
   - ○ fixmbr

7. **Which system recovery tool restores a system image created by the user?**
   - ○ System Restore
   - ○ System Image Recovery
   - ○ Memory Diagnostic
   - ○ Startup Repair

8. **Which is the best description of the Startup Repair utility?**

- ○   Restores a system image created by the user
- ○   Checks the system's memory for errors
- ○   Restores computer settings and system files to a user-defined time
- ○   Repairs system files that are missing or corrupted

9. Close the command prompt.

TOPIC D

Windows Security Settings

In the last topic, you identified some command line tools that you can use to manipulate some elements of the operating system. Another critical aspect of configuring and supporting the operating system is managing the security settings that control the access to data and files within the environment. In this topic, you will identify Windows security settings.

As an IT professional, your responsibilities are likely to include configuring and maintaining operating systems for many employees within the organization. Knowing the Windows security settings and how to properly configure them enables you to ensure that users have the proper access to only the data and files that are applicable and appropriate to their employment status.

This topic covers all or part of the following CompTIA® A+® (2012) certification objectives:

- Exam 220-802, Objective 1.2: Given a scenario, install and configure the operating system using the most appropriate method.
- Exam 220-802, Objective 1.8: Explain the differences among basic OS security settings.
- Exam 220-802, Objective 2.3: Implement security best practices to secure a workstation.

Types of User Accounts

Windows includes several built-in user accounts to provide you with initial access to a computer.

User Account	Provides
Administrator	Complete administrative access to a computer. This is the most powerful account on a computer and should be protected with a strong password. In some situations, you might also consider renaming this account.
Power User	Fewer access privileges than administrators, but more access privileges than standard users. Power Users might be able to install most software and updates, but they will be restricted from making changes that affect security or the core operating system. This account is available *only* in Windows XP.
Standard User	Access to use most of the computing software on the computer. However, higher permission is required to uninstall or install software and hardware. This account also limits the configuration of security settings, operational settings, and deletion of necessary system files. This account is sometimes referred to as a non-privileged user account.
Guest	Limited computer access to individuals without a user account. By default, the **Guest** account is disabled when you install the operating system. You enable this account only if you want to permit users to log on as a guest.

User Account Control

User Account Control (UAC) is an enhanced security feature of Windows 7 and Vista that aims to limit the privileges of a standard user unless a computer administrator decides otherwise. The intent is to limit accidental changes to the computer to reduce exposure to malware. Administrators can control access by managing privilege levels, which are not the same as permissions. A user might have administrator permissions, but still needs to be explicitly granted the privilege of running an application.

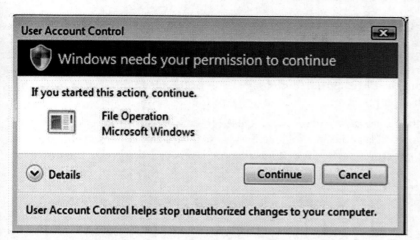

Figure 2-9: The UAC.

 Note: Complaints from end users against Windows Vista's UAC are common because many tasks that users were able to perform on their own in previous Windows versions require additional privileges in Vista. However, in Windows 7, this issue has been addressed and UAC is now less intrusive.

Changing UAC Settings

If the UAC is too restrictive for you or for your users, the settings can be changed. Open the Microsoft Management Console (MMC) and open the **Local Security Policy** settings. You must be logged on to the administrator account to modify:

- Whether the UAC is enabled or disabled.
- What the UAC behavior is for administrator or Standard Users.
- Application-specific behavior.

Tasks Requiring a UAC Prompt

Tasks that are preceded by the **Security Shield** icon will invoke the UAC.

Group Accounts

Windows includes several built-in group accounts that you can use to control basic system security.

Group Account	Description
Administrators	Users in the **Administrators** group can perform all administrative tasks on the computer.
	When an account is created during the installation of Windows, it is automatically added to this group by default.
Power Users	Available only in Windows XP. Users in the **Power Users** group can run pre-Windows 2000 applications, modify some system-wide settings (such as the time), install some programs, and manage some local accounts.
Standard Users	Users in the **Standard Users** group can run applications and perform other day-to-day computer tasks for which the group has been granted permissions. In the various Windows user interfaces, the **Standard Users** groups are referred to simply as **Users.**
Guests	Users in the **Guests** group can perform any tasks for which the group has permissions.

(handwritten: user access Rights)

System Files and Folders

System files are the files that are required for the operating system to function to its fullest capabilities. These files are typically hidden because their deletion can prevent the computer from working properly. For system files, both the file extension and the location of the file in the system hierarchy are important, as they help the computer recognize it as a system file.

In the file system hierarchy, the terms *folder* and *directory* are used interchangeably to describe a container that is used to organize files and other folders. System software and applications usually create standardized directory structures at the time of installation. Users can also create their own directory structures.

Figure 2-10: A folder in the system hierarchy.

 Note: In Windows, the maximum depth of a folder structure is restricted by the 255-character limit in the overall file path, including the character representing the drive and any file name and extension. Otherwise, there is no set limit on the length of a particular file or folder name.

Creating a File

The most common way for a file to be created is to start a new file within a specific application and then save it to a directory. But you can also create a file without opening an application.

- Display the pop-up menu for the Windows desktop and select **New,** and then select what kind of blank file you would like to save to the desktop.
- In Windows Explorer, display the pop-up menu for the view pane of a particular folder and select **New→[filetype].**
- From a Windows command prompt, you can also use the `copy con [filename]` command, which creates an empty file and allows you to edit it immediately, without leaving the command prompt. After typing the contents of the file, press **Ctrl+Z** and then press **Enter** to save and exit the file.
- In a UNIX system, users can create files at the command line by using the `touch [filename]` command, where [filename] is the name of the file.
- UNIX users can also create files by using the `cat > [filename]` command. Like `copy con`, the `cat` command (which is short for "concatenate") creates the file, opens it within the

command prompt window, and allows a user to edit the file's contents. To save and exit the file, type **Ctrl+D.**

Windows Explorer

Windows Explorer is a graphical tool that enables users to manage files and folders on a computer, including the contents of hard disks, floppy disks, CDs, DVDs, USB devices, and any other storage devices attached to the computer. On the left side of Windows Explorer, the **Explorer** bar displays the folder hierarchy tree by default, and the right pane displays the contents of the selected item.

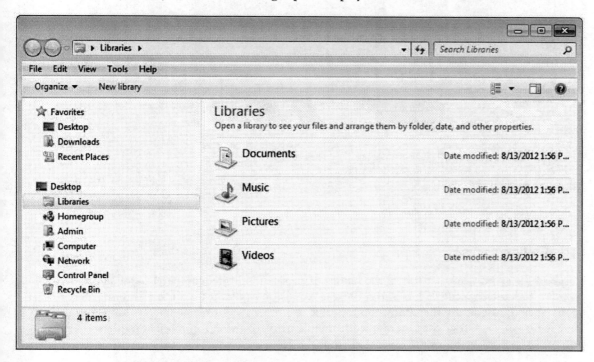

Figure 2-11: Windows Explorer in Windows 7.

Note: You can run Windows Explorer in Windows 2000, Windows XP, Windows Vista, and Windows 7 from the **Accessories** group on the **Start** menu. In Windows XP, you can also open Windows Explorer by displaying an object's pop-up menu and selecting **Explore.** Windows Explorer open with the object selected in the folder hierarchy. For example, if you display the pop-up menu for the **Start** menu and select **Explore,** Windows Explorer opens and displays the contents of the Start Menu folder on the disk.

Note: In Windows XP and Windows 2000, you can choose to display other contents in the **Explorer** bar. In Windows Explorer, select **View→Explorer Bar** and then select **Search, Favorites, History, Research,** or **Folders.**

Computer/My Computer

Like Windows Explorer, **Computer,** or **My Computer** as it is called in Windows XP, is used to manage files and folders on a computer and on any storage devices attached to the computer. In Windows 7, **Computer** is a two-pane window, with a Windows Explorer-like navigation bar on the left side. You can open **Computer** from an icon on the Windows desktop or from the **Start** menu.

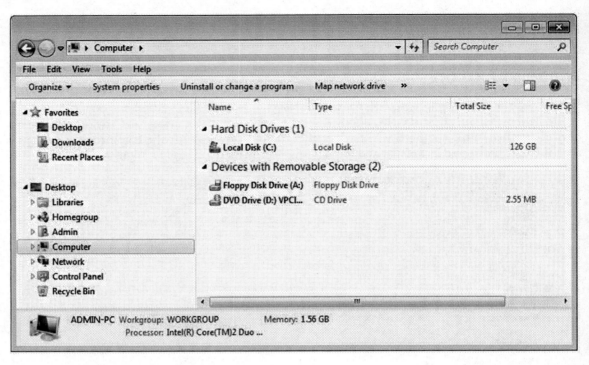

Figure 2-12: Computer in Windows 7.

File Extensions

Standard file extensions that follow the names of files can indicate whether a particular file is a program file or a data file. If it is a data file, the extension can indicate the application category that might be used to edit the file. Many common file extensions are three characters long, although there is no longer a strict character limit for the file name or extension in most modern operating systems. A period separates the extension from the file name itself.

Common File Extensions

The following table lists a number of common file extensions. Because Windows uses the file extension to determine how the system will use a file, if you alter a file name extension, you might find that a program file will not execute properly or that a data file will not automatically open in the associated application.

File Extension	Typically Indicates
.txt	A plain text file that contains no formatting other than spaces and line breaks. You can open .txt files in any text editing program, such as Notepad, or word processing programs, such as Microsoft® Word.
.rtf	Rich Text Format (RTF), or a text file that includes a limited amount of formatting such as bold and italic. You can open .rtf files in various applications, such as common word processors or Microsoft's WordPad accessory.
.doc	A data file created in a word processing program, such as Microsoft Word or WordPad. You might also see .docx, which is an Office 2010 format.
.bat	A batch file; a small text file containing a list of system commands that execute in a "batch," rather than requiring the user to enter each command in succession.
.bin	A binary file, containing only binary data (1s and 0s), which cannot typically be opened and read by a user application.
.com	A command file or compiled application file.

(handwritten notes: "Note Pad Text Editor", "Mac + Windows need File Extensions", "Executable File")

File Extension	Typically Indicates
.exe	Executable files that launch programs and applications.
.dll	A Dynamic Link Library (DLL) file, containing additional application settings or functions that are loaded by executable files, as needed.
.hlp, .chm	Help files used by various applications.
.htm, .html	HyperText Markup Language (HTML) files, used to indicate web pages.
.inf	Setup configuration settings for operating systems and applications. (Info file)
.ini	Configuration settings for software and hardware components.
.msi	A Windows Installer package; a file that can specify installation parameters for an application.
.sys — driver	System files. System files are typically hidden, as their deletion can prevent the computer from working properly. With system files, it is not only the extension that is important because it helps the computer recognize it as a system file, but the location as well.
.tif, .jpg, .jpeg, .gif, .bmp, .png	Graphic image files in various formats.
.xls, .ppt, .mdb	Data files created in Microsoft® Excel®, Microsoft® PowerPoint®, and Microsoft® Access®, respectively. Office 2007 and Office 2010 file formats include .xlsx, .pptx, and .mdbx files.

Note: By default, the folder view options in **Computer** and Windows Explorer are set so that common file extensions do not display. You can display the extensions by unchecking **Hide extensions for known file types** on the **View** page in the **Folder Options** dialog box.

ACTIVITY 2-4
Viewing File Extensions

Scenario

In this activity, you will view the file extensions for the files that are stored on your Windows 7 system.

1. Open the folder that contains the Windows system files.
   a) Select **Start→Computer.**
   b) Double-click the **C** drive.
   c) Double-click the **Windows** folder.

2. Display the file extensions.
   a) On the menu bar, select **Organize→Folder and search options.**
   b) Select the **View** tab.
   c) Uncheck **Hide extensions for known file types** and select **OK.**

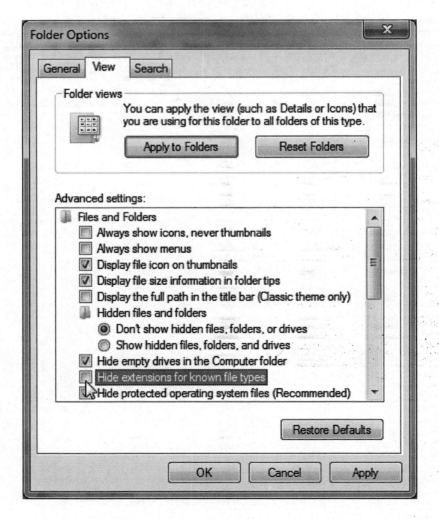

3. Examine the file extensions.

a) Scroll down to view the files. The first few files in the window have a number of different extensions.

b) To see all of the files in a list format, right-click in an open area and select **View→List**.

c) To see similar extensions grouped together, right-click in an open area and select **Sort by→Type**.

d) To return to the default view, right-click in an open area and select **Sort by→Name**.

e) Close the window.

File Attributes

File attributes are characteristics that can be associated with a file or folder that provide the operating system with important information about the file or folder and how it is intended to be used by system users.

There are several standard attributes that can be enabled for files or folders on Windows systems.

File Attribute	Description
Archive (A)	Indicates that a file has not been backed up. Windows automatically sets the **Archive** attribute on any file you create or modify. When you back up data, you can choose to back up only the files on which the Archive attribute is set.
Hidden (H)	Hides a file from view in file management tools such as Windows Explorer, **Computer** in Windows Vista and Windows 7, or **My Computer** in Windows XP.
Read-Only (R)	Enables users to read the contents of a file or execute it if it is a program file, but prevents users from changing the contents of a file.
System (S)	Indicates that a file is used by the operating system. Some applications use this attribute to restrict user access to these files. The System attribute in Windows automatically hides the file or folder. *Same as hidden will appear transparent*
Index (I)	This Windows-specific attribute enables the Windows **Indexing Service** to create an index of the file to speed up the Search function.

Viewing and Changing Attributes

You can view or change most attributes of a file or folder object by opening the properties of the object in Windows Explorer. You can view and manage the System attribute at the command line by using the `attrib` command. For information on the functions and syntax of the `attrib` command, see the Windows Help system.

Windows File System Types

A *file system* is an inherent organizational structure that is used to organize and store data and information in a logical manner on the system's storage device. It enables the system to retrieve and update data efficiently when it needs to be accessed and manages the space available on the storage device where the data will be stored. The file system is created when the storage device or drive is formatted.

Windows supports a number of different file systems.

File System	Description
File Allocation Table (FAT)	An older file system that is best suited for use with drives smaller than 4 GB in size. The primary advantages of the FAT file system are its extremely low disk overhead (less than 1 MB), and its compatibility with many different operating systems, including all versions of Windows and MS-DOS and UNIX systems. You might use the FAT file system if you want to dual-boot a computer

Fat 12 - Floppy disks

Fat 16 - Spinning disks
896

(handwritten margin notes: Ex Fat — Fat 64 / For larger Partition / Max file Size 4gb / ISO 9660)

File System	Description
	between a version of Windows and another operating system. It is primarily used for formatting floppy disks.
FAT32	An enhanced version of the FAT file system that was designed to overcome the size limit of FAT. It scales better to large hard drives (up to 2 TB in size) and uses a smaller cluster size than FAT for more efficient space usage.
NT File System (NTFS)	The recommended file system for today's Windows-based computers. NTFS was introduced with the Windows NT operating system. NTFS provides many enhanced features over FAT or FAT32, including file- and folder-level security, file encryption, disk compression, and scalability to very large drives and files.
Media file systems	Windows also supports various types of special media file system formats, such as CD File System (CDFS) for CD-ROM devices.

Disk Clusters and File System Types

When you format drives, you organize the drive into individual data storage areas called *sectors*. Sectors are grouped together into larger units called *clusters* or *allocation units*. A cluster is the smallest unit that the system will use to store a file. If a file does not fill a cluster, the extra space in the cluster remains empty.

The size of sectors and clusters is determined by the file system that was used to format the drive. Smaller allocation units reduce unused space on the disk, but they can reduce disk read/write performance because there are more locations to access on the disk. The smaller cluster sizes that FAT32 offered were of more benefit when disk space was costly and most drives used FAT; very large hard drives are now relatively inexpensive. In any case, you should generally use NTFS on Windows partitions to gain the available security benefits.

Permissions

In a Windows environment, *permissions* are security settings that control access to individual objects, such as files or folders. Permissions determine which specific actions users can perform on a given object. You can assign permissions by modifying an object's properties.

Figure 2–13: Permissions.

 Note: In UNIX and Linux systems, the terms "permissions" and "rights" are used interchangeably.

NTFS File Permissions

There are five standard NTFS permissions that you can assign to files.

Permission	Enables the User To
Read	Read the file and view file attributes, ownership, and permissions.
Write	Overwrite the file and change file attributes.
Read & Execute	Run applications and perform Read tasks.
Modify	Modify and delete the file.
Full Control	Change permissions, take ownership, and perform all other tasks.

Special Permissions

Each of the standard NTFS permissions is made up of several more granular permissions called special permissions. Standard permissions are the most frequently assigned groups of permissions; special permissions provide you with a finer degree of control.

For example, the standard Read permission is made up of the following special permissions:

- List Folder/Read Data.
- Read Attributes.
- Read Extended Attributes.
- Read Permissions.

File Permissions in Windows XP Home

The Classic security model is not available in Windows XP Home, so you will not be able to set individual NTFS permissions on Windows XP Home computers. However, when Simple File Sharing is active, both Windows XP Professional and Windows XP Home provide a rudimentary mechanism for protecting or sharing local files when multiple users use the same computer.

- To protect files, individual users can mark user profile folders such as My Documents as **Private.** Other local users will not be able to access these folders.
- To share files, users can place files and folders in the Shared Documents folder in **My Computer.** All local users will be able to access the contents of Shared Documents. The Shared Documents folder is also shared on the network and can be accessed by users at other computers.

File Compression and Encryption

File compression and file encryption are two special features of the NTFS file system that are implemented as advanced attributes.

- File compression is a way to save disk space by removing blank or repeated characters within files. Windows file compression is rarely used, partly because disk space on most systems today is relatively plentiful, and partly because there are other ways to reduce file size, such as with a file-compression utility like WinZip®, which creates a new, compressed file that you can copy to other media or email to other users.
- File encryption is an NTFS security measure that scrambles the contents of a file so that only the person who encrypted the file can open it, even if the disk containing the file is physically removed from the computer and loaded into a different computer system. File encryption is a good way to protect data on portable devices such as laptop computers.

NTFS Folder Permissions

There are six standard NTFS permissions that you can assign to folders or to drives.

Permission	Enables the User To
List Folder Contents	View the names, attributes, and permissions of subfolders in the folder, but only see the names of files within the folder.
Read	View names, attributes, permissions, and contents of files and subfolders in the folder.
Write	Create new files and subfolders in the folder, and change their attributes.
Read & Execute	Perform the same functions as Read and List Folder Contents tasks, as well as execute files.
Modify	Delete the folder and perform Write and Read & Execute tasks.
Full Control	Change permissions, take ownership, delete subfolders and files, and perform all other tasks.

Permissions Inheritance

Permissions that you assign to a folder are inherited by files and folders within that folder. It is generally most efficient to group similar files together in a folder and assign permissions to the folder, rather than to the individual files. Inherited permissions are indicated by gray background check marks in the file or folder's security properties.

Permissions Propagation

If you modify the permissions for a parent folder, you can choose whether or not to propagate the changes downwards, which means to apply those permissions changes to all of the subfolders within the folder.

ACTIVITY 2–5
Exploring NTFS Permissions

Scenario

In this activity, you will examine NTFS file and folder permissions.

---

1. Turn off the **Sharing Wizard.**
   a) Open **Computer,** and select **Organize→Folder and search options.**
   b) Select the **View** tab. Scroll to the bottom of the **Advanced settings** list.
   c) Uncheck **Use Sharing Wizard (Recommended)** and select **OK.**

2. Examine the NTFS permissions on a drive.
   a) Select the **C** drive, and select **Organize→Properties.**
   b) Select the **Security** tab.
   c) In the **Group or user names** list, select the **Administrators** group.
   d) Determine the permissions assigned to the **Administrators** group.
   e) Select the **Users** group.
   f) Determine the permissions assigned to the **Users** group and select **Cancel.**

3. What level of permissions did the administrators group have?
   - ○ Full Control
   - ○ Modify
   - ○ Write
   - ○ Read & Execute

4. What level of permissions did the Users group have?
   - ○ Full Control
   - ○ Modify
   - ○ Write
   - ○ Read & Execute

5. Examine NTFS folder permissions.
   a) Double-click the **C** drive. Select the **LocalData** folder, and then select **Organize→Properties.**
   b) Select the **Security** tab.
   c) Select the **Administrators** group.
   d) Determine the permissions assigned to the **Administrators** group.
   e) Select the **Users** group.
   f) Determine the permissions assigned to the **Users** group, and then select **Cancel.**

6. How were the permissions in the LocalData folder different from the permissions on the C drive?
   - ○ Administrators did not have Full Control to the LocalData folder.
   - ○ Users could not read files in the LocalData folder.
   - ○ The permissions on the C drive were set explicitly; the permissions on the LocalData folder were inherited from the C drive.
   - ○ The available permissions were different.

7. Examine NTFS file permissions.
   a) Double-click the **LocalData** folder.
   b) Select the **New Text Document** file, and then select **Organize→Properties.**
   c) Select the **Security** tab.
   d) Select the **Administrators** group.
   e) Determine the permissions assigned to the **Administrators** group. Verify that the permissions of the New Text Document file is the same as that of the **C** drive and the LocalData folder.
   f) Select the **Users** group.
   g) Determine the permissions assigned to the **Users** group, and then select **Cancel.**
   h) Close the window.

8. **True or False? The permissions in the New Text Document file were inherited from the LocalData folder permissions.**
   ☐ True
   ☐ False

Shared Files and Folders

A *share* is any network resource that is available to other computers or users on the network. Typical shares include folders, printers, and drives. Because shares enable users to access a computer system from a remote location, you should secure all shared resources against unauthorized access.

There are two kinds of shares: *administrative shares* and *local shares*.

- Administrative shares are hidden shares that are created and shared by default on every Windows system. They are displayed with a "$" to indicate that they are hidden files. Although you can delete these administrative shares, the system will re-create them every time the system restarts. Anyone with administrator access to the system can interact with administrative shares.
- Local shares are folders that are created on the local network by system users and then shared with other network users by using shared folder permissions. Users, including administrators, can delete local shares, and they are not automatically created upon restart.

File Sharing with Windows

On Windows systems, you can share a folder by modifying the folder's properties. When you share a folder, you assign it a share name that can be different from the underlying folder name. You can share the folder more than once using different names.

Users can connect to the shared folder by browsing to the computer in **Network,** or by selecting **Start→Run** and entering the Universal Naming Convention (UNC) path to the folder, in the form **\\computername\sharename.**

Viewing Shares on the System

You can see all shares on a system, including administrative shares, by opening **Computer Management,** expanding **Shared Folders,** and selecting the **Shares** node. You should see the following administrative shares on every Windows system:

- The root of each drive on the system is shared with its drive letter. Thus, the C drive is shared administratively as C$, the D drive is shared as D$, and so on.
- The folder where Windows is installed, usually the C:\Windows folder, is shared as ADMIN$.
- An InterProcess Communication (IPC) network object is created and shared as IPC$. This does not represent a local folder, but it enables computers to establish network sessions using the IPC mechanism.

File Sharing with OS X

When you use OS X, you can share files in the Public folder for your user account with up to 10 other network users. (Sharing with more users requires OS X Server.) You will need to make the

AppleTalk service active, assign a network name to your computer, and start the file sharing service. Other OS X users on your local network can then connect to your system by choosing **Connect To Server** from the **Go** menu and browsing for your computer's name. They can access files in your Public folder, and place files in your Drop Box folder.

For more information about file sharing in OS X, including information on how to make other folders public, share files with remote users on the Internet, and share with computers running different operating systems, see the technical document "Mac 101: File Sharing" on the Apple website at **http://support.apple.com/kb/HT1549**.

File Sharing with UNIX or Linux

UNIX and Linux are typically used as centralized network file servers, rather than for ad hoc peer-to-peer resource sharing. These systems generally use the Network File Sharing (NFS) protocol to share files with other UNIX and Linux systems. NFS enables clients to see the files on the shared system as if they were part of the client's own local file system.

The specific steps for implementing file sharing with NFS will vary depending on the operating system version, and also depending on whether you use shell commands or your system's GUI to configure the service. This is also true for the commands or steps that the clients will need to use to mount the file systems that NFS exports.

For a sample discussion of exporting and mounting NFS file systems on Red Hat Enterprise Linux, see the Red Hat Enterprise Linux 6 Storage Administration Guide: Chapter 12, Network File System (NFS). Go to **https://access.redhat.com/knowledge/docs**, select **Red Hat Enterprise Linux,** scroll down until you see **Storage Administration Guide,** select an available format, and in the Storage Administration Guide, navigate to Section 12.1.

For additional information about Samba, see the Samba Wiki at **https://help.ubuntu.com/community/Samba**.

Share Permissions

You can set three different levels of permissions on shared files and folders in Windows.

Permission	Enables Users To
Read	• View file and subfolder names. • View file contents and file attributes. • Run program files. The Read permission is granted by default to the Everyone group when a folder is shared and to new users when they are added to the **Permissions** list.
Change	• Perform all Read permission tasks. • Add files and subfolders. • Change file contents. • Delete subfolders and files.
Full Control	• Perform all Read and Change tasks. • Change NTFS permissions on files and folders inside the shared folder.

NTFS vs. Share Permissions

NTFS permissions apply to the actions that users can take on a file or folder either on the network or locally. Share permissions apply only to the folders (and possibly subfolders and files) that have been shared with other users and are being accessed over the network. Using both NTFS and share permissions on the same files and folders may seem like overkill, but they are often used together, and it is important to understand the differences between the two permissions and how they interact with one another.

In Windows, a shared folder has two sets of permissions: the NTFS permissions (which are on the **Security** tab of that folder's **Properties**) and the share permissions (which are on the **Shared** tab of that folder's **Properties**). The security permissions do not automatically change once a folder is designated as a share, and there is no propagation between the two. A folder can have NTFS permissions assigned, and then be shared and have share permissions assigned. When a user accesses the folder over the network, both the share and NTFS permissions are applicable, and the most restrictive of the two sets of permissions applies. So, if the network user has the Full Control NTFS permission but only the Read share permission, the user will have only the ability to read the contents of the folder.

 Note: When a user accesses a file on the local system, however, only the NTFS permissions apply. The fact that the folder is shared is not relevant when you are accessing the folder locally.

Permissions Considerations

There are some important considerations that you should keep in mind when applying permissions to files and folders.

NTFS vs. Share Property	Function and Description
Allow vs. Deny	When choosing whether to allow or deny an action using permissions, you need to choose carefully between the two. Deny is more restrictive than Allow. If the Deny property is applied on either a file or a folder, it will override any Allow permissions that may have been granted to the user. Therefore, use of the Deny permission should be done sparingly. You should deny permissions (using explicit Deny) only to a specific user when it is necessary to override permissions that are otherwise allowed for the group to which this user belongs.
	When establishing permissions, administrators can specify whether the entry being added should have access (Allow) or not have access (not Allow) to the resource. It is more practical to clear all the Allow check boxes for a group or a user, in effect denying them access to the resource without using the absolute Deny option. "Not-Allow" access in this way is easier to troubleshoot, manage, and configure.
Moving vs. copying files and folders	When permissions have been applied, moving a file or folder and copying that file or folder will have different results. It is important to consider those results when choosing whether to move or to copy your files or folders.
	When you move a file or folder from one folder to another on the same partition, it retains the permissions that were applied to it in its original location. When you copy a file or folder from one directory to another, it inherits the permissions of the folder or directory to which it has been copied.
	When you move a file or folder between partitions, the result is similar to copying the file or folder: it will inherit the target folder's permissions.
File attributes	You can set file attributes on files and folders, and these attributes can affect the actions a user can have on that specific file or folder, regardless of the permissions that have already been set. If a file or folder has the Read-Only attribute, the attribute will override the permissions applied to users who are accessing that file or folder.

User Authentication

User authentication is a network security measure in which a computer user or some other network component proves its identity in order to gain access to network resources. There are many possible authentication methods; one of the most common is a combination of a user name and a password.

Most authentication schemes are based on the use of one or more authentication factors. The factors include:

- Something you know, such as a password.
- Something you have, such as a key or an ID card.
- Something you are, including physical characteristics, such as fingerprints.

SSO

Single sign-on (SSO) is an access control property that you can use to provide users with one-time authentication to multiple resources, servers, or sites. Users log in once with a single user name and password to gain access to a number of different systems, without being asked to log in at each access point. Different systems may use different mechanisms for user authentication, so SSO has to use different credentials to perform authentication. With the widespread use of SSO, it is important to ensure that user authentication is strong for the login; with one potential user name and password providing access to a host of systems, it is critical that this single access point is being properly secured.

User Access Process

There are three phases in the user access process that a person or system must perform in order to gain access to resources:

- Identification: The claim of identity made by the user when entering a user name and password.
- Authentication: The verification of that claim.
- Authorization: The action taken as a result of verifying the claim.

One–, Two–, and Three–Factor Authentication

An authentication scheme with just one factor can be called single-factor authentication, while a two- or three-factor authentication scheme can simply be called *multi-factor authentication*.

TOPIC E

Windows Operating System Tools

In the previous topic, you identified Windows security settings that you can use to control access to data and files stored in the operating system. With so many files and features available in the operating system, a working knowledge of the toolset that is used to manage the operating system is crucial to your success as a computer technician. In this topic, you will identify some of the fundamental Windows operating system tools.

As an IT professional, you will need to be prepared to act on varying requests for supporting Windows systems, from installation to configuration and beyond. The Windows operating system provides a great many tools to assist you in supporting your Windows users. By identifying Windows operating system tools, you can be better prepared to select the appropriate tool for the job at hand.

This topic covers all or part of the following CompTIA® A+® (2012) certification objectives:

- Exam 220-802, Objective 1.1: Compare and contrast the features and requirements of various Microsoft Operating Systems.
- Exam 220-802, Objective 1.4: Given a scenario, use appropriate operating system features and tools.

Administrative Tools

In Windows 7, Windows Vista, and Windows XP, the Administrative Tools folder includes several tools that advanced users and system administrators can use to help manage the system. In Windows 7 and Windows Vista, you can access the Administrative Tools folder by selecting **Start→Control Panel→System and Maintenance.** In Windows XP, select **Start→Control Panel.** The following table describes the contents of the Administrative Tools folder.

Administrative Tool	Description
Component Services	*Component Services* is the GUI that developers and administrators can use to configure and administer Component Object Model (COM) components.
Computer Management	*Computer Management* is the primary administrative tool you will use to manage and configure a Windows XP or Windows 7 computer. **Computer Management** combines several administrative utilities into a single console to provide easy access to the most common system tools, including **Event Viewer, Performance Monitor, Disk Defragmenter, Disk Management,** and more.
Data Sources (ODBC)	*Data Sources* uses Open Database Connectivity (ODBC) to move data between different databases on the system.
Event Viewer	You can use the *Event Viewer* to view the contents of event logs, which contain information about significant incidents that occur on your computer. Examples of events that might be contained in an event log include a program starting or stopping and security errors.
iSCSI Initiator	You can use the *iSCSI Initiator* to configure connections between network storage devices.
Local Security Policy	You can use the *Local Security Policy* to view and edit the security settings for the local computer.

Administrative Tool	Description
Performance Monitor	*Performance Monitor* is a software tool that monitors the state of services or daemons, processes, and resources on a system. **Performance Monitor** tracks one or more counters, which are individual statistics about the operation of different objects on the system, such as software processes or hardware components.
Print Management	You can use *Print Management* to view and manage all of the printers and print servers installed on a network.
Services	You can use *Services* to view all of the services that run in the background on a system. For each service, you can view a description of the service, and for some services, you can perform certain actions such as starting, pausing, stopping, or restarting the service.
System Configuration MSCONFIG	You can use *System Configuration* to identify and manage issues that may be causing the system to run improperly at startup.
Task Scheduler crontab	You can use the *Task Scheduler* to create and manage certain system tasks that will be automatically carried out by your computer at predetermined times.
Windows Firewall with Advanced Security	You can use *Windows Firewall with Advanced Security* to manage advanced firewall settings for the computer and any remote computers that are connected to the network.
Windows Memory Diagnostic	You can use the *Windows Memory Diagnostic* to check the RAM on the system and verify that it is functioning appropriately and efficiently.

The Microsoft Management Console

Many of the administrative tools, such as **Computer Management,** are snap-in tools for the MMC interface. The MMC interface provides a standard framework for a wide variety of administrative tools within Windows, so that tools with many different functions have a similar look and feel and so that you can access them from within a common application. All Windows XP MMC consoles have a two-pane structure with a hierarchical console tree view on the left and a details pane view on the right; a third **Actions** pane was added in Windows Vista and Windows 7. **Computer Management** is just one of several preconfigured MMC consoles that are included with Windows XP, Windows Vista, and Windows 7; you can also create custom MMC consoles by adding snap-in tools into the MMC interface. See Windows Help for more information on creating and saving a custom MMC console.

Event Logs in Windows XP

There are three default event logs available in the **Event Viewer** on Windows XP computers:

- The Application log records Information, Warning, or Error messages generated by specific applications, and by some Windows services. The application developer determines whether or not a particular application will post entries to the log.
- The Security log records Success Audit or Failure Audit events if an administrator has configured security auditing on the system. If you have not configured an audit policy, this log will be empty.
- The System log records Information, Warning, or Error messages generated by system components. For example, this log will show you if a driver or service has failed to load.

Event Logs in Windows Vista and Windows 7

Windows Vista and Windows 7 include two additional event logs in the **Event Viewer:** :

- The Setup log stores events relating to installation of new applications.
- The Forwarded Events log stores event IDs from other computers.

Additional Event Logs

In certain circumstances, additional logs may also be available; for example, a DNS server will also have a DNS log. To access **Event Viewer** from the command line, enter `eventvwr.exe`

ACTIVITY 2-6
Exploring Administrative Tools

Scenario

In this activity, you will explore some of the options available in the **Administrative Tools Control Panel**.

1. Open the **Administrative Tools Control Panel**.
   a) Select **Start→Control Panel**.
   b) Select **System and Security**.
   c) Select **Administrative Tools**.

2. Examine the options available in the **Administrative Tools Control Panel**.

3. Examine system performance by using the **Performance Monitor**.
   a) Double-click **Performance Monitor,** and in the console tree, select **Performance Monitor**.
   b) The default configuration does not contain a counter. To add a counter, select the **Add** icon.
   c) In the **Select counters from computer** drop-down list, verify that **Local computer** is selected.
   d) Scroll and expand the **Memory** object.
   e) With the **Memory** performance object expanded, check **Show description**.
   f) View the explanations for other performance counters.
   g) Click **Memory** and verify that all objects are highlighted under the **Memory** performance object, and then select **Add.**

   All of the **Memory** performance objects are transferred to the **Added counters** pane and are marked with an asterisk.
   h) Select **OK.**

4. Change the **Performance Monitor** report type.
   a) On the toolbar, select **Change graph type→Report.**
   b) Verify that the default line graph is replaced by a text-based report.
   c) Select the **Freeze Display** button, to freeze the display.

   When you freeze the display, the counters no longer update in real time.
   d) Select the **Unfreeze Display** button to resume the counters.

5. Change the rate at which the system collects performance data.
   a) Press **Ctrl+G** to change the graph type back to a line graph. Observe the time increments on the horizontal axis.
   b) Select **Action→Properties.**
   c) In the **Performance Monitor Properties** dialog box, on the **General** tab, in the **Graph elements** section, in the **Sample every** text box, select the text and type *5*
   d) In the **Duration** text box, select the text and type *90*
   e) Select **OK.**
   f) Watch the screen for 10 seconds and verify that the sampling rate has been changed to every 5 seconds and that the graph now displays 90 seconds of information at a time. When you have finished, close **Performance Monitor**.

Local Users and Groups

You can use *Local Users and Groups* to create and manage user and group accounts on the local system. To access **Local Users and Groups,** open **Computer Management,** and expand **System Tools.**

Device Manager

You can use *Device Manager* to manage and configure hardware devices. In Windows 7, there are several ways to access **Device Manager:**

- Select **Start→Control Panel→System and Security→Device Manager.**
- At a command prompt, enter the mmc devmgmt.msc command.
- In the navigation pane of **Computer Management,** select **Device Manager.**

You can use **Device Manager** to:

- View a list of all devices attached to the system.
- See the status of a device. An exclamation point means there is a problem with a device; a yellow question mark means the device has been detected but a driver is not installed, or there is a resource conflict.
- Enable or disable a device. A disabled device appears with a red X.
- Determine the device driver a device is using; upgrade a device driver; roll a device driver back to a previous version.
- Determine any system resources that the device is using, such as interrupt request lines (IRQs) or Direct Memory Access (DMA) ports.
- Uninstall or reinstall devices.

Device Manager Log On Options

No matter which option you use to access **Device Manager,** if you are logged on as the built-in administrator account, **Device Manager** opens immediately. If you are logged on as a member of the **Administrators** group, the **User Account Control** dialog box opens, and you can select **Continue** to open **Device Manager.** If you are logged on as a standard user, you are notified that you are restricted from changing device settings, and **Device Manager** opens in read-only mode.

ACTIVITY 2–7
Using Computer Management and Device Manager

Before You Begin

The **Administrative Tools Control Panel** is open.

Scenario

In this activity, you will use **Computer Management** and **Device Manager** to check the status of the various functions and devices installed in your computer.

1. Examine the **Computer Management** console.
   a) Double-click **Computer Management.**
   b) To view the categories of log files that Windows maintains, select **Event Viewer.**
   c) If necessary, scroll down to view the **Log Summary** section. To view the contents of a log file in the **Log Summary** list, select **System,** and in the **Actions** pane, select **View events in this log.**
   d) To view the tools for managing shared network folders, in the console pane, select **Shared Folders.**
   e) To see the shared folders on the system, in the console pane, expand **Shared Folders,** and then select **Shares.**
   f) To view the tools for managing local computer accounts, in the console pane, select **Local Users and Groups.**
   g) To see the local users on the system, expand **Local Users and Groups,** and then select **Users.**

2. View device status in the **Device Manager.**
   a) In the console pane, expand **Performance,** and select **Device Manager.**
   b) Expand the **Keyboards** node.
   c) Verify that the **Keyboard Device** icon appears normal, and double-click the icon to open the keyboard's property sheet.
   d) Select the **Driver** tab.
      You can view details about the driver, update or roll back the driver, or disable or uninstall the device on the **Driver** page.
   e) Select the **Details** tab.
   f) On the **Details** tab, select a property, and view the corresponding details. Select **Cancel.**
   g) Expand other categories, and view the status and properties of other devices.
   h) Close **Computer Management** and the **Administrative Tools** and **Control Panel** windows.

3. Did any devices have problems?

Task Manager

Windows Task Manager is a basic system diagnostic and performance monitoring tool included with Windows XP, Windows Vista, and Windows 7. You can use **Task Manager** to monitor or terminate applications and processes, view current CPU and memory usage statistics, monitor network connection utilization, set the priority of various processes if programs share resources, and manage logged-on local users.

Task	Description and Purpose
Applications	Displays all of the applications currently running on the system and their status (running, not responding, etc.). Users can use the **Task Manager** to end an application that is running, switch to a different open application, or start a new application.
Processes	Displays all of the processes currently running on the system, including the CPU and memory usage for all processes. Users can choose to end a process from the **Task Manager**.
Performance	Displays the current CPU and physical memory usage statistics for the system in a graphical format and numerical format for an overall view of the current system performance.
Networking	Displays the networks that the system is currently connected to, and graphically displays current connection utilization for all network connections.
Users	The **Users** tab was added in Windows Vista and is still available in Windows 7. It displays all of the users currently logged on to the system. Users can select another user's account and connect to that user's session, send them a message, or disconnect or log off the user via the **Task Manager.**

Viewing the Task Manager

You can view **Windows Task Manager** by right-clicking the taskbar and choosing **Start Task Manager,** or by selecting **Ctrl+Alt+Del** and selecting **Start Task Manager.** By default, **Windows Task Manager** will always remain on top of other applications.

ACTIVITY 2-8
Using Task Manager

Scenario

In this activity, you will use the **Task Manager** utility to examine your system's status.

1. Display the pop-up menu for the taskbar, and select **Start Task Manager.**
   The **Applications** tab is blank because there are no application windows open.

2. Run an application.
   a) To start an application, select **New Task** to open the **Create New Task** dialog box.
   b) In the **Open** text box, type *notepad* and select **OK.**
      Notepad opens in the background and the **Untitled - Notepad** task appears on the **Applications** tab.

3. Use **Task Manager** to review the system's status.
   a) Verify that a running process count, CPU usage percentage, and committed memory value all appear on the **Task Manager** status bar.
   b) On the **Applications** tab, display the pop-up menu for the **Notepad** application and select **Go To Process.**
      There are various processes running on the system. Some are running in the background, not in their own windows, and so they do not appear on the **Applications** tab.

4. From within **Task Manager,** close Notepad.
   a) To close Notepad, verify that the **Notepad** process is selected, and select **End Process.**
   b) Select **End process** to confirm that you want to close the application.

5. Select the **Services** tab, and examine the services that are running independently on the system.

6. Select the **Performance** tab.
   The **Performance** tab provides a graphical report on system performance statistics.

7. Select the **Networking** tab.
   The **Networking** tab provides a graphical report on network activity.

8. Select the **Users** tab.
   This tab lets you see the other users who may be logged on to Windows 7.

9. Close **Task Manager.**

Disk Management

Disk Management is a snap-in utility for the MMC that you can use to manage all of the drives installed on the system, including hard disk drives, optical disk drives, and flash drives.

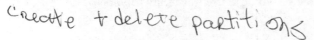
Create + delete partitions

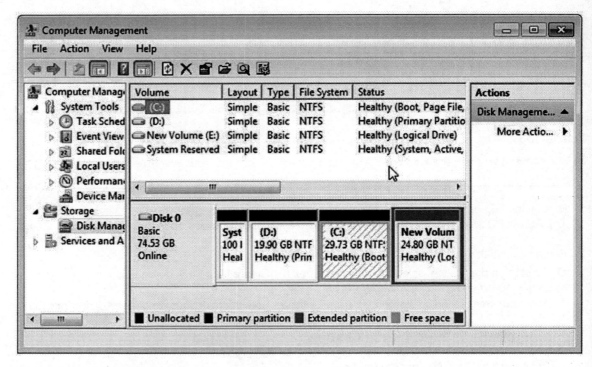

Figure 2-14: The Disk Management utility in Windows 7.

 Note: Although any user can access **Disk Management** and view information about their drives, only an administrator can use the other disk management tools available through this utility.

Action	Description
Views	Displays all of the drives on the system, the drive letter assigned, the total capacity of the drive and how much free space is available, and the current status of the drive. It also displays the partitions for each drive.
Assign a drive letter	Can be used to assign or change a drive letter for any hard drives, optical drives, or flash drives being used by the system. The drive letter for the partition that Windows is installed on cannot be changed.
Mount a drive	Can be used to create a mounted drive or partition, in which the drive is mapped to a NTFS-formatted folder on the hard drive and is assigned a folder path name rather than a drive letter.
Extend partitions	Can be used to create a container for logical partitions in order to extend the volume of an existing partition, if more than four partitions are desired.
Split partitions	Can be used to shrink or divide a partition on the drive to make room for another partition to be created. In Windows Vista and Windows 7, you can reduce the partition volume to a desired size to make free space for a new partition to be created.
Add a drive	Can be used to add a drive/disk to the machine. Once the drive has been installed and depending on the history of the drive (already partitioned, never been used, etc.), you can use this utility to initialize the disk or set an offline disk to online.
Add an array	Can be used to create and add an array to the system, including assigning the drive a drive letter, mounting it to a folder, and formatting the volume. An array is more than one physical drive on the machine that is combined and managed as a single logical drive in the disk management utility.

Accessing Disk Management Directly

You can access **Disk Management** by using an MMC snap-in, but you can also access it directly by selecting **Start→Run,** and then entering the `diskmgmt.msc` command.

Migration Tools

There are a number of tools available through the Windows operating system to assist in migrating user information between systems, including files and settings.

Migration Tool	Description
User State Migration Tool	The *User State Migration Tool (USMT)* is a command line utility that copies files and settings from one Microsoft Windows computer to another, including user accounts, files, folders, Windows settings, email messages, and more. USMT can support the transfer of files and settings for Windows 2000, Windows XP, Windows Vista, and Windows 7. Not all versions of the USMT can support all source or destination operating systems.
Easy Transfer	*Easy Transfer* is a built-in data-migration utility in Windows Vista and Windows 7 that helps transfer files, data, and settings from one personal computer to another. If the computer isn't running Windows 7, the user will need to download and install a version of **Easy Transfer** for Windows Vista or Windows XP before beginning the migration process. **Easy Transfer** replaced the **Files and Settings Transfer Wizard** from Windows XP. It was upgraded with Windows 7 to include a file explorer for easy selection of files to transfer and provides a report of any files that were not migrated to the new system.
Files and Settings Transfer Wizard	The *Files and Settings Transfer Wizard* is a system tool that is available in Windows XP and earlier versions of Windows. It transfers files and settings from an old computer to a new computer. In the tool, the user can choose what to migrate (files only, settings only, or both files and settings) and how the selected items should be migrated (via a storage device like a disk or other removable media device, via a direct connection between the computers, or via a drive on a network). The files created using the **Files and Settings Transfer Wizard** are not supported in Windows Vista or Windows 7. However, to work around this problem, a user running Windows XP who needs to transfer files to a computer running Windows Vista or Windows 7 can download and install a version of **Easy Transfer** for Windows XP, and then migrate data by using the **Easy Transfer** tool.

UDMT

The Windows NT **User Data Migration Tool (UDMT)** is a legacy tool that was used with the Microsoft Windows NT operating system to copy files and settings from one system to another. In the later versions of NT derivatives, from Windows 2000 and on, it was replaced by the **USMT**.

The Registry

The *Registry* is the central configuration database where Windows stores and retrieves startup settings, hardware and software configuration information, and information for local user accounts. Logically, the Registry is divided into five sections called subtrees; each subtree is further divided into keys that contain individual data items called value entries. The Registry is stored on the disk as a group of files.

Note: For additional information, check out the LearnTO **Use the Registry** in the LearnTOs for this course on your LogicalCHOICE Course screen.

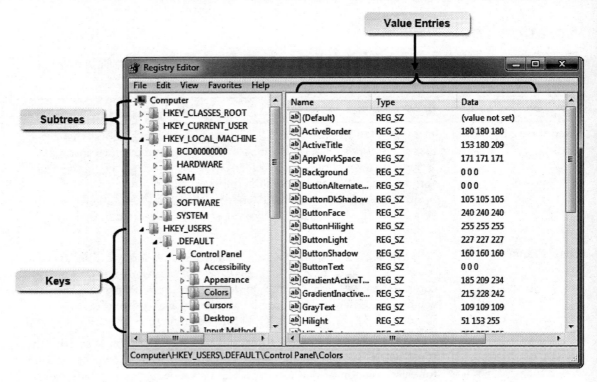

Figure 2-15: The Registry.

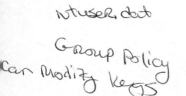

Editing the Registry

You can view and edit the contents of the Registry directly using the **Registry Editor** tool, regedit.exe. However, most changes to the Registry are made automatically by the system, by hardware devices, and by applications. It is rarely necessary to edit the Registry directly. If you ever need to do so, use extreme caution and back up the Registry files first, because incorrect changes can cause irrecoverable problems with Windows.

Windows 2000 offered an alternate version of the **Registry Editor,** regedt32.exe, that had a slightly different user interface. On Windows XP and the recent versions of Windows, if you enter the regedt32.exe command, regedit.exe will launch.

Registry Files

The Registry consists of five files stored in the \Windows\System32\Config folder: Default, SAM, Security, Software, and System. Plus, there is a Registry file named Ntuser.dat, which is unique for each user who logs on to the computer. This file is stored in each user's profile folder.

Registry Value Entries

An individual Registry value entry consists of a name, a data type, and the actual data stored in the value. The data types can be various types of alphanumeric strings, binary data, or hexadecimal data.

Registry Subtrees

The Registry consists of five subtrees, which are sometimes called "hives." Some of the subtrees are temporary pointers to information stored permanently in another Registry location. The following table lists and describes the subtrees.

Subtree	Contains
HKEY_CLASSES_ROOT	All the file association information. Windows uses this information to determine which application it should open whenever you double-click a file with a specific extension. For example, Windows automatically opens Notepad whenever you double-click a file with the extension .txt.
	In Windows 95 and later, HKEY_CLASSES_ROOT displays merged information from other hives such as HKEY_LOCAL_MACHINE and HKEY_CURRENT_USER To gain accurate configuration information, refer to those hives.
HKEY_CURRENT_USER ~~must be~~	The user-specific configuration information for the user currently logged on to the computer. For example, information about the user's selected color scheme and wallpaper is stored in this subtree. These settings take precedence over the default settings for the local machine.
HKEY_LOCAL_MACHINE - must be Admin	All the configuration information for the computer's hardware. For example, this subtree contains information about any modems installed in the computer, any defined hardware profiles, and the networking configuration. These settings will be used when there are no settings specified in HKEY_CURRENT_USER.
HKEY_USERS	User-specific configuration information for all the users who have ever logged onto the computer.
HKEY_CURRENT_CONFIG	Information about the current configuration of the computer's hardware. Windows operating systems support Plug and Play (PnP), a set of industry-standard device specifications, originally developed by Intel Corporation, which enables computers to automatically detect and install various types of devices without user intervention.

Run Line Utilities

The **Run** line appears in the **Start** menu by default in Windows XP. In Windows Vista and Windows 7, the **Search** function in the **Start** menu can be used in the same manner as the **Run** line, or the **Run** line can be added to the **Start** menu by customizing the properties. In all versions, you can also access the **Run** line via the keyboard shortcut **Windows key + R**.

You can use the **Run** line to access various system components and utilities by entering specific commands. These commands and their outcomes are the same for Windows XP, Windows Vista, and Windows 7.

Run Command	Description and function
cmd	Opens a new instance of the command interpreter/command prompt interface.
dxdiag	Opens and runs the **DirectX Diagnostic** tool, which displays hardware specifications and can be used to test that hardware's suitability for use with DirectX software, which handles multimedia tasks on Windows platforms. The report generated by running dxdiag can be used to view a list of all hardware, drivers, codecs, and system information for a computer, and can be a useful diagnostic tool.
explorer	Opens Windows Explorer in whatever the default view is for the system.
mmc	Opens the MMC.

Run Command	Description and function
`[command].msc`	Opens the management console for that entry (if one is available) when the .msc extension is added to the command. For example, `diskmgmt.msc` opens the **Disk Management** console, and `services.msc` opens the **Services Control Panel.**
`msconfig`	Opens the **System Configuration** utility.
`msinfo32`	Opens the **System Information** utility, which displays a summary of the hardware, software, and other system components in the environment.
`mstsc`	Opens the **Remote Desktop Connection** utility.
`notepad`	Opens an instance of Notepad.
`regedit`	Opens the **Registry Editor,** where the user can view or modify the contents of the Registry.
`services.msc`	Opens the **Services** console, where the user can manage all of the services and installed software on the system. Must be used with the .msc extension to open the management console.

 Note: You can use the **Run** line to open programs, folders, documents, Internet resources, or any other system component if there is an appropriate command to use.

Using .msc Extensions in the Run Line

There are a number of management consoles that can be accessed via the **Run** line using the .msc extension. When `[command].msc` is entered in the **Run** line, it will open the management console for that utility if one is available. For example:

- `devmgmt.msc` opens the **Device Manager** console.
- `diskmgmt.msc` opens the **Disk Management** console.
- `compmgmt.msc` opens the **Computer Management** console.

MSConfig

MSConfig is a system utility that is specifically used to troubleshoot issues that can arise during system startup. You can use it to view and manage which files or programs are processed on startup, including temporarily disabling and re-enabling software, programs, device drivers, or services that run automatically upon startup.

 Note: MSConfig.exe is called **System Configuration** in Windows Vista and Windows 7, but was called the **Microsoft System Configuration Utility** in earlier versions.

Within the **MSConfig** utility, there are five areas that can be accessed and modified.

Option	Description
General	Provides the options to choose from for startup configuration modes:
	• Normal startup. Windows will start in the normal manner. This is the default configuration or is selected once the other two modes have been used to troubleshoot an issue.

Option	Description
	• Diagnostic startup. Use this mode to troubleshoot issues by ruling out potential problem files. Windows will start running only basic services and drivers. • Selective startup. Use this mode to troubleshoot issues by running only the basic services and drivers at startup, but allowing the user to launch selected programs after startup. This enables you to begin to rule each program out as the potential cause of the problem.
Boot	Provides configuration settings for the boot process and advanced debugging configurations. Basic **Boot** options include: • Safe boot mode, including Minimal, Alternate shell, Active Directory repair, or Network modes. • No GUI boot. • Boot log. • Base video. • OS boot information. • Make all boot settings permanent. Advanced options include: • Number of processors. • Maximum memory. • PCI lock. • Debug. • Global debug settings. • Debug port. • Baud rate. • Channel. • USB target name.
Services	Displays all of the services that begin running at startup and their current status (running or stopped) and can be used to temporarily disable or re-enable specific programs or services to begin to determine which are potentially causing the problem at startup.
Startup	Displays all of the applications that begin running at startup, including the publisher of the application, the path to the .exe for the application, and the location of the shortcut or registry key for the application. You can temporarily disable or re-enable applications upon startup to begin to determine which application may be causing the startup issue.
Tools	Displays all of the diagnostic and advanced troubleshooting tools that are available on the system to help identify and fix the problem.

System Configuration Utility in Windows XP

While the functions were largely the same, the layout of the **System Configuration Utility** was rather different in Windows XP. It previously had six tabs:

• **General**
• **SYSTEM.INI**
• **WIN.INI**
• **BOOT.INI**
• **Services**

- **Startup**

MSConfig vs. Services

The **MSConfig** tool is frequently used to test various configurations for diagnostic purposes, rather than to permanently make configuration changes. Following diagnostic testing, permanent changes would typically be made with more appropriate tools, such as **Services,** to change the startup settings of various system services.

ACTIVITY 2-9
Exploring System Configuration Settings and Information

Scenario

In this activity, you will use the **MSConfig** and **MSINFO** tools to examine the system configuration settings and information.

---

1. Examine the system configuration settings with **MSConfig**.
   a) Select **Start**.
   b) In the **Search programs and files** text box, enter *msconfig*

      System Configuration is a diagnostic and troubleshooting utility that can help automate routine troubleshooting steps. The **General** page controls overall startup behavior.
   c) Select the **Boot** tab.

      System Configuration provides another way to define how you want to boot the computer.
   d) Select the **Services** tab.

      You can use **System Configuration** to enable or disable services that start when your computer boots.
   e) Select the **Startup** tab.

      You can view and manage items that are configured to load at system startup.
   f) To close **System Configuration,** select **Cancel.**

2. Examine the system information with msinfo32.
   a) Select **Start**.
   b) In the **Search programs and files** text box, enter *msinfo32*
   c) In the **System Information** dialog box, in the right pane, verify that the system is running Microsoft Windows 7 Professional.
   d) In the left pane, expand **Hardware Resources.**
   e) To view the assigned interrupts, select **IRQs.**
   f) Collapse **Hardware Resources.**
   g) Expand **Components** and select **CD-ROM** to view information about your CD-ROM drive.
   h) Collapse **Components.**
   i) Expand **Software Environment** and select **System Drivers** to view all the drivers installed on your computer.
   j) Collapse **Software Environment.**
   k) Close **System Information.**

Summary

In this lesson, you identified the fundamental components and functions of personal computer operating systems. Understanding the basics of what operating systems are, including their various versions, features, components, and technical capabilities, is knowledge that you can use to build a successful career as an IT support representative or PC service technician, interact confidently with other professionals, and perform your job duties properly and efficiently.

What operating systems do you have personal experience with? What operating systems would you like to learn more about, and why?

Which of the Windows system components and tools discussed in this lesson were familiar to you? Which ones were new?

 Note: Check your LogicalCHOICE Course screen for opportunities to interact with your classmates, peers, and the larger LogicalCHOICE online community about the topics covered in this course or other topics you are interested in. From the Course screen you can also access available resources for a more continuous learning experience.

3 | Operational Procedures

Lesson Time: 1 hour, 20 minutes

Lesson Objectives

In this lesson, you will identify the operational procedures that should be followed by professional PC technicians. You will:

- Identify basic maintenance tools and techniques for personal computer systems.

- Identify the best practices for PC technicians to follow to promote electrical safety.

- Identify best practices for PC technicians to follow to promote environmental safety and proper handling of materials.

- Identify best practices for PC technicians to use to communicate appropriately with clients and colleagues to conduct business in a professional manner.

Lesson Introduction

In the previous lessons, you gained fundamental knowledge about personal computer hardware components and operating systems. In addition to that information, every PC technician also needs a working knowledge of tools, safety and environmental precautions, and when professional conduct is important in the workplace. In this lesson, you will identify the operational procedures that you should follow to ensure a safe working environment.

As an A+ technician, you will be asked to install, configure, maintain, and correct problems with a variety of PC components. To work with these components without damaging them or causing physical injury to yourself or others, there are several tools to use and operational procedures to follow in order to get the job done quickly, safely, and correctly.

This lesson covers all or part of the following CompTIA® A+® (2012) certification objectives:

- Topic A:
  - Exam 220–801: Objectives 5.1, 5.2
  - Exam 220-802: Objective 1.6
- Topic B:
  - Exam 220–801: Objective 5.1
- Topic C:
  - Exam 220–801: Objectives 5.1, 5.2

- Topic D:
  - Exam 220–801: Objectives 5.3, 5.4

TOPIC A

Basic Maintenance Tools and Techniques

In this lesson, you will identify the operational procedures that can help ensure your success as an A + certified professional. To begin, it's critical to select the right tool or technique for the job. In this topic, you will identify common hardware and software tools, maintenance techniques, and resources that are used by professional PC technicians.

When it comes to computer maintenance, having the right tool will save time, trouble, and money. Having a good collection of software and hardware tools at your disposal, a foundational knowledge of maintenance techniques, and access to documentation or resources when you need assistance is essential to help you perform your job tasks efficiently.

This topic covers all or part of the following CompTIA ®A+® (2012) certification objectives:

- Exam 220–801: Objective 5.1 Given a scenario, use appropriate safety procedures.
- Exam 220–801: Objective 5.2 Explain environmental impacts and the purpose of environmental controls.
- Exam 220-802: Objective 1.6 Setup and configure Windows networking on a client/desktop.

Types of Hardware Toolkits

Because of the complexity of personal computers, there are several types of hardware toolkits that are commonly used in PC maintenance and repair.

Toolkit Name	Description and Contents
Basic	This toolkit should contain the tools necessary to remove and install computer components. Each tool should be demagnetized, and the tools should be stored in a case to protect and organize them.
	A basic toolkit should include:
	• Pen and/or pencil
	• Phillips screwdrivers (small and large, #0 and #1)
	• Flat-blade screwdrivers (small and large, 1/8-inch and 3/16-inch)
	• Flashlight
	• Container for screws
	• Nut driver
	Basic toolkits can also include:
	• Additional sizes of drivers and screwdrivers
	• Torx driver (size T8, T10, and T15)
	• Tweezers
	• Three-prong retriever
	• Ratchets
	• Allen wrenches
	• Cotton swabs
	• Batteries
	• Anti-static cleaning wipes
	• Anti-static wrist band
	• Compressed air canister
	• Mini vacuum
	• Pen knife

Toolkit Name	Description and Contents
	• Clamp • Chip extractor • Chip inserter • Multimeter • Soldering iron and related supplies • Spare parts container • Circuit tester • Drive adapters (USB to IDE/SATA and SATA/PATA/IDE to USB)
Network	Specialized tools, in addition to those listed previously, are needed to make and install network cables. Kits containing these tools are available, but the prices vary widely depending on the quality of the tools. A network toolkit typically includes: • Cable crimper with dies for a variety of cable styles • Wire stripper for flat and coax cable • Precision wire cutters • Cable tester • Punchdown tool • Curved forceps • Multi-network Local Area Network (LAN) cable tester • Digital multimeter
Circuit board	Usually circuit boards are replaced, not repaired. However, sometimes you can fix an obviously loose connection or replace a jack with a broken pin. A circuit board toolkit typically includes: • 30-watt (W) ceramic soldering iron • Desoldering braid • Desoldering pump • Soldering iron stand with sponge • Solder • Miniature pliers and wire cutters • Heat sink

Software Diagnostic Tools

A *software diagnostic tool* or utility is a computer repair program that can analyze hardware and software components and test them for problems. Some software diagnostic tools can repair software problems and optimize settings. Most operating systems include several software diagnostic tools integrated into them. In addition, most computer stores have at least one aisle dedicated to utility software that has been developed by other software manufacturers.

Microsoft® Windows® 7 provides a few different software diagnostic tests that you can use to identify and repair computer hardware and software issues. For example, you can run the **Automatically fix file system errors** tool on any of your system drives by accessing the drive's **Properties,** selecting the **Tools** tab, and pressing **Check now.**

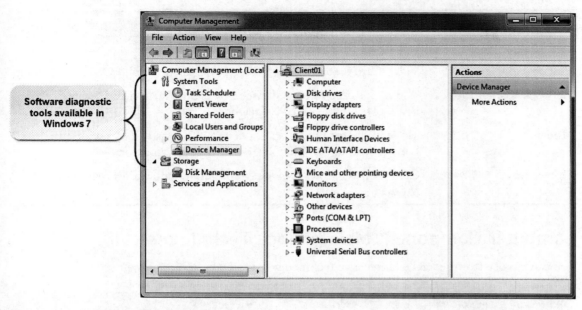

Figure 3–1: Software diagnostic tools.

Hard Drive Self–Tests Smart - System monitoring analysis Reporting Tool)

Most hard disk drive manufacturers provide a diagnostic tool that enables the drive to test itself when you start up a PC. Some of these hard drive self-tests are built into the firmware for the hard disk drive, while others are separate utilities that are available for download from the drive manufacturer's website. Make sure that you download the test utility that was designed to be used with your hard disk drive.

Software Diagnostic Tests

Software diagnostic tests are available from many different manufacturers, and they vary widely in their capabilities, but they can all assist you in detecting, repairing, and preventing hardware and software problems. The Windows operating systems also come with their own sets of diagnostic tools that can help you detect problems.

Examples of Software Diagnostic Tests

There are many applicable software diagnostic tests that you can use to troubleshoot computer problems.

Hardware Component	Examples of Software Diagnostics Test
Entire system	PC-Doctor Service Center, PC-Diag, Norton™ SystemWorks, QuickTech Pro, McAfee® System Mechanic, CheckIt Diagnostics, DirectX Diagnostic Tool, Windows **Device Manager**, Windows **Performance Monitor** There are many additional antivirus and anti-malware software solutions provided that detect and remove viruses, malware, and spyware.
Motherboard	Motherboard Diagnostic Toolkit, Power-On Self Test (POST), Basic Input/Output System (BIOS) setup
Central processing unit (CPU)	x86test, POST, BIOS setup
Memory	Memtest86+, DocMemory Diagnostics, POST, BIOS setup

Hardware Component	Examples of Software Diagnostics Test
Fan	SpeedFan, BIOS setup
Video adapter card	Video Card Stability Test, DirectX Diagnostic Tool, POST, BIOS setup
Network adapter card	3Com Dynamic Access Managed PC Boot Agent (MBA), Intel® PROset II Utility, DirectX Diagnostic Tool
Modem	Modem Doctor Diagnostics, DirectX Diagnostic Tool, Windows **Device Manager,** Windows **Performance Monitor**
Optical drive	CDRoller, Windows **Device Manager,** Windows **Performance Monitor**

Computer Component Maintenance Techniques

You can choose from several maintenance techniques to maintain PC components.

Maintenance Technique	Description
Use proper power devices.	Use a surge protector or *uninterruptible power supply (UPS)* to protect the computer from power surges, spikes, brownouts, and power failures.
Clean peripheral components.	Use to prevent problems with the computer's peripherals resulting from dust buildup.
Clean internal system components.	Use to prevent problems with internal computer components resulting from dust buildup.

Cleaning Compounds and Materials

 Note: For additional information, check out the LearnTO **Clean a Desktop Computer** in the LearnTOs for this course on your LogicalCHOICE Course screen.

Cleaning materials for computers range from standard household cleaning supplies to supplies specifically designed for computers and electronics.

Cleaning Supply	Description
Wipes and cloths	There are several types of wipes and cloths that you can use to clean displays, keyboards, and other equipment.
	• Monitor cleaning wipes are alcohol-based, lint-free, pre-moistened wipes for cleaning monitor screens. Use these only on cathode ray tube (CRT) or TV monitors and not on plastic-coated liquid crystal display LCD screens.
	• Keyboard cleaning wipes are pre-moistened wipes for cleaning keyboards.
	• You can use microfiber cloths to lightly remove dust and smudges from LCD displays. You can also use an LCD cleaning solution with the cloth to remove particles and smudges that are stuck to the screen.
	• If you choose not to use pre-moistened wipes, you can use rubbing alcohol applied to a lint-free cloth to wipe down screens and keyboards. You can also use this to clean other components.

Cleaning Supply	Description
	• A toner cloth is a special cloth that you stretch that picks up toner particles that are either in the printer or around the printer. Be careful if you are using it inside the printer so that the cloth does not get caught on any components and leave fibers behind.
Cleaning solutions	There are a variety of cleaning solutions that you can use to clean displays, keyboards, and other equipment.
	• You can use rubbing alcohol on cotton swabs or lint-free cloths to clean many components.
	• You can use mild household cleaner to keep the exterior of computer components clean. This helps prevent dirt and debris from getting inside the equipment. Never spray the cleaner directly on the equipment. Avoid using ammonia-based cleaners around laser printers; the ammonia may react chemically with the toner.
	• For older monitors, especially plastic monitors, read the device's manual to determine the cleaning method recommended by the manufacturer. While some recommend water or isopropyl alcohol (IPA), others claim it is acceptable to use volatile chemicals such as hexane or petroleum benzene, a soft detergent such as Palmolive and water, no suds, or nothing but a dry soft cloth. While some recommend a top-down motion, others subscribe to the circular method.
	• For flat screens such as LCDs, light emitting diodes (LEDs), and plasmas, you can use distilled water, or an equal ratio of water and vinegar on a microfiber or lint-free cloth. There are also specialized cleaners available for flat screens, but make sure to check the manufacturer's instructions before use.
	• In some cases, you can use standard household window cleaner on components if you spray it on a lint-free cloth first. You can use this to clean smudges from optical disks. Never use window cleaner on plastic monitor screens, and even on glass screens; this cleaner might strip off the anti-glare protection. The best option is a damp, clean, soft cloth with water or a cleaner specifically made for monitors (or one that states it is safe for use with monitors) and will not damage anti-glare finishes.
Cleaning tools	Several tools are optimal for cleaning computer components.
	• Tightly wound cotton swabs are useful in getting cleaning solution into tight places. They are also useful when used dry to get dust and debris out from between keys and around buttons or other tight areas.
	• Toothpicks come in handy in getting dirt out from around keys, buttons, and other tight spaces. They are also useful for removing the debris that builds up on the rollers inside of a mouse.
	• You can use a small paint brush to remove dust from between keys on a keyboard. If the brush has long bristles, they can reach under the keys where other cleaning objects would not be able to reach.
Compressed air canister	A canister with a nozzle that can be aimed at components to blow dust out. This is often used when removing dust from the interior of a computer or laptop. Be sure to blow the dust away from the power supply and drives. You can also use it to blow dust out of the power supply fan area, from keyboards, and from the ventilation holes on various components.

Cleaning Supply	Description
	Use caution when working with compressed air. Read the instructions on the can and follow them carefully. Tipping the can too much, which is easy to do when you are trying to maneuver the can into place, can cause the propellant to leave the can in liquid form and at sub-freezing temperatures. The freezing could easily damage components, particularly those that may still be hot from use. There is also the issue of the corrosiveness of the chemical damaging components later on. Also, some delicate components on the motherboard can be damaged (literally blown off the board) if compressed air is used too close to a component.

If you use compressed air, take the equipment to a different location, preferably outside, so that the dust does not simply disperse into the air in the work area and settle back on the computer equipment or other devices. |
| Computer or electronics vacuum | A non-static vacuum that you can use on system components such as the power supply, fans, and in printers. (Regular vacuum cleaners can create static, which will damage computer equipment.) The vacuum should have a filter and bag fine enough to contain toner particles so that you can use it to clean up toner spills from laser printers or photocopiers. These vacuums can often be used to blow air as well as for suction, so they can replace the need for compressed air canisters for blowing dust out of machines. Sucking the dust up is usually better, though, since blowing the dust can cause it to get onto or into other components. Sucking it up into a vacuum cleaner bag gets it out of the system without the chance of it getting into something else. |
| Mask and gloves | A mask that fits over your mouth and nose should be worn when you are using a compressed air canister or working around toner spills. This will keep the particles out of your body. You should also wear latex gloves when cleaning up a toner spill. |

Documentation and Resources

There are several types of documentation and resources that you might find helpful when you are dealing with common hardware and operating system problems. You can also share documentation and resources with users as a means of assisting and educating them.

Method	Description
User/installation manuals	User and installation manuals can provide you with basic guidance for installing, configuring, and troubleshooting hardware and software.

By providing users with various user and installation manuals, users can fix minor issues and problems before requesting additional assistance from a technician. Examples include installing company-specific applications, installing network printers, and mapping drives. |
| Internet/web-based resources | Internet and web-based resources can provide a wealth of information on installing, configuring, and troubleshooting hardware and software. Many hardware and software manufacturers maintain knowledge bases and wikis to share information about |

Method	Description
	both common and unusual issues that can arise with PC hardware and software.
	Internet and web-based materials can also provide users with quick reference materials for dealing with everyday issues on their own. Some organizations provide a web page or wiki with user-specific information and reference materials.
Training materials	Most major hardware and software manufacturers provide training materials on how to install and use their products. These materials can be helpful for both new and experienced technicians.
	You can provide training materials for various tasks that users may need to complete on their own, such as virus scans, computer maintenance tasks, and PC clean-up tasks. By providing training materials, you empower users to be proactive in maintaining their systems.

Compliance and Government Regulations

In the United States and many other nations, your employer is obligated to comply with government regulations that apply to its specific business. The most common regulations are those issued by the federal government, such as the Occupational Safety and Health Administration (OSHA), and state standards regarding employee safety. OSHA-compliant employers must provide:

- A workplace that is free from recognized hazards that could cause serious physical harm.
- Personal protective equipment designed to protect employees from certain hazards.
- Communication—in the form of labeling, Material Safety Data Sheets (MSDSs), and training about hazardous materials.

Your responsibility—to yourself, your employer, your coworkers, and your customers—is to be informed of potential hazards and to always use safe practices.

Protection of the environment is another area that is regulated by the federal and local governments in the United States and many other nations. Many municipalities have regulations that control the disposal of certain types of computer equipment. Your responsibility is to be aware of any environmental controls that are applicable to your workplace, and to be in compliance with those regulations.

ACTIVITY 3-1
Examining Basic Maintenance Tools and Techniques

Scenario

In this activity, you will examine the various tools and techniques used to maintain computer equipment and the workplace environment.

1. You are asked to repair a motherboard in a customer's PC. Which set of tools would be best suited for the task?
   - Phillips screwdriver (#0), torx driver (size T8, T10, and T15), tweezers, and a three-prong retriever
   - 30-W ceramic solder iron, miniature pliers, wire cutters, and a soldering iron stand with sponge
   - Wire strippers, precision wire cutters, digital multimeter, and cable crimper with dies
   - Chip extractor, chip inserter, ratchet, and Allen wrench
   - Anti-static cleaning wipes, anti-static wrist band, flashlight, and cotton swabs

2. You are asked to correct a network cabling problem at a customer site. Which set of tools would be best suited for the task?
   - Phillips screwdriver (#0), torx driver (size T8, T10, and T15), tweezers, and a three-prong retriever
   - 30-W ceramic solder iron, miniature pliers, wire cutters, and a soldering iron stand with sponge
   - Wire strippers, precision wire cutters, digital cable tester, and cable crimper with dies
   - Chip extractor, chip inserter, ratchet, and Allen wrench
   - Anti-static cleaning wipes, anti-static wrist band, flashlight, and cotton swabs

3. You suspect that contaminants from the environment have prevented the fan on a PC from working optimally. Which set of tools would be best suited to fix the problem?
   - Phillips screwdriver (#0), torx driver (size T8, T10, and T15), tweezers, and a three-prong retriever
   - 30w ceramic solder iron, miniature pliers, wire cutters, and a soldering iron stand with sponge
   - Wire strippers, precision wire cutters, digital multimeter, and cable crimper with dies
   - Chip extractor, chip inserter, ratchet, and Allen wrench
   - Anti-static cleaning wipes, anti-static wrist band, flashlight, and cotton swabs

4. True or False? Windows includes software diagnostic tests that help you find and correct hardware problems.
   - ☐ True
   - ☐ False

5. Examine the tools that are available to you in class. Discuss how and when they may be used to repair, fix, or maintain computer equipment.

TOPIC B

Electrical Safety

In the previous topic, you identified basic maintenance tools and techniques that you will use as a PC technician. In addition to these basic maintenance practices, you need to be aware of specific tools and techniques that are available to promote electrical safety. In this topic, you will identify the best practices for PC technicians to follow to promote electrical safety.

The most prevalent physical hazards that computer technicians face are electrical hazards. Electricity is necessary to run a computer, but it can also damage sensitive computer equipment, and in some cases, pose a danger to humans. Following established best practices for promoting electrical safety will protect not only the computer equipment that you work on, but also your personal safety and the safety of others.

This topic covers all or part of the following CompTIA® A+® (2012) certification objectives:

- Exam 220–801: Objective 5.1 Given a scenario, use appropriate safety procedures.

Static Electricity

Static electricity is a build-up of a stationary electrical charge on an object. It is called "static" because the charge cannot escape the charged body until it comes in contact with another object. Static electricity is often caused by friction; rubbing one object against another causes a transfer of electrons between the two. Using friction to create a static charge is called *triboelectric generation*. The amount of static that can be built up in this manner depends on various factors, including the types of materials, their surface area and texture, and the ambient humidity. If you have ever shuffled your feet on a carpet and then gotten a small shock when you touched a doorknob or other metal object, you have used triboelectric generation.

 Note: Static charges can be as small as the sparks that come off a dry blanket in the wintertime or as massive as a lightning strike, with its millions of volts.

ESD

Electrostatic discharge (ESD) occurs when a path is created that allows electrons to rush from a statically charged body to another with an unequal charge. The electricity is released with a spark. The charge follows the path of least resistance, so it can occur between an electrical ground, such as a doorknob or a computer chassis, and a charged body, such as a human hand. ESD can damage sensitive computer equipment.

Static Electricity and Voltage

Because air has very high resistance, a static electric discharge usually requires contact with the statically charged object. For a static discharge to arc through the air, it requires a very high voltage, and no other path to the ground with lower resistance. You can feel a static discharge starting at around 3,000 volts (V). The drier the air, the greater the resistance, which is why static shocks on dry winter days can fall within the range of 10,000 to 20,000 V. Keeping a room humidified is one way to reduce the risk of static electricity.

If 120 V from a household electrical outlet can kill you, why does a static spark of 20,000 V just startle you? Because, while the voltage might be high, the current is very low; very few total electrons are transferred in a static spark. All the energy of all the electrons in a spark added together cannot hurt you, even though it may surprise you. Each electron in a static discharge has extremely high energy, but the human body is just too big for the very small number of electrons involved in the spark to cause widespread damage. A few cells in your fingertip may be damaged, but they easily grow back.

ESD Prevention Techniques

Charges as low as 10 V can damage or destroy sensitive electronic circuits and components. This is why ESD is such an enemy of integrated circuits. Static charges can build up on both conductors and insulators, as well as in the human body. When you work with computer equipment, you must take steps to protect against ESD.

There are several prevention techniques that you can use to protect yourself and equipment when you are working with computer components.

Prevention Technique	Description
Eliminate activities and tasks.	By eliminating unnecessary activities that create static charges and by removing unnecessary materials that are known charge generators, you can protect against ESD-related damage and injuries.
Use self-grounding methods.	Use grounding conductive materials and self-grounding methods before touching electronic equipment. You can prevent ESD injuries by using ESD straps that can be attached to your ankle or wrist.
Use equipment grounding methods.	Grounding equipment made up of *dissipative material* can also be used to avoid a static shock. A dissipative material is a conductor, but with high resistance. It loses its electrical charge slowly, so when you touch it, the electron flow is spread over time and you do not feel a shock. Prevent ESD damage to equipment by: • Using anti-static vacuums for cleaning computer components (such as system units, power supplies, and fans). • Using ESD mats and materials such as electric grounded flooring, work benches, or surfaces. • Using anti-static bags to store computer components that are particularly sensitive to ESD, such as RAM and power supplies.
Maintain air quality.	You can maintain air quality and prevent a high-ESD work environment by: • Using an air ionizer, which releases negative ions into the air. They attract positively charged particles and form neutrally charged particles. • Humidifying the air to speed up the static discharge from components. When the air is extremely dry, more static is likely. A higher humidity is best for ESD prevention. A rate of 50 to 60 percent is comfortable for both computers and technicians.

Anti-static Bags

Anti-static bags that are used for shipping components actually conduct electricity, so keep them away from equipment that is powered on.

EMI

Electromagnetic interference (EMI) occurs when a magnetic field builds up around one electrical circuit and interferes with the signal being carried on an adjacent circuit, causing network communication interference issues. All current-carrying devices generate magnetic fields, and fluctuating magnetic fields generate electrical current in nearby wires. While ESD is the primary electrical danger to computer equipment, EMI also causes problems with microcomputer circuitry and data transmissions between computing devices.

Magnets

EMI-related issues can be a result of magnets being placed too close to computer systems. Magnets can be harmful to computer components, and components should not be placed in close proximity to any magnets or items that contain magnets. It's important that you inform users to keep magnets away from their computer equipment.

EMI Prevention Techniques

There are many different methods that you can use to prevent EMI damage to the internal circuitry of devices and systems. *Use metal cases.*

Method	Description
Twisted-pair implementations	Twisted-pair cables are made with both sending and receiving conductors twisted together within the same cable. This method of manufacturing cable minimizes the chances of EMI interference because the conductors within the wire cancel each other out. For extra protection in multi-pair cables, such as Ethernet, each pair is twisted together at a different rate, and the multiple twisted pairs are then twisted together.
Cautious wiring techniques	The types of cables you use and how you place them can prevent certain devices and wires from interfering with each other. Fluorescent lights and alternating current (AC) electrical cables, for example, emit signals that are a source of EMI, so when you are running network cable in or along walls or ceilings, avoid running them near fluorescent fixtures, and try to cross electrical cables at right angles, rather than follow them. This minimizes the "cross-section" of interference from these sources. Electronic components themselves may generate or be susceptible to EMI; however, their leads serve as the antennae that radiate or receive such interference.
SMD technology implementation	Surface Mount Devices (SMDs) are electronic components that are designed to be soldered directly onto circuit boards without legs. This technology minimizes EMI transmissions to and from such devices.
Electromagnetic shielding	Shielding is used to prevent electromagnetic transfers from cables and devices by creating a conductive material protective barrier. For example, a shielded cable contains electromagnetic shielding within the cable that directly protects the inner core conductor from producing electromagnetic discharge.

Network Interference

Network interference is the disruption of normal data transmissions over a network. EMI can cause intermittent network issues and can be avoided by applying EMI prevention techniques such as shielding, wiring techniques, and using twisted pair cables to connect network components.

An ESD Toolkit

Some people who work on computer equipment never use a single piece of ESD safety equipment. They discharge themselves by touching an unpainted metal part of the computer case before touching any components. In other instances, a company policy might require that you use a properly equipped ESD-free work area. The minimum equipment in this case would be a grounded wrist ESD strap. Other ESD-protection equipment includes leg ESD straps, anti-static pads to cover the work surface, and grounded floor ESD mats to stand on. The mats contain a snap that you connect to the wrist or leg strap. Anti-static bags for storing components might also be included in an ESD toolkit. If the technician's clothing has the potential to produce static charges, an ESD smock, which covers from the waist up, can be helpful.

To ensure that the ESD equipment remains effective, you should test it frequently. A minor shock that you cannot feel can compromise ESD-sensitive equipment.

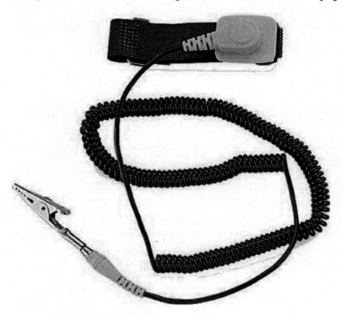

Figure 3–2: An ESD strap.

Electrical Hazards

Because computers are powered by electricity, there are some common potential electrical hazards that you should be aware of when you are servicing them.

Electrical Hazard	Description
Electric shock	If you touch a high-voltage source, and if you are either grounded or in contact with another electrical circuit, your body may complete an electrical circuit, permitting electrons to flow through you. Water is a better conductor than air or dry skin, so touching an electrical contact with wet hands reduces resistance and increases the current flow even more. Depending on the conditions, this may cause pain, burns, or even death.
Electrocution (fatal shock)	Electrocution results when the body is exposed to a lethal amount of electrical energy. For death to occur, the body must become part of an active electrical circuit with a current capable of overstimulating the nervous system or damaging internal organs. The extent of injuries received depends on the current's magnitude (measured in amperes), the pathway through the body, and the duration of flow. The resulting damage to the human body and the emergency medical treatment determine the outcome.
Burns	Contact with a source of electrical energy can cause external and internal burns. Exposure to higher voltages will normally result in burns at the sites where the electrical current entered and exited the body. High-voltage contact burns may display only small superficial injuries; however, the danger of these deep burns is destruction of internal tissues.

CRt -
Cathode Ray Tube

Electrical Hazard	Description
	Electricity can hurt you even if you are careful and avoid becoming part of an electrical ground circuit. The heat generated by an electric arc or electrical equipment can burn your skin or set your clothes on fire.
Collateral injuries	Collateral injuries occur when involuntary muscle contractions caused by the shock cause the body to fall or come in contact with sharp edges or electrically live parts. You instinctively pull your hand back from the doorknob when you get a static shock. Electricity flowing through your body can also cause your muscles to twitch uncontrollably. These motions can cause you to hurt yourself on objects around you.

Power Supplies and Electrical Hazards

Most of the internal circuitry in a computer is low voltage (12 V or less) and low current, so there is not much of a threat to your personal safety. However, there are exceptions to this, and these exceptions can be very dangerous. The main exceptions that you need to be aware of are power supplies.

- The computer's power supply outputs a relatively low voltage, but the high-voltage input can be hazardous. PC technicians who have diagnosed a bad power supply should simply replace it, rather than open it to troubleshoot the internal components.
- The power supply in older CRT computer monitors increase the voltage, because CRT monitors contain circuits that require 35,000 V with a high current. In any power supply, the current is stored on capacitors that do not discharge, even when the component is turned off or unplugged. Even after months of inactivity, the capacitors may have enough stored electrical energy to kill you. Today, it is less likely than in the past that you will be working with CRT monitors, but if you find yourself in a situation where repair or maintenance is needed, leave the internal workings of the monitor to specialists who have the extra training and special equipment that are required to safely remove a monitor cover and make repairs. In most cases, it is less costly and faster to simply replace a defective monitor.

Laser Printer Electrical Safety

Laser printers contain high-voltage electronic components inside the case, and these components can be harmful if not handled properly. Components such as the rollers and wires can hold a charge, and you should avoid contact with them. Follow proper cleanup and safety guidelines to prevent electrical shock when you are working with laser printers.

ESD and Electrical Hazards

All of the precautions that you use to prevent ESD *increase* your danger when you work near high voltages. An anti-static wrist band is specifically designed to provide a low-resistance path for electricity to a ground. If there were ground problems or shorts, your body and your static protection equipment could provide a path from the problem device to ground—the circuit would be completed through your body, causing electrocution.

This is precisely why you must unplug devices that you are servicing. Even when devices are turned off, the power supplies in most devices continue to produce voltage if the device is plugged into an outlet. You and your anti-static devices could provide a better path to ground than the device's wiring, leading to your electrocution. If there is a chance of coming in contact with a high-voltage source, you are advised to insulate yourself from ground by wearing rubber-soled shoes or standing on a rubber mat, and avoiding contact with any other grounded mass.

Power Inverter Electrical Safety

A power inverter converts direct current (DC) voltage to AC voltage. For example, you can use a power inverter in a car to provide a normal wall-style outlet for a laptop. The power inverter unit has no user-serviceable parts within it, so after you determine that the inverter is a problem, there is no need for further diagnosis and troubleshooting; the unit must be replaced.

Electrical Safety Precautions

Working on a computer can be safe and enjoyable if you protect yourself from electrical hazards by using some common sense and by taking appropriate precautions.

Category	Guidelines
Personal safety	• Make sure that you disconnect the power before repairing computer equipment. • Do not attempt repair work when you are tired; you may make careless mistakes, and your primary diagnostic tool, deductive reasoning, will not be operating at full capacity. • Do not assume anything without checking it out for yourself. • Remove jewelry or other articles that could accidentally contact circuitry and conduct current. • Wear rubber-soled shoes to insulate yourself from ground.
Environment conditions	• Suspend work during an electrical storm. • Do not handle electrical equipment when your hands or feet are wet or when you are standing on a wet surface. Perform as many tests as possible with the power off.
Anti-static equipment	• Prevent static electricity from damaging components by standing on a totally insulated rubber mat to increase the resistance of the path to ground. In some cases, workstations are located in areas with grounded floors and workbenches, so static electricity has a low-resistance, non-destructive path to ground. • When removing circuit boards, place them on a dissipative ground mat or put them in an anti-static bag. • Use an anti-static wrist strap when you are handling static-sensitive components such as system boards, sound cards, and memory chips.
Disassembly safety	• After cleaning a keyboard, be completely sure it is dry before powering it up. • Label wires and connectors as you detach them, and make sure you that plug them back into the proper sockets in the proper order. • When you replace the computer's case, make sure that all of the wires are inside. The case may have sharp edges that can cut through exposed cables.
Power supply safety	• Power supplies have a high voltage in them any time the computer is plugged in, even if the computer power is turned off. Before you start working inside the computer case, disconnect the power cord and press the power button to dissipate any remaining power in the system circuitry. Leave the power off until you are done servicing the system unit.

Category	Guidelines
	• Never stick anything into the power supply fan to get it to rotate. This approach does not work, and it is dangerous.
CRT monitor safety 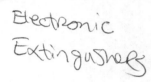	• Do not take the case off a monitor. The risk to your life is not worth any repairs you might make. • Do not tap or bang on the monitor screen with your tools; an implosion will propel shards of glass in every direction. • To clean the monitor, turn it off and unplug it; do not wear an anti-static wrist strap. Use isopropyl alcohol, rather than a general-purpose cleaner; alcohol does not create a safety hazard if small amounts are dripped inside the case, as it will evaporate rapidly. Use an anti-static cleaner to clean the glass on the monitor. • Follow proper disposal guidelines if the CRT monitor cannot be repaired.
Electrical fire safety	Electrical fires in computer facilities are especially dangerous. The damage done to computers is extremely expensive, and the chemicals used in the machines may emit toxic substances. It is not practical to fight these fires with small extinguishers or to douse fires with water. Special gases should be used to extinguish fires in computer facilities. To prevent electrical fires: • Check the electrical wiring of computer systems and components regularly. • Implement a strategy to make sure any old, worn, or damaged cables, network appliances, and computer systems are checked and replaced regularly. • Verify that smoke detectors are installed to sense the presence of smoke. • Use heat sensors that are triggered either when a target temperature is reached or when there is a high rate of increase in temperature. • Use flame detectors with optical sensors to record incoming radiation at selected wavelengths. Commercial fire detection systems should be connected to a central reporting station where the location of the suspected fire is indicated. In some cases, the detection system or monitoring station is connected directly to a fire department.

[Handwritten note near CRT monitor safety: "do Not want to Be gRounded on CRt"]

[Handwritten note near Electrical fire safety: "Electronic ExtinguisheR"]

ACTIVITY 3–2
Identifying Electrical Safety Issues

Scenario
In this activity, you will identify electrical safety issues.

1. True or False? If you are using an anti-static ESD floor mat, you do not need any other ESD safety equipment.
   ☐ True
   ☐ False

2. Electrical injuries include electrocution, shock, and collateral injury. Would you be injured if you are not part of the electrical ground current?

3. Which computer component presents the most danger from electrical shock?
   ○ System boards
   ○ Hard drives
   ○ Power supplies
   ○ System unit

4. Have you had any personal experience with any of the electrical hazards covered in this topic? What safety precautions could have prevented the incident?

TOPIC C

Environmental Safety and Materials Handling

In the previous topic, you identified best practices for safely dealing with electricity. Electrical safety is just one factor that you need to consider to ensure a safe work area. In this topic, you will identify best practices for promoting environmental safety and proper materials handling.

In addition to electrical issues, there are other environmental issues that computer technicians must deal with on a regular basis. The health and safety of you and those around you should always be your highest priority. Recognizing potential environmental hazards and properly dealing with them in a safe manner is a critical responsibility for an A+ technician.

This topic covers all or part of the following CompTIA® A+® (2012) certification objectives:

- Exam 220–801: Objective 5.1 Given a scenario, use appropriate safety procedures.
- Exam 220–801: Objective 5.2 Explain environmental impacts and the purpose of environmental controls.

Environmental Considerations and Controls

Certain environmental conditions can be extremely dangerous to you and those around you.

Consideration	Description and Controls
Ozone gas	Laser printers produce ozone gas, usually when the corona wire produces an electrical discharge during printing. Depending on the levels, ozone can be a mild-to-severe irritant. Regulatory agencies have established limits regarding the amount of ozone that employees can be exposed to. Be sure that your laser printers operate in a well-ventilated area. Some laser printers have a filter to control ozone emissions.
Temperature and humidity	Computer equipment and performance are both affected by temperatures and humidity levels. • Too much moisture can be problematic and cause physical damage to equipment. On the other hand, low humidity can contribute to more electrostatic charge into the air. High humidity levels can also have an effect on tapes and paper media. • Extreme temperatures can also be an issue. Low temperatures can cause condensation on computer system components that generate heat while turned on, while high temperatures can cause the components to overheat. Proper ventilation systems must be used to help prevent overheating of computer systems. Be aware of the humidity level and temperatures of the environment where devices will be installed and running to prevent these types of issues.
Dust and debris	Dust can be a more subtle hazard. The buildup of dust particles over time can cause problems with different types of equipment. Dust buildup causes resistance in moving parts, such as fans, drives, and printer motors. Dust buildup on circuit boards, heat sinks, and vents creates insulation that reduces heat dissipation. Dusting equipment often with compressed air and vacuums can prevent these types of issues. Make sure that printers and paper products are kept in a

Consideration	Description and Controls
	separate area from computer equipment to prevent paper dust from getting into the equipment.
Airborne particles	The conditions surrounding computer equipment can be an issue when there is a large number of airborne particles flowing in and around various devices. Contaminants can be either gaseous, such as ozone; particles, such as dust; or organic, which comes from industrial processing of fossil fuels, plastics, etc. All these contaminants can cause damage to computer equipment, such as corrosion and overheating. To protect your computing environment from airborne particles, you can: • Install computer equipment enclosures that will prevent contaminants from entering the devices. • Install air filters throughout the facility to catch excess particles as the air flows through the heating, ventilation, and air conditioning (HVAC) system.

Workplace Safety Issues

Various workplace situations can be a hazard to you and your coworkers.

Safety Issue	Description
Falling and tripping	Within your work area alone, a number of things can cause you to fall or trip. While working with computer equipment, you need to keep in mind the location of hardware, cables, and devices.
Equipment storage	CPUs and other hardware should not be stacked on top of one another. Make sure the equipment is secure, whether it is on the floor or on a desk or shelf.
Component handling and protection	Whenever you are handling computer equipment, you must follow the proper handling guidelines. Use an anti-static bag to store any computer component that can carry ESD. For example, when you are removing or replacing RAM, motherboards, or CPUs from inside a computer, immediately place the component in an anti-static bag until it is either replaced or disposed of.
Cable management	In office environments where there are many computers, there can also be many cables and power cords. If these cords and cables are lying on the floor, they could possibly cause a person to trip on them.
Lasers	Lasers are used in printers, CD drives, DVD drives, and Blu-ray drives and players. "Laser" is an acronym for Light Amplification by Stimulated Emission of Radiation. A laser produces an intense, directional beam of light by stimulating electronic or molecular transitions to lower energy levels. This powerful beam can cause damage to the human eye or skin. Lasers have many uses and, like other tools, are capable of causing injury if improperly used. The most likely injury is a thermal burn that will destroy retinal tissue in the eye. Because retinal tissue does not regenerate, the injury is permanent.
Repetitive strain injury (RSI)	Repetitive strain injuries involve damage to muscles, tendons, and nerves caused by overuse or misuse. Computer users suffer mostly from repetitive strain injuries to the hand, wrist, and arm. Unlike strains and sprains, which usually result from a single incident—called acute trauma—

Safety Issue	Description
	repetitive strain injuries develop slowly over time. The type of injury depends on whether the muscle, tendon, tendon sheath, or nerve tissue has been irritated or damaged. Any or all of the following symptoms may appear in any order and at any stage in the development of an injury of RSI: • Aching, tenderness, and swelling • Pain, crackling, and tingling • Numbness and loss of strength • Loss of joint movement and decreased coordination
Eye strain	Many computer tasks are done at a close working distance, requiring the eyes to maintain active focusing. This can cause stress and strain on the eyes and the muscles that control them. A very common health problem reported by users of computer monitors is eye strain—including the following symptoms: • Blurred vision • Difficulty focusing • Double vision • Tiredness • Headaches • Burning, sore, or itchy eyes Dry eyes can also be a concern for computer operators. The eye surface becomes dry because computer users tend to blink less and tears evaporate faster during monitor use. Symptoms associated with dry eyes are redness, burning, and excess tearing.
Radiation *Radio waves*	Radiation is a broad term used to describe energy in the form of waves or particles. Electromagnetic radiation comes from both natural and manufactured sources, including CRT computer monitors. Circuits within the monitor are responsible for the horizontal and vertical movements of the electron beam. This movement occurs tens of thousands of times each second (Very Low Frequency, or VLF) for the horizontal scan, and 50 to 60 times each second (Extremely Low Frequency, or ELF) for the vertical scan. The VLF and ELF field intensities have been extensively evaluated in many different models of monitors for possible biological effects. CRT computer monitor users have expressed concerns about the possible health effects from the electromagnetic radiation that monitors produce. While the research continues, current scientific information does not identify a health risk from exposure to these electromagnetic fields. With CRT monitor use decreasing, concerns about radiation exposure have also declined.
Noise	Noise levels produced by computers and most printers are well below those that cause adverse health effects. The equipment has minor noise sources such as the hum of cooling fans and the clicking of keys. Excessive noise from a computer may indicate an internal malfunction. Certain industrial high-speed line printers may produce noise at a level which is uncomfortable for prolonged exposure; in these cases, sound-deadening covers are often used.
Hot components	Hot computer components within the system unit can be problematic. For example, any component carrying a high electrical voltage can get very hot and could cause burns. High-speed processors are also known heat generators; heat sinks and fans keep them cool enough to prevent a

Safety Issue	Description
	burnout, but they may still be uncomfortably hot to touch. You must exercise caution when working with any part of a computer or printer that may be hot to the touch, or that might be holding an electrical charge.
Food and drink	Eating and drinking around computer equipment can be problematic. Food particles and liquids can get inside and harm the inner mechanics of the hardware. Your employer may have policies in place that prohibit eating and drinking around computer equipment for these reasons.
Moving equipment	Lifting and moving computer equipment can be one of the more strenuous parts of your job. For example, when you need to work on a CPU, you may have to lift and relocate the machine to your work area. Always assess the situation first to determine if you can lift or move items safely.

Laser Safety Standards

To provide a basis for laser safety, standards are established for Maximum Permissible Exposure (MPE). Lasers and laser systems and devices are grouped into classes:

- Class 1 lasers do not emit harmful levels of radiation and are exempt from control measures.
- Class 2 lasers are capable of creating eye damage through chronic, continuous exposure; this class includes bar code readers.
- Class 3 lasers pose severe eye hazards when viewed through optical instruments (for example, microscopes) or with the naked eye.
- Class 4 lasers pose danger to eyes and skin, and are fire hazards.

Frequently, lasers are embedded in laser products or systems with a lower hazard rating. For example, laser printers, CD drives, and DVD drives are Class 1 laser products; however, they contain Class 3 or Class 4 lasers. When the printer or drive is used as intended, the controls for the device's class (Class 1) apply. When the system is opened—for example, for service—and the embedded laser beam is accessible, precautions must be based on the classification of the embedded laser (Class 3 or 4).

Environmental Safety Best Practices

To minimize the personal safety issues associated with computing environments, follow the recommended safety best practices and use the appropriate repair tools at all times.

Best Practice	Safety Precautions
Cords and cables	If cords and cables must traverse a floor area where people need to walk, it is recommended that cord protectors be used to shield the cords and cables from being damaged by pedestrian traffic, as well as to minimize the chance of someone tripping on the cords and cables. You can also use cable management techniques and tools to group and organize cables together to keep them out of the way and hidden from the general working space.
Lasers	Precautions include the following: • Never point a laser beam in someone's eyes. • Never look directly at a laser beam. • Never disable safety mechanisms when servicing a device with an embedded laser.
RSI	If an individual has even mild RSI symptoms, action should be taken. If symptoms are allowed to progress, a person with RSI can develop

Best Practice	*Safety Precautions*
	chronic symptoms. The key to RSI management is to remove an individual from the exposure that causes injury. A period of time away from the keyboard and mouse is followed by a gradual return to keying in an ergonomically correct work setting. Occasionally, a physician will prescribe a medication to help reduce symptomatic inflammation and pain. People with more severe forms of RSI may be referred by their medical provider to an occupational therapist who can do further evaluation and recommend a program of localized treatments, stretches, and exercises. Referral to an orthopedic hand specialist may be needed to determine treatment options. If the individual displays symptoms even at rest, splints may be recommended; while these are useful in the first stages of recovery, they are not the long-term solution. The best treatment for RSI, of course, is prevention through proper arrangement of computer workstations and reasonable project design.
Eye strain	A vision examination is recommended. A specific eyeglass prescription for computer use may help compensate for the strain involved in looking at a close and fixed point for periods of time. Artificial tears—used to supplement the eye's natural tear film and lubricate the dry surface—alleviate dry-eye symptoms for some computer users.
Noise	Impact printers and even the paper handling mechanisms on other industrial high-speed printers can be noisy and should be placed in rooms away from operators, where possible. Noise reduction hoods are recommended.
Lifting techniques	Before lifting anything: • Know your own strengths and weaknesses. You need to be aware of what your weight limitations are. • When you lift, bend at your knees and not at your waist. This will prevent strain on your back muscles and pressure on your spine. • Assess the equipment you are moving. If you feel that physically the equipment is too heavy or awkward for you to move alone, then get help from a coworker, or use a cart to relocate the equipment. If you use a cart, make sure the equipment is tightly secured during transport. • The equipment may be unstable for lifting. You may need to take special precautions and may require help moving it to a cart. • Equipment should never be stacked too high while moving to avoid hardware falling and breaking on the floor. This can cause damage to other devices or to you. • Plan ahead. While moving equipment from one area to another, be aware of narrow doorways or columns that you will encounter on the way. Also, make sure to prep the space before delivering the equipment so that you are not trying to reconfigure the space with all the equipment in the way.

General Power Issues

Power issues can cause a number of problems for computer equipment and the working environment. Computer equipment, printers, network devices, and other resources require power, so any disruption in electricity will present a number of issues. There are several power problems that can occur.

Power Problem	Description
Blackout	A *blackout* involves a complete loss of power.
Brownout	A *brownout* is a temporary power reduction that is often used by electrical power companies to deal with high power demands. It is called a brownout because the lights dim during the event.
Sag	A *sag* is a momentary low-voltage power failure.
Spike	A *spike* is a short-term, high-voltage power malfunction.
Surge	A *surge* is a long-term, high-voltage power malfunction.
In-rush	An *in-rush* power problem is a surge or spike that is caused when a device that uses a large amount of current is started.

(handwritten: decrease — Sag; increase — Surge)

Power Protection Systems

There are several protection systems that can restore power to some operational capacity, decrease failures, or monitor power sources.

Power Protection System	Description
UPS or battery backup	An *uninterruptible power supply (UPS)*, also referred to as a *battery backup*, is a device that continues to provide power to connected circuits when the main source of power becomes unavailable. Depending on the design, UPSs can be battery operated, AC powered, or both. They are meant for temporary use and are intended to support computer systems until they can be powered off normally. Power is likely to be interrupted when the batteries or other power sources are discharged.
Generators	A *generator* creates its own electricity through the use of motors. Generators provide long-term power and are often started while a UPS system supports equipment through the initial power loss. Generators can fail when motor fuel runs out or when a mechanical failure occurs.
Surge suppressor	A *surge suppressor* is a device that provides power protection circuits that can reduce or eliminate the impact of surges and spikes.

UPS Types

Depending on the needs of an organization, different types of UPSs might be used. Common types include:

* A standby UPS, which is primarily AC-powered, until the power source fails. When the power source fails, it switches to the backup power source or battery. This UPS is used most often with personal computers.
* A line interactive UPS is commonly used in smaller business settings to provide power through a constant AC connection. When the AC power fails, the inverter switches to battery power. This UPS is unique in that while the AC power is available, it is used to also charge the battery.

Liquid Hazards

There are many different professional situations when you may come in contact with a hazardous liquid. Some such compounds are used to clean or condition equipment, including the computer's case, adapter card contacts and connections, and glass surfaces. They may present safety or environmental problems. Make sure you read the labels and follow the instructions carefully when you are disposing of hazardous materials.

(handwritten: acetone is also used to clean a computer)

Chemical Hazards

Working with personal computers can cause you to come in contact with some chemical hazards.

Chemical Hazard	Description
Laser printer toner	Made of fine particles of iron and plastic, toner presents its own set of problems due to its reactions with heat. If you spill toner, do not clean it up with a regular vacuum; the particles will get into the motor and melt. Do not use warm water to wash toner off your hands or arms; the toner could fuse to your skin. Instead, brush off as much as you can with a dry paper towel, rinse with cold water, and then wash with cold water and soap. In addition, do not use ammonia-based cleaners on or around laser printers, as the ammonia may react chemically with the toner.
Batteries	Batteries maintain the data in complementary metal oxide semiconductor (CMOS) chips and supply power to remote controls, portable computers, and other devices. These batteries may contain mercury, cadmium, and lithium, as well as other dangerous chemicals.
Capacitors	Capacitors store electricity by using two or more conducting plates separated by an insulator. There are capacitors in various personal computer components, including microprocessors. The electrolytes in capacitors are very caustic; treat them as you would any hazardous chemical. Thoroughly wash your hands after handling ruptured capacitors.

 Caution: The capacitors in power supplies and monitors do not discharge when they are turned off or unplugged, and contain enough charge to kill you. Do not open or attempt to service internal components of power supplies or monitors.

MSDS Documentation

A *Material Safety Data Sheet (MSDS)* is a technical bulletin that is designed to give users and emergency personnel information about the proper procedures for the storage and handling of a hazardous substance. This applies to any situation in which an employee is exposed to a chemical under normal use conditions or in the event of an emergency. The manufacturers supply MSDSs with the first shipment to a new customer and with any shipment after the MSDS is updated with significant and new information about safety hazards. You can get MSDSs online; the Internet has a wide range of free resources. OSHA regulations govern the use of MSDSs and the information an MSDS must contain.

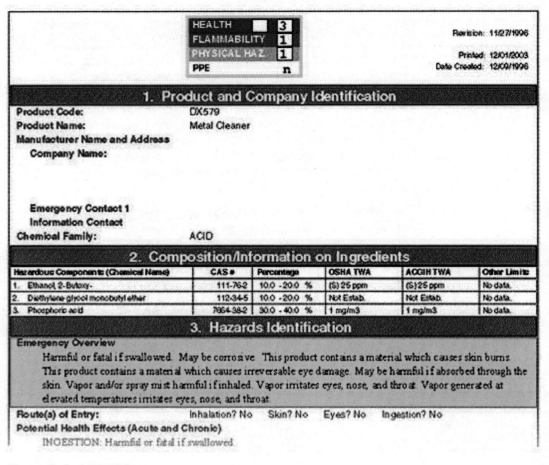

Figure 3-3: An MSDS.

Required Information in an MSDS

Every MSDS is required to include information about the following items:

- Physical data
- Toxicity
- Health effects
- First aid
- Reactivity
- Storage
- Safe-handling and use precautions
- Disposal
- Protective equipment
- Spill/leak procedures

Incident Reports

An *incident report* is a record of any instance where a person is injured or computer equipment is damaged due to environmental issues. The report is also used for accidents involving hazardous materials, such as chemical spills, that could have an impact on the environment. Any time an accident occurs at a work site, you should submit an incident report. Reporting these occurrences is often part of company policy and can help provide protection against liability.

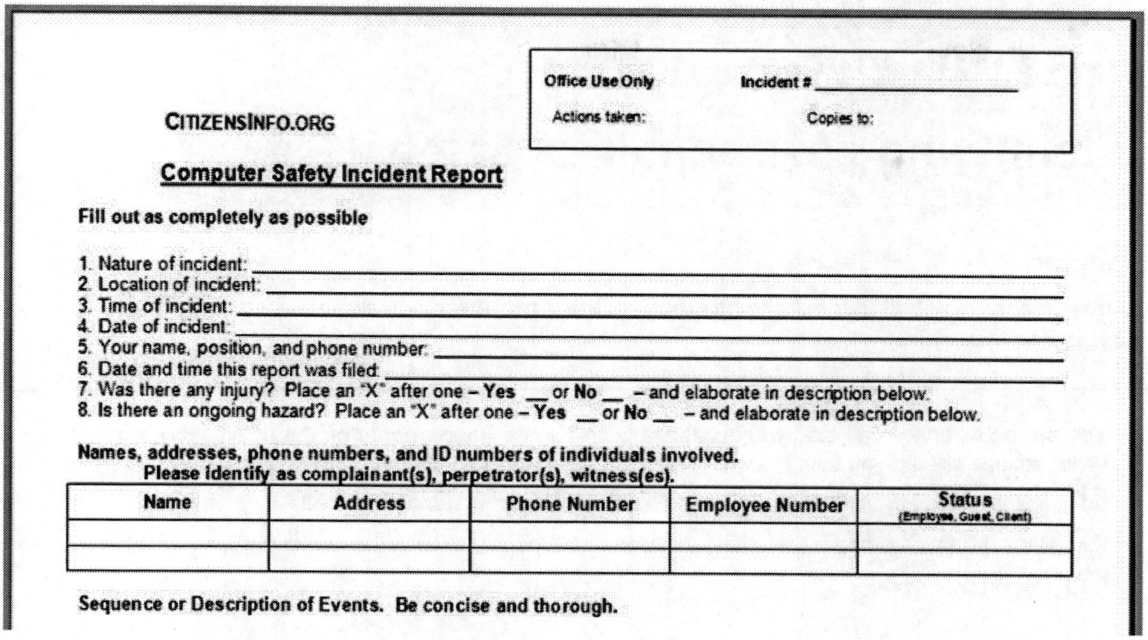

CITIZENSINFO.ORG

Office Use Only	Incident # ____________
Actions taken:	Copies to:

Computer Safety Incident Report

Fill out as completely as possible

1. Nature of incident: ____________
2. Location of incident: ____________
3. Time of incident: ____________
4. Date of incident: ____________
5. Your name, position, and phone number: ____________
6. Date and time this report was filed: ____________
7. Was there any injury? Place an "X" after one – **Yes** __ or **No** __ – and elaborate in description below.
8. Is there an ongoing hazard? Place an "X" after one – **Yes** __ or **No** __ – and elaborate in description below.

Names, addresses, phone numbers, and ID numbers of individuals involved.
Please identify as complainant(s), perpetrator(s), witness(es).

Name	Address	Phone Number	Employee Number	Status (Employee, Guest, Client)

Sequence or Description of Events. Be concise and thorough.

Figure 3-4: Sample incident report.

Hazardous Material Disposal Procedures

Proper disposal of hazardous materials is an essential part of maintaining a safe work environment.

Hazardous Material	*Disposal Recommendations*
Liquid cleaning materials and empty containers	Follow your company's guidelines for disposing of liquid cleaning materials and their containers. Each municipality has its own disposal regulations that you must learn and follow. You can find out about these regulations by contacting your local government's environmental office or department for trash disposal and recycling.
Toner	Empty toner cartridges should not be discarded in the trash because of the damage that the residual chemicals can do to the environment. Used toner cartridges should be refilled or returned to the manufacturer for recycling and/or disposal. Follow your company's guidelines for disposal procedures.
Display devices	The CRTs in older computer monitors contain lead, which is considered a hazardous material. Follow your company's guidelines for disposing of display devices. Many municipalities have regulations for disposal and recycling of old monitors and television sets; contact your local government's environmental office or department for trash disposal and recycling to determine if there are specific rules you need to follow.
Ozone filter	Follow the manufacturer's recommendations for replacement and disposal of a laser printer's ozone filter.
Batteries	Used batteries should not be discarded in the trash; they should be recycled or disposed of following your company's guidelines.

ACTIVITY 3-3
Identifying Environmental Safety Issues

Scenario

In this activity, you will identify the best practices for promoting environmental safety and proper handling of materials.

1. **You are on a service call, and you accidentally spill some liquid cleaner on the user's work surface. What actions should you take?**

    ☐ Refer to the MSDS for procedures to follow when the material is spilled.

    ☐ Wipe it up with a paper towel and dispose of the paper towel in the user's trash container.

    ☐ Report the incident.

2. **Ozone is classified as an environmental hazard. Which device produces ozone gas?**

    ○ Laser printer

    ○ CPU

    ○ Laptop

    ○ Power supply

3. **What item reacts with heat and ammonia-based cleaners to present a workplace hazard?**

    ○ Capacitor

    ○ Laser

    ○ Toner

    ○ Battery

TOPIC D

Professionalism and Communication

So far in this lesson, you have identified best practices for working directly with computer equipment. On almost every service call, you will also need to interact with users who are experiencing problems. In this topic, you will identify best practices for PC technicians to use to communicate appropriately with clients and colleagues and to conduct business in a professional manner.

You are a representative of your profession, as well as your company. Working with customers is a fundamental job duty for every A+ technician. How you conduct yourself will have a direct and significant impact on the satisfaction of your customers, and your level of professionalism and communication skills can directly affect whether or not you will do business with them again in the future.

This topic covers all or part of the following CompTIA® A+® (2012) certification objectives:

- Exam 220–801: Objective 5.3 Given a scenario, demonstrate proper communication and professionalism.
- Exam 220–801: Objective 5.4. Explain the fundamentals of dealing with prohibited content/ activity.

Communication Skills

Using the proper communication skills when dealing with clients and colleagues creates a professional environment that is conducive to solving the problem at hand.

Communication Skill	Description
Use proper language	• Use clear, concise, and direct statements. This will help you get to the crux of the matter more quickly, and it will help the user understand what you are saying.
	• Avoid using jargon, abbreviations, acronyms, and slang. Many users will not have the same level of technical knowledge as you and your colleagues, and using terminology that is beyond their level of knowledge can confuse or upset them.
	• Use timing to set the pace of a conversation. A pause may be more valuable than an immediate answer, as it allows you time to formulate your response. If a situation escalates and your customer becomes agitated, you may ask him or her to slow down so that you can get all the information. When a customer is having difficulty ending a call to the help desk, you may gently step up the pace to indicate your need to move on.
Non-verbal communication	• Be aware of the non-verbal clues you use, whether you are talking or listening. Body language communicates more than actual words. Studies show that up to 70 percent of a message is conveyed through actions. Even when you are talking on the phone, non-verbal characteristics—such as tone of voice—will add meaning to your message and help you interpret your customer's concerns.
	• Use the proper level of eye contact. You and your customer will make, maintain, and break eye contact as you talk with each other. When attention is directed to the problem at hand, eye contact may be minimal. Avoid staring directly at your customer—a form of

Communication Skill	Description
	invading personal space—or letting your gaze wander, which indicates disinterest, or even worse, inappropriate interest. • Use gestures and facial expressions to reinforce your spoken message. Broad, friendly gestures indicate being open to the conversation, while sharp or jabbing gestures usually mean anger. The variety, intensity, and meaning of facial expressions are almost endless. You and your customer read each other's faces to gain insight into the spoken words. Your expression must match the content of your words; if there is a mismatch, your customer will believe the message in your face, rather than what you say. • Use non-verbal encouragement to gather information. Encourage your customer to continue with "Mm-hmm" and a slight nod of your head. You convey that you are listening and want to know more. • Be aware of physical positioning and posture. Respect your customer's personal space. Depending on the circumstances, you may be from 1.5 to 4 feet away from your customer. If the customer backs up, you are too close. You may be working in close quarters; ask permission before you move into your customer's personal space—for example, sitting in the office chair. Messages are conveyed by body position. Slouching indicates: "I am bored with this conversation." Holding one's arms across the chest says: "I am closed off to what you are saying." Watch your body's signals, as well as those of your customer. • Be aware of the effect of tone of voice, which can indicate many internal moods: excitement, boredom, sarcasm, fear, or uncertainty. A rise in your voice at the end of a sentence makes it sound like a question, implying lack of assurance instead of competence. Listen to your customer's tone. Volume—loudness or softness—colors the spoken message. If your customer's agitation escalates, try lowering your volume to re-establish a sense of calm. • Use the appropriate level of physical contact. A firm handshake is appreciated and may be expected in some business dealings. Other forms of touching are generally unnecessary, inappropriate, and risky.
Listening skills	• Listen and do not interrupt the customer. If your attention drifts or you interrupt, you run the risk of missing some important information that can help you solve the problem. • Allow the user to complete statements—avoid interrupting. This will convey the message that you respect the user and want to hear what he or she is saying. • Employ passive listening techniques. Your message is: "I am listening. Tell me more." You are alert, attentive, and accepting, but do not participate actively in the conversation. Your silence may help your customer to collect his or her thoughts, especially if he or she is upset or angry. Listen for factual data and be alert for feelings and attitudes, which are conveyed non-verbally. It may be difficult to keep from jumping in with a question or a "Yes, but..." Resist the temptation by writing down your thoughts to refer to later. • Employ active listening techniques. When your customer is describing the problem, listen actively to elicit as much information as you can. Clarify user statements by asking pertinent questions.

Active Listening

Active listening techniques can enhance your communications skills. These techniques may feel awkward at first, so you might want to try them out in a situation outside your job. With practice, you will use active listening skills more easily and creatively.

Action	Description
Questioning	Ask questions to gain information, clarify what you have heard, and direct the conversation. Open-ended questions can elicit a lot of information. Close-ended questions limit the amount of information by giving a choice of answers. Yes/no questions further limit the information exchange and can be used when you need to get closer to a conclusion. Examples of each of these question styles are: • Open-ended: "What happened after you pressed Ctrl+Alt+Delete?" • Close-ended: "What kind of a printer do you have, laser or inkjet?" • Yes/no: "Are you on a network?" What if the answer to your open-ended question is "I do not know" or "I am not sure"? Go down the list—using close-ended and then yes/no —until you reach the customer's level of expertise. Examples of less helpful question styles: • Confusing multiple questions: "What did you do next? Did you try...? What happened?" • Accusations: "What did you do that for?"
Empathizing	Let your customer know that you perceive and support what they are feeling. Try to be specific in naming the emotion and link it to the customer, using "you," not "I." Examples of helpful empathetic responses include: • "This delay is frustrating for you." • "You are afraid you will lose business while your computer is down." • "You must be worried about the cost." Examples of less helpful empathetic responses include: • "I know how you are feeling." • "I can identify..."
Paraphrasing	Restate what the customer says in your own words to make sure that you interpreted correctly, to bring order to the customer's thoughts, and to relay that their message is important. Use statements, not questions, and do not add or change anything. Examples of starters for paraphrasing include: • "You are saying that..." • "It sounds like..." • "I am hearing you say..."
Summarizing	Outline the main points of your conversation to summarize what has been said. You can begin by summarizing your understanding of the problem and then checking for clarification. During the conversation, you can re-establish the focus by listing the important facts. Bring closure by summing up the work performed. If a follow-up plan is needed, restate the responsibilities and timeline. Helpful starters for summarizing include:

Action	Description
	<ul><li>"Let's see what we have so far."</li><li>"Why don't we back up a minute and go through that again?"</li><li>"Let's go over our plan."</li></ul>

Organizational Policies and Procedures for Appropriate Use

Organizational policies are documents that convey the corporate guidelines and philosophy to employees. Policies can be either high-level corporate documents distributed to the entire organization, or lower-level operational documents that affect only certain departments, divisions, individuals, or roles in an organization. For example, most organizations will have an *acceptable use policy (AUP)* that includes practices and guidelines that management expects all employees to follow when they are using and accessing company-owned computer equipment and information-related resources.

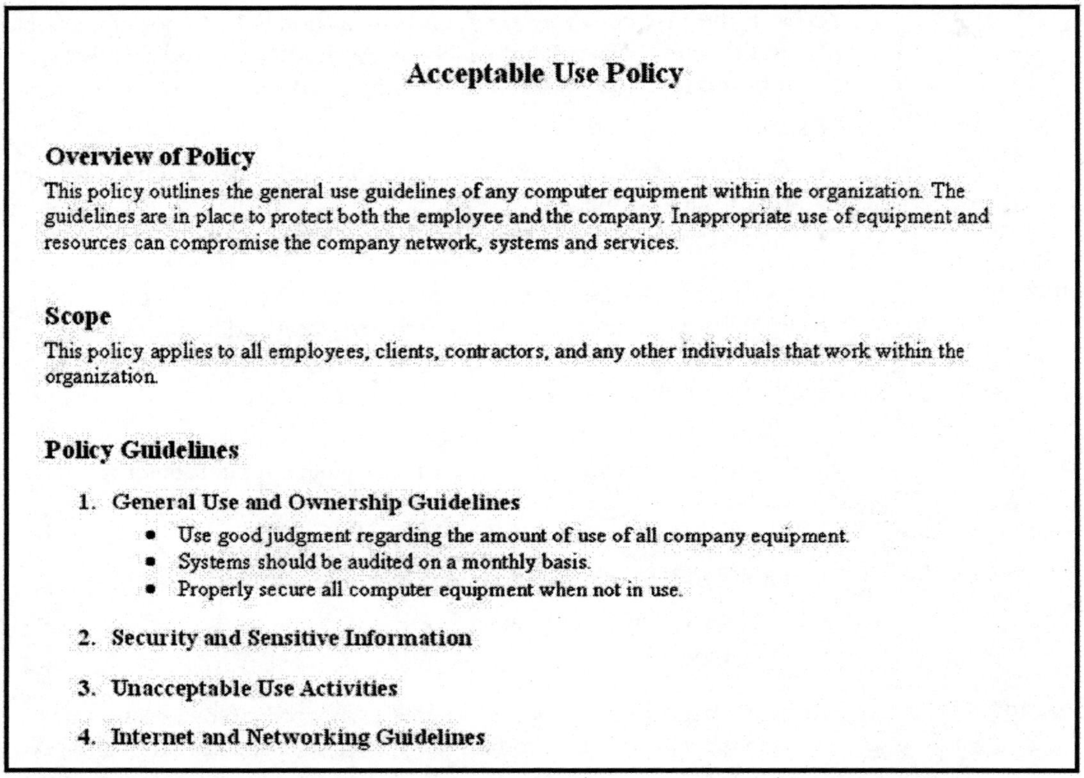

Acceptable Use Policy

Overview of Policy

This policy outlines the general use guidelines of any computer equipment within the organization. The guidelines are in place to protect both the employee and the company. Inappropriate use of equipment and resources can compromise the company network, systems and services.

Scope

This policy applies to all employees, clients, contractors, and any other individuals that work within the organization.

Policy Guidelines

1. General Use and Ownership Guidelines
   - Use good judgment regarding the amount of use of all company equipment.
   - Systems should be audited on a monthly basis.
   - Properly secure all computer equipment when not in use.

2. Security and Sensitive Information

3. Unacceptable Use Activities

4. Internet and Networking Guidelines

Figure 3-5: An AUP.

Professional Conduct

Acting in a professional manner when dealing with colleagues and clients provides a work environment where problems can be solved efficiently.

Facet	Description
Appearance	Exhibit a professional appearance. Your work environment may be in a repair shop, at a help desk, or on-site at the customer's business. Whatever the situation, you will want to present a neat, clean, business-like appearance. On-site work may take you into many settings, from muffler repair shops to executive offices. You may be asked to remove

Facet	Description
	your shoes or put on a hard hat. Be aware of the corporate culture and respond accordingly.
Respect	Be respectful of the customer and the environment in which you are working. <ul><li>Maintain a positive attitude when talking with users. Avoiding arguing or getting defensive with users will make it easier for you to solve the problem to the user's satisfaction.</li><li>Be culturally sensitive. Always be conscious of who you are working with, and how your actions can be conveyed.</li><li>Do not minimize the customer's problem. What seems simple to you could be a mission-critical problem to the user.</li><li>Never insult a customer or call the customer names. No matter how frustrating a service call might become, rudeness is never the answer.</li><li>When you are dealing with customers, avoid distractions and interruptions. Repeatedly answering a mobile phone, talking to coworkers, or attending to any other personal distractions while you are supposed to be working on a problem sends the message that the user's problem is unimportant to you.</li><li>Ask open-ended questions and try and narrow the scope of the problem. Restate the issue or question to verify understanding. This will show the customer that you are listening and care about resolving the issues at hand.</li><li>Be sure to keep your work area at the customer site neat. Do not pile materials on your customer's books and files. Clean up after yourself. When you are on-site, ask where to dispose of materials; find out where the recycling bin is for printer test-run paper.</li><li>Be on time. Tardiness can give the customer a negative impression of you. If you are going to be late, always call and communicate with the customer.</li><li>Be respectful of the property at the customer site. Always ask permission before entering an office or workspace, using the telephone, sitting down at a computer, or adjusting the workspace.</li></ul>
Accountability	Be accountable. Do not misrepresent your credentials, competence, or training. Take responsibility for your actions, and admit your mistakes. In questions of conflict of interest between your company and the customer, refer to your supervisor or follow your company's procedures. Be aware of your company's policy for accepting gifts or samples, and for socializing with customers.
Confidentiality	Treat any information located on a desktop, a computer, or a printer that pertains to your customer's business as confidential. Know your company's policies concerning confidential information—and follow them. Many fields—including medicine, social work, and special education—are regulated by federal and state laws concerning the confidentiality of their customers, consumers, or clients. All companies have personal information about their employees. Many corporations have sensitive information about the development of their products or services.
Honesty	Be forthright with your customers about what is occurring and the actions you will take. Clients have a right to understand the process you are following and how it will affect them.

Facet	Description
	Discourage software pirating. Software copyright infringement, or pirating, relates to the legal issues surrounding the distribution and use of software. The Federal Copyright Act of 1976 protects the rights of the holder of a copyright. Typically, a backup copy of software is allowed and a site license allows for the use of multiple copies at one facility. You are responsible for upholding the law by complying with the license agreements that both your company and your customer hold. Learn your company's policies and adhere to them. Pirating carries penalties and risks, including fines, imprisonment, corrupted files, virus-infected disks, discontinued technical support, and upgrade unavailability.
Prioritizing	Set priorities. You will often need to set priorities and make judgment calls. You will recommend whether your customer should repair or replace equipment. You will rank the urgency of your customers' needs. Base your decisions on common courtesy, fundamental fairness, and keeping promises. Be familiar with your company's policies and follow them.
Expectations	You should set and meet customer expectations up front. Set a timeline and a communication plan that both you and the customer agree to at the start of the business relationship. Always communicate repair and replacement options, and provide the proper documentation needed for the services provided. Always follow up and get customer feedback on the work completed. This information allows you to improve customer satisfaction.
Ethics	Practice ethical conduct. You have an obligation to take responsibility for ethical conduct within your delivery of service. Ethical issues are complex and ever-changing in the computer industry. An unethical practice may become so routine that it is falsely assumed to be acceptable behavior. Learn your company's policies and adhere to them.

Prohibited Content

As an A+ technician, you may come across situations when you may encounter prohibited activities, such as viewing pornography on work-issued devices by users either within your organization or by a customer. There are different levels of prohibited content, which can be described as distasteful, inappropriate, or illegal. Every organization will have different guidelines and restrictions based on the type of content. For example, some organizations will discourage access to social networking sites, or websites that contain questionable words or phrases, but will not explicitly forbid it. On the other hand, restrictions on content or data that can be categorized as inappropriate or illegal, such as pornography, will be enforced heavily, and accessing such content will have immediate consequences. In each of these cases, it is your responsibility to follow organizational procedure to report the incident. When reporting potentially illegal activities, you must follow the organization's policy on reporting, collecting, and documenting the specifics of the situation and what evidence was found.

Best Practices Related to Prohibited Content or Activity

The process of identifying and reporting prohibited content or activity can be complicated, especially when an organization does not have sufficient policies and documented guidelines. There are some fundamental methods that can be applied to help properly report, document, and resolve issues.

Phase	Description
First response	*First response* refers to the immediate actions that follow an incident, as well as the individual or individuals who perform these actions. There are a few actions that take place during the first response to an incident: • Identifying the data and/or hardware. • Reporting the details of the discovery and evidence through the proper channels. This will vary depending on the specific organization's policies and reporting instructions. • Preserving the data and/or device as evidence. This can sometimes be also be called computer forensics.
Chain of custody	The *chain of custody* is the record of tracking evidence from collection through presentation in court. The evidence can be hardware components, electronic data, or telephone systems. The chain of evidence reinforces the integrity and proper custody of evidence from collection, to analysis, to storage, and presentation in a court of law. Every person in the chain who handles evidence must log and document the process, methods, and tools they used.
Documentation	In the process of identifying and reporting incidents with prohibited content, you should follow the organization's documented procedures to ensure that you are carrying out the correct response tasks and guidelines. You must also be aware of any changes made to the documentation so that you are always following the right procedures in handling incidents, managing evidence, and reporting findings to the appropriate individuals.

Computer Removal

When computer crimes are reported, one of the first response activities is removing computers from the crime location. They are tagged with a chain of custody record to begin the process of making the evidence secure for future presentation in court.

Computer Forensics

Computer forensics is the practice of collecting and analyzing data from storage devices, computer systems, networks, and wireless communications and presenting this information as a form of evidence in a court of law. Primarily, forensics deals with the recovery and investigation of potential evidence. Computer forensics is a fairly new field, so there is little standardization or consistency in practicing it across organizations and courts. Basically, computer forensics is a blend of the elements of law with computer science in analyzing evidence in a way that is permissible in the court of law.

Basic Forensic Response Procedures for IT

Forensic response procedures for IT help security professionals collect data evidence in a form that is admissible in a court of law.

Forensic Response Procedure	Description
Capture system image	One of the most important steps in computer forensic evidence procedures is to capture exact duplicates of the evidence, also known as forensic images. This is accomplished by making a bit-for-bit copy of a piece of media as an image file with high accuracy.
Examine network traffic and logs	Attackers always leave behind traces; you just need to know how and where to look. Logs record everything that happens in an intrusion

Forensic Response Procedure	Description
	prevention system (IPS) or intrusion detection system (IDS), and in routers, firewalls, servers, desktops, mainframes, applications, databases, antivirus software, and virtual private networks (VPNs). With these logs, it is possible to extract the identity of hackers and provide necessary evidence.
Capture video	Video forensics is the method by which video is scrutinized for clues. Tools for computer forensics are used in reassembling video to be used as evidence in a court of law.
Record time offset	The format in which time is recorded against a file activity, such as file creation, deletion, last modified, and last accessed, has developed to incorporate a local time zone offset against GMT. This makes it easier for forensic examiners to determine the exact time the activity took place, even if the computer is moved from one time zone to another or if the time zone has deliberately been changed on a system.
Take hashes	Federal law enforcement agencies and federal governments maintain a list of files such as files relating to components of Microsoft® Windows® and other application software. The hash codes generated by a file or software can be compared to the list of known file hashes and hacker tools if any are flagged or marked as unknown.
Take screenshots	You should capture screenshots of each and every step of a forensic procedure, especially when you are retrieving evidence by using a forensic tool. This will ensure that data present on a compromised system is not tampered with and also provides the court with proof of your use of valid computer forensic methods while extracting the evidence.
Identify witnesses	Courts generally accept evidence if it is seconded by the testimony of a witness who observed the procedure by which the evidence was acquired. A computer forensics expert witness is someone who has experience in handling computer forensics tools and is able to establish the validity of evidence.
Track man hours and expense	When the first incidents of computer crimes occurred, it would usually take less than 40 man hours to complete a forensic investigation because incidents usually involved single, standalone computers. Now, with advances in technology and the advent of new digital media such as voice recorders, cameras, laptop computers, and mobile devices, computer forensics procedures can require a much greater amount of time and expense. Also, the increase in storage device capacities and encryption affect the amount of man hours that it can take to assess any damage, and consequently increase the expenses incurred in any computer forensics investigation. Capturing this expense is part of the overall damage assessment for the incident.

ACTIVITY 3-4
Examining Professionalism and Communication Techniques

Scenario

In this activity, you will examine different professionalism and communication techniques.

1. **What is an example of verbal communication skills? What is an example of non-verbal communication skills?**

2. Select the correct response.

   Which is a good example of listening skills?
   - ○ Maintain a neat and clean appearance.
   - ○ Keep sensitive customer information to yourself.
   - ○ Interrupt the customer to ask for more details.
   - ○ Let your eyes wander around the room as the customer is speaking.
   - ○ Allow the customer to complete statements without interrupting.

3. **While answering a service call on a computer that is located in a common area of the office, you come across information showing that some unauthorized websites have been viewed. The activity has been linked to a particular user account. What is the appropriate action to take?**

4. **When a service technician does not share sensitive customer information with others, which skill or behavior is being practiced?**
   - ○ Confidentiality
   - ○ Ethical behavior
   - ○ Respect
   - ○ Active listening

5. **You have received an off-site service call to service a network printer at a customer location. When you arrive, the user is at the printer and starts talking about how the printer is not working properly, and he cannot get his reports handed in on time. As a result, you start asking more clarifying questions to gather more information, so you can identify the specific issue with the printer. What type of technique are you using to gather information?**
   - ○ Passive listening
   - ○ Non-verbal communication
   - ○ Active listening

6. **Which are examples of displaying respect during a service call?**

☐   Asking permission before changing display settings

☐   Asking "What happened just before you noticed the problem?"

☐   Sitting in a user's chair without permission

☐   Silencing your pager or mobile phone

Lesson Summary

In this lesson, you identified best practices that are followed by professional PC technicians. With the proper tools, awareness of safety and environmental issues, and basic communication skills, you are prepared to do your job in a safe, effective, and professional manner.

Which of the best practices discussed in this lesson apply in your workplace?

Have you ever been in a situation where you uncovered inappropriate conduct or prohibited activity?

 Note: Check your LogicalCHOICE Course screen for opportunities to interact with your classmates, peers, and the larger LogicalCHOICE online community about the topics covered in this course or other topics you are interested in. From the Course screen you can also access available resources for a more continuous learning experience.

4 | Peripheral Components

Lesson Time: 2 hours, 15 minutes

Lesson Objectives

In this lesson, you will install and configure peripheral components. You will:

- Install and configure display devices.

- Install and configure input devices.

- Install and configure expansion cards

- Install and configure multimedia devices.

Lesson Introduction

So far in this course, you have identified the hardware and software that makes up a personal computer system and examined some general best practices for working with them. Now that you have a solid base of background information, it is time to roll up your sleeves and start working with some of those hardware components. In this lesson, you will install and configure peripheral computer components.

Much of the work that you will perform as a PC technician will involve installing and configuring various hardware and software components. As an IT professional, you will often find yourself setting up end-user workstations or helping those end users with the hardware they need to make their daily lives easier. Installing and configuring peripheral components—like display devices, keyboards and mice, or even more specialized devices—are some of the more common tasks that you will perform.

This lesson covers all or part of the following CompTIA® A+® (2012) certification objectives:

- Topic A:
  - Exam 220–801: Objective 1.10
- Topic B:
  - Exam 220–801: Objective 1.12
- Topic C:
  - Exam 220–801: Objective 1.4
- Topic D:
  - Exam 220–801: Objective 1.12

TOPIC A

Install and Configure Display Devices

In this lesson, you will install and configure peripheral components. Generally, one of the most common peripherals that you will be asked to install is the display device. In this topic, you will install and configure display devices.

The display device provides visual output from the computer system. Without the display device, you can't see any images on screen to guide your interactions with programs or see the results of your input. Correctly installing and configuring the display device enables you to meet the basic user need to see what they are working on.

This topic covers all or part of the following CompTIA® A+® (2012) certification objectives:

* Exam 220–801: Objective 1.10: Given a scenario, evaluate types and features of display devices.

Display Device Types

There are several different types of display devices that you might be asked to install or configure.

Display Device	Description
CRT	*Cathode ray tube (CRT)* displays use electron beams within a vacuum tube to create images on a fluorescent screen. The intensity of three electron beams, one for each primary color (red, blue, and green), are manipulated to display the image on the screen.
	CRT monitors are larger, heavier, and boxier than their more modern counterparts due to the components used to build them, especially the thick glass used for the screen. The screen may be curved or flat, but CRTs are not considered flat-panel monitors.
	CRT monitors have for the most part been replaced by more modern and efficient displays like LCD, LED, or plasma screens, though many may still be in use in organizations who have yet to upgrade their devices.
LCD	Liquid crystal display (LCD) flat-panel displays are a compact, lightweight alternative to traditional CRT displays.
	LCDs consume much less energy than CRTs and do not emit nearly as much electromagnetic radiation as CRTs do. LCD monitors use a *cold cathode fluorescent lamp (CCFL)* as the backlight source. CCFLs use electrodes and mercury vapor to create ultraviolet light that is used as the light source.
	Depending on the LCD screen, the user may need to sit directly in front of the screen to see the display properly.
	A unique feature of LCD displays is that the screen auto centers. There is typically no center alignment needed.
LED	*Light emitting diode (LED)* displays utilize the same screen as an LCD display, but use a different backlighting technique/technology. Instead of the CCFLs used in LCD, LED screens use one of two types of light emitting diodes as a backlighting source: dynamic RGB LEDs, which are located behind the panel; or white edge-LEDs, which are located around the edge of the screen and use a diffusion panel to evenly distribute the light source.
	LED displays consume even less power than LCD displays. However, LED displays are currently more expensive to purchase.

[Handwritten annotations: "Can't run off direct current", "Invert DC to Alternating C", "Power hungry", "Very Power Effect", "Can be powered via DC"]

Display Device	Description
OLED	*Organic light emitting diode (OLED)* displays utilize the same technology as LED displays, but use organic compounds that emit light when subjected to an electric current as the light source.
	However, OLED screens can be used in a larger variety of dimensions than LED screens, and are currently utilized in computer monitors, television screens, tablets, and mobile phones.
Plasma	*Plasma displays* use xenon and neon rays and a flat panel of glass to provide visuals with high contrast, brightness, and vibrant colors that can be viewed from a multitude of angles.
	However, plasma displays can suffer from image burn-in from repeated, long-term use. They are currently only available in very large dimensions, typically 40 inches or more, and are mostly marketed and utilized as television displays. They can also be incredibly heavy and cumbersome due to the technology.
Projector	Video projectors are often used to display the video output onto a whiteboard or other surface so that a larger audience can see it.

(Handwritten notes: OLED pros: Flexible display, light weight, smart phones use OLED. Plasma - Burn In. Con: Short life span, Hard to make w small pixel size, grainy appearance, does not scale well to large sizes, expensive)

Other Display Devices

There are a number of other display device types that you may encounter in your personal or professional experience:

- Touch screen monitors enable input by touching images on the screen. This technology is used in bank ATMs, some point-of-sale terminals at fast food restaurants, and other situations where a separate keyboard for input is not appropriate. Touch screens are also found on many smartphones, tablets, and laptops sold for general public use.
- Virtual reality games and special-purpose imaging needs led to the development of glasses/goggles that substitute for a monitor.
- Video display systems can be used to display one image to several monitors (often used in training situations) or to display an image covering a huge screen (often used at trade shows).

Display Device Settings and Features

You can configure several features and settings for a display device, either through the **Control Panel** utility in the Windows® system or through controls on the physical device.

Display Setting or Feature	Description
Resolution	The number of *pixels* that make up the dimensions of a display. The resolution value is given as the number of horizontal pixels by vertical pixels, or width by height, traditionally in the ratio of 4:3. For wide screen displays, the ratio is 16:10. Common resolutions are 640 x 480, 800 x 600, 1024 x 768, and 1600 x 1200. The higher the resolution, the more objects or information you can fit on the screen at once. Just as widescreen televisions have become popular, video monitors with higher aspect ratio are also becoming more common.
Native resolution	A fixed resolution for LCD or other flat panel display devices. Unlike a CRT, which can change resolution to match that of the signal being received, display devices with native resolution will only display the best quality image when the input signal and the native resolution are the same. Other resolutions may display on a device where that signal input

Display Setting or Feature	Description
	is not the same as the native resolution, but it will result in image quality loss.
Refresh rate	The number of times per second that the entire monitor is "refreshed," or scanned to illuminate the pixels. Each scan is referred to as a frame. The rate is expressed in *hertz (Hz)*. Typical refresh rates are 60 to 70 Hz or 60 to 70 times per second. Any setting lower than 60 Hz usually produces noticeable flickering.
Brightness	The amount of light that is being emitted from a display device. Brightness is measured in *lumens*, which is the unit of measurement for visible light that is being emitted from a light source. On a display device, brightness can be increased or decreased for the display. If the brightness is set too high, you might get an "aura" effect displayed on the screen. If it is set too low, you might not see anything on the screen.
Multiple displays	Many users choose to use more than one display device to increase the amount of display space. The typical setup is two displays, though more than two displays can be configured with the appropriate expansion card that can support that setup. Multiple displays are most commonly used for either a professional computer workstation or for gaming environments, where an extended desktop is useful.
	Within the monitor's display properties, you can designate one of the two monitors as the primary monitor, which controls where the desktop administrative features (**Start** menu, taskbar, etc.) appear. The other monitor would contain extra desktop space. While it is far more common to have the desktop span both monitors and contain a different window in each, it is also possible to have the two monitors display the same image, which is useful for presentations.
Analog vs. digital	Depending on the type and make of the display device, it may support either analog or digital inputs. Most devices providing the input signals (like a computer) are inherently digital. CRT display devices are analog, and will need a video card and VGA cable to receive the digital input and convert it to analog. Newer display devices such as LCD or LED can innately support digital input signals, and do so via Digital Video Interface (DVI) connections between the input device and the display device.
Privacy/antiglare filters	Privacy or antiglare filters are physical accessory screens that can be attached onto or over a display device and provides a number of benefits: • Reduces glare from the screen for the user sitting in front of the display device. • Protects the display device screen from scratches or dust. • Prohibits others not sitting in the front of the device from viewing information being displayed, protecting confidentiality and providing privacy.
Color depth (quality)	The number of bits used to store the color of a pixel: the more bits per pixel, the more colors can be displayed.
Font	A size and style of typeface. Computers use fonts to display text on the screen. Common font faces include Arial (which is a sans serif font),

[handwritten notes in margin: "— Flicker Based", "— Store + Hold", "Clear type"]

Display Setting or Feature	Description
	Times (which is a serif font), and Courier (which looks like legacy computer output).
Contrast	The difference in intensity between adjacent colors in an image. If the contrast is not set correctly for the display device and the lighting conditions in the room (for example, a really bright or really dark room), you might not be able to see anything on the screen, or you might get strange results.
Image position	The location or size of the display in relation to the physical device. Sometimes the image is not centered on the display screen. Other times the image does not fill the screen, leaving a black band around the edge. Or, part of the image can scroll off the screen. There are usually separate buttons or menu options to adjust each of these issues.
Distortion control	Distortions can appears as curves, waves, or moiré patterns in the video image. These are typically caused by electromagnetic interference or a defect with hardware, usually with the video card or video cable. If lines do not appear straight on the screen, you might need to adjust settings. Electromagnetic issues, however, are resolved by eliminating the source of interference. Refer to the display device documentation for how to resolve such issues. Distortion control is configured on the display device itself, not through a system utility.

Seen on Projectors & CRT's (handwritten note)

Aspect Ratio

The aspect ratio is the ratio of width to height of a display. Most software expects a 4:3 ratio, and the display will appear to be distorted if other ratios are used. The aspect ratio is found by determining the proportion of the number of pixels across the screen to the number of pixels down the screen. For example, a resolution of 640 x 480 has a 4:3 aspect ratio.

Resolution	Number of Pixels	Aspect Ratio
320 x 200	64,000	8:5
640 x 480	307,200	4:3
800 x 600	480,000	4:3
1,024 x 768	786,432	4:3
1,280 x 1,024	1,310,720	5:4
1,600 x 1,200	1,920,000	4:3

Note: For a demonstration, check out the LearnTO **Adjust Display Output Settings** in the LearnTOs for this course on your LogicalCHOICE Course screen.

Device Drivers

A *device driver* is a type of software that enables the operating system and a peripheral device to communicate with each other. Also referred to as simply a driver, a device driver takes generalized commands from the system software or an application and translates them into unique programming commands that the device can understand. It also provides the code that allows the device to function with the operating system, and it is generally installed as part of the installation process for a new piece of hardware. Device drivers can be generic for a class of device or specific to a particular device.

Where to Get Device Drivers

Device drivers can be:

- Included with the operating system. New operating systems include thousands of drivers that allow them to work with all current, popular devices. Peripherals that are designed after the operating system comes out must supply their own drivers.
- Supplied with the device on a CD-ROM when you purchase the hardware.
- Downloaded from the Internet from an operating systems vendor's site, such as Windows Update, or from the hardware manufacturer's website.

Display Device Selection Tips

There are hundreds, if not more, of display devices from which you can choose, depending on your needs. Selecting the display device to use may depend on a number of things.

Criteria	Description
Size	Depending on the space available for the display or a user's personal preferences, you may choose a display based on the physical size or footprint of the device. Because they take up less space, flat-panel devices like LCD, LED or OLED, may be preferred or needed for small work spaces. Plasma screens are still rather large, and may not be practical for a workstation.
Technical needs	Depending on what the display device will be used for, technical requirements for programs, or personal preferences, a specific type of display device may be required or desired. LCD, LED/OLED, and plasma monitors support high resolutions, which make them a better choice for users who work in high-end graphics applications such as Adobe® Photoshop®. However, some users still prefer CRT monitors because their display is brighter.
Efficiency	As the technology used in display devices evolves, the devices tend to be more energy efficient than its predecessors. LEDs consume less energy than LCDs, which may make them preferable if you are trying to be more energy efficient and cost efficient.
Cost	The newer the technology, the more expensive the device. LCDs are still fairly low cost, as the most common and in-demand type of display. LEDs and OLEDs are more expensive, but as they become more common, the cost is decreasing as well. Plasma displays are currently the most expensive option.

Display Device Installation Considerations

When you are ready to install a display device, keep the following considerations in mind:

- Do you have the necessary cables and connectors available to connect the display device to the machine?
- Do you have the necessary expansion cards, such as a video card, installed on the machine to support the display device you have selected?
- Do you have the necessary drivers for the display device installed on the machine?
- Do you have a power source available for the display device?

Note: For a demonstration, check out the LearnTO **Install a Display Device** in the LearnTOs for this course on your LogicalCHOICE Course screen.

Access the Checklist tile on your LogicalCHOICE course screen for reference information and job aids on How to Install and Configure Display Devices

ACTIVITY 4-1
Examining Display Devices

Scenario

In this activity, you will examine display devices.

---

1. **What step should you complete first when you are installing a monitor?**
   ○ Secure the monitor to the port by tightening the screws on each side of the connector.
   ○ Turn off the computer.
   ○ Plug in the monitor power cord.
   ○ Locate the monitor port on the computer.
   ○ Align the pins on the monitor cable with the holes in the adapter port and plug in the monitor.

2. **What kind of video is component video?**
   ☐ Analog
   ☐ Digital
   ☐ HD
   ☐ Brightness only

ACTIVITY 4–2
Installing Display Devices

Before You Begin

You have a working monitor with either a 15-pin VGA-style monitor cable and a computer equipped with a VGA port, or you have a digital flat-panel monitor (LCD or LED) that uses the 29-pin DVI connector, High-Definition Multimedia Interface (HDMI) connector, or a universal serial bus (USB) display. The computer is turned off and the monitor is unplugged.

Scenario

The marketing department of your company is moving to new offices, and you have been assigned the task of setting up the computers in their new offices. The computers and monitors have been delivered to each office. Employees want to begin using their computers as soon as possible.

---

1. Install the monitor.
   a) Verify that the power is off at the computer.
   b) Locate the monitor cable and examine the connector.
   c) If you have a standard VGA CRT monitor, locate the VGA adapter port on the computer. If you have an LCD display, locate the VGA, 29-pin DVI, or the USB port on the computer.
   d) Insert the monitor connector into the appropriate port, being sure to align the pins carefully.
   e) Tighten the screws. Do not over-tighten them.
   f) Plug in the monitor.

2. Check whether the monitor is functional.
   a) Turn on the computer power.
   b) Turn on the monitor power.
   c) After the system has started to boot, verify that the power light on the monitor is green and is not flashing.
   d) Watch the monitor and verify that the display is clear.

ACTIVITY 4-3
Configuring Display Devices

Before You Begin

Your instructor has altered the display settings for your monitor. The computer is running and the **Welcome** screen is displayed.

Scenario

An employee recently had to move the location of his workstation. The employee reports that, since the move, the display does not appear in the center of the monitor. The images are too dark, making them difficult to see, and he cannot see as much on the screen as he would like. The employee needs you to resolve these issues so that he can get back to work.

---

1. Adjust the monitor display.
   a) Referring to the monitor's documentation as necessary, locate the physical controls to adjust the brightness of the display image.
   b) Adjust the brightness so that the monitor is comfortable to view.
   c) Adjust the contrast so that you can view all the screen elements easily.

2. Change the resolution.
   a) To open the Screen Resolution window, right-click the desktop and select **Screen resolution.**
   b) In the **Resolution** section, select the current resolution to display the drop-down list.
   c) In the Screen Resolution window, drag the slider or click to select the appropriate resolution.
   d) Select **OK.**
   e) In the **Display Settings** message box, select **Keep changes** to set the new resolution.

3. Adjust the horizontal and vertical positions of the image.
   a) Referring to the documentation as necessary, locate the controls to adjust the size and centering of the display image.
   b) Adjust the vertical display position so that the display is centered top-to-bottom on the screen.
   c) Adjust the horizontal display position so that the display is centered side-to-side on the screen.
   d) Adjust the height and width of the image so that there is either no border or the smallest border allowed.

TOPIC B

Install and Configure Input Devices

In the previous topic, you examined display devices and how to install and configure them so that users can see the computer system's output. Users also need to be able to interact with the computer system by using input devices. In this topic, you will install and configure input devices.

Computers need user input such as directions or commands and user interaction with the programs that are included in order to produce something of use. Keyboards and pointing devices are the standard input devices for personal computers these days, but there is an ever-growing number of input devices available for the user to interact with in a variety of ways. As an A+ technician, part of your responsibilities will include installing and configuring all types of input devices.

This topic covers all or part of the following CompTIA® A+® (2012) certification objectives:

• Exam 220–801: Objective 1.12: Install and configure various peripheral devices.

Standard Input Device Types

Common input devices include mice and keyboards, but even these two components come in a variety of implementations.

Input Device	Description
Standard keyboard 	Standard keyboards are rectangular in shape, and have 84, 101, or 104 keys. • The original PC keyboard, the XT, has 84 keys. A numeric pad is integrated to the right of the alphabetical keys. Function keys are along the left side of the keyboard. • The AT keyboard also has 84 keys and is very similar to the original PC keyboard. However, on the AT keyboard, the numeric pad is separate from the alphabetical keys. • The AT Enhanced keyboard has 101 keys. The function keys are integrated across the top. Arrow keys have been added, as well as a set of six keys—**Insert, Delete, Home, End, Page Up,** and **Page Down.** There are also additional command keys such as **Esc** and **Ctrl.** • The Windows 104-key keyboard is similar to the AT Enhanced keyboard, but adds two **Windows** keys and a **Menu** key. The **Windows** keys are analogous to clicking the Windows **Start** button and the **Menu** key performs the same functions as right-clicking the mouse.
Ergonomic keyboard	Natural or ergonomic keyboards usually split the keyboard in half so each hand can comfortably use its own set of keys. Built-in wrist rests are common, and some ergonomic keyboards also have an integrated pointing device such as a trackball or touch pad.

Input Device	Description

Dvorak keyboard

Dvorak keyboards rearrange the keys into a more efficient arrangement that makes faster typing possible for users who have become familiar with it.

Mouse

A mouse is a small object that runs across a flat surface and has at least one, but typically two or three, buttons that send electronic signals to the graphical user interface (GUI). Its name is derived from its appearance—a small rounded rectangle shape with a single cord attached at one end. Mice can be:

- Mechanical—A ball on the underside runs along a flat surface. Mechanical rollers detect the direction the ball is rolling and move the screen pointer accordingly.
- Optical—A laser detects the mouse's movement. Optical mice have no mechanical moving parts, and they respond more quickly and precisely than other types of mice.

Trackball mouse

A trackball is basically an upside down mouse. The ball is mounted on the top of the case instead of the bottom and signals are sent to the computer by moving the ball with your thumb, fingers, or palm instead of by rolling the ball across a flat surface. Like a mouse, a trackball has at least one button that is used to send electronic signals to the computer.

Touch pad

A touch pad is a small, touch-sensitive pad where you run your finger across the surface to send electronic signals to the computer to control the pointer on the screen. Touch pads can have buttons like a mouse or trackball, or the touch pad can be

Input Device	Description
	configured to detect finger taps on its surface and process those signals like button clicks.
Trackpoint	A *trackpoint*, or pointing stick, is most commonly found on laptops. Located in the center of the keyboard, the trackpoint is a small joystick-like button that responds to user force in all directions in order to move the mouse pointer on screen.

Specialty Keyboards

Specialty keyboards include:

- Keyboards for children or users with special needs. These may have enlarged or specially constructed keys.
- Foreign language keyboards, which have a variety of different keys.
- Custom application keyboards, which can have multimedia access buttons, video/audio editing software buttons, and gaming devices.

Ports, Cables, and Connections

Keyboards and mice can use several types of ports and connections:

- Serial (now largely obsolete)
- Standard DIN (5-pin, and largely obsolete)
- PS/2 (6-pin mini-DIN)
- USB
- Wireless infrared
- Wireless radio frequency (RF)
- Bluetooth

Function Keys

Function keys, typically positioned horizontally along the top length of the keyboard, allow a user to do two things: they launch operating system commands, and they allow a user to customize the input from the keyboard. For example, when booting a PC, a user can change Basic Input/Output System (BIOS) settings by choosing certain function keys. A user can also customize how certain programs interpret function keys. On smaller devices, such as laptops, a user might notice a key labeled "Fn." This key is usually labeled in a different color from the rest of the keyboard, and is used in conjunction with other keys to increase the number of distinct inputs a keyboard can offer. Many of the **Fn** inputs control video or sound settings since there are not usually separate monitor buttons on a laptop.

Biometric Input Device Types

Biometrics is an automated method of recognizing a person based on a physiological or behavioral characteristic unique to the individual, such as a retina pattern, fingerprint, or voice pattern. Biometric technologies are becoming the foundation of an extensive array of highly secure identification and personal verification solutions. Biometric input devices can add an additional layer of physical security or information security by verifying the identity of the person attempting to gain access to a location or device.

Several types of biometric input devices might be used in an organization.

Biometric Device	Description
Fingerprint scanner/reader 	Scans a person's fingerprint(s) and matches it against a database of fingerprints to verify that person's identity. Once verified, that person will be able to access a building, location, or device or can be used with point-of-sale applications to complete a transaction. If not hard-wired into a system (such as a security system), fingerprint scanners/readers used with smaller devices like a personal computer typically connect via a USB connection. Some laptops have a fingerprint scanner integrated into the system as well, which is usually placed near the keyboard area of the laptop. The scanner is used to verify the identity of the user and grant them the ability to use the laptop.
Retina scanner 	Scans a person's retina or iris and matches it against a database of retina scans to verify the person's identity. Once verified, that person will be able to access a building, location, or device. If not hard-wired into a system (such as a security system), a retina scanner used with a smaller device like a personal computer typically connects via a USB connection.
Voice recognition	Uses a spoken phrase called the "pass phrase" and compares it against a person's "voice print," a recorded and stored version of that person saying the pass phrase, to verify identity. Once verified, that person will be able to access a building, location, or device.

Biometric Device	Description
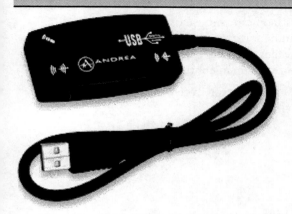	If not hard-wired into a system (such as a security system), a voice recognition system used with a smaller device like a personal computer typically connects via a USB connection.
Signature recognition 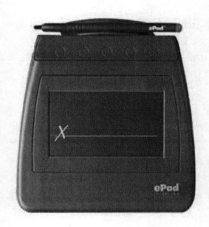	Uses a signature pad and a database of approved signatures. A user signs the signature pad, and the recognition system analyzes the individual behavior of the person signing, such as the strokes used and the pressure applied while signing, to verify the identity of the user. If not hard-wired into a system (such as a security system), a signature capture pad used with a smaller device like a personal computer typically connects via a USB connection.
Keyboard 	Using a biometric keyboard, only authorized users would be able to use the keyboard, and only once their identity was verified through the verification program. The keyboard and a special program monitor the individual's typing behaviors, such as key press duration or pressure, key strokes, and so forth, to create a baseline for normal typing for the individual. The program can challenge a user to verify identity by typing, and compares the keystroke behavior of the typist to that stored in a database for the user. Most biometric keyboards connect via a USB connection.
Mouse	Using a biometric mouse, only authorized users would be able to use the mouse and access or navigate the computer system, and only once their identity was verified through the verification program.

Biometric Device	Description
	A biometric mouse uses biometric authentication, typically a built-in fingerprint reader, to verify the identity of the user and provide them control over the mouse. Most biometric mice connect via a USB connection.
Storage devices	Using a biometric storage device, such as flash drive or hard drive, only authorized users would be able to access files or data stored on the storage device. Biometric flash drives or hard drives use another kind of biometric authentication, typically a built-in fingerprint reader, to verify the identity of the user and provide them access to the flash drive files. Most biometric storage devices connect via a USB connection.

Biometric devices will need to be installed and configured, and then initialized for the specific end user that will be using the device. The initial biometric authentication "object" for the user (be it a fingerprint, retina scan, pass phrase, etc.) must first be captured and stored. Then the user will have to test the device to make sure that it accurately verifies his or her identity against the authentication object, permitting them access to the location or device.

Specialized Input Device Types

Although keyboards and mice are the most popular of the input devices for personal computers, there are some specialized input devices that you might encounter in your workplace.

Input Device	Description
Touch screen	Touch screens enable users to enter inputs by touching areas on a monitor screen. They can be activated by a finger touch or a stylus touch. Touch screens are composed of: • Touch sensors. The sensors can be a panel that lays over a standard monitor or can be built into a special touch screen monitor where the user actually touches the glass on the monitor. • A controller. If using an overlay panel, the controller connects to the panel and then to a PC port. Many use a COM or USB port, although there are special instances where the controller connects to a drive or other device or port. For touch screens with built-in touch sensors, the controller is built into the monitor. In this case, the monitor contains two cables—one to the monitor port and one to the COM or USB port (or other port). • A device driver or specialized software. This enables the operating system to receive and interpret information from the touch screen device.

Input Device	Description
Scanner	A scanner is used to take a photo-identical copy (scan) of a physical hard copy of any kind of document, such as a piece of paper or a photo, and create a digital-format copy of the document.
	A scanner is similar to a photocopy machine or copier, but with a much smaller footprint. Scanners can be attached directly to a personal computer to import scanned copies of documents. With the proper software or program installed, scanned versions can be manipulated and edited once they have been imported.
	A scanner typically uses a USB or high-speed USB connection to connect between devices.
Barcode reader	Barcodes provide a simple and inexpensive method of encoding text information that is easily read by inexpensive electronic readers. A barcode reader decodes a barcode by scanning a light source across the barcode and converting the pattern of reflected light to an electronic signal that is decoded back to the original data by electronic circuits. There are currently four different types of barcode readers available: pen-type readers (or barcode wands), laser scanners, Charge Coupled Device (CCD) readers, and camera-based readers.
	Barcode scanners or readers connect to a device via a USB connection or are wireless.
Microphone	Microphones record any type of sound and convert it to a electronic or digital format. Once in this format, the recorded sounds can be manipulated or edited, and used in a variety of ways.
	Microphones typically connect to a device through a MIC jack, although some connect with a USB connection. Some laptops may have a built-in microphone.
Gamepad	A gamepad is a game controller used to interact with a video game console or program, typically held and manipulated with two hands. It uses a number of buttons and toggles, each of which controls a different action within the game program.
	The latest versions of many gamepads also include sensors and pointing devices that sense directions of movement and rotation, and use a combination of these movements to control actions within the game program.
	Gamepads typically connect to a device via a USB connection. The latest technology in gamepads is unique in its wireless capabilities: many gamepads do not attach to a device via a connector, but rather transmit inputs wirelessly to the receiving device or console.
Joystick	A joystick is a pivoting stick or lever attached to a base that is used to control movement on a device. It typically also includes push buttons, toggles, or switches that control other actions associated with the program or device that the input is controlling. The joystick inputs the angle and direction of a desired movement.
	Joysticks are most commonly used to control video games or other computer programs, but are also used to control machines and devices such as cranes and unmanned vehicles.
	Legacy joysticks connected to a computer via a game port, a device port designed specifically for connecting this input device. However, most modern joysticks connect to the device via a USB connection.

Input Device	Description
Digitizer	A digitizer is any device that performs digitization, which is the conversion of any type of analog signal into its digital form. This includes images, objects, text, and so forth. However, the term is most commonly used in reference to the device used to convert audio and video data into a digital format that can be edited, manipulated, and viewed on a computer, television or other device. A digitizer typically uses a USB or high speed USB connection to connect between devices. Some older versions may use an S-Video and Composite-to-USB connection.
Interactive whiteboard	An interactive whiteboard looks similar to a traditional whiteboard; however, it connects to a computer using a wired USB cable, or connects wirelessly through a Bluetooth® connection. A projector is typically used with it to display the computer's desktop, and it can be used as an input device once the correct device drivers are installed on the computer. You can manipulate the computer directly on the whiteboard using a special stylus or by using your finger. Interactive whiteboards are used in many schools today, and have become a very popular teaching tool.

[handwritten note next to Digitizer row: Ex- Artwork]

Touch Screen Technologies

Touch screens can gather input through a number of different technologies:

- Capacitive: Uses electrical conductors to manipulate the screen. The screen is coated with a conductor and, as the human body is also a conductor, contact on the surface of the screen by a finger or other body part results in a change to the screen's electrostatic field. The change in the field provides a horizontal and vertical coordinate, pinpointing the location of the touch on the screen.
- Resistive: Uses electrically resistive layers to comprise the screen. When the touch object (finger or stylus) pushes down on the first outer layer, it depresses and touches the second layer, creating an electrical charge between the two layers that provides a horizontal and vertical coordinate, determining the location of the touch on the screen.
- Surface Acoustic Wave: Uses ultrasonic waves that are disrupted when the screen is touched. The change in the wave is absorbed and registers where the screen was touched, determining the location of the touch on the screen.
- Infrared: Uses infrared LEDs and photodetectors that are disrupted when the screen is touched. The LED beams are set up in a cross-hatch pattern that are disrupted when the screen is touched, and determine the location of the touch on the screen.
- Optical imaging: Uses image sensors placed around the screen that detect the touch on the screen based on the shadow that is created when the screen is touched. The image sensors compare the information about the shadow to determine the location of the touch on the screen.
- Dispersive signal: Uses sensors that detect vibrations that occur when the screen is touched. The vibrations created by the touch are analyzed to determine the location of the touch on the screen.
- Acoustic pulse recognition: Uses unique acoustic sounds that are associated with a specific location on the screen to determine the exact location of the touch on the screen.

Specialized Input Devices in Everyday Life

Many people might encounter specialized input devices during a trip to the grocery store. It is increasingly common to see the cashier use a barcode scanner to account for the item's price, and to use a touch screen to enter any additional information (such as whether there is more than one item at that price, or to enter the correct produce code). Additionally, most grocery stores use a touch screen device to capture the customer's credit card number and accept any additional user input, such as a PIN. Finally, the touch screen device often has a stylus attached so that the customer can sign the screen; there will be no paper at all in this entire transaction.

KVM Switches

A *keyboard, video, mouse (KVM) switch* is a device that enables a computer user to control multiple computers with a single keyboard and mouse, with the display sent to a single monitor. This feature is particularly useful in managing multiple test environments, or in accessing multiple servers that have no need for dedicated display or input devices. KVM switches are available with PS/2 or USB connections, and come in desktop, inline, or rack-mount varieties. Higher-end rack-mount models can be uplinked to connect dozens of computers.

Figure 4–1: A KVM switch.

Input Device Selection Tips

Windows operating systems support a variety of input devices, so you should select an input device based on user requirements.

Input Device	Description
Keyboard	When selecting a keyboard for a user, in addition to considering its ergonomics, you should also consider whether the keyboard offers additional features (such as customizable hot keys and scrolling) as well as wireless connectivity. Many users now prefer to use a wireless keyboard as it gives them the freedom to locate the keyboard anywhere on their desks. In some cases, users might be able to use a Bluetooth-enabled keyboard to communicate with both their desktop computers and a mobile device such as a tablet or a smartphone. Be sure to determine the potential keyboard's connector requirements; if the keyboard uses USB, you will need to make sure the user's computer has an available USB port.
Pointing device	When selecting a mouse for a user, most users prefer optical mice because they are less susceptible to problems such as dirt interfering with the rollerball. As with keyboards, you will also find that users prefer wireless mice over wired mice because of the freedom it gives them to move around while working. Besides these factors, choosing between a mouse, a trackball, and a touch pad comes down to the personal preference of the user.
Biometric device	Whether or not a biometric device is being deployed will likely be a decision made based on an organizational security policy or standard. If biometric devices will be deployed at individual workstations, you will need to determine the specific biometric device's connector requirements; as most use a USB connection, you will need to make sure that the user's computer has an available USB port to connect the device.
Specialty device	Using a specialty device will be determined by two main factors: is the device needed by the end user as a matter of productivity (to complete job tasks)? Or is the device desired by the end user as a personal preference?

[handwritten: FoR Security]

Input Device	Description
	If any specialty devices will be deployed on the system, you will need to determine the device's connector requirements. Most specialty input devices use a USB connection, so you will need to make sure that the user's computer has an available USB port or ports if multiple specialty devices will be connected.

Input Device Installation Considerations

Before you attempt to install an input device, you should consider certain factors.

Factor	Considerations
Drivers	Be sure that you have the most current drivers for the input device for the operating system of the computer on which you plan to install it. If you install a USB device, you might get a HID message (which stands for "Human Input Device"). Either let the PC find the right driver, or restart the computer and see if the issue resolves itself. If that does not work, you will need to find a driver for the device.
Ports	Make sure that the computer has an available port to which you can connect the device. Input devices can use a variety of ports, including PS/2, serial, parallel, USB, infrared, and FireWire/IEEE 1394. If a large number of input devices will be connected using the same connector type, you may need to consider using a hub, splitter, or extender that creates multiple accessible ports via one port on the device. For example, a USB hub expands one USB port into several available USB ports, using an upstream port that connects to the device USB port and multiple downstream ports on the hub.
Manufacturer's instructions	Review the manual or quick start guide that came with the device. In some cases, the manufacturer might require you to install the device drivers before connecting the device to the computer.

 Access the Checklist tile on your LogicalCHOICE course screen for reference information and job aids on How to Install and Configure Input Devices

ACTIVITY 4-4
Installing Input Devices

Before You Begin
For this activity, you will need a replacement keyboard and mouse or other pointing device.

Scenario
You have received a service call to replace a user's mouse and keyboard.

1. Replace the keyboard.
   a) Shut down the computer.
   b) Determine the connection type used by the replacement keyboard.
   c) Unplug the old keyboard from the system unit.
   d) Plug the new keyboard into the appropriate PS/2 or USB port.

2. Replace the mouse or pointing device.
   a) Determine the connection type used by the replacement mouse.
   b) Unplug the old mouse from the system unit.
   c) Plug the new mouse into the appropriate PS/2 or USB port.
   d) Start the computer.

3. Test the installed devices.
   a) Use the keyboard to access the **Start** menu.
   b) Move the mouse around to verify that it is working properly.

ACTIVITY 4-5
Configuring Input Devices

Scenario

You just replaced a user's mouse and keyboard. The user is left-handed and prefers a slow-blinking cursor. She also has a hard time distinguishing the mouse pointer from other screen elements, and asks if you can adjust the pointer to something more easily discernible.

1. Configure the keyboard settings.
   a) Select **Start→Control Panel.**
   b) In the Control Panel window, in the **Adjust your computer's settings** section, from the **View by** drop-down list, select **Large icons.**
   c) Select the **Keyboard** link.
   d) In the **Keyboard Properties** dialog box, on the **Speed** tab, reduce the cursor blink rate by dragging the **Cursor blink rate** slider to the left.

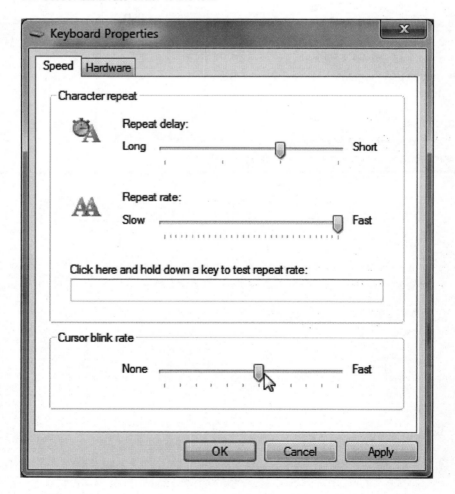

   e) Select **Apply.**
   f) Select **OK.**

2. Configure the mouse settings.

a) In the Control Panel window, select the **Mouse** link.

b) In the **Mouse Properties** dialog box, on the **Buttons** tab, check the **Switch primary and secondary buttons** check box.

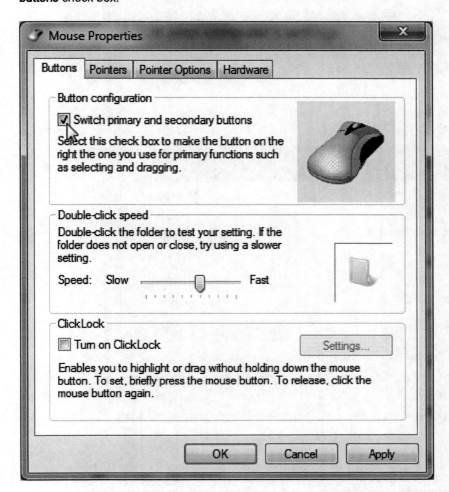

c) To verify that the right mouse button is now the primary button, right-click the **Pointers** tab.

d) Right-click the **Buttons** tab.

e) Select the **Pointers** tab.

f) From the **Scheme** drop-down list, select **Magnified (system scheme).**

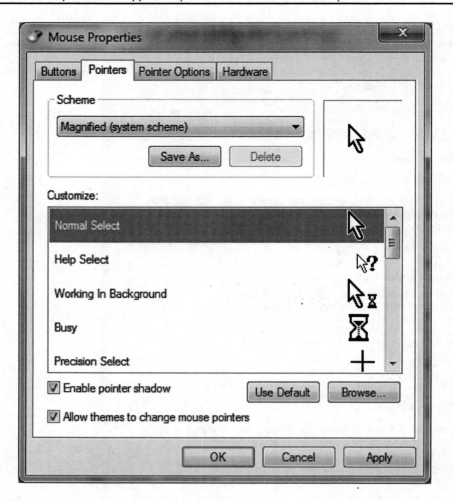

g) Select **OK**.

3. Reconfigure the mouse settings to suit your personal preferences, and close the **Control Panel**.

TOPIC C

Install and Configure Expansion Cards

In the previous topic, you installed input devices, such as mice and keyboards, that are most commonly connected and used on a computer system. These devices typically connect using standard ports that are available on most machines, such as a USB port. You can expand the functionality of your computer by adding expansion cards that provide additional ports for a variety of peripheral devices. In this topic, you will install and configure expansion cards.

Display devices, keyboards, and other pointing devices are the most common devices you are likely to install and configure; these devices are typically included in a standard workstation environment when a PC is requested. When a user needs to connect a peripheral component that doesn't have an existing interface, like a multimedia device, you will need to install an expansion card. As an A+ technician, your responsibilities are likely to include upgrading users' computers by installing a variety of components, including expansion cards.

This topic covers all or part of the following CompTIA® A+® (2012) certification objectives:

*   Exam 220–801: Objective 1.4: Install and configure expansion cards.

Expansion Card Types

Expansion cards extend the capabilities of a computer. There are many different types of expansion cards, each of which provide different capabilities.

Expansion Card Type	Description
Sound cards	A sound card or audio card provides the interface necessary for the input and output of audio signals both to and from the computer.
Video cards	A video card, sometimes called a display card or graphics card, provides the interface necessary to generate the visual output that is sent to the display device.
Network cards	A network card, sometimes called a network interface card (NIC), provides the interface necessary for network communications, whether for wired or wireless connectivity.
Serial and parallel cards	A serial or parallel card provides the interface necessary for the computer to recognize and interact with any devices that connect to the computer via a serial or parallel connection. Devices that utilize serial or parallel connections include modems, display devices, barcode scanners, point of sale devices, and more.
USB cards	A USB card provides the interface necessary for the computer to recognize and interact with all devices that connect to the computer via a USB connection. Devices that utilize USB connections include keyboards, flash drives, cameras, and more.
FireWire cards	A FireWire card provides the interface necessary for the computer to recognize and interact with all devices that connect to the computer via a FireWire connection. FireWire is mainly used for high-speed data transfer. Devices that use FireWire connections include external hard drives, video and audio recording devices, and more.
Storage cards	A storage card provides the interface for the computer to recognize and interact with a storage device such as a disk. Systems with multiple disk drives, especially of different types, may require multiple storage

Expansion Card Type	Description
	cards to manage the communication between the disks and the system board.
Modem cards	A modem card provides the interface necessary for remote communications over phone or data lines that have been provided by a cable or Internet service provider.
Wireless/cellular cards	A wireless or cellular card provides the interface necessary for remote communications, such as Internet over mobile phone or wireless data lines such as Wi-Fi, 3G, or 4G Internet that have been provided by a cellular service provider.
TV tuner cards	A TV tuner card provides the interface necessary for the computer to receive television signals and display the output on a display device.
Video capture cards	A video capture card provides the interface necessary for the computer to input video feeds, including digital video, and interact with the software necessary to process and edit video.
Riser cards	A riser card provides the interface necessary for adding expansion cards to a system board while saving space within the system case. A riser card allows the cards to stack horizontally rather than vertically within the system.

[handwritten: Slot used to change the orientation of the card]

Extended Capabilities for Sound Cards

Because so many computer manufacturers now build sound capabilities into motherboards, many sound card manufacturers add extended features to their cards in order to justify their purchase. These features might include digital output so that you can integrate the computer into a home entertainment system, or FireWire connections so that you can play MP3 recordings directly from an MP3 device.

Card Selection Tips

Before selecting an expansion card for a computer, you must verify that its bus type is compatible with the computer. In addition, you must also make sure that the expansion card's drivers are compatible with the computer's operating system. Typically, most expansion cards on the market today support Plug and Play (PnP) standards. PnP is a functionality of many buses that automatically detects new hardware, and automatically assigns resources for the device, without the need for manual configuration. If you plan on using PnP when adding expansion cards, make sure that the computer's BIOS and operating system support it.

Card Installation Considerations

Before you attempt to install an expansion card, verify that the computer has an available slot that matches the expansion card's bus type and that you have the device's latest drivers for the computer's operating system. Be sure to unplug the computer and discharge any static electricity before installing the card. If you are installing a card that has its own cooling system, such as a fan, make sure there is enough room for the card's airflow system to function properly.

Expansion Card Configuration

Once the expansion card is installed, there are a number of means for configuring the expansion card. Depending on the type and manufacturer, you may need to use one or a combination of these methods.

Configuration Method	Description
PnP installation	If the expansion card, the device, the BIOS, and the operating system (Windows® 95 and newer) are all PnP compatible, the expansion card will be automatically configured and the system will automatically assign resources to the card when the system starts.
Manufacturer driver	If Windows does not automatically detect an expansion card, you can manually install a driver from the manufacturer.
The **Add Hardware** wizard	You can use the **Add Hardware** wizard to install and configure PnP devices, although to install most unrecognized devices, you will typically just run a setup program provided by the manufacturer.
Hardware scan	When using the wizard, you should initially let Windows try to scan for new hardware (this is the default selection).
Device list	If Windows cannot find the device, you can then choose the device from a list of devices offered by Windows and Windows will install the appropriate driver.

Note: Read the installation instructions for the expansion card to determine if any software is required prior to the installation. Failure to do so could cause the installation to fail or the card and system to behave erratically.

Note: For additional information, check out the LearnTO **Install Expansion Cards** in the LearnTOs for this course on your LogicalCHOICE Course screen.

Access the Checklist tile on your LogicalCHOICE course screen for reference information and job aids on How to Install and Configure Expansion Cards

ACTIVITY 4-6
Examining Expansion Cards

Scenario
In this activity, you will examine expansion cards.

1. Which expansion card provides interfaces necessary to connect Small Computer Systems Interface (SCSI) devices?
   - ○ Input/output card
   - ○ Multimedia card
   - ○ Video card
   - ○ Modem card

2. True or False? Before attempting to install an expansion card, verify that the computer has an available slot that matches the expansion card's bus type.
   - ☐ True
   - ☐ False

3. What is the first step in installing an expansion card?
   - ○ Turn off power to the system and unplug the power and peripheral cables.
   - ○ Remove the system cover and access the slots on the system board.
   - ○ Remove the slot cover from an empty slot.
   - ○ Read the quick start guide to see if drivers or other software should be installed before or after installing the card.

ACTIVITY 4-7
Installing Expansion Cards

Before You Begin

You have open expansion slots on the system board. You have been given one or more expansion card types and device drivers.

Scenario

You have been asked to install several expansion cards on a user's system. The appropriate drivers for the cards are also available to you should you need them.

---

1. Open the system cover and access the slots.
   a) Turn off the system power.
   b) Unplug the computer from the electrical outlet.
   c) Unplug peripherals from the system.
   d) Remove the cover.
   e) Determine if you need to move or remove any components in order to access the slots.

2. Insert the card in an available slot.

> **Note:** Some manufacturers suggest installing a driver prior to inserting the adapter card. It is therefore important to read the manufacturer's instructions before installing the card.

   a) Locate an open slot.
   b) Remove the slot cover.
   c) Firmly press the card into the slot.

> **Caution:** Do not rock the card side to side when installing or removing it.

   d) Secure the card to the chassis with the screw from the slot cover. Normally, you would now secure the cover back on to the system, but because you will be doing more work inside the system, leave it off.

3. Configure the card for the computer.
   a) Reconnect the peripherals and cables that you disconnected in step 1.
   b) Power on the system.
   c) Install any required drivers.

4. Check whether the card is functioning properly.
   a) Connect any devices to the card that are required for testing the card functionality.
   b) Access or use the device connected to the card.
   c) In **Device Manager,** verify that the device's properties show that the device is working properly and that there are no conflicts, and then select **Cancel.**

TOPIC D

Install and Configure Multimedia Devices

In the previous topic, you installed and configured expansion cards to support additional computer functionality. Once you have the right expansion cards in place, you can add peripheral components such as multimedia devices that provide users with additional and expanded capabilities such as recording music. In this topic, you will install multimedia devices.

As an A+ technician, you might support corporate users, such as marketing or sales representatives, who will need to create multimedia business presentations. Or, you might work for a retail computer outlet, supporting home users who like to play music and games on their PCs. Add to that the sheer number of multimedia devices that are now available for personal computer systems, and you will likely be tasked at some point with connecting and configuring a variety of multimedia devices for various types of end users.

This topic covers all or part of the following CompTIA® A+® (2012) certification objectives:

- Exam 220–801: Objective 1.12: Install and configure various peripheral devices.

Multimedia Devices

A *multimedia device* is a computer peripheral or internal component that transfers sound, images or a combination of both to or from a personal computer. Multimedia devices can be input devices or output devices.

Figure 4–2: Multimedia devices.

Common Multimedia Devices

Common multimedia devices include different types of cameras and sound devices.

Multimedia Device	Description
Digital camera	A digital camera uses electronic signals to capture and store photographic images or video images. The resulting files are often stored on embedded memory cards, removable memory cards, or optical disks. Connecting the digital camera or its removable memory card to a PC enables you to save, transfer, print, and otherwise work with the images.

Multimedia Device	Description
	If the digital camera has a removable memory card, the card itself may need to be connected to a computer through a media reader. Most digital cameras also offer USB and FireWire cables and connections.
Camcorder	A video recording camera captures and stores visual images and sounds in the form of either analog or digital signals. Video files are stored either on an internal storage device or on removable memory cards.
	Most digital camcorders available for personal (commercial) use also offer USB and FireWire cables and connections. If the camcorder has a removable memory card, the card itself may need to be connected to a computer through a media reader. Professional-grade cameras are more likely to use tapes or disks that will need an alternate transfer method, often including digitizing.
Webcam	A web camera, or webcam, is used to send periodic images or continuous frames to a website for display. Webcam software usually captures the images as JPEG or MPEG files and uploads them to a web server. Webcam images can also be accessed using some instant messaging software and by some video applications. Some corporations use webcams as a security measure.
	Webcams commonly use USB or FireWire cables and connectors.
MIDI-enabled device	The Musical Instrument Digital Interface (MIDI) connection enables you to connect and control musical devices such as electric keyboards, synthesizers, guitars, drum kits, and mixers. Sound cards usually include built-in synthesizers as well, to produce MIDI sounds. MIDI devices can be connected to each other and then to the computer.
	MIDI devices can connect to the computer using a number of ports. MIDI to USB interface, MIDI to serial, or MIDI to FireWire connections are most commonly used, allowing for faster communication between the musical instrument and the computer or controller device.
Microphone	A computer microphone is used to input audio into the device, either for recording the audio as data or for use in real-time, such as the audio input that accompanies a webcam or video conferencing chat.
	Microphones can be connected to the microphone port or jack of any sound card. If the card is color-coded, it will be pink. Otherwise, it will be labeled MIC or have a picture of a microphone. Many microphones have a 1/8-inch phono plug built into the attached cable.
Speakers	Speakers can be attached to the device to play the audio out loud, without the need for headphones.
	Speakers are connected to the line out port or jack on the sound card. Some speaker sets are permanently connected to each other. Other speaker sets are connected by the user to each other or to a subwoofer. A cable runs from one of the speakers to the line out port to connect both speakers to the computer. If the card is color-coded, the speaker port will be lime. The port might be labeled as Line Out, Out, Spkr, or Speaker, or it may have an image with an arrow indicating the direction of the audio (out).
	Speakers typically have a 1/8-inch phono plug built into the attached cable.

Line In

On many devices, there will be a third auxiliary port available: line in. Most PCs will have at least one line in jack, which provides a connection for a music player or other audio input device. If the sound card is color-coded, the line in port will be light blue. The port might be labeled as Line In or In, or it may have an image with an arrow indicating the direction of the input (in).

 Note: Most desktop computers will have three auxiliary jacks available: microphone, line out, and line in. Most laptops don't have a line out or line in jack, but will typically have a microphone jack and a headphone jack.

Media Readers

A media reader functions as an interface between a removable memory card and a PC. Commonly connecting to the computer via a USB cable, a media reader is a small device that a user inserts a memory card into if that card does not have an interface of its own. For example, a Secure Digital (SD) card cannot be inserted directly into a computer, but by inserting the SD card into a media reader and then connecting the media reader to the computer, the computer will recognize the SD card as another external storage device.

Multimedia Device Selection Tips

You will need to select a multimedia device that meets the user's needs and that can be supported on the user's machine. Depending on the multimedia device, there are a number of criteria to consider when making a selection.

Multimedia Device	Considerations
Digital camera	Determine what type of output the user needs from the camera. If the user plans to use the images only for viewing online, you can select a lower quality (fewer megapixels) camera. If the user also wants to print the images, particularly if the user wants large prints (such as 11-inch x 17-inch and higher), you should select a camera with as many megapixels as the user can afford.
	Keep in mind that you also need to have a means for the user to move photos off the device and onto the computer. Common techniques you can use include:
	• Connecting the camera directly to the computer via a USB or FireWire port.
	• Connecting the camera's memory card directly to the computer via a memory card slot. Not all computers have this feature, but many home PCs do.
	• Using a memory card reader that connects to a USB or FireWire port.
	Determine if you have the appropriate cables or connectors available that will be needed to connect the camera. Depending on the connector needed, make sure that there is also a port available on the device to connect the camera.
Camcorder	Determine what type of recording format/output the user needs from the camcorder. The format (analog or digital) can determine the cost of the device, the type and cost of any additional storage devices used with the device, how much video can be recorded, and the quality of the recordings and copies. Specifically, converting analog recordings to digital formats can be time consuming and usually results in degradation of quality.

Multimedia Device	Considerations
	You should also consider the additional costs for the tapes or disks that will be used to record videos. which will vary depending on the manufacturer or type of device used.
	Determine if you have the appropriate cables or connectors available that may be needed to connect the camcorder. If the camcorder does not have external or removable storage, you may also need to have a solution for moving video files from the device and onto the computer, such as a FireWire cable.
	If a camcorder that records analog signals is being used, the user will likely need a digitizer (and the accompanying cables and connectors) to convert the files to digital format.
Webcam	Ensure that the user's computer has the necessary hardware, operating system, and memory required to support the device. Older computers may not meet the requirements.
	Different webcams offer different features: image quality can vary, lens quality and focus (manual versus automatic) can vary, they can be color or monochrome, some come with audio integrated and some need an external microphone. Determine what the user needs to do with the webcam and what features are indispensable.
	You will also need to determine if you have the appropriate cables or connectors available that may be needed to connect the webcam. You may also need to install an expansion card if the required port is not available on the computer.
	Many laptops will have a built-in webcam that is integrated into the system already.
MIDI-enabled device	Determine what kind of device is needed based on what the user needs or wants to do with the device. Once you know what kind of device they need, ensure that the user's computer has the necessary hardware and software to support the device.
	Determine if you have the appropriate cables or connectors available that may be needed to connect the device. You may also need to install an expansion card if the required port is not available on the computer.
Microphone	Users use microphones to complete tasks such as making phone calls through their computers and dictating to the computer using voice recognition software. For such users, the higher the quality of the microphone, the better they will be able to accomplish these tasks.
	Determine if you have the appropriate cables or connectors available that will be needed to connect the microphone. You will also need to make sure that there is an available port or jack available on the device to connect the microphone.
	Many laptops will have a built-in microphone that is integrated into the system already.
Speakers	If users plan to listen to music or play games on a computer, it is important to help them select higher-quality speakers. Key speaker standards include:
	• Stereo: Specifies a left and right speaker that connects directly to a single jack in a sound card. These types of speakers are usually the least expensive.

Multimedia Device	Considerations
	• 2.1 Systems: Specifies a pair of stereo speakers plus a subwoofer. These systems do not support surround sound. • 5.1 Systems: Specifies five channels of sound: front-left, front-center, front-right, rear-left, and rear-right speakers, plus a subwoofer. • 7.1 Systems: Specifies seven channels of sound: front-left, front-center, front-right, middle-left, middle-right, rear-left, and rear-right speakers, plus a subwoofer. Determine if you have the appropriate cables or connectors available that will be needed to connect the speakers. You will also need to make sure that there is an available port or jack available on the device to connect the speakers.

Multimedia Device Installation Considerations

There are some considerations you should be aware of when installing multimedia devices.

Consideration	Description
Expansion card slots	If the device requires a specific expansion card, do you have an available slot on the motherboard? Also, try to place this expansion card in such a way as to avoid reducing the airflow in the computer.
Device drivers	Do you have the appropriate device drivers for the computer's operating system? If not, download them before starting the installation.
Cables and connectors	Do you have the necessary cables and connectors to connect devices, such as speakers, and place them where the user wants them?
Cameras and card readers	Although you can connect a digital camera directly to a computer to download its photos, you can use a memory card reader instead. The user will also see faster download performance when downloading photos using a memory card reader.

 Note: Read the installation instructions for the device to determine if any software is required prior to the installation. Failure to do so could cause the installation to fail or the device and system to behave erratically.

 Note: For additional information, check out the LearnTO **Install Multimedia Devices** in the LearnTOs for this course on your LogicalCHOICE Course screen.

Multimedia Device Configuration

You can use multimedia device-specific software and either the **Device Manager** or the appropriate utility in the **Control Panel** to configure multimedia devices. Options you can configure for these devices include:

• Enabling and disabling a device.
• Selecting a default device for performing certain tasks, such as audio playback.
• Viewing and configuring features and properties for specific devices.

• Updating the device's driver.

 Access the Checklist tile on your LogicalCHOICE course screen for reference information and job aids on How to Install and Configure Multimedia Devices

ACTIVITY 4-8
Examining Multimedia Devices

Scenario

In this activity, you will examine multimedia devices.

1. If you want to watch TV on your PC, but you do not need to record the transmission on your hard drive, which multimedia adapter should you use?

   ○ TV tuner card

   ○ Capture card

   ○ Video card

   ○ NIC

2. True or False? When you are installing a sound card, you do not have to worry about the available slots on the motherboard.

   ☐ True

   ☐ False

ACTIVITY 4–9
Installing Multimedia Devices

Before You Begin

If your computer does not have integrated (onboard) sound support, a sound card has been installed. You have speakers, a microphone, and possibly other MIDI devices available to install.

Scenario

A group in the marketing department is responsible for creating and presenting audio-visual presentations. These users have sound cards installed on their systems. They all have speakers and microphones connected to their sound cards. Some of them also have MIDI instruments and instruments that connect through an 8-inch stereo jack. The users have just received these sound devices and want to begin using them.

1. Connect the speakers to the computer.
    a) Determine if you need to connect the speakers to each other, and if so, connect them to each other.
    b) Locate the speaker jack on the computer and plug the speaker cable into the jack.
    c) Test the speakers to ensure they are working properly.

2. Connect a microphone to the MIC jack.
    a) Locate the MIC jack on the computer and connect the microphone to the MIC jack.

3. Test the microphone.
    a) To test the microphone, select **Start→Control Panel→Sound.**
    b) Select **Sound Recorder.**
    c) In the Sound Recorder window, select **Start Recording.**
    d) Speak a few words into the microphone.
    e) Select **Stop Recording.**
    f) Save the file as *Test Audio*
    g) Browse to the folder where the audio file is saved.
    h) Open the **Test Audio** file.

4. If you have a MIDI device, connect the MIDI device through the USB-to-MIDI device or a MIDI expansion card.
    a) Locate the appropriate port and connect the MIDI adapter to the appropriate port.
    b) If necessary, connect MIDI cables to the MIDI adapter.
    c) Connect the MIDI cable to the MIDI instrument.
    d) If necessary, install drivers for the MIDI instrument.
    e) Test the MIDI device by playing a few notes to ensure that it is working properly.

5. If you have another external multimedia device, connect it to the Line In jack.
    a) Locate the line in jack and connect an 1/8-inch stereo jack from the device to the computer.
    b) Test the device to ensure that it is working properly.

6. Close **Sound Recorder.**

Summary

In this lesson, you installed and configured various types of peripheral computer components, including input and output devices and the expansion cards that may be necessary to connect them. As an IT professional, having the ability to successfully install and configure these components is an integral part of a your daily work life, as you will be expected to set up workstations or assist users in installing anything that they may need to perform their job duties effectively.

What types of peripheral components do you anticipate having to install and configure most often in your current job role?

Will there be any specialty input devices that you will need to install or configure at your workplace? How might this affect your day-to-day activities as an IT professional?

Note: Check your LogicalCHOICE Course screen for opportunities to interact with your classmates, peers, and the larger LogicalCHOICE online community about the topics covered in this course or other topics you are interested in. From the Course screen you can also access available resources for a more continuous learning experience.

5 Managing System Components

Lesson Time: 4 hours, 35 minutes

Lesson Objectives

In this lesson, you will manage system components. You will:

- Identify motherboard installation and replacement methods.
- Select CPUs and cooling systems.
- Select and install power supplies.
- Identify the characteristics of RAM.
- Install and configure storage devices.
- Configure the system BIOS.

Lesson Introduction

In the previous lesson, you worked with peripheral components such as display devices, input devices, expansion cards, and multimedia devices. As an A+ technician, you are not only responsible for the components outside the system unit, but all the internal components as well. On the job, you may be asked to connect peripheral components for a user, or you may be asked to swap out a motherboard. In this lesson, you will explore the components that reside within a computer system.

A large part of your time as an A+ technician will be helping users to install and configure new software and hardware components. Having the knowledge and skills to properly install and configure the internal system components is crucial because, in most cases, users will not have the knowledge or the experience to install the components themselves. It will be your professional responsibility to know the technical specifications for these components and how to manage them appropriately.

This lesson covers all or part of the following CompTIA® A+® (2012) certification objectives:

- Topic A:
  - Exam 220–801: Objectives 1.2, 1.3
- Topic B:

- Exam 220–801: Objectives 1.2, 1.6
- Topic C:
  - Exam 220–801: Objective 1.8
- Topic D:
  - Exam 220–801: Objective 1.3
- Topic E:
  - Exam 220–801: Objective 1.5
- Topic F:
  - Exam 220–801: Objective 1.1

TOPIC A

Motherboards

In this lesson, you will dive inside the computer system and take a closer look at the internal components that enable the computer to run successfully. In this topic, you will start by examining motherboards.

The most important system component in a computer system is the motherboard. Although you can argue a case for almost any system component as being most important, without the motherboard, the computer simply cannot run. As an A+ technician, you must be knowledgeable about motherboards and their purpose within the computer system.

This topic covers all or part of the following CompTIA® A+® (2012) certification objectives:

- Exam 220–801: Objective 1.2: Differentiate between motherboard components, their purposes, and properties.
- Exam 220-801: Objective 1.3: Compare and contrast RAM types and features.

Motherboard Sizes/Form Factors

Motherboards come in several different sizes. This is often referred to as the board's *form factor*. The form factor describes the size, shape, and configuration of the motherboard.

System Board	Form Factor
ATX	ATX boards are an older motherboard standard that was introduced by Intel® in 1995 to provide better I/O support, lower cost, easier use, and better processor support than even earlier form factors. Some of the features of the ATX board are as follows: • Power supply with a single, keyed 20-pin connector. Rather than requiring Voltage Regulator Modules (VRMs) to reduce voltage down from 5 volts (V) to 3, 3 VDC is available directly from the power supply. • The central processing unit (CPU) is closer to the cooling fan on the power supply. Also, the cooling circulation blows air into the case instead of blowing air out of the case. • Input/output (I/O) ports are integrated into the board along with PS/2 connectors (instead of 5-pin DIN connectors). • You can access the entire motherboard without reaching around drives. This was accomplished by rotating the board 90 degrees. • This board cannot be used in Baby AT or LPX cases. • The board is 12 inches by 9.6 inches.
Mini-ATX	The mini-ATX board has a maximum size of 11.2 inches by 8.2 inches. The main difference between the mini board and the full-size ATX board is its smaller size. For example, it uses the same power supply form factor and case mounting holes as the full-size board.
microATX	The microATX board introduced in late 1997, is often written as μATX, and has a maximum size of 9.6 inches by 9.6 inches. MicroATX boards with integrated graphics are often used by system board manufacturers as a basis for small form factor and home entertainment PCs. MicroATX boards are backward compatible with the full size ATX boards and often use the same chipsets, so they can usually use the same components. However, because the cases are generally smaller, there

(handwritten margin note next to ATX: "7 Expansion Slots")

(handwritten margin note next to microATX: "4 Expansion Slots")

System Board	Form Factor
	are fewer I/O ports available than in ATX systems, so it might be necessary to use external USB hard drives, CD burners, and so forth.
mini-ITX	The mini-ITX motherboards are small, compact boards that fit the same form factor as the ATX and the micro-ATX boards. They have a maximum size of 6.7 inches by 6.6 inches. ITX boards were developed by a company named VIA technologies in 2001 to provide a compact board that does not drain system power. The boards are unique in that they are uniquely designed to consume less power while providing adequate processing power. Because of this, the board itself does not demand excessive cooling components. Due to their small size, and low power consumption, the boards can be implemented in a number of cases and electronics, and are popular among the industries that purchase motherboards in bulk to be incorporated into a number of different products.

Legacy System Boards

There are also a number of older model system board form factors that you might encounter on the job while supporting or repairing legacy systems. This information may be helpful to you in those situations and can be used as a reference.

System Board	Form Factor
Full-size AT	This form factor is usually used in older tower systems. Originally, it was designed from an even older system, the original XT motherboard, which itself was designed for use in the second version of the IBM® PC, released in 1983. These original full-size systems took up a large amount of desktop space. Vertically oriented tower systems using the AT board can stand on the floor and not take up desktop space, and they can still use the full-size system board. The board is 12 inches by 13.8 inches. A transfer bus of 16-bit or better is required. It uses complementary metal oxide semiconductors (CMOS) to retain configuration settings. It has a 5-pin DIN keyboard connection.
Baby AT	This form factor is usually used in older desktop systems. In an effort to free up desk space, manufacturers wanted to build a computer that was smaller than systems with full-size AT motherboards. The popular AT motherboard was scaled down to create the Baby AT motherboard. It fits into a smaller case than the full-size AT board, but it is otherwise the same. It works in any case except for those considered low profile or slimline. This was an extremely popular design. This board is usually 13 inches by 8.5 to 9 inches. It was never developed as a standard, so there are variations on the size of this particular board.
LPX	Slimline and low-profile cases, which are today's typical desktop cases, were being developed about the same time as the Baby AT motherboard was introduced. However, these smaller cases could not use even the Baby AT board. The LPX and Mini-LPX motherboards were developed for these cases. A riser card is used to plug expansion cards into the motherboard. This riser card enables the expansion cards to lie sideways, in the same orientation as the system board. Thus, the case does not have to be as high as the card. Another difference in this board is that it uses a PS/2-style keyboard connector rather than the 5-pin DIN connector used on the AT boards. Video, parallel, and two serial ports were placed at the rear of the board in standard locations. This board is 9 inches by 11 to 13 inches. A mini-LPX board was also designed, which was 8 to 9 inches by 10 to 11 inches.

System Board	Form Factor
NLX	The NLX system board was developed to replace the LPX system board initially in 1997. It is a small form factor designed around the Pentium II processor. It supports advances in memory and graphics technology such as dual in-line memory modules (DIMMs) and accelerated graphics port (AGP). This board was designed to fix all the known issues with the LPX board and still fit slimline design systems. The board is 8 to 9 inches by 10 to 13.6 inches. The use of the NLX system board never really gained any headway with computer system manufacturers and was later replaced by the micro-ATX, FlexATX, and Mini-ITX boards.
BTX	Intended to be the replacement for the ATX system board form factor in 2005, the BTX form factor was designed to fix some of the issues that arose from using newer technologies (which often demand more power and create more heat) on system boards compliant with the circa-1996 ATX specification. BTX features include: • A low profile: The backplane is inches lower than the ATX. • Thermal design: The BTX layout establishes a straighter path of airflow with fewer obstacles, resulting in better overall cooling capabilities. • Structural design: The emerging need for heat sinks, capacitors, and other components dealing with electrical and thermal regulation has resulted in devices that can physically strain some motherboards. The BTX standard addressed this issue by specifying better locations for hardware mounting points. For example, the chips that make up the system's chipset are located closely to each other and to the hardware they control to reduce delays in data transfer. The BTX was discontinued by Intel in 2006.
MicroBTX (µBTX)	The MicroBTX is similar to the standard BTX system board, measuring 10.4 by 10.5 inches. The main difference between the standard board and the micro board is the smaller size and that the micro board has fewer expansion slots.
PicoBTX	The PicoBTX system board form factor is a smaller version of the standard BTX board measuring 10.5 inches by 8 inches. The pico board is designed with the same rear panels as the standard board and is used for half height or riser cards applications. Pico boards usually include only one or two expansion slots.

ACTIVITY 5–1
Identifying Motherboards

Scenario

In this activity, you will analyze and identify common motherboards in use today.

1. Examine the graphic and answer the following question.

What type of motherboard is displayed here, and what characteristics did you use to help you identify the board type?

2. Examine the graphic and answer the following question.

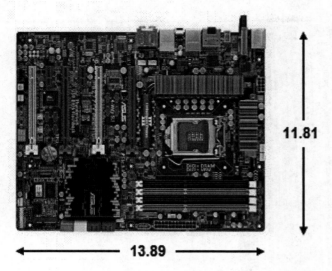

11.81

13.89

What type of motherboard is displayed here, and what characteristics did you use to help you identify the board type?

3. Take the case off of the computer you are using for this course to identify the type of motherboard installed in the system. Use the descriptions presented in this topic to help you.

Expansion Slots

Expansion slots allow you to add expansion cards to your motherboard in order to extend the capabilities of a computer system. Motherboards generally include several of these slots so that the adapters can transfer data to and from the different computer components that have been installed in a system.

Expansion Slot Type	Description
PCI	The *Peripheral Component Interconnect (PCI)* expansion slot is the most common expansion slot used on system motherboards. The specifications include: • Physical characteristics of cards: 33 or 66 MHz. 133 MBps throughput at 33, 66, or 133 MHz. Up to eight functions can be integrated on one board. • Configuration: Supports up to five cards per bus and a system can have two PCI buses for a total of 10 devices per system. Can share interrupt requests (IRQs). Uses Plug and Play (PnP). • Used for all current adapters in client and server systems. • Number of data lines: 64-bit bus often implemented as a 32-bit bus. • Communication method: Local bus standard; 32-bit bus mastering. Each bus uses 10 loads. A load refers to the amount of power consumed by a device. The PCI chipset uses three loads, while integrated PCI controllers use one load. Controllers installed in a slot use 1.5 loads.

(handwritten notes in left margin: 3.3 Volts or 5 Volts   Para lel Bus)

Expansion Slot Type   Description

N/A ded PCI-X
SeRveR only
Technology
Speeds are different
FRom PC‡

PCI-eXtended (PCI-X) is a motherboard expansion slot that improves upon some of the PCI expansion capabilities and is the latest version of PCI technology. The specifications include:

- Provides increased bandwidth and faster speeds by doubling the bus width from 32 bits to 64 bits.
- Clock rate ranges from 66 megahertz (MHz) to 133 MHz, depending on the card.
- Commonly found in server machines to provide faster transfer rates required.

Rotated
PCIe
seRial
Bus
Bandwoth is calculated by lanes

The *PCI Express (PCIe)* slot and bus is an implementation of the PCI bus that uses a faster serial physical-layer communications protocol. It is the most common system bus found in PCs today. There are four versions of

| Expansion Slot Type | Description |

the PCIe standard—1.x, 2.x, 3.x, and 4.x. PCIe version 3.x is the current standard, which will eventually be replaced by version 4.x.

- Used for high-speed graphics cards and high-speed network cards.
- Number of data lines: Each device has a serial connection consisting of one or more lanes. The data rate depends on the PCIe version.
    - PCIe version 1.x: Each lane offers up to 250 MBps of throughput. An x16 slot (16 lanes) can handle 4 GBps of bandwidth in one direction.
    - PCIe version 2.x: Each lane offers up to 500 MBps of throughput. An x16 slot (16 lanes) can handle 8 GBps of bandwidth in one direction.
    - PCIe version 3.x: Each lane offers up to 1 GBps of throughput. An x16 slot (16 lanes) can handle 16 GBps of bandwidth in one direction.
    - PCIe version 4x: Specifications are not expected to be released until 2014, but the transfer rates are targeted to reach 16 gigatransfers per second (GT/s).
- Communication method: Local serial interconnection.

MiniPCI   *Laptops*   MiniPCI is a standard that was based on the PCI specification 2.2. It was specifically for use in laptops to implement a number of devices. The cards are attached to the motherboard and are not accessible from the outside of the laptop. There are three card form factors available:

- Type I: Uses a 100-pin stacking connector
- Type II: Uses a 100-pin stacking connector
- Type III: Uses a 124-pin edge connector

CNR   A Communications/Networking Riser (CNR) supports audio, modem, and local area network (LAN) functionality.

- Physical characteristics of cards: Two rows of 30 pins, with two possible pin configurations. CNR Type A uses an 8-pin network interface, while Type B uses a 16-pin interface. Both types carry USB and audio signals. The slot is often brown and is usually located in the back-left corner of the system board.
- Used for connecting audio, network, and modem cards, but is being phased out in favor of on-board components.

Expansion Slot Type	Description

AGP

*only for
Video*

The *Accelerated Graphics Port (AGP)* bus was developed by Intel® specifically to support high-performance video requirements, especially fast 3D graphics.

- Physical characteristics of cards: Brown slot on the system board. AGP 1.0 is a 1x/2x slot. This is the shortest of the AGP slots with a small separator that divides it into two sections. AGP 2.0 is a 2x/4x slot that has extra pins at one end. There is also an AGP Pro slot. See **http://en.wikipedia.org/wiki/AGP** for more information.
- Have their own processors and cooling units attached.
- Used for video cards.
- Number of data lines: 32 bits wide with a throughput of 266 MBps for AGP 1x. Faster modes with throughput of 533 MBps are available on AGP 2x, 1.07 GBps for AGP 4x, and 2.1 GBps for AGP 8x.
- Communication method: Directly accesses Random Access Memory (RAM) rather than needing to transfer data to video RAM first.

ACTIVITY 5-2
Identifying Expansion Slots

Scenario

In this activity, you will examine and identify the expansion slots on your system's motherboard.

---

1. With the case removed from your computer, examine the expansion slots on your motherboard.

2. Try to identify the different types of expansion slots.

RAM Slots

RAM slots come in several form factors, and each module will connect to the system board through a RAM slot of a compatible type.

RAM Form Factor	Description
SIMM	Generally found in older systems, Single In-line Memory Modules (SIMMs) have a 32-bit data path. Because most processors now have a 64-bit bus width, they required that SIMMs be installed in matched pairs so that the processor could access the two SIMMs simultaneously. SIMMs generally have 8 memory chips per module. Only SIMMs can be installed into SIMM slots on the system board.
DIMM	Dual In-line Memory Modules (DIMMs) are found in many systems, and they have a 64-bit data path. The development of the DIMM solved the issue of having to install SIMMs in matched pairs. DIMMs also have separate electrical contacts on each side of the module, while the contacts on SIMMs on both sides are redundant. DIMMs generally have 16 or 32 chips per module.
SODIMM	Small Outline Dual In-line Memory Modules (SODIMMs) are half the size of DIMMs, and therefore cannot fit into a DIMM slot. SODIMMs are most often seen in laptops, small networking devices (such as routers), and PCs with smaller system boards. They have either 32- or 64-bit data paths.
RIMM	Rambus Inline Memory Modules (RIMMs) have a metal cover that acts as a heat sink. Although they have the same number of pins, RIMMs have different pin settings and are not interchangeable with DIMMs. RIMMs can be installed only in RIMM slots on a system board.

ACTIVITY 5-3
Identifying RAM Slots

Scenario

In this activity, you will examine and identify the RAM slots on your system's motherboard.

---

1. With the case removed from your computer, examine the available RAM slots on your motherboard.

2. How many RAM slots are on your motherboard? Are they all being used?

Integrated I/O Port Types

System boards can include any or all of a number of integrated input/output controllers or ports: sound, video, network, modem, USB, serial, IEEE 1394/FireWire, parallel, and PS/2.

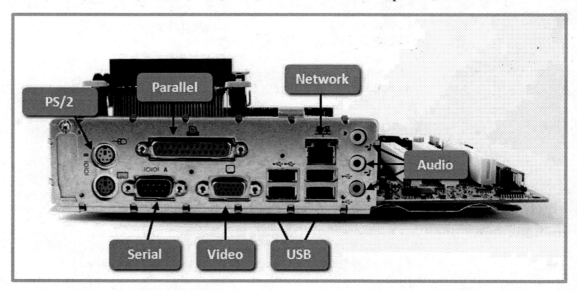

Figure 5-1: I/O ports on a motherboard.

Chipsets

The *chipset* is the collection of chips and integrated circuits that support basic functions of the computer. PC chipsets are housed on one to four chips and include built-in controllers for the system board's buses and all the integrated peripherals.

The chipset architecture, including the number, function, name, and placement of the various chips in a chipset, will vary depending on the type and manufacturer of the system board. For example, on many Intel Pentium computers, the two main chips in the chipset are known as the Northbridge and the Southbridge.

- The *Northbridge* controls the system memory and the AGP video ports, and it may also control cache memory. The Northbridge is closer to the processor and communicates directly with it using the system bus.

Ich

- The *Southbridge* controls input/output functions, the system clock, drives and buses, advanced power management (APM), and various other devices. The Southbridge is further from the CPU and uses the PCI bus to communicate with the Northbridge.

Newer Intel systems employ the Intel Hub Architecture (IHA) chipset. This also has two main chips, now named the Graphics and AGP Memory Controller Hub (GMCH) and the I/O Controller Hub (ICH), which perform functions roughly analogous to the Northbridge and Southbridge, but the communication between the two new chips is designed to be faster.

Figure 5–2: A chipset on a system board.

CMOS Battery

The *complementary metal-oxide-semiconductor (CMOS)* battery is a small battery on the motherboard that provides power to the real-time system clock when the computer is turned off. You may find cases when the CMOS battery fails, which will result in a CMOS Battery Failure message (or possibly a CMOS Read Error). Replacing a CMOS battery is not difficult, but it is not always necessary. Start by leaving the computer on for a day, and see if this helps the battery recharge. If this does not work, and you need to replace the battery, immediately write down all of your CMOS settings, as you will need to re-enter them later after replacing the battery. Note that not all motherboards can have their CMOS batteries replaced; in these cases you can add a new CMOS battery, but not remove the old one. Consult the documentation for your motherboard.

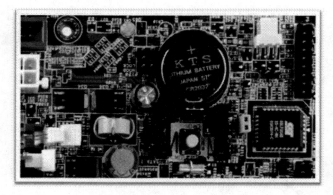

Figure 5–3: A CMOS battery.

CMOS Settings

CMOS settings can be changed if needed in the system setup program that is loaded from the BIOS setup utility. The CMOS battery supports the Basic Input/Output System (BIOS) utility by providing enough power to save critical system settings.

CMOS Setup Setting	Description
System date and time	You can set the system's real-time clock using DOS date and time commands, or by setting the clock in Windows, which will adjust the real-time clock.
Password	You can specify whether a user or administrator password is required to start up the system.
Boot sequence	You can specify the order that Power-On Self Test (POST) checks drives for an operating system.
Memory	Some systems require you to specify in CMOS how much RAM is installed on the system. You might also be able to specify whether the system uses parity memory or non-parity memory. Most modern systems automatically detect and report the installed RAM.
Hard drive	You can specify the number, type, and size of the hard drives attached to the system.
Floppy drive	You can adjust the speed and density settings for the floppy drive. You can also disable or enable a floppy drive.
Display	You can specify the monitor type and port.
Parallel/LPT ports	You can specify settings such as unidirectional or bidirectional printing, Enhanced Capability Port (ECP) options, and Enhanced Parallel Port (EPP) options. You can also disable or enable a parallel port. If you know that a parallel or serial port will not be used, you can disable the port, thereby freeing up the resources for use by other devices. Conversely, if you connect a device to a port and the device will not work at all, you might want to check the CMOS to ensure that the port has not been disabled.
Serial/COM ports	You can specify settings such as what memory addresses and interrupts are used by a port. You can also disable or enable a serial port.
Power management	In most modern computers, you can specify settings such as powering down components (such as the monitor, video card, and hard drives) when the components have not been used for a specified time period,

CMOS Setup Setting	Description
	as well as options and time limits for standby and suspend modes. You can also disable or enable global power management.

ACTIVITY 5-4
Identifying Other Motherboard Components

Scenario

In this activity, you will locate and identify various components on the motherboard of your system.

1. Look closely at the I/O ports on your system board and try to identify each one. You may need to look on the back of the system unit to identify all the ports.

2. On the motherboard, identify the chipset. How is it configured? Can you see the Northbridge and Southbridge chips? Or does this computer have the newer GMCH/ICH chipset?

3. Try to find the CMOS battery on the motherboard.

Jumpers and DIP Switches

Jumpers and dual in-line package switches (more commonly called *DIP switches*) are used to configure older system boards by shutting off an electrical circuit located on the motherboard. Using jumpers, this is accomplished by sliding a jumper shunt over the jumper pins on the *jumper block* of the motherboard. When using DIP switches, the numbered notches located on the switch can be moved to cut off the electrical circuit it is attached to. Newer motherboards are being designed to use software to configure these values (through the BIOS Setup program) instead of jumpers and DIP switches.

Front Panel Connectors

Many different components connect to the motherboard. It is important to understand where each component is supposed to be attached. Always check the manufacturer's information for your motherboard before you disconnect or reconnect a component to the pins on the various panels of the board.

Motherboard headers	Description
USB header	The USB header contains the pins that the USB cable connects to. This connects the USB drive installed in the computer case directly to the motherboard. USB headers will have one pin missing from the second row on the end. This can be a visual guide when identifying the different headers.

Motherboard headers	Description

Front panel header   The front panel header of the motherboard contains many system connection pins that are used to connect components installed in the computer case to the motherboard. Most front panel headers will include:

- Power switch
- Power light emitting diode (LED)
- Reset switch
- Hard drive LED
- Speaker

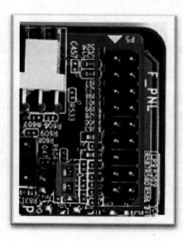

Audio header   The audio header contains the pins to connect the system audio cable to the motherboard.

Motherboard headers	Description

Fan Connectors

There are a number of uses for fans within a computer. The components installed and how much heat they produce will determine what type of fans are installed. Full size desktop systems will generally have a case fan that will pull the hot air out, letting the cooler air circulate through the chassis. There is no current standard that dictates the size and form factor of the fan connector. Common connectors include:

- A 3–pin Molex KK connector, commonly used to connect a fan directly to the motherboard.
- A 4–pin Molex KK connector is similar in function to the 3–pin KK connector, except that it has an extra pin to provide the ability to control the speed of the fan.
- A 4–pin Molex connector that connects directly to the system's power supply.

ACTIVITY 5–5
Identifying the Front Panel and Fan Connectors

Scenario

In this activity, you will identify the front panel connectors on the system board and any fan connections within the system unit.

1. On the motherboard, try to identify the front end connectors.

2. Check for any fans installed within the system. Locate the case fan and see how it is connected to the motherboard. Also check for any fans connected directly to the motherboard, and identify where the connections are made.

Bus Speeds

The motherboard bus speed determines how fast circuits will carry data simultaneously from one area of the motherboard to another. Speed can vary based on the capacity of the specific bus. The bus speed will depend on what components are installed in the computer.

Motherboard Power Connectors

The modern ATX power supply connection to the system board is a keyed connection that enables the power supply to provide power to the internal components of the system. Keyed connectors are designed so that the plug and socket have notches that must line up in order for the plug to fit into the socket. Older AT power supplies used two connectors, labeled P8 and P9. Be sure not to switch them when you plug them in or you could damage the system board. Most systems today have a single, keyed connector that can be inserted only one way, which prevents damage to the system board.

Power supplies have connections to other internal components as well. There are Berg and Molex connections, and older AT power supplies also had a connection to the power switch for the system.

Notch for keyed connector

A Single Keyed Connector

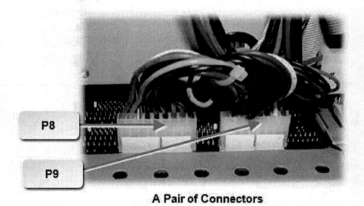

P8

P9

A Pair of Connectors

Figure 5–4: System board power supply connectors.

Specific Connectors

There are specific connectors, depending on the motherboard requirements, usually tied to the CPU type. There is the 20-pin (ATX), a 24-pin ATX connector, and the 20+4 combo (which you can separate, or not, depending on the motherboard). This includes a 20-pin for the main power, plus a 4-pin connector for additional CPU power. This 4-pin is sometimes known as the Intel® Pentium® 4 connector. There is also an 8-pin CPU connector that requires an ATX 2.02 or an EPS12V PSU.

Motherboard Selection Tips

You will most likely select a motherboard based on what components you will need within the system. Use the table to help identify the system components you need and what impact that may have on the type of motherboard you choose.

System Component	Questions To Ask
Clock speed	Does the motherboard operate at a high enough frequency to support the processor you want to use?
CPU	What type of processor can you install? Can you install more than one CPU?
Drive interfaces	Does the motherboard include drive interfaces? If not, does it have enough available expansion slots to accommodate the user's hard disk requirements?
Expansion slots	How many expansion slots will the user need? What types of slots does it include? What type of expansion cards will you be installing?
Form factor	Will the motherboard fit inside the case of the computer?

System Component	Questions To Ask
Ports	Does the motherboard have the necessary ports to meet the user's needs? Specifically, does it have the parallel, serial, or multiple USB ports, and possibly FireWire ports needed?
RAM	Does the motherboard support enough Random Access Memory (RAM) to meet the user's needs?

Motherboard Installation Considerations

When you are replacing a motherboard, there are specific system requirements such as form factor, power needs, and component connections, that need to be considered. The process can be challenging based on a number of different requirements. The type of board you choose can also depend on the manufacturer's requirements for the system and you need to make sure you get one that fits your case. Cases will all have predetermined holes for the system board to line up to secure screws to the case.

Configuration and Optimization Requirements

When replacing and installing a new motherboard, you must ensure that it is properly configured to match the processor that it will host. In essence, you must configure the system board so that the internal and external frequencies of the processor are compatible. You can accomplish this by specifying a frequency multiple. Most system boards operate at a specific speed, but some enable you to select the speed via DIP switches, jumpers, or the BIOS setup software.

Note: For additional information, check out the LearnTO **Remove and Install Motherboards** in the LearnTOs for this course on your LogicalCHOICE Course screen.

Access the Checklist tile on your LogicalCHOICE course screen for reference information and job aids on How to Install and Configure Motherboards

TOPIC B

CPUs and Cooling Systems

In the last topic, you identified the various types of motherboards used in computer systems. Now that you understand the purpose of the motherboard, you can take a closer look at the components that make up the board. Two of these components are the central processing unit, or CPU, and the cooling systems that service it. In this topic, you will examine CPUs and cooling systems.

Much like the motherboard, the CPU is another important component of the computer system that actually carries out all the tasks requested by the applications installed in the computer. The CPU is a heat generator, so part of understanding the CPU includes understanding how to manage heat inside the computer case by managing the airflow and temperature. Keeping the system cool is an easy but important way to maintain or even increase its productivity. A computer that runs too hot risks damaging its own components. As an A+ technician, you need to be familiar with these essential components of the computer system.

This topic covers all or part of the following CompTIA® A+® (2012) certification objectives:

- Exam 220–801: Objective 1.2: Differentiate between motherboard components, their purposes, and properties.
- Exam 220–801: Objective 1.6: Differentiate among various CPU types and features and select the appropriate cooling method.

CPU Sockets

CPUs use either sockets or slots to connect to the motherboard. Older slot-based processors plugged into a system board in much the same way as an expansion board, while socketed processors plug into a system board using a pin grid array (PGA). Modern CPUs usually fall into either the AMD or Intel category. While there are other CPU manufacturer brands available, Intel and AMD technologies tend to dominate in the marketplace.

Intel CPU Socket Types

While you may encounter older socket types on the job, most computers will use more recent socket types and processors. Common Intel CPU sockets include the following.

Socket Type	Description
LGA 775	The land grid array (LGA) 775 CPU is also referred to as Socket T.
	• Uses 775 copper pins with no socket holes to attach to the motherboard's pins. The CPU is connected via a load plate that the CPU attaches to and is lowered onto the board by a lever.
	• Proper cooling is accomplished by the design of the CPU connection to the motherboard. By using the load plate to connect, the CPU is properly seated into place and is perfectly level. This ensures that the CPU is making full contact with the heat sink or liquid cooling method.
	• Commonly used in consumer desktop computers.
	• Used for Pentium 4, Celeron D, Pentium Extreme Edition, Core 2 Duo, and Core 2 Extreme processors.
LGA 1156	The LGA 1156 is also referred to as Socket H or H1.

Socket Type	Description
	• Uses 1,156 copper pins to attach to the processor pads on the motherboard. • Commonly used in consumer desktop computers. • Designed to replace the LGA 775 socket type. • Used for Core i3, Core i5, Core i7, Xeon, Celeron, and Pentium processors.
LGA 1155	The LGA 1155 is also referred to as Socket H2. • Uses 1,155 copper pins to attach to the processor pads on the motherboard. • Designed to replace the LGA 1156 socket type. • Used for Intel's Sandy Bridge and Ivy Bridge microprocessors.
LGA 1366	The LGA 1366 is also referred to as Socket B. • Uses 1,366 copper pins that connect to the bottom of the processor. • Commonly used in higher-end desktop systems that require high performance. • Used for Intel's X58 processor.
LGA 2011	The LGA 2011 is also referred to as Socket R, and was designed to replace LGA 1366. • Uses 2,011 copper pins that connect to bottom of the processor. • Commonly used in higher-end desktop computers and servers. • Used for Intel's Sandy Bridge and Ivy Bridge microprocessors.

AMD CPU Socket Types

Similarly to the Intel socket types, there will be, on occasion, an older socket and processor used, but in more cases, you will be supporting computers that contain newer-model AMD sockets and processors.

Socket Type	Description
940	The 940 was designed primarily for use in 64–bit server machines. Commonly found used with the Opteron and Athlon 64 FX processors.
AM2	The AM2 is similar to the 940 in design with the exception that it uses a DDR2 controller, instead of DDR used by the 940. This socket replaces the older Socket 939 and 754. This socket is commonly used with Athlon 64, Sempron, Athlon 64 X2 and Athlon 64 FX.
AM2+	The AM2+ was designed to replace the AM2. They are similar in design and are, in some cases, interoperable with the processors they support.
AM3	The AM3 was designed to replace AM2+. The socket is not compatible with the previous versions AM2 and AM2+ because of the pin layout being slightly different than the older models. The AM3 has 941 pins, while the AM2+ has 940.
AM3+	The AM3+, also referred to as AM3b, is designed to be more efficient and use less power.
FM1	FMI is AMD's next generation socket type that is designed to be used with the Fusion and Athlon II processors.

F - For Servers only

Socket Type	Description
F	An older model socket type that was designed specifically for the Operton and Athlon 64 FX processors that used the LGA connection method.

Cache

Cache memory, or CPU cache, is a type of memory that services the CPU. It is faster than the main memory, is physically located closer to the processor, and allows the CPU to execute instructions and read and write data at a higher speed. Instructions and data are transferred from the main memory to the cache in blocks to enhance performance. Cache memory is typically static RAM (SRAM) and is identified by level. Level 1 (L1) cache is built directly into the CPU chip. Level 2 cache (L2) feeds the L1 cache. L2 can be built into the CPU chip, reside on a separate chip, or be a separate bank of chips on the system board. If L2 is built into the CPU, then a level 3 cache (L3) may also be present on the system board.

CPU Cache Types

There are three main types of cache found in modern computer systems:

- Instruction cache, which is used to retrieve and execute instructions faster.
- Data cache, which is used quickly retrieve and store data.
- Translation lookaside buffer (TLB), which is used to provide faster address translation for both data and instruction cache.

CPU Operational Characteristics

There are many different characteristics and technologies that can affect a CPU's performance.

CPU Characteristic or Technology	Description
Architecture	The CPU architecture is a description of the width of its front-side bus. A CPU's front-side bus width is either 32 or 64 bits.
Clock speed	The number of processing cycles that a microprocessor can perform in a given second. Some CPUs require several cycles to assemble and perform a single instruction, whereas others require fewer cycles. The clock speed is a technical rating; actual performance speeds can vary from the published clock speed rating. The clock speed is typically referred to as the processor performance.
Overclocking	Overclocking is configuring your system board to run at a speed greater than your CPU is rated to handle. Doing so can cause the CPU to overheat, produce random results, or be damaged or destroyed.
CPU speed	CPU speed is an umbrella term for the overall rate at which instructions are processed. There are two factors that affect the CPU speed. One is the core clock speed, which is the internal speed at which instructions are processed within the CPU. The other is the bus clock speed, which is the actual speed at which instructions are transferred to the system board.
Throttling	Used to adjust CPU speed. A CPU throttle is typically used to slow down the machine during idle times to conserve the battery or to keep the system running at a lower performance level when hardware problems have been encountered.

CPU Characteristic or Technology	Description
Hyperthreading (HT)	A feature of certain Intel chips that makes one physical CPU appear as two logical CPUs. It uses additional registers to overlap two instruction streams to increase the CPU's performance by about 30 percent.
Integrated GPU	The graphics processing unit (GPU) is integrated within the die of the CPU to provide an alternative to having a dedicated graphics card.
Virtualization support	Most modern CPUs are virtualization compatible, meaning that they have virtualization software built into the chipset of the CPU. Both Intel and AMD have CPU virtualization built into their chips. This allows the CPU to process instructions from multiple operating systems quickly and efficiently.
Cores	CPU cores read and execute instruction data sent from computer applications. A single chip that contains two or more distinct CPU cores that process simultaneously is called a multi-core. Options include dual-core (two CPUs), triple-core (three CPUs) and quad-core (four CPUs), though octo-core chips are becoming more common. Once you start adding tens or hundreds of CPUs, the terminology changes from "multi-core" and becomes "many-core."
Cache	Dedicated high-speed memory for storing recently used instructions and data.
VRM	A voltage regulator module (VRM) is a replaceable module used to regulate the voltage fed to the CPU.
MMX	Multimedia Extensions (MMX) is a set of additional instructions, called microcode, to support sound, video, and graphics multimedia functions.

CPU Selection Factors

Selecting a CPU for a computer can be a complicated process. Consider the factors provided to help you identify the requirements for both the CPU and motherboard.

Factor	Considerations
Compatibility	Start by checking the motherboard within the computer system. The design of the computer's motherboard determines the type of CPU you can install. For example, you cannot install an AMD processor into a system board designed to support an Intel processor. You should review the documentation for the computer's system board to determine its compatibility with other CPUs. Keep in mind that most original equipment manufacturers (OEMs) do not typically provide you with the system board's documentation. To obtain this documentation, try contacting the computer's manufacturer or the manufacturer of the system board. You can typically identify the manufacturer of the system board by examining it. It is critical that the motherboard is configured to properly support the new CPU. Most importantly, you might need to configure the system board to use the correct voltage. This is done by using the jumper settings on the system board or the computer's CMOS setup program. Setting the voltage on the system board too high can destroy the CPU.
Performance	In addition, you should keep in mind that there is a trade-off between price and performance when selecting a CPU. The greater the performance requirements of the user, the more powerful CPU you should select. And more powerful

Factor	Considerations
	CPUs are simply more expensive. When selecting a CPU for a user, you should ask the user his budget for the purchase. This budget can help you narrow down the choices for selecting a processor.

Cooling System Types

Having the right cooling method can be crucial to reach the optimal performance of the system's CPU. Many cooling systems will be directly attached to the CPU.

Cooling System	Description
Fans	Computer fans provide cooling by simply blowing regular air across heated components. It is common to see case fans, power supply fans, adapter card fans, and CPU fans.
Vents	Computer cases are designed with vents to facilitate airflow through the case and across all components. A common implementation is to include air vents near the bottom of the front of the case and to place a fan near the top of the rear of the case to pull cooler air through the system.
Heat sinks	A heat sink is designed to provide direct cooling to a system's CPU. Modern CPUs have enormous processing power that requires instant cooling that is attached right the CPU itself. Heat sinks have metal fins to increase their surface area to aid in heat dissipation. Cool air is blown past it by a fan, removing the heat from the processor.
Thermal paste	Thermal paste is used to connect a heat sink to a CPU. At the microscopic level, when two solids touch, there are actually air gaps between them that act as insulation; the liquid thermally conductive compound gel fills these gaps to permit a more efficient transference of heat from the processor to the heat sink.
Liquid-based	CPUs can also be kept cool using a device to circulate a liquid or liquefied gas, such as water or freon, past the CPU. Like an air conditioner, heat from the CPU is absorbed by the cooler liquid, and then the heated liquid is circulated away from the CPU so it can disperse the heat into the air outside the computer. Liquid cooling systems are not as prevalent as heat sinks in most desktop systems or low-end servers.

Cooling System Selection Factors

When selecting a cooling system for a computer you must make sure that the following factors have been considered:

- What components need to be cooled?
- Will the cooling system fit within the computer case? Cooling systems come integrated within the computer case, while some can be installed externally.
- Do you need multiple cooling methods? Decide if you will need more than one cooling method installed. Most CPUs will have their own cooling system attached, so if you are in need of additional cooling, you should verify that a proper case fan is used as well.
- What size fan should be installed? The larger the fan, the more cooling power provided, so check what the maximum size fan opening is within your computer case before choosing the fan.

Computer Cases and Cooling

Although it might seem to be a good idea to remove the chassis cover to provide additional cooling, it is not recommended. Most PC cases have been designed to provide an airflow path, with fans positioned to keep the air moving and blow hot air away from heat-sensitive components. The PC case must be closed for this airflow path to work properly. If the case cover is removed, the fans will be less efficient, blowing air around at random.

 Access the Checklist tile on your LogicalCHOICE course screen for reference information and job aids on How to Install and Configure CPUs and Cooling Systems

ACTIVITY 5-6
Selecting Cooling Systems

Scenario
In this activity, you will select cooling systems.

---

1. When might you need more than one cooling system in a computer?

2. When would liquid cooling systems be more appropriate than adding a fan?

TOPIC C

Select and Install Power Supplies

In the previous topic, you examined CPUs and cooling systems. The next logical step is to select and install the power supply in the system unit. In this topic, you will take a closer look at the computer's power supply and its connections to the other system components.

The computer's power supply is the main source of power for all components installed within the system unit. Understanding the power requirements of all the components and the maximum power supplied is crucial in managing the overall computer system power needs. Whether you are upgrading or replacing faulty components, you need to effectively manage the capacity of the current power supply.

This topic covers all or part of the following CompTIA® A+® (2012) certification objectives:

*   Exam 220–801: Objective 1.8: Install an appropriate power supply based on a given scenario.

Power Supply Specifications

Each component in a personal computer has different power requirements that are required from the power supply. The specification provided will help in determining the right levels of power supplied to all internal computer components.

Specification	Description
Size	Hardware manufacturers across the globe strive to standardize the power supply unit specifications in terms of dimensions and layout to make computer users' lives simpler. This has resulted in a range of power supply unit types that are accepted worldwide. The key to replacing and installing a power supply is to make sure that the form factor matches the case and the motherboard it will connect to. Form factors available today are: • AT, which is used in AT form factor cases and with AT or Baby AT system boards. Dimensions are 213 mm x 150 mm x 150 mm. It is a legacy form factor found in older desktops and towers. • ATX, which can be used in ATX and NLX cases and with ATX and NLX motherboards. Dimensions are 150 mm x 140 mm x 86 mm. Found in desktops and towers. ATX power supplies do not have a pass-through outlet, but instead usually have a physical on-off switch. • Micro ATX is essential the same form factor as standard ATX, only with smaller wattage and physical size. • Proprietary, which include motherboards that do not conform to standards. It is likely that these proprietary system boards will require nonstandard power supply form factors as well, although you might be able to use an ATX power supply.
Connector styles	There are generally three types of connectors used to connect different devices in a computer to the power supply: • Berg, a square shaped connector used to supply power to floppy disk drives and some tape drives. • Molex, a round shaped connector used to supply power to Parallel ATA drives, optical drives, and SCSI drives. • SATA, used to supply power to Serial ATA drives.

Specification	Description
Wattage	Power supply specifications are given in watts. Watts are volts times amps (voltage x current). Older systems typically had power supplies under 200 watts (W) and often even under 100 W. Newer power supplies typically have wattages ranging from 200 to 500 W. Because of their increased power demands, high-powered servers or computers designed for gaming can have power supplies with wattages from 500 W up to 1 kilowatt (kW).
Voltage	All system components require specific voltages. Some devices have different voltage requirements depending on use. This is particularly true of some memory chips, which vary in voltage requirements from 1.8 volts (V) to 3.3 V, and some can actually function at different voltages (voltage range). You must verify that the power supply used can provide the volts demanded by the system.
	Some power supplies are dual-voltage power supplies. They can contain multiple channels that provide discrete voltages, with 5 V, 12 V, 15 V, and 24 V being the most common.
	In order to calculate whether your power supply meets your power needs, you will need to add up the maximum power you might use at one time. A range of maximum power consumption for various components has been established. Most components use much less than the maximum, so by using the published requirements as a guide, you are overestimating the power usage, and therefore making it more likely that you never test the capacity of the power supply. You can check the documentation for the component to determine how much power it actually will use.
	Even some of the most powerful current CPUs, such as the Intel Core 2 Extreme and the AMD Opteron Dual Core, only use 1.1 to 1.3 V. The necessary voltage for CPU and RAM is usually detected by the motherboard (BIOS) and configured appropriately, but sometimes you have to manually configure it by accessing the BIOS and entering the appropriate values. The power supply will supply 3.3 V for the CPU, RAM, and other devices, but the motherboard regulates how much they actually get.

 Note: Although most devices require specific voltages, some devices have different voltage requirements depending on use. This is particularly true of some memory chips, which vary in voltage requirements from 1.8 V to 3.3 V, and some can actually function at different voltages, or in a voltage range.

Power Supply Connections

One of the first things you will notice about a power supply is the cable that connects it to the components within a computer because there are so many different colored wires and connectors. Every device uses one of several types of connectors to connect to the computer's power supply.

Connector Type	Description
SATA	The 15-pin Serial Advanced Technology Attachment (SATA) connector connects peripheral components to the power supply and has a maximum wattage of 54. The SATA connector provides power at three voltages: • +3.3 • +5 • +12

Connector Type	Description

| 4/8–pin 12 V | The 4-pin and 8-pin connectors are similar in that they both provide 12 volts of power to the CPU on the motherboard. The 8-pin was designed to provide power to multiple CPUs in the system. The 4-pin has a maximum wattage of 192, and the 8-pin has a maximum wattage of 336. |

| PCIe 6/8–pin | The Peripheral Component Interconnect Express (PCIe) 6-pin and 8-pin connectors provide power to PCIe slots on the motherboard. Both connectors provide power at 12 V. The 6-pin has a maximum wattage of 75, while the 8-pin has a maximum wattage of 150. |

| Main power connectors | The main power connector to the motherboard is either a 20-pin or 24-pin ATX connector. The 24-pin connector contains four additional pins to support the requirements for PCI Express slots on the motherboard. The 20-pin connector has a maximum wattage of 72, while the 24-pin has 144. Both connectors provide power at three voltages:
 • +3.3
 • +5
 • +12 |

Connector Type	Description

Floppy

The floppy connector is a Berg connector and was used to connect floppy drives to the power supply. The connector has only four pins and provides power at +5 and +12 V with a maximum wattage of 36.

ACTIVITY 5–7
Identifying Power Supply Connections

Scenario

In this activity, you will identify the various power supply connections within your system.

---

1. Locate the power supply within your system.

2. Trace the connections from the power supply to the motherboard and identify the type of connections made.

Power Supply Safety Recommendations

Power supplies can be very dangerous to work with. You should take careful security measures when working with power supplies.

Safety Precaution	Explanation
Check for certification	Be sure to purchase power supplies that are certified by the Underwriters Laboratories, Inc. (UL). UL standard #1950, the "Standard for Safety of Information Technology Equipment, Including Electrical Business Equipment, Third Edition," regulates computer power supplies (along with other components). When it comes to electricity, you do not want to take a chance with a non-certified power supply. The risk of electrocution or fire from a malfunctioning power supply is simply not worth saving a few dollars by purchasing a low-quality power supply.
Replace instead of repair the power supply	You run the risk of electrocution if you open a power supply to attempt to repair it. Even when you unplug a computer, the power supply can retain dangerous voltage that you must discharge before servicing it. Because power supplies are relatively inexpensive, it is easier (and safer) to simply replace a failed power supply rather than attempting to repair it.
Keep the computer case on	Make sure that you run computers with their cases on. The fans inside power supplies are designed to draw air through the computer. When you remove the cover, these fans simply cool the power supplies and not the computer's components. Leaving the case open puts the computer at risk of overheating.
Protect the power supply	Use a power protection system such as an uninterruptible power supply (UPS) or surge suppressor to protect each computer's power supply (and thus the computer) from power failures, brownouts, surges, and spikes. You should also make sure that the computer's power cord is plugged into a properly grounded electrical outlet. (Three-pronged outlets include grounding; never use an adapter to plug a computer's power cord into a two-pronged electrical outlet.) You can buy a socket tester (available at hardware stores) to test your outlets if you suspect that they are not properly grounded.

Note: You should also make sure to cover empty slots in the system board with filler brackets. If you do not install a filler bracket, you reduce the efficiency of the power supply's fan and increase the chances of the computer overheating.

Selecting the Right Power Supply

Selecting the right power supply can be overwhelming, as effective performance depends on all of the components you plan on installing in the system. If you are building a computer from scratch, then selecting a power supply is a bit more tedious than just installing a replacement that meets the manufacturer's requirements. Each system component has its own power needs and requirements, so selecting the right power supply will enable all these components to function properly. Things you should consider include the total system requirements for power, the form factor for the unit, and whether there is adequate cooling within the system. When determining the cooling requirements, some power supplies can be examined to see the revolutions per minute (RPMs) of the power supply fan. You can then adjust the fan speed to run at only the speed needed to cool your system. This can reduce power consumption and save fan wear and tear.

Note: For additional information, check out the LearnTO **Install a Power Supply** in the LearnTOs for this course on your LogicalCHOICE Course screen.

Access the Checklist tile on your LogicalCHOICE course screen for reference information and job aids on How to Select and Install Power Supplies

ACTIVITY 5-8
Calculating Power Requirements

Scenario

In this activity, you will calculate the power required by the computer you are using for this course. As a guide, you can refer to the following table that includes common component types and example specifications and required wattages.

Component Type	Example Specification	Example Wattage Required
CPU	Intel Core i7-970, 3.2 GHz	130
Memory	4GB DDR3-1600	8
Video card	NVIDIA GeForce 8800 GTS	220
Motherboard	ASUS P6X58D Premium LGA	36
Hard drive	1 TB SATAII 7200 RPM	6
Optical drive	6x Blu-ray	32
NIC	10/100/1000 Mbps PCI-Express	14
Sound card	SoundBlaster X-Fi Titanium	23
USB wired keyboard	Yes/No	4
USB wired mouse	Yes/No	4
USB flash drive	Yes/No	5
Other external devices	External DVD+R drive	External DVD+R drive: 5

1. Examine your computer, and complete the **Specifications** row of the table in step 2. If you have different or additional components in your PC, revise the table accordingly.

2. Determine the power required by each component, and complete the following table. Again, example values have been provided for your reference.

Component Type	Specification	Wattage Required
CPU		
Memory		
Video card		
Motherboard		
Hard drive		
Optical drive		
NIC		
Sound card		
USB wired keyboard		
USB wired mouse		
USB flash drive		
Other external devices		

3. Calculate the total wattage required for your system. Compare this value with the maximum wattage output listed on the power supply. Does this power supply need to be upgraded?

4. Add a buffer of 30 percent to the total wattage required for your system. Will the existing power supply continue to supply enough power if additional components are added to the system?

ACTIVITY 5-9
Replacing a Power Supply

Scenario

After calculating the power needed for all the components added to a user's system, you have determined that it exceeds the capacity of the installed power supply. You have ordered and received a replacement power supply and now you need to install it.

1. Remove the existing power supply.
   a) Shut down and turn off the system.
   b) Unplug the power cord from the electrical outlet.
   c) On AT systems, to discharge any remaining electricity stored in the computer's capacitors, toggle the power switch on the computer on and off.
   d) Remove any components necessary in order to access the power supply and its connection to the system board.
   e) Unplug all power connections from devices, marking where each connection went to as you go.
   f) Unplug the power supply from the system board.
   g) Unscrew the power supply from the case.
   h) Remove the power supply from the case.

2. Install the replacement power supply.
   a) Insert the power supply into the case. Align the guides on the base of the supply with the base.
   b) Secure the power supply to the case.
   c) Plug all power connections into the devices.
   d) Plug the power supply into the system board.
   e) Reinstall any components you removed to access the power supply.
   f) Plug the power cord from the power supply to the electrical outlet.

3. Test the power supply.
   a) Turn on the system.
   b) Test all components.

TOPIC D

RAM Types and Features

In the previous topic, you examined the requirements of the system's power supply. Providing sufficient electrical power is one way to ensure that system components run at an acceptable performance level, but it is not the only solution you should consider. In this topic, you will examine RAM.

Just as some people say you can never be too rich or too thin, you can never have too much memory. Adding memory is one of the simplest and most cost effective ways to increase a computer's performance, whether it is on a brand-new system loaded with high-performance applications or an older system that performs a few basic tasks. Upgrading the memory is a common task for any PC technician.

This topic covers all or part of the following CompTIA® A+® (2012) certification objectives:

*   Exam 220-801: Objective 1.3: Compare and contrast RAM types and features.

RAM Modules

A *RAM module*, or *memory module*, is a printed circuit board that holds a group of memory chips that act as a single memory unit. Memory modules reside in slots on the motherboard, and they are removable and replaceable. Memory modules are defined by their design, and by the number and type of chips they contain.

Figure 5-5: A memory module.

Single-Sided vs. Double-Sided Memory

Single-sided RAM does not refer to the literal number of sides that a RAM module has, but rather it means an expansion bank of RAM has all of its available memory accessible by the computer. Double-sided RAM might have two banks of memory, but only one can be accessed at a time by the computer.

[handwritten notes in left margin:] Single 64 bit memory Bus, double 2/64 bit memory bus

Note: Whether a RAM module has chips on one side or two, if the computer can access all of its memory at once, the RAM module is considered to be single-sided.

Single- and Double-Sided Media

Single-sided and double-sided have two meanings when discussing computer memory, depending on the media type. Single-sided removable media refers to a disc (floppy, CD, or DVD) that can be read and written to one side only. Double-sided discs or DVDs can be read from and written to both sides, thus doubling the storage capacity of the media.

RAM Configurations

There are three different chipset configurations used in RAM that will determine how fast data can be transferred between the chips on the board. The slowest is the single channel because it is limited to only one channel for communication. On the other hand, double channel can transfer data twice as fast as single, because it has two channels in which to send and receive data. The fastest configuration is called triple channel, and it uses three channels for data transfer and is three times as fast as single channel.

Intel has recently introduced a fourth RAM configuration that can support a quadruple channel architecture, but there are restrictions based on the limitations from system components within the system.

Types of RAM

There are several types of RAM.

Type of RAM	Description
SRAM	Static RAM (SRAM) is used for cache memory, which is high-speed memory that is directly accessible by the CPU. It does not need to be refreshed to retain information. It does not use assigned memory addresses. It is faster than Dynamic RAM, but it is also more expensive.
DRAM	Dynamic RAM (DRAM) is used on single and dual in-line memory modules (SIMMs and DIMMs). It is the most common type of RAM. It needs to be refreshed every few milliseconds. It uses assigned memory addresses and can be implemented using Synchronous DRAM, Direct Rambus DRAM, or Double Data Rate SDRAM.
DRDRAM	Direct Rambus DRAM (DRDRAM) is implemented on a RIMM memory module. It is a type of synchronous, dynamic RAM.
SDRAM	Synchronous DRAM (SDRAM) runs at high clock speeds and is synchronized with the CPU bus. SDRAM was originally packaged on a 168-pin DIMM.
DDR SDRAM	Double Data Rate SDRAM (DDR SDRAM) transfers data twice per clock cycle. It is a replacement for SDRAM. DDR uses additional power and ground lines and is packaged on a 184-pin DIMM module.
DDR2 SDRAM	DDR2 chips increase data rates over those of DDR chips. DDR2 modules require 240-pin DIMM slots. Although DDR2 chips are the same length as DDR, they will not fit into DDR slots.
DDR3 SDRAM	DDR3 chips transfer data at twice the rate of DDR2, and use 30 percent less power in the process, Like DDR2, DDR3 chips use 240-pin connections, but cannot be used interchangeably because of differences in notch location and electrical requirements.

8x per Clock Cycle

Types of ROM

ROM is memory that is non-volatile. The original ROM chips could not be altered after the program code was placed on the ROM chip. As time went on, though, users needed the ability to update the information stored on ROM chips. Over the years, various chips have been created that perform the function of ROM, but can be updated one way or another. These are referred to as programmable ROM (PROM). Types of ROM include:

- PROM: A blank ROM chip that is burned with a special ROM burner. This chip can be changed only once. After the instructions are burned in, it cannot be updated or changed.
- EPROM (erasable PROM): Like PROM, except that the data can be erased through a quartz crystal on top of the chip. After removing the chip from the system, an ultraviolet (UV) light is used to change the binary data back to its original state, all ones.
- EEPROM (electronically erasable PROM): A chip that can be reprogrammed using software from the BIOS or chip manufacturer using a process called flashing. Also known as Flash ROM. The chip does not need to be removed in order to be reprogrammed.

Memory Standard Specifications

The following table summarizes the memory standard specifications.

Standard	Characteristics
PC100	• Clock speed: 100 megahertz (MHz) • Bus width: 8 bytes • Voltage: 3.3 V • Form factor: 168-pin DIMM and 144-pin SODIMM • Transfer rate: 763 MBps • Backwards-compatible with PC66
PC133	• Clock speed: 133 MHz • Bus width: 8 bytes • Voltage: 3.3 V • Form factor: 168-pin DIMM and 144-pin SODIMM • Transfer rate: 1,015 MBps • Backwards-compatible with PC100
DDR-333 or PC2700	• Clock speed: 166 MHz • Bus width: 8 bytes • Voltage: 2.5 V • Form factor: 184-pin DIMM • Transfer rate: 2,533 MBps • Backwards-compatible with slower DDR SDRAM DIMMs
DDR-400 or PC3200 *MBps*	• Clock speed: 200 MHz • Bus width: 8 bytes • Voltage: 2.6 V • Form factor: 184-pin DIMM • Transfer rate: 3,052 MBps • Backwards-compatible with slower DDR SDRAM DIMMs
DDR2–667, PC2-5300, or PC2-5400	• Clock speed: 166 MHz • Bus width: 8 bytes • Voltage: 1.8 V • Form factor: 240-pin DIMM • Transfer rate: 5,066 MBps

Standard	Characteristics
DDR3–1600 or PC3-12800	• Backwards-compatible with slower DDR2 SDRAM DIMMs • Clock speed: 200 MHz • Bus width: 8 bytes • Voltage: 1.5 V • Form factor: 240-pin DIMM • Transfer rate: 12,207 MBps

ECC

Error Correcting Code (ECC) is an error correction method that uses several bits in a data string for error checking. A special algorithm is used to detect and then correct any errors it finds. ECC is used only in upper-end systems such as high-end workstations and servers; other desktop systems use non-ECC memory. Non-ECC memory usually employs *parity* to ensure that errors are detected within the data, but does not have the functionality to correct them.

Parity

Parity is an error-checking method that is sometimes used in RAM modules to detect errors that may occur during data transmission. When parity is used, a data transmission contains 8 bits of data with the ninth bit being the parity bit. The parity bit is used to determine whether a piece of data is equal to another piece of data. The parity bit value can be either true, or a 1, or it can be false, or 0. An error is detected if the parity bit values of two data strings do no match. When an error is detected, the system simply tries again after discarding the data. Parity memory is rarely used; however, there are usually other system components that are relied on to verify that the data contained in memory is accurate when non-parity memory is used. You will typically find this type of memory used in servers.

RAM Characteristics

There are several factors you should consider when purchasing RAM for a computer.

RAM Characteristic	Questions to Ask
Compatibility	Is the RAM compatible with the system's motherboard? What is the maximum RAM size supported by the computer's motherboard? What channel architecture does the RAM support? What architecture is desired based on the requirements of the system's motherboard?
Speed	What is the current speed of the RAM in the computer? What is the bus speed of the computer? RAM speed is the time needed to read and recharge a memory cell, and is measured in nanoseconds (ns). A nanosecond is one-billionth of a second. The smaller the number, the faster the RAM. For example, 10 ns RAM is faster than 60 ns RAM. All of the RAM in the system runs at the lowest common speed. It is backward-compatible, so it can run at the lower speed if it finds slower RAM. Some systems will not run with mixed RAM speeds, but these are not common. Also, the RAM will not run any faster than the system board's bus speed.
System board configuration	Do you need to install RAM in pairs of memory modules? What is the size of the connector for RAM chips?

RAM Speed

Older Ferroelectric Random-Access Memory (FPRAM) was often 60- to 70-nanosecond (ns) speed RAM. Modern RAM that you are likely to find runs at clock speeds of 100 MHz and 133 MHz. The 100 MHz RAM has a RAM speed of 10 ns. The 133 MHz RAM has a RAM speed of 6 ns. The SDRAM used in 168-pin DIMMs has access times in the 6 to 12 ns range.

Determine and Upgrade Your RAM

If you wish to upgrade your computer's RAM, some vendors (such as Crucial: **www.crucial.com/index.aspx**) have a downloadable utility that scans your computer and tells you what kind of upgrade is compatible with your machine.

ACTIVITY 5-10
Comparing RAM Types and Features

Scenario

In order to choose the right type of RAM for a computer system, you typically will compare the various types and features.

1. When selecting a new RAM module, how do you determine the maximum running speed of the RAM once it has been installed?

2. On a typical system with RAM that runs at 10 ns, what RAM can you add? (Select all that apply.)
   - ☐ RAM that runs at 10 ns
   - ☐ RAM that runs at 12 ns
   - ☐ RAM that runs at 6 ns
   - ☐ RAM that runs at 8 ns

3. When selecting a RAM module, when would you choose RAM enabled with ECC as opposed to RAM with only parity?

TOPIC E

Install and Configure Storage Devices

In the previous topics, you identified a number of system components that you may have to install and configure on a computer system. Storage devices such as hard disks are one of the most common system components you will install. In this topic, you will install and configure storage devices.

Users rely on local storage devices to keep their applications and data current and available. As an A + technician, your responsibilities are likely to include installing and configuring different types of storage devices to provide your users with the data-storage capabilities that they need to perform their jobs.

This topic covers all or part of the following CompTIA® A+® (2012) certification objectives:

- Exam 220–801: Objective 1.5: Install and configure storage devices and use appropriate media.

Media Capacity

There are several media types available to users for storing their data. The capacity for any type of media will depend on what the capacity is. Each media type has a limit to the amount of data it can store.

Media	Capacity
CD/CD-RW	The capacity for CD-ROMs ranges from 700 to 860 MB.
DVD/DVD-RW	- Single-sided (single-layer): 4.7 GB - Single-sided (double-layer): 8.7 GB - Double-sided (single-layer): 9.4 GB - Double-sided (double-layer): 17.08
Blu-ray	Blu-ray discs have a capacity of up to 128 GB, depending on the number of layers. Each layer on the disc has a capacity of 25 GB. Newer discs have the capability of holding up to four layers of storage.
Tape	Tapes are generally used to backup data. Higher-end tapes can store up to 5 TB of digital data.
Floppy	Floppy disks are rarely used any longer. Regular 3.5 inch floppy disks had a capacity of 720 KB or 1.44 Mb. Super floppy disks are rarely used today and only have a capacity ranging from 100 to 200 MB.
DL DVD	Dual layer (DL) DVDs have a capacity of 8.5 GB.

RAID Standards

The *Redundant Array of Independent Disks (RAID)* standards are a set of vendor-independent specifications for improvements in performance and/or fault-tolerant configurations on multiple-disk systems. In a fault-tolerant configuration, if one or more of the disks fails, data may be recovered from the remaining disks.

RAID can be implemented through operating system software, but hardware-based RAID implementations are more efficient and are more widely deployed. Hardware-based RAID requires a card, or controller, to show the different disks to the computer as a single drive. These cards are usually a PCI or PCIe card, but can also be already built into the motherboard. There are several

RAID levels, each of which provides a different combination of features and efficiencies. RAID levels are identified by number; RAID 0, RAID 1, and RAID 5 are the most common.

 Note: The original RAID specifications were titled Redundant Array of Inexpensive Disks. As the disk cost of RAID implementations has become less of a factor, the term "Independent" disks has been widely adopted instead.

Common RAID Types

RAID 0, 1, 5, and 10 are the most common implementations.

RAID Type	Description
RAID 0	RAID level 0 implements *striping*, which is the process of spreading data across multiple drives. Striping can dramatically improve read and write performance. Striping provides no fault tolerance, however; because the data is spread across multiple drives, if any one of the drives fails, you will lose all of your data. You must have at least two physical disk drives to implement striping, and the largest size RAID-0 partition that can be created is equal to the smallest available individual partition times the number of drives in the set. For instance, combining a 37 GB drive and a 100 MB drive in a RAID 0 set would result in a 200 MB partition; the balance of the 37 GB drive could not be included in the set (although it would remain available for use in other partitions).
RAID 1	In RAID level 1, data from an entire partition is duplicated on two identical drives by either mirroring or duplexing. In *mirroring*, the two disks share a drive controller. In *duplexing*, each disk has its own drive controller, so the controller card is not a single point of failure. Data is written to both halves of the mirror simultaneously. This redundancy provides fault tolerance and provides for quick failure recovery, but the storage overhead consumes half the available space. The work of reading the data can be split between both drives, improving performance. However, with the increased read speed, a RAID 1 implementation loses some write speed.
RAID 5	RAID level 5 spreads data byte by byte across multiple drives, with parity information also spread across multiple drives. You need at least three physical disk drives that have the same capacity and are the same type. If one drive fails, the parity information on the remaining drives can be used to reconstruct the lost data. In the event of a drive failure, data recovery is not instantaneous (as it is in RAID 1); the bad drive needs to be replaced, and then the missing data needs to be reconstructed. With RAID 5, disk performance is enhanced because more than one read and write can occur simultaneously. However, the parity calculations create some write-performance overhead. Storage overhead is at a ratio of one to the number of drives in the set (for example, 1/3 overhead in a three-drive set or 1/10 overhead in a 10-drive set), so the more drives that are in the set, the less overhead, and the better performance. In the event of multiple drive failures, all data will be irrecoverable.
RAID 10	RAID 10, or RAID 1+0, combines two RAID levels into one. It uses RAID 1 and RAID 0 to provide both mirroring from level 1 and striping from level 0. RAID 10 uses a minimum of four disks, in two disk mirrored blocks. This configuration gives you better performance and system redundancy.

(Handwritten annotation in left margin next to RAID 0: "No Fault Tolerance")

Internal Storage Device Considerations

There are several things to consider when you are installing an internal storage device in a computer system. It is not as simple as just plugging the device into the slot inside the case. Make sure you consider each factor before installation.

Consideration	Details
Does the computer have existing internal storage devices?	If it does, what interfaces do these devices use (PATA, SCSI, or SATA)? Is there room on the controller of these devices for an additional device? For example, if the computer uses devices with the SATA interface, are there already two devices connected to the controller? If there are, you will need to purchase an additional SATA controller before you can add another SATA device. If you do not have room on the controller for an additional storage device, you must purchase both the storage device and a controller. In addition, make sure that the computer has an available slot for the controller.
Does the device need additional drivers installed?	Make sure that you have the appropriate operating system device drivers to install the new storage device on the computer. If necessary, download the device drivers from the device manufacturer's website.
Does the computer have an available power supply cable to supply power to the device?	If not, you can purchase splitters to enable two (or more) devices to be connected to a single power connection, but be aware of power consumption. The number of connectors approximates the available power, so make sure that the storage device will not cause the computer to exceed the capacity of its power supply.
Does the computer have an available drive bay for the storage device?	Most hard drives require a 3.5-inch drive bay; most tape drives and optical drives require a 5.25-inch drive bay. If you want to install a hard drive in a 5.25-inch drive bay, you will need *drive rails*. Make sure you place the storage device where it will get good air flow to avoid overheating the device. Consider the placement of the drives inside the bays with the cable configurations. You may need to adjust the placement of the drives to match the order of cable connectors.
Do you have the necessary data cables to connect the storage device to the controller?	SCSI devices require unique SCSI IDs. *SCSI IDs* are assigned to each device connected to the bus. The ID numbers range from 1 to 15, and determine the device priority. Some storage devices require you to configure this ID using a jumper or the device's installation software. PATA (IDE): Internal PATA hard drives must be jumpered properly. If the drive is the only drive in the computer, you must jumper it as a single drive. If the drive is the second drive in the computer, you must jumper the drive as the second (slave) drive in a two-drive configuration and the first drive as the master drive.
Does the placement of the device interrupt the air flow of the case?	Make sure there is enough total air flow to handle whatever heat the new storage device will add to the computer.

External Storage Device Considerations

External storage devices have a whole set of different considerations than internal devices. Make sure to verify all the factors before selecting and installing a new device.

Consideration	Details
What interface does the external storage device require (USB, FireWire, or SCSI)?	• If the external storage device uses USB 2.0, does the computer support it?

Consideration	Details
	• If the external storage device uses FireWire, is there an available FireWire port in the computer? If not, you must buy and install a FireWire controller. Make sure the computer has an available slot for the FireWire controller before purchasing one. • If the external storage device uses SCSI, is there room on the SCSI chain for an additional device?
Do you need a cable to connect the external storage device to the computer?	Depending on the type of interface used, you will need to make sure that you have a compatible cable to connect to the computer. Common cable connections include: • USB • FireWire • eSATA • Ethernet
Do you have an available source of power for the storage device?	Some external storage devices will require an additional power source from the computer. For example, eSATA requires an additional power connection to function.

USB Performance Factors

To get the best possible performance from a storage device that uses USB as a connection method, connect it to a port or hub that supports USB 3.0. Keep in mind that many hubs drop all ports down to the slower USB 1.1 speed if you connect any USB 1.1 devices. Try not to connect a slower-speed device to the same hub in which you plan to connect a USB 3.0 storage device.

Note: For additional information, check out the LearnTO **Install Storage Devices** in the LearnTOs for this course on your LogicalCHOICE Course screen.

Access the Checklist tile on your LogicalCHOICE course screen for reference information and job aids on How to Install and Configure Storage Devices

ACTIVITY 5-11
Installing an Internal Storage Device

Before You Begin

To complete this activity, you will need the following hardware components. If you do not have these available, you can remove and reinstall the existing hardware:

- A second hard drive and an empty drive bay. If you have a PATA drive, you will also need an available connection on the PATA cable. If you have a SCSI drive, you will also need an installed SCSI HBA.
- An available power connection for the device you are adding to the system.
- Optionally, rails to allow smaller drives to fit into larger drive bays.

Scenario

You have been assigned the task of refurbishing a computer for a client. This computer has a single functioning hard drive, and the user needs a significant amount of local storage space.

---

1. Locate the available bay and the power and data connections for the new hard disk drive.
   a) Power off the system, unplug all the peripherals and power cord, and open the computer case.
   b) Locate an available drive bay and determine if the bay is the same form factor as the drive. If you are using a 5.25-inch drive bay and a 3.5-inch drive, you will need to install the drive using rails to adapt the drive to the larger bay.
   c) Locate an available data connection on the data cable. If necessary, connect a PATA data cable to the PATA controller connection on the system board.
   d) Locate an available power connector. If necessary, connect a power splitter to an existing power connection.

2. Prepare the drive for installation.
   a) If you are installing a PATA drive, set the jumpers or switches to Cable Select or slave.
   b) If you are installing a SCSI drive, set the SCSI ID to an unused ID number. If the drive is at the end of the SCSI chain, terminate the device and, if necessary, remove termination from the previously terminated device.
   c) If necessary, attach rails to the drive to fit in the bay.

3. Install the hard disk drive into the system.
   a) Slide the drive into the bay.
   b) Connect the data cable to the drive.
   c) Connect the power cable to the drive.
   d) Secure the drive to the bay chassis with screws.

4. Check whether the drive is accessible.
   a) Plug all the peripherals back into the system.

   > **Note:** You can leave the case open until the end of the activity.

   b) Restart the computer.
   c) If necessary, access CMOS, enable the disk, and then exit CMOS and save your settings.

5. Partition and format the new drive as an NTFS drive.

a) Log on to Windows as *Admin##* with *!Pass1234* as the password.

b) Select **Start,** right-click **Computer,** and select **Manage.**

c) In the left pane, select **Disk Management.**

d) If the **Initialize Disk** window is displayed, select **MBR** if the new drive is smaller than 2 TB or **GPT** if the drive is larger than 2 TB. Select **OK.**

e) If necessary, maximize the **Disk Management** window to view the new drive. It may be labeled **Disk 1 Unallocated.**

f) Right-click the unallocated space for the new disk.

g) Select **New Simple Volume.** The **New Simple Volume** wizard starts.

h) Select **Next.**

i) In the **Simple volume size in MB** text box, type *20000*

j) Select **Next.**

k) From the **Assign the following drive letter** drop-down list, select **S.**

l) Select **Next.**

m) On the **Format Partition** page, verify that **NTFS** is selected and select **Next.**

 Note: To save time during class, you can check the **Perform a Quick Format** option.

n) Select **Finish.**

o) Close the new drive window.

p) Close **Computer Management.**

q) In the **Auto Play** dialog window, click **Open folder** to view files.

r) Close the **New Volume (s:)** window.

TOPIC F

Configure the System BIOS

In the previous topics, you focused on the basic internal storage devices that enable a computer to run, but what about how the computer communicates with all these devices? In this topic, you will configure settings in the system BIOS.

How does the computer know when to start devices within the computer? Without the system BIOS managing the system components within the computer system, the devices simply would not be accessible. As an A+ technician, you must fully understand how the system BIOS operates and how to configure it to enable a customized computing environment for users.

This topic covers all or part of the following CompTIA® A+® (2012) certification objectives:

* Exam 220–801: Objective 1.1 Configure and apply BIOS settings.

BIOS Memory / CMOS

BIOS memory stores information about the computer setup that the system BIOS refers to each time the computer starts. The BIOS information is stored in non-volatile *Electrically Erasable Programmable Read-Only Memory (EEPROM)*, or flash memory chips. Because you can write new information to BIOS memory, you can store information about system changes, such as new components that you add to your system. The computer will look for the component each time it is turned on.

BIOS Components

When the BIOS is activated on startup, it determines which components are present and when they are accessed during the boot process. Any time you change a hardware component, you should check the BIOS settings to see if they also need to be changed for the system BIOS to recognize the new hardware. Also, you can configure BIOS memory without needing to open the chassis. Several system components can be configured through the system BIOS:

* RAM
* Hard drives
* Optical drives
* CPU

Firmware Upgrades

Most modern motherboards contain a number of BIOS chips that contain the system firmware that runs the system BIOS. This firmware may need an upgrade from time to time depending on the manufacturer. When the manufacturer issues an update, then the firmware will need to be updated. These updates contain security patches, updates to the performance, and updates to address any known issues. The updates can be installed in a number of ways, but most commonly can be downloaded from the manufacturer's website and then either burned to CD, or copied to a flash drive.

BIOS Configuration Options

BIOS configuration options can be altered at any time by changing the settings within the BIOS configuration utility. Many times when you replace or change a hardware component, the BIOS configuration will need to be changed so that the system BIOS can recognize the newly installed hardware. System BIOS settings can be configured without having to physically open the system case of the computer. The extent to which you can use BIOS to configure a computer depends heavily on the manufacturer of the particular BIOS; however, in most cases, you should be able to configure at least the following—and possibly much more—from the keyboard by using the BIOS configuration utility.

Configuration Option	Description
General	General settings include: • Motherboard information, including the manufacturer, brand, and CPU vendor. • System date and time. You can use the BIOS Setup program to set the PC's real-time clock. (You can also use DOS date and time commands to reset the real-time clock.) • Boot sequence. You can specify the order that drives are checked for the operating system. • BIOS version. This can be used when looking for firmware updates for the BIOS chip.
Security settings	You can specify a number of security functions: • Manage passwords, including both administrator and system passwords. • Enable and disable the trusted platform module (TPM) security feature. When enabled, the BIOS will load the TPM and make it available within the operating system. • In some laptop computers, laptop-tracking software such as LoJack® for Laptops can be configured to help recover lost or stolen laptops.
Memory	Some systems require you to specify in BIOS how much RAM is installed on the system. You might also be able to specify the type of memory used.
Enabling and disabling devices	Many devices can be configured by modifying the BIOS settings. You can:: • Specify the type and size of the hard disk drives attached to the system. • Enable and disable advanced drive settings, such as RAID settings. • Specify the preferred default monitor. • Specify settings such as unidirectional or bidirectional printing, Extended Capabilities Port (ECP) options, Enhanced Parallel Port (EPP) options, and what memory addresses and interrupts are used by a port. You can also disable or enable the ports. If you know that a parallel or serial port will not be used, you can disable the port, thereby freeing up the resources that would otherwise be unusable by other devices. Conversely, if you connect a device to a port and the device will not work at all, you might want to check the BIOS to ensure that the port has not been disabled. • Specify settings such as powering down components (like the display device, video card, and hard drives) when the components have not been used for a specified time period, as well as options and time limits for standby and suspend modes. You can also disable or enable global power management.
Clock speed	The clock speed for the CPU can be adjusted in the BIOS. In some modern systems, the CPU type and speed is automatically adjusted, but in older systems, you will verify that the clock speed is optimized for the CPU installed on the motherboard.
System configuration	Allows you to configure various system components such as integrated network interface cards (NICs), USB controllers, parallel ports, and serial ports.

Configuration Option	Description
Video	Allows you to change the video controller settings when more than one video card is installed.
Performance	Allows you to change CPU settings such as enabling or disabling multicore support and changing processor modes.
Virtualization support	If the CPU supports virtualization, then you can use the BIOS setup utility to enable or disable the various virtualization settings available. Virtualization support within the BIOS is dependent on the OEM model. Most modern systems will support virtualization.
Power management	Allows you to configure different power options available, such as how the system will recover from a power loss and other advanced power options.
Maintenance	Allows you to verify and set service and asset tags used when a computer needs further maintenance from an outside vendor. The asset tag is used to identify the computer within the BIOS. It is usually a four or five digit number.

 Note: For additional information, check out the LearnTO **Work with the System BIOS** in the LearnTOs for this course on your LogicalCHOICE Course screen.

BIOS Diagnostics

Most BIOS systems come with a built-in diagnostics utility that can be used to troubleshoot issues and verify proper functionality. Most diagnostic tools allow you to test the system memory and the entire system. The tool will thoroughly test each system component and display test results which are usually a pass or fail. This will help you to identify which component is having issues. Most utilities will run tests on the following components:

- Video cards
- System memory
- Hard drives
- Optical drives

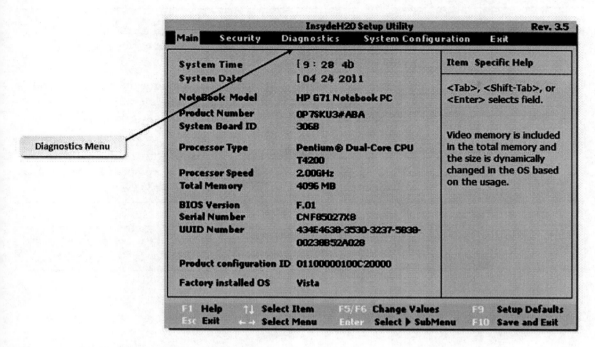

Figure 5-6: A sample BIOS diagnostic utility.

BIOS Monitoring Capabilities

Most BIOS have monitoring capabilities built in and can allow you to check a number of system activities for issues. To access the monitoring options, you must enter the system BIOS during start up, by pressing one of the function keys. The specific function key will depend on the type of motherboard installed, so verify the key you need to press on startup to access the BIOS.

Monitoring Capability	Description
Temperature	The temperature of the CPU, motherboard, and overall system can usually be checked within the system BIOS. You can use this options to check for overheating and to verify that the CPU is running within its safe temperature range.
Fan speeds	Within the BIOS, you can verify the fan speed for your CPU, and any system fans installed in the computer. Keep in mind that you must balance the rotations per minute (RPM) speed of the fans with the temperature of the CPU and motherboard.
Intrusion detection	Most modern BIOS will have some security functions built in. This includes system intrusion detection. The intrusion detection is implemented using a sensor that alerts the system BIOS when the case cover of the system has been removed.
Voltage	The system voltage settings are strictly based on the specific hardware you have installed in the system, such as type of motherboard and CPU. The BIOS allows you to change the voltage configuration for each device installed. Once in the BIOS, you will look for: • Vcore, or VCC, which is the CPU voltage reading. • Memory voltage, which displays the RAM voltage settings. • VDD voltage, which displays the motherboard's voltage. This rating is driven by the Northbridge chip of the board. • If there is a graphics card installed, then you will see the AGP voltage setting displayed.

Monitoring Capability	Description
Clock	You can verify that the BIOS clock is accurate by verifying the time within the system BIOS.
Bus speed	In some cases, you may find the need to monitor the bus speed, and to make sure that the overall CPU speed is in line with the bus speed. Bus speeds are usually set by the manufacturer at a natural clock rate or an enhanced clock rate. For an example, when you have a processor with a CPU speed of 1.82 GHz clock speed, you would need to set the bus speed to 166 MHz with the multiplier of 11. (166 MHz x 11 = 1.826 GHz).

 Access the Checklist tile on your LogicalCHOICE course screen for reference information and job aids on How to Configure System BIOS Settings

ACTIVITY 5-12
Exploring and Configuring the System BIOS

Scenario

In this activity, you will explore the configuration options available to you in the system BIOS utility.

---

1. Explore the system BIOS utility.
   a) From the **Start** menu, restart your computer system.
   b) As the computer restarts, press the BIOS access key. You might want to record this key for later use.
   c) Navigate to the **System Setup** menu option.
      Depending on the BIOS installed on your computer, this menu might have a different name.
   d) Browse through the available BIOS configuration options.
   e) Locate the motherboard settings and record the BIOS version.
      This information can be helpful if you ever have to update the BIOS to solve a hardware issue.

2. Change the boot order.
   a) Navigate to the **Boot Sequence** setting.
      Depending on the BIOS installed on your computer, this setting might have a slightly different name.
   b) Examine the current boot order.
      In older systems, the floppy drive was often configured as the primary boot device. In newer systems, a USB storage device or the internal hard disk might be configured as the primary boot device.
   c) Change the boot order to the following:
      * Optical drive
      * Internal hard disk 1
      * Internal hard disk 2
      * USB storage device
   d) Save the change.

3. Update the system date and time.
   a) Navigate to the **Date and Time** setting.
      Depending on the BIOS installed on your computer, this setting might have a slightly different name.
   b) Examine the current setting. If the date and time appear to be correct, you can skip this and the next substep. If the date and time are not correct, adjust them to match the current date and time.
   c) Save your changes.

4. Examine system monitoring options.
   a) Navigate to the **Hardware Monitoring** menu option.
      Depending on the BIOS installed on your computer, this setting might have a different name, such as **PC Health, CPU Temperature,** or some other name.
   b) Examine the CPU temperature reading.
      Normal CPU temperatures range from 30 to 60 degrees Celsius.

5. Verify the BIOS changes.
   a) Exit the BIOS utility.
   b) Log on to Windows.

c) If you changed the date and time, verify that the system date and time has been updated in the taskbar.

Summary

In this lesson, you installed and configured internal system components. In your role as an A+ technician, you will be responsible for helping users with installing motherboards, RAM, CPUs, and storage devices, so having the skills to install and configure them correctly will be crucial to assisting users.

In your current job role, what system components have you worked with the most?

In future job roles as an A+ technician, what system components do you think you will be working with the most?

 Note: Check your LogicalCHOICE Course screen for opportunities to interact with your classmates, peers, and the larger LogicalCHOICE online community about the topics covered in this course or other topics you are interested in. From the Course screen you can also access available resources for a more continuous learning experience.

6 Installing and Configuring Operating Systems

Lesson Time: 3 hours, 10 minutes

Lesson Objectives

In this lesson, you will install and configure operating systems. You will:

- Implement virtualization.

- Install Microsoft Windows.

- Perform a Windows Upgrade.

- Perform preventive maintenance with common tools and techniques.

Lesson Introduction

So far in this course, you have learned in general about hardware and software, and have installed and configured many of the hardware components required for a computer system. Now it is time to install the most important software component—the operating system— so that all the hardware you've assembled so far can function together. In this lesson, you will install and configure operating systems.

Because so many computers today come with operating system software installed by the vendor, an ordinary user might never need to install an operating system. As an IT professional, however, you might be called upon to install and configure operating systems for a variety of reasons: if the original installation does not meet a user's needs; if the system needs to be upgraded; if you are redeploying a system from one user to another; or even if you need to complete a brand new build and construct a computer entirely from scratch. In all of these cases, you will need to be able to install, configure, and optimize the computer's operating system.

This lesson covers all or part of the following CompTIA® A+® (2012) certification objectives:

- Topic A:

    - Exam 220–802: Objective 1.9
- Topic B:

- • Exam 220–802: Objectives 1.2, 1.6
- Topic C:
  - • Exam 220–802: Objective 1.1
- Topic D:
  - • Exam 220–802: Objective 1.7

TOPIC A

Implement Virtualization

In this lesson, you will install and configure the Windows® operating system. One or more of those operating systems can be leveraged using virtualization to improve performance or increase productivity for one or more machines. In this topic, you will implement virtualization.

As organizations grow in size and scope, there is an increased need for more resources, especially when it comes to computing. Virtualization can help ease the growing pains of an organization by providing the opportunity to leverage one machine and one operating system for use over many machines, and save valuable time and resources when it comes to hardware, software, and personnel. As an A+ technician, you may need to know what is needed to set up a virtualized environment.

This topic covers all or part of the following CompTIA® A+® (2012) certification objectives:

* Exam 220–802: Objective 1.9: Explain the basics of client-side virtualization.

What is Virtualization?

Virtualization is the technological process of creating a virtual version of a computing environment by separating the elements of the computing environment—the applications, operating system, programs, documents, and more—from each other and from any physical hardware by using an additional software application. Virtualization can provide flexibility and scalability for organizations where the costs for hardware and software and the IT infrastructure needed to maintain them both continue to increase. It can increase resource utilization by allowing those resources to be pooled and leveraged as part of a virtual infrastructure, and it can provide for centralized administration and management of all the resources being used throughout the organization.

Types of Virtualization

 Note: For additional information, check out the LearnTO **Identify Server-side vs. Client-side Virtualization** in the LearnTOs for this course on your LogicalCHOICE Course screen.

There are two main types of virtualization being used today: server virtualization and client-side virtualization. The main difference between the two types is determined by where the virtualization takes place.

* *Server (or server-side) virtualization* takes place centrally at the server or data center. Server virtualization utilizes one logical device, typically the server, to act as the host machine for the guest machines that virtually use the applications and programs provided by the host. A software application is used to divide the single physical device into multiple isolated virtual devices.
* *Client-side virtualization* takes place at the endpoints, the desktop environments themselves. Client-side virtualization separates the elements of a user's logical desktop environment—the applications, operating system, programs, and more—and divides them from each other and from the physical hardware or a physical machine. With desktop virtualization, a single user can run multiple operating systems on one machine simultaneously and seamlessly; a single user can interact with their computer and all of their applications remotely from a mobile device; or numerous users can access and maintain their own individual desktop environments via a single and centrally-managed physical device which can either be co-located to the virtualized environments or operate from a remote location. This type of virtualization environment allows multiple virtualized machines to run on a single device with no impact on the host's file system, registry and OS.

Components of a Virtual Environment

A virtual environment is made up of three components:

- The *host machine,* which is the computer or server on which the elements of the virtual environment are installed and which manages the machines or desktops accessing or running the environment virtually.
- The *hypervisor,* which is a software application that is installed on the host machine and is used to configure and manage all the machines or desktops running virtually from the host.
- And the *virtual machines* or VMs, which are the software implementations or emulations of the host machine, and which run programs just like a physical machine. The VMs are created by the hypervisor and run independently from the host in which they are installed.

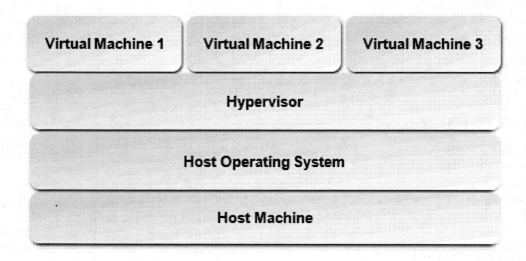

Figure 6–1: Components of a virtual environment.

Virtual Desktop Infrastructure

In a *Virtual Desktop Infrastructure (VDI),* the personal computing environment is separated from a physical machine using desktop virtualization. It can include hardware, applications, operating systems, or a combination of these pieces. Although this sounds like client-side virtualization, it is actually server-side virtualization.

The desktop operating system and any necessary applications are run inside the virtual machines, which are hosted on servers in the data center. These VMs running the desktop operating systems are called *virtual desktops.*

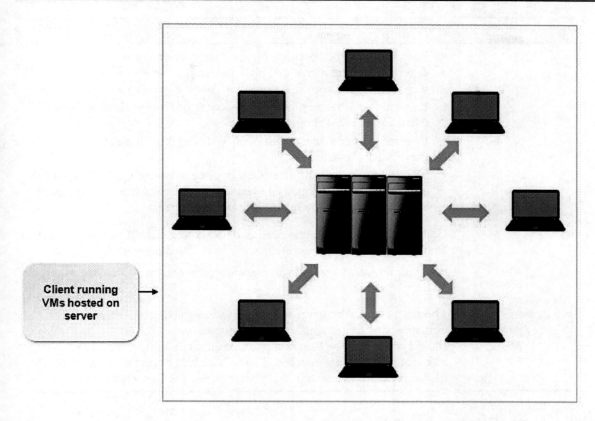

Figure 6-2: VDI.

Virtualization Requirements

In order to run a virtualization environment on a client computer securely, certain requirements must met. There are generally four areas that should be addressed.

Area	Requirements
Emulator	In a client-side virtualization environment, the *emulator* is the software installed that allows the computer to virtually run another operating system, or another instance of the same operating system. Each emulator manufacturer will have specific hardware and processor requirements that the client machine must have in order to be able to run the emulation software.
	Client-side virtualization capabilities are still growing to meet consumer needs. Recent advances include mobile device hypervisors that give the devices the ability to access corporate resources without having to manage each device individually.
Security	Security requirements will primarily be based on an organization's security policy. There are however, general security guidelines that should be followed when configuring a VM:
	• Ensure that the VM has been equipped with appropriate antivirus software that is designed to protect both the physical client computer and the VM. Not all antivirus software packages can properly protect against malware on a VM. Always check with the manufacturer of the software before you install any program files on a VM. Issues can arise when the client machine running VM gets infected and there is no control in place to prevent the virus from propagating to the VM.

Area	Requirements
	• Restrict users from copying files and applications from a traditional desktop machine to a VM. This vulnerability can lead to issues if infected files are copied, or sensitive data is copied to a shared VM. • Regularly update and manage the security patches for both the physical client and the VM running on it. • Enforce proper management of all VMs installed in client machines to prevent data leakage. • Ensure that security measures are in place to isolate the VMs from the hypervisor. This prevents any viruses or infections from being spread between VMs and the hypervisor and vice versa.
Network	Generally for client computers running VMs, the normal network activity load will also suffice for running any VM-initiated network functions. Network requirements will vary depending on the hardware used to run the VDI.
Resource	The resource requirements for virtualization will depend on what virtualization components will be supported within the environment. You should verify that the host computer has the required hardware and software components installed. This can include having enough RAM and hard drive capabilities and CPU power to run the virtualization software.

Windows Client Virtualization Solutions

There are several virtualization solutions available for installing VMs on a personal computer, depending on what version of Windows the PC is running.

Client Virtualization Solution	Description
Windows Virtual PC	Enables you to install Windows® 7, Windows Vista®, and Windows® XP VMs on a Windows 7 computer. Freely downloadable from **www.microsoft.com/windows/virtual-pc/download.aspx.** You also have the option of downloading only Windows Virtual PC or Windows Virtual PC and Windows XP Mode.
Windows XP Mode	Consists of a VM package that contains an installed and licensed version of Windows XP Professional with Service Pack 3. Free for licensed Windows 7 Professional, Windows 7 Enterprise, and Windows 7 Ultimate.
Microsoft Virtual PC 2007	Enables you to install VMs on a Windows Vista or Windows XP computer. Freely downloadable from **www.microsoft.com/windows/virtual-pc/support/virtual-pc-2007.aspx.**

Integration Components

Windows client virtualization solutions provide *integration components* that enable you to work more effectively within the VM environment. Integration components enable you to share the mouse between the host and the VM, as well as sharing other physical components and exchanging data without the need for a virtual network connection. Integration components are installed by default if you are using Windows XP Mode; otherwise, you need to install them manually.

For more information about integration components, visit **About integration features** at **http:// technet.microsoft.com/en-us/library/ee449432(v=ws.10).aspx.**

 Access the Checklist tile on your LogicalCHOICE course screen for reference information and job aids on How to Implement Virtualization

ACTIVITY 6-1
Creating a VM on Windows 7

Scenario

You have recently been hired as a PC technician at a local business. One of your primary responsibilities will be to install and upgrade operating systems. To prepare for your new job responsibilities, you have decided that you will create a VM on your Windows 7 computer so that you can practice installing Windows 7 without affecting the files stored on your computer.

---

1. Download Windows Virtual PC.
   a) Navigate to **www.microsoft.com/windows/virtual-pc/download.aspx**.
   b) Select **Download Windows Virtual PC without Windows XP Mode**.
   c) In the **Select system** drop-down list, select **Professional 32-bit** or **Professional 64-bit,** depending on your system.
   d) In the **Select language** drop-down list, select **English**.
   e) Select **Download**.

   If your version of Windows 7 is not activated, you may be prompted with additional validation downloads.
   f) In the **Windows validation required** window, select **Continue**.
   g) In the **Windows validation was successful** window, select **Continue**.
   h) When you are prompted to open or save the file, select **Save**.
   i) When the download is complete, select **Open folder**.

2. Install Windows Virtual PC.
   a) In the **Admin##>Downloads** folder, open the file you just downloaded.
   b) When you are prompted to install the Windows software update, select **Yes**.
   c) Accept the license agreement.
   d) When the installation is complete, select **Restart Now**.
   e) When the computer restarts, log on to Windows.

3. Create a VM named *Win7test##*
   a) Select **Start→Windows Virtual PC**.
   b) In the **Admin##>Virtual Machines** folder, select **Create virtual machine**.
   c) For the VM name, type *Win7test##* where ## corresponds to the number in your user name. Accept the default location, and select **Next**.
   d) Accept the default memory and network settings, and select **Next**.
   e) Accept the default of creating a new dynamic virtual hard disk, and select **Create**.

4. Start the VM by double-clicking it.
   After a few moments, you should receive a message that states: "Reboot and Select proper Boot device" or "Insert Boot Media in selected Boot device." This happens because there is no operating system installed on the VM yet.

5. Close the VM.
   a) Select **Action→Close**
   b) In the **What do you want the virtual machine to do?** drop-down list, select **Turn off,** and then select **OK**.
   c) Verify that the VM's **Machine status** setting is **Powered down**.

TOPIC B

Install Microsoft Windows

In this lesson, you will install and configure operating systems. The fundamental installation method is to install the operating system from scratch. In this topic, you will perform a fresh installation of Microsoft® Windows®.

Being able to perform a fresh installation of Windows can be important if you have built a custom computer system from scratch, if the system you purchased from a vendor did not have the correct system installed, or if you are completely redeploying existing hardware from one system to another. The skills and information in this topic will help you plan and perform a fresh installation properly, for whatever your technical and business requirements might be.

This topic covers all or part of the following CompTIA® A+® (2012) certification objectives:

*   Exam 220–802: Objective 1.2: Given a scenario, install and configure the operating system using the most appropriate method.
*   Exam 220–802: Objective 1.6: Set up and configure Windows networking on a client/desktop.

Windows System Requirements

Before installation, you must make sure that your hardware meets or exceeds the minimum requirements for the version of Windows you will install.

Operating System	Requirements
Windows® 7 Home Premium, Professional, or Ultimate	• 1 GHz 32-bit (x86) or 64-bit (x64) processor. • 1 GB RAM (32-bit) or 2 GB RAM (64-bit). • 40 GB hard disk with a minimum of 20 GB of available space. • Support for DirectX 9 graphics; some programs may require support for DirectX 10 graphics or higher to provide optimal performance.
Windows Vista® Home Premium, Business, or Ultimate	• 1 GHz 32-bit (x86) or 64-bit (x64) processor. • 1 GB of RAM. • 40 GB hard disk with a minimum of 15 GB of available space. • Support for DirectX 9 graphics and 128 MB of graphics memory available.
Windows Vista® Home Basic	• 1 GHz 32-bit (x86) or 64-bit (x64) processor. • 512 MB of RAM. • 20 GB hard disk with a minimum of 15 GB of available space. • Support for DirectX 9 graphics and 32 MB of graphics memory available.
Windows XP® Home Edition or Professional	• 233-MHz minimum processor required; 300 megahertz (MHz) or higher recommended. (Intel® Pentium®/Celeron® family, AMD K6/Athlon™/ Duron™ family, or compatible processor recommended). • 64 MB of RAM required; 128 MB recommended.

Operating System	Requirements
	• At least 1.5 GB of space available on the hard disk. • Video adapter and monitor with Super VGA 800 x 600 resolution or higher.

Windows XP Media Center Edition System Requirements

Windows XP Media Center Edition is intended for installation on a specially configured media-ready Media Center PC that will connect to and interact with other home media devices such as a TV, music center, or game system. Media Center PCs are available from many major retailers and computer manufacturers.

For information about the different Media Center PC models and options as well as purchasing information, see the Media Center web page at **http://windows.microsoft.com/en-US/windows/products/windows-media-center.**

Apple OS System Requirements

The system requirements for OS® X Lion are:

• A Mac computer with an Intel Core 2 Duo, Core i3, Core i5, Core i7, or Xeon processor.
• 2 GB of RAM.
• At least 7 GB of available hard disk space.
• OS X version 10.6.6 or later (10.6.8 recommended) and the Mac® App Store installed.

Linux System Requirements

The hardware requirements for installing Linux will depend upon the distribution of Linux you choose. Linux is a portable operating system, which means it can run on a variety of hardware platforms. There are versions available for many different processor types, including Intel x86 and Pentium, Itanium, DEC Alpha, Sun Sparc, Motorola, and others. In general, a basic installation of Linux on a workstation might require as little as 16 or 32 MB of memory and 250 MB of disk space, but you might need several gigabytes of disk space for complete installations including all utilities.

Hardware Compatibility

Prior to installing any versions of Windows, you should check to make sure that your system meets the system requirements and that all your hardware is compatible with the version of Windows you plan to install.

If you plan on installing or upgrading to Windows 7, Microsoft offers a number of ways to check to see if your existing hardware is compatible.

• The Microsoft Windows 7 Upgrade Advisor: For single systems or for home computers, you can download and run the Windows 7 Upgrade Advisor, available at **http://windows.microsoft.com/en-us/windows/downloads/upgrade-advisor.** The Upgrade Advisor will scan your hardware and any connected devices to determine if you can upgrade to Windows 7 with your current hardware configuration.
• The Windows 7 Compatibility Center: The Windows 7 Compatibility Center is a one-stop-shop where you can find out which hardware and software components are compatible with Windows 7. You can visit the Compatibility Center at **www.microsoft.com/windows/compatibility/windows-7/en-us/default.aspx.**
• The Microsoft Assessment and Planning (MAP) Toolkit: The MAP Toolkit is the appropriate tool to use to assess an organization-wide or network-wide migration to a Windows operating system. It allows you to check the hardware configuration of all the systems on your network The toolkit can generate details about those systems that can be readily upgraded to Windows 7 using their present configuration. It also provides details about the hardware that needs to be upgraded for the other systems to run Windows 7. The toolkit is freeware, and can be

downloaded from the Microsoft Download Center at **www.microsoft.com/download/en/details.aspx?id=7826.**

Macintosh Hardware Compatibility

If your Macintosh® computer meets the minimum requirements for OS X installation, the hardware should all be compatible with the operating system. You can verify that your hardware is supported by examining the technical specifications, by product, at **http://support.apple.com/specs/.**

Linux Hardware Compatibility

Because Linux is a portable operating system, it is compatible with a wide range of hardware. You will need to check with the vendor or provider of your Linux distribution to verify if your particular system hardware is supported by that distribution.

Some web resources you can use to research general Linux hardware support include:

- The Linux Hardware Compatibility HOWTO website at **http://tldp.org/HOWTO/Hardware-HOWTO/index.html.**
- The Linux Questions website's hardware compatibility list at **www.linuxquestions.org/hcl/.**
- Linux hardware and driver support lists at **www.linux-drivers.org.**

Boot Methods

The operating system comes loaded onto a boot device, which is connected to the computer and can be used to either launch the OS or, in some cases, install the OS files onto the computer. There are a number of boot methods that can be used to install the operating system.

Boot Method	Description
USB	The operating system files and all necessary support files are loaded onto a USB device, such as a flash drive. The USB is connected to the computer and the operating system is booted and launched via the files on the USB.
CD-ROM/DVD	The operating system files and all necessary support files are loaded onto an optical disk, such as a CD-ROM or DVD. The disk type used will be dependent upon the size of the files on the disk: DVDs can hold more files and larger files than a CD-ROM. Regardless of the type, the disk is inserted into the optical drive of the computer and the operating system is booted and launched via the files on the disk.
PXE	The operating system files and all necessary support files can be accessed from a Preboot Execution Environment, or PXE (pronounce as "pixie"). With PXE, the operating system and all necessary supporting files are loaded onto a server. The operating system is then booted and launched over a network interface, accessing the operating system files on the server, instead of using a local drive. This method is often used for booting multiple computers that are being managed centrally and accessed by more than one user, such as public computers at a library or school.

Factory Configuration

Most computers are factory-configured to boot from CD-ROM or DVD-ROM first, and changing them to boot from hard disk speeds up the startup process. It also reduces the risk of contracting viruses by accidentally booting from an infected disk.

Device Priority

The BIOS allows a user to specify disk boot order and to provide device priority. By default, the computer might look to boot from the hard disk or a DVD-ROM first. If you prefer to boot from an operating system contained on a USB device, you can instruct the computer to look to that device first. To change the settings, wait until the computer has performed its POST, press the key (usually a function key, such as **F12**) indicated onscreen, and follow the instructions.

Imaging

Imaging is the process of creating a computer image from one main computer, called the *reference computer,* and copying that image onto one or more other computers, called the *target computers,* as a method of installing an operating system and other programs. A *computer image* is essentially a replica of the reference computer's hard disk and contains the operating system software, such as Windows XP Professional or Windows 7, and any other desired applications, files, desktop settings, and user preferences.

Problems can arise from differences in the hardware between the reference computer and the target computer. Not everyone has the same exact computer throughout a company, so it is not uncommon for slight variances in network and video cards to exist. For these systems, the best thing to do is to create the image without these drivers installed, then install them after the machine is imaged. Bigger concerns that are difficult to overcome deal with differences at the motherboard level, which can cause the installation to fail. This would necessitate different images for each system type.

Installation Types

There are several methods available for installing a Windows operating system.

Installation Method	Description
Clean install	A clean install is used to install the operating system on a brand new computer or to replace the operating system on an older computer in which the hard drive has been completely wiped.
	If the computer is new or once the old hard drive has been wiped, you can install the operating system using the boot method of your choice. Typically a clean installation will be performed with a local source, likely an installation disc.
	A clean install on an old system is particularly helpful if the system has been plagued by problems; erasing the hard drive and starting with a clean install can eliminate viruses and corrupted files and allow the computer to work more efficiently. However, it is important to remember that all the settings, preferences and files will be lost with a clean install to replace an existing system. Some of these settings or files can be migrated after the install using a migration tool.
Unattended installation	An unattended installation is an automated installation method that is most often used to roll out an installation or upgrade of the operating system to multiple systems and with minimal user interaction. An administrator is needed to start the installation, but then tasks that would usually require user input during installation are carried out automatically using an answer file. An answer file is a simple text file that contains all of the instructions that the Windows Setup file will need to install and configure the OS without any administrator intervention, including the product key.
	Using unattended installation allows for multiple installations to occur simultaneously, can prevent errors during installation and create more consistency between installations in a large-scale rollout,

Installation Method	Description
	all while lowering overhead costs and decreasing installation time and effort.
Repair installation	A repair installation is used to fix or repair the operating system that is currently installed on the computer and is experiencing issues. A repair install will replace the system files currently on the system with a fresh set of system files, essentially overwriting the existing system files. A repair install will only work if you are replacing the same version of the operating system; you cannot upgrade in this manner.
	With a repair installation you can install the operating system using the boot method of your choice.
	It is important to back up any data that you do not want to lose during the repair install to another disk partition, separate hard drive, or to an external storage device.
Upgrade	An upgrade is used when an operating system is already installed, but the user needs or wants a newer version of the operating system. Upgrades are often provided on a disk or via a download from a vendor's website.
	It is recommended that you back up any data that you do not want to lose during the upgrade to another disk partition, separate hard drive, or to an external storage device. It is also recommended that files for the upgraded system are placed in a separate directory folder, preserving the current OS files, to ensure that everything is working properly.
Multiboot	Multiboot or dual boot refers to installing more than one operating system on a machine. This may mean more than one type of OS made by different vendors (such as Windows and Unix or Linux OS) installed on a single machine, or could mean having a newer and an older version of the same OS (such as Windows XP and Windows 7) on a single machine.
	Multiboot installation requires that the machine either has multiple hard disks or that the hard disk has been partitioned, with a separate partition available for each operating system.
	Multiboot installations can be completed using the boot method of your choice.
Remote network installation	With remote network installation, copies of the necessary operating system installation files are placed on a server that supports remote installations, and an administrator can remotely initiate the installation over the network onto one or more client computers.
	Installing an operating system remotely requires the use of PXE as the boot method.
Image deployment	Image deployment provides a rapid way to install a standardized version of an operating system on one or many target computers. The operating system is first installed and configured with any additional software, security settings or general user settings on a reference computer. A computer image is made of the reference computer's hard disk, including the operating system and all

Handwritten note in left margin: "Recovering The OS"

Installation Method	Description
	associated files, and then replicated onto the specified target computers.
	More than likely, the image will be too large to be placed on a CD or DVD, and it will need to be saved to a large flash drive. This installation will likely be completed using a USB drive as the boot method.

Note: If your network environment supports Microsoft Active Directory®, you can use Microsoft's Windows Deployment Services (WDS) to deploy Windows automatically on multiple computers. WDS uses disk imaging (the Windows Imaging format). It will now fully automate the installation of Windows XP, Windows Server 2003, Windows Server 2008, Windows Vista, and Windows 7. WDS is a replacement of the old Remote Installation Services (RIS).

ACTIVITY 6-2
Examining Installation Methods

Scenario

Based on the scenario given, choose the most appropriate installation method.

---

1. **A user has had Windows 7 for several months, but a virus attack has corrupted some files.**
   - ○ Unattended
   - ○ Upgrade
   - ○ Repair
   - ○ Multiboot

2. **Several identical PCs need their operating systems upgraded.**
   - ☐ Unattended
   - ☐ Clean
   - ☐ Repair
   - ☐ Image deployment

3. **A user has Windows XP and needs both Windows XP and Windows 7.**
   - ○ Clean
   - ○ Repair
   - ○ Remote network
   - ○ Multiboot

Third Party Drivers

The installation files for your operating system should include the necessary drivers for the hardware components of the system. However, if you have hardware that has been released more recently than the operating system or have added hardware components to the system that are not traditionally part of the environment, such as a wireless card or printer, then you may need to load alternate third party drivers for these devices during the installation process.

Partitioning

Partitioning is the process of dividing a single hard disk into multiple isolated sections that function like separate physical hard drives, known as *disk partitions*. Partitions enable you to create a logical disk structure to organize hard drives. You can set up and format one or more disk partitions during installation. If you make an entire disk one partition, you cannot re-partition the disk later without either reinstalling the operating system or using a third-party disk utility. After you create a partition, you must format it to be able to store data on that partition.

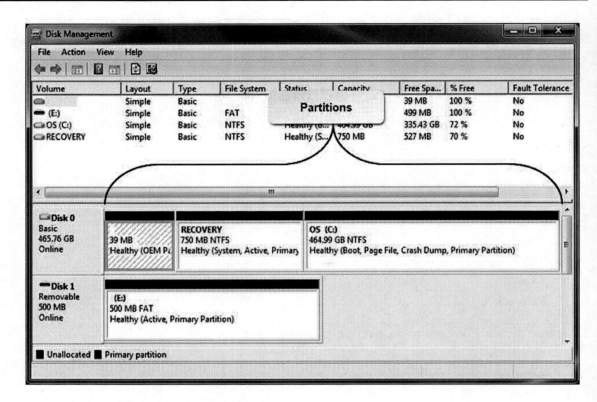

Figure 6-3: Disk partitioning in Windows 7.

Partitioning Types

There are several types of partitions and disks used to create sections on a hard disk.

Partition Type	Description
Logical	A part of a physical disk drive that has been partitioned and allocated as an independent unit and functions as a separate drive.
Primary	A partition that contains only one file system or logical drive.
Extended	An extended partition can be subdivided into several file systems or logical disks/drives. Extended drives can be assigned a new drive letter.

Disk Type	Description
Basic	A basic disk contains a primary partition, logical drives, and possibly an extended partition. These partitions have been formatted with a file system and are used as a volume for storage. Up to four partitions can be made on a basic disk. Basic disks are the most commonly used storage type in a Windows environment.
Dynamic	A dynamic disk contains dynamic volumes, which are volumes that can span multiple disks. On a dynamic disk, up to 2,000 volumes can be created, though a maximum of 32 volumes is recommended.

only understood by windows

Volumes

A *volume* is a single storage unit made up of free space that can reside on a single disk or partition or across multiple disks or partitions. However, a volume must be located on a single file system. The term "volume" may be used in place of the term "drive" to refer to a drive that is not a physical disk.

Types of Volumes

There are two main types of volumes: basic or simple volumes and dynamic volumes. Within dynamic volumes, there are different ways of expanding storage space over multiple disks.

- Basic (Simple) volume: A volume where the free space on a single disk or partition is used for storage space. It can be extended on the same disk or onto an additional disk; if extended onto an additional disk, it becomes a spanned volume.
- Spanned volume: A volume where the free space from multiple disks or partitions, which have been linked together, is used for storage space. A maximum of 32 disks can be linked together on a spanned volume.
- Striped volume: A volume where the free space from two or more physical disks is alternately utilized for storage space. The data is stored equally and alternately on each of the physical disks. It is sometimes referred to as a RAID-0 volume.
- Mirrored volume: A volume where the free space is used on two physical disks to store duplicate copies of the same data. The data from the volume on one disk is duplicated another physical disk to provide data redundancy. It is sometimes referred to as a RAID-1 volume.
- RAID-5 volume: A volume that is a combination of hard drives that are configured to write data across three or more drives.

File System Types

During installation, you can choose to format the hard disk with the appropriate file system.

Type	Description
NTFS	For a typical Windows setup, it is recommended that you choose the NTFS file system. This file system is used in newer Windows operating systems and can handle larger size partitions greater than 32 GB.
FAT	The FAT file system is a legacy formatting option that should only be used if running an older operating system such as Windows 95 or 98. The FAT file system is less secure and has a limit to size of partition it can support. If FAT32 is chosen, the size of the partition being formatted will determine the FAT file type used. If the partition is larger than 2 gigabytes, Windows automatically uses the FAT32 file system; smaller than 2 GB, FAT16 is used. If the partition is larger than 32 GBs, FAT is not an option
CDFS	*Compact Disc File System (CDFS)* CDFS is a very limited file system that was developed for optical disc media, typically for open source operating systems. Multiple operating systems support CDFS, including Windows, Apple® OS, and Unix-based systems. By supporting multiple platforms, CDFS allows for data and files to be exchanged without compatibility issues between the various operating systems.

Format Options

Whether your needs are to support older operating systems with FAT, or newer systems with NTFS, there are two options available for formatting during setup: full format and quick format. During a full format, any existing files on the partition being formatted are removed and the disk is scanned for any potential bad sectors. This scan can be time consuming, which is why the quick format option is available. During a quick format, the existing files on the partition are removed, but the hard disk is not scanned for bad sectors. While the quick format may indeed be quicker, it is suggested that quick format is used only if the hard disk was previously formatted and you are sure there are no damaged sectors.

Format Types

There are two types of formatting for hard disks:

- *Low-level formatting* is the process of writing track and sector markings on a hard disk. This level of formatting is performed when the hard disk is manufactured.
- *High-level formatting* is an operating system function that builds file systems on drives and partitions. It tests disk sectors to verify that they can be reliably used to hold data. It marks any unreliable sectors as bad sectors that cannot be used.

Workgroups

A *workgroup* is a Microsoft peer-to-peer network model in which computers are grouped together with access to shared resources for organizational purposes. Members of a workgroup can access folders, files, printers, or other connections over the network. The computers that make up a workgroup appear together when you browse the list of networked devices in either the **Network** folder or **My Network Places.** Each computer in the workgroup maintains its own user account database. This means that if a user wants to log on at any computer within the workgroup, you must create an account for the user on each computer in the workgroup.

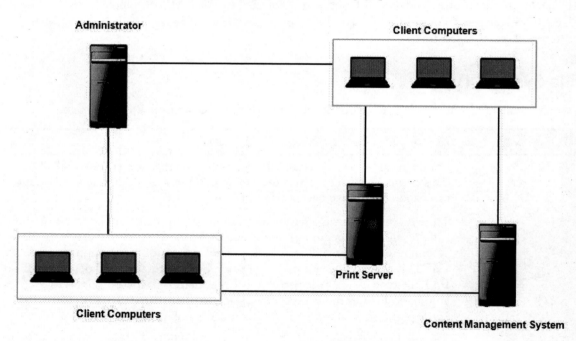

Figure 6–4: A workgroup.

Homegroups

In Windows 7, a homegroup is a peer-to-peer networking scheme where computers on a home network are grouped together for the purpose of sharing files and other resources such as printers. Computers on a home network must belong to a workgroup, but they can also belong to a homegroup.

When you install Windows 7, a homegroup is created automatically, if one does not already exist on your home network. The homegroup is automatically assigned a password by Windows. If you want to add computers to the homegroup, you will need to enter the password to join.

The homegroup provides easy resource sharing with security options such as:

- Excluding files and folders from being shared.
- Specifying whether or not others can change the files that you share.

The **HomeGroup Control Panel** contains options to manage your homegroup.

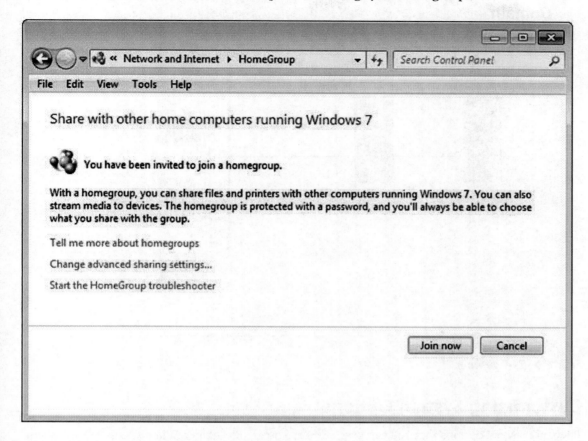

Figure 6–5: The HomeGroup Control Panel.

Domains

A *domain* is a Microsoft client/server network model that groups computers together for security and to centralize administration. Computers that are members of a domain have access to a shared central user account database, which means that an individual can use a single user account to log on at any computer within the domain. Administration is centralized because you need to create the user accounts only once in the domain, not on each computer. Domains require a specially configured server computer called a *domain controller,* where the centralized user account database is stored. Like a workgroup, computers that are members of a domain appear together when you browse the network.

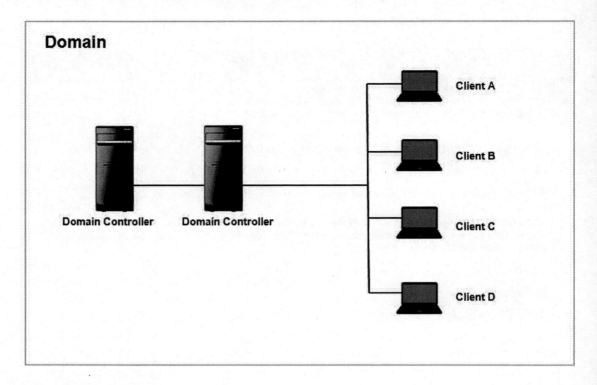

Figure 6-6: A domain.

Customizing System Options

There are several options that you can customize as you are installing a Windows operating system.

 Note: These options can be set during or after installation. They do not have to be configured during installation; if they are not set up during the installation, they can be changed at any time, typically through a Control Panel utility.

Option	Description
Regional and language settings	The default for a Windows system is the English language, with the location set to the United States. However, these settings can be customized to reflect region- or language-specific options. You can select the date and time for a specific location and choose appropriate regional settings, such as the manner in which numbers or currencies are displayed.
Computer name	During installation, you can provide the computer with a descriptive name and the organization to which you or the computer belongs.
Date and time	If you are within the United States and did not customize the regional and language settings, you can set the correct date and time, and choose the appropriate time zone for your region. If desired, you can choose to have Windows automatically adjust the time for Daylight Savings Time.
Network configuration	If Windows detects a network adapter during installation, you can decide how you want to configure networking settings for the computer. You can accept a Typical configuration or you can configure Custom settings that are appropriate to your environment. Otherwise, you can install your network adapter settings after the installation.
Workgroup vs. Domain setup	During installation, you can decide if you want the computer to be a member of a domain or a member of a workgroup. If the computer is not

Option	Description
	on a network or on a network without a domain, you can select or create a workgroup for the computer to belong to. If the computer is part of a network with a domain, you can select the domain to which the computer will be added as a member.

Creating Local User Accounts During Installation

For Windows XP, if you are installing into a workgroup, you can create local user accounts during installation. You can create additional local users and groups after installation.

For Windows 7, you create local users and groups after the installation is complete.

Creating a Homegroup

If you are installing Windows 7 on a computer that is connected to a home network, the homegroup will be created when you configure the network settings.

Updates

As operating systems constantly evolve with the many changes in the technological world, there is always the possibility that you may need to update your operating system immediately after installing it. You will also need to maintain the system over time as changes and improvements are made. Updates fall into one of three categories: critical updates, including Service Packs and security-related system patches; optional software updates that provide new tools and functionality; and optional hardware updates such as new device drivers.

Windows XP uses the Microsoft Update website or the Microsoft Update utility within the **Help and Support Center** to obtain any updates needed for the operating system. Windows Vista and Windows 7 uses the Windows Update Control Panel utility, a centralized location where you can check to see if your system is up to date and if there are any updates available, and configure the settings for updating your system. Regardless of the version you are running, the Microsoft Update website can provide updates for other Microsoft products that may have updates available.

Note:

The Windows Update website is located at **www.update.microsoft.com/microsoftupdate**. You can run either an Express or Custom update; if you run a Custom update, you will be able to choose from updates in each of the three main categories.

Service Packs and Patches

Patches are targeted operating system updates that Microsoft releases on an as-needed basis to provide enhancements to the operating system or to address security or performance issues. *Service Packs* are comprehensive updates that generally include all prior patches and updates, but which can also include important new features and functions. Windows XP SP2, for instance, included firewall changes; SP3 included support for Statements of Health and Digital Rights Management.

Windows Genuine Advantage

Every time you access the Microsoft Update website, it goes through a process of validating your installation. If Microsoft deems the install to be invalid, you will not be able to proceed with updates and will be instructed to contact Microsoft.

Factory Recovery Partition

Sometimes a computer may be experiencing problems that require you to recover it to the factory settings in order for it to work properly. In these instances, you may need to restore the computer to its initial state as provided from the manufacturer. You can use the *factory recovery partition,* a hidden partition on the computer's hard disk containing all of the original files and settings for the operating system and other pre-installed applications in their initial state, to restore the computer to it's factory settings.

The steps you use to perform this type of recovery are manufacturer-specific. You should always review the documentation that came with the computer to determine how to perform the recovery for the specific computer you are restoring. Regardless of how you perform the restore, it is always recommended that you back up any important data from the computer onto an external storage device, as all data will be lost when the system is restored to factory settings.

Recovery Partition or Recovery CD?

Depending on the manufacturer of your computer, you may have been supplied with either a recovery partition or CD-ROM (sometimes called a Recovery CD, or a Recover CD) that you can use to restore the computer to the configuration it was in when it shipped from the manufacturer. Some computers may allow you to create your own recovery CDs from the factory partition proactively, in case the hard drive should ever fail and you can't access the recovery partition to restore the computer.

Microsoft Product Activation

Microsoft Product Activation for Windows XP or Volume Activation for Windows 7 is an anti-piracy technology that verifies that software products are legitimately purchased. Product activation reduces a form of piracy known as casual copying. For example, you must activate Windows 7 within a given number of days after installation. After the grace period, users cannot access the system until they activate Windows. Volume Activation automates the activation process.

Activation Methods

For individual installations of Windows, you can activate the installation over the Internet. If you do not have an Internet connection, you can activate over the phone, although this takes a little longer. If you wish, you can postpone product activation and activate later in the activation grace period.

In large organizations, you can use a Volume License Product Key, which eliminates the need to individually activate each installation of Windows. You can also activate Windows as part of an automated installation.

 Access the Checklist tile on your LogicalCHOICE course screen for reference information and job aids on How to Install Microsoft Windows

ACTIVITY 6-3
Installing Microsoft Windows

Before You Begin

There is a VM named **Win7test##** installed on your computer that you can use to install Windows 7 Professional, and your instructor has provided you with installation DVDs or the instructions to use another installation method, as well as a valid product key.

Scenario

You have created a VM named **Win7test##** on your Windows 7 computer so that you can practice installing Windows 7 for a new job opportunity.

---

1. Configure the VM to access the Windows 7 Professional setup program.

   a) If you have a physical installation DVD, insert the Windows 7 Professional installation DVD into the optical drive of the computer.

   b) In the **Virtual Machines** window, display the pop-up menu for **Win7test##** and select **Settings.**

   c) In the left pane, select **DVD Drive.**

   The **DVD Drive** settings enable you to specify a physical drive, such as an optical drive, or you can browse for and select an ISO image to access.

   d) If you have a physical installation DVD, verify that **Access a physical drive** is selected.

   e) If you have an ISO image of the installation DVD, browse to the location of the ISO image and select **Open.**

   f) Select **OK.**

2. Run the Windows 7 Professional setup program in the **Win7test##** VM.

   a) Start the VM.

   b) When you are prompted, press **Spacebar** to boot from the DVD drive or ISO image.
   The Setup program starts, and begins loading the files needed for setup.

3. Run the **Installation** wizard for Windows 7 Professional.

   a) In the **Install Windows** dialog box, examine the selections for **Language to install, Time and currency format,** and **Keyboard or input method.** If necessary, adjust the selections for your locale. Select **Next.**

   b) Click **OK** in the **Mousepointer will be captured by the Virtual machine** dialog box.

   c) Click **Next.**

   d) Select **Install now.**

   e) When the license terms are displayed, review them, check **I accept the license terms,** and select **Next.**

   f) On the **Which type of installation do you want?** screen, select **Custom (advanced).**

   g) On the **Where do you want to install Windows?** screen, select **Drive options (advanced).**

   h) Select **Disk 0 Unallocated Space,** and select **Next.**

   i) The VM will automatically restart after a few minutes. Remove the DVD before the VM restarts.

   j) Observe as the VM restarts, Registry settings are updated, services are started, and the installation is completed.
   When the installation is completed, Windows restarts, prepares the computer for first use, and checks video performance.

4. Configure Windows.

   a) In the **Set Up Windows** dialog box, type *Admin##* for the user name and *VMWin##* for the computer name. Select **Next.**

You are prompted to set a password for the new account.

b) Type and confirm *!Pass1234* as the password and as the password hint, and then click **Next.**

c) Type the product key provided by your instructor, and select **Next.**

d) On the **Help protect your computer and improve Windows automatically** screen, select **Use recommended settings.**

e) On the **Review your date and time settings** screen, select the correct **Time zone, Date,** and **Time** for your locale. Select **Next.**

f) On the **Select your computer's current location** screen, select **Work network.**
Windows connects the VM to the network and prepares the desktop.

TOPIC C

Windows Upgrades

In the previous topic, you installed Microsoft Windows on a personal computer system. Upgrades are one method for installing Windows, but are more commonly utilized to migrate from one version of Windows to a different or newer version. In this topic, you will perform a Windows upgrade.

Software vendors such as Microsoft are constantly coming out with new operating system versions, and it can sometimes be more economical to upgrade existing systems when possible rather than to purchase new computer hardware with the new version pre-installed. Whether you are upgrading for an individual user or as part of a company-wide migration plan, the skills in this topic should help you upgrade from older versions of Windows to the current version successfully.

This topic covers all or part of the following CompTIA® A+® (2012) certification objectives:

- Exam 220–802: Objective 1.1: Compare and contrast the features and requirements of various Microsoft Operating Systems.

In-Place Upgrades

An *in-place upgrade* is the process of installing a newer version of an operating system without first removing the existing operating system that is currently installed on the computer. In-place upgrades also eliminate the need to perform the most tedious tasks involved with a clean install of an operating system: saving or backing up data that has been saved on the computer, wiping the hard drive, migrating or transferring saved data back to the machine, and reinstalling any programs that had been added to the system. In essence, an in-place upgrade can overwrite the existing, older operating system with the new version without disruption to the end user's environment.

In-Place Upgrade vs. Clean Install

In-place upgrades have been known to cause problems when upgrading to a version of the operating system that is significantly different from the existing version. In-place upgrades are only recommended when moving between operating systems that are one version apart, such as from Windows Vista to Windows 7. When there is a larger gap in the differences between the systems, such as migrating from Windows XP to Windows 7, a clean install is recommended rather than an in-place upgrade.

Supported Upgrade Paths

Existing Windows operating systems that are installed on a machine can be upgraded to another version of Windows, but these upgrades can only follow specific and supported upgrade paths.

Current Operating System	Can Be Upgraded To
Windows XP Home Edition	• Windows XP Professional • Windows Vista Home Basic • Windows Vista Home Premium • Windows Vista Business • Windows Vista Ultimate
Windows XP Professional	• Windows Vista Business • Windows Vista Ultimate

Current Operating System	Can Be Upgraded To
	Windows XP can be upgraded to Windows Vista Home Basic and Home Premium, but to do so requires a clean installation.
Windows Vista Home	Windows Vista Home Basic can be upgraded to: • Windows Vista Home Premium. • Windows Vista Ultimate. • Windows 7 Home Basic. • Windows 7 Home Premium. • Windows 7 Ultimate. Windows Vista Home Premium can be upgraded to: • Windows Vista Ultimate. • Windows 7 Home Premium. • Windows 7 Ultimate.
Windows Vista Business/ Enterprise/Ultimate	Windows Vista Business can be upgraded to: • Windows Vista Ultimate. • Windows 7 Professional. • Windows 7 Enterprise. • Windows 7 Ultimate. Windows Vista Enterprise can be upgraded to Windows 7 Enterprise. Windows Vista Ultimate can be upgraded to Windows 7 Ultimate.
Windows 7 Starter	• Windows 7 Home Premium • Windows 7 Professional • Windows 7 Ultimate
Windows 7 Home	Windows 7 Home Basic can be upgraded to: • Windows 7 Home Premium. • Windows 7 Professional. • Windows 7 Ultimate. Windows 7 Home Premium can be upgraded to: • Windows 7 Professional. • Windows 7 Ultimate.
Windows 7 Professional	Windows 7 Professional can be upgraded to Windows 7 Ultimate.

Upgrade Support

There are many upgrade paths that are not supported, whether because of the vast differences in functions between the operating systems, or if your operating system is no longer commercially available. To see a full list of all of the supported or unsupported upgrade paths for Windows XP, Windows Vista, and Windows 7, please visit the following links:

* Windows XP: **http://support.microsoft.com/kb/292607**
* Windows Vista: **http://windows.microsoft.com/en-us/windows7/help/upgrading-from-windows-vista-to-windows-7**
* Windows 7: **http://windows.microsoft.com/en-US/windows7/products/home**

Compatibility Tools

When upgrading to a different version of Windows, you will need to check to ensure that the existing hardware is compatible with the new operating system and that your existing software applications will run properly on the new version of Windows. Applications written for earlier versions of Windows might not always work with your new OS version, but you may be able to select an appropriate application compatibility mode for the application after you have upgraded the operating system.

 Note: To access the Upgrade Advisor, you can visit **http://windows.microsoft.com/en-US/ windows/downloads/upgrade-advisor.**

Windows Compatibility Center

The Windows Compatibility Center is a central location where you can find out if your hardware or software is compatible with the latest version of Windows. From the Compatibility Center, you can also download and launch the Upgrade Advisor, which will scan your computer in its current configuration, including any peripheral devices, to see if all parts are compatible with the operating system's requirements. Upgrade Advisor is only available for the most current version of Windows available; it will not support a compatibility check for older versions. However, the Setup program included with Windows XP, Windows Vista, and Windows 7 will automatically run a compatibility check during the upgrade process, and should find any compatibility issues.

 Note: To access the Compatibility Center, visit **www.microsoft.com/windows/ compatibility/windows-7/en-US/.**

Network Compatibility Considerations

As part of the hardware compatibility check, you should verify that drivers are available for the existing network adapter card that are compatible with the new version of Windows.

Application Compatibility Modes

The Windows XP application compatibility modes are Windows 95, Windows® 98/Windows® Me, Windows NT® 4.0, Windows 2000, 256 colors, and 640 x 480 screen resolution. You can set the appropriate mode for a particular application by running the **Program Compatibility** wizard from Windows XP **Help and Support Center.** See the article "Windows XP Application Compatibility Technologies" at **www.microsoft.com/technet/prodtechnol/winxppro/plan/ appcmpxp.mspx** for more information.

The Windows 7 application compatibility modes are Windows 95, Windows 98/Windows Me, Windows NT 4.0 (Service Pack 5), Windows 2000, Windows XP (Service Pack 2), and Windows Server® 2003 (Service Pack 1). You can set the appropriate mode for a particular application by right-clicking the program's executable, choosing **Properties,** selecting the **Compatibility** tab, and then choosing the desired OS from the drop-down list.

Macintosh Software Compatibility

Applications that ran in previous releases of Mac OS X should be supported when you upgrade to any current release.

If you need to use Mac OS 9 applications on a Mac OS X system, you can do so in the Classic environment in Mac OS X. To use the Classic environment, you must have a Mac OS 9 System Folder installed on your computer, either on the same hard disk as Mac OS X, or on another disk or disk partition. For more information on Mac OS X technical specifications, see **http:// support.apple.com/specs#macos.**

Apple also provides tools to enable IBM® PC users to transfer files and software when migrating from an IBM Windows PC to a Macintosh. For more information on moving from Windows to Macintosh, see **www.apple.com/macosx/compatibility/.**

Linux Software Compatibility

Check your Linux vendor's website and read the technical documentation for the distribution of Linux you plan to upgrade to in order to determine if your existing applications will be supported under the new version. You can also check the resources at **www.linux.org/apps** for lists of Linux-compatible applications in various categories from a number of vendors. You can also register as a user at **www.linux.org/user** and post questions about particular applications in the online user forums.

ACTIVITY 6-4
Discussing Windows Upgrades

Scenario

In this activity, you will discuss Windows upgrades.

1. **When is the best time to use an in-place upgrade?**
   - ○ Upgrading from Windows XP Professional to Windows 7 Professional.
   - ○ Upgrading from Windows Vista Home to Windows 7 Starter.
   - ○ Upgrading from Windows Vista Business to Windows 7 Professional

2. **Where can you go to find out if your hardware and software will work properly if you upgrade to Windows 7?**

3. **Have you had experience with upgrading operating systems, either at home or at work? Share your experiences with the rest of the participants.**

TOPIC D

Windows Optimization and Preventive Maintenance

In the previous topics, you installed, configured, and upgraded Microsoft® Windows®. Once the system has been installed, you will need to maintain it on an ongoing basis and set up some basic preventive maintenance procedures to keep the system running. In this topic, you will identify preventive maintenance tools and techniques.

Maintaining an operating system might not seem as exciting or interesting as performing a new installation or replacing a hard disk, but it is actually one of the most crucial tasks for a support technician. System maintenance is important for two reasons; first, proper maintenance can prevent system problems from arising. Second, proper maintenance of the system, including the creation of appropriate backups, can make recovery or troubleshooting operations much easier in the event that problems do arise. As an A+ technician, you can use the skills and information in this topic to perform preventive maintenance as part of your ongoing job tasks.

This topic covers all or part of the following CompTIA® A+® (2012) certification objectives:

*   Exam 220–802: Objective 1.7: Perform preventive maintenance procedures using appropriate tools.

Virtual Memory

Using *virtual memory* is a way for the computer to accomplish more than the limits of what its physical memory can perform. The computer system uses a portion of the hard disk as if it was physical RAM. When all physical memory is filled, the OS can transfer some of the least-recently-used data from memory to a file on the hard disk called the *pagefile,* thereby freeing up an equivalent amount of space in main RAM for other purposes. When the original data is needed again, the next least-recently-used data is moved out of RAM onto the hard drive to make room to reimport the needed data. In Windows systems, the *Virtual Memory Manager* (VMM) manages the memory mappings and assignments.

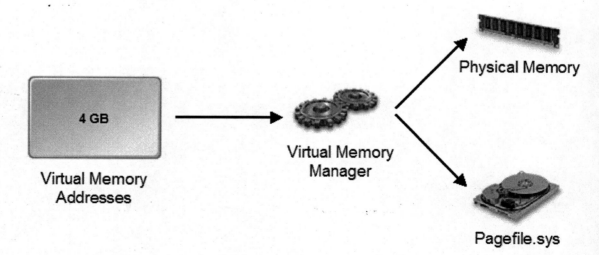

Figure 6–7: Virtual memory.

Virtual Memory and RAM Speed

Virtual memory is not nearly as fast as actual memory. Modern SDRAM DIMMs read/write speeds are measured in nanoseconds, whereas hard drive seek, read, and write times are measured in milliseconds. If your computer is frequently exceeding its physical RAM and having to resort to using a pagefile on disk, adding more physical RAM may be the most economic way of effecting a noticeable change in performance.

The Virtual Memory Process

When data is stored in virtual memory:

1. An application loads and requests memory from the system.
2. The VMM assigns it a *page* of memory addresses from within the virtual memory space.
3. The application stores information in one or more of the virtual memory locations.
4. The VMM maps the virtual address the application uses to a physical location in RAM.
5. As physical RAM becomes full, the VMM moves inactive data from memory to the pagefile in a process called *paging* or *swapping*.

When data is retrieved from virtual memory:

1. An application requests data from its virtual memory location.
2. The VMM determines which physical RAM location was mapped to this virtual memory address.
3. If the VMM finds that the data is not present in the RAM location, it generates an interrupt called a *page fault*.
4. The VMM locates the data in the pagefile, retrieves the data from the hard disk, loads it back into RAM, and updates the virtual-to-physical address mapping for the application. If necessary, the VMM swaps other data out of RAM to release space.
5. The application retrieves the data from RAM.

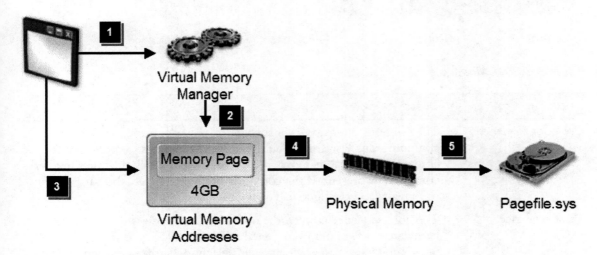

Figure 6–8: Storing and retrieving virtual memory data.

Pagefile Optimization

When you install Windows, the system automatically creates a pagefile named Pagefile.sys at the root of the drive. The size of the pagefile varies within a range determined by the pagefile's initial size value and maximum size value. The system sets the size values of the pagefile using an algorithm that takes into account the amount of physical memory and the space available on the disk. When the system starts, the pagefile is set to the initial size; if more virtual memory space is needed, the system adds it to the pagefile until it reaches the maximum size. An administrator can alter the initial and maximum size values to optimize the pagefile and virtual memory performance. In modern systems, there is rarely a severe shortage of either physical RAM or disk space, so optimizing the pagefile might not be an issue, but you can consider the following tips:

- Although Microsoft recommends an initial pagefile size of 1.5 times the amount of RAM, the more RAM you have, the smaller a pagefile you need.
- If the initial size of the pagefile is too low, the system will waste time as it adds more space to the pagefile. Adding space to the pagefile after startup also increases disk fragmentation. Consequently, it is often a good idea to set the initial size to the same value as the maximum size. If the initial size is too high, however, the pagefile will be mostly empty, which wastes disk space.
- If you get a lot of "low virtual memory" errors, increase the maximum size of the pagefile.
- If you have multiple drives, you can move the pagefile off the drive that contains the Windows system files, so that the computer can access system files and pagefile information simultaneously. Put the pagefile on the fastest drive that does not contain Windows.
- If there is not a noticeable speed difference between drives, create additional pagefiles on multiple drives. This speeds access time because the system can read and write from multiple drives simultaneously. However, there is no performance advantage to putting the pagefile on different partitions on the same disk.

 Access the Checklist tile on your LogicalCHOICE course screen for reference information and job aids on How to Optimize Virtual Memory

The Windows Boot Process

There are five major sequences that occur during the Windows boot process.

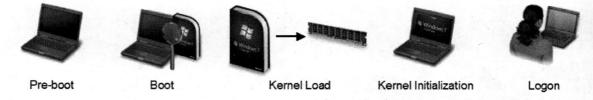

Pre-boot   Boot   Kernel Load   Kernel Initialization   Logon

Figure 6–9: The Windows boot process.

Sequence	Description
Pre-boot sequence	The pre-boot sequence begins when the power is turned on. The computer runs Power-On Self Test (POST) routines to determine the amount of physical memory and to identify and check the other hardware components present. If the computer has a PnP BIOS, the hardware is recognized and configured. The comp
Boot sequence	The boot sequence is when the operating system is selected, and the hardware configuration is detected and loaded. It has four subphases: initial boot loader, operating system selection, hardware detection, and configuration selection. In Windows 7, this is accomplished by the winload.exe and Windows Boot Manager components. In Windows XP and earlier operating systems that use the NT kernel, this was done with NTLDR (NT Loader) and the boot.ini file.
Kernel load sequence	During the kernel load sequence, the operating system components are loaded into memory.

Sequence	Description
Kernel initiation sequence	In the kernel initiation sequence, the Windows kernel takes control of the system. At this point, the Microsoft Windows logo appears, along with a status bar.
Logon sequence	During the logon sequence, Winlogon.exe starts the Local Security Authority (LSA), and the **Logon** screen or **Logon** dialog box appears. Users can now log on, while Windows continues to load low-level drivers and services in the background. The boot process is considered complete when a user successfully logs on. The Clone control set built is copied to a new control set called LastKnownGood, thus preserving a copy of the settings in the successful boot sequence.

Windows XP Startup Settings and the Boot.ini File

Boot.ini is a text file stored in the root of the Windows system partition. In some editions of Windows, it may be hidden or read-only. It has been replaced in Windows 7 and Windows Vista by the Boot Configuration Editor, but is used in all other NT kernel-based Windows operating systems. The Boot.ini file has two functions: to store the load paths to the operating system or systems installed on the computer, and, if there are multiple operating systems installed, to build and display the **Please Select The Operating System To Start** menu during the boot process. (Note that it is uncommon to boot multiple operating systems on a single computer, and therefore it is seldom necessary to edit the startup settings in Boot.ini to optimize boot performance on multi-boot systems. Currently, a more common way to host multiple operating systems on a single physical system is to employ virtualization technologies such as VMware® or Microsoft Virtual PC.)

 Note: The **Please Select The Operating System To Start** menu is also known as the **Boot Loader** menu and the **OS Choices** menu.

There are two sections in the Boot.ini file.

- The [boot loader] section contains the `timeout` parameter, which determines how long the **Please Select The Operating System To Start** menu is displayed. The default value is 30 seconds. It also contains the `default` parameter, which stores the path to the default operating system, which loads if no other operating system is selected.
- The [operating systems] section lists the path to each operating system installed on the computer. Each entry includes descriptive text, which is displayed as the choice for that operating system on the **Please Select The Operating System To Start** menu. The path also includes any special boot switches to use for that operating system. The path to a Windows installation appears in Advanced RISC Computer (ARC) syntax, and tells the system which disk controller, disk, disk partition, and folder contains the operating system.

You can edit the Boot.ini file to change the list of operating systems that appears on the **Please Select The Operating System To Start** menu, adjust the amount of time the menu is displayed, change a boot switch for an operating system, or change the boot partition for an operating system.

- You can edit the file directly by opening it in Notepad.
- You can modify boot settings from the **Advanced** page of the **System Properties** dialog box. Under **Startup And Recovery,** select **Settings.**

Windows 7 and the Boot Configuration Data Editor

In Windows 7, the Boot.ini file was replaced with the Boot Configuration Data Editor (BCD). Instead of editing the Boot.ini file, you can now use the bcdedit.exe command-line tool. BCDedit is located in the %WINDIR%\System32 folder, and requires administrator privileges to use. For information on the bcdedit command, enter `bcdedit /?` in a command window.

Data Backup and Restoration

Data backup is a system maintenance task that enables you to store copies of critical data for safekeeping. Backups protect against loss of data due to disasters such as file corruption or hardware failure. *Data restoration* is a system recovery task that enables you to access the backed-up data. Restored data does not include any changes made to the data after the backup operation. Data backups can be accomplished simply by copying individual files and folders to a local or network location or by using dedicated software and hardware to back up large amounts of data.

Maintenance Tools

There are a number of tools within the Windows environment that can be used to perform preventive maintenance tasks.

Maintenance Tool	Description
Backup Utility (Windows XP)	The Windows Backup Utility, sometimes referred to as NTBackup, was included with Windows XP and earlier versions of the operating system. The Backup Utility is a system tool that can save copies of your data onto recordable optical media or to a network folder, from which you can then restore the data if needed. This tool allows you to use either the Backup and Restore Wizard to quickly and easily create an immediate backup of your data, or use the Advanced Mode to create scheduled backups or restore the data you saved.
	The Backup Utility was not automatically included with installations of Windows XP Home Edition, but can be installed from the installation CD.
Backup and Restore (Windows Vista and Windows 7)	Backup and Restore was introduced with Windows Vista and is included with Windows 7 installations. It is a system utility that allows you to save copies of files, schedule backups, and restore saved files as needed. Backup files are saved as zip files, and can be stored on newer media types including CDs, DVDs, and Blu-ray disc. USB storage devices can be used, but they must be formatted with NTFS.
	Backup and Restore can either save full file backups of all files, incremental file backups of only files that have changed since a previous backup, or a full system image backup.
Check Disk	You can run a Check Disk (or chkdsk if using a command prompt) to scan the hard disk for any potential file system errors or bad sectors on the disk.
	Using Check Disk, you can:
	• Scan only for file system errors and view a report of any drive errors.
	• Scan for file system errors and attempt to automatically fix file system errors.
	• Scan for bad sectors and attempt recovery of the bad sectors.
	• Scan for both file system errors and bad sectors, and attempt to automatically fix both types of problems.
Disk Cleanup	Disk Cleanup is a system utility available in all versions of Windows that frees up space on the hard disk that is being used to store unnecessary temporary files, such as Temporary Internet Files. Disk

Maintenance Tool	Description
	Cleanup scans the hard disk for these temporary files and will remove them with minimal user input.
Disk Defragmenter	*DEFRAG (Disk Defragmenter)* is a system utility available in all versions of Windows that scans and analyzes how file fragments are arranged and accessed on the hard disk. The tool arranges stored data on a disk into contiguous blocks to improve access speed, system startup, and overall system performance. Because individual files are stored on disks in multiple separate blocks, the used and empty storage areas on a disk can become fragmented and scattered. This utility is commonly used in older versions of Windows.
Recovery Image	Once you have your Windows environment installed and configured to your preferences, you can create a recovery image, or a copy of your full system, to use as a backup reference point should your computer ever crash.
	For Windows XP and earlier versions, a third-party disk image program was needed to make a recovery image. With the introduction of the Backup and Restore utility in Windows Vista and Windows 7, you can create a full system image, called the Windows Complete PC Backup image, directly through the utility.
System Restore	System Restore is a system utility included with all versions of Windows that allows you to roll back your computer to a previous state, called a restore point, if the computer is experiencing serious issues, such as a system malfunction or failure. System Restore returns the computer to a more stable state, keeping all of your installed programs, settings, and even recent files intact.
	Though your computer automatically saves restore points, you can use the System Restore utility to forcibly create a restore point. This is helpful and advisable to do if you are going to make a significant change to the system that could result in performance issues, such as installing an application or program.

Note: You can access the Backup Utility in Windows XP from the command line using the `ntbackup.exe` command. For Windows Vista and Windows 7, you can use the command prompt `wbadmin` to perform backup and restore tasks through a command line utility.

Note: There are also many third-party backup utilities available for backing up and restoring data on Windows computers.

Backup Types Supported by Windows Backup

Windows Backup supports a variety of backup types.

Backup Type	Backs Up
Copy	Selected files, without marking them as backed up by clearing the Archive file attribute.
Daily	Files modified the day the backup is performed, without marking them as backed up.
Differential	Files changed since the last normal or incremental backup, without marking them as backed up.

Backup Type	Backs Up
Incremental	Files changed since the last normal or incremental backup, marking them as backed up.
Normal	Selected files, marking them as backed up. (This type of backup is also known as a full backup.)

 Note: For additional information, check out the LearnTO **Perform Preventive Maintenance** in the LearnTOs for this course on your LogicalCHOICE Course screen.

Scheduling Tasks

Many of the preventive maintenance tools included with the Windows environment also provide you with the option of scheduling and automating the tasks they perform. Scheduling preventive maintenance tasks ensures that your data is safe and your computer is performing optimally.

Different organizations and even different administrators within an organization may have differing opinions on what preventive tasks should be performed automatically and how often. There are best practices for any organization or individual user when it comes to performing scheduled tasks.

Scheduled Task	Description
Scheduled backup	Backups should be performed systematically and on a regular basis for the best protection against data loss. For large organizations that have important business data, scheduled backups are likely to be performed nightly for all users or for specific data housed in specific locations, and will be planned and scheduled by IT administrators. For smaller businesses or even individual users, backups can be scheduled to run automatically via the backup utility provided with the version of Windows. Users can choose what information will be saved, how it is saved (full or incremental), where it is saved to, and how often the backup will occur.
Scheduled check disk	Over time, the errors on the hard disk can build up and cause a computer to perform slowly or poorly. Scheduling a check disk to run regularly will keep these errors from accumulating on the hard disk. As with all scheduled tasks, you can choose when and how often the check disk will be performed, but it is recommended that you run the Check Disk utility weekly to scan and resolve any disk errors.
Scheduled disk defragmentation	Your computer automatically breaks large files into fragments and stores them in various locations, only piecing them together when the file is accessed. The more large files you access and are fragmented by Windows, the more fragments accumulate on the hard disk; the more fragments that accumulate on the hard disk, the slower your computer accesses files and processes commands. Scheduling Disk Defragmenter to run automatically and regularly can keep fragmenting to a minimum, optimize the space on the hard disk, and improve the overall performance of your computer. Like all scheduled tasks, you can choose when and how often to defragment the hard disk, but it is recommended that you schedule Disk Defragmenter to run once a week.

Backup Schemes

Most large organizations will implement a structured backup scheme that includes a backup schedule and specifications for which files are backed up, where the backup is stored, and how it can be retrieved. The backup scheme will specify the backup *rotation method*, which determines how many backup tapes or other media sets are needed, and the sequence in which they are used and reused. Designated administrators will have the responsibility for designing and managing the backup scheme and for restoring data when needed.

Patch Management

Patch management is the practice of monitoring for, obtaining, evaluating, testing, and deploying integral fixes and updates for programs or applications, known as *patches*. As the number of computer systems in use has grown over recent years, so has the volume of vulnerabilities and corresponding patches and updates intended to address those vulnerabilities. However, not every computer within an organization will necessarily be compatible with a certain patch, whether it be because of outdated hardware, different software versions, application dependencies, and so on. Because of the inconsistencies that may be present within the various systems, the task of managing and applying patches can become very time-consuming and inefficient without an organized patch management system. In typical patch management, software updates are evaluated for their applicability to an environment and then tested in a safe way on non-production systems. If the patch is validated on all possible configurations without causing more problems, only then will the valid patch be rolled out to all computers throughout the entire organization.

A patch management program might include:

- An individual responsible for subscribing to and reviewing vendor and security patches and updating newsletters.
- A review and triage of the updates into urgent, important, and non-critical categories.
- An offline patch-test environment where urgent and important patches can be installed and tested for functionality and impact.
- Immediate administrative push delivery of approved urgent patches.
- Weekly administrative push delivery of approved important patches.
- A periodic evaluation phase and full rollout for non-critical patches.

Patch Management Policies

Many organizations have taken to creating official patch management policies that define the who, what, where, when, why, and how of patch management for that organization.

Managing Updates

Managing updates is an important part of preventive maintenance, to ensure that all computers under your care are up to date with the most current software or applications available. Having a plan in place for how you will manage updates will help to make sure that your computers are protected against all of the possible threats, vulnerabilities, and functionality issues that arise as the technologies evolve and change.

How an organization or individual chooses to manage updates as part of preventive maintenance will vary depending on needs or personal preferences. There are, however, some best practices to follow when it comes to managing updates, especially for integral components of the computer system.

- Windows updates: Updates released from Microsoft should be tested and implemented on a test machine before rolling out to user computers.
- Driver/firmware updates: Driver and firmware manufacturers often develop updates to address known functionality issues. By updating device drivers and firmware, you can avoid many potential operational problems.

- Antivirus updates: All anti-virus updates from the manufacturer should be installed automatically on all company computers and devices to protect against the latest security threats and vulnerabilities.

 Access the Checklist tile on your LogicalCHOICE course screen for reference information and job aids on How to Perform Preventive Maintenance

ACTIVITY 6-5
Performing Preventive Maintenance

Scenario

You have been refurbishing a PC for a user, and you are just about ready to return the computer to its owner. Before you release it, however, you decide to ensure optimal performance by cleaning up the primary hard disk, creating a restore point, and scheduling disk defragmentation.

---

1. Run the **Disk Cleanup** utility on the primary hard disk.
    a) Select **Start→All Programs→Accessories→System Tools→Disk Cleanup.**
    b) When you are prompted as to which disk you want to clean up, select the **C** drive and select **OK.**
        Disk Cleanup automatically begins scanning the disk to determine the free space.
    c) When the scan is complete, examine the information in the **Disk Cleanup for (C:)** dialog box. View the amount of free space Disk Cleanup can provide and view the files to be deleted.
    d) If necessary, check and clear dialog boxes until only **Downloaded Program Files, Temporary Internet Files, Temporary Files,** and **Recycle Bin** are selected. Select **OK.**
    e) When you are prompted to confirm the cleanup action, select **Delete Files.**
        When the cleanup operation is complete, **Disk Cleanup** closes automatically.

2. Create a restore point.
    a) In the **Start** menu, right-click **Computer** and select **Properties.**
        The **Control Panel→All Control Panel Items→System** window opens.
    b) In the left pane, select **System protection.**
        The **System Properties** window opens.
    c) Select the **System Protection** tab, and select **Create.**
    d) For the description of the restore point, type *Second drive added* and then select **Create.**
    e) When you are notified that the restore point was successfully created, select **Close** and then select **OK.**
    f) Close the open **Control Panel** window.

3. Schedule disk defragmentation for every Monday at 5 pm.
    a) Select **Start→All Programs→Accessories→System Tools→Disk Defragmenter.**
    b) Select **Configure schedule.**
    c) In the **Disk Defragmenter: Modify Schedule** dialog box, adjust the settings so that **Frequency** is **Weekly, Day** is **Monday, Time** is **5:00 PM,** and **Disks** is set to defragment all disks.
    d) Select **OK.**
    e) Select **OK** and then select **Close.**

Summary

In this lesson, you installed and configured operating systems. Whether you are upgrading, installing from scratch, or redeploying a system, you will need the skills that enable you to install, configure, and optimize computer operating systems to meet your business needs.

Do you have experience installing operating systems? Do you feel you will be able to perform installations more efficiently as a result of the information presented in this lesson?

How often do you expect to be able to perform in-place upgrades instead of clean installs at your workplace?

 Note: Check your LogicalCHOICE Course screen for opportunities to interact with your classmates, peers, and the larger LogicalCHOICE online community about the topics covered in this course or other topics you are interested in. From the Course screen you can also access available resources for a more continuous learning experience.

7 Customized Client Environments

Lesson Time: 45 minutes

Lesson Objectives

In this lesson, you will identify the hardware and software requirements for client environment configurations. You will:

- Identify the requirements of a standard client.

- Identify the hardware and software needs for custom computing environments.

Lesson Introduction

At this point in the course, you have identified the different components that make up a standard workstation, and the operating systems available for installation. With this information, you are ready to take a look at the hardware needs and requirements for different client configurations. In this lesson, you will identify the different hardware and software needs based on job tasks and functions.

As an A+ technician, you must be knowledgeable in many different areas of information technology. This may include supporting a wide variety of client configurations, such as gaming, audio and video workstations. You must be prepared to fully support any type of environment including more specialized hardware and software configurations based on job roles and tasks.

This lesson covers all or part of the following CompTIA® A+® (2012) certification objectives:

- Topic A:
  - Exam 220–801: Objective 1.9
- Topic B:
  - Exam 220–801: Objective 1.9

TOPIC A

Standard Clients

Now that you have identified the main components of a personal computer, you can start to take a look at what requirements are needed to install and configure a standard client. In this topic, you will identify the hardware and software needs to install a thin client, a thick client, or virtualization workstation.

When installing and configuring user workstations, it is important to identify what the specific needs are of the user that will be using the workstation to perform job tasks. Standard clients are a good starting point for any installation and must be examined to verify that it fits the requirements of the job function.

This topic covers all or part of the following CompTIA® A+® (2012) certification objectives:

• Exam 220–801: Objective 1.9: Evaluate and select appropriate components for a custom configuration, to meet customer specifications or needs.

What is a Standard Client?

Standard clients are user-end computers that are administered and managed centrally by a server. Clients will typically include various hardware features and applications that suit the specific needs of the user. Client machines are generally referred to as either thin or thick, depending on the requirements. A *thin client* is a system that relies heavily on another system, typically a server, to run most of its programs, processes and services. On the other hand, a *thick client,* also referred to as a fat client, performs most or all computing functions on its own.

Client Requirements

Client setup requirements will be specific to a user's needs and will most likely be based on a job role. There are however general requirements for each type of client:

Thin Client Requirements	Thick Client Requirements
The system must meet the minimum requirements to run a Windows operating system.	The system must meet the standard requirements for running a Windows operating system.
The system uses basic applications that can be accessed over the Internet. The applications do not get installed on the computer and do not use up any hard drive space. RAM is used to run the application from the server.	Full application versions are installed and run directly from the client machine using its own resources. The applications are installed using traditional methods and are stored on the hard drive.
Must have a fast network connection to access the server that is hosting the applications.	If data is stored locally, then access to storage locations is a required with a consistent pathway to data.
Might require specialized software in order to access the applications hosted by the server.	If data is stored on the network, then a consistent path should be established to the storage location with proper security implementations.
May require a specific browser in order to run any web-based applications.	Hardware should be robust enough to run all required applications.

Virtualization Workstation

A virtualization workstation is a system that utilizes both hardware virtualization and client virtualization resources to provide a single virtualized workstation for users. The virtualized workstation is configured to use the system's hardware functions such as access to the graphics card, Random Access Memory (RAM), and Network Interface Card's (NIC's), as well as run the software that provides multiple virtual machines (VMs). Organizations may use virtualization workstations to reduce the use and cost of hardware and to provide employees with a wide variety of OS specific applications from a single workstation. Virtualization provides users with a variety of applications and resources by offering multiple platforms within a single system.

Common virtualization workstation software offerings include:

* VMWare®: **http://www.vmware.com/**
* Oracle®'s VirtualBox: **https://www.virtualbox.org/**
* Microsoft®'s Virtual PC: **http://www.microsoft.com/windows/virtual-pc/**
* Microsoft's Hyper-V® hypervisor (running on the server)

Virtualization Workstation Requirements

Virtualization software vendors will all have specific hardware and system requirements based on their actual software needs, but in most cases will require a virtualization workstation to have:

* The maximum RAM the motherboard can support.
* Maximum central processing unit (CPU) cores.
* Virtualization operating system (OS) if the local personal computer (PC) will be the VM host or virtualization client software installed on the PC if the VM is hosted on a server.
* Fast network connection for server-side VM hosting.

ACTIVITY 7-1
Identifying Standard Client Components

Scenario

You have been asked by your manager to evaluate the hardware and software needs for all the clients within the Human Resources (HR) department of your organization. There was a recent reorganization of the department and some of the job roles and functions have changed. Based on the recent changes, you need to review the job functions and identify what type of client workstation will meet those needs.

1. The manager of the Human Resources department needs to be able to access the central employee data repository to run reports, but will not need access to the data entry application used to create, edit, and manage the employee data. The employee data is managed on a server that can be accessed with a log in. What type of client is best in this case?

   ○ Thin client

   ○ Virtualization workstation

   ○ Thick client

2. June has recently been put in charge of making updates to the Human Resource employee benefits website. She will be publishing a monthly newsletter and posting company wide announcements, among other small updates and changes on a regular basis. All changes to the website must be tested on a number of platforms and web browsers to verify that the changes are correct regardless of the operating system and browser. What type of client setup would you suggest for her?

3. In order to properly support the HR employee benefits website, a new server running client VMs has been installed so that the environment that the application requires can be strictly administered by IT staff. Current PCs will be used to access the Client VM environment that is configured on the VM Server. What needs to be present at all PCs that will be accessing this new server and application??

   ☐ Appropriately configured VM Client.

   ☐ Fast network connection to server hosting the VM environment.

   ☐ Upgrade to video cards.

4. True or False? The HR manager's client computer must meet the recommended requirements to run Windows 7 so that she can access and use all of the HR related applications used by the organization. In this case, the best client option is a thick client.

   ☐ True

   ☐ False

TOPIC B

Custom Client Environments

The next logical step in examining custom computing environments, is to take a closer look at some of the more specialized environments based on a specific function. In this topic, you will identify the hardware and software needs for various custom computing environments.

There are a wide variety of job functions within the job force, and you may find yourself having to support more specialized computer hardware and software installations. This may include media, audio, and even home entertainment systems. As an A+ technician, you must have the knowledge to provide support in any computing environment.

This topic covers all or part of the following CompTIA® A+® (2012) certification objectives:

* Exam 220–801: Objective 1.9: Evaluate and select appropriate components for a custom configuration, to meet customer specifications or needs.

Media Design Workstations

Media design workstations are configured to support the needs of graphic designers, Engineers, architects, 3D media developers, and other design driven job roles. The workstation's hardware and software needs will be dependent on the specific programs and computing tasks required by the job role.

Figure 7-1: A media design workstation.

Media Design Workstation Requirements

Media design workstations require a specific set of requirements. Actual hardware and software requirements will depend on the user's specific job role and function, but most media design workstations will require a similar set of tools and components.

Common hardware components include:

* A powerful processor.
* A high-end video/graphics card with integrated *Graphics Processing Unit (GPU)*.
* Large flat panel display, or multiple monitors.
* Maximum RAM supported by the motherboard and CPU.

Common software applications include:

* Adobe's Creative Suite.
* 3D Studio Max.

- Computer aided design (CAD) programs.
- SharePoint.

GPUs

The GPU (graphics processing unit) is an electronic circuitry unit that alters and controls the memory of a computer to meet the immediate needs of rapidly changing computer graphics and detailed visual images displayed on the display device. There are a number of ways GPUs are implemented within a computing device depending on the specific needs of the user and applications. Most modern PCs, laptops, and some mobile devices come with a GPU already installed on either the motherboard or the CPU. The most powerful GPUs are considered to be high-end specialized units that come already installed on the video card and have various output methods and capturing devices.

CAD Design Workstations

CAD workstations are unique in that they require both the hardware and the software on a system to meet certain requirements to produce complex 3D designs. CAD workstations require a high-end graphics card and monitor, and specialized input devices such as, a digitizing tablet and light pen. Industries that use CAD created design specifications include the automotive companies, aerospace, and architectural firms.

CAM Design Workstations

Computer aided manufacturing workstations are a type of workstation that is set up with specific hardware and software that can control machine tools found in manufacturing environments. Specialized controller cards may be required as well as specialized connections and software. CAM machines may be installed in harsh environments—such as manufacturing buildings and automotive factories—so the environments may need to be hardened machines that will not be aversely affected by harsh working environments.

Audio/Video Editing Workstations

An *audio/video editing workstation* is a powerful computer setup that supports editing of audio and video recordings. These systems must be able to support the demanding editing programs that audio/video technicians use in post production editing functions. Most professional videos taken today include special effects and CGI (computer generated imagery) that is all applied after the digital video is taken. Common applications found on an audio/video editing workstation include:

- Sony's Vegas Pro.
- Apple's iMovie.
- WavePad.
- Corel's VideoStudio Pro X5.
- Adobe's Premiere Elements.
- AVS Audio Editor.
- MAGIX Movie Edit Pro and Music Maker.
- CyberLink's PowerDirector.

Figure 7-2: An audio/video editing workstation.

Audio Video Editing Hardware Requirements

The hardware and software requirements for each individual audio/video editing workstation will differ depending on what specific tasks the job role will need to do. Most stations will require the following hardware components:

- A specialized audio and video card to support CGI and 3D post production effects.
- A large fast hard drive.
- A high-end general processing unit (GPU).
- Large flat panel or multiple displays.

Gaming PCs

A *gaming PC* is a computer that comes equipped with powerful graphics capabilities, fast processing capabilities and a large amount of memory. The main difference between a gaming PC and other consumer workstations is that they are specifically designed and built to support the demanding computing requirements by gaming software applications. All gaming PCs will require a high-end GPU to support the detailed 3D graphics and realistic imagery presented in PC games today. Gaming platforms are also popular today and provide gamers with a number of application options, message boards, and files sharing via an online portal, such as Steam™ and Origins™.

Figure 7–3: A gaming PC.

Popular gaming software applications include:

- Diablo® III
- StarCraft® II: Heart of the Swarm
- Dota™ 2
- Guild Wars® II

Gaming PC Requirements

There is such a wide variety of gaming software applications, so each gaming PC will have specific requirements based on the needs of the user and the applications used. Gaming PC's require very specific components in order to support the demands of gaming software. Common requirements include:

- A powerful processor.
- A high-end video/specialized GPU unit.
- A high quality sound card.
- High-end cooling such as a water cooling system.
- Maximum RAM that is supported by the motherboard.
- Fast Internet connection for interactive gaming needs.
- Real-time video and audio input/output capabilities.
- In some cases, HDMI output.

Gaming Peripherals

There are many different peripherals used within the gaming world. The most common ones include the mouse and keyboard, but there are others that may be used depending on the type of game played:

* Gaming mice that are wireless and include many buttons and different ergonomic form factors.
* Customized keypads, with moveable keys.
* Steering wheels used for auto racing games.
* 3D glasses.
* Specialized gaming mouse pads.
* Specialized audio system.
* PC video camera.

Home Theater PC

A *home theater PC (HTPC)* is a computer system that is dedicated and configured to store and stream digital movies, either from the local hard drive or through an online subscription such as Netflix. Other capabilities include connecting and managing surround sound audio and speakers and DVR, or digital recording functions. The HTPC is usually equipped with specific entertainment software that can be used to manage the music and video files stored on the computer. The PCs are generally located near the TV and other home entertainment devices and have a HTPC form factor, which is aesthetically appealing and designed to look similar to other home entertainment devices. They are also designed to be less noisy that a traditional PC, with more compact quieter cooling methods and the addition of sound dampening foam or padding to limit excessive noise generated by the fan and hard drive.

Figure 7-4: A home theater PC.

Home Theater PC Requirements

Home Theater Personal Computers (HTPCs) are built specifically for home theater purposes, so most of the required elements are built right into the actual system. They generally include:

* A TV tuner card that allows the computer to display high-definition (HD) digital output and attach the cable provider's cable TV wire directly to the system.
* A cable card, that provides authentication and encryption services to connect with the cable set top box provided by the cable company.
* Optical disk player that supports both DVD and Blu-ray.
* Maximum RAM supported by the motherboard.
* Video card with both GPU and HD capabilities.

• Bluetooth® or wireless capabilities when using specialized remotes or input devices.

Movie Players

There are a number of software applications available for playing HD movies on a HTPC including:

• Cyberlink PowerDVD.
• XBMC Media Center.
• Windows Media Center.
• Boxee.

Home Server PC

A home server PC is a server for your house that is connected to multiple computing devices within the home to store videos, music, and pictures. It also provides central access to all stored files and is often used for file and print sharing with other computing devices in the home. The home setup generally includes a wireless network that all devices can connect to provided by a home wireless router. This allows any device to access the server within the home.

Figure 7–5: A home server.

Home Server Requirements

Each home server PC will have a variety of features and functions, but when it comes to requirements they all have common requirements for providing a home with necessary functions:

• Media streaming capabilities to access and play digital movies.
• File sharing for all home users to access the file system on the server.
• Print sharing.
• A gigabit NIC to provide the speeds necessary to perform large file transfers over the wireless network.
• Router that is compatible with the gigabit speed required by the NIC in the server.
• Redundant Array of Independent Disks (RAID) array to provide redundancy.

ACTIVITY 7-2
Selecting a Custom Client Configuration

Scenario

You are a support technician for a local business that specializes in consulting, purchasing and installing home computing solutions for consumers. You are responsible for fulfilling all the orders that have come in overnight through the business' website.

1. Customer 1 is using a desktop PC to play home movies and to set up slide shows to show his family their vacation photos and is having difficulty with the computer freezing during the movies. He is looking for a solution that will allow him to store and play his movies seamlessly through a computer. He also wants his wife to be able to access the pictures and movies from her laptop within the house. What type of computer setup would you suggest for this customer? What specific questions might you ask this customer about additional component needs?

2. Customer 2 is from a small real estate office who has recently hired a Graphic Designer to produce informational pamphlets and other marketing materials for the agency such as, property drop sheets and circular layout designs. The office manager has asked your company to determine the hardware and software needs for the designer's workstation so that it can be ordered and set up before their scheduled start date in two weeks. What hardware and software requirement you would suggest for the Graphic Designer's workstation?

3. Customer 3 is looking to make the switch from a traditional cable box, DVD player to a home theater PC, so that she can stream Netflix and DVR shows and movies from her TV. She already purchased a HTPC from a local home entertainment store but cannot figure out how why she cannot connect the cable TV wire into the HTPC. What required component might be missing that would enable her to make the connection?

Summary

In this lesson, you identified all the different components needed to provide a custom computer setup that is based on specific user needs. There is a wide variety of job functions within the corporate world today, so identifying specific hardware and software needs based on a users job role will only help you in providing the right level of support within your organization.

Have you had any experience with any of the workstation or server setups presented in this lesson?

What types of custom client setups do you think you will encounter the most in your role as an A+ technician?

 Note: Check your LogicalCHOICE Course screen for opportunities to interact with your classmates, peers, and the larger LogicalCHOICE online community about the topics covered in this course or other topics you are interested in. From the Course screen you can also access available resources for a more continuous learning experience.

8 | Networking Technologies

Lesson Time: 3 hours, 15 minutes

Lesson Objectives

In this lesson, you will identify network technologies. You will:

- Identify the fundamental components that make up a computer network.

- Identify the properties and characteristics of TCP/IP.

- Identify network connectivity technologies.

- Examine common ports and protocols.

- Set up and configure Windows networking.

- Examine networking tools.

Lesson Introduction

In this course, you are learning to support a wide range of computing device features and functions. A key factor in device communication is how they are connected and how they transfer data to one another. In this lesson, you will identify a number of networking technologies.

Just about very digital device on the planet today is connected to external resources via some kind of network, whether it is a small office/home office network, a corporate wide area network (WAN), or directly to the Internet itself. The ability to connect, share, and communicate using a network is crucial for running a business and staying connected to everything in the world, so as an A+ support technician, you will need to understand the technologies that underlie both local and global network communications to ensure that the organization you support stays connected.

This lesson covers all or part of the following CompTIA® A+® (2012) certification objectives:

- Topic A:
  - Exam 220–801: Objectives 1.7, 1.11, 2.1, 2.2
- Topic B:
  - Exam 220–801: Objectives 2.3, 2.4

- Topic C:
  - Exam 220–801: Objectives 2.7, 2.8, 2.9
- Topic D:
  - Exam 220–801: Objective 2.4
- Topic E:
  - Exam 220–802: Objective 1.6
- Topic F:
  - Exam 220–801: Objective 2.10

TOPIC A

Physical Network Connections

In this lesson, you will identify various networking technologies. In order to do so, you will need to understand a few basic concepts and the connections used to implement computer networks and their components. In this topic, you will identify the physical network connections that make up most computer networks.

No matter what types of networks you support in your professional career, they will all share some fundamental characteristics as well as basic physical components. As a computer support technician, dealing with these components will need to be as natural to you as handling a scalpel is to a surgeon. The information in this topic will familiarize you with the physical network connections and components that you will deal with on a daily basis as a support technician.

This topic covers all or part of the following CompTIA® A+® (2012) certification objectives:

- Exam 220–801: Objective 1.7: Compare and contrast various connection interfaces and explain their purpose.
- Exam 220–801: Objective 1.11: Identify connector types and associated cables.
- Exam 220–801: Objective 2.1: Identify types of network cables and connectors.
- Exam 220–801: Objective 2.2: Categorize characteristics of connectors and cabling.
- Exam 220–801: Objective 2.4: Explain common TCP and UPD ports, protocols, and their purpose.

Networks

A *network* is a group of connected computers that communicate and share resources such as files, printers, Internet connections, and databases. Whether wired or wireless, most networks will include network media, such as a cable to carry network data; network adapter hardware to translate the data between the computer and the network media; an operating system to enable the computer to recognize the network; and a network protocol to control the network communication. All these components work together to enable a fully functioning computer network. Any computing device that will communicate with a network will also include a *network interface card (NIC)* that is usually built into most devices. Older devices may require an adapter card that can be inserted into an expansion port or slot.

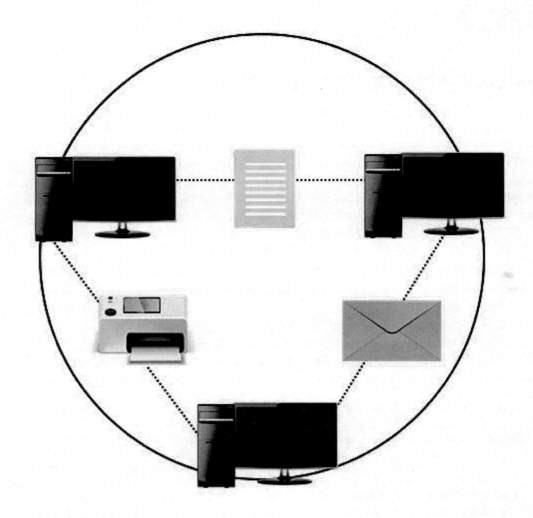

Figure 8-1: A network.

Network Models

There are two primary network models, which are design specifications for how the computers and other *nodes* on a network can interact.

Network Model	Description
Client-server	A *client/server network* is a network in which computer functionality is divided into two roles: *server* computers, which provide services and control network operations, and *client* computers, which use the services provided by the servers. Typically, there is at least one server providing central authentication services. Servers also provide access to shared files, printers, hardware, and applications. In client/server networks, processing power, management services, and administrative functions can be concentrated where needed, while clients can still perform many basic end-user tasks on their own. Microsoft® Windows Servers® support a client/server network type known as a domain.
Peer-to-peer	A *peer-to-peer network* is a network in which resource sharing, processing, and communications control are completely decentralized. All clients on the network are equal in terms of providing and using resources, and users are authenticated by each individual workstation. Peer-to-peer networks are easy and inexpensive to implement. However, they are practical only in very small organizations, due

Network Model	Description
	to the lack of central data storage and administration. In a peer-to-peer network, user accounts must be duplicated on every workstation from which a user accesses resources. Such distribution of user information makes maintaining peer-to-peer networks difficult, especially as the network grows. Consequently, peer-to-peer networks should not exceed 10 computers. A Windows® workgroup is an example of a peer-to-peer network.

Network Interface Card Characteristics

Network interface cards have some special characteristics that distinguish them from other types of adapter cards.

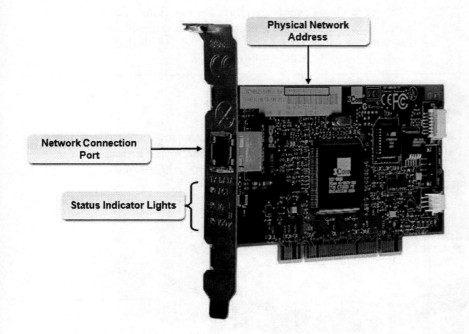

Figure 8-2: A network interface card.

Network interface card characteristics are described in the following table.

Characteristic	Description
Network connection port	Network adapter cards will have one or more ports that are configured to connect specifically to a given type of network cable. Some older cards had several types of ports so that they could connect to several different types of network cable. Network connections today are standardized and almost all use one port type.
Physical network address	Each network adapter has a globally unique *physical address* burned onto the card by the card manufacturer. The physical address uniquely identifies every individual card that connects to the network cable or media. For this reason, the physical address is also called the *Media Access Control (MAC) address*. MAC addresses are six bytes long. A typical MAC address might appear as **00-00-86-47-F6-65,** where the first three bytes are the vendor's unique ID and the next three uniquely identify that card for its vendor.

Characteristic	Description
Status indicator lights	Network adapters, including those built into most network devices, typically have one or more light emitting diode (LED) status lights that can provide information on the state of the network connection.

- Most adapters have a *link light* that indicates if there is a signal from the network. If the link light is not lit, there is generally a problem with the cable or the physical connection.
- Most adapters also have an *activity light* that flickers when packets are received or sent. If the light flickers constantly, the network might be overused or there might be a device generating network noise.
- Some multi-speed adapters have a *speed light* to show whether the adapter is operating at 10 Mbps (Ethernet), 100 Mbps (Fast Ethernet), or 1000 Mbps (Gigabit Ethernet).
- Some types of equipment combine the functions of more than one light into dual-color LEDs. For example, a green flickering light might indicate normal activity, while an orange flickering light indicates network traffic collisions.

Twisted Pair Cables

Twisted pair is a type of cable in which four pairs of insulated conductors are twisted around each other in pairs and clad in a protective and insulating outer jacket. There may be multiple pairs depending on the type and size of cabling. Shielding can be added around the bundle of twisted pairs to reduce electronic interference.

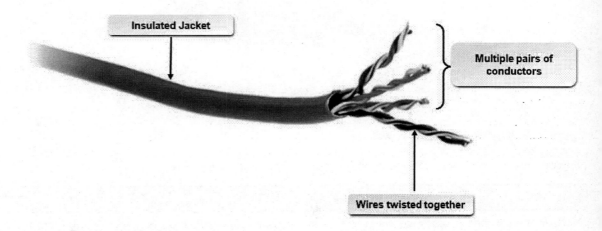

Figure 8-3: Twisted pair cable.

Types of Twisted Pair Cable

Twisted pair cable comes in two basic types: unshielded twisted pair (UTP) and shielded twisted pair (STP). As the name implies, STP includes shielding, typically a foil wrapper, around its conductors to improve the cable's resistance to interference and noise. It tends to be more expensive than UTP and is installed only when needed.

UTP cable comes in different grades, called categories, which support different network speeds and technologies. A cable's category is typically printed on the cable itself, making identification easy.

Category	Network Type and Maximum Speed
CAT 3	• Network Type: Telephone or Ethernet • Maximum speed: 10 Mbps CAT 3 is currently used for telephone wiring
CAT 5	• Network Type: Fast Ethernet Maximum speed: CAT 5 supports a signaling rate up to 100 Mbps
CAT 5e	• Network Type: Gigabit Ethernet Maximum speed: CAT 5e supports a signaling rate of 350 Mbps
CAT 6	• Network Type: Gigabit Ethernet • Maximum speed: 1 Gbps CAT 6 supports a signaling rate of 250 MHz
CAT 6a	• Network Type: Gigabit Ethernet • Maximum speed: 1 Gbps CAT 6a supports a signaling rate of 500 MHz
CAT 7	• Network Type: Gigabit Ethernet. • Maximum speed: 1 Gbps+ CAT 7 supports a signaling rate of 1 GHz

PVC Cable vs. Plenum Cabling

Polyvinyl chloride (PVC) is an inexpensive and flexible rubber-like plastic used to surround some twisted pair cabling. However, when PVC burns, it gives off noxious or poisonous gases.

Plenum cable jacketing does not give off noxious or poisonous gases when it burns. Fire codes require that you install this special grade cabling in the *plenum,* which is a building's air handling space between the structural ceiling and any suspended ceiling, under raised floors, and in firebreak walls.

Twisted Pair Connectors

The RJ45 connector is used on twisted pair cable. RJ45 is an eight-position connector that uses all four pairs of wires. Be careful not to confuse the RJ45 connector with the similar, but smaller, RJ11 connector. The RJ11 connector is a six-position connector that uses just one pair of wires. It is used in telephone system connections and is not suitable for network connectivity. The RJ in RJ11 or RJ45 is an abbreviation for "registered jack."

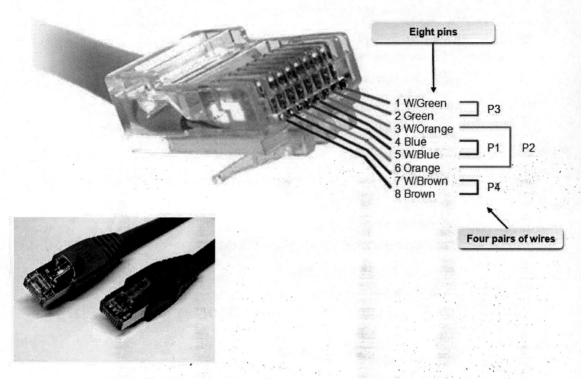

Figure 8–4: Twisted pair connectors.

Twisted Pair Wiring Standards

The *Telecommunications Industry Association (TIA)* and the *Electronic Industries Alliance (EIA)* developed the 568 Commercial Building Telecommunication Cabling standard. This standard defines the regulations on designing, building, and managing a cabling system that utilizes structured cabling according to specified performance characteristics to create a system of unified communications.

TIA/EIA releases recommendations for how network media may best be installed to optimize network performance:

- T568A is a legacy standard that was used in commercial buildings and cabling systems that support data networks, voice, and video. It further defines cable performance and technical requirements.
- T568B defines the standards for preferred cable types that provide the minimum acceptable performance levels including:
    - 100 ohm twisted pair cable.
    - Shielded twisted pair cable.
    - Optical fiber cable.
- T568C is the latest standard released by TIA/EIA that is designed to be used in commercial buildings and in multiple locations and to provide full support for all modern and future communications needs.

Coaxial Cables

Coaxial cable, or *coax*, is a type of copper cable that features a central conductor surrounded by braided or foil shielding. An insulator separates the conductor and shield, and the entire package is wrapped in an insulating layer called a jacket. The data signal is transmitted over the central conductor. The outer shielding serves to reduce electromagnetic interference.

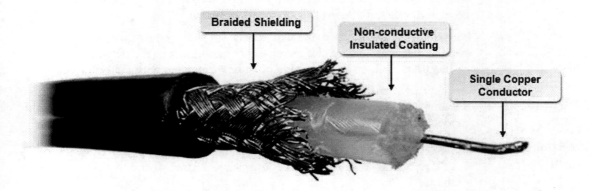

Note: Coaxial cable is so named because the conductor and shield share the central COmmon AXis or are co-axial. This arrangement helps prevent electromagnetic interference from reaching the conductor.

Braided Shielding

Non-conductive Insulated Coating

Single Copper Conductor

Figure 8-5: Coaxial cable.

Coaxial Cable and Connector Types

Coaxial cable comes in various thicknesses that use different connector types.

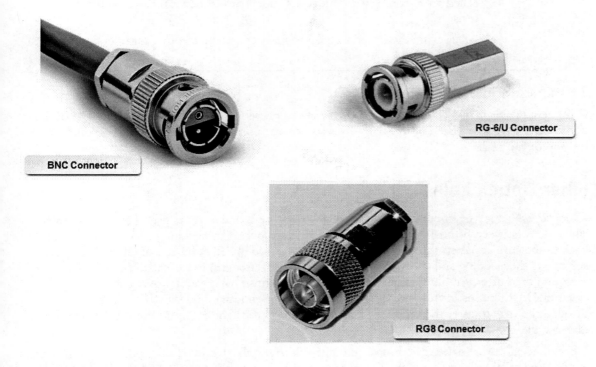

BNC Connector

RG-6/U Connector

RG8 Connector

Figure 8-6: Typical Thinnet connectors.

The different types of coaxial cable are described in the following table.

Coaxial Cable Type	Description
5 mm/0.25 inch ("Thinnet")	RG-58/U and RG-58A/U, also known as thinnet, are older types of media used for networking. RG-59 is used for cable television transmission. The specifications include a maximum transmission speed is 10 Mbps using baseband transmission up to 185 meters in length.
	Thinnet connections are made with a twist-lock connector called a Bayonet Neill-Concelman (BNC) connector. Devices connect to the network with T-connectors. Each end of the cable must be terminated with a 50-ohm resistor.
	Another coax connector type is the *F-connector*, which is used to connect cable TV and FM antenna cables. Today, F-connectors are also used to connect cable modems to the CATV network.
6.91 mm/ 0.35 inch	RG-6/U has been replacing RG-59 in recent years as the preferred cable for CATV networks. Like RG-59, F-connectors are used to connect cable modems to the CATV network.
10 mm/0.5 inch ("Thicknet")	RG8 is a thicker type of coaxial cable often referred to as thicknet. It is seldom seen today due to its expense and stiffness, but was popular at one time as a backbone cable in coaxial network installations. The specifications include a maximum transmission speed is 10 Mbps using baseband transmission up to 500 meters in length.
	Connections between Thicknet segments are made with a screw-type connector called an N-connector. Thicknet segments must be terminated with a 50-ohm resistor.
	A legacy method used to quickly connect a computer to a thicknet wire is called a vampire tap.

[handwritten note: Cable modem]

Termination

Coax network segments typically must be *terminated* to prevent signal reflections off the end of the cable. Cables are terminated by installing a resistor of an appropriate rating, typically 50 ohms, on the end of the cable.

Fiber Optic Cables

Fiber optic cable is a type of network cable in which the core is one or more glass or plastic strands. The core is between 5 and 100 microns thick and is surrounded by cladding, which reflects light back to the core in patterns determined by the transmission mode. A buffer, often made of plastic, surrounds the cladding and core. To add strength (or pull strength) to the cable, strands of Kevlar® surround the buffer. An outer jacket, sometimes called armor, wraps and protects the whole assembly. Light pulses from a laser or high-intensity light-emitting diodes (LEDs) are passed through the core to carry the signal. The cladding reflects the light back into the core, increasing the distance the signal can travel without being regenerated.

Fiber optic cables are expensive, fragile, and difficult to install. However, fiber optic transmissions are fast and reliable over extremely long distances, so they are used frequently in backbone wiring solutions. Also, fiber optic cables are impervious to electromagnetic interference.

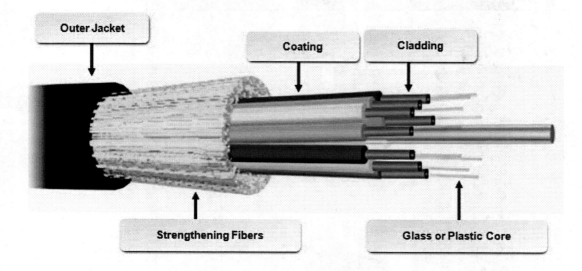

Figure 8-7: A fiber optic cable.

Fiber Optic Cable Types

There are two types of fiber optic cables: single-mode or multimode fiber.

Mode Type	Description
Single-mode fiber *Glass*	Carries a single optical signal, and has a small core that allows only a single beam of light to pass. A laser, usually operating in the infrared portion of the spectrum, is modulated in amplitude (intensity) to transmit the signal through the fiber.
Step index multimode fiber *Plastic used leds*	Contains a core surrounded by cladding, each with its own uniform index of refraction. When light from the core enters the cladding, a step down occurs due to the difference in the refractive indices. Step-index fiber uses total internal reflection to trap light.
Graded index multimode fiber	Possesses variations in the core glass to compensate for mode path length differences. It provides up to 2 GHz of bandwidth, which is significantly more than step-index fiber.

Fiber Optic Connector Types

There are various connector types used with fiber optic cable.

Connector	Description
Straight Tip (ST)	Used to connect multimode fiber, ST connectors look like BNC connectors. They have a straight, ceramic center pin and bayonet lug lockdown. They are often used in network patch panels. ST connectors are perhaps the most popular type of fiber connector.

Connector	Description
 Subscriber Connector or Standard Connector (SC)	Box-shaped connectors that snap into a receptacle. SC connectors are often used in a duplex configuration where two fibers are terminated into two SC connectors that are molded together. SC is used with single-mode fiber.
 Face Contact (FC)	Similar to SMA connectors, FC connectors use a heavy duty ferrule in the center for more mechanical stability than SMA or ST connectors. These connectors are more popular in industrial settings where greater strength is required.
 Fiber Distributed Data Interface (FDDI)	The FDDI connector is a push/pull type, two-channel snap-fit connector used for multimode fiber optic cable. Also called a MIC (Media Interface Connector).
 Mini-BNC	A bayonet-style connector using the traditional BNC connection method.

Connector	Description
Biconic	The biconic connector is a screw-on type connector with a tapered sleeve that is fixed against guided rings and screws onto the threaded sleeve to secure the connection. When the connector is inserted into the receptacle, the tapered end of the connector locates the fiber optic cable into the proper position. The biconic connector is one of the earliest connector types and is, for the most part, no longer in use. 
Local Connector (LC)	The LC is a small form factor ceramic ferrule connector for both single-mode and multimode fiber. It is about half the size of the SC or ST. The LC uses an RJ45-type latching and can be used to transition installations from twisted pair copper cabling to fiber. 
Sub Multi Assembly or Sub Miniature type A (SMA)	Similar to ST connectors, SMA connectors use a threaded ferrule on the outside to lock the connector in place. These are typically used where water or other environmental factors necessitate a waterproof connection, which is not possible with a bayonet-style connector. 
Mechanical Transfer Registered Jack (MT-RJ)	The MT-RJ connector, sometimes called a Fiber Jack connector, is a compact snap-to-lock connector used with multimode fiber. The MT-RJ is easy to use and similar in size to the RJ45 connector. Two strands of fiber are attached with one connector. 

Wireless Connections

Wireless connections are network connections that transmit signals without using physical network media. Instead, signals are transmitted as electromagnetic energy, such as radio waves, satellite microwave, or infrared light. Most general office wireless implementations use radio. Wireless communication enables users to move around while remaining connected to the network.

 Note: Wireless communication permits connections between areas where it would be difficult or impossible to install wires, such as in hazardous areas, across long distances, or inside historic buildings. It is also extremely popular in standard business and home installations because of the mobility and flexibility it provides, as well as the simplicity of media-free installation.

Figure 8-8: Wireless connections.

Wireless Signal Strength

The ability to communicate via wireless network is highly dependent upon the local signal strength. Signal strength can vary in relation to a number of factors, including interference and distance from the Wireless Access Point (WAP). Most wireless devices will provide some kind of indicator regarding the strength of the current wireless signal. For example, in Windows, a wireless network card will display a message on screen when signal strength is low and connectivity is limited as a result.

Wi-Fi

Wireless radio communications following the IEEE 802.11g Wi-Fi standard are the most common choice for ordinary wireless LAN connectivity for portable computers inside homes, offices, and, increasingly, public buildings. Choose Wi-Fi when you need to connect portable computer systems to a wired or wireless Ethernet LAN and enable users to move from place to place freely without a line of sight to the WAP. Wi-Fi provides good performance within the WAP coverage area, barring any signal interference.

Additional Network Connection Methods

In addition to coax, twisted pair, and fiber optic, you can use other types of cables and methods to make network connections, including USB, FireWire®, and RS-232 null-modem cable. You can also make wireless connections using radio, infrared, or satellite transmissions. Physical network cable connections are often referred to as a group as bounded media. Wireless connection types that transmit signals through the air without a cable are collectively called unbounded media.

RS-232 Null-Modem Connections

RS-232 is a standard serial interface that was used to connect serial devices, particularly modems. These connections have been primarily replaced by the faster Ethernet, but can be found in some cases to connect devices for debugging and to connect devices in close proximity of one another. When you use an RS-232 null-modem cable to create network connections between computers, it mimics the presence of a modem connection between the two systems. There are some types of network connections, such as a dial-up Internet connection, that use telephone media. So, with an RS-232 null-modem cable connected to two computers' serial ports, you can, in effect, create a simulated dial-up connection directly between the two systems.

ACTIVITY 8–1
Identifying Network Cables and Connectors

Scenario
In this activity, you will identify the various types of cables and connectors used to make network connections.

1. Look at the cables and connectors on the back of your computer, and identify what cables are used and what their purpose is.

2. What type of cable is used to connect your computer to the network?

3. Are there any LED lights on the cable ports indicating activity?

TOPIC B

TCP/IP

Now that you are familiar with the basic components that make up a network, you can start to take a closer look into how Transmission Control Protocol/Internet Protocol (TCP/IP) addressing and data delivery methods are used to implement TCP/IP on a network. In this lesson, you will identify the properties and characteristics of TCP/IP.

As an A+ technician, you must be able to identify the components of a system in order to provide the right level of support to your organization. Because all networks are different, you still need to be able to identify the components and how they are connected. Understanding how everything is connected and functioning within the network will allow you to properly support TCP/IP within the network.

This topic covers all or part of the following CompTIA® A+® (2012) certification objectives:

- Exam 220–801: Objective 2.3: Explain properties and characteristics of TCP/IP.

What is TCP/IP?

Transmission Control Protocol/Internet Protocol (TCP/IP) is a nonproprietary, routable network protocol that enables computers to communicate over all types of networks. TCP/IP is the native protocol of the Internet and is required for Internet connectivity. TCP/IP is a suite of related protocols that work together to provide network addressing and naming, and data delivery. In this suite, IP provides addressing, TCP provides connection-oriented message transmission, and User Datagram Protocol (UDP) provides connectionless, best-effort message transmission.

 Note: For additional information, check out the LearnTO **Interpret IP Address** in the LearnTOs for this course on your LogicalCHOICE Course screen.

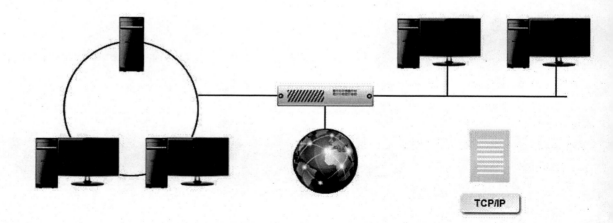

Figure 8-9: TCP/IP.

Nonproprietary, Routable Protocols

Nonproprietary means that no one group or organization owns or controls the protocol. You do not have to purchase software from a particular vendor or pay any kind of licensing fee to use TCP/IP.

Routable means the protocol can be used to communicate between different network sections. Thus, TCP/IP communications are not confined to a single network segment. To be routable, a protocol must provide addresses that identify individual network segments as well as network *hosts*.

Broadcast, Unicast, and Multicast

Broadcasts are network communications that are sent to all the computers on the network at once. Compare this to unicast transmissions, which are sent to a specific address or addresses, or multicast transmissions, which use a single address to transmit to a group of systems.

IPv4 Addresses

An *IPv4 address* is a 32-bit number assigned to a computer on a TCP/IP network. Some of the bits in the address represent the network segment; the other bits represent the computer, or node, itself. For readability, the 32-bit IPv4 address is usually separated by dots into four 8-bit octets, and each octet is converted to a single decimal value. Each decimal number can range from 0 to 255, but the first number cannot be 0. In addition, all four numbers in a host address cannot be 0 (0.0.0.0) or 255 (255.255.255.255).

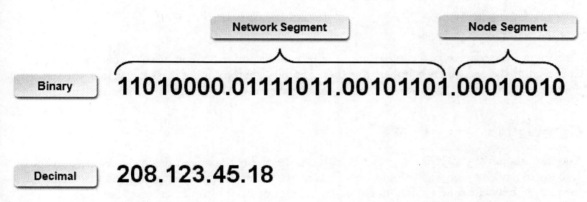

Figure 8-10: An IPv4 address.

Network Names

Systems on a network are typically assigned a host name, in addition to the numeric address. The host name is the descriptive name you see assigned to computers on the Internet, but systems on local networks have them as well. On the Internet, these host names appear to the left of the domain name. Host names can be up to 63 characters long.

Binary and Dotted Decimal Notation

TCP/IP uses binary numbering. Binary is a base 2 numbering system in which any bit in the number is either a zero or one. An IP address might appear in binary as 11001011.01111011.00101101.00010010.

Although the underlying IPv4 addresses are binary numbers, for readability, TCP/IP addresses are usually displayed in dotted decimal notation. Dotted decimal notation consists of four decimal numbers separated by three dots. Each decimal number is called an octet because it represents eight binary bits. When pronouncing a dotted decimal number, include the separator dots. For example, the IPv4 address 192.168.1.18 is pronounced one ninety-two dot one sixty-eight dot one dot eighteen.

Subnet Masks

A *subnet mask* is a 32-bit number that is assigned to each system to divide the 32-bit binary IP address into network and node portions. This makes TCP/IP routable. A subnet mask uses a binary operation to remove the node ID from the IP address, leaving just the network portion. Subnet masks use the value of eight 1s in binary, or 255 in decimal, to mask an entire octet of the IP address.

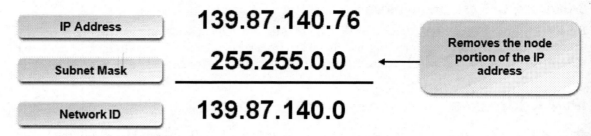

Figure 8-11: The subnet mask.

Binary ANDing

The binary logical operation applied to the subnet mask and the IP address is called binary ANDing. There are two rules in the binary AND operation:

- Zero AND any value equals zero.
- One AND one equals one.

To apply a subnet mask, you convert both the IP address and the subnet mask to binary. You AND each digit of the two binary numbers together. The zeros in the subnet mask convert all the bits in the node portion of the IP address to zeros, leaving the network portion of the address intact.

Gateways

A *gateway* is a device, software, or a system that has the ability to convert data between incompatible systems or devices. Gateways can translate data between different operating systems, or email formats, or between totally different networks. A gateway can be implemented as hardware, software, or both. You can also install gateways as software within a router, allowing the router to act as a gateway when required, and eliminating the need for separate hardware.

The Default Gateway

When TCP/IP communications need to be routed to systems on other networks, the protocol directs the packets to a special address known as the default gateway. The default gateway is different from a typical gateway in that the address is typically that of a network router that connects the local network to other external networks. A default gateway address is not a required component of a TCP/IP address assignment, but without a default gateway, the computer will only be able to communicate on the local network segment.

IP Address Classes

The designers of the TCP/IP suite defined five ranges of addresses, called address classes, for specific network uses and sizes. Changes in the Internet since the early 90s have rendered classful addresses all but obsolete. One of the final remnants of classful addressing is the use of the terms "Class A," "Class B," and "Class C" to describe common subnet masks.

Class and Subnet Mask	Description
Class A 255.0.0.0	*Class A* subnet masks provide a small number of network addresses for networks with a large number of nodes per network: • Number of nodes per network: 16,777,214 • Network ID portion: First octet • Node ID portion: Last three octets Used only by extremely large networks, Class A addresses are far too big for most companies. Large telephone companies and ISPs leased most Class A network addresses early in the development of the Internet.

0 - 127

Class and Subnet Mask	Description
Class B 255.255.0.0 *128 - 192*	*Class B* subnet masks offer a larger number of network addresses, each with fewer nodes per network: • Number of nodes per network: 65,534 • Network ID portion: First two octets • Node ID portion: Last two octets Most companies leased Class B addresses for use on Internet-connected networks. In the beginning, there were plenty of Class B addresses to go around, but soon they were depleted.
Class C 255.255.255.0 *192 - 223*	*Class C* subnet masks offer a large number of network addresses for networks with a small number of nodes per network: • Number of nodes per network: 254 • Network ID portion: First three octets • Node ID portion: Last octet Because there can be more Class C networks than any other type, they are the only addresses still generally available.

Classless Addressing

Because the traditional IP address classes have limitations on the number of available addresses in each class, there are now various implementations that utilize classless addressing. In these schemes, there is no strict dividing line between groups of addresses, and the network address/node address division is determined entirely by the number of 1 bits in the subnet mask.

IPv6 Addresses

IP version 6, or *IPv6,* is an Internet standard that increases the available pool of IP addresses by implementing a 128-bit binary address space. IPv6 also includes new efficiency features, such as simplified address headers, hierarchical addressing, support for time-sensitive network traffic, and a new structure for unicast addressing. One of the goals of IPv6 is to keep the IP headers as small as possible to make access to the address more efficient and quicker. Non-essential information in IPv6 headers is moved to optional extension headers. In IPv6, address blocks are automatically assigned hierarchically by routers. Top-level routers have top-level address blocks, which are automatically divided and assigned as routers and segments are added. This divides the address space logically instead of randomly, making it easier to manage.

IPv6 is not compatible with IPv4, so now, it is narrowly deployed on a limited number of test and production networks. Full adoption of the IPv6 standard will require a general conversion of IP routers to support interoperability. IPv6 makes use of an Institute of Electrical and Electronics Engineers (IEEE) standard called Extended Unique Identifier (EUI). A host computer implemented with EUI-64 can assign itself a 64-bit IPv6 interface identifier automatically.

 Note: For more information on IPv6, see the IETF's IP Version 6 Working Group charter at **www.ietf.org/html.charters/ipv6-charter.html.**

The IPv6 Address Format

An *IPv6 address* has 128 bits or 16 bytes and is denoted as eight hexadecimal blocks separated by colons. The byte on the left has the highest order, and the byte on the right has the lowest order. To make the representation easier, some abbreviation techniques are used. For example, one abbreviation technique used replaces all zero hexadecimal values with a single zero and removes the leading and trailing zeros of all nonzero values.

For example, in the IPv6 address **2001:DB8:0000:0056:0000:ABCD:EF12:1234,** the third, fourth, and fifth bytes contain consecutive zeros and, therefore, they can also be represented as **2001:DB8:0:56:0:ABCD:EF12:1234** without the unnecessary zeros.

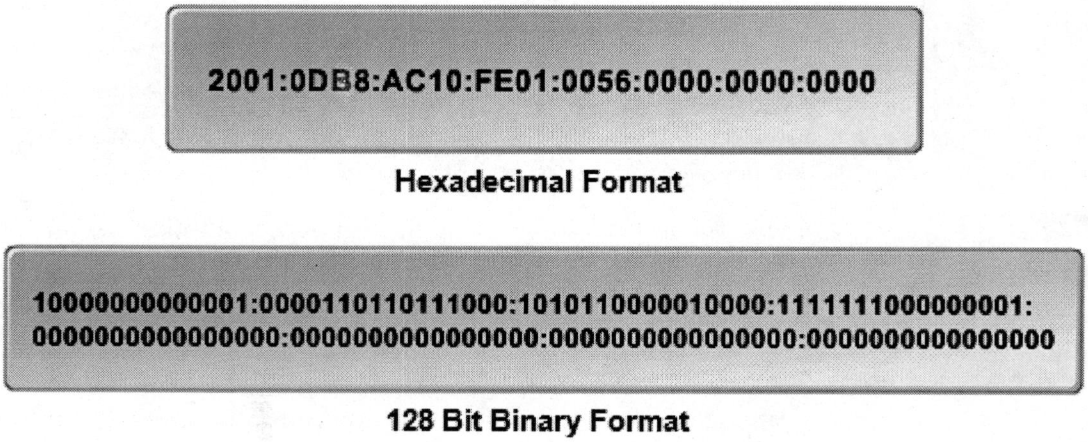

```
2001:0DB8:AC10:FE01:0056:0000:0000:0000
```

Hexadecimal Format

```
10000000000001:0000110110111000:1010110000010000:1111111000000001:
0000000000000000:0000000000000000:0000000000000000:0000000000000000
```

128 Bit Binary Format

Figure 8-12: An IPv6 address.

Another technique used replaces all consecutive zero values or consecutive leading or trailing zeros with a double colon. However, the double colon can be used only once in an address. This is because when a computer comes across a simplified address, it replaces the double colon symbol with as many zeros as required to make it 128 bits long. If an address contains more than one double colon, the computer cannot determine the number of zeros for each place.

For example, the IPv6 address **2001:DB8:0000:0056:0000:ABCD:EF12:1234** can also be represented as **2001:DB8::56:0:ABCD:EF12:1234** or **2001:DB8:0:56::ABCD:EF12:1234** after replacing any one of the consecutive zeros with a double colon.

IPv4 vs. IPv6

IPv4 addresses use 32 bits as opposed to the 128 bits used in IPv6 addressing. While implementing IPv4 addresses, IPSec is optional. However, IPSec is not optional in IPv6 addresses. The header information structure is different between IPv4 and IPv6 addresses. IPv6 is not compatible with IPv4, so now, it is narrowly deployed on a limited number of test and production networks. Full adoption of the IPv6 standard will require a general conversion of IP routers to support interoperability.

Addressing Schemes

When assigning addresses to hosts on your network, you must assign an address in the right scheme based on the type of network and access is given to that host.

Scheme	Description
Private	*Private IP addresses* are addresses that organizations use for nodes requiring IP connectivity within enterprise networks, but not requiring external connections to the global Internet. IP addresses in each of the Classes A, B, and C are reserved as private IP addresses. When an Internet router receives a data packet bound for one of these reserved IP addresses, it recognizes the address as nonroutable and does not forward it outside the network. Private IP addresses can be used freely on internal networks.

Scheme	Description
	Because they are not routable, private IP addresses do not cause duplicate IP address conflicts on the Internet.
	Any organization that opts to use private IP addresses can do so without contacting the ICANN or an Internet registry. Because these addresses are never injected into the global Internet routing system, the address space can simultaneously be used by many different organizations. Problems arising due to the shortage of IP addresses are resolved by private IP addresses.
Public	*Public IP addresses* are addresses that get shared on the Internet. In order to keep internal addresses private, *Network Address Translation (NAT)* is used to conceal internal private IP addresses from external networks. A router is configured with a single public IP address on its external interface and a private address on its internal interface. A NAT service running on the router or on another system translates between the two addressing schemes. Packets sent to the Internet from internal hosts all appear as if they came from a single IP address, thus preventing external hosts from identifying and connecting directly to internal systems.
APIPA	*Automatic Private IP Addressing (APIPA)* is a feature of Windows that enables a Dynamic Host Configuration Protocol (DHCP) client computer to configure itself automatically with a random IP address in the range of 169.254.0.1 to 169.254.255.254 if there is no DHCP server available. APIPA enables DHCP clients to initialize TCP/IP and communicate with other local APIPA-configured machines, even in the absence of an active DHCP scope. APIPA addresses are not routable, so computers with APIPA addresses cannot communicate outside their local subnet. APIPA can be a useful configuration method on small home networks because computers can initialize TCP/IP and connect without any administrative configuration. On larger networks, however, a computer with an APIPA-range address is usually nothing more than a symptom, to the technician, of a DHCP problem that requires resolution.

Static vs. Dynamic Addressing

On a TCP/IP network, you can assign IP address information statically to nodes by manually entering IP addressing information on each individual network node. Or, *dynamic addressing* can be used to assign IP addresses using the Dynamic Host Configuration Protocol (DHCP) service.

Static addressing involves configuring TCP/IP statically on a network and requires that an administrator visit each node to manually enter IP address information for that node. If the node moves to a different subnet, the administrator must manually reconfigure the node's TCP/IP information for its new network location. In a large network, configuring TCP/IP statically on each node can be very time consuming and prone to errors that can potentially disrupt communication on the network. Static addresses are typically only assigned to systems with a dedicated functionality, such as router interfaces, network-attached printers, or servers that host applications on a network.

DHCP

Dynamic Host Configuration Protocol (DHCP) is a network service that provides automatic assignment of IP addresses and other TCP/IP configuration information on network systems that are configured as DHCP clients. DHCP requires a DHCP server computer configured with at least one active DHCP scope. The scope contains a range of IP addresses and a subnet mask, and can contain other options, such as a default gateway address or *Domain Name Server (DNS)* addresses. When the

udp Port 67 & 68

service is enabled, it automatically leases TCP/IP configuration information to DHCP clients for a defined lease period.

DNS

[handwritten margin note: Converts friendly names to an IP Address Ex. YAhoo.com Operates on Port 53]

Computers on TCP/IP networks are assigned both a host name and an IP address. Users generally access systems by their descriptive names, and the network needs to translate, or resolve, those names into the relevant systems' IP addresses. The *Domain Name System (DNS)* is the primary name resolution service on the Internet as well as private IP networks.

DNS is a hierarchal system of databases that map computer names to their associated IP addresses. DNS servers store, maintain, and update the databases and respond to DNS client name resolution requests to translate host names to IP addresses. The DNS servers on the Internet work together to provide global name resolution for all Internet hosts. For example, the IP address 209.85.165.99 might map to **www.google.com.**

Hosts Files

Another way to resolve machine names to IP addresses is to provide each computer on the TCP/IP network with a hosts file. The hosts file is a text file that contains a list of computer names and their associated IP addresses. The use of hosts files predated the development of DNS and they are no longer commonly used, because this manual name-resolution method is practical only on very small and very stable networks. Adding a new computer, for example, requires that the hosts file of every computer that might need to reach it be manually updated with the new information.

However, a TCP/IP system will still use entries in the hosts file if the file is present, and the hosts file actually takes precedence over DNS name resolution. This can make the hosts file useful for testing purposes. However, if the hosts file is configured incorrectly, it can cause connectivity problems even when the DNS configuration is correct. Because altering the hosts file is a simple way to disrupt communications, the hosts file can be a target of attacks or malware. Be sure to check it when you troubleshoot name resolution and connectivity.

Client-Side DNS

Client-side DNS can be implemented by running a DNS service on a client computer. The client can quickly use the client resolver cache to lookup host names for resolution. This enables the client to perform basic DNS lookups without having to connect to a DNS server. In cases where the lookup is out of scope for the client resolver, the DNS servers that store, maintain, and update databases will respond to any resolution requests that may be out of scope for client-side DNS services to handle. In this case, the client-side DNS service will communicate directly with multiple DNS servers to resolve name requests made from the client machine.

ACTIVITY 8-2
Identifying Your Computer's TCP/IP Information

Scenario

In this activity, you will examine the configuration settings on your computer that enables it to connect to the network.

1. Determine the protocol in use on your system.
   a) Select **Start→Control Panel**. In the **Search Control Panel** text box, type *network connections*
   b) Under **Network and Sharing Center,** select **View network connections.**
   c) Examine the contents of the **Network Connections** window.
      One of the connections that is displayed in this window is the connection to the class network.
   d) Display the pop-up menu for the network connection, and select **Properties.**
   e) In the **This connection uses the following items** list, verify that **Internet Protocol Version 4 (TCP/IPv4)** is listed.
   f) Close the **Properties** dialog box without making any changes.

2. View the TCP/IP information assigned to your network adapter.
   a) Display the pop-up menu for the network connection, and select **Status.**
   b) Select **Details.**
   c) In the **Network Connection Details** dialog box, examine the information for the IPv4 address, subnet mask, and default gateway.

3. In the **Network Connection Details** dialog box, examine the information for DHCP.

4. **If DHCP is enabled on your computer, when does the lease expire?**

5. In the **Network Connection Details** dialog box, examine the information for DNS.

6. **How many DNS servers are listed?**

7. Return to the network connection properties, and examine the **Internet Protocol Version 4 (TCP/IPv4)** properties.
   a) Select **Close.**
   b) Select **Properties** to return to the network connection properties.
   c) In the **This connection uses the following items** list, select **Internet Protocol Version 4 (TCP/IPv4),** and then select **Properties.**
   d) Select **Advanced.**
   e) Select the **DNS** tab.
   f) Select **Cancel** three times, and then select **Close.**
   g) Close the **Network Connections** window.

TOPIC C

Network Connectivity

In the previous topics, you identified network communication technologies and the components of TCP/IP. To complete your understanding of network concepts, you will need to examine the technologies that connect multiple nodes and networks together. In this topic, you will identify network connectivity technologies.

Putting together a network is like putting together a huge puzzle. There are physical pieces, such as network adapters and network clients, and conceptual pieces, such as protocols and addresses. To understand how the pieces all fit together, however, you need to be able to see the overall picture. Examining the large structures and techniques that provide network connectivity between and within network locations will help you see the big picture of network implementation and support.

This topic covers all or part of the following CompTIA® A+® (2012) certification objectives:

- Exam 220–801: Objective 2.7: Compare and contrast Internet connection types and features.
- Exam 220-801: Objective 2.8: Identify various types of networks.
- Exam 220-801: Objective 2.9: Compare and contrast network devices, their functions, and features.

LANs

A *Local Area Network (LAN)* is a self-contained network that spans a small area, such as a single building, floor, or room. In a LAN, all parts of the network are directly connected with cables or short-range wireless media.

Figure 8–13: LANs within a building.

WANs

A *Wide Area Network (WAN)* is a network that spans multiple geographic locations. WANs typically connect multiple LANs using long-range transmission media. Such a network scheme facilitates communication among users and computers in different locations. WANs can be private, such as those built and maintained by large, multinational corporations, or they can be public, such as the Internet.

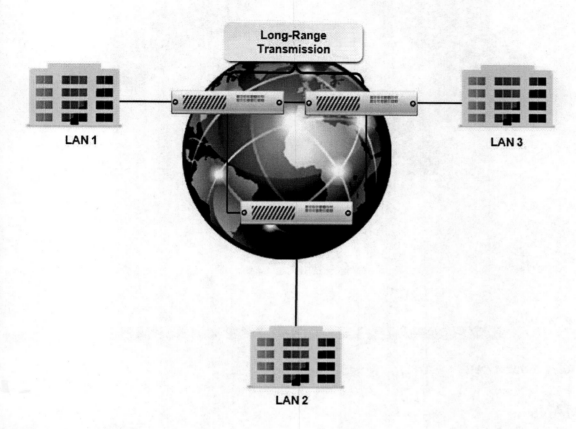

Figure 8-14: A WAN.

PANs

(handwritten: wifi network)   *(handwritten: Network adapter to Network adapter)*

A *Personal Area Network (PAN)* connects two to three devices together for use by one person using a router with cabling; most often seen in small or home offices.

A *Wireless Personal Area Network (WPAN)* is a network that connects wireless devices in very close proximity but not through a Wireless Access Point (WAP). Infrared and Bluetooth are some technologies used for connecting devices in a WPAN.

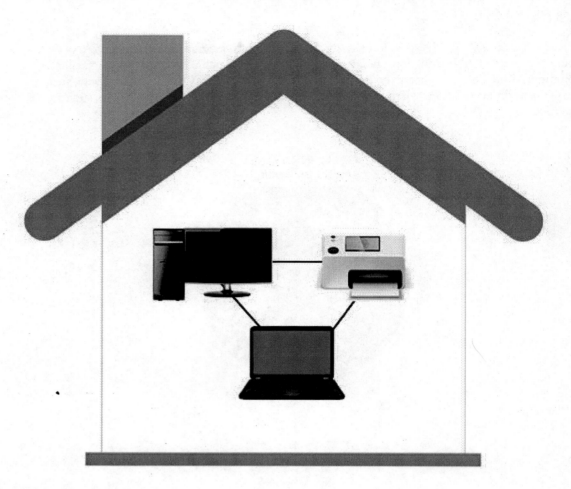

Figure 8–15: A PAN.

MANs

A *metropolitan area network (MAN)* covers an area equivalent to a city or other municipality. In many cases the MAN connects multiple LANS.

City

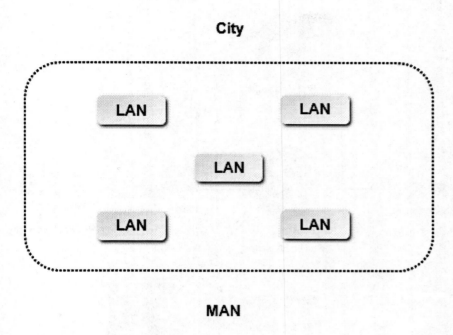

MAN

Figure 8-16: A MAN.

Additional Network Types

While on the job, you may come across several other loosely defined network categories, named according to the geographic areas they cover. These include:

- A *campus area network (CAN)*, which covers an area equivalent to an academic campus or business park. A CAN is typically owned or used exclusively by one company, school, or organization.
- A *global area network (GAN)*, which is any worldwide network.

VPNs

A *virtual private network (VPN)* is a private network that protects communications sent through a public network, such as the Internet. VPNs provide secure connections between endpoints, such as routers, clients, or servers, by using tunneling to encrypt data. These connections are established either between two LANs or between a user and a LAN over the Internet. Special *VPN protocols* are required to provide the VPN *tunneling*, security, and data encryption services.

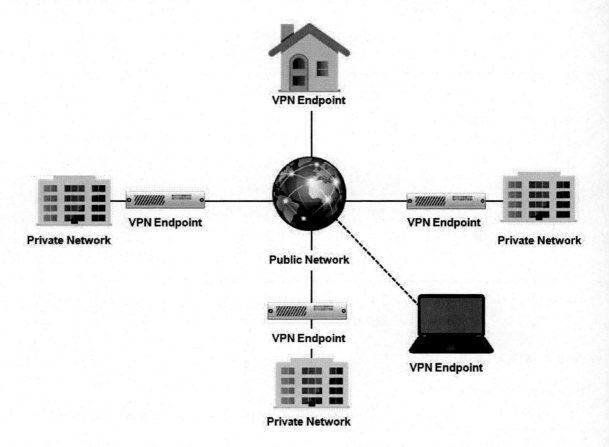

Figure 8-17: A VPN.

Ethernet

An *Ethernet* network is a popular LAN implementation that uses Ethernet network adapters, contention-based media access, and twisted pair, coax, or fiber media. Xerox® corporation first developed Ethernet in the 1970s. Later, the IEEE used Ethernet as the basis of the 802.3 specification, which standardized Ethernet and expanded it to include a wide range of cable media. The 802.3 family of specifications also determines transmission speed (10 Mbps, 100 Mbps, or 1000 Mbps) and signal method (baseband or broadband).

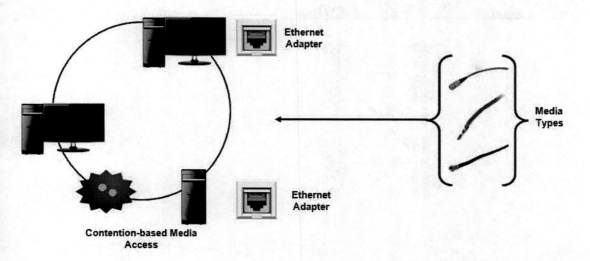

Figure 8-18: Ethernet.

Ethernet WAN

To implement an Ethernet WAN, in most cases, you establish a connection to the Internet by using Ethernet technology on the LAN and a broadband Internet connection such as a cable modem or digital subscriber line (DSL) modem. After you connect to the Internet, you can then connect to your organization's LAN using a VPN. Use Ethernet WANs when you want to enable users to connect remotely to the Internet, your company's VPN, or both.

Network Topologies

A *network topology* is a specification that determines the network's overall physical layout and transmission and flow patterns. There are a number of different topologies used to configure networks.

Topology	Description
Mesh	A *mesh topology* is a network topology in which each node is directly connected to every other node, similar to the physical point-to-point topology. This configuration allows each node to communicate with multiple nodes at the same time. Since all nodes have dedicated links with other nodes, there is no congestion on the network and data travels very fast. Since no node can be isolated from the network, this topology is extremely reliable. It is also difficult to implement and maintain because the number of connections increases exponentially with the number of nodes. Mesh topologies typically provide reliable connections between separate independent networks.

Pan

Topology	Description

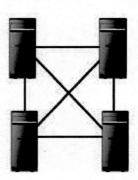

Ring

Physical + logical Side is Identical Fddi fiber

A *ring topology* is a network topology in which each node is connected to the two nearest nodes: the upstream and downstream neighbors. The flow of data in a ring network is unidirectional to avoid collisions. All nodes in the network are connected to form a circle. There is no centralized node to control network traffic and each node handles every data packet that passes through it. Data transmission moves in one direction to each node that scans data packets, accepts packets destined for it, and forwards packets destined for another node.

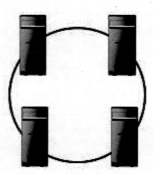

Bus

ViA Coax

A *bus topology* is a network topology in which nodes receive the data transmitted all at the same time, regardless of the physical wiring layout of the network. Data flow propagates in a single, continuous stream.

Tw.sted Pair Ethernet

Star

A *star topology* is a network topology that uses a central connectivity device, such as a hub or a switch, with individual physical connections to each node. The individual nodes send data to the connectivity device, and the device then either forwards data to the appropriate destination node, as in the case

Topology	Description
	of a switch, or simply passes it through to all attached nodes, as in the case of a hub. Star topologies are reliable and easy to maintain as a single failed node does not bring down the whole network. However, if the central connectivity device fails, all nodes on that device fail to communicate.

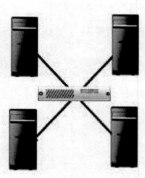

Hybrid	A *hybrid topology* is any topology that exhibits the characteristics of more than one standard topology. Each section of the network follows the rules of its own topology. They can be complex to maintain because they typically incorporate a wide range of technologies. Most of the large networks consist of several smaller subnetworks, and each subnetwork may have a different topology.

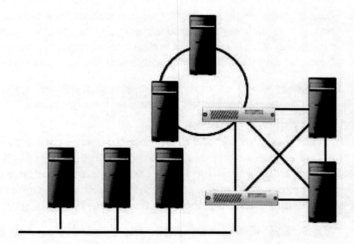

Network Device Types and Features

Computers attached to a network need to have their data mediated by a network device, and there are several kinds of network devices.

Network Device	Description
Hub	A *hub* is a device that connects multiple Ethernet or twisted pair devices together. By this connection, multiple devices can act as a single network segment. Hubs can either simply receive data transmitted from a device on one port and broadcast it out to the devices connected on all other ports, or

Network Device	Description
	they can perform the same receive-then-broadcast action but regenerate or boost the signal. Hubs are generally inexpensive and easy to manage; however, they do not provide the best performance in high-traffic or latency-sensitive situations. Hubs have largely been replaced by switches, but many dedicated hubs still remain in use. Troubleshooting a hub is made easier by the use of status lights for the various ports.
Switch	A *switch* is a network hardware device that joins multiple computers together within the same LAN. Unlike a hub, switches forward packets to only the destination port based on MAC addresses. Because of this, they are slightly "smarter" than hubs, and are more common. Switches can also be connected to other switches, thus increasing the number of devices on a LAN without sacrificing performance. Troubleshooting a switch is made easier by the use of status indicator lights on the various ports.
Router	A *router* is a networking device that connects multiple networks that use the same protocols. Traffic from one network to another does not always have to travel between the same routers. On the Internet, for example, traffic is routed according to the best available path at the time. Troubleshooting a router is made easier by the use of status indicator lights on the various ports.
Bridge	A *bridge* is a network device that divides a logical bus network into segments. Bridges examine the MAC address of each packet. If the packet is destined for a node connected to a different port, the bridge forwards the packet. If the packet is addressed to a node on its own segment, the bridge does not forward the packet. This arrangement reduces traffic between segments and improves overall network performance.
Access Point	An *access point (AP)* is a device or software that facilitates communication and provides enhanced security to wireless devices. It also extends the physical range of a WLAN. The AP functions as a bridge between wireless STAs (stations) and the existing network backbone for network access.
Modem	A *modem* is a device that modulates and demodulates digital data to an analog signal that can be sent over a telephone line. Its name is a combination of *mo*dulate and *dem*odulate.
	Use a modem to connect to the Internet and to translate digital information to and from your computer. Depending on the type of connection used, you will use either a cable modem, a DSL modem, a wireless modem, a voice modem, or a radio modem. A laptop modem can be an internal device, or can be added to a system using a PC Card or an ExpressCard.
NAS	A *network-attached storage (NAS)* appliance is a data storage device that can be connected to a network to provide direct data access and file sharing to multiple computing devices attached to the network.
Firewall	A firewall is a software program or hardware device that protects networks from unauthorized data by blocking unsolicited traffic. Firewalls allow incoming or outgoing traffic that has specifically been permitted by a system administrator and incoming traffic that is sent in response to requests from internal systems. Firewalls use complex filtering algorithms that analyze incoming network data based on destination and source addresses, port numbers, and data type.
VoIP phones	*Voice over IP (VoIP)* phones can transmit voice signals over IP data networks. With VoIP, the phone system and IP network translate between voice and network signals and between phone numbers and IP addresses. You can make a telephone call and the signal will be transmitted over your network

Network Device	Description
	connection and transferred to the standard phone system if the called party does not have VoIP service. Conversely, when a caller dials a phone number that maps to a VoIP device, VoIP routes the call to the IP host.
Internet appliance	An *Internet appliance* is a device that allows quick easy access to the Internet. It can be connected to a number of computing devices for allowing access to Internet services.

Ex. Smart TV.s

ISPs

An *Internet Service Provider (ISP)* is a company that provides Internet access to individuals and to businesses. Most ISPs charge a fee for this connection. Customers receive logon information, access to servers that provide name resolution and email services, dynamic or static IP configurations, and a method for connecting to the ISP. Once connected to the ISP, the customer can access the Internet.

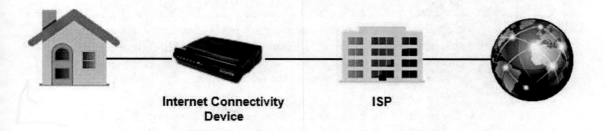

Internet Connectivity Device   **ISP**

Figure 8–19: An ISP.

Broadband Communications

Broadband is a general term for a category of network transmission technologies that provide high throughput by splitting communications into multiple channels transmitted simultaneously over the network media. Today's common broadband network communications technologies are typically employed to provide affordable high-speed Internet access to homes and businesses.

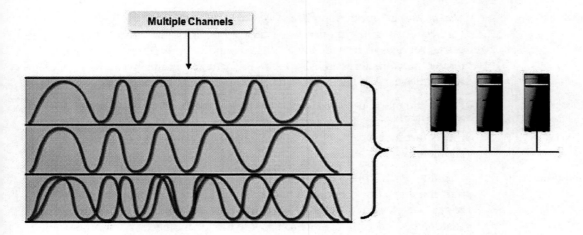

Multiple Channels

Figure 8–20: Broadband transmission.

Baseband vs. Broadband

The opposite of broadband is *baseband*. In baseband transmissions, a single signal sends data using the entire bandwidth of the transmission media. Devices cannot simultaneously send and receive data.

Neither baseband nor broadband is inherently faster or slower, but broadband is effectively faster on large public networks, notably the Internet, where multiple clients are trying to send and receive data simultaneously. For this reason, in common usage, broadband networks have become synonymous with fast networks, although not all fast networks use broadband signaling. There is no single common definition of the minimum data rate for a technology to be fast enough to qualify as broadband in this sense, although a one-way transmission rate in the range of at least 1.5 Mbps is typical.

Internet Connection Types and Features

Internet connections can be accomplished in a wide variety of ways today. Each method has unique connection technology that is used to connect computing devices to the Internet.

Method	Description
Cable	*Cable* or *cable modem* transmissions use a cable television connection and a specialized interface device known as a cable modem to provide high-speed Internet access to homes and small businesses. Cable access arranges users in groups around nodes that split the television and data signals at the cable provider's end.
	The speed of the network varies depending on how populated the group on each node is. Download speeds can vary by more than 1 Mbps in different areas. Most cable companies try to guarantee at least a 768-Kbps download speed; however, speeds of 3.0 to 7.0 Mbps are common, and speeds of 20 Mbps or more are possible.
DSL	*Digital Subscriber Line (DSL)* is a broadband technology that transmits digital signals over existing phone lines. It has become a popular way to connect small businesses and households to the Internet because it is affordable and provides a relatively high download speed—a typical maximum is 1.5 Mbps for basic DSL and 7 Mbps for high-end DSL. However, distance from the phone company's switching station and the quality of the lines affect the total bandwidth available to a customer.
Dial-up	*Dial-up lines* are local loop *Public Switched Telephone Network (PSTN)* connections that use modems, existing phone lines, and existing long-distance carrier services to provide low cost, low bandwidth WAN connectivity, and remote network access. Dial-up lines are generally limited to 56 Kbps, and are sometimes used as backups for higher bandwidth WAN services.
Fiber	*Fiber* is a method used to connect devices to the Internet using fiber optic cable. Fiber is mostly used in smaller areas to connect computing devices to a router. It provides a fast data exchange rate over distances of several kilometers.
Satellite	Orbiting *satellites* provide extremely long-range wireless network transmissions. For broadband network access, satellites can be employed to relay network signals from the network service provider to individual customers. This can be a way to provide broadband network communications in rural or remote areas where cable service or viable DSL lines are not available. However, satellite Internet communications are comparatively expensive and some only operate one-way; satellite transmissions provide the downstream communication, but another media (typically telephone) is

Method	Description
	needed for upstream communication. For remote or mobile locations, true two-way satellite-only communication is also available, but aligning a dish for upstream communication to a satellite requires a certain degree of precision and skill.
ISDN	*Integrated Services Digital Network (ISDN)* is a digital transmission technology that carries both voice and data over digital phone lines or PSTN wires. Connections are made on demand by dialing another ISDN circuit's telephone number.
	ISDN and DSL are very similar technologies because they both use existing phone lines to transmit digital signals. However, ISDN technology predates DSL and has largely been superseded by DSL for the home and small business market. ISDN requires a specialized client adapter called a Terminal Adapter, which DSL does not. ISDN is also slower than DSL, being limited to a data rate of approximately 128 Kbps for basic rate ISDN, and thus barely qualifies as broadband. (Primary rate ISDN, which was commonly used for network backbone communications before fiber optic cable, provides more bandwidth and has higher speeds.)
Cellular	*Cellular* technology uses radio signals to transmit network data over the cellular telephone system. Cellular-enabled computers have a cellular radio built in. Coverage can be regional, national, or global, depending on the service chosen and the capabilities of the cellular service provider. Signal fidelity will vary depending on interference and the distance from a cell tower.
	Some of the cellular transmission technologies and standards in use include Code-Division Multiple Access (CDMA) and the Global System for Mobile Communications (GSM). CDMA is a spread-spectrum implementation that uses the full frequency spectrum for each channel rather than assigning specific frequencies to particular users. It separates the calls using digital encoding. GSM uses time-division multiplexing (TDM), which transmits multiple calls on the same frequency by dividing each call into separate time slices.
	Use a cellular *Wireless WAN (WWAN)* when you have users that have no other way to connect to the Internet, your company's VPN, or both. Cellular WWANs are typically more expensive than Ethernet WANs.
WiMAX *IEEE Wireless*	*Wireless Interoperability for Microwave Access (WiMAX)* is a packet-based wireless telecommunication technology that provides wireless broadband access over long distances. Based on the *IEEE 802.16* standard, it is intended for wireless MANs. WiMAX provides fixed as well as mobile broadband access. It covers a range of about 30 miles for fixed stations and 3 to 10 miles for mobile stations. WiMAX also provides line of sight and non-line-of-sight communication, and can provide connection speeds of about 70 Mbps. WiMAX operates in the wireless frequency ranges of between 2 and 11 GHz of the wireless spectrum.
	Line of sight communication is a method used when distances between devices can be seen by the human eye. In wireless networking this term can be used to determine whether an access point is within a certain distance and is within an acceptable range of connecting devices. There are a few terms used when referring to line of sight factors:
	• *Line-Of-Sight (LOS):* Wireless signals that travel over a direct visual path from a transmitter to a receiver.

Method	Description
	• *Non-Line-Of-Sight (NLOS):* Wireless signals that reach a receiver through reflections and obstructions within the visual path in the environment.
Bluetooth	Bluetooth® is a wireless radio protocol that is used to communicate from one device to another in a small area, usually less than 30 feet. Bluetooth is commonly used to enable communication between small personal electronic devices, such as between a cellular phone and a wireless earpiece or between an electronic organizer and a personal computer.
	Bluetooth uses the 2.4 GHz spectrum to communicate a 1 Mbps connection between two devices for both a 232 Kbps voice channel and a 768 Kbps data channel (technically, Bluetooth detects other devices in the 2.4 GHz spectrum and avoids the frequencies they use by "hopping" to an available frequency). Bluetooth 2.0 is an improved version of Bluetooth, has a range up to 100 meters, offers faster data transfer speeds (up to 3 Mbps), and also uses less power to extend battery life. Bluetooth 2.0 is backwards-compatible with earlier versions of Bluetooth, but the connection between devices is governed by the slowest device; in other words, connecting a Bluetooth 1.2 device to a Bluetooth 2.0 device means the data transfer is at the rate of Bluetooth 1.2. Bluetooth 3.0 is available but not yet widely adopted, though it boasts speeds up to 24 Mbps.

Bluetooth Naming and Addressing

Each Bluetooth device has its own unique 48-bit address. But instead of requiring you to connect via this address, most Bluetooth devices also have their own Bluetooth names. By default, manufacturers set the Bluetooth name for devices to the name of the manufacturer and model of the device. If you have several users you support that are in close proximity to each other and have the same devices, these default Bluetooth names can cause problems. In this scenario, you should be sure to rename each user's Bluetooth device.

Bluetooth Pairs

Most Bluetooth devices require you to establish a trusted relationship between two devices (referred to as pairing). This trusted relationship is established through the use of an encrypted shared secret or passkey. After the relationship is established, the pair of devices can encrypt the data transmissions they exchange. However, most Bluetooth printers permit all devices to use their services without requiring pairing.

ACTIVITY 8-3
Discussing Network Connectivity

Scenario

In this activity, you will discuss network connectivity.

---

1. The transmission method that allows multiple signals to be carried separately on the same media at the same time is called _____

   ○ Baseband.

   ○ Broadband.

   ○ Modulated.

   ○ Multicast.

2. Which broadband communication method uses existing telephone lines to transmit digital signals?

   ○ Cable modem

   ○ DSL

   ○ ISDN

   ○ Fiber

   ○ Satellite

3. Which broadband communication method uses the same physical media to provide high-speed transmission of data and television signals?

   ○ Cable modem

   ○ DSL

   ○ ISDN

   ○ Fiber

   ○ Satellite

4. Which broadband communication method uses light to carry signals?

   ○ Cable modem

   ○ DSL

   ○ ISDN

   ○ Fiber

   ○ Satellite

5. Which are wired connection technologies?

   ☐ Bluetooth

   ☐ ISDN

   ☐ Dial-up connections

   ☐ Wi-Fi

6. Which are wireless connection technologies?

   ☐ Bluetooth

☐ Fiber optic

☐ Cellular WAN

☐ Twisted-pair

7. Which wireless technology provides broadband Internet coverage in rural or remote areas?

○ Cellular WAN

○ Satellite

○ Wi-Fi

○ Infrared

○ Bluetooth

8. Which wireless technology is a short-range connection method requiring direct line of sight?

○ Cellular WAN

○ Satellite

○ Wi-Fi

○ Infrared

○ Bluetooth

9. When would some of the different Internet connection types be used and when do you think you might encounter them within the workplace?

10. If you have remote employees that need to connect to the corporate network but they are located in a remote area with no access to broadband Internet service, what do you think is the best Internet connection method to use in this situation?

TOPIC D

Ports and Protocols

In the previous topic, you explored the different network types and how they are connected. Now that you have a good understanding of how a network can be structured physically, you are ready to examine the various ports and protocols that are used to ensure data transmission is successful and secure. In this topic, you will examine common TCP and UDP ports and protocols.

Properly configuring the ports of a network device and selecting the right protocol will ensure that data gets transmitted over the network. As an A+ technician, you must understand how ports and protocols are implemented within a network and how they function to provide the right level of data transmission while keeping data secure.

This topic covers all or part of the following CompTIA® A+® (2012) certification objectives:

- Exam 220–801: Objective 2.4: Explain common TCP and UPD ports, protocols, and their purpose.

Ports

In TCP/IP networks, a *port* is the endpoint of a logical connection. Client computers connect to specific server programs through a designated port. All ports are assigned a number in a range from 0 to 65,535. An international agency, the Internet Assigned Numbers Authority (IANA), separates port numbers into three blocks: well-known ports, which are preassigned to system processes by the IANA; registered ports, which are available to user processes and are listed as a convenience by the IANA; and dynamic ports, which are assigned by a client operating system as needed when there is a request for service.

TCP vs. UDP

The TCP/IP protocol suite includes two Transport-layer protocols: *Transmission Control Protocol (TCP)* and *User Datagram Protocol (UDP)*. TCP is a connection-oriented, guaranteed-delivery protocol used to send data packets between computers over a network such as the Internet. It is part of the Internet protocol suite along with the *Internet Protocol (IP)*. TCP is responsible for breaking up data into datagrams, reassembling them at the other end, resending data lost in transit, and resequencing data. It sends data, waits for an acknowledgement, and fixes erroneous data. IP is responsible for routing individual datagrams and addressing.

The User Datagram Protocol (UDP), also known as the Universal Datagram Protocol, is a connectionless Transport-layer protocol in the Internet protocol suite. A connectionless, best-effort delivery protocol, UDP is used with IP like TCP. It transmits data and ensures data integrity as TCP does. UDP, however, lacks reliability, flow-control, and error-recovery functions. It is less complex than TCP, and since it is a connectionless protocol, it provides faster service.

Port Ranges

There are three recognized blocks of port numbers.

Block	Range	Description
Well-known ports	Port range: 0 to 1,023.	Well-known ports are pre-assigned for use by common, or well-known, services. Often the services that run on these ports must be started by a privileged user. Services in this range include HTTP

Block	Range	Description
		on TCP port 80, IMAP on TCP port 143, and DNS on UDP port 53.
Registered ports	Port range: 1,024 to 49,151.	These ports are registered by software makers for use by specific applications and services that are not as well known as the services in the well-known range. Services in the registered port range include SOCKS proxy on TCP port 1080, QuickTime® Streaming Server administration on TCP port 1220, and Xbox® Live on TCP and UDP port 3074.
Dynamic or private ports	Port range: 49,152 to 65,535.	These ports are set aside for use by unregistered services and by services needing a temporary connection.

Common Ports

This table lists some of the most common well-known TCP and UDP port numbers. Additional well-known ports and other port number assignments are available online at **www.iana.org/assignments/port-numbers**.

DhCP
67 - 68   *20 →*

Port	Type	Service Name	Purpose
21	TCP	FTP	File transfers
22	TCP/UDP	SSH *eCRypted*	Secure shell for secure data transmission
23	TCP/UDP	TELNET *unecRypted*	Telnet services
25	TCP	SMTP	Simple mail transfers
53	TCP/UDP	DNS	Domain name system
80	TCP	HTTP	Hypertext transfer protocol
110	TCP	POP3 *Pulls from server*	Post office protocol *Retreival of Email*
143	TCP/UDP	IMAP *Leaves on seru*	Internet message access protocol
443	TCP	HTTPS	HTTP secure combines HTTP with SSL/TLS protocols.
3389	TCP/UDP	RDP	Remote desktop protocol

LDAP

Lightweight Directory Access Protocol (LDAP) is a protocol that defines how a client can access information, perform operations, and share directory data on a directory server. It was designed for use specifically over TCP/IP networks and on the Internet in particular. In most implementations, LDAP relies on the DNS service. First, DNS enables clients to find the servers that host the LDAP directory, and then the LDAP servers enable clients to find directory objects. Most common network directories are LDAP-compliant.

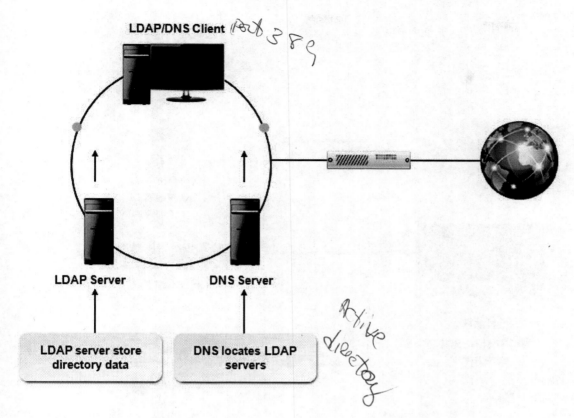

Figure 8–21: LDAP.

SNMP

Simple Network Management Protocol (SNMP) is an Application-layer protocol used to collect information from network devices for diagnostic and maintenance purposes. SNMP includes two components: management systems and agent software, which are installed on network devices such as servers, routers, and printers. The agents send information to an SNMP manager. The SNMP manager can then notify an administrator of problems, run a corrective program or script, store the information for later review, or query the agent about a specific network device.

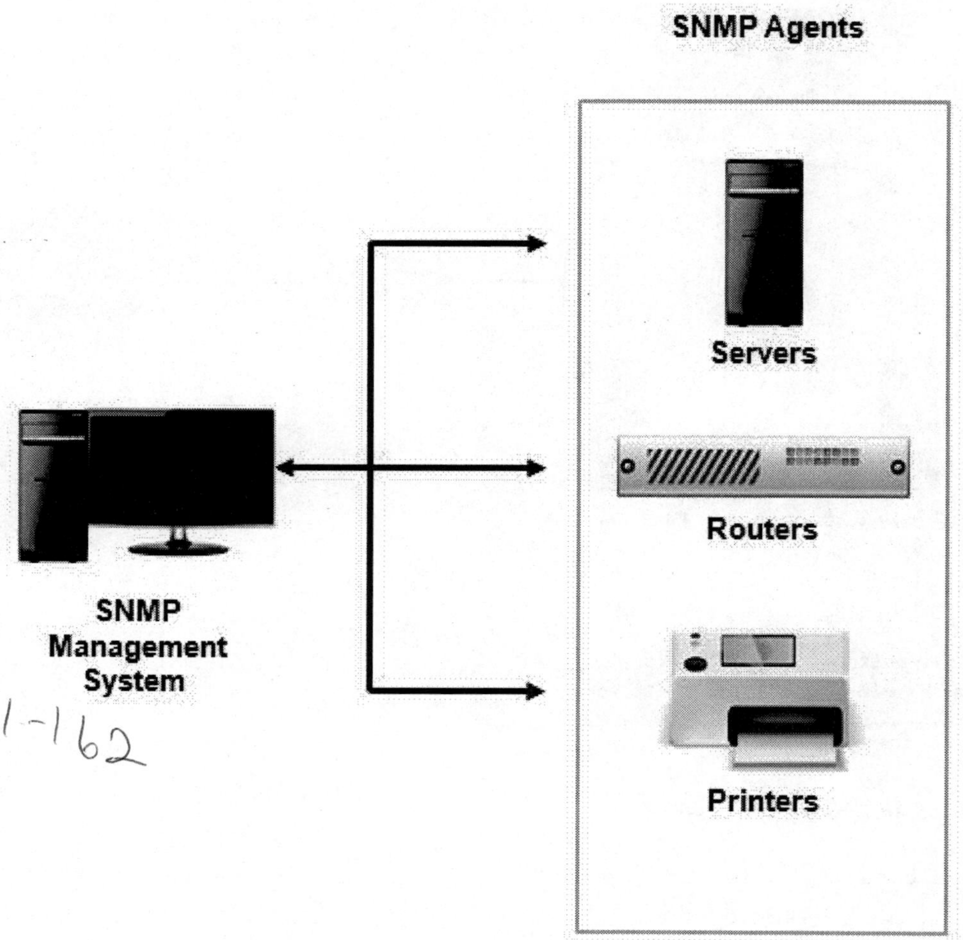

Figure 8–22: SNMP collects information from network devices for diagnostic purposes.

SSH

Secure Shell (SSH) is a protocol that enables a user or application to log on to another computer over a network, execute commands, and manage files. It provides strong authentication methods and secure communications over insecure channels. It is a more secure version of remote connection programs that transmit passwords unencrypted, such as Telnet. With the SSH `slogin` command, the entire login session, including the password, is encrypted and protected against attack.

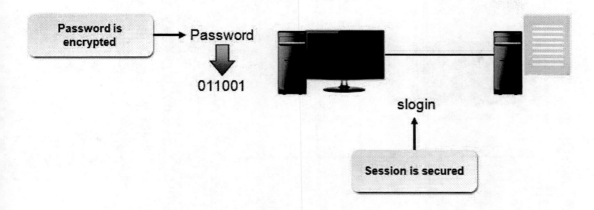

Figure 8–23: SSH.

SSH1 and SSH2

There are two versions of Secure Shell available: SSH1 and SSH2. They are two different protocols and encrypt different parts of a data packet. To authenticate systems, SSH1 employs user keys, to identify users; host keys, to identify systems; session keys, to encrypt communication in a single session; and server keys, which are temporary keys that protect the session key. SSH2 is more secure; it does not use server keys. Because they are different protocol implementations, SSH1 and SSH2 are not compatible with each other.

SFTP

Secure FTP (SFTP) is a more secure replacement for FTP that uses the SSH protocol to manage, transfer, and access files over a secure connection.

 Note: Note that the acronym SFTP is used both for Secure File Transfer Protocol as well as for the now obsolete Simple File Transfer Protocol.

SMB

The *Server Message Block (SMB)* is a protocol that works on the Application layer and helps share resources such as files, printers, and serial ports among computers. In a TCP/IP network, NetBIOS clients, such as Windows systems, use NetBIOS over TCP/IP to connect to servers, and then issue SMB commands to complete tasks such as accessing shared files and printers.

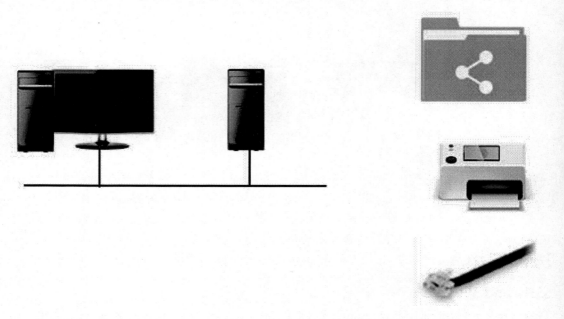

Figure 8-24: Resource sharing using SMB.

TOPIC E

Set Up and Configure Windows Networking

In the previous topics, you focused on the network infrastructure and how it all works together. Now you can take a look at how the operating system is configured to run on the hardware systems. In this topic, you will setup and configure Windows networking.

Once all the hardware and connections are made in a networking environment, you will need to make sure that the operating system is configured to use the hardware successfully. It is important to fully understand not only the hardware and the connections within a network, but how Windows will need to be setup and configured to accomplish connectivity with the resources of a network.

This topic covers all or part of the following CompTIA® A+® (2012) certification objectives:

*   Exam 220–802: Objective 1.6: Set up and configure Windows networking on a client/desktop.

Directory Services

A *network directory,* or *directory service,* is a centralized database that includes objects such as servers, clients, computers, user names, and passwords. The directory is stored on one or more servers and is available throughout the enterprise. The directory provides centralized administration and centralized authentication.

 Note: There are many directory services available from different network vendors. Some directory services include Microsoft's Active Directory Domain Services, Open LDAP, and Novell's eDirectory, although eDirectory is now less common.

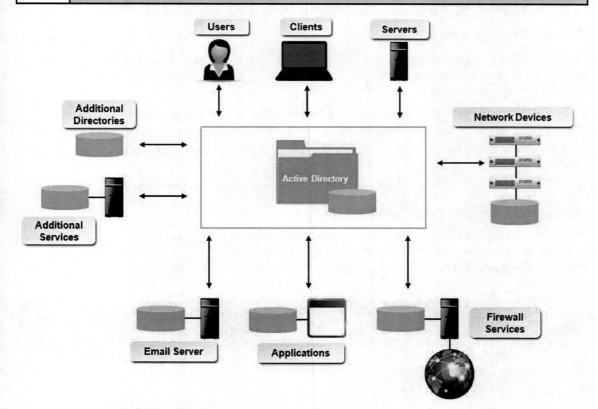

Figure 8–25: A network directory.

Novell eDirectory and Novell Directory Services

Novell® eDirectory™ is Novell's standards-based, enterprise-level directory service. It is an object-oriented database organized as a hierarchical tree. The eDirectory is LDAP-compliant and supports HTTP and SSL. It is portable to Windows, Linux, and UNIX platforms and supports the grafting and moving of directory trees. The eDirectory is an evolution of earlier versions of Novell's directory service, which was called Novell Directory Services (NDS). NDS was one of the first standards-based directory services, and it predated Microsoft's Active Directory. NDS directories comply with X.500, an International Telecommunication Union (ITU) standard for hierarchical object-based enterprisewide directories and are LDAP compliant.

Windows Networking Options

There are three available networking options available in Windows:

- Homegroups
- Workgroups
- Domains

Comparing Networking Options

Domains, homegroups, and workgroups are different organizational and security models for Windows networking.

- Domains require a specially configured Windows Server computer called a domain controller and are most often used in corporate environments with centralized administration.
- Workgroups are unstructured named collections of individual computers and are usually deployed in homes and small offices.
- Homegroups provide easy file and printer sharing, but are available only for Windows 7 computers.

Effects of Domain Membership

Domain controllers run the Microsoft Active Directory® directory service. To fully participate in the benefits of an Active Directory domain, client computers must become members of the domain. Domain membership means:

- The computer has a computer account object within the directory database.
- Computer users can log on to the domain with domain user accounts.
- The computer and its users are subject to centralized domain security, configuration, and policy settings.
- Certain domain accounts automatically become members of local groups on the computer.

Prestaging Computer Accounts

In Windows Server 2012, as well as other versions of Windows Server, you can create the computer accounts in Active Directory before you join the computer to the domain. This process is called pre-staging, and requires administrative privileges to add Active Directory objects.

 Access the Checklist tile on your LogicalCHOICE course screen for reference information and job aids on How to Join a Computer to a Domain

ACTIVITY 8-4
Joining a Computer to a Domain

Scenario

In this activity, you will examine the current networking configuration for your computer and for the VM you created. Then, you will join your computer to the **APLUS-CLASS** domain, and re-examine the networking configuration settings to see how they changed.

1. Determine the network configuration for your computer.
   a) Select **Start,** display the pop-up menu for **Computer,** and select **Properties.**
   b) In the **Computer name, domain, and workgroup settings** section, observe the **Computer name, Full computer name,** and **Workgroup** settings for the computer.
   c) Minimize the **System Control Panel.**

2. Determine the network configuration for the **Win7test##** virtual machine.
   a) Start the **Win7test##** VM, and log on to Windows.
   b) Determine the **Computer name, Full computer name,** and **Workgroup** settings for the **Win7test##** VM.
   c) Close the **System Control Panel** within the VM.

3. Join your computer to the **APLUS-CLASS** domain.
   a) Switch back to the **System** window for the physical computer.
   b) Select **Change settings.**
   c) In the **System Properties** dialog box, on the **Computer Name** tab, select **Change.**
   d) Select the **Domain** radio button, type *APLUS-CLASS* and select **OK.**
   e) In the **Windows Security** dialog box, for **User name,** type *Admin##* and for **Password,** type *! Pass1234* and then select **OK.**
   f) Acknowledge the welcome message, and then restart the computer when you are prompted to do so.
   g) When the computer restarts, press **Ctrl+Alt+Del,** select **Switch User** and select **Other User.** For **User name,** type *aplus-class\admin##* and for **Password,** type *!Pass1234* and select **Enter** to log on to the APLUS-CLASS domain.

4. Examine the changes to the networking configuration.
   a) Open the **System Control Panel.**
   b) In the **Computer name, domain, and workgroup settings** section, examine the **Computer name, Full computer name,** and **Workgroup** settings for the computer.
   The settings should reflect a change to the **Full computer name,** where the name should resemble **Client##.aplus-class.com** and the **Workgroup** setting should have been replaced with the **Domain** setting, where the **Domain** is **aplus-class.com.**
   c) Close the **System Control Panel.**

Network Shares

A *network share* is any network resource that is available to other computer users on the network. Typical shares include folders, printers, and drives. Because shares enable users to access a computer system from a remote location, you should secure all shared resources against unauthorized access. Users can map drives to any shared resource on the network to access files quickly and efficiently.

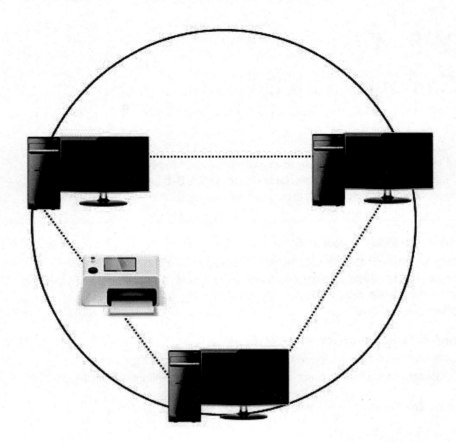

Figure 8-26: Shared resources.

On Windows systems, you can share folders by modifying the folders' properties. When you share a folder, you assign it a share name that can be different from the underlying folder name. You can share the folder more than once using different names.

Users can connect to the shared folder by browsing to the computer in **Network,** or by choosing **Start→Run** and entering the Universal Naming Convention (UNC) path to the folder, in the form *computername**sharename.* Be aware that a shared folder has two sets of permissions: the NTFS permissions (which are on the **Security** tab of that folder's **Properties**) and the share permissions (which are on the **Shared** tab of that folder's **Properties**). The security permissions do not automatically change once a folder is designated as a share, and there is no propagation between the two.

File Sharing with Mac OS X

When you use Mac OS X, you can share files in the Public folder for your user account with up to 10 other network users. (Sharing with more users requires Mac OS X Server.) You will need to make the AppleTalk® service active, assign a network name to your computer, and start the file sharing service. Other Mac® OS X users on your local network can then connect to your system by choosing **Connect To Server** from the **Go** menu and browsing for your computer's name. They can access files in your Public folder, and place files in your Drop Box folder.

For more information about file sharing in Mac OS X, including information on how to make other folders public, share files with remote users on the Internet, and share with computers running different operating systems, see the technical document "Mac 101: File sharing" on the Apple Computer website at **http://support.apple.com/kb/HT1549.**

File Sharing with UNIX or Linux

UNIX and Linux are typically used as centralized network file servers, rather than for ad hoc peer-to-peer resource sharing. These systems generally use the Network File Sharing (NFS) protocol to share files with other UNIX and Linux systems. NFS enables clients to see the files on the shared system as if they were part of the client's own local file system.

The specific steps for implementing file sharing with NFS will vary depending on your operating system version, and also depending on whether you use shell commands or your system's Graphical User Interface (GUI) to configure the service. This is also true for the commands or steps the clients will need to use to mount the file systems that NFS exports.

Windows Administrative Shares

Certain folders are shared by default on every Windows system. These administrative shares can be deleted, but by default, the system will re-create them every time it restarts (unlike local shares, which do not get re-created if they are deleted). The administrative shares are hidden shares, which means that they have a dollar sign ($) appended to the share name. (You can create your own hidden shares by doing the same thing.) You can connect to hidden shares by entering a Universal Naming Convention (UNC) path, but otherwise, the shares are not visible on the network.

You can see all shares on a system, including administrative shares, by opening **Computer Management,** expanding **Shared Folders,** and selecting the **Shares** node. You should see the following administrative shares on every Windows system:

- The root of each drive on the system is shared with its drive letter. Thus, the C drive is shared administratively as C$, the D drive is shared as D$, and so on.
- The folder where Windows is installed, usually the C:\Windows folder, is shared as ADMIN$.
- An InterProcess Communication (IPC) network object is created and shared as IPC$. This does not represent a local folder, but enables computers to establish network sessions.

 Access the Checklist tile on your LogicalCHOICE course screen for reference information and job aids on How to Create a Network Share

ACTIVITY 8–5
Creating a Network Share

Scenario

In this activity, you will create a network share.

1. Navigate to the C: drive and create a folder named **Share#** with the # being your student number.

2. Share the **Share#** folder with **Everyone,** and grant **Read/Write** share permissions.
   a) Select the folder, display its pop-up menu, and select **Share with.**
   b) Select **Specific people** to open the **File Sharing** wizard.
   c) On the **Choose people to share with** page, select the down arrow next to the text box and select **Find people.** In the **Select Users or Groups** dialog box, type *everyone.* Select **Check Names** and then select **OK.**
   d) In the list, select **Everyone,** and then select the down arrow under **Permission Level.** Select **Read/Write.**
   e) Select **Share.**
   f) In the **User Account Control** dialog box, in the user name text box, type *APLUS-CLASS/Administrator##.*
   g) In the **Password** text box, type *!Pass1234* and select **Yes.**
   h) Select **Done.**

Network Connection Types

Connecting various devices to a network can be done in a number of ways. How devices will communicate with one another is determined by the connection method:

- Virtually, using a virtual private network (VPN) connection.
- Using a dial-up connection.
- Wirelessly, through Bluetooth, infrared, or a WAP.
- Wired, using Ethernet cabling.
- Using a WWAN cellular connection.

Proxy Settings —middle man/ Facilitator a communicates

In computer networking, a *proxy* is a system that acts as an intermediary for requests for resources.

Client proxy software, such as Microsoft's MSP Client, can be installed on any client machine to add an additional level of security between the client machine and the proxy server. Data requests sent from the client get routed from the client side proxy through a back channel directly to the proxy server. The key part of this relationship is the additional metadata attached to the request by the client proxy that aids with identification once it hits the proxy server. So in essence the client proxy and the server proxy work together to provide quick identification and access to resources.

When configuring a client computer, use the following settings:

- Set the proxy server settings to the correct IP address.
- Exceptions can be set to include ranges (for example, you can bypass a proxy server if you access anything in the 192.168.x.y scope).

- Proxy settings can be set so that all HTTP or FTP connections use a proxy server, but no other connections.

 Access the Checklist tile on your LogicalCHOICE course screen for reference information and job aids on How to Configure Proxy Settings

Remote Desktop

Remote Desktop is used to operate a Windows computer from a remote location as if you were in front of it. Depending on the permissions you define, you will have full access to all resources, including printers, storage devices, and the network to which the machine is attached. You are even capable of accessing multiple machines at once or hopping to multiple machines in a chain, by running Remote Desktop on each machine on the daisy chain. In other words, Computer01 has a Remote Desktop connection to Computer02, and Computer02 has a Remote Desktop connection to Computer03. Computer01 has access to Computer03 through the open window that displays Computer02's desktop.

The biggest limitation of Remote Desktop on Windows is that only one person can be logged in to the machine at once, so once you log in using Remote Desktop, the monitor at the local computer will go to the login screen. If a local user logs in, the remote user will be disconnected. Remote Desktop is not really a remote diagnostic and troubleshooting tool as much as a management tool.

Network Location Settings

Windows 7 is configured to recognize three different network locations depending on what type of network you are connecting to. Network settings can be determined during the Windows 7 installation, or they will be set the first time the device is connected to a network.

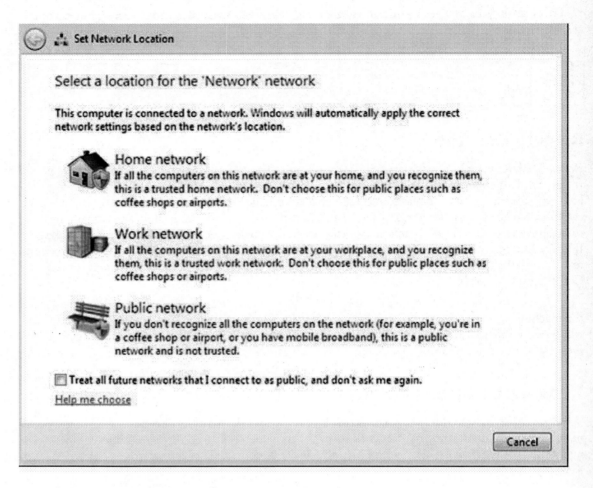

Figure 8-27: Network settings in Windows 7.

The following table describes each of the network location settings available in Windows 7.

Location	Description
Home	The Home network setting is used for small home networks where devices are trusted. All devices connected in a home network must be part of a workgroup or part of a homegroup. This allows all devices to recognize and see one another within the network using the network discovery function.
Work	The Work network setting is used for small private business networks. In this configuration all devices are part of a workgroup and can see one another as peers, but cannot join as a homegroup.
Public	The Public setting is used when devices connect to a network in a public space. This setting automatically applies security settings for that location and protects your device from unauthorized access via the public network.

Firewall Settings

Windows client firewalls can be configured for networking to ensure that they are secure against unauthorized access attempts and attacks. Consider the following settings when setting up the firewall:

- Enabling or disabling port security on certain ports.

- Inbound and outbound filtering. The user can set up rules or exceptions in the firewall settings to limit access to the web.
- Reporting and logging activity.
- Malware and spyware protection.
- Pop-up blocking.
- Port assigning, forwarding, and triggering.
- Enabling or disabling the Windows Firewall when necessary.

Windows Firewall is a software-based firewall that is included with Windows 7, Windows Vista, Windows XP with Service Pack 2, Windows Server® 2003 with Service Pack 1 or later, and Windows Server 2008. Once an operating system is installed, Windows Firewall is automatically installed and enabled. By default, the firewall blocks unsolicited incoming traffic on all ports. You can open blocked ports and configure other firewall settings by using the Windows Firewall program in the **Control Panel** or through Windows Security Policy Settings. In Windows 7, Windows Vista, and Windows Server 2008, Windows Firewall offers more security options and can be configured to drop outgoing traffic as well as incoming traffic.

Access the Checklist tile on your LogicalCHOICE course screen for reference information and job aids on How to Configure Windows Firewall Settings

Alternative IP Address Configuration Methods

In some cases you may need to configure an alternative IP address for your client computer. By configuring a static backup addressing scheme, you can ensure connectivity when DHCP is unavailable. Make sure to assign an appropriate IP address, subnet mask, and gateway, as well as at least one DNS server address.

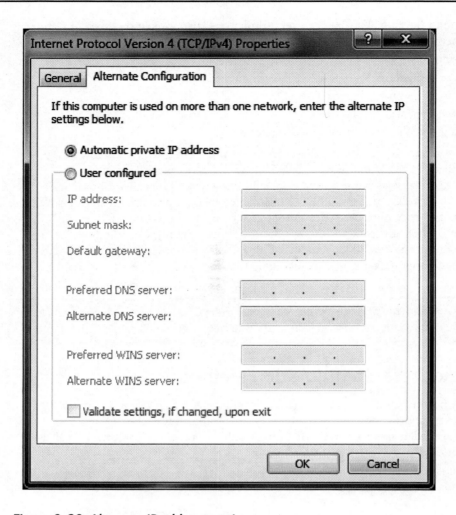

Figure 8–28: Alternate IP address settings.

Network Card Properties

A computing device's network card can be configured for optimal performance and specific network requirements.

Property	Description
Speed and duplex settings	The speed and duplex of the NIC can determine how efficient data transmissions are sent. The speed can range from 10 MB to 100 MB and can run in three different modes: • *Half duplex* permits two-way communication, but only in one direction at a time. • *Full duplex* permits simultaneous two-way communication. • *Auto negotiation* is used to negotiate a speed that is compatible with the network router or switch. In this process the NIC can respond quickly with a speed that meets the requirements of the network device.
Wake-on-LAN	*Wake-on-LAN (WOL)* is a networking capability that is built into a device's NIC circuitry that allows a device to turn on, or power up when a network message is received by another computing device. You can check if your NIC has this functionality by booting up the system BIOS and checking the NIC card properties.

Property	Description
PoE	*Power over Ethernet (PoE)* is a technology standard that enables both power and data to be transmitted over an Ethernet cable. NICs that are PoE compliant will allow both power and data to be sent as long as the device itself is also PoE compliant. PoE is commonly used to power and transmit data for APs that are installed in locations where AC outlets are not available.
QoS	*Quality of service* is a set of parameters that controls the level of quality provided to different types of network traffic. QoS allows NICs to prioritize data traffic in order to fully support the networking needs for all devices connected.

(handwritten note next to PoE: "Switch or VoIP Phones")

TOPIC F

Networking Tools

Now that you have covered all the different network types, configurations, and connection methods, you are ready to take a closer look at tools used to properly install, configure, and maintain all parts of a network.

Working with networks can be challenging depending on the size, location, and environment. In order to properly and safely work with networking components, you must understand how networking tools are used and how they can be used to fix common issues found in networks.

This topic covers all or part of the following CompTIA® A+® (2012) certification objectives:

* Exam 220–801: Objective 2.10: Given a scenario, use appropriate networking tools.

Cable Testers

A *cable tester,* also called a *media tester,* is an electrical instrument that verifies if a signal is present on a network cable. A simple cable tester will determine whether a cable has an end-to-end connection and can detect shorts or opens, but it cannot certify the cable for transmission quality.

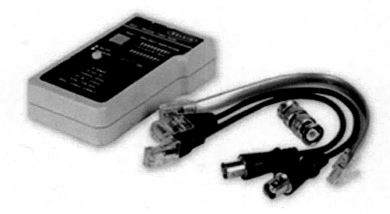

Figure 8–29: A cable tester.

Crimpers

A *wire crimper* is a tool that attaches media connectors to the ends of cables. You can use it if you need to make your own network cables or trim the end of a cable. There are different crimpers for different types of connectors, so select the one that is appropriate for the type of network media you are working with. A *wire stripper* is often part of a wire crimper, allowing the user to strip wires of their protective coating, and then use the crimping tool to attach a media connector.

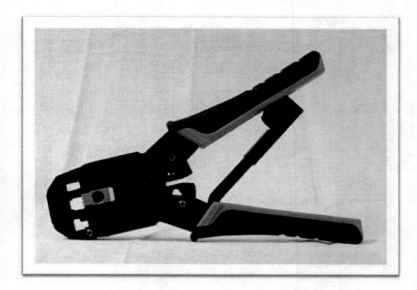

Figure 8-30: A wire crimper.

Multimeter

A *multimeter* is an electronic instrument used to measure voltage, current, and resistance. It usually has two probes with leads, one red and one black, that are plugged into two sockets on the meter. To switch between measuring volts, ohms, and amps, the leads can be moved to different sockets, or there may be a selector switch. Digital meters have a screen that displays the numeric value of what you are measuring. Analog meters have a thin needle that swings in an arc and indicates the value of what you are measuring. Many meters also have specific settings for testing circuit continuity, diodes, or battery charges. Multimeters are sometimes called volt-ohm meters.

 Note: Use a digital multimeter whenever possible. It is much more difficult to read and interpret an analog multimeter accurately.

Figure 8-31: Multimeters.

Toner Probe

A digital toner and toner probe traces and locates voice, audio, and video cabling on a network. In addition to confirming the cable location, a toner and probe can verify continuity and detect faults.

Labeling
Cable Runs

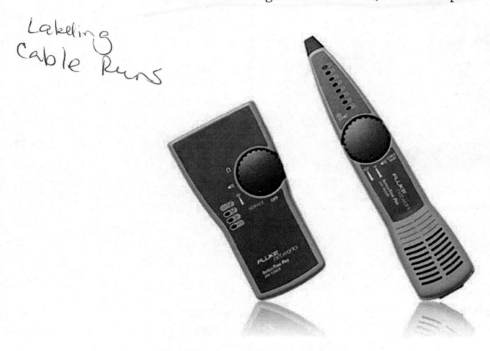

Figure 8-32: A toner probe.

Loopback Plug

A *loopback plug* is any tool that causes the device to transmit a signal back to itself. It is typically used for diagnosing transmission problems that redirects electrical signals back to the transmitting system. It typically plugs into a port and crosses over the transmit line to the receive line. Many times technicians will construct their own device based on their specific needs, but it can be used to test Ethernet network interface cards (NICs).

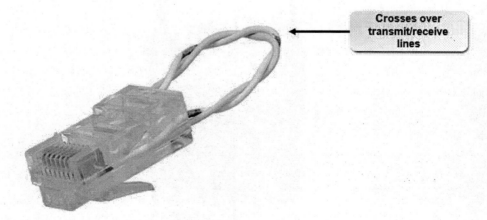

Crosses over transmit/receive lines

Figure 8-33: A loopback plug.

Punch Down Tool

A *punch down tool* is used in a wiring closet to connect cable wires directly to a patch panel. The tool strips the insulation from the end of the wire and embeds the wire into the connection at the back of the panel. The punch down tool makes connecting wires to a patch panel easier than it would be to connect them by hand. Without the punch down tool, you would have to strip the wire manually and connect it by twisting it or tightening it around a connection pole or screw.

 Note: The technical name for a punch down tool is an Insulation Displacement Connector (IDC).

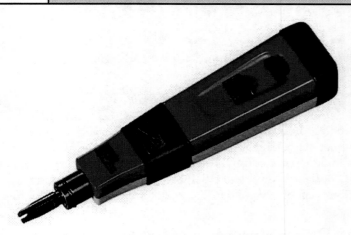

Figure 8–34: A punch down tool.

Networking Utilities

Microsoft includes a variety of tools in its Windows operating systems that you can use to troubleshoot TCP/IP.

Tool	Use To
ipconfig	Verify the configuration of TCP/IP and to release or renew DHCP IP address leases. (Other operating systems use different commands rather than ipconfig. For example, Linux uses ifconfig.)
ping	Test TCP/IP communications. With the -t switch, you can ping the indicated host until the request gets interrupted; with the -l [number] switch, you can send a ping of a specified buffer size.
nslookup	Verify that the computer can connect to a DNS server and successfully find an IP address for a given computer name.
tracert	Determine and test all points along the route the computer uses to send a packet to a destination. If tracert is unsuccessful, you can use the results generated to determine at what point communications are failing.
netstat	Show the status of each active network connection; netstat will display statistics for both TCP and UDP, including protocol, local address, foreign address, and the TCP connection state. Because UDP is connectionless, no connection information will be shown for UDP packets.
net	Manage Microsoft network resources from a command line. With the use option, you can connect or disconnect the computer from a shared resource. You can also retrieve information about current network connections. To see all of the available commands in this suite, type net /? at a command line.

Tool	Use To
Device connection status	Depending on whether you are using a wired or wireless network connection, the connection status might be called something like *Local Area Connection* or *Wireless Network Connection.* Verify that the device is connected to the network and able to send and receive data.
Network troubleshooters	Walk you through the resolutions to various common network problems. There are several network-related troubleshooters in the **Help and Support Center** that can help.

Ipconfig Options

The ipconfig command provides several options that are helpful for network maintenance and troubleshooting.

Command	Enables You To
ipconfig /all	View the computer's host name, DNS domain name, network card driver, IP address, subnet mask, default gateway, DNS server(s), and WINS server(s). In addition, you can use this display to determine whether the computer was configured through DHCP or APIPA. If the computer obtained its addressing through DHCP, you also see the IP address of the DHCP server.
ipconfig /release	Release the IP addressing information assigned to the computer by the DHCP server or APIPA.
ipconfig /renew	Lease IP addressing information from a DHCP server or APIPA. If the computer already has a good IP addressed leased, it will not renew unless you release the address first.
ipconfig /flushdns	Clear DNS information on the client so that client updates with new configuration information more quickly.
ipconfig / registerdns	Register the client with its DNS server.

ACTIVITY 8-6
Identifying Networking Tools

Scenario
In this activity, you will identify networking tools.

---

1. **You need to determine if a cable is carrying a signal. Which networking tools might help you?**
   - ☐ Crimpers
   - ☐ Cable testers
   - ☐ Multimeters
   - ☐ Toner probe
   - ☐ Punch down tool

2. **You need to connect cable wires to a patch panel. Which networking tool might help you?**
   - ○ Crimpers
   - ○ Loopback plug
   - ○ Punch down tool
   - ○ Toner probe

3. Open a command prompt.
   a) Select **Start.**
   b) In the **Search programs and files** text box, enter *cmd*
   c) Select **cmd.**

4. Display and examine the TCP/IP configuration information for your computer.
   a) Enter *ipconfig /all*
   b) Scroll through the results of the command as your instructor describes the information that is displayed.

5. Verify network connectivity with the **APLUS-DC** server.
   a) Enter *ping 192.168.1.10*
   b) Examine the results. Were you able to reach the target computer?

6. Examine the status of network connections on your computer.
   a) Enter *netstat*
   b) Examine the results as your instructor describes them.

7. View help for the `net` command.
   a) Enter *net /?*
   b) Enter *net help*
   c) Examine the results as your instructor describes them.
   d) Select at least one of the `net help` commands (such as `net help view`) and display detailed help information. Share your findings with the rest of the class.

8. Close the command prompt.

Summary

In this lesson, you identified many different network technologies. Networking is at the heart of any type of business. Without it, a business simply cannot function in today's world. It is your job to ensure that the networks behind the business are running properly and managed correctly.

What do you think are the most important network concepts covered in this lesson?

Do you have any experience working with any of these technologies?

 Note: Check your LogicalCHOICE Course screen for opportunities to interact with your classmates, peers, and the larger LogicalCHOICE online community about the topics covered in this course or other topics you are interested in. From the Course screen you can also access available resources for a more continuous learning experience.

9 Installing, Configuring, and Maintaining SOHO Networks

Lesson Time: 1 hour, 30 minutes

Lesson Objectives

In this lesson, you will install, configure, and maintain SOHO networks. You will:

- Install and configure a SOHO network.

- Implement SOHO network security.

Lesson Introduction

In the last lesson, you identified basic networking technologies. As an A+ technician, you might be asked to implement these technologies in a small office or home office (SOHO) situation, rather than in a corporate enterprise setting. In this lesson, you will install, configure, and maintain SOHO networks.

Small businesses, whether located in a commercial building or in an individual's home, can benefit greatly from being able to share files and other resources. SOHO networks generally contain anywhere from two to ten computers, though there can be exceptions to this guideline. As an A+ technician, you might be called upon to implement SOHO networks as part of your job duties.

This lesson covers all or part of the following CompTIA® A+® (2012) certification objectives:

- Topic A:
  - Exam 220–801: Objectives 2.5, 2.6
  - Exam 220-802: Objective 2.3
- Topic B:
  - Exam 220–802: Objectives 2.3, 2.5, 2.6

TOPIC A

Install and Configure SOHO Networks

In the last lesson, you covered basic networking concepts, the Transmission Control Protocol/ Internet Protocol (TCP/IP) addressing scheme, and how networks are connected. In this topic, you will use that knowledge to install and configure a SOHO network.

SOHO networks are much like the larger corporate networks, just on a much smaller scale. No matter what the size or location of the network, you are still responsible for understanding how it is structured and configured. A+ technicians must understand the needs and complexities of SOHO wired and wireless networks.

This topic covers all or part of the following CompTIA® A+® (2012) certification objectives:

- Exam 220–801: Objective 2.5: Compare and contrast wireless networking standards and encryption types.
- Exam 220-801: Objective 2.6: Install, configure, and deploy a SOHO wireless/wired router using appropriate settings.
- Exam 220–802: Objective 2.3: Implement security best practices to secure a workstation.

What is a SOHO Network?

A *SOHO network* is a network that provides connectivity and resource sharing for a small office or home office. Generally limited to fewer than 20 computers or nodes, a SOHO network often facilitates sharing of files and printers, as well as services such as email, faxing, and so forth. A SOHO network can contain a combination of wired and wireless computer connections, and all of the computing devices in a SOHO network usually share the same physical location.

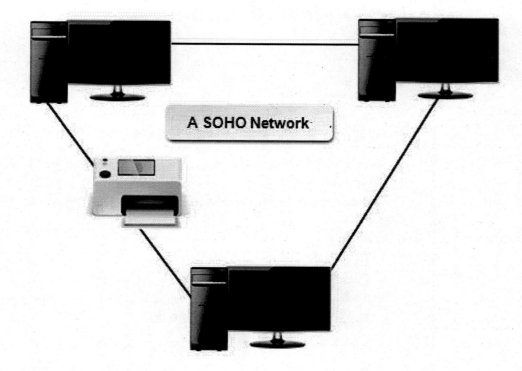

Figure 9–1: A SOHO Network.

How Small is Small?

SOHO networks can range in size, and there is no real consensus as to the maximum number of nodes that can be in a SOHO network. Some sources cite the maximum as 10 nodes, while others say that four or five nodes is the maximum.

Firewalls and SOHO Networks

A firewall is a software program or hardware device that protects networks from unauthorized access by blocking unsolicited traffic. Firewalls allow incoming or outgoing traffic that has specifically been permitted by configuring settings. Firewalls use complex filtering algorithms that analyze incoming network data based on destination and source addresses, port numbers, and data type. In many cases a firewall will be the first stop in defending unauthorized access attempts in a SOHO network. Because of the small network size a SOHO the firewall installed must provide the right level of security for the size of the office and the number of connected computing devices.

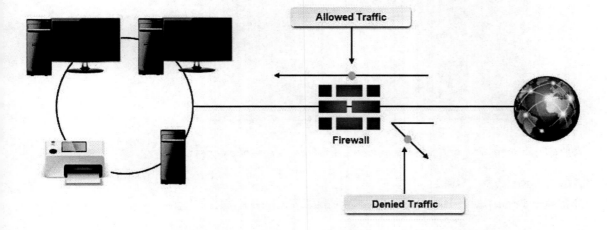

Figure 9–2: A firewall in a SOHO network.

Software Firewalls

In some cases a software firewall can be useful for SOHOs. The firewall provides many features that can be configured to suit various computing needs. Some features include:

- Enabling or disabling port security on certain ports.
- Inbound and outbound filtering. The user can set up rules or exceptions in the firewall settings to limit access to the web.
- Reporting and logging activity.
- Malware and spyware protection.
- Pop-up blocking.
- Port assigning, forwarding, and triggering.

Hardware Firewalls

A hardware firewall is a hardware device, either stand-alone or built into most routers, that protects computers on a private network from unauthorized traffic. They are placed between the private network and the public network to manage inbound and outbound traffic and network access.

DMZs

A *demilitarized zone (DMZ)* is a small section of a private network that is located between two firewalls and made available for public access. A DMZ enables external clients to access data on private systems, such as web servers, without compromising the security of the internal network as a whole. The external firewall enables public clients to access the service whereas the internal firewall prevents them from connecting to protected internal hosts.

In small offices, DMZs are commonly used to protect any client-facing webservers. This security method prevents any hackers from seeing the private internal IP scheme.

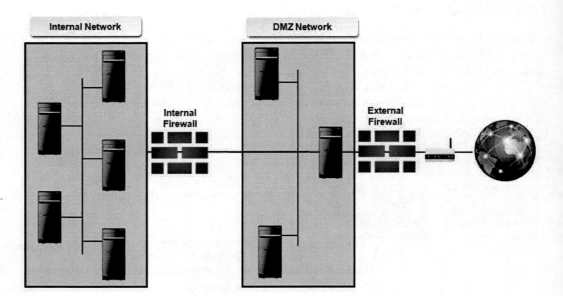

Port 80
open

Figure 9–3: A section of a private network available for public access.

Other Names for DMZs

DMZs might also be referred to as perimeter networks or screened subnets.

NAT Implementations

Network address translation (NAT) can be implemented as software on a variety of systems or as hardware in a dedicated device such as a router. Internet Connection Sharing (ICS) in Windows systems includes a simple software-based NAT implementation, but requires a separate device, such as a modem, to provide actual Internet connectivity. Hardware-based NAT devices, such as cable modems and DSL routers, often have extended functionality and can double as Internet access devices.

 Note: A vast internal network can be configured with a single public address, which makes NAT both secure and cost-efficient.

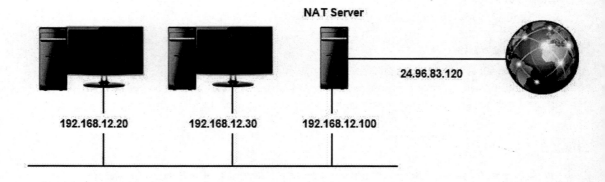

Figure 9–4: NAT Implementation.

Static vs. Dynamic NAT

In static NAT, each internal address is mapped to a single specific public address. In dynamic NAT, there is not a one-to-one ratio of internal to external addresses; any number of internal addresses can share a pool of external addresses.

WPS

Wi-Fi-Protected Setup (WPS) is a newer standard that was released in 2007 by the Wi-Fi Alliance to enable an easy yet secure setup of small home networks. The goal of the standard was to ease the setup and complicated configuration settings of wireless routers designed for use in SOHO networks. WPS is a service that comes installed on some routers to support quick secure setups for routers; however, recently the standard has been tainted. The standard has been cracked by brute force attacks and has been reported to be less secure. It is important to fully understand the technology installed on network devices before you connect and install them within your network. In most cases routers come with WPS enabled by default, so you may need to turn it off once the router is connected.

Basic QoS

The amount of data being transmitted over networks is rising every day. Also, the type of data being transferred is changing. Traditional applications such as file transfer protocol (FTP) and Telnet are now outnumbered by real-time multimedia applications such as IP telephony, multimedia applications, and videoconferencing. FTP and Telnet are very sensitive to packet loss but are tolerant to delays in data delivery. The reverse is applicable to multimedia applications; they can compensate for some amount of packet loss, but are very sensitive toward delays in data delivery. Therefore, an optimum usage of bandwidth becomes very critical while dealing with multimedia applications. Low bandwidth may result in a bad quality transmission of real-time applications, leading to dropouts or hangs. In small offices, this issue can be a major problem due to the small network and need to access the Internet. To avoid this, certain parameters were developed to prioritize bandwidth allocation for real-time applications on networks such as the Internet and guarantee a specific QoS.

Quality of Service (QoS) is a set of parameters that controls the quality provided to different types of network traffic. QoS parameters include the maximum amount of delay, signal loss and noise that can be accommodated for a particular type of network traffic; bandwidth priority; and CPU usage for a specific stream of data. These parameters are agreed upon by the transmitter and the receiver, the transmitter being the ISP and the receiver being the subscriber. Both the transmitter and receiver enter into an agreement known as the *Service Level Agreement (SLA)*. In addition to defining QoS parameters, the SLA describes remedial measures or penalties to be incurred by an ISP in the event that the ISP fails to provide the QoS promised in the SLA.

Relevance for SOHO Networks

In SOHO networks, network performance degradation can occur when several users are running multiple applications or processes (such as downloads) that consume a lot of network bandwidth. Often, the effects of this are markedly slow Internet connections or connectivity issues with Voice over IP (VoIP) phones. By implementing basic QoS to prioritize services such as VoIP over file downloads and Internet surfing, you can ensure that the services that you decide to prioritize are getting the bandwidth they need.

802.11 Wireless Standards

The *802.11* standard is a family of specifications developed by the IEEE for wireless LAN technology.

802.11 Standard	Description
802.11a	*802.11a* is an approved specification for a fast, secure, but relatively expensive wireless protocol. 802.11a supports speeds up to 54 Mbps in the 5 GHz frequency band. Unfortunately, that speed has a limited range of only 60 feet, which, depending on how you arrange your access points, could severely limit user mobility.
802.11b	*802.11b* (also called *Wi-Fi,* short for "wireless fidelity") is probably the most common and certainly the least expensive wireless network protocol. 802.11b provides for an 11 Mbps transfer rate in the 2.4 GHz frequency. Some vendors have increased the rate on their devices. 802.11b has a range up to 1,000 feet in an open area, and a range of 200 to 400 feet in an enclosed space (where walls might hamper the signal). It is not compatible with 802.11a. This standard supports up to 14 channels, but the available channels depend on local regulations. For instance, in areas where the FCC governs, the available channels are channel 1 through channel 11.
802.11e	*802.11e* is a wireless standard for home and business implementations. It adds Quality of Service (QoS) features and multimedia support to 802.11a and 802.11b, and is compatible with those standards.
802.11g	*802.11g* is a specification for wireless data throughput at the rate of up to 54 Mbps in the 2.4 GHz band. It is compatible with 802.11b, and is replacing it due to its faster speed.
802.11n	*802.11n* is a recent specification for wireless data throughput. Even before approval, many "Draft N" or "Pre-N" products were already being produced and sold, compliant with the specification. The specification increased speeds dramatically with data throughput up to 600 Mbps in the 2.4 GHz or 5 GHz ranges.

Handwritten annotations in left column:
- 802.11a: *Low supply*, *5 GHz*
- 802.11b: *Wifi*, *11mps ~2.4*
- 802.11e: *QoS into wifi*
- 802.11g: *54 Mps in 2.4Gh*
- 802.11n: *dual Band*, *Beng*

 Note: Home-based Wi-Fi networks are often susceptible to interference from microwave ovens, which also operate in the 2.4 GHz frequency range.

WAPs

A *Wireless Access Point (WAP)* is a device that provides connection between wireless devices and enables wireless networks to connect to wired networks. A WAP is sometimes called just an AP or a WLAN-AP. WAPs have a network interface to connect to the wired network and a radio antenna or infrared receiver to receive the wireless signals. Many include security features that enable you to specify which wireless devices can make connections to the wired network.

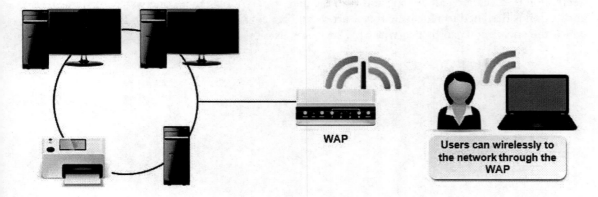

Figure 9-5: A Wireless Access Point.

SSID

The *Service Set Identifier (SSID)* is a 32-bit alphanumeric string that identifies a WAP and all devices that connect to it. Since a wireless client device must provide the SSID in order to connect to the WAP, the SSID functions as a sort of password for the wireless network. However, because the WAP typically broadcasts the SSID in plain text, it does not provide any security. It is more realistic to think of the SSID as a network name that is applied to the grouping of the WAP and the devices currently connected to it. The administrator can accept a device's default SSID or specify an SSID manually to more clearly identify the device.

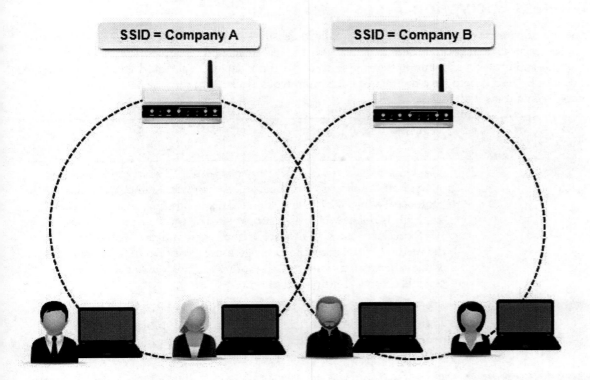

Figure 9-6: SSID.

What is Encryption?

Encryption is the process of converting data into a form that is not easily recognized or understood by anyone who is not authorized to access the data. Only authorized parties with the necessary decryption information can decode and read the data. Encryption can be one-way, which means the encryption is designed to hide only the cleartext and is never decrypted, or it can be two-way, in which the encryption can be decrypted back to cleartext and read.

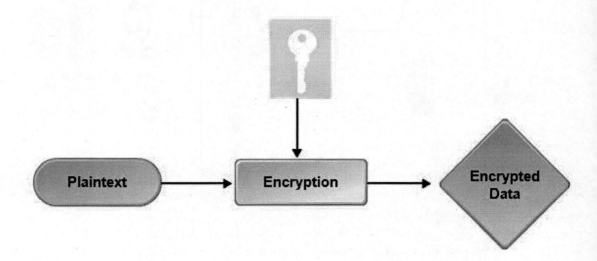

Figure 9–7: Encryption.

Wireless Encryption Types

The use of wireless computing devices is rapidly increasing every day. This also increases the risk of wireless security attacks on devices to gain access to secure data and resources. *Wireless encryption* conceals and protects data during transmission so that if the data were accessed during transmission it cannot be read. There are a number of encryption types available to provide encryption over wireless data transmissions.

Wireless Encryption Type	Description
WEP Broken	*Wired Equivalent Privacy (WEP)* provides 64-bit, 128-bit, and 256-bit encryption for wireless communication that uses the 802.11a and 802.11b protocols. While WEP might sound like a good solution at first, it ironically is not as secure as it should be. The problem stems from the way WEP produces the keys that are used to encrypt data. Because of a flaw in the method, attackers could easily generate their own keys by using a wireless network capture tool to capture and analyze network data and crack WEP in a short period of time.
WPA	*Wi-Fi Protected Access (WPA)* is a security protocol that was introduced to address some of the shortcomings in the WEP protocol during the pending development of the 802.11i IEEE standard. It uses strong authentication and data encryption mechanisms.
WPA2 or 802.11i	*802.11i* is a complete wireless standard that adds strong encryption and authentication security to 802.11 and relies on 802.1x as the authentication mechanism. 802.11i is sometimes referred to as WPA2. • WPA provides improved data encryption through the *Temporal Key Integrity Protocol (TKIP)*, which is a security protocol created by the IEEE 802.11i task group to replace WEP. It is combined with the

Wireless Encryption Type	Description
	existing WEP encryption to provide a 128-bit encryption key that fixes the key length issues of WEP.
	• In addition to TKIP, WPA2 adds *Advanced Encryption Standard (AES)* cipher-based Counter Mode with Cipher Block Chaining Message Authentication Code Protocol (CCMP) encryption for even greater security and to replace TKIP. It provides a 128-bit encryption key.
	• Both standards have been extended to include several types of user authentication through EAP, which is considered poor in WEP. WEP regulates access to a wireless network based on a computer's hardware-specific MAC address, which is relatively easy to figure out, steal, and use (that is, sniff and spoof). EAP is built on a more secure public key encryption system to ensure that only authorized network users can access the network.

Router Settings and Configurations

Most routers available today can be configured for wired and wireless networks. Depending on the router installation, there are a number of settings that can be configured to ensure connectivity, security, and access.

Setting	Description
Basics	Basic settings apply to both wired and wireless routers and can include the ability to: • Secure your router or access point administration interface. • Change default administrator passwords (and user names). • Disable remote administration. • Secure/disable the reset switch/function. • Change the default SNMP parameter. • Regularly upgrade the Wi-Fi router firmware to ensure you have the latest security patches and critical fixes.
SSID	When installing a wireless router, change the default Service Set Identifier (SSID) and verify that you are not broadcasting out to the network.
MAC filtering	Apply MAC address filtering to both wired and wireless routers. By configuring a wireless access point (WAP) to filter MAC addresses, you can control which wireless clients may join your network.
Channels	Change the default channel on wireless routers. By changing the router channel, you can optimize data transmission and reduce interference with other routers in close proximity. If your router is dual channel, then you can easily change from the default channel to the other channel available. To help determine what channel is not being used there are utilities available that can scan the local area and display used channels. This can be very helpful in choosing a different less used channel for your router.
DHCP	Depending on the needs of your network, turn on DHCP on both wired and wireless routers to automatically connect and assign an IP address, or turn it off and enter a static IP address.

Port Forwarding and Triggering

If your router has NAT, then you can also configure port forwarding, which forwards a network port from one network node to another, and port triggering, which automates port forwarding by specifying ports (triggering ports) to automatically and dynamically forward inbound traffic to.

 Access the Checklist tile on your LogicalCHOICE course screen for reference information and job aids on How to Install and Configure SOHO Networks

TOPIC B

SOHO Network Security

In the last topic, you installed and configured a SOHO network. As with any other computer network, SOHO networks need to be secured to prevent unauthorized access and other threats. In this topic, you will examine how security controls are implemented to secure both wired and wireless SOHO networks.

Securing your network is critical to keeping data, systems and resources safe from unauthorized access. You must understand what the security implications are when a network is improperly secured. Security controls and implementations restrict access to sensitive data and system resources. As the A+ technician, it's your job to make sure that the right security controls are implemented and functioning as expected.

This topic covers all or part of the following CompTIA® A+® (2012) certification objectives:

- Exam 220–802: Objective 2.3: Implement security best practices to secure a workstation.
- Exam 220–802: Objective 2.5: Given a scenario, secure a SOHO wireless network.
- Exam 220–802: Objective 2.6: Given a scenario, secure a SOHO wired network.

SOHO Security Methods

When implementing and configuring a SOHO network, you must ensure that the proper security measures have been taken to prevent any unauthorized access.

Method	Description
Change default user name and password	Change the default user name and password for all devices connected to the network. Use strong password guidelines when assigning the new passwords.
Enable MAC filtering	MAC address filtering provides a simple method of securing a network. Typically, an administrator configures a list of client MAC addresses that are allowed to join the network. Those pre-approved clients are granted access if the MAC address is known by the network.
Assign static IP addresses	When implementing a small network, you can assign each device on the network a static IP address. When each device has a designated IP address, you remove the plug-in-and-go capability that DHCP provides, so only those devices with IP addresses that are in the same range as the static addresses will be able to connect to the network.
Disable ports	Disabling unused network ports can prevent unauthorized access to your network. Attackers look for open ports on networks to launch an attack.
Apply physical security controls	Depending on the location of the network, you may need to ensure that the devices and network components cannot be accessed by unauthorized users. This may be as simple as making sure that all the entrances have proper security controls installed. This could be anything from locked doors, surveillance systems, to installing a biometric identification system.
Perform assessments	Perform regular security assessments to determine if current controls are meeting the needs of the organization.

Wireless Security

Wireless security is any method of securing a wireless local area network (LAN) to prevent unauthorized network access and network data theft. You need to ensure that authorized users can connect to the network without any hindrances. Wireless networks are more vulnerable to attacks than any other network system. For one thing, most wireless devices such as laptops, mobile phones, and other mobile devices search and connect automatically to the access point offering the best signal, which can be coming from an attacker. Wireless transmissions can also be scanned or sniffed out of the air, with no need to access physical network media. Such attacks can be avoided by using relevant security protocols.

SOHO Wireless Security Methods

There are a number of security methods you can use to ensure that your wireless network is secure from unauthorized access.

Method	Description
Configure the network settings	• Secure your wireless router or access point administration interface. • Disable remote administration. • Secure/disable the reset switch/function. • Change the default SNMP parameter. • Change the default channel. • Regularly upgrade the Wi-Fi router firmware to ensure you have the latest security patches and critical fixes. • Use the Remote Authentication Dial-In User Service Plus (RADIUS+) network directory authentication where feasible. • Use a VPN. • Perform periodic rogue wireless access point scans.
Configure the SSID	• Disable the Service Set Identifier (SSID). • Change the default SSID broadcast.
Setting encryption	• Enable WPA2 encryption. • Change the default encryption keys. • Avoid using pre-shared keys (PSK).
Properly place the antenna and access point	• Position the router or access point and antennae safely. The radio frequency range of each access point should not extend beyond the physical boundaries and layout of the organization's facilities. • Adjust the radio power level controls on routers and access points as needed to help minimize power consumption within the wireless network. It can be difficult to manage the radio power of wireless to reduce the power used, while providing the right level of radio power to operate the network.
Secure the wireless access point	Specific procedures for implementing security options on wireless devices, as well as the options your devices support, will vary. Always check the documentation from your wireless device manufacturer before implementing any security configurations. Common methods include: • Implementing some form of user authentication. • Implementing a security protocol that requires over-the-air data encryption.

Method	Description
	• Updating firmware on the device to implement any manufacturer security patches and enhancements. • Restricting unauthorized devices from connecting to the WAP by filtering out unauthorized MAC addresses. • Implementing a firewall. For a small office or home office, enable a firewall on the WAP, and then also on the host computer to further secure your network. • Configuring vendor-recommended security settings on your wireless router or access point.
Configure the workstation	• Do not auto-connect to open Wi-Fi networks. • Enable firewalls on each computer and the router. • Assign static IP addresses to devices to prevent inadvertent broadcasting of IP addresses to unauthorized parties.

Wireless Client Configuration Options

You have several options for increasing the security on your wireless clients, however specific procedures for implementing security options on wireless clients, as well as the options your devices support, will vary. Consult the documentation for your wireless client devices.

• Implement a security protocol that requires over-the-air data encryption.
• Install antivirus software and/or adware and spyware blockers.
• Update clients regularly with any software security patches.

ACTIVITY 9-1
Discussing Wireless SOHO Security Methods

Scenario

In this activity, you will identify some commonly used wireless security methods.

What security methods do you think a SOHO organization is most likely invest in and implement? What methods do you think they are less likely to implement?

Summary

In this lesson, you installed, configured, and maintained SOHO networks. These skills can help you support users in smaller networking environments so that they can communicate and share resources in a secure manner.

Do you have any experience working with SOHO networks? What do you expect to support in future job functions?

What do you think is the most important SOHO network security measure?

Note: Check your LogicalCHOICE Course screen for opportunities to interact with your classmates, peers, and the larger LogicalCHOICE online community about the topics covered in this course or other topics you are interested in. From the Course screen you can also access available resources for a more continuous learning experience.

10 | Supporting Laptops

Lesson Time: 1 hour

Lesson Objectives

In this lesson, you will support laptops. You will:

- Describe laptop hardware and components.

- Install and configure laptop hardware components.

Lesson Introduction

In the previous lessons, the focus has been on installing system components, operating systems, and establishing network connectivity. In this lesson, the focus will be on laptop components and how they differ from the standard system components. As an A+ technician, you will also require a robust knowledge of portable computing principles. In this lesson, you will install and configure various system components and explore the components that make up the laptop.

Laptops are everywhere today. Because of their portability and powerful computing capabilities they are prominent in most workplaces. So, as a certified A+ technician, you will be expected to configure, maintain, and troubleshoot laptop computing devices. With the proper information and the right skills, you will be ready to support these devices as efficiently as you support their desktop counterparts.

This lesson covers all or part of the following CompTIA® A+® (2012) certification objectives:

- Topic A:
  - Exam 220–801: Objectives 1.3. 3.1, 3.2, 3.3
- Topic B:
  - Exam 220–801: Objective 3.1

TOPIC A

Laptop Hardware and Components

You have examined the components of desktop machines in the previous lessons. Similarly, laptops have many of the same components that are configured to fit into a portable format. In this topic, you will examine the hardware components of a laptop.

As a certified A+ technician, you already know a lot about the components of desktop systems. However, you will also be expected to support laptops, and the components are not always the same as their desktop counterparts. Having a solid understanding of laptop hardware components is essential for you to be able to implement and support them properly. The information in this topic should give you the foundation you need to understand the components in the various types of laptops you might be called upon to support.

This topic covers all or part of the following CompTIA® A+® (2012) (2012) certification objectives:

- Exam 220–801: Objective 1.3: Compare and contrast RAM types and features.
- Exam 220–801: Objective 3.1: Install and configure laptop hardware and components.
- Exam 220–801: Objective 3.2: Compare and contrast the components within the display of a laptop.
- Exam 220–801: Objective 3.3: Compare and contrast laptop features.

Laptops

A *laptop* is a complete computer system that is small, compact, lightweight, and portable. All laptops have specialized hardware designed especially for use in a smaller portable system, use standard operating systems, can run on battery or AC power, and can connect to other devices. Laptops and their components can vary by the following factors:

- Size of the device. Smaller models are referred to as notebooks or sub-notebooks and typically have fewer features.
- Display size, quality, and technology.
- Keyboard size, number of keys, and additional options.
- Pointing device used.
- Power supply type.
- Battery type used.
- Length of battery support time.
- How long it takes to recharge the battery.
- Power cord connection and power source options.
- Docking solutions.
- Connections for external peripherals.
- The power button can be located inside or outside of the closed case. It is more often located inside so that it is not accidentally turned on when it is in the user's briefcase or being transported in some other bag.
- Bays or connections for additional drives such as optical drives.

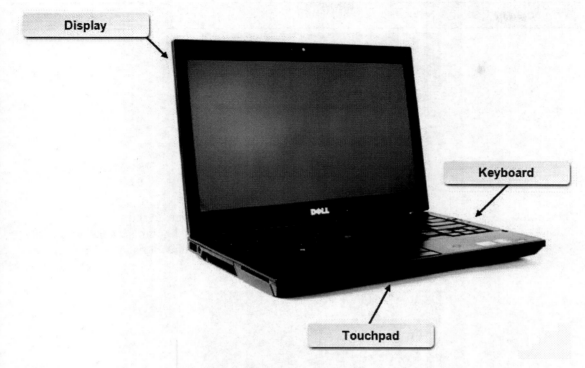

Figure 10–1: A laptop.

Laptop Hardware Components

A laptop has many different hardware components that each have unique characteristics and features.

Component	Description
Keyboard	The keyboard is an integrated component on a laptop. Not all laptop keyboards can be replaced, so you should check the manufacturers documentation to verify that it can be repaired or replaced. 
Touchpad	A touchpad is a small, touch-sensitive pad where you run your finger across the surface to send electronic signals to the computer to control the pointer on the screen. Touchpads can have buttons like a mouse or trackball, or the touchpad can be configured to detect finger taps on its surface and process those signals like a mouse button.

Component	Description

Trackpoint

A *trackpoint*, or pointing stick, is most commonly found on laptops. Located in the center of the keyboard, the trackpoint is a small joystick-like button that responds to user force in all directions in order to move the mouse pointer on screen.

Plastics

The *plastics* are the hard surfaces that cover the internal components of the laptop. They are typically secured together using small screws or pressure tabs.

Speaker

The speakers are located in a number locations depending on the style and manufacturer of the laptop. Newer model laptop speakers are just as powerful as the desktop versions.

Component	Description

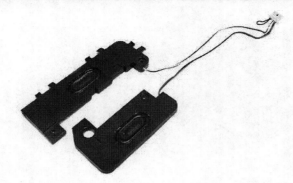

Battery	The battery designed for laptops is rechargeable and can easily be removed or replaced. Most batteries will last between one and six hours per charge while extended life batteries have a wide range of limitations based on the manufacturer and what the user is doing with the laptop. Programs that require more computing power and screen updates such as multimedia applications are likely to deplete the battery faster than working on simple word processing documents. Some laptops offer extra battery packs that can be inserted in place of other removable devices, such as optical drives, allowing users to easily reconfigure their laptops for various travel and working situations. Rechargeable batteries are used in most portable computing devices. They are usually packaged in a battery pack. Before replacing a laptop battery you should verify what the system requirements are. New batteries must be compatible with the system.

DC jack	The direct current (DC) jack on a laptop provides power through the power cord. Most laptop DC jacks are specific to the manufacturer and even the laptop model, so make sure to check the documentation for power requirements and compatible power cords.

Component	Description

Screen	The screen is the visual display of a laptop and is typically hinged at the bottom and swings down to form the cover for the laptop. It latches to the body of the computer to secure it for transport.

Integrated Peripherals

Integrated peripherals include the screen, keyboard, and touchpad devices. Not all peripherals can be replaced. Check with the manufacturer of the laptop for guidelines on what components can be replaced and what components cannot.

Types of Laptop Displays

Traditionally, laptop displays used CCFL with an inverter cable. Newer laptops use LCD or LED displays.

Contrast Ratio

The contrast ratio is a metric of a display system, defined as the ratio of the luminosity of the brightest and the darkest color the system is capable of producing. High contrast ratio is a desired aspect of any display.

Laptop Display Components

Within the display unit of a laptop, there are several specialized components, with a unique function.

Component	Description
Inverter	An *inverter* is used to convert DC power to AC power for the display. When an inverter fails, depending on the laptop model, it may be

Component	Description
	appropriate to simply replace the display rather than replace the inverter. Replacement of the inverter requires an exact match, both electrically and mechanically (connectors, size/shape, and mounting).
Backlight	A *backlight* is the typical form of illumination used in a full-sized LCD display. Backlights differ from frontlights because they illuminate the LCD from the side or back, where frontlights are in front of the LCD. *Frontlights* are used in small displays such as on MP3 players to increase readability in low light conditions.
Wi-Fi antenna	The Wi-Fi antenna is typically placed inside the display section of the laptop. The cables are run along the sides of the display unit and connects to the network card inside the main unit of the laptop. It sends and receives wireless signals and transmissions to the WAP.

Internal Laptop Components

The internal components of a laptop are similar to full size desktop computers except that they are much smaller and more compact to fit inside the case.

Component	Description
Motherboard	From a technical viewpoint, a laptop system board is very similar to the system boards found in desktop systems. The main difference is that the components are often compressed to squeeze into a smaller space. Other major differences include reduced power consumption and more common integration of items such as video, sound, USB/FireWire®, wired and wireless network connections, and so on. Laptop system boards often contain power management and throttling options to help in preserving battery life. These features allow for the machine to adjust the power to the processor and other components as necessary.
	The integration of all the features on the motherboard limits customization options and necessitates replacement of the entire board when one of the integrated features fails. However, you may be able to use an alternative slot or port and add an adapter card or an external device to substitute for the failed integrated component.
CPU	Laptop CPUs are designed to use less power and to generate less heat than desktop CPUs, and often are designed to be used without a CPU fan, which, again, saves on size and weight, as well as reducing power consumption to maximize battery life. CPUs can be surface-mounted devices, soldered directly to the motherboard, or attached via a socket on the motherboard. CPUs that are soldered onto the motherboard are not replaceable. It is best to determine how a laptop CPU is attached before trying to replace it.
Hard drive	Portable computer drives are specially designed to fit in portable computers. Drives can be unique to a manufacturer and sometimes even to the computer model. All laptop computers have an internal hard drive. Hard drives come in two main form factors: 2.5 inch and 3.5 inch. The 3.5 inch HDD tends to be too big for laptops, so in most laptops the hard drives the 2.5-inch HDD. Because of their smaller size, the 2.5 inch platters tend to run at slower speeds than the 3.5 inch desktop HDDs.
	Some internal hard drives are difficult to remove and require dismantling of the computer. Others have a slide lock to unlock them from the case, so that

Component	Description
	you can slide the drive out. If it is too difficult to remove the internal drive from the notebook you are working on, then you might consider using alternate hard drive solutions such as USB or FireWire hard drives that can be connected externally.
Memory	Portable devices use memory that was specifically designed for those devices. Since it is not produced in as high quantities as desktop memory, it tends to be more expensive. While some laptops use SODIMM modules, which are about half the size of standard desktop DIMMs, or *MicroDIMMs,* many require non-standard proprietary memory that must be ordered from the manufacturer. Other portable computing devices and some notebooks use flash memory modules rather than regular RAM. Be sure to check the documentation for your device so that you purchase the correct type of memory. Before you replace the memory in a laptop, you must verify that it is compatible with the system. Always check the manufacturer's documentation or website to verify the form factor and types of compatible memory.
Optical drive	Optical drives in laptops are similar in function to the full size desktop models except that they are small and more compact. When replacing a drive, the first thing to do is check with the manufacturer to verify that it can be replaced and with what type of drive. You need to make sure that the drive you install in compatible with the laptop.
Wireless card	In some laptops, the wireless card and video card can be upgraded to improve performance. However, replacement is dependent on whether the card is an integrated component of the mobile system board. In this case, you cannot upgrade or replace the card. If the card is independent of the system board, then you should refer to the manufacturer's documentation to verify what components can be replaced and upgraded. Some components may be covered under a system's warranty, so refer to the manufacturer's policies to determine what can be upgraded without breaking the warranty guidelines.

Laptop Memory Package Specifications

The following table lists some of the technical specifications for laptop memory packages.

Memory Package	Description
SODIMM	Small Outline Dual Inline Memory Module. Used in some notebook systems and Apple® iMac® systems. Measures about 2 inches by 1 inch and has 144 pins. Capacity ranges from 16 to 256 MB per module.
MicroDIMM	Micro Dual Inline Memory Module. Used in small, sub-compact notebooks. Measures about 1.5 inches long and has 144 pins. Capacity ranges from 512 MB to 1 GB.

Laptop Expansion Options

Laptop systems offer many different options to expand system functionality. Slots and ports located on the outside of the case can allow you to add compatible expansion cards to the system. There are a number of different expansion cards available.

Expansion Card	Description
PC Cards	Designed by the *Personal Computer Memory Card International Association (PCMCIA)*, these cards were originally referred to as PCMCIA Cards. *PC Cards* are credit-card-sized expansion cards that are used in portable computers rather than the full-sized expansion cards used in desktop systems. PC Card expansion slots provide additional functionality to laptop systems. Cards are 4 mm wide by 85.6 mm long, and have a female 68-pin connector that plugs into a 68-pin male connector inside a slot in the side of the computer. There are currently three types of approved cards: • Type I: 3.3 mm thick, with a 16-bit interface. Typically used for memory devices. • Type II: 5.0/5.5 mm thick, with a 16- or 32-bit interface. Typically use a *dongle* to connect to a full-size connector. • Type III: 10.5 mm thick, with a 16- or 32-bit interface. Hard disk drive cards are Type III.
ExpressCards	*ExpressCards* are mobile expansion cards designed by the PCMCIA to replace traditional PC Cards. The ExpressCard slot on mobile devices provides PCI Express and USB 2.0 connectivity. The two form factors available for the ExpressCard are the ExpressCard/34 (34 mm wide) and ExpressCard/54 (54 mm wide). ExpressCard slots are a bit smaller than the PC Card slots and are usually located on the side of the laptop. ExpressCards can be used to provide many additional functions such as wireless network access, USB ports, and others. The ExpressCard technology has many advantages over the PC Card, including reduced voltage usage, increased bandwidth, and a maximum throughput of 2.0 Gps through PCI Express and 480 Mbps through USB 2.0. Some manufacturers are providing both PC Card slots along with ExpressCard slots to comply with both standards.
Mini-PCIe	Some portable systems include a PCI Express Mini Card (Mini-PCIe) slot. A *Mini-PCIe* card is an extremely small expansion card, often just a few centimeters in length. Unlike PC Cards, Mini-PCIe cards are internal and are installed by the computer manufacturer. Mini-PCIe cards are most often used to increase communication abilities by providing network adapters or modems and supports various connections and buses: • USB 2.0. • Diagnostic wiring that provides LED for wireless network connectivity. • System management Bus (SmBus).
SODIMM and Flash memory	Portable devices use memory that was specifically designed for those devices. Since it is not produced in as high quantities as desktop memory, it tends to be more expensive. While some laptops use SODIMM modules, which are about half the size of standard desktop DIMMs, or MicroDIMMs, many require non-standard proprietary memory that must be ordered from the manufacturer. Other portable computing devices and some notebooks use *flash memory* modules rather than regular RAM. Flash memory is a type of non-volatile storage method that provides devices with quick access to data.

Expansion Card	Description
	Be sure to check the documentation for your device so that you purchase the correct type of memory.

Special Function Keys

Laptops are all so different and the features can vary based on the manufacturer. A common feature included in most devices are the special function keys. The specific keys available will depend on the size, shape, and overall design of the laptop but most systems will provide the basic keys. The special keys are typically positioned horizontally along the top length of the keyboard and allow users to launch operating system commands, and manage laptop settings from their keyboard in many ways:

- Switching between single and dual displays.
- Turning the wireless on and off.
- Changing the volume of the speakers.
- Managing the screen brightness.
- Turning the Bluetooth® on and off.
- Configuring the keyboard backlight.

Figure 10-2: Special function keys.

Laptop Docking Solutions

One of the most attractive features of laptops is that they are so portable. They can be docked and undocked quickly for transport. Docking solutions provide users with a power source and full size peripherals with a similar feel to a full size desktop computer. There are a few different docking options depending on the specific needs of the user.

Docking Solution	Description
Docking station	A *docking station* is used when a laptop computer replaces a desktop computer. This technology is rarely used today and is considered to be legacy hardware. The laptop is connected to the docking station through a docking port located on the back or bottom of the laptop. Docking stations typically extend the capabilities of the laptop by providing additional interfaces for the laptop. In addition, there are often slots for desktop PCI or ISA expansion cards, drive bays for additional mass storage devices, and possibly additional ports and connectors, such as extra USB or wireless connections.

Docking Solution	Description
Port replicator	A *port replicator* is a scaled-down version of a docking station that presents the interfaces that the laptop already has. It contains connections for the standard ports, such as power, keyboard, mouse, and display, but it generally does not support additional expansion cards or drive bays, although some port replicators will contain extra USB or wireless connections.
Media/accessory bay	Some portable computing devices offer media/accessory bays to allow a user to expand the functionality of the device. Such bays often accept optical drives, secondary hard drives, or secondary batteries. These bays are typically proprietary and the accessories for the bays must be ordered directly from the device manufacturer. Most laptops today will utilize wireless peripherals and USB attached drives, so USB hubs and media bays are not used as much anymore.

Laptop Locks

Because laptops are so portable, they are easily lost or stolen. Another feature of laptops is the ability to attach a physical laptop lock or a cable lock. A physical cable lock attaches to the laptop using one of the compatible slots. The cable is then secured around a permanent object. The lock is usually accessed using a combination or a key. Depending on the lock, it may attach to the VGA or printer port. The locks come with special screws that secure the lock in place. The Kensington lock is a cable lock that inserts into a specifically designed port on the laptop. After the Kensington cable was released, laptop manufacturers named the special port the Kensington lock port.

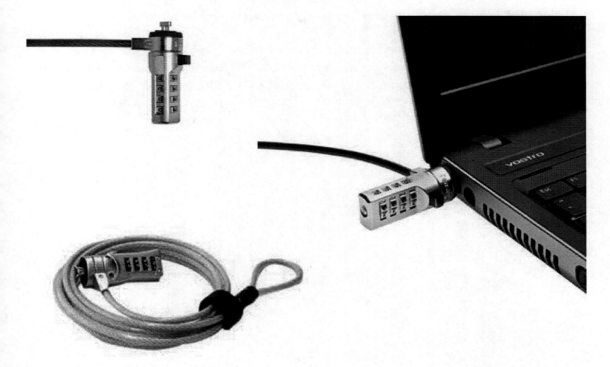

Figure 10-3: Kensington laptop locks.

Laptop Power Supplies and Batteries

Laptops can use either AC power sources (alternating current from an electrical outlet) or DC power sources (direct current from a battery). While the laptop is in its portable state, it uses batteries. When the device is used as a desktop computer or peripheral, it can use either batteries or AC power.

AC power connectors vary from device to device. It is important that a laptop not be used with a power cord other than the one provided by the manufacturer. When the laptop is not being used as a portable device, it is usually plugged in using the AC power cord that matches the computer. The battery is also recharged through this connection.

Auto-Switching and Fixed Input Power Supplies

Power supplies with voltage selector switches are called fixed-input power supplies. The voltage selector switches generally have two settings—for example, 220 and 110—depending on the manufacturer. If you set the switch to a higher voltage than supplied by the power source, the system will not receive enough power and will not function properly. However, if you set the switch to a lower setting than supplied by the power source—for example, if you set the switch to 110V while connected to a 220V outlet—you run the risk of burning out the power supply, damaging system components, or more seriously, creating a fire or electrocution hazard.

Auto-switching power supplies do not have a manual voltage switch, but detect the voltage level supplied by the outlet and set themselves to the correct voltage automatically. This can be convenient and safe for people who travel to various countries with portable computers.

Laptop Cooling Considerations

Heat can be a considerable problem with laptops due to their compact size and integrated design. The components are all within close proximity and can generate a lot of heat. There are a number of cooling methods and considerations used to keep the devices within a safe heat range for operation:

- Laptop CPUs are engineered to draw less power and thus run cooler than their similarly rated desktop counterparts.
- Fans are used to move the hot air out from the inside of the laptop case.
- Limit the use of the laptop battery as much as possible. The battery itself can be a heat source.
- Laptop cooling pads are accessories that are designed to sit under the laptop to protect a user from getting a burn from a device overheating. The cooler is placed underneath the laptop to move the air away from the device.

ACTIVITY 10–1
Identifying Laptop Components

Scenario

In this activity, you will examine a laptop and identify its components.

---

1. Examine a laptop and identify the external components such as the keyboard, display, track point or touch pad.

2. What type of screen display does the laptop have?

3. Locate the battery. Is it visible from the outside, or is it an internally mounted battery?

4. What special function keys does the laptop have?

5. Does the laptop have a Kensington cable lock port?

6. What expansion options are available on the laptop?

TOPIC B

Install and Configure Laptop Hardware Components

In the previous topic, you identified the internal and external components of laptops. Now that you understand how all these components fit together, you are prepared to install and configure them. In this topic, you will install and configure laptop hardware components.

Laptops are extremely popular in the business, personal, and recreational markets. With these devices now so prevalent, having the skills to install, configure, and support the various components is very important. As an A+ technician, you will use the skills and information in this topic to install and configure laptop components.

This topic covers all or part of the following CompTIA® A+® (2012) certification objectives:

- Exam 220–801: Objective 3.1: Install and configure laptop hardware and components.

General Laptop Support Guidelines

There are some general guidelines that can be helpful when supporting laptops within the workplace. With the increased use of smaller laptop devices, you should be aware of the issues and best practices applied when working with the hardware components:

- Verify that there are adequate cooling methods installed and used. Overheating is a serious issue when operating laptops.
- Be aware of the device's warranty restrictions and guidelines. You never want to break a warranty by opening the case or replacing an integrated component that may have been fully covered by a warranty.
- Be careful of the wires that pass through the hinges of a laptop. They can be easily damaged when replacing a display, or screen.

 Note: For additional information, check out the LearnTO **Install RAM in a Laptop** in the LearnTOs for this course on your LogicalCHOICE Course screen.

Note: For additional information, check out the LearnTO **Replace a Laptop Battery** in the LearnTOs for this course on your LogicalCHOICE Course screen.

Access the Checklist tile on your LogicalCHOICE course screen for reference information and job aids on **How to Power and Dock a Laptop**

Access the Checklist tile on your LogicalCHOICE course screen for reference information and job aids on **How to Install or Replace a PC Card**

Access the Checklist tile on your LogicalCHOICE course screen for reference information and job aids on **How to Install an Express Card**

Access the Checklist tile on your LogicalCHOICE course screen for reference information and job aids on **How to Install and Replace RAM in a Laptop**

Access the Checklist tile on your LogicalCHOICE course screen for reference information and job aids on **How to Replace Laptop Components**

Access the Checklist tile on your LogicalCHOICE course screen for reference information and job aids on **How to Replace a Laptop Motherboard**

ACTIVITY 10–2
Installing Laptop Components

Scenario

In this activity, you will examine the internal components of a laptop.

1. Following the manufacturer's instructions or your instructor's guidance, remove the outer case from the laptop.

2. Locate the memory module.

3. Locate the hard drive.

4. Locate the fan.

5. Reassemble the laptop.

Summary

In this lesson, you supported laptop computers by identifying the basic components and installing and configuring external and internal hardware components. With these skills you will be ready to provide the right level of support to your clients or organization in the future.

What is your experience with replacing laptop components?

What type of laptop support do you foresee having to provide to clients in the future?

Note: Check your LogicalCHOICE Course screen for opportunities to interact with your classmates, peers, and the larger LogicalCHOICE online community about the topics covered in this course or other topics you are interested in. From the Course screen you can also access available resources for a more continuous learning experience.

11 Mobile Computing

Lesson Time: 1 hours, 25 minutes

Lesson Objectives

In this lesson, you will configure mobile computing devices. You will:

- Identify mobile device technologies.

- Configure mobile devices.

Lesson Introduction

Just like laptops, mobile computing devices have specialized hardware and system configurations that can be used to optimize functionality. In this lesson, you will configure mobile computing technology, and discover the potential of mobile device use within the professional community.

Today, mobile devices are used in just about every workplace. Because of the portability and functionality they provide, use within the workplace is on the rise. As an A+ technician, you may be expected to not only support desktop and laptop computers, but mobile devices too. It is crucial that you understand the basic features, networking and email settings, and security methods used when setting up and configuring mobile devices.

This lesson covers all or part of the following CompTIA® A+® (2012) certification objectives:

- Topic A:
  - Exam 220–802: Objectives 3.1, 3.4
- Topic B:
  - Exam 220–802: Objectives 3.2, 3.3, 3.5

TOPIC A

Mobile Device Technologies

Up until this point in the course, your primary focus has been on the more traditional system hardware components and laptop technologies. In this next topic, you will dive into the mobile computing realm and will take a closer look at the capabilities and technologies that they employ to provide optimal performance.

Not only has mobile technology reached a new level of performance and portability, but the use of these devices is on the rise every day. As a certified A+ technician, you will be expected to understand how these devices work and how they should be deployed within the workplace.

This topic covers all or part of the following CompTIA® A+® (2012) certification objectives:

- Exam 220–802: Objective 3.1: Explain the basic features of mobile operating systems.
- Exam 220–802: Objective 3.4: Compare and contrast hardware differences in regards to tablets and laptops.

What is Mobile Technology?

Mobile technology is fast-paced and changing daily. Mobile technology enables instant wireless communications between users, resources, and computing devices. There are a number of devices that employ mobile technology to connect to the Internet, cellular networks, and other mobile users. There are four general types of mobile devices used today:

- *Smartphones* are high-end mobile devices that provide users with a wide range of functions, such as portable media players, video cameras, GPS, high-resolution touch screens, high-speed Wi-Fi, web browsers, and mobile broadband, along with phone service.
- *Tablet PCs* are mobile computers that function similarly to a full-sized desktop computer that come with an integrated touchscreen and virtual on-screen keyboard.
- *Carputers* are wireless computing devices that are specifically designed for cars. Many devices include features such as a global positioning system (GPS), media players, universal serial bus (USB), and Bluetooth® communications. Common brands are Xenarc, HP, and Lilliput.
- *PDAs (Personal Digital Assistants)* are mobile devices used to manage personal information, such as address books, calendars, and emails.

Mobile Carriers

Mobile carriers, also referred to as mobile providers, mobile network carriers, or wireless carriers, provide wireless phone and data access to mobile devices. Each carrier provides different phone and data plans that provide devices with an allotted amount of phone-call minutes, texts, and Internet access. Common carriers include:

- Verizon Wireless
- T-Mobile
- AT&T Mobility

Mobile Operating Systems

There are two primary operating systems utilized in most mobile devices today: Android™ and Apple® iOS. *iOS* is the base software that allows all other applications to run on an iPhone®, iPod touch®, or iPad®. The iOS user interface supports direct touch, multitouch, and using the *accelerometer*. Interface control elements consist of switches, buttons, and sliders. The response to user input is immediate and provides a fluid interface that includes swiping, tapping, pinching, and reverse pinching, all of which have specific definitions within the context of the iOS operating system and its multitouch interface.

Android, on the other hand, is a layered environment built on the Linux® kernel foundation that includes not only the operating system, but middleware, which provides additional software for the operating system (OS), and additional built-in applications. The Android OS was developed by the *Open Handset Alliance* and is owned by Google. It supports open source-developed applications and functions and comes with basic operating system services, message passing, and so on. The major difference between Android and iOS is that iOS runs on Apple products only, where the Android OS is used by many different mobile device manufacturers and is more widespread across a number of different mobile devices. Android also enables manufacturers to overlay a suite of applications that they support.

Additional mobile operating systems are available but are not used nearly as much as Android and iOS, such as the BlackBerry® OS, Microsoft® Windows® Phone 8, and HP® webOS. Carputers tend to be a separate category and mainly use either one of Microsoft's operating systems or an open-source OS, such as Linux.

Smartphones

New smartphones are emerging almost every day. The market is expanding and demand for powerful mobile devices has never been higher. While Android and iOS dominate the smartphone device marketplace, there are many other technologies and devices available.

As an A+ technician, it can be challenging to keep up with the mobile device market as it is constantly changing and there are so many different smartphones all with unique features and functions. The most popular devices used in the marketplace include:

Mobile Smartphone	Description
iPhone	iPhones are a combination of a phone, an Internet gadget, and a widescreen iPod, which runs on the iOS operating system. Apart from the more common features of a telephone, music player, camera and games, the latest iPhone includes features such as video conferencing and Siri®—a voice-controlled software assistant to perform various tasks and run other applications through a multitouch interface. iPhone applications utilize innovative iOS technology to facilitate Wi-Fi Internet connectivity with *General Packet Radio Service (GPRS)*, an intuitive user interface, GPS, the accelerometer, audio, video and graphic capabilities, and other advanced features.
Android smartphones	Android-based smartphones have similar functions to the iPhone, except that the Android OS allows multiple applications to run simultaneously without interruption. Popular Android-based smartphones include: • Samsung™ Galaxy S® III • MOTOROLA® DROID RAZR M • HTC One™ X • HTC One™ S
BlackBerry smartphone	BlackBerry phones are primarily used by professionals to conduct business operations and tasks. The BlackBerry OS directly supports corporate business requirements with functions such as synchronizing with Microsoft® Exchange, IBM® Lotus® Domino®, or Novell® GroupWise® emails, contacts, and tasks by maintaining a high level of security.
Windows smartphone	Windows smartphones run on the Windows Phone OS, which is maintained and developed by Microsoft. Features include a suite of Microsoft® Office®

Mobile Smartphone	Description
	applications, Outlook® Mobile, web browsing, Windows Media® Player, and other advanced features.

Tablet PCs

Mobile devices that fall into the tablet PC category range from larger tablets that look like a traditional laptop but have a touch screen to small notebook-sized mobile devices that operate similarly to a smartphone, but are a bit larger and have more computing power. Just like smartphones, tablet PCs can run a number of different operating systems depending on the manufacturer:

- Apple's iPad and iPod touch both run on iOS.
- The Android OS is used in a number of different tablet PCs including Amazon™ Kindle Fire™, Samsung™ Galaxy tablets, Toshiba Excite™.
- The Windows® 7 Home OS runs on Acer® ICONIA TAB, ASUS Eee Slate, and Samsung™ Series 7 tablet.
- Microsoft® Surface™ running the Windows® RT OS, which is a tablet version of Windows® 8.
- BlackBerry® PlayBook™, which runs the BlackBerry OS.

For a complete list of Tablet PCs and operating systems visit **www.tabletpccomparison.net**.

Tablets vs. Laptops

Laptops and tablets both offer a wide variety of hardware features that allow for better portability and ease of use, but there are also some major differences that should be considered.

 Note: For additional information, check out the LearnTO **Identify Laptops vs. Tablets** in the LearnTOs for this course on your LogicalCHOICE Course screen.

Characteristic	Laptops	Tablets
Repairs	The hardware components of a laptop can be fixed and replaced when issues arise. This is still fairly common with newer laptops as well.	There are no field-serviceable parts in a tablet. When something breaks, in most cases, the entire tablet needs to be replaced.
Upgrades	The hard drive and central processing unit (CPU) can be upgraded, if needed, to meet OS requirements or to add more functionality to the laptop.	Tablets are not typically upgradeable, unless it is software-related. The storage components cannot be upgraded.
Touch interface	Most laptops do not come with a touch interface component. You can purchase specific laptops that have the feature, but it is not common.	All tablets come with touch interface technology. The touch technology allows the user to interact with the tablet. It is also the primary input method used for tablets. Tablets utilize a touch interface that allows interaction between the user and the OS. *Multitouch* is the technology used on the surface of the touch screen on tablets and other mobile devices. The technology can recognize more than one contact on the

Characteristic	Laptops	Tablets
		surface at one time. This allows users to pinch and zoom the screen to make images or text larger and smaller. **Note:** Touch Flow or (*TouchFLO*) is an older touch technology that was used on HTC phones before the HTC Sense interface was developed.
Storage	Most laptops will have a mobile version of a traditional mechanical hard drive that has a higher storage capacity than solid state drives (SSDs).	Most tablets will come equipped with SSDs. Because of the space limitations and the portability of the tablet computers, SSDs make sense. They have no moving parts to maintain and provides a more stable mechanical design. The SSDs are made up of a number of flash chips that can retrieve data much faster than a standard hard drive that needs to start a motor and move the arm to read data.
OS	Laptops can run a number of different operating systems including versions from Microsoft, Linux, and UNIX.	Tablets can only run the mobile OS that the device was manufactured to run. The actual mobile OS will depend on the specific tablet due to the CPU architecture versus the ARM architecture.

Mobile Operating System Features

The features and advanced functions of a mobile device are what makes them so popular with consumers and professionals. Each mobile operating system will have its unique features that stand out from the rest, but most functions tend to be pretty similar.

Feature	Description
Open/closed source	The programming code used to develop mobile apps can be either open source code or closed source code, depending on the platform. *Open source* refers to application code, operating systems, and programming languages that are developed, published, and shared among the developer and professional community. This process also promotes collaboration among developers to build various apps and software programs. The Android mobile operating system was developed using open source methods and is free to customize. *Closed source* refers to any application code, programming code, or operating system code that is not published or shared with the community. Apple's iOS operating system is an example of a closed source OS.
App source	There are mobile apps for just about everything these days. Ranging from games, calorie counters, virtual sticky notes, to recipes, and many more. These apps are developed for personal and professional use and are intended to make life easier, to entertain, or to connect businesses with consumers. Some apps come preloaded on smartphones; others can be downloaded for free or a small fee. Apple apps can be accessed and downloaded from the App Store, or for Android devices from Google Play.

| CompTIA® A+® Certification: A Comprehensive Approach (Exams 220-801 and 220-802)

Feature	Description
Screen orientation	The screen orientation on most mobile devices will change automatically with the position of the device. This is function is possible using advanced mobile OS technology which includes an *accelerometer* and *gyroscope*. The accelerometer reads and measures the orientation of the device using a sensor that can measure the acceleration of the direction the device is moving in order to reposition the screen. This technology works when the device is in motion and upright. When the device is flat on a surface, the gyroscope changes the orientation of the device by reading the x and y coordinates as the device is moved to quickly update the orientation of the screen. These technologies work together to provide an instant update to the screen in all environments.
GPS and geotracking	Most mobile operating systems today use *Global Positioning System (GPS)* technology to determine the location, weather, and time zone information of a device using the satellite navigation system. Users can enter their starting location and final destination to start the phone's built-in GPS. Depending upon the phone and application, the navigator will provide directions or step-by-step instructions or assistance. GPS technology is also used by certain smartphone applications to let users check and share their location with others. This practice is often referred to as *geotracking*. Geotracking uses the GPS mobile technology component to constantly track and update a device's location with applications that share and use positioning information. If mobile devices do not use GPS technology, they will probably use Wi-Fi triangulation to provide location services.
Screen calibration	*Screen calibration* is a mobile operating system function typically used on older PDAs and pen-based interfaces to update the sensors on the device to respond quicker and more effectively to tapping, swiping, and pinching actions on the touch screen. On most devices, the calibration settings will be located in the device settings menu. If it is not, then it may not be available, so refer to the manufacturer's documentation.
Voice recognition	Voice recognition capabilities built in to the mobile operating system is quickly on the rise. Apple's Siri was the first in a growing trend to use voice recognition software in a mobile device that can not only recognize and interpret a user's voice, but can respond and react to the instructions given. Android has recently added a voice component called Voice Actions that functions similarly to Siri.

 Note: The CompTIA® exam objectives specifically refer to Android 4.0.x versus iOS 5.x.

ACTIVITY 11-1
Exploring iOS and Android Devices

Scenario
In this activity, you will examine mobile devices and their operating systems.

---

1. Examine an iOS device, and examine an Android device.

2. Compare the interfaces and settings, and share your findings with the rest of the class.

TOPIC B

Configure Mobile Devices

Now that you are more familiar with the different mobile device technologies available, you are ready to learn how they can be configured for optimal performance while maintaining an acceptable level of security. In this topic, you will configure mobile devices.

Mobile devices can be used for a number of functions within the professional workplace. Knowing that, you must be able to provide basic level support to your users, such as configuring security settings, configuring email, and setting up basic network connections.

This topic covers all or part of the following CompTIA® A+® (2012) certification objectives:

- Exam 220–802: Objective 3.2: Establish basic network connectivity and configure email.
- Exam 220–802: Objective 3.3: Compare and contrast methods for securing mobile devices.
- Exam 220–802: Objective 3.5: Execute and configure mobile device synchronization.

Mobile Security

Mobile devices today can do just about anything a laptop or desktop computer can do when it comes to end-user productivity such as making and receiving phone calls, emailing, capturing and editing photos and videos, accessing the Internet, and in some cases, remotely accessing data and resources on a private or public network. With all these functions, you can assume all the same threats related to desktop computers and laptops will apply. For example, viruses and spam can infect mobile devices as they would desktop and wireless devices by email or downloaded applications and due to the portability, small size, and always-connected state, threats such as loss, theft, and damage due to dropping are prominent.

Mobile Device Security Techniques

Securing a mobile device is a necessary task that should be required and enforced by any employer or user. There are a number of security methods that can be implemented to provide the right level of security while still providing access to desired resources and applications.

Security Control	Description
Enable screen lock and passcode settings	The screen lock option on all mobile devices should be enabled with a passcode, and strict requirements on when the device will be locked. You can specify how long the device is active before it locks, which typically ranges from 1 minute to 5 minutes. Once the device is locked, it can only be accessed by entering the passcode that has been set up by the user. This security control prevents access to the device if it is misplaced or stolen.
	On some devices, you can configure the passcode settings to erase all data stored on the device after a certain number of failed logon attempts.
	Often, enabling screen lock can be a requirement in an organizational security policy, no matter if the mobile device is provided by the employer or the individual.
	Be aware of pattern passcodes that require a user to complete a specific action on the touch screen to activate the device. Most of the time, the smudge pattern is visible on the surface and can be re-created to gain access to the device. Using a numeric pin or a password is considered more secure.

Security Control	Description
Configure device encryption	When available, all mobile devices should be configured to use data encryption to protect company-specific and personal data that may be stored and accessed on the device. This method is effective as long as the hardware cannot be accessed to steal the data. Along with device encryption, data encryption should also be used so when data is accessed by physically taking the device apart, the data remains secured.
	Device encryption can also be a requirement in an organizational security policy.
Require remote wipes	*Data wiping* is a method used to remove any sensitive data from a mobile device and permanently delete it.
	Remote wiping is also available for some devices, so you can perform these functions remotely in case the phone is lost or stolen. Wipe and sanitization guidelines and requirements might be included in an organization's security policy if mobile devices are issued to employees for professional use. In some cases, Admins will have rights to remote in to any device that is supported by the organization.
Enable location services and applications	GPS tracking service functionality is available on a number of mobile devices and can be added in most cases when required for business reasons. This feature is used as a security measure to protect and track mobile devices that may be lost or stolen.
	If a mobile device does not have the locating functionality built in, then you can download a locator application that can track and locate a lost or stolen device.
Enable remote backup	Depending on the type of mobile device, there are remote backup services available through the OS. For example, Apple offers remote backup services to its iCloud® through the **General Settings** of the device. From there, you can specify what application data to back up. Android offers remote backup using Google Drive. Both these services offer the first 5 GB of data for free, then you can purchase more backup space as needed. These features allow you to recover your data when a device is either lost or stolen.
Install antivirus software	There are many different options when it comes to mobile antivirus solutions. Organizations that allow mobile devices to connect to the network and transfer data should require that antivirus get installed to prevent unauthorized access to data, systems, and resources. There are a number of solutions available: • BullGuard Mobile Security • Kaspersky Mobile Security • ESET Mobile Security • Lookout Premium • Trend Micro Mobile Security • Webroot Secure Anywhere Mobile
Install updates and patches	Mobile device updates are similar to other computing devices updates and patches. Verify that devices are set up to automatically install updates from the manufacturer. Updates and patches can resolve security issues and systems flaws that present a security risk.

ACTIVITY 11-2
Examining Mobile Security

Scenario

In this activity, you will examine mobile security components and measures.

 Note: For additional information, check out the LearnTO **Secure a Mobile Device** in the LearnTOs for this course on your LogicalCHOICE Course screen.

1. How can the use of mobile devices by employees affect the security of an organization as a whole?

2. Examine some of the features on a mobile device. Using the main menu, open the security settings for your device. What specific security settings are available?

3. Now, pair up with a partner who has a different mobile device and examine the security features on that device. Use the main menu to open the security settings. Are the security settings similar? Are there different options available?

4. Tap to open the various options and check out the security settings that can be customized, such as the screen lock feature, device encryption options, and GPS tracking features. Compare the available settings on a couple different devices.

Smartphone Network Configuration Settings

Most smartphones have the functionality to connect to both a cellular network and a Wi-Fi network. Both modes allow web browsing, email, and a variety of push notifications from apps, and can be enabled or disabled in the general settings for the device.

Cellular data networks are subscribed to through a mobile carrier such as Verizon and GSM networks. Users can subscribe to an appropriate wireless data plan that typically comes with usage and bandwidth restrictions based on the chosen plan. On the other hand, connecting to Wi-Fi networks provides users with unlimited use of network resources.

To connect to a Wi-Fi network, you must first verify that the mode is enabled on the smartphone. Once its enabled, the phone will automatically detect local area networks (LANs) within the discoverable range of the device. If the network is open to the public, then you can simply connect, but if the network has been secured, you will need the wireless password to establish a secure connection.

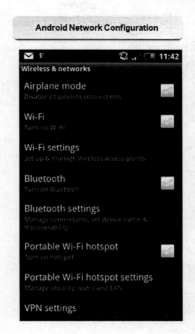

Figure 11-1: Smartphone network settings.

Bluetooth Configuration Methods

Bluetooth enables mobile devices to connect wirelessly to various devices such as headsets, carputers, laptops, MP3 players, and gaming consoles. Newer computers come with a Bluetooth radio built right into the system, while older computers require an adapter, such as a USB-enabled Bluetooth adapter. Devices in *discovery mode* will transmit their Bluetooth-friendly name, which is in most cases is the manufacturer's name. Once the name has been transmitted, the device can be paired with another device also transmitting a signal. Using Bluetooth technology, mobile devices can establish a connection through a process called *pairing*. When two devices pair, they share a secret key in order to establish a wireless connection.

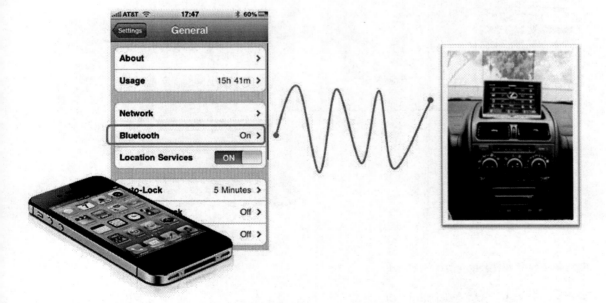

Figure 11-2: Pairing.

The Bluetooth Pairing Process

The pairing process involves devices sharing a secret key in order to create a working relationship. The basic steps in this process include:

1. Enable Bluetooth on the mobile device through system settings.
2. Enable pairing on the device.
3. On your mobile device, find a device for pairing.
4. Once the device is found, it will ask for a PIN code.
5. Depending on the type of device, the PIN code will be sent via a text, or will be a standard code, such as "0000" used for wireless headsets.
6. Verify that a connection message has been displayed.
7. Test the connection by using the two devices together to either make a phone call, transfer data, or play music.

Data Synchronization

Data synchronization is the process of automatically merging and updating common data that is stored on multiple devices. For example, a user can access his email contacts list from both his mobile device and his laptop computer. Synchronization is established when the devices are either connected via a cable or wirelessly, or over a network connection. In some cases, you may need to install synchronization software on the devices you choose to synchronize. The sychronization rate can be controlled and limited to allowing and restricting push and pull notifications from the cloud over the Internet. There are many types of data that can be synchronized:

- Contacts
- Programs
- Email
- Pictures
- Music
- Videos

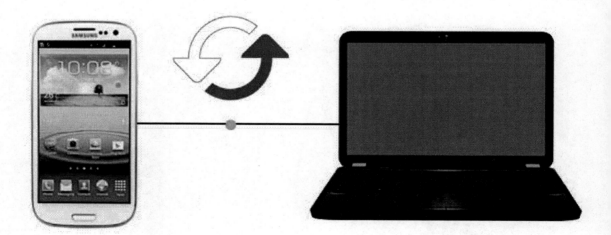

Figure 11-3: Data synchronization.

Microsoft has its own synchronization protocol called *Exchange ActiveSync (EAS)* that enables mobile devices to connect to an Exchange Server to access mail, calendars, and contacts. Exchange administrators can control what devices can connect and synchronize with the server and which ones are blocked.

Synchronization Requirements

Synchronization requirements will vary and will be specific to each mobile device. There are a number of factors to consider when enabling data synchronization on a mobile device:

- You might need to use a specific system account to enable synchronization.
- You might require an email account.
- If you are using Microsoft Exchange, then control may be given to the Admin.
- Organizations may have specific requirements to synchronize data.
- Certain devices might require additional software to enable synchronization.

Email Configuration Methods

Once you've established a network connection with your mobile device, you can set up and configure your email. Mobile devices can be configured to automatically update your email account information and manage mail. Mobile devices support a number of different email providers such as Yahoo! Mail, Microsoft Exchange, Windows Live, Gmail, and Hotmail.

Email can be accessed in one of two ways on a mobile device: web-based or client-based. Web-based access is accomplished by installing the email provider's application available in the mobile devices store. This method requires you to enter your user name and password to access the web-based email application. On the other hand, client-based email access is a bit more complicated and requires more information to access email services. Microsoft Exchange is a client-based email system that allows mobile devices to sync with the server. Before you can set up your mobile device's email, you need to determine the type of email account you will be configuring.

Email Server and Configuration Settings

Depending on which email provider you use, there may be additional settings that you need.

Server Information	Description
Protocol	Your email server will be configured to support either POP3 or IMAP.
	Post Office Protocol version 3 (POP3) is a protocol that enables an email client application to retrieve email messages from a mailbox on a mail server. With POP3, the email messages wait in the mailbox on the server until the client retrieves them, either on a schedule or manually. Once the messages are retrieved and downloaded to the client, they are generally deleted from the server. The client then stores and works with the email messages locally.
	Internet Mail Access Protocol version 4 (IMAP4) is a protocol that enables a client to retrieve messages from a mail server. With IMAP4, messages generally remain on the server while the client works with them as if they were local. IMAP4 enables users to search through messages by keywords and to choose which messages to download locally. Messages in the user's mailbox can be marked with different status flags that denote states such as "deleted" or "replied to." The messages and their status flags stay in the mailbox until explicitly removed by the user. Unlike POP3, IMAP4 enables users to access folders other than their mailbox.
Security	In order to establish secure authentication to and from an email server, a security protocol should be used. There are two main security protocols used: • *Secure Sockets Layer (SSL)* is a security protocol that combines digital certificates for authentication with public key data encryption. SSL is a server-driven process; any web client that supports SSL, including all current web browsers, can connect securely to an SSL-enabled server.

Server Information	Description
	• *Transport Layer Security (TLS)* protects sensitive communication from eavesdropping and tampering by using a secure, encrypted, and authenticated channel over a TCP/IP connection. TLS uses certificates and public key cryptography for mutual authentication and data encryption using negotiated secret keys. TLS is very similar to SSL, but the two protocols are not compatible.
Ports	Email servers use different ports for incoming and outgoing mail. Before you can configure any Exchange email settings, you will need to determine the specific port numbers used. The email provider and the type of protocol used determines the port number used. You should check the email provider's website for protocol and port information.

Android Email Configuration Requirements

In order to fully configure an email account on an Android mobile device, you may need additional email provider server information. Common required settings include:

- The email domain which is the @_____ portion of your full email address.
- Your email authentication information.
- The access domain, which is the unique hostname that is assigned to the email provider's server. You may need to visit your email provider's website to verify the hostname.

 Note: For additional information, check out the LearnTO **Configure Email on a Mobile Device** in the LearnTOs for this course on your LogicalCHOICE Course screen.

 Access the Checklist tile on your LogicalCHOICE course screen for reference information and job aids on How to Configure Mobile Devices

Summary

In this lesson, you worked with mobile computing devices. You examined mobile device technologies including the operating systems for smartphones and tablets. You also examined how to configure mobile devices to be secure when connecting to a network, connecting via Bluetooth, synchronizing data, and using email.

In your professional experience, have you supported mobile devices? If not then, what kind of experience do you have with them?

What type of technical support do you think will be expected of an A+ technician as mobile devices become even more prominent within the workplace?

Note: Check your LogicalCHOICE Course screen for opportunities to interact with your classmates, peers, and the larger LogicalCHOICE online community about the topics covered in this course or other topics you are interested in. From the Course screen you can also access available resources for a more continuous learning experience.

12 | Supporting Printers

Lesson Time: 1 hour

Lesson Objectives

In this lesson, you will support printers. You will:

• Identify printer components.

• Install, configure and maintain printers.

Lesson Introduction

In previous lessons, you have installed, configured, and managed system hardware for desktops, laptops, and mobile devices, as well as the basic operating software and networking components on all three systems. The next logical step is to examine some of the most common external devices in use on personal computer systems: printers. In this lesson, you will support printers.

Despite predictions that computers would bring about a paperless office environment, the need to transfer digital information to paper or back again remains as strong as ever. Therefore, printing and scanning are among the most common tasks for users in almost every home or business environment. As an A+ certified professional, you will often be called upon to set up, configure, and troubleshoot printing environments, so you will need to understand printer technologies as well as to perform common printer support tasks.

This lesson covers all or part of the following CompTIA® A+® (2012) certification objectives:

• Topic A:
   • Exam 220–801: Objective 4.1
• Topic B:
   • Exam 220–801: Objectives 4.2, 4.3

TOPIC A

Printer Technologies

In this lesson, you will support printers. Before you can provide the right level of support, you must fully understand how these systems are used in a production environment. You need to understand how the various printer components work within a printer to provide the desired outputs. In this topic, you will identify printer technologies.

As a professional support technician, you might be supporting the latest cutting-edge technology, or you might be responsible for ensuring that legacy systems continue to function adequately. So, you must be prepared for either situation and be able to provide the right level of support to users and clients. Having a working knowledge of the many printer technologies and components will help you to support users' needs in any technical environment.

This topic covers all or part of the following CompTIA® A+® (2012) certification objectives:

- Exam 220–801: Objective 4.1: Explain the differences between the various printer types and summarize the associated imaging process.

Printers

A *printer* is a device that produces text and images from electronic content onto physical media such as paper, photo paper, and labels. A printer is one of the most popular peripheral devices in use in most computing environments. Printers employ a range of technologies; the quality of the print output varies with the printer type and generally in proportion to the printer cost. A printer output of electronic documents is often referred to as "hard copy." Printers can connect to computers using a variety of connection types, with the most popular methods being USB, networked, and wireless.

Figure 12–1: Printers.

Microsoft Printing Terminology

Some Microsoft technical content makes a firm distinction between the software components that represent the printer, and the physical printer itself. You may find that Microsoft refers to the software representation of the printer as the "printer object," "logical printer," or simply "printer," and refers to the printer itself as the "print device" or "physical printer." However, Microsoft sometimes also uses the word "printer" as in common usage, to mean the physical print device. Be aware of the context usage of the terms.

MFDs

A *multi-function device (MFD)* is a piece of office equipment that performs the functions of a number of other specialized devices. MFDs typically include the functions of a printer, scanner, fax machine, and copier. However, there are MFDs that do not include fax functions. Although the multi-function device might not equal the performance or feature sets of the dedicated devices it replaces, multi-function devices are very powerful and can perform most tasks adequately and are an economical and popular choice for most home or small-office needs.

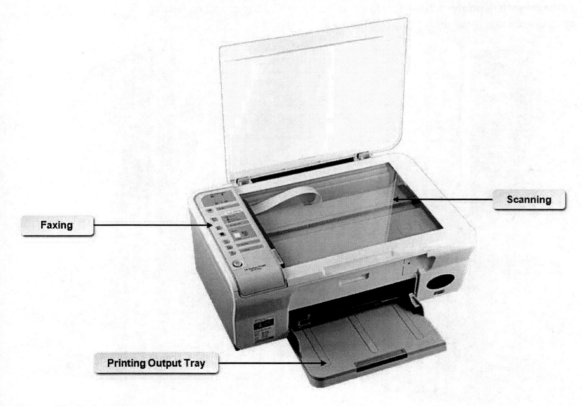

Figure 12-2: An MFD.

Types of MFDs

MFDs can be broadly classified into three types, based on their size, cost, and functions.

Type of MFD	Description
All-in-one (*AIO MFD*)	These MFDs are small in size and include basic features of printing, scanning, and copying that are required for home users. Interestingly, some of them include features such as *PictBridge* and smart card readers that are not available on high-end MFDs. They have limited or no fax features and do not support networking.

Type of MFD	Description
SOHO MFD	These MFDs are medium sized and are designed specifically for small and home offices. They can be connected to a network and can perform tasks at a faster pace than AIOs. They usually have enhanced faxing capabilities and some high-end models are loaded with additional time-saving features, such as an automatic document feeder, duplex printing, *duplex scanning*, extra paper trays, and stapling.
Heavy-duty MFD	As the name suggests, these MFDs are large, network-enabled machines that can cater to the documentation needs of an entire office. They may not include a fax. They are built to handle large volumes of printing, scanning, and copying. Additional features such as automatic document feeder, duplex printing and scanning, and enhanced storage space are available by default.

Laser Printers

A *laser printer* is a printer that uses a laser beam to form images and toner to print the images on a printing medium, such as paper or photo paper.

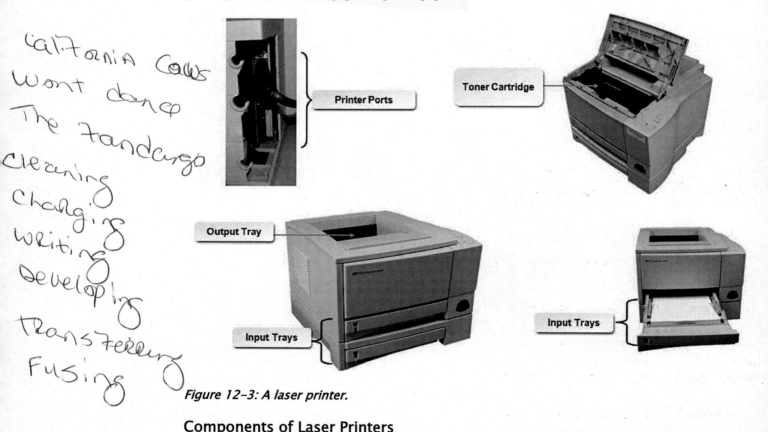

Figure 12–3: A laser printer.

Components of Laser Printers

Laser printers include some specialized components not found in other printer types:

- *Toner* cartridge. This is a single, replaceable unit that contains the fine powder used to create images as well as additional components used in image production. Frequently, the EP drum is also incorporated in this cartridge.
- Laser scanning assembly. This is the unit that contains the laser.
- High-voltage power supply. This component converts the supplied current to optimal voltage for specific components and also converts the supplied alternating current (AC) to direct current (DC) for specific internal parts of the printer.

- Paper transport mechanism. This includes the transfer belt and separator pads that move the paper through the laser printer. If the printer is equipped with a duplexing assembly, then the rollers and motors will flip the paper and feed it through to the imaging drum twice.
- *Electrostatic Photographic drum (EP drum)*, or imaging drum. This component carries an electrical charge that attracts the toner. It then transfers the toner to the paper.
- Transfer *corona* assembly. This is a component that contains the corona wires; it is responsible both for charging the paper so that it pulls the toner off the drum and also for charging the drum itself.
- *Fuser assembly*. This unit, also known as the fuser, applies pressure and heat to the paper to adhere the toner particles to the paper.
- Formatter board. This unit exposes and processes all of the data received from the computer and coordinates the steps needed to produce the finished page.

LED Printers

LED printers are similar to laser printers but use the latest printing technology, namely Light Emitting Diodes (LEDs), to replace the laser beam. Some LED printers can print 420 pages per minute.

The Laser Print Process

In the laser printing process, laser printers print a page at a time using a combination of electrostatic charges, toner, and laser light. The laser print process follows the steps detailed in the table.

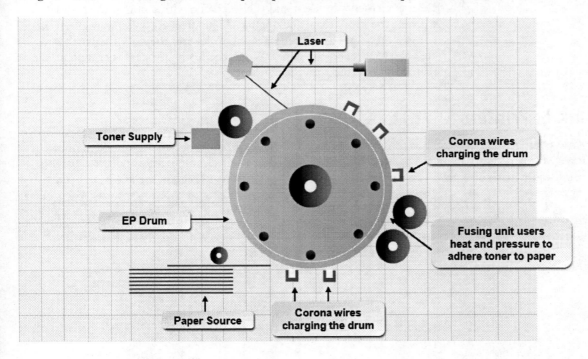

Figure 12-4: The laser print process.

Process Step	Description
1. Cleaning	The EP drum is cleaned with a rubber squeegee blade.
2. Erasing	Charges are removed from the EP drum in preparation for the next image.
3. Charging (conditioning)	The imaging drum is prepared by charging it with a charge roller. The roller is connected to a high-voltage power supply unit to produce negative charges. The roller then applies these negative charges, up to

Process Step	Description
	-600 volts (V), on the surface of the drum. This process is known as conditioning. A finely tuned laser beam, which consists of positive charges, is cast on the negatively charged drum. A multi-faced mirror that rotates reflects the laser beam onto the drum.
4. Writing	A laser beam writes to the EP drum, giving portions of the drum a weaker negative charge.
5. Developing	Toner is attracted to the areas of the drum that were hit by the laser light. In this step, the invisible image is now ready to be developed. Inside the toner cartridge, a thin layer of toner is applied to the surface of the drum. A thin blade, called a wipe blade, then spreads the toner evenly on the surface of the drum, leaving behind the toner only on the regions written by the laser beam.
6. Transferring	In the next phase, positively charged papers are fed into the printer by the pickup rollers. The positively charged paper attracts the negatively charged toner sticking on the drum. The transferred toner sticks loosely on the paper's surface, bound by the charges.
7. Fusing	In the final stage, the toner is melted and fused with the paper permanently. There are two transfer rollers, closely placed to each other, with almost no clearance between them. The heating roller at the top has heating elements inside it and is also coated with a non-stick material to prevent the toner from sticking to it. The pressure roller at the bottom presses the paper against the heating roller and together they melt and fuse the toner with the paper. When the fusing process is complete, the printed paper rolls out of the printer.

Inkjet Printers

An *inkjet printer* is a printer that forms images by spraying liquid ink from an ink cartridge out of nozzles aimed carefully on the printer. Inkjet printers have a self-cleaning cycle and will park the printhead when not in use. The printer can use heat or vibrations to release the ink.

 Note: Canon refers to their inkjet printers as "BubbleJet," and HP refers to theirs as "DeskJet."

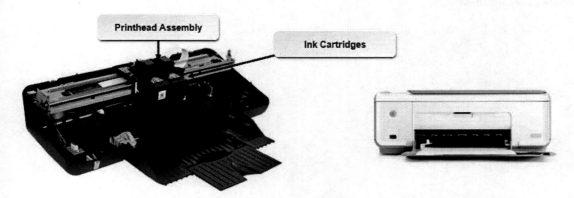

Figure 12-5: An inkjet printer.

Inkjet Printer Capabilities

Inkjet printers are very versatile. Inkjet printers vary by:

- The media they can print on. This includes the following:
  - Inexpensive copier paper
  - Bright paper made specifically for inkjet printers
  - Photo paper
  - Transparencies
  - Labels
  - Card stock
  - Envelopes
- Whether they produce black and white or color output.
- Whether they have duplexing capabilities.
- The cartridge design and the cost of cartridges.
- The speed at which they print.
- Whether the printhead is part of the printer or whether it is packaged together with the ink tanks in a print cartridge.
- The paper path. Some printers have a straight-through paper path and others turn the paper over as it passes through the printer.
- The resolution in dots per inch (DPI).
- How the ink is released. It could be by:
  - The piezoelectric method, used in Epson printers. This uses a vibration to release a droplet of ink from the cartridge.
  - The thermal method, used in most other printers. This method releases a droplet of ink by heating up the ink.
- The volume of the ink drop, expressed in picoliters (10^{-12} liters). The smaller the drop, the less grainy the print output.

Solid Ink Printers

Solid ink printers are somewhat of a cross between inkjet and laser printers except that they use ink from melted solid-ink sticks. The melted ink is forced into a printhead, where it is transferred to a drum, which then transfers the image to the paper as it rolls over the drum. Solid ink printers can produce an image with a clear, fine edge on a wide variety of media, such as standard paper or transparency film.

The Inkjet Print Process

In the inkjet print process, inkjet printers spray ink on paper to form images. The inkjet print process follows these steps:

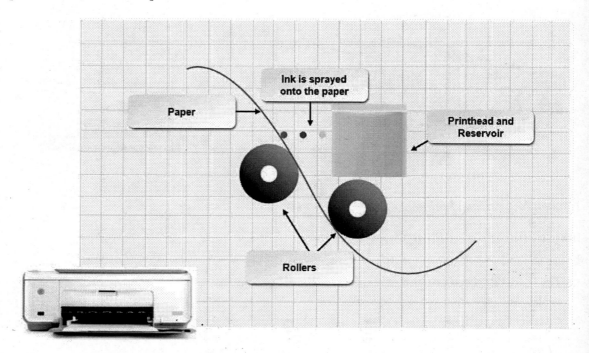

Figure 12–6: The inkjet printing process.

Process Step	Description
1. Preparation	When the print process is initiated, a motor and belt mechanism moves a printhead across the printer. Another stepper motor along with gears advance the paper into the printer.
2. Ink dispersion	As the printhead moves across the paper, images are formed by heat or vibration forcing liquid ink out of carefully aimed nozzles onto the paper. The printhead does not touch the paper. If the printer has double-sided printing capabilities, then the duplexing assembly will move the paper or other printing media through the printer twice.
3. Ink deposit	The printhead moves back and forth across the paper, printing one row of the image at a time. Each row is several dots wide. The amount of ink shot onto the page is determined by the driver software that controls where and when each nozzle deposits ink. The printhead typically produces at least 300 distinct DPI. Some printers can print at up to 1,200 DPI or more.
4. Paper advance	The paper advances using rollers and feeders after every row until the page is covered.

Thermal Inkjet Printers

Thermal inkjet printers use heat to release the ink from the nozzle.

1. The ink in the printhead is heated to a specified temperature.

2. Once the ink is heated, bubbles are formed in the cartridge that burst and shoot ink onto the media.
3. The heat is turned off and the element cools.
4. More ink is sucked into the nozzle when the bubble collapses. Each thermal printhead has about 300 to 600 nozzles that shoot spheres of ink that can create dots about 60 microns in diameter.

Piezoelectric Inkjet Printers

Some inkjet printers use piezoelectric technology. Piezoelectric technology uses a piezo crystal that flexes when current flows through it. When current flows to the crystal, it changes shape just enough to force a drop of ink out of the nozzle and onto the paper.

Duplexing

Duplexing is the process that enables automatic printing and scanning on both sides of printing media, such as paper and envelopes. This function can be found in both inkjet and laser printers, and also in MFDs, and in some cases can be installed as an add-on to provide the duplexing functionality to printers that do not have the function installed. The printer component that is responsible for duplexing is referred to as the *duplexing assembly*. Its primary function is to reverse the media inside the printer so that both sides can be moved through the imaging function of the printer. In some higher-end commercial printers, the duplexing function can print both sides simultaneously, without having to flip the media over.

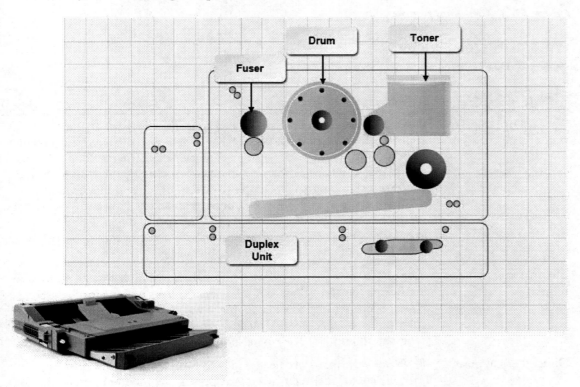

Figure 12-7: The duplexing assembly.

Thermal Printers

A *thermal printer* is a general term for any printer that uses a heating element to create the image on the paper with dye, ink from ribbons, or directly with pins while the feed assembly moves the media through the printer. There are several types of thermal printers that use significantly different technologies and are intended for different uses. The most sophisticated types of thermal printers can produce professional photo-quality images. There are also thermal printers for everyday office use and for special-purpose applications. Most thermal printers will require special *thermal paper* that contain chemicals designed to react and change color as it is heated by the heating element within the printer to create images. These printers are commonly used with cash registers to print receipts.

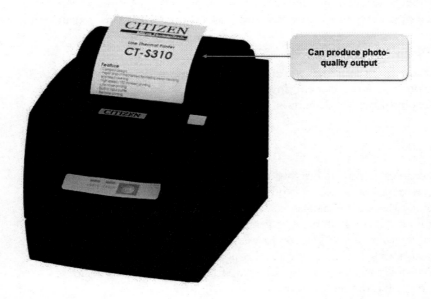

Can produce photo-quality output

Figure 12–8: A thermal printer.

Types of Thermal Printers

There are three basic categories of thermal printers.

Thermal Printer Type	Definition
Thermal dye transfer printer	A *thermal dye transfer printer*, also called a *dye sublimation printer*, is a sophisticated type of color printer that uses heat to diffuse dye from color ribbons onto special paper or transparency stock. The resulting continuous-tone image is similar in quality to photographic printing, and professional photographers employ them to produce prints quickly without having to send them to a photographic lab. However, the printers themselves are expensive and slow, and the special media is also expensive. Newer and less-expensive *snapshot printers* produce snapshot-sized images of acceptable photographic quality.
Thermal wax transfer printer	*Thermal wax transfer printers* have a thermal printhead that melts wax-based ink from a transfer ribbon onto the paper. These printers can be used in typical office settings as an economical way to produce color copies or color prints at an acceptable quality but at lower cost than dye sublimation printers. They are also used for standard text-based printing.
Direct thermal printer	*Direct thermal* printers use heated pins to form an image directly onto specially coated thermal paper. Early personal computer printers, such as Apple's first printer, the SilenType, were thermal printers. However, direct thermal printers are found today only in special-purpose printing devices such as cash registers and some fax machines.

Thermal Print Processes

There are several different print technologies grouped together in the general category of thermal printers. Each specific thermal printer type uses a unique print process:

- A thermal dye transfer printer, or dye sublimation printer, uses a heating element to diffuse dye from color ribbons onto special thermal paper or transparency stock.
- A thermal wax transfer printer uses the heating element to melt wax-based ink from a transfer ribbon onto special thermal paper as it moves through the printer by the feed assembly.
- A direct thermal printer has a heating element with heated pins to create the image directly on the paper as it gets passed through the printer by the feed assembly.

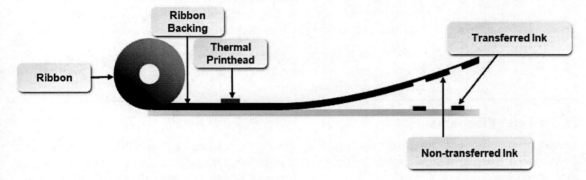

Figure 12-9: The wax thermal print process.

Impact Printers Dot, Matrix - To Make carbon copy

An *impact printer* is any type of printer that strikes a component directly against the ink ribbon to create characters on impact paper. The strike can be made with a group of pins or with a preformed type character. Impact printers tend to be noisy and slow compared to other printers and have largely been superseded by other printer technologies. The most common use is for printing carbon or carbonless multi-part forms such as receipts or invoices.

Figure 12-10: An impact printer.

Types of Impact Printers

There are several terms used to categorize impact printers.

Impact Printer Type	Description
Dot-matrix printer	A *dot-matrix printer* is a type of impact printer that uses a set of pins to strike the ribbon. Dot-matrix printers create printed characters by using various combinations of dots. The printhead contains a vertical column of small pins that are controlled by an electromagnet. Because it uses an array of pins to form images, this type of printer can produce graphics as well as text.

Impact Printer Type	Description
Formed-character printer	A *formed-character printer* is any type of impact printer that functions like a typewriter, by pressing preformed characters against the ink ribbon to deposit the ink on the page.
	The printhead might be shaped like a golf ball, with the type distributed around the ball, or it might be in the form of a wheel with the characters around the perimeter of the wheel. Because of this type of printhead's resemblance to flower petals, they are referred to as daisy-wheel printers.
Line printer	A *line printer* is any type of impact printer that can print a full line of text at a time, rather than printing character by character. These are the fastest type of impact printers.

Paper Feed Mechanisms

Impact printers can use either tractor feed when printing on continuous-roll impact paper, or friction feed when printing on individual cut sheets of paper. Tractor feed uses pairs of wheels with pins evenly spaced around the circumference at a set spacing. Continuous-roll paper with matching holes in the edges fits over the pins. The wheels turn and pull the paper through the printer. There are usually just two wheels, but there might be additional wheels or pin guides that the paper is latched to. There is usually a lever or other setting on the printer that needs to be engaged in order to use the tractor feed.

Friction feed uses two rollers placed one on top of the other. The rollers turn to force individual cut sheets of paper or envelopes through the paper path. This is used to print on individual sheets of paper (cut-sheet paper) and envelopes. Be sure to set the printer lever or other setting to the cut-sheet mode when printing using friction feed.

The Impact Print Process

The impact print process consists of four steps.

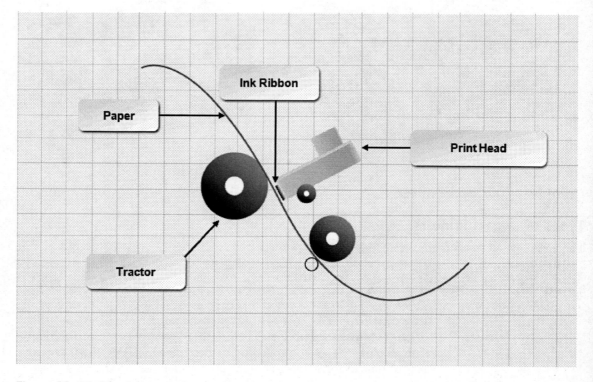

Figure 12–11: The impact print process.

Process Step	Description
Pin strike	The printhead has a vertical column of small pins that are controlled by an electromagnet. The pins shoot out of the printhead and strike an ink-coated ribbon. The dots created on the page become the printed text or graphics. More, smaller pins create better quality images. Printers come in 9-pin or 24-pin varieties.
Ink transfer	The impact of the pin transfers ink from the ribbon to the printed page. This physical impact is responsible for the printer's ability to print multiple-layer forms.
Printhead move	After a set of pins has fired, an electromagnet pulls them back in, the printhead moves a fraction of an inch across the page, and another set of pins is fired.
Letter quality pass	Near Letter Quality (NLQ) printers usually use two or more passes over a line of text to increase the number of dots used per letter. This connects the dots to form sharper and clearer letters.

ACTIVITY 12–1
Identifying Printer Technologies

Scenario

In this activity, you will identify various types of printers.

---

1. What printer process is displayed here?

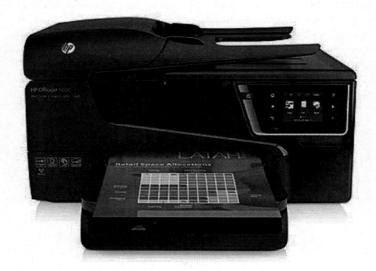

- ○ Laser
- ○ Impact
- ○ Inkjet
- ○ Thermal

2. What printer is displayed here?

○ Inkjet

○ Thermal

○ Laser

○ MFD

3. **True or False? The fuser assembly is a component of a laser printer.**

☐ True

☐ False

4. Identify any available printers that may be within your workspace for taking this class. See how many of the components you can identify inside the printers.

TOPIC B

Install, Configure, and Maintain Printers

In the previous topic, you examined printer technologies, components, and processes. You can use this basic understanding when you install and configure printers on laptop and desktop systems. In this topic, you will install, configure, and maintain printers.

Because printers are such a fundamental component of almost every computing environment, it is almost a guarantee that you will be called upon to set up and configure printing on devices no matter what professional environment you are working in. The skills you will learn in this topic should prepare you to install, configure, and maintain a wide range of printer types efficiently and correctly.

This topic covers all or part of the following CompTIA® A+® (2012) certification objectives:

*   Exam 220–801: Objective 4.2: Given a scenario, install and configure printers.
*   Exam 220–801: Objective 4.3: Given a scenario, perform printer maintenance.

Technical Printer Components

Printer types can vary, but there are many common technical components that are used to provide a number of common functions within the printer.

Component	Description
Printer memory	Printers typically come with their own installed memory to store information about the current device settings as well as the print jobs in the queue. Different devices will have a different amount of memory installed by default; you may be able to upgrade the memory. Upgrading the memory can enable a printer to handle higher-resolution jobs and to buffer more of each print job to increase throughput.
	Printers store current print jobs in volatile Random Access Memory (RAM); they typically store device settings in flash-based non-volatile RAM. Consult your device documentation for the memory amounts and types your device supports, as well as procedures for installing or upgrading device memory.
Printer drivers	Like all hardware devices, printers require appropriate software drivers in order to enable the device to communicate with the computer system and function correctly. The driver controls all device-specific functions, including print resolution and quality choices, color rendition, contrast and brightness, and finishing options such as two-sided printing, collation, stapling, and so on. If you open a device's property sheet, you can see the driver functions on the **Advanced** page and on any custom pages the driver adds. Printers might also include management software that is separate from the low-level driver interface and provides sophisticated control over device settings and functions.
Printer firmware	Many printers include built-in firmware that provides the on-board device management interface. This enables you to configure printer functions, monitor and manage print jobs, select output options, and run diagnostic tests from a console on the device itself, rather than indirectly through a computer operating system. The firmware type and the functions provided by the firmware will vary depending upon your device. Check with your device vendor for any available firmware updates.

Component	Description
Printer interfaces	Printers have been traditionally connected to computers using parallel or sometimes serial cables and ports. However, those connection methods are considered obsolete. Most printers and multifunction devices used today use USB and wireless technologies, or are directly connected to the network via a network cable.

Centronics Ports and Connectors

One of the few places you will come across a Centronics connector is with printers. The Centronics standard describes a type of parallel port used to connect printers. It is named after the company that designed the original interface. The Centronics standard uses a 36-pin Centronics connector to connect to the printer and a DB-25 (25-pin) connector to connect to the PC.

Printer Supplies and Media

There are a number of additional printer supplies and media that are necessary for a printer to function properly.

Supply or Media	Description
Printer toner	Laser printer toner is a fine powder made of particles of iron, carbon, and resin. Laser printers require a toner cartridge, which is a single, replaceable unit that contains toner as well as additional components used in image production. You will need to maintain a supply of the proper toner cartridges for your printer model. Refill or recycle empty toner cartridges; do not dispose of them in regular trash.
	Users can change toner cartridges, but everyone should follow proper handling procedures, which are usually printed right on the cartridge. Toner particles can stain clothing or skin, especially when exposed to heat. Toner rarely spills, but when it does, clean it up with an electronics vacuum that has a fine filter and bag to contain the material. Using a regular vacuum can melt the toner if it gets on the vacuum motor. Use a dry paper towel, toner spill cloths, or cool water to clean toner from skin or clothing. Do not rub the area, because the heat from friction will make it harder to remove.
Ink and ink cartridges	Inkjet printers require ink cartridges to supply black or colored ink. You will need to maintain a supply of the ink cartridges for your printer model. Ink cartridges vary by:
	• The size of cartridges and how much ink each cartridge contains.
	• Whether black is produced using a separate cartridge or by combining the cyan, yellow, and magenta inks into a composite black output.
	• Whether there are separate cartridges for each color or if they are all in one unit. The black cartridge is separate on almost all printers, except for some very low-end printers. If the colors are in one unit and one color runs out, the entire cartridge needs to be replaced.
	Solid ink printers require you to supply solid ink sticks designed for your particular printer model.
Paper and other media types	Depending upon your printer, you may be able to print to a variety of media types, including:
	• Standard-quality copier paper in a variety of form sizes, such as letter, legal, tabloid, and so on.
	• Bright paper made specifically for inkjet printers.

Supply or Media	Description

- Photo paper.
- Transparencies.
- Labels.
- Card stock.
- Envelopes.

You will need to install paper trays that accommodate the media stock you select for your printer. You can also select paper trays in different orientations, whether letter or landscape. Some media sizes and types might need to be fed into the printer manually.

Most printer outputs goes to an output bin on top of the printer, but there might be an additional or alternate straight paper path through a drop-down door, called a bypass tray, on the rear of the printer that you can use for specialized media, such as transparencies.

Maintain an appropriate media stock on hand. Users can typically refill paper trays themselves if the correct stock is available.

Printer Driver Types

There are several types of drivers you might encounter when supporting printers. In Windows, each of these drivers is normally composed of several files. A typical driver will contain a configuration file (.dll), a driver file (.drv), a data file (.ppd), a .help file (.hlp), and one or more dependent files (.ntf).

Driver Type	Description
PostScript printer description (PPD)	A printer driver used to render print jobs into the PostScript printer language and provide device capability information to the user. It displays specific information about the printer itself, such as whether the printer is a color printer. It also contains options that can be modified by the user, such as paper size, resolution, and print job information. PPD files can be used on Windows®, Mac®, or LPD (Line Printer Daemon) clients.
Printer control language (PCL)	A print driver protocol used to render print jobs into the PCL printer language and transfer data from the central processing unit (CPU) to the printer. It has become a standard used mostly by Hewlett-Packard printers. This protocol can be found for laser, thermal, and dot matrix printers. Sometimes seen as Printer Command Language.
Universal print driver (UPD)	UPDs are designed to support multiple printers and MFDs with one driver. The universal drivers may only be available for some printer brands. For example, Hewlett-Packard developed a UPD that can support almost all Hewlett-Packard printers and MFDs.
Raster/bitmap	A universal driver type that supports raster/bitmap printing to most printers.
Plotter/vector	Renders print jobs into specialized plotter language, for making large-scale drawings based on X and Y coordinates.

Print Driver Compatibility

Before you can start sending print jobs to a printer, you must verify that the print driver is installed. Print drivers must be compatible with the operating system running on your computer and the type of printer you have installed. You can view the driver files for any installed printer on your system by opening the printer properties window to see the driver files in use by that printer. Print drivers are generally available on installation discs provided with the printer. Updated print drivers are usually available for download from the printer manufacturer's website. However, in most cases, the majority of print drivers will be available as part of the operating system.

Local and Network-Based Printers

There are two general types of printers you can install on a Windows system.

- *Local printers* are managed by and may be physically or wirelessly connected to the local computer. The local computer holds the *print queue*, which contains the print jobs waiting to print.
- *Network-based printers* are shared print devices that are managed by a network computer, called a *print server.* The print server holds the print queue.

  Network-connected printers have built-in network adapter cards and connect directly to a network cable or via a wireless network interface. Print jobs are sent over the network using a network protocol such as Transmission Control Protocol/Internet Protocol (TCP/IP). Some network-connected printers have on-board print server software so they can be installed on the network directly and manage the print queue without requiring a separate print server computer.

Print Device Sharing

Depending on an organization's infrastructure, printers can be shared with computers, networks, or other devices using a number of methods. Both local and network printers can be shared with other computers and devices.

Method	Description
Wired	With the increased use of USB and Ethernet cables over the years, parallel and serial cables and ports are just about obsolete. Most wired printers and MFDs found today will connect to devices using a USB port or are directly connected to a network via an Ethernet cable.
Wireless	Wireless printers offer many capabilities such as flexible printer locations. Printers can be connected to a wireless network using: • Bluetooth® • 802.11x • Infrared (IR) technology
Print server	Print servers hold the print queue for a number of printers connected to the same network. The server manages print jobs that come from client computers or devices, and sends the jobs on to the desired printer. You may also come across occasions when the print server is built into a printer, or is a component of an appliance that also provides additional functions, such as a firewall.
Operating system	Printers can be shared with other devices on the network by assigning print permissions that apply to local users and to users of a shared network printer. Permissions can be allowed or denied within the operating system settings, but if you deny a user the print permission, the user will have no access to the printer. Available permissions include: • The print permission, which enables you to print to the shared printer. Assigned by default to Everyone. • Manage this printer, which enables you to print to the printer and fully administer the printer. Assigned by default to administrators and Power Users.

Method	Description
	• Manage documents, which enables you to manage other users' documents. This permission includes the ability to manage all the jobs in the print queue.
	• Special permissions, which is generally only used by the system administrator to manage printer owner settings.

Workgroup Security Models and Print Permissions

To assign permissions to printer objects on a Windows® 7 computer in a workgroup, you need to turn off **File Sharing** and enable **Classic authentication** so that local users can authenticate as themselves. In the **Network and Sharing Center,** select **Change advanced sharing settings** from the left pane and then select the **Turn on file and printer sharing** option.

 Note: In Windows® XP, use Simple File Sharing to change the share permissions.

Once you do this, the **Security** tab will be available in the printer's property sheet.

Printer Configuration Options

Depending upon your particular printer, you will have various options for configuring and optimizing printer performance.

Printer Configuration Option	Description
Device calibration	The printer manufacturer should provide documentation and tools for calibrating device-specific settings on the physical print device. For example, the cartridges on inkjet printers often require alignment after changing the cartridge (this often happens automatically, or may be done manually through the print driver interface). Or, you may need to calibrate the color overlays so that the colors align properly and do not create shadows.
Tray assignments	Each physical printer has different numbers and sizes of media and paper trays that can accommodate different paper and media forms and weights. Once you have installed the appropriate paper trays, you should verify that the appropriate media form type is assigned to each tray. Configure form-to-tray assignments on the **Device Settings** page of the printer's property sheet.
Tray switching	If you have installed multiple trays that use the same media size and type, most printers can use automatic tray switching to switch a job to a different tray when the default tray is empty. See your printer's documentation for information on configuring tray switching.
Print spool settings	You can configure how an individual printer will spool print jobs. The printer can print as soon as a page is spooled, or it can hold the job until the entire document is spooled. You can also configure the printer to bypass spooling and print directly to the device. Set spooler options on the **Advanced** tab of the printer's property sheet.
Printer availability	You can use the printer's availability schedule to postpone printing of long documents or low-priority documents to off-hours or other convenient times. Users can send jobs to the print queue at all times; the print server holds the jobs until the available hours, and then produces the output. To configure availability, open the properties of the printer and select the **Advanced** tab. Select **Available From** and set the time range in the boxes.

Printer Configuration Option	Description
Color management	The settings on the **Color Management** page control how Windows will select color settings for the printer based on the media type and printer configuration.
Printer ports	You can use the **Ports** tab to configure the printer to print to local parallel or serial ports, or to a network port address.

 Note: For additional information, check out the LearnTO **Install and Configure a Printer** in the LearnTOs for this course on your LogicalCHOICE Course screen.

Printer Maintenance

Proper printer maintenance will extend the life of a printer and will help prevent mechanical issues in the future.

Device	Maintenance
Inkjet printer	• Use the printer often to prevent the ink from drying out and clogging the nozzles. • Run the printer's cleaning utility to clean the printhead. • Run the printer's nozzle test.
Impact printer	• Regularly clean the paper path and the ribbon path using a dry, soft cloth. • Replace the printhead, ribbon, and paper when needed. • Regularly vacuum the dust from the wheels in the tractor feed assembly. • To avoid overheating the printhead, be mindful of the printer's location. Make sure it is clear of clutter and other machines.
Laser printer	• Replace the toner cartridge once it gets low. • Clean excess toner out of the printer each time you replace the cartridge to avoid buildup inside the printer. • Be mindful of the printer's location. Keep it well ventilated with proper spacing from other devices.
Thermal printer	• Replace the paper when needed. • The heating element may need cleaning to prevent buildup and smudging. • Remove debris from inside and outside printer to prevent unwanted particles from getting into the printer components.

 Access the Checklist tile on your LogicalCHOICE course screen for reference information and job aids on How to Install, Configure, and Maintain Printers

ACTIVITY 12-2
Installing and Sharing a Local Printer

Scenario
One of your clients has just asked you to install a refurbished printer that he purchased online. He would like to use this printer on his Windows 7 computer as his default printer. He has also asked that you make the printer available to other users in the company. Even though your client has not yet received the printer, he would like you to configure his computer so that all he will need to do is plug in the printer when it arrives.

1. Start the **Win7test##** VM.
    a) Select **Start→Windows Virtual PC→Win7test##**.
    b) Enter *IPass1234* to log onto Windows.

2. Install the printer on the **Win7test##** VM.
    a) In the **Win7test##** window, select **Start→Control Panel**.
    b) Under **Hardware and Sound**, select **View devices and printers**.
    c) Select **Add a printer** and then select **Add a local printer**.
    d) From the **Use an existing port** drop-down list, select **USB001 (Virtual printer port for USB), LPT1** or **LPT2**, and then select **Next**.
    e) On the **Install the printer driver** page, from the **Manufacturer** list, select a printer manufacturer.
    f) From the **Printers** list, select a printer and select **Next**.
    g) In the **Printer name** text box, type *My Local Printer*
    h) Select **Next**.
    i) Select **Finish**, and close the **Devices and Printers** window.

3. Share the printer.
    a) Open the **Control Panel**.
    b) Under **Network and Internet**, select **Choose homegroup and sharing options**.
    c) Select the **Change advanced sharing settings** link.
    d) Under the **File and printer sharing** section, select the **Turn on file and printer sharing** option and then select **Save changes**.
    e) Close the **Advanced sharing settings** window.

4. Create a print job on the local printer.
    a) Open the **Control Panel**.
    b) Under **Hardware and Sound**, select **View devices and printers**.
    c) Display the pop-up menu for **My Printer** and select **Printer properties**.
    d) Select **Print Test Page**.
    e) Select **Close**.
    f) Select **OK**.
    g) Select **See what's printing**.
    h) At least one print job should appear in the queue. Close the print queue window and the **Devices and Printers** window.

5. Log off and shut down the **Win7test##** VM.

Summary

In this lesson, you supported printers. Because printers enable users to transfer digital information to paper, they are among the most commonly used devices in almost every type of computing environment. As an A+ certified professional, you can use the skills and knowledge from this lesson when you are called upon to install, configure, or troubleshoot printers

What types of printer have you had experience with in your current job role?

In your experience, what printer maintenance tasks are you most familiar with?

 Note: Check your LogicalCHOICE Course screen for opportunities to interact with your classmates, peers, and the larger LogicalCHOICE online community about the topics covered in this course or other topics you are interested in. From the Course screen you can also access available resources for a more continuous learning experience.

13 | Security

Lesson Time: 3 hours, 20 minutes

Lesson Objectives

In this lesson, you will implement concepts and techniques used to secure computing devices and environments. You will:

- Describe security fundamentals.

- Identify common security threats and vulnerabilities.

- Identify security protection measures.

- Describe workstation security best practices.

Lesson Introduction

So far in this course, you have installed and configured a wide variety of computer components. The next step in completing the full installation and configuration process is to protect those systems from threats and vulnerabilities. In this lesson, you will implement security concepts and best practices used to secure computing devices.

Every computing device within an organization is at risk for an attack. It does not take much for an attacker to gain access to a device and access sensitive data or launch an attack. So, it is crucial to understand how security should be applied to the organization as a whole and to individual devices. If you understand the concepts of computing security, you will be prepared to take the necessary steps to prevent an attack.

This lesson covers all or part of the following CompTIA® A+® (2012) certification objectives:

- Topic A:
  - Exam 220–801: Objectives 2.1, 2.3
- Topic B:
  - Exam 220–801: Objective 2.2
- Topic C:
  - Exam 220–801: Objective 5.4
  - Exam 220-802: Objectives 2.1, 2.4
- Topic D:
  - Exam 220–801: Objective 2.6

- Exam 220-802: Objective 2.3

TOPIC A

Security Fundamentals

In this lesson, you will identify security concepts that can be applied to both organizations and individual computing devices. Security best practices and concepts can be applied to all security implementations. In this topic, you will identify security fundamentals.

Security is always a primary concern for organizations due to the costs that result from security incidents. In order to perform the necessary security tasks needed to establish a strong defense against potential attacks, you should understand the business of security from the ground up. Security implementations need to be carefully planned, implemented, and maintained. This topic will help you understand the fundamentals of security so that you can use them as the foundation for implementing and maintaining security within an organization.

This topic covers all or part of the following CompTIA® A+® (2012) certification objectives:

- Exam 220–802: Objective 2.1: Apply and use common prevention methods.
- Exam 220–802: Objective 2.3: Implement security best practices to secure a workstation.

Corporate Security Policies

A corporate *security policy* is a formalized statement that defines how security will be implemented and managed within a particular organization. It describes the tasks the organization will undertake to protect the confidentiality, availability, and integrity of sensitive data and resources, including the network infrastructure, physical and electronic data, applications, hardware, computing devices, and the overall physical environment of an organization. It often consists of multiple individual policies that relate to separate security issues, such as password requirements and acceptable use of hardware guidelines. All security measures and controls should conform with all of the security policies enforced by an organization.

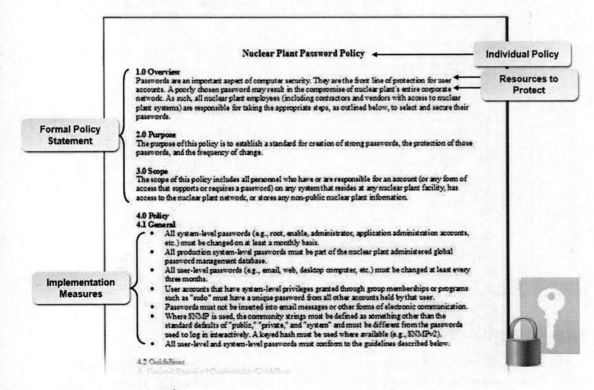

Figure 13-1: A security policy.

Security Compliance

Security compliance refers to an organization's efforts to enforce its security policies. To ensure data sensitivity and security, many organizations will include the following guidelines in a security policy:

*   Patch management guidelines.
*   User account and group management.
*   Access Control List (ACL) verification.
*   Auditing of both systems and data.
*   Security testing.
*   User education materials, such as documentation, resources, and training schedules.

Security Incident Reports

A security *incident report* is a method used to document and communicate a possible or confirmed security incident and any actions already taken in response to the incident. Timely and accurate incident reports enable security staff to respond appropriately to possible security breaches in progress, to audit for patterns of security problems, and to determine if staff members are following proper security procedures. An incident report can be as minor as an informal help desk call from a concerned user, to a more detailed electronic or paper form completed by security or IT personnel. For example, if a security incident indicates a possible breach of civil law, the security incident report can be a first step towards completing a police report and the beginning of a full criminal investigation. Incident reporting tasks will vary depending on the organization, but the specific tasks should always be documented in an organization's security policy.

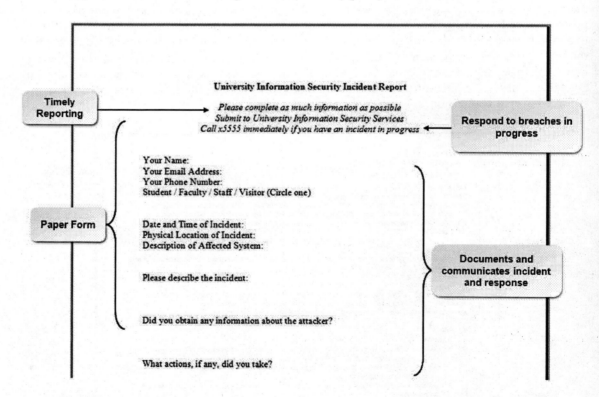

Figure 13-2: An incident report.

The Principle of Least Privilege

The principle of *least privilege* dictates that users and software should only have the minimal level of access that is necessary for them to perform the duties required of them. This level of minimal access includes facilities, computing hardware, software, and information. Where a user or system is given access, that access should still be only at the level required to perform the necessary task.

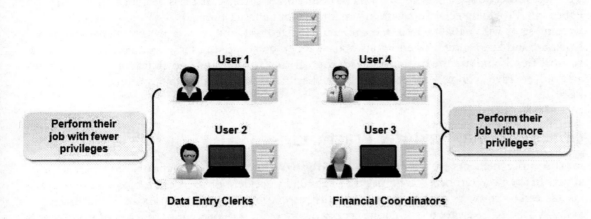

Figure 13-3: Least privilege.

Strong Passwords

A *strong password* is a password that meets the complexity requirements that are set forth by a system administrator and documented in a security policy or password policy. Strong passwords increase the security of systems that use password-based authentication by protecting against password guessing and other password attacks.

Strong password requirements should meet the security needs of an individual organization, and can specify:

*   The minimum length of the password.
*   Required characters, such as a combination of letters, numbers, and symbols.
*   Forbidden character strings, such as the user account name, personal identification information, or words found in a dictionary.

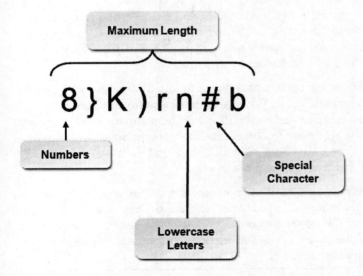

Figure 13-4: Strong password requirements.

User Education

The best protection against *malicious software* or any other security threat is user awareness and education. Providing end users with information about common threats, hoaxes, and security warning signs will enable them to recognize and delete hoax email messages, avoid unauthorized software, and keep antivirus definitions updated. You must support and encourage users to follow security trends and use the organization's resources to stay up-to-date on all recent security incidents and preventative actions. User education is the best defense against data compromise or system damage.

Common User Security Practices

Most security incidents are a result of a user error or unauthorized user action. User errors do not always happen on purpose; sometimes they happen by accident or users are fooled by an attacker. Users need to be aware of their specific security responsibilities and habits. As an A+ technician, you will need to be aware of common security practices used to prevent both types of user security incidents so that you can make sure that all hardware and software implementations support common goals.

Security Area	Employee Responsibilities
Physical security	Employees should not allow anyone in the building without an ID badge. Employees should not allow other individuals to "tailgate" on a single ID badge. Employees should be comfortable approaching and challenging unknown or unidentified individuals in a work area. Access within the building should be restricted to only those areas an employee needs to access for job purposes. Data handling procedures of confidential files must be followed. Employees must also follow clean desk policies to ensure that confidential documents and private corporate information are secured and filed away from plain sight.
System security	Proper password behaviors can be crucial in keeping systems resources secure from unauthorized users. Employees must use their user IDs and passwords properly and comply with the ID and password requirements set forth by management. Password information should never be shared or written down where it is accessible to others. All confidential files should be saved to an appropriate location on the network where they can be secured and backed up, not on a hard drive or removable media device.
Device security	Employees must follow the correct procedures to log off all systems and shut down computers when not in use. Wireless communication and personally owned devices must be approved by the IT department and installed properly. These devices can be a gateway for attackers to access corporate information and sensitive data. Portable devices, such as laptops and mobile devices, must be properly stored and secured when not in use.
Social networking security	Employees must be made aware of the potential threats and attacks that target social networking applications and websites. The use of these applications can lead to potential breaches in security on an organization's network. Security policies should include guidelines and restrictions for users of any social networking application or website.

Authentication Methods

Most organizations will employ a variety of authentication methods in order to prevent unauthorized access to the physical building, infrastructure, and resources. Common authentication methods include the following.

Authentication Method	Description
User name and password	In this system, a user or computer must have a valid user name and an associated secret password. The user submits the user name/password combination to an authenticating system such as a network directory server, which validates the credentials against a database and verifies the user's identity. The security of the system can be breached if the authentication database is altered or compromised, whether accidentally or maliciously, or if the credentials, particularly the password, are lost, stolen, or guessed by a third party.
Biometrics	Biometrics are authentication schemes based on individuals' physical characteristics, such as fingerprints or vocal patterns. Biometrics require specialized equipment and software to store, access, and verify the physical information. As biometric authentication becomes less expensive to implement, it is becoming more widely adopted.
Tokens	*Tokens* are physical or virtual objects, such as *RSA tokens,* smart cards, and ID badges that store authentication information. Tokens can store personal identification numbers (PINs), information about the user, or passwords. For example, a *smart card* is a plastic card containing an embedded computer chip that can store different types of electronic information. The contents of the card are read with a special device called a smart card reader, which can be attached to a PC. When used for authentication, the smart card will store user credentials or private information such as a password or PIN. The user must present the smart card as a token of the user's identity, and so smart cards are sometimes classified as a form of token-based authentication.
Multi-factor authentication	*Multi-factor authentication* is any authentication scheme that requires verification of two or three authentication factors. It can be any combination of what you are, what you have, and what you know. System designers determine what specific factors are required during the design phase. If a user is required to pass a fingerprint scan as well as to enter a password to gain access to a secure facility, this would combine the "who you are" and "what you know" factors. Multi-factor authentication enhances the security of using any single factor alone. Token-based or biometric-based authentication are rarely deployed alone; more frequently, they are used on top of user name and password authentication.
Mutual authentication	*Mutual authentication* is a security mechanism that requires that each party in a communication verify its identity. First, a service or resource verifies the client's credentials, and then the client verifies the resource's credentials. Mutual authentication prevents a client from inadvertently submitting confidential information to a non-secure server. Any type or combination of authentication mechanisms can be used.

Biometric Authentication Methods

Biometrics are used often in high security areas where there is a restricted security clearance, such as in government offices and financial institutions. There are several categories of biometric authentication.

Biometric Authentication Method	Description
Fingerprint scanner	A user's fingerprint pattern is scanned and stored. To authenticate, the user scans a finger again and the print is compared to the stored image in

Biometric Authentication Method	Description
	the authentication database. The fingerprint scanner can be a small separate hardware device, and is even built into some laptops, mice, and universal serial bus (USB) flash drives.
Hand geometry scanner	An individual's hand geometry can also be used for authentication. Hand scanners have pegs between which users insert their fingers. Once the initial scan is stored, and then used to authenticate, subsequent scans are compared to the stored scan in the authentication database.
Retinal scanner	The pattern on a user's retina is scanned and stored. To authenticate, the user scans an eye again and the pattern is compared to the authentication database.
Voice recognition	The user provides a speech sample that is analyzed with voice-recognition software and stored. To authenticate, the user speaks again and the speech patterns are analyzed by the software and compared against the stored sample in the authentication database.
Face recognition	A digital image of the user's face is analyzed with face-recognition software and stored. To authenticate, the user's face is scanned digitally again and the facial appearance is compared against the stored image in the authentication database.
Biometric authentication tokens	Biometric user data can be scanned and encoded once and then stored on a chip on some form of portable electronic security token, such as a smart card or a digital key fob. To authenticate, the user presents the token instead of submitting to another biometric scan. Because the token could be lost or stolen, it is best to combine this type of authentication with a password or PIN, or at least to include a user photograph on the card for visual confirmation of the user's identity.

ACTIVITY 13–1
Identifying Security Concepts

Scenario
In this activity, you will identify common security concepts.

---

1. Katie works in a high-security government facility. When she comes to work in the morning, she places her hand on a scanning device in her building's lobby, which reads her handprint and compares it to a master record of her handprint in a database to verify her identity. This is an example of:

   ○ Biometric authentication

   ○ Multi-factor authentication

   ○ Data encryption

   ○ Tokens

2. How does multi-factor authentication enhance security?

3. While assigning privileges to the accounting department in your organization, Cindy, a human resource administrative assistant, insists that she needs access to the employee records database in order to fulfill change of address requests from employees. After checking with her manager and referring to the organization's access control security policy, Cindy's job role does not fall into the authorized category for access to that database. What security concept is being practiced in this scenario?

   ○ The use of strong passwords.

   ○ User education.

   ○ The principle of least privilege.

   ○ Common user security practices.

TOPIC B

Security Threats and Vulnerabilities

In the previous topic, you identified the fundamental security concepts and methods that can be used to ensure your organization's infrastructure is secure. The next step is to zero in on the all the specific threats and vulnerabilities that you must protect your organization from. In this topic, you will identify common security threats and vulnerabilities.

How can you implement and enforce a good security solution if you don't know what it is your are protecting against? A full understanding of common security threats and vulnerabilities will enable you to customize security solutions based on the specific issues presented within an organization.

This topic covers all or part of the following CompTIA® A+® (2012) certification objectives:

- Exam 220–802: Objective 2.2: Compare and contrast common security threats.

Malware

Malware is any unwanted software that has the potential to damage a system, impede performance, or create a nuisance condition. The software might be introduced deliberately or inadvertently and might or might not be able to propagate itself to other systems.

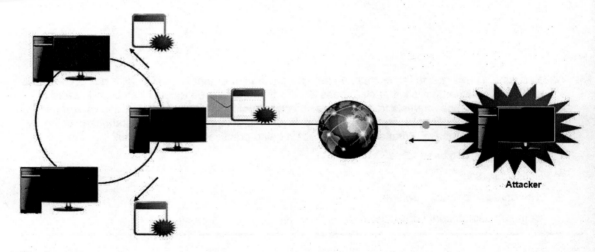

Figure 13–5: Malware.

Types of Malware

There are a number of malicious code attacks you should be aware of that fall into the general malware category.

Malware Type	Description
Virus	A piece of code that spreads from one computer to another by attaching itself to other files. The code in a virus executes when the file it is attached to is opened. Frequently, viruses are intended to enable further attacks, send data back to the attacker, or even corrupt or destroy data.
Worm	A piece of code that spreads from one computer to another on its own, not by attaching itself to another file. Like a virus, a worm can enable further attacks, transmit data, or corrupt or erase files.

[handwritten note:] Needs a host to spread it.

[handwritten note:] Self Replicate

Malware Type	Description
Trojan horse	An insidious type of malware that is itself a software attack and can pave the way for a number of other types of attacks. There is a social engineering component to a Trojan horse attack since the user has to be fooled into executing it.
Logic bomb	A piece of code that sits dormant on a target computer until it is triggered by a specific event, such as a specific date. Once the code is triggered, the logic bomb "detonates," and performs whatever actions it was programed to do. Often, this includes erasing and corrupting data on the target system.
Spyware	Surreptitiously installed malicious software that is intended to track and report the usage of a target system, or to collect other data the author wishes to obtain. Data collected can include web browsing history, personal information, banking and other financial information, and user names and passwords.
Adware	Software that automatically displays or downloads advertisements when it is used. While not all adware is malicious, many adware programs have been associated with spyware and other types of malicious software. Also, it can reduce user productivity by slowing down systems and simply by creating annoyances.
Rootkit	Code that is intended to take full or partial control of a system at the lowest levels. Rootkits often attempt to hide themselves from monitoring or detection, and modify low-level system files when integrating themselves into a system. Rootkits can be used for non-malicious purposes such as virtualization; however, most rootkit infections install backdoors, spyware, or other malicious code once they have control of the target system.
Spam	Spam is an email-based threat that presents various advertising materials, promotional content, or get-rich-quick schemes to users. The messages can quickly fill a user's inbox and cause storage issues. Spam can also carry malicious code and other types of malware.

Handwritten margin notes:
- *Logic bomb:* on a specific Anniversary or date
- *Spyware:* used by
- *Adware:* Random Pop ups
- *Rootkit:* Fully compromise the machine + can hide themselves
- *Trojan horse (right margin):* Appears to be harmless; keylogging; Remote Admin Tool; can use up webcam against you

Social Engineering

A *social engineering attack* is a type of attack that uses deception and trickery to convince unsuspecting users to provide sensitive data or to violate security guidelines. Social engineering is often a precursor to another type of attack. Because these attacks depend on human factors rather than on technology, their symptoms can be vague and hard to identify. Social engineering attacks can come in a variety of methods: in person, through email, or over the phone. Social engineering typically takes advantage of users who are not technically knowledgeable, but it can also be directed against technical support staff if the attacker pretends to be a user who needs help. Social engineering attacks can be prevented with effective user education.

Types of Social Engineering

There are various types of social engineering attacks.

Social Engineering Type	Description
Shoulder surfing	This is a human-based attack where the goal is to look over the shoulder of an individual as he or she enters password information or a PIN. Shoulder surfing can happen in an office

Social Engineering Type	Description
	environment, a retail environment, at an ATM or at the entryway of a secure physical facility.
Spoofing	This is a human-based or software-based attack where the goal is to pretend to be someone else for the purpose of identity concealment. Spoofing can occur in Internet Protocol (IP) addresses, network adapter's hardware (Media Access Control [MAC]) addresses, and email. If employed in email, various email message headers are changed to conceal the originator's identity.
Impersonation	This is a human-based attack where an attacker pretends to be someone he is not. A common scenario is when the attacker calls an employee and pretends to be calling from the help desk. The attacker tells the employee he is reprogramming the order-entry database, and he needs the employee's user name and password to make sure it gets entered into the new system.
Hoax	This is an email-based or web-based attack that is intended to trick the user into performing undesired actions, such as deleting important system files in an attempt to remove a virus. It could also be a scam to convince users to give up important information or money for an interesting offer.
Phishing	This is a common type of email-based social engineering attack. In a phishing attack, the attacker sends an email that seems to come from a respected bank or other financial institution. The email claims that the recipient needs to provide an account number, Social Security number, or other private information to the sender in order to "verify an account." Ironically, the phishing attack often claims that the "account verification" is necessary for security reasons. Individuals should never provide personal financial information to someone who requests it, whether through email or over the phone. Legitimate financial institutions never solicit this information from their clients. A similar form of phishing called *pharming* can be done by redirecting a request for a website, typically an e-commerce site, to a similar-looking, but fake, website.
Vishing	This is a human-based attack where the goal is to extract personal, financial, or confidential information from the victim by using services such as the telephone system and IP-based voice messaging services (Voice over Internet Protocol [VoIP]) as the communication medium. This is also called voice phishing.
Whaling	This is a form of phishing that targets individuals who are known to possess a good deal of wealth. It is also known as *spear phishing*. Whaling targets individuals that work in Fortune 500 companies or financial institutions whose salaries are expected to be high.
Spam and *spim*	Spam can also be categorized as a type of social engineering because it can be used within social networking sites such as Facebook and Twitter. Spim is an Internet messaging (IM)-based attack similar to spam that is propagated through IM instead of through email.

Physical Security Threats and Vulnerabilities

Physical security threats and vulnerabilities can come from many different areas. Threats and vulnerabilities can come from inside the organization, or can come from an external source. It is important to understand all aspects of physical security and where issues can arise.

Threat Type	Description
Internal	Internal threats come from inside the organization, such as a disgruntled employee.
External	External threats are difficult to secure against, but risks posed by external power failures may be mitigated by implementing devices such as an Uninterruptible Power Supply (UPS) or a generator.
Natural	Natural threats pose a significant threat to the physical security of a facility. Buildings and rooms that contain important computing assets should be protected against likely weather-related problems including tornadoes, hurricanes, snowstorms, and floods.
Man-made	Man-made threats have the potential of causing a lot of damage. Whether intentional or accidental, people can cause a number of physical threats.

Common Wireless Security Threats

Wireless networks have an increasing number of specific vulnerabilities.

Wireless Threat and Vulnerability	Description
Rogue access point	This is an unauthorized wireless access point on a corporate or private network. Rogue access points can cause considerable damage to an organization's data. They are not detected easily, and can allow private network access to many unauthorized users with the proper devices. A rogue access point can allow man-in-the-middle attacks and access to private information. Organizations should protect themselves from this type of attack by implementing techniques to constantly monitor the system, such as installing an IDS.
Evil twins	These are rogue access points on a network that appear to be legitimate. Although they can be installed both in corporate or private networks, typically they are found in public Wi-Fi hotspots where users do not connect transparently and automatically as they do in a corporate network, but rather select available networks from a list. Evil twins can be more dangerous than other rogue access points because the user thinks that the wireless signal is genuine, making it difficult to differentiate from a valid access point with the same name.
Interference	In wireless networking, this is the phenomenon by which radio waves interfere with the 802.11 wireless signals. It usually occurs at home because of various electronic devices, such as microwaves, operating in a bandwidth close to that of the wireless network. When this occurs, it causes the 802.11 signals to wait before transmitting and the wait can be indefinite at times.
Bluejacking	This is a method used by attackers to send out unwanted Bluetooth® signals from mobile devices, tablets, and laptops to other Bluetooth-enabled devices. Because Bluetooth has a 30-foot transmission limit, this is a very close-range attack. With the advanced technology available today,

[handwritten note next to Rogue access point: Mimic your originally access point]

[handwritten note next to Evil twins: Near an existing wifi in a business loaded w spyware]

Wireless Threat and Vulnerability	Description
	attackers can send out unsolicited messages along with images and video. These types of signals can lead to many different types of threats. They can lead to device malfunctions, or even propagate viruses, including Trojan horses. Users should reject anonymous contacts, and should configure their mobile devices to non-discoverable mode.
Bluesnarfing	This is a method in which attackers gain access to unauthorized information on a wireless device using a Bluetooth connection within the 30-foot Bluetooth transmission limit. Unlike bluejacking, access to wireless devices such as tablets, mobile phones, and laptops by bluesnarfing can lead to the exploitation of private information including email messages, contact information, calendar entries, images, videos, and any data stored on the device.
War driving and *war chalking*	War driving is the act of searching for instances of wireless networks using wireless tracking devices such as tablets, mobile phones, or laptops. It locates wireless access points while traveling, which can be exploited to obtain unauthorized Internet access and potentially steal data. This process can be automated using a GPS device and war driving software. War chalking is the act of using symbols to mark off a sidewalk or wall to indicate that there is an open wireless network which may be offering Internet access. This threat is not as common now that there are so many open networks to connect to.
IV attack	In this attack, the attacker is able to predict or control the *initialization vector (IV)* of an encryption process. This gives the attacker access to view the encrypted data that is supposed to be hidden from everyone else except the authentic user or network.
Packet sniffing	This can be used as an attack on wireless networks where an attacker captures data and registers data flows, which allow the attacker to analyze the data contained in a packet. In its benign form, it also helps organizations monitor their own networks against attackers.

Handwritten notes: Involves 2 people External wifi + an antenna. Chalking is when you've found your access point. To reveal a key in a wep Network.

ACTIVITY 13–2
Identifying Common Security Threats and Vulnerabilities

Scenario

In this activity, you will identify common security threats and vulnerabilities.

---

1. Recently there has been a number of issues within your organization due to the reorganization of a few departments and the reassignment of job roles. As a result, a disgruntled employee removes the UPS on a critical server system and then cuts power to the system, causing costly downtime. This physical threat is what type of threat?

2. John is given a laptop for official use and is on a business trip. When he arrives at his hotel, he turns on his laptop and finds a wireless access point with the name of the hotel, which he connects to for sending work-related communications. This leaves him open for which type of wireless threat?

3. Lucy wants to use "password1" as her system login password. This new password meets all strong password requirements. What do you think of the password she chose?

TOPIC C

Security Protection Measures

In the previous topic, you identified various security threats and vulnerabilities that can cause damage to many aspects of an organization. Once you have identified the types of threats and vulnerabilities that can impact your systems, you can build on that knowledge by identifying general security measures you can employ. In this topic, you will identify security protection measures.

The next layer in your understanding of a computer security infrastructure is to build on basic security concepts by identifying protection measures you can implement. The measures you will select in any given situation will vary depending upon the source of the threat or vulnerability, so you should understand the wide range of security measures available for you to implement.

This topic covers all or part of the following CompTIA® A+® (2012) certification objectives:

- Exam 220–801: Objective 5.4: Explain the fundamentals of dealing with prohibited content/activity.
- Exam 220–802: Objective 2.1: Apply and use common prevention methods.
- Exam 220–802: Objective 2.4: Given a scenario, use the appropriate data destruction/disposal method.

Physical Security

Physical security refers to the implementation and practice of various security control methods that are intended to restrict physical access to facilities. One case where physical security is important is when there is a need to control access to physical documents, password records, and sensitive documents and equipment. One successful unauthorized access attempt can lead to financial losses, credibility issues, and legalities. In addition, physical security involves increasing or assuring the reliability of certain critical infrastructure elements such as electrical power, data networks, and fire suppression systems. Physical security may be challenged by a wide variety of events or situations, including:

- Facilities intrusions.
- Electrical grid failures.
- Fire.
- Personnel illnesses.
- Data network interruptions.

Physical Security Measures

There are a number of physical access controls available to ensure the protection of an organization's physical environment.

Security Measure	Description
Lock doors	There are a number of different locks that can be used to restrict unauthorized access to information resources: • Bolting door locks are a traditional lock-and-key method that requires a non-duplicate policy for keys to access a door. • Combination door locks, or cipher locks, use a keypad or dial system with a code or numeric combination to access a door. • Electronic door locks use an access ID card with an electronic chip or token that is read by the electronic sensor attached to a door.

Security Measure	Description
	• Biometric door locks are commonly used in highly secure environments. This method uses an individual's unique body features to scan and identify the access permissions for a particular door. For example, retinal scanners are used to read the unique patterns of a person's eye to authorize access. • Hardware locks can be attached to a laptop, hard drive, or file cabinet to secure it from being opened or turned on.
Logging and visitor access	Logging should be used at all entrances that are open to the general public. This method requires all visitors to sign in and out when entering and leaving the building. Logging requirements will vary depending on the organization, but should include the following: • Name and company being represented. • Date, time of entry, and time of departure. • Reason for visiting. • Contact within the organization. When possible, one single entry point should be used for all incoming visitors. This decreases the risk of unauthorized individuals gaining access to the building and tailgating.
Identification systems	Identification systems can use a number of different tokens and methods to identify an authorized person and allow them physical access to buildings, room, and grounds. Systems can use a number of different tokens and methods to validate access: • *Badges*, or security cards, can be used to swipe through an identification system or can be configured as a proximity card with radio-frequency identification (RFID) technology that is activated automatically when the card is within a specified distance from the system. *RFID badges* are security cards that contain a tag that reacts with the radio frequency of the identification system to allow or deny access. • *Key fobs* are security devices small enough to attach to a key chain that contain identification information used to gain access to a physical entryway. A user places the fob next to an identification system for validation and then access. • *RSA tokens* are small devices that include cryptographic keys, a digital signature, or even biometric information that is verified against an identification system to allow or deny access to a physical location, system, or network location. RSA tokens are the most common form of token and are generated by RSA Security Solutions. Security cards, such as swipe cards, proximity cards, and badges, provide identity information about the bearer, which is then checked against an appropriate access list for that location. The cards can be used along with a proximity reader to verify identification and grant access. A security card can also include a picture or some other identification code for a second authentication factor. Security cards should be required for all employees and should be visible at all times.
Video surveillance	Video or still-image surveillance can be put in place to deter or help in the prosecution of unwanted access. These systems can be placed inside and outside the building. All video recording should be saved and stored in a secure environment.

Security Measure	Description
Security guards	Human security guards, armed or unarmed, can be placed in front of and around a location to protect it. They can monitor critical checkpoints and verify identification, allow or disallow access, and log physical entry occurrences. They also provide a visual deterrent and can apply their own knowledge and intuition to potential security breaches.
Physical barriers	The location of highly secure resources, such as a server room, should not have windows or be visible from the outside of a building. This creates a more secure barrier from the outside. Examples of physical barriers include fencing and true floor-to-ceiling wall architectures. Other types of physical barriers can be implemented to restrict viewing of a user's computer display. For example, privacy filters can be installed on a computer's display to decrease the physical viewing area of the display so that only the authorized user sitting directly in from of it can see the full screen.
Alarms	Alarms activated by an unauthorized access attempt require a quick response. Locally stationed security guards or police may respond to alarms. These responding individuals may trigger access control devices in the facility to automatically lock.

Digital Security

Digital security refers to the idea that any information or data that is created, stored, and transmitted in digital form is secured to the desired level. This concept applies to many components of the digital world, such as the Internet, cloud-based computing, networks, mobile devices, tablets, laptops, and standard desktop computers. There are a number of prevention methods used to manage and control security issues surrounding digital data. These include:

- Antivirus software
- Anti-spyware software
- Firewalls
- User authentication and strong passwords
- Directory permissions

Antivirus Software

Antivirus software is an application that scans files for executable code that matches patterns, known as *signatures* or *definitions*, that are known to be common to viruses. The antivirus software also monitors systems for activity that is associated with viruses, such as accessing the boot sector. Antivirus software should be deployed on various network systems as well as on individual computers, and the signature database and program updates should be downloaded and installed on a regular basis as well as whenever a new threat is active. Antivirus software does not usually protect against spam, but it can identify malware symptoms and can provide protection from adware and spyware.

Antivirus updates must be managed as they are made available. Antivirus engine updates can include enhancements, bug fixes, or new features being added to the software engine, improving the manner in which the software operates. Updates can be implemented automatically or manually depending on the software. Automatic updating refers to software that periodically downloads and applies updates without any user intervention, whereas manual updating means that a user must be involved to either initiate the update, download the update, or at least approve installation of the update.

Anti-Spyware Software

Anti-spyware software is specifically designed to protect systems against spyware attacks. Some antivirus software packages include protection against adware and spyware, but in most cases, it is necessary to maintain anti-spyware protection in addition to antivirus protection. Some examples of anti-spyware include Webroot's Spy Sweeper and STOPzilla Anti-Spyware.

Firewalls

A firewall is a software program or hardware device that protects networks from unauthorized access by blocking outgoing and incoming unsolicited traffic. Firewalls allow incoming or outgoing traffic that has specifically been permitted by a system administrator and incoming traffic that is sent in response to requests from internal systems. Firewalls use complex filtering algorithms that analyze incoming network data based on destination and source addresses, port numbers, and data types.

There are two common firewall types:

*   *Host or personal firewalls* are installed on a single computer and are used to secure most home computers.
*   *Network-based firewalls* are dedicated hardware/software combinations that protect all the computers on a network behind the firewall.

Software Firewalls

Software firewalls can be useful for small home offices and businesses. The firewall provides many features that can be configured to suit various computing needs. Some features include:

*   Enabling or disabling port security on certain ports.
*   Inbound and outbound filtering. The user can set up rules or exceptions in the firewall settings to limit access to the web.
*   Reporting and logging activity.
*   Malware and spyware protection.
*   Pop-up blocking.
*   Port assigning, forwarding, and triggering.

Hardware Firewalls

A hardware firewall is a hardware device, either stand-alone or built into most routers, that protects computers on a private network from unauthorized traffic. They are placed between the private network and the public network to manage inbound and outbound traffic and network access.

Windows Firewall Configuration

Windows® Firewall is a software-based firewall that is included with all current Windows operating system client and server versions. You can configure the firewall by using the Windows Firewall program in **Control Panel**, or through **Group Policy Settings**, although most versions of Windows will provide a wizard. You can use the Windows Firewall with Advanced Security console to monitor the rules that control the flow of information to and from the system, specify new rules, modify existing rules, or delete rules. For more information, see the Windows Firewall entries in the **Help and Support Center**, and the "Windows Firewall Technical Reference" on the Microsoft Technet website.

Social Engineering Prevention Techniques

The most effective way to prevent damage from social engineering attacks is to educate users. Social engineering is human-based and can be prevented if users are able to recognize and respond to these attacks properly. Follow these guidelines to prevent social engineering attacks:

- Users should not automatically believe everything they see, hear, or read, particularly on the Internet.
- Organizations should implement security policies and train users to follow them.
- Users should report possible attacks.
- Users should not give out passwords over the phone or in email.
- Users should not comply with phone or email requests for personal or company information or access to company resources.
- Users should transfer phone callers who make unusual requests to a system operator.
- Above all, users must employ common sense. If anything sounds forced, too good to be true, or otherwise unusual, it is best to err on the side of caution.

Hard Drive Sanitation

The next step in fully securing an organization's assets is to focus on the physical-based attacks and how they can be prevented. *Hard drive sanitation* is the method used to repeatedly delete and overwrite any traces or bits of sensitive data on a hard drive. There are a few different ways you can sanitize a hard drive to ensure the security of the data stored on the drive:

- Degaussing magnetizes the disk in order to scramble the data. To effectively sanitize the drive, this process needs to be done multiple times.
- Overwriting, or data wiping, is a process used to repeatedly write over existing data on a hard drive until the original data cannot be recovered. This is the most common method of sanitizing hard drives.
- Physically destroying the drive by damaging the platters inside the hard drive. This can be done by burning, breaking, or pulverizing them.
- Recycle hard drives using a reputable recycling company.

Formatting Hard Drives for Disposal

Disk formatting is the process of deleting file systems from a computing device in order to clean the computing device for reuse. Proper formatting should be conducted to prevent any data remnants from being accessed on the device. This process can be done in two ways:

- *Low level formatting* is the process of writing track sector markings on a hard disk. This level of formatting is performed when the hard disk is manufactured.
- *Standard formatting*, also called *high-level formatting*, is an operating system function that builds file systems on drives and partitions. It tests disk sectors to verify that they can be reliably used to hold data. It marks any unreliable sectors as bad sectors that cannot be used.

As a security best practice, standard formatting should be done to ensure that all data is removed from a device.

Physical Destruction Methods for Computer Media

Physical destruction of computer media components ensures that the data is unrecoverable. Effective methods include using a shredder, drill, or smashing the platters completely to change the physical makeup of the component so that it cannot be reassembled or recognized. Other methods include using a degausser to demagnetize the internal components of the device so that they are unreadable or using electromagnetic waves to alter the magnetic components inside the device so that they are unreadable and unrecoverable.

ACTIVITY 13-3
Identifying Security Protection Measures

Scenario
In this activity, you will identify security protection measures.

---

1. Your organization has issued a new security policy that states that any laptop, desktop, or mobile device that is replaced must be completely sanitized to ensure that all sensitive data is removed. What sanitation method would you suggest to ensure that the data cannot be recovered?

2. What is the difference between a host-based and network-based firewalls?

3. What physical security measures are familiar to you and how have they been implemented?

TOPIC D

Workstation Security

In the previous topic, you examined various security methods used to ensure that your network is protected from unauthorized access. Network security will restrict unauthorized access through a network connection, but what if an unauthorized user comes in through the front door and sits down at a company computer? In this topic, you will examine methods used to secure workstations.

Each day, the number and complexity of threats against computer security increases. In response to these threats, there are more and more security tools and techniques available to increase the level of protection you can configure on a system. As a computer support professional, your organization and your clients will all be looking to you to ensure that the computing environment provides the appropriate level of security, without compromising performance or data access.

This topic covers all or part of the following CompTIA® A+® (2012) certification objectives:

- Exam 220–801: Objective 2.6: Install, configure, and deploy a SOHO wireless/wired network using appropriate settings.
- Exam 220–802: Objective 2.3: Implement security best practices to secure a workstation.

Windows Security Policies

Windows security policies are Windows configuration settings that control the overall security behavior of the system. The security policy consists of hierarchical groupings of related policy nodes, which contain individual policy entries you can enable, configure, or disable. The **Local Security Policy** is a subset of the comprehensive local policy object used to configure the general behavior of each Windows system.

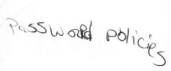

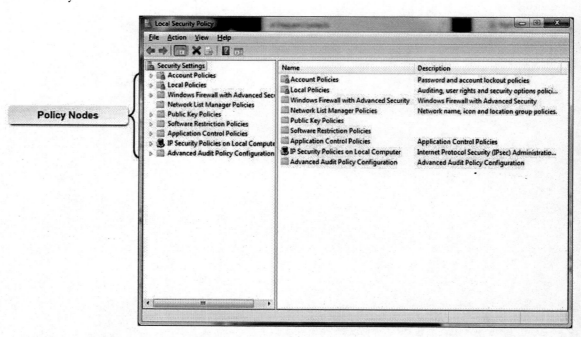

Figure 13–6: Windows security settings.

Local Policy Settings and Group Policy Settings

In Windows workgroups, all policies, including security policies, are set in the local policy object on each individual system. To view the full set of local policies, you can open the Microsoft Management Console (MMC) object. You can find the security policy settings under **Computer**

Configuration→Windows Settings→Security Settings. The **Local Security Policy** utility in the **Administrative Tools** group enables you to access the **Security Settings** node alone.

When Windows computers are members of a centralized Windows domain, an administrator can also manage policies for all computers by using **Group Policy.** The structure of domain-based **Group Policy** objects and the local policy object are similar.

Windows Firewall

Windows Firewall is a software-based firewall that is included with Windows 7, Windows Vista®, Windows XP with Service Pack 2, Windows Server® 2003 with Service Pack 1 or later, and Windows Server 2008. Once an operating system is installed, Windows Firewall is automatically installed and enabled. By default, the firewall blocks unsolicited incoming traffic on all ports. You can open blocked ports and configure other firewall settings by using the Windows Firewall program in the **Control Panel** or through Windows Security **Policy Settings.** In Windows 7, Windows Vista, and Windows Server 2008, Windows Firewall offers more security options and can be configured to drop outgoing traffic as well as incoming traffic.

 Note: For more information, see the Windows Firewall entries in the **Help and Support Center,** and the "Windows Firewall Technical Reference" on the Microsoft Technet website.

Software Firewall Configuration Settings

There are many different firewall applications available. Although all firewalls follow the same basic principles, the specific features and configuration tools available can vary considerably. Consult the documentation for the particular firewall application you need to support. Running more than one different firewall application at the same time is not recommended. Most software-based firewalls offer configuration settings for common security options.

Security Option	Description
Global security level	Settings usually range from denying applications' inbound and outbound access to other networks to allowing all traffic through the firewall, in which case the firewall is disabled.
Program filters	You can configure network access rules and exceptions for each application individually. For example, allowing an application to have an outbound connection only without inbound connections.
Security log	You can configure different options for logging information concerning unsolicited traffic on your network.
Unsolicited traffic blocking and filtering	Most software firewalls have many options for blocking unsolicited traffic, including: • Preventing specific IP addresses from accessing your network. • Blocking specific data, such as File Transfer Protocol (FTP). • Blocking traffic on specific ports. • Configuring open and closed ports.
Port forwarding and triggering	Port forwarding and triggering are options you can configure on Network Address Translation (NAT)-enabled routers. • Port forwarding is used to forward a network port from one network node to another. Port forwarding is used to provide remote computers access to a specific computer inside a private LAN. • Port triggering is used to automate port forwarding by specifying ports (triggering ports) to automatically and dynamically forward inbound traffic to.

Workstation Security Best Practices

When you select and apply computer security measures, you must make security adjustments that protect the workstation and the applications and data on it, while ensuring that the system runs appropriately for legitimate users.

Some steps you might take to apply security measures include the following.

Steps	Description
Manage user authentication	• Change the default user name and password on each workstation device. • Require all users to create strong passwords and to protect the passwords from others. • In high-security environments, implement multi-factor authentication that can include smart cards or biometric authentication systems.
Install updates and patches	• Install the latest operating system service packs and security update patches. • Install the latest application patches for utilities that are included in the operating system as well as for web browsers and third-party application software.
Manage user accounts	• Use policy settings to disable or delete guest accounts or other unnecessary accounts, and rename default accounts, so attackers cannot use known account names to access the system. • Restrict user permissions so that only those users who absolutely need access are allowed into the system. • Disable the guest account on all machines to prevent unauthorized access to any shared files and folders on the workstation.
Educate users	• Educate users to follow best security practices, such as recognizing and avoiding hoaxes, phishing attacks, and potential malicious software sources.
Apply workstation security measures	• Implement antivirus software to protect against malicious software. • Block pop-ups in your web browser. • Install a firewall and configure the appropriate open and closed ports and the program filtering settings. • Implement warning messages or banners displayed at user login to warn users that only authorized use is allowed. These banners could be important in future civil litigation or criminal prosecution, and they can put all users on notice that their activities might be monitored. All warning banners should comply with the legal requirements of your jurisdiction. • Disable autorun to prevent malware and other viruses from being loaded automatically with a device, such as a USB drive. Disabling the autorun features will restrict any infected files from automatically loading. • Enable the screensaver and password functionality to lock systems when idle. • Enable automatic operating system updates through the **Control Panel.** • Limit the number of shared resources on a system. Use share and file system permissions to restrict access to file and print resources.

ACTIVITY 13-4
Securing a Workstation

Scenario

Scott recently bought a new computer and has asked you to implement some of the security features provided in Windows 7 Professional. You decide to encrypt a folder that contains sensitive data, add more restrictive user account control settings, and make sure that the SmartScreen Filter is active in Internet Explorer®.

---

1. Encrypt the Encrypt folder.
   a) Open **Computer,** and navigate to **Local Disk (C:)\datafiles.**
   b) Locate and select the **Encrypt** folder, and display its pop-up menu.
   c) Select **Properties.**
   d) On the **General** tab, select **Advanced.**
   e) Check **Encrypt contents to secure data.**
   f) Select **OK** twice.
   g) In the **Confirm Attribute Change** dialog box, verify that **Apply changes to this folder, subfolders and files** is selected, and select **OK.**
      A message is displayed in the status bar prompting you to back up your EFS certificate.
   h) Select **Back up your file encryption key.**
   i) Select **Back up later.**
   j) Examine the Encrypt folder.
      The Encrypt folder name is now green to indicate that it and its contents are encrypted.
   k) Close **Computer.**

2. Adjust the User Account Control settings to always notify the user when administrative-level changes are made to the computer.
   a) Open **Control Panel,** and enter *uac* in the **Search Control Panel** text box.
   b) Select **Change User Account Control settings.**
   c) If prompted, by **UAC Credentials,** type *Admin##* with a password *!Pass1234*
   d) Move the slider bar to **Always Notify.**
   e) Select **OK.**
   f) Select **Yes.**
   g) Close **Control Panel.**

3. Verify that the Internet Explorer **SmartScreen Filter** is enabled.
   a) Open **Internet Explorer.**
   b) Select **Safety→SmartScreen Filter,** and examine the menu options.
      The menu should contain the option **Turn off SmartScreen Filter.**
   c) Close the **Safety** menu without selecting any commands, and close **Internet Explorer.**

Summary

In this lesson, you implemented and described many concepts and techniques that can be used to establish the desired level of security within an organization. Every organization will have different security requirements based on the type of business they conduct. It is your job to understand those requirements and know how security controls should be implemented to directly support those needs.

What security concepts have you come across in your experience?

What physical security controls have you had experience with? What controls do you think are the most common?

 Note: Check your LogicalCHOICE Course screen for opportunities to interact with your classmates, peers, and the larger LogicalCHOICE online community about the topics covered in this course or other topics you are interested in. From the Course screen you can also access available resources for a more continuous learning experience.

14 Troubleshooting Hardware Components

Lesson Time: 2 hours

Lesson Objectives

In this lesson, you will troubleshoot hardware components.

- Describe troubleshooting theory.
- Troubleshoot video and display devices.
- Troubleshoot hard drives and RAID arrays.
- Troubleshoot system hardware components.
- Troubleshoot laptops.
- Troubleshoot printers.

Lesson Introduction

In the previous lessons, you installed, configured, and maintained the hardware, software, and other components that make up the computer system to ensure that they work properly. But what happens when one of those components stops working or breaks? In this lesson, you will troubleshoot hardware components.

Installing and configuring computer systems for an organization is an important task, as more and more companies and even the general public become more tech savvy. But, the increased use of technology inevitably invites problems: broken hardware, user accidents, and natural wear and tear on resources. As an A+ technician, it is part of your responsibilities to troubleshoot these issues as they arise within your organization.

This lesson covers all or part of the following CompTIA® A+® (2012) certification objectives:

- Topic A:
  - Exam 220–802: Objective 4.1
- Topic B:
  - Exam 220–802: Objective 4.4
- Topic C:

- • Exam 220–802: Objective 4.3
- • Topic D:
  - • Exam 220–802: Objective 4.2
- • Topic E:
  - • Exam 220–802: Objective 4.8
- • Topic F:
  - • Exam 220–802: Objective 4.9

TOPIC A

Troubleshooting Theory

In this lesson, you will troubleshoot various hardware components used in computers and printers. Before you can even begin to troubleshoot a physical problem with a piece of hardware, you need to understand the basics of troubleshooting and some best practices used. In this topic, you will apply troubleshooting theory.

The most elaborate toolkit and expensive diagnostic software can be useless if you do not have a consistent plan of attack for solving problems. Even experienced technicians can sometimes overlook obvious problems or solutions. Troubleshooting can be extremely challenging and not always easy, but if you follow common best practices and basic troubleshooting procedures, you will often be able to determine the specific cause of a problem, as well as possible solutions to the problem.

This topic covers all or part of the following CompTIA® A+® (2012) certification objectives:

- Exam 220–802: Objective 4.1: Given a scenario, explain the troubleshooting theory.

Troubleshooting Theory

A logical, methodical approach to troubleshooting usually leads to quicker solutions, so there are certain general factors that will apply in any troubleshooting situation.

Factor	Description
Identify the problem	Identify the issue or problem. Ask questions and try and extrapolate key information that will help you identify any anomalies.
	Make sure to perform backups before making any changes. This will allow you to restore any information that may be lost during the troubleshooting process.
	Use open-ended questions when working with users to help identify the issue behind the symptoms. For example, instead of asking if the user can start the computer, try asking what happens when the user tries to start the computer. Use following questions to help identify the problem:
	• *Were you able to complete this task before?* If not, maybe the system is simply unable to perform the task without additional hardware or software.
	• *If you could do the task before, when did you notice there was an issue?* If you can identify what happened immediately before the problem, then it could lead you right to the issue.
	• *What types of changes have you noticed since the last time you completed this task?* If you cannot get a specific answer from the user, then you may need to follow up with a few more targeted questions such as "Did something get added to the computer?" or "Did you follow the exact same procedure or did you do this task differently?"
	• *Were error messages displayed?* If you can get the exact text of any error messages displayed, you can try searching the manufacturer's website (or just a general Internet search) to get an explanation of the message and to see if any problem reports have been logged related to this message.
Establish a theory	Establish a theory. Verify anything that may seem too obvious. Make no assumptions and check everything that may seem too simple and easy. Always

Factor	Description
	verify that components are plugged in, connected, and powered on. Oftentimes, problems are the result of simple things.
	• If applicable, try to re-create the issue so that you can experience it for yourself and can see exactly what the results are. If you can, observe the user as they complete the steps to verify that they are following the proper procedures.
	• Depending on the issue, develop a theory and determine how the problem may be corrected. Use your personal experiences, refer to support websites and online forums, and discuss theories with your colleagues to build possible resolutions and how they may be implemented.
Test the theory	Test the theory to determine the cause by testing related components; inspecting connections, hardware and software configurations; and consulting vendor documentation, to solve the problem or identify a likely solution.
	Once the theory is confirmed, if the problem is not resolved, then determine what the next steps will be. If the theory is not confirmed, then determine what the next steps are to resolve the problem. In some cases, you may need to escalate the issue to a designated party or individual.
Establish a plan	Establish a plan of action to resolve the problem and implement the solution. You may need to conduct further research and establish new ideas and determine priorities. Research and planning may result in using a different approach that may need detailed planning. You may also end up with more than one plan depending on what the possible causes are, so prioritize and execute each plan carefully. During this process, you need to make sure that productivity does not suffer and that any downtime is limited.
Verify	When the issue is resolved, verify full system functionality and, if applicable, implement preventative measures. This part of the process may also involve consulting with colleagues or vendors to communicate known issues, solutions, and preventative measures. Preventative measures might include applying system updates and installing antivirus software.
	Once the issue has been resolved, make sure that the solution implemented is actually working the way you intended and did not cause any additional or new issues. Always make sure that the user or customer is completely satisfied with the results.
Document	Document your findings, actions, and outcomes. Documentation of computer problems and their solutions can be a helpful part of the overall documentation plan for your company's computers. Not only will this provide you with an ever-growing database of information specific to the computers you are responsible for, it also will be valuable reference material for use in future troubleshooting instances.

Troubleshooting Models

Troubleshooting models are used to support computing devices and networks. There are a number of different models in use by technicians, so you may come across a variety of approaches over the course of your professional career. Using a model, or standardized approach, can provide you with a systematic way to tackle an issue or problem. While there is no surefire method that will work every single time, since troubleshooting requires you to make intuitive guesses based on your own experience and those of other professionals, using a model will help you break down each phase of the process in order to identify causes and solutions in areas where you do not have the required type of experience. Ultimately, the troubleshooting process that you use will probably be a mix of more standardized models, plus your own processes and methods that you've used in the past.

Troubleshooting Template Forms

Creating a template form will ensure that all necessary information get included in any reports. This provides an organization with consistent trouble reports for creating policies and adjusting procedures based on findings from the troubleshooting process. Many organizations will use some sort of help desk software or similar forms or tools that allow users and technicians to enter information. Key components that you should consider including in a troubleshooting template or help desk form are:

- A general section, listing a description of the issue, the date and time the issue was received, the person who reported the problem, and the person who has the problem (if the report was made by someone else).
- A description of the conditions and specifics of the issue, such as the type of device, details about any other devices connected, the OS, any applications being used on the device, and if the device is connected to the network, and what type of connection. For example, a laptop running Windows® 7 connecting to the corporate wireless network.
- The problem identified while troubleshooting.
- Whether or not the problem can be reproduced. If it can be reproduced, then take the necessary steps.
- The possible cause or causes identified during troubleshooting.
- Any solutions or corrections made during troubleshooting.
- The results of implementing the solutions and corrections.
- All testing results.
- Any external resources that were used, such as vendor assistance, support websites or forums, contact information for other technicians that provided help, and information for any third-party service providers used.
- Customer sign-off on the resolved issue. This will ensure that the customer is completely satisfied with the outcome.

TOPIC B

Troubleshoot Video and Display Devices

In the previous topic, you examined troubleshooting theory and general troubleshooting tips. Now, you can start working with those theories and put those tips and tricks to work. In this topic, you will troubleshoot common video and display devices issues.

It's simple: the display device is a user's window into the computer system. Without a fully functioning display, you will not be able to interact with the device. Its crucial to understand common display issues and how they can be resolved so that users can get back to work quickly. It is your job to respond quickly and be as timely as you can to resolve the issues and so users can complete their tasks.

This topic covers all or part of the following CompTIA® A+® (2012) certification objectives:

- Exam 220–802: Objective 4.4: Given a scenario, troubleshoot common video and display issues.

Common Video and Display Issues

When it comes to display devices, you will encounter a number of issues that are fairly common and can be resolved quickly. Common issues and solutions include the following.

Issue	Possible Problems and Solutions
Dark screen	A dark screen, or an indicator light that is not lit, can indicate general power problems, such as the power is not turned on, the power cable is disconnected, or the power is on but the display is plugged into a power strip, surge protector, or uninterruptible power supply (UPS) that is not turned on.
	To correct the problem, turn on the power or power strip and reconnect the cables and cords at both ends. If a circuit breaker has tripped, reset it. Press or jiggle the power button on the monitor itself.
Dim image or no image in screen	If there is no power light, check for and correct power problems.
	The data cable to the Video Graphics Array (VGA), Digital Video Interface (DVI), High-Definition Multimedia Interface (HDMI), or display port on the PC may be disconnected. Except on very old displays, you will see an On Screen Display (OSD) message in this case, indicating a signal problem. Connect or re-seat the cables and connectors. If the cable is disconnected, and you do not see an OSD message, the display may be bad.
	Brightness or contrast may be adjusted improperly. Adjust the settings using the display controls. (The OSD message is not affected by brightness or contrast.)
	The display may be in power saving mode. The power light will typically change from green to solid or blinking orange. Press a key or move the mouse to wake up the monitor.
Flickering or distortion	The display cable may need to be adjusted so that is it more securely connected to the video port. This might also imply that there are bent or broken pins. Try to straighten any bent pins and re-connect the cable. Use caution; a severely bent pin may break, in which case you will need to replace the monitor. Sometimes the cable is removable, in which case you can replace it.

Issue	Possible Problems and Solutions
	This could also be an incorrect display adapter used with incorrect device drivers. If you can see the Power-On Self Test (POST), but the image goes black when the system starts up, try booting the device into VGA Mode and verify that the correct adapter and device drivers are being used.
	The refresh rate may be too low or too high. The refresh rate should be set to as high as the display and the adapter card can support. If the rate is set too high, then you risk damaging the display.
	If the display is placed in close proximity to other electronic or magnetic equipment, then interference may cause damage. In this case, move the equipment so that there is adequate space between devices.
	Check the color depth setting on the display device. The settings may be incorrect. If needed, make the necessary adjustments to the color depth settings for the display.
Display turns itself off	In this case, power management may be enabled. You can adjust this in complementary metal oxide semiconductor (CMOS) settings or in the operating system's display properties.
	Another reason might be that the display's video card is overheating. You can replace the card with one that has a better cooling system, or you can install additional fans to cool the entire system.
Application problems	If the screen goes blank, flickers, or acts erratically when a specific application is active, the application may require different color depth or screen resolution. Right-click in a free area on the desktop and choose *Screen Resolution*. Adjust the settings on this page to suit the user's requirements.
Defective pixels	The pixels that make up a liquid crystal display (LCD) output sometimes to do not display as they should. There are generally two types of pixels issues: • *Dead pixels* are pixels that do not display the light as expected. This is shown visually when the LCD is displaying a picture, and there are black spots shown with no light. • *Stuck pixels* are pixels that only show light, so they appear out of place when the display is on. Light colors can vary from red, to blue or green. Fixing defective pixels can be difficult to repair. It is recommended that you contact the display manufacturer to check for warranty information. If the LCD unit is an older one, you can attempt to fix the pixels in a number of different ways: • Using pressure against the screen using the blunt end of an object. • Using heat to apply pressure to the defective pixels. You must protect yourself with gloves and protect the screen by placing a hot, wet cloth within a plastic bag before placing it on the screen. • Using defective pixel software utility, such as JScreenFix, Dead Pixel Tester 2.20, and PixelRepairer.
Color issues	If the color patterns are incorrect on the display, then you may need to adjust the tint in the display settings. If you notice discoloration of the display, then that could be a sign that you need to degauss the monitor.
Physical damage	If there is noticeable physical damage to the display device or you know of internal physical damage, you may not be able to repair it. In general, most damaged display devices will need to be replaced rather than repaired.

Issue	Possible Problems and Solutions
Video card issues	There are a number of specific problems that can cause a number of specific symptoms: • *Visual artifacts* are errors or anomalies in the visual display of a picture. • A Windows® system stop error (known as the Blue Screen of Death, or BSOD) can be a indicator that there is an issue with your graphics card. • Distortions, such as curves, waves, or other patterns show in the video image. Additional troubleshooting steps to take in the case of a video card issue include: • Check to make sure that the actual video card is seated correctly on the motherboard. • Always verify that you are running the latest drivers for the video card and the chipsets on the motherboard. • Check for interference with other devices within a close proximity. Try removing devices that you suspect may be causing issues. • Check to make sure you are not overclocking the system beyond the capabilities of the card. • Check the power supply and make sure that all connections are secure. • Check to make sure that the fans are operating.

 Access the Checklist tile on your LogicalCHOICE course screen for reference information and job aids on How to Troubleshoot Video and Display Devices

ACTIVITY 14-1
Troubleshooting Video and Display Devices

Before You Begin
Your instructor might ask you to take a short break so that issues can be introduced into your computer systems.

Scenario
Several users are having issues with their displays. You have been assigned to get to each workstation and resolve the problems appropriately.

---

1. The first user's LCD display is not coming on. The power light is not lit. The user has checked that the display is plugged in and the display is connected to the system. Follow the appropriate actions to resolve this issue.
   a) Unplug the display from the electrical outlet and plug in a lamp or other device to verify that the display is plugged into a working outlet. If the device works, plug the display back into the outlet. If the device does not work, contact an electrician to fix the outlet and plug the display into another outlet.
   b) If the outlet is on a UPS, surge protector, or power strip, verify that the unit is turned on.
   c) Verify that the connections of the power cord and display cable are secure on the display as well as on the PC and electrical outlet.
   d) Try to turn on the display again.
   e) If the display still does not come on, replace the display with a known good monitor.

2. When you arrive at the next user's workstation, you can hear that the display is making noises.
   a) Determine whether the noise is a crackling or whining noise.
   b) If it is a crackling noise, clean the display and try to vacuum or blow dust out of the display vents. Do not open the display. If necessary, send it out for more in-depth cleaning.
   c) If it is a whining noise, try the following to fix it: move the display or change the refresh rate. If it will not stop whining, send it out for adjustment and replace the display with a quieter one.

3. The next user's older CRT monitor is flickering and the display is distorted.
   a) Verify that the monitor cable is firmly plugged into the monitor and to the computer.
   b) If available, press the **Degauss** button.
   c) Check the monitor cable for any bent pins and straighten them, if necessary.
   d) Move the monitor away from florescent light, speakers, other monitors, or other electronic devices with powerful motors.

4. The next user's display power light is on, but there is no picture.
   a) Verify that the display cable is connected to the display and to the PC.
   b) Adjust the contrast using the buttons on the display.
   c) Adjust the brightness using the buttons on the display.
   d) If it still is not working, swap the display with one that you know works to determine if the problem is with the display or the video card.

5. At the last user's workstation, the LCD screen is blank with an error message that reads "Out of Frequency."
   a) Restart Windows and select **F8** before Windows is loaded.
   b) Start Windows in Safe Mode.
   c) Display the pop-up menu for the desktop and select **Personalize.**

d) Select **Display Settings.**

e) In the **Display Settings** dialog box, change the resolution to the next lower resolution by dragging the **Resolution** slider to the left.

f) Select **Apply,** select **OK,** and then close the **Personalization** window.

g) Restart Windows in normal mode.

h) If the error message "Out of Frequency" appears again, repeat the steps to change the resolution to a lower resolution until the monitor is recognized by the operating system.

i) Once the monitor is recognized, the error message disappears. Configure the monitor resolution to the original setting.

TOPIC C

Troubleshoot Hard Drives and RAID Arrays

In the previous topic, you examined troubleshooting for video and display devices. While input devices like video and display devices are essential for the end user to be able to interact with the system, hard drives and arrays are important components in the system as well. In this topic, you will troubleshoot hard drives and Redundant Array of Independent Disks (RAID) arrays.

End users rely on the hard drive in their systems to store important system information and personal or professional data and files. Without a hard drive that works properly, the computer system is essentially worthless. As an A+ technician, you will likely be called upon to fix or troubleshoot common problems with hard drives. In this topic, you will troubleshoot hard drives and RAID arrays.

This topic covers all or part of the following CompTIA® A+® (2012) certification objectives:

- Exam 220–802: Objective 4.3: Given a scenario, troubleshoot hard drives and RAID arrays with appropriate tools.

Drive and Array Troubleshooting Tools

To resolve hard drive and RAID array problems, there is a variety of different physical tools and software utility tools available.

Tool	Description
Screwdriver	In order to repair a faulty hard drive, you will need a screwdriver to remove the drive from the drive bay within the computer case.
External enclosures	*External enclosures* protect the hard drive by providing a strong barrier typically made of plastic all the way around the disk. Most enclosures also provide power to the drive through an external connection, typically through a universal serial bus (USB) port.
CHKDSK	This utility is also referred to as Check Disk. It is used to verify the logical integrity of a file system. With the /f switch, chkdsk.exe can repair the file system data. Enter chkdsk "drive letter" /f in the **Run** dialog box or at the command line. With the /r switch, chkdsk can locate bad sectors on the disk and recover any readable information. Entering chkdsk /? displays a list of all available switches.
FORMAT	The format utility can be used to format partitions to a selected file system. You can run the format command right from the command line, or right-click any drive letter in Windows® Explorer and choose the **Format** option.
FDISK	Use to create and manage partitions on a hard disk. You can run the fdisk command at the command line to open the utility. The tool can be used to not only create partitions, but to change, delete, and view current partitions.
File recovery software	*File recovery software* is used to recover deleted files from your computer system. In many cases, files that have were moved to the recycle bin, then emptied, can still be recovered. Some files may still live on the hard disk. There are a number of free software programs that will provide recovery functions:

Tool	Description
	• Recuva • Glary Undelete • Pandora Recovery

Common Hard Drive Symptoms

When you are troubleshooting hard drives, you will run into a number of different issues with numerous potential solutions.

Hard Drive Symptom	Possible Problems and Solutions
Failure to boot	If you receive an error that says "Not Ready—System Halted" then the drive is damaged, is not configured to be a master or Cable Select to suit the system, or a data cable is not connected properly. You should check the drive for physical damage and verify that the connections are properly attached to the drive.
POST error	POST errors in the 17xx range could indicate a number of different issues including: • 1701: Drive not found • 1702: Hard drive adapter not found • 1703: Hard drive failure • 1704: Hard drive or adapter failure • 1780, 1790: Hard drive 0 failed • 1781, 1791: Hard drive 1 failed • 1782: Hard drive controller failed You should check for damage to the connections and reconnect drive. You may need to replace any component that has failed.
Drive not recognized	If your hard drive is not recognized by the system when it boots up, then verify that the system has been set to boot from the hard drive in the system Basic Input/Output System (BIOS) settings in the boot priority list. You may also need to verify that the correct drivers for the hard drive are installed.
Drive read/write failure	The drive might have been infected with a virus. Run an antivirus utility to find and remove any infections. If you suspect that the drive is not writing and reading data properly, then it could mean that there are bad sectors on the drive, the drive has failed, or the drive has been infected by a virus. Sometimes, issues that seem to be device-specific are actually virus infections that can cause physical damage as well, but in most cases, the damage is limited to the data stored on the device. Start by running CHKDSK to attempt to recover data from any damaged sectors of the drive. Use **Device Manager** to resolve any resource conflicts and indications of drive failure.
Computer will not boot	If the computer will not boot up, then it could be a sign that the drive is disconnected, is damaged, is not recognized by the system BIOS, or is not configured properly by the system BIOS. Start by enabling the drive in the CMOS setup utility and check the startup settings, then visually inspect the drive for damage and reconnect it to the system.
Grinding noises	If you hear grinding noises coming from the system, then it could be a sign that the drive is physically damaged. If there is data that needs to be recovered, then

Hard Drive Symptom	Possible Problems and Solutions
	power down the system immediately because powering the drive at all will make the damage worse. Next, remove the damaged drive and send it to a suitable recovery facility, where it will be rebuilt in a cleanroom, and the data can be extracted.
Loud clicking noises	Loud clicking noises can be a sign that the drive is trying to park the drive head but cannot park the head. You can try turning off power management to the drive. This will allow the drive to only park its head when the device is shut down.
Possible data corruption	If you suspect that the data is corrupted, then the system may not have been shut down properly or the drive is either in the process of failing or has been infected with a virus. In this case, all you can really do is educate users to be aware of this and make sure that they are shutting the system down properly every time. In the event that it may be a virus, run antivirus software to clean the computer of all infected files.
Slow performance	Slow hard drive performance can mean that the drive is too full or fragmented, the controller is too slow, or the wrong cable type was used to connect the drive. To resolve these issues: • Delete all unneeded files. • Defragment the drive. • Verify and replace the hard drive cable, if necessary.
External drive issues	External drives come with their own types of issues, including: • The cable connecting the hard drive to the PC may be bad, so check it for physical damage. • The USB port may not be functioning, so try connecting to another USB port and make sure the connection is successful. • If the drive requires an external power supply, then supply an external power source to the drive.
Removable drive issues	Removable drives can be problematic if the jumper settings on the drive are not configured properly, or the hard drive bay cable is not connected securely to the system board. In some cases, issues can arise due to a power issue. Start by verifying that the jumper settings are set to **Cable Select**. Then check the connections of the hard drive and that the drive is seated properly within the drive bay. Finally, make sure that the drive has power by verifying that the power cable is connected securely to the bay and confirm that the keylock on the drive is in the locked position.
OS not found	An "Operating system not found" or "Missing Operating System" error can be common after an operating system is either reinstalled or has been reconfigured. In this case, the system BIOS does not detect the hard drive or the hard drive may be damaged or has been corrupted. Verify that the system BIOS settings are correct and that the hard disk is recognized within the system, or replace the defective hard drive. This may also be a symptom of a Master Boot Record (MBR) problem. The MBR is specific to each operating system, so you will need to check the manufacturer's documentation and website for possible solutions.
BSOD	*BSOD*, or often referred to as the "Blue Screen of Death," is a system *stop error* that is severe enough to stop all processes and shut the system down without

Hard Drive Symptom	Possible Problems and Solutions
	warning. BSOD errors can be a sign that the hard drive is damaged or is not working properly.

Common Solid State Device Issues

Solid state storage device issues can include:

- Limited and slower erase-write cycles. Flash memory devices do not last as long as traditional hard drives and often performance will suffer because of this. Usually at around 100,000 cycles, the devices will begin to break down.
- Power consumption. Solid State Drive (SSD) devices do not have their own power source and will consume power from the system, so if the main device or system cannot provide the right amount of power, then the SSD will not be accessible.

Common RAID Array Issues

When configuring RAID arrays, you may come across a number of issues that prevent proper functioning of the drives.

RAID Array Symptom	Possible Problems and Solutions
RAID not found	If RAID is not found when the computer boots up, it could be a sign that either RAID is not configured within the system BIOS or that the motherboard does not recognize RAID. You must verify that the motherboard installed in the system does in fact support RAID. You may want to refer to the manufacturer's documentation.
RAID stops working	If RAID stops working suddenly, then that could mean that the settings have changed within the system BIOS. If you have made other configurations or replaced a component in the computer, then those configurations may have conflicted with the RAID settings.
	In the system BIOS, verify that the drive configuration is set to RAID. Also check the motherboard documentation to see if RAID is fully supported by the board installed in the computer.
	If there is a non-system board RAID controller used, then check the BIOS specific to the controller and verify that the settings are properly configured.

SATA Troubleshooting Tips

There are several points to keep in mind when troubleshooting Serial Advanced Technology Attachment (SATA) drive problems.

SATA Issue	Description
Controller card	Not all SATA controller cards are supported on all operating systems. Check the vendor specifications for the operating system or software you are using. *Put in Ide Compatibility Mode*
Controller driver	SATA drives themselves do not require drivers, but the SATA controller does. Ensure that you are using the latest version.

SATA Issue	Description
Drive not detected	If you install a fresh copy of your operating system and the SATA drive is not detected, then restart the setup process and press **F6** when prompted to install the driver.
Drive size limitation	If the SATA controller drivers are not loaded during the operating system installation, then the drive will only report the 137 GB capacity supported natively by the operating system.
Speed limitation	1.5 gigabytes per second (GBps) SATA cards do not always auto negotiate with newer 3.0 GBps drives. Use jumper settings on the drive to limit the transfer rate to 1.5 GBps.

PATA Troubleshooting Tips

There are some important points to keep in mind as you troubleshoot Parallel ATA (PATA) drive problems.

PATA Issue	Description
Configuring single drives	If you have one drive on a channel, depending on the manufacturer, it might need to be configured as single—not master or slave. Alternatively, set it to Cable Select and plug it into the PATA cable connector furthest from the motherboard. Check your manufacturer's documentation for the proper procedures and settings for your drive.
Configuring two drives	With two drives on a channel, set both to Cable Select or configure them both manually, setting one to master and the other to slave. Do not mix these settings by setting one to be Cable Select and the other as either master or slave. Make sure both are not set to master or slave.
Removing a drive	If you remove the second PATA hard disk from a computer with two drives installed, verify that the disk that remains in the computer is set as single. The master/slave setting should be used only when there is more than one hard disk in a system; otherwise, a disk-controller error will occur when you restart the computer.
Moving to another system	If you need to move a PATA drive from one computer to another, you likely will not run into problems. However, especially if there is a great difference in age between the computers, you might run into problems. The BIOS of another computer might not support logical block addressing (LBA) or Large (Extended CHS [ECHS]), or the computer might not be set up for it. In that case, data on the hard drive would be lost if you install it in that system. You can change the mode for a hard drive (from LBA to Large, or vice versa), but this poses a risk of data loss. Typically, you should set the mode only when you first install the disk. If you do need to change it, make sure you have a working backup of all of the data on the disk before doing so.

[Handwritten notes in margin: "Set one to Primary t the other to Secondary", "Change the Jumpers", "Validate the Jumpers"]

SCSI Troubleshooting Tips

Keep some basic points in mind as you troubleshoot Small Computer Systems Interface (SCSI) drive problems.

[Handwritten note: "Every device has a unique Id"]

SCSI Issue	Description
IDs and termination	The vast majority (up to 95 percent) of problems with SCSI disks are due to incorrect ID settings and improper termination. Verify that all SCSI devices have unique SCSI ID numbers and are properly terminated.
Resetting system	When a SCSI system is booted or reset, SCSI controllers generally need to renew all SCSI device connections before activating the devices, causing a delay during POST.
Cables	SCSI cables should be handled carefully to minimize problems. For instance, rolling SCSI cable onto itself can cause crosstalk and impede the signal. Running long lengths of it past power supplies can also cause errors due to signal impedance.
SCSI BIOS	If you intend for a SCSI disc to be bootable after you install it, you must enable the SCSI BIOS by using jumper settings or software configuration.
Connectors	If you are installing an additional SCSI hard drive into a computer where only one connector is available on the SCSI cable and the cable itself is terminated, remove and replace the cable with one that has multiple connectors.

 Access the Checklist tile on your LogicalCHOICE course screen for reference information and job aids on How to Troubleshoot Hard Drives and RAID Arrays

ACTIVITY 14-2
Troubleshooting Hard Drive Problems

Scenario

In this activity, you will troubleshoot a number of different issues relating to hard drives.

---

1. **Problem #1: Grinding Noises**

   A user has reported that there are grinding noises coming from her computer case. Once you take a closer look, you suspect that it is the hard drive. What is the possible cause and solution to this type of issue?

   ○   The hard drive is physically damaged, probably due to a head crash, so the drive must be replaced.

   ○   A virus has attacked the hard drive, so use antivirus software to mitigate the issues.

   ○   Data is corrupt on the drive, and has not been shut down correctly.

2. **Problem #2: A Computer Won't Start** A user has reported that her computer cannot boot and is getting an error message at POST. Diagnose and correct the issue.

   a) Perform a cold boot.
   b) Verify that BIOS lists the correct drive settings.
   c) Listen to the drive or touch the drive to determine if it is spinning during POST.
   d) Using your multimeter, verify that power connection readings are +12 V for Pin 1 and +5 V for Pin 4. Pins 2 and 3 should be grounded.
   e) Verify that the data cable is correctly oriented.
   f) Check the drive settings: PATA should be: Master, slave, or Cable Select, or SCSI should be: Termination and device ID
   g) If nothing else corrects the problem, replace the drive.

3. **Problem #3: A Second Hard Drive is Not Recognized**

   You recently installed a second hard drive into a user's system. He is now reporting that the drive is not showing up or is not recognized. You know that one of the things you forgot to check when you first performed the installation is CMOS settings for the drive. What in particular do you need to check in CMOS for this problem?

4. **Problem #3: A Second Hard Drive is Not Recognized** (Continued)

   Another thing you should check when a second hard drive is not recognized is that the drive was installed correctly. What exactly should you be checking?

5. **Problem #4: The Drive Letter for a Second Hard Drive is Not Accessible**

   A second hard drive was properly installed, but you cannot access it by its drive letter. What should be your next step?

6. Problem #5: Hard Drive Data Access Issues

   A user is encountering the following problem: Her computer boots fine and everything works until the user tries to access data on the second hard drive, the D drive. The message "Can't Access This Drive" is displayed when she tries to access the D drive. The user would also like an explanation about what the error message means. List some of the steps you might take to resolve this problem.

7. Problem #5: Hard Drive Data Access Issues (Continued)

   When a user tries to access the hard drive containing his data, the system locks up and makes a clicking sound. From the command prompt, he can change to drive D, but when he tries to access a file or list the files on the drive, it locks up and begins clicking again. What steps might you take to attempt to resolve this problem? What is the most likely cause of the problem?

8. Problem #5: Hard Drive Data Access Issues (Continued)

   A user reports that some of his folders have begun disappearing and some folder and file names are scrambled with strange characters in their names. What steps might you take to attempt to resolve this problem? What is the most likely cause of the problem?

9. Problem #5: Hard Drive Data Access Issues (Continued)

   A user is questioning the difference between the sizes in GB and bytes. Why is there such a big difference? The disk reports in some places as 9.33 GB and in others as 10,025,000,960 bytes. Why is it not 10 GB?

TOPIC D

Troubleshoot System Components

In the previous topics, you examined troubleshooting for some very important hardware components in the computer system: the display device and the hard drive. Without these components, the user would have no way of seeing what they are working on or saving the work they are doing. Equally essential to the system are the hardware components that are vital to all user interactions. In this topic, you will troubleshoot system hardware components.

It is only a matter of time before a personal computer's internal system hardware components experience problems, and generally these are problems users themselves cannot fix. As an A+ technician, many of the service calls that you respond to will involve troubleshooting system hardware components, and your ability to quickly and effectively diagnose and solve the problems will be essential in maintaining the satisfaction level of the users you support.

This topic covers all or part of the following CompTIA® A+® (2012) certification objectives:

- Exam 220–802: Objective 4.2: Given a scenario, troubleshoot common problems related to motherboards, RAM, CPU, and power with appropriate tools.

Common System Troubleshooting Tools

Troubleshooting system devices can be challenging when the problem is not visually detected or obvious. To help you determine where the problem stems from within a computer, you can use a few different tools each with a unique function that will enable you to fix the defective hardware component:

- A *power supply tester* is a tool that connects to the power supply's 24-pin connector that tests the functionality of the unit. These testers can be used to test various power connectors including Berg, Molex, AT, and ATX. You can also use them to test the power supply under load. Some advanced testers can even test the functionality of other drives such as hard drives, optical drives, and floppy drives.
- A multimeter can be used to verify correct voltage ranges for a system's power supply.
- A loopback plug can be used to test data transmissions between components.
- A *POST card* is a card that can be plugged directly into the motherboard in an available expansion card slot that can read and display any error codes that get generated during the POST process of a computer. This tool can be extremely useful for determining why a computer will not boot up. The specific error codes will differ depending on the BIOS version and the specific manufacturer. You may need to refer to the manufacturer for an updated error code list before you start using the card in the computer.

Common CPU Issues

When troubleshooting central processing units (CPUs), you must be aware of common issues and how to manage them effectively.

Problem	Description
Overheating and failure	Most problems with CPUs can be attributed to overheating or outright failure. The main solution to CPU problems is to replace the CPU. In some cases, you may be able to add additional cooling units to prevent the CPU from overheating and prevent further damage from occurring. Other times, it may be possible to simply pro-actively optimize the existing cooling system, such as by clearing dust from chips, heat sinks, and fans.

Problem	Description
Slot and socket compatibility	Before you replace a processor, you need to make sure you select a processor that matches the type of socket on the system board. Most sockets today use a pin grid array (PGA) that enables the chip to drop in and ensures that Pin 1 on the processor is properly aligned with Pin 1 on the socket. This method prevents you from bending the pins when removing or inserting the processor. The chip fits easily into the socket and does not need to be forced. Once the chip is in place, the retaining clip is secured.
	The land grid array is another type of socket that contains pins that connect to pads located on the bottom of the processor package. When examining CPU issues, confirming the socket type may help you to identify any possible CPU connection issues.
Cooling system issues	Because CPUs are prone to damage from overheating, you should always consider the cooling system components when you are troubleshooting CPU issues. For instance, if a user is experiencing intermittent problems during operation, there could be inadequate airflow within the computer chassis that can be corrected by providing space in front of the vents and fans. Also, dust can often accumulate on the CPU's heatsink, and can reduce the efficiency of the heatsink, possibly causing the CPU to overheat.
	When thermal problems cause a system to shut down or fail to boot, it could be that the overall system cooling is inadequate, a cooling device has failed, or the processor is overclocked, whether intentionally or not.
	• If you suspect the cooling system is a problem, you can add more cooling devices, upgrade to more efficient devices, or clean or replace failed devices.
	• If you suspect the CPU is overclocked, use BIOS or jumper settings to reduce the CPU speed. If you have an advanced system BIOS, then you may be able to see the actual CPU temperature readings.
Excess power consumption	Power consumption is a major factor for manufacturers when designing CPUs. When troubleshooting possible CPU issues, keep in mind that because some CPUs operate at higher clock frequencies, they require more power. If not properly cooled, this can result in the CPU overheating. In this case, you may need to either reduce the clock frequency of the processor using *Power Management*, or install additional cooling devices.

 Access the Checklist tile on your LogicalCHOICE course screen for reference information and job aids on How to Troubleshoot CPU Problems

ACTIVITY 14-3
Troubleshooting CPU Issues

Scenario

You are attempting to resolve problems for a user who has been reporting intermittent but severe system errors, such as frequent unexpected shutdowns. The problems have been getting more frequent, and you have been unable to pinpoint a cause within the system software, power supply, memory, or any adapter cards. You are starting to suspect that there is a bad CPU, and you need to proceed accordingly to get the user back to work with as little downtime and cost as possible.

---

1. A user has reported intermittent but severe system errors, such as frequent unexpected shutdowns. The problems have been getting more frequent, and you have been unable to pinpoint a cause within the system software, power supply, memory, or any adapter cards. You are starting to suspect that there is a bad CPU, and you need to proceed accordingly to get the user back to work with as little downtime and cost as possible.

   What initial steps should you take to identify and resolve a potential CPU problem?

   ☐ Replace the CPU with a known-good processor.

   ☐ Verify that the CPU fan and other cooling systems are installed and functional.

   ☐ Replace the motherboard.

   ☐ If the CPU is overclocked, throttle it down to the manufacturer-rated clock speed.

2. **All other diagnostic and corrective steps have failed. You need to verify that it is the CPU itself that is defective. What should you do?**

   ○ Replace the CPU with a known-good chip.

   ○ Remove all the adapter cards.

   ○ Reinstall the operating system.

   ○ Replace the motherboard.

Common Cooling System Issues

There are a few issues common to computer cooling systems.

Issue	Solution
Dust buildup	Over time, dust will build up on components inside the computer. Dust can act as a thermal insulator once it has gathered on a system's heat sinks and fans. In this case, the dust can act as an insulator and keep heat from escaping from the components, and can inhibit proper airflow within the system. As a result, system components will not perform to capacity and can burn out quicker than expected. Make sure to keep system components clean and free of dust.
Poor airflow	When system components are not properly placed inside the computer's case, the result can be reduced airflow within the system. This can happen when system board components are placed too close together and create too much heat. Another cause for concern is when there is more than one fan used in the cooling system. Both of these examples can create irregular airflow and can

Issue	Solution
	also create small pockets of hot air inside the case. Always check the manufacturer information for your system before adding additional components including core cooling devices such as CPUs and case fans.
Poor heat transfer	Thermal compounds are used to aid in the cooling of computer devices. Thermal compounds are often used in conjunction with a heat sink to maximize the cooling effect. In cases when the thermal compound is not applied properly, heat transfer may not be effective and can result in heat damage to the components instead of the heat being properly dissipated.

Access the Checklist tile on your LogicalCHOICE course screen for reference information and job aids on How to Troubleshoot Cooling System Issues

Common Motherboard Issues

Motherboard problems can be among the most difficult to recognize and diagnose. Typically, the computer will not boot, or the computer will display erratic behavior, or there may be intermittent device failures that cannot be resolved otherwise. If you have eliminated all other hardware components, applications, and the operating system as the source of the problem, then you should check to see if the system board is the cause.

Causes of System Board Problems

Common sources of system-board-related problems include:

- Computer viruses infecting the system, including the BIOS.
- Loose connections between system components and the system board. For example, front panel connectors may not be secure.
- Out-of-date BIOS. Check the BIOS firmware and the advanced BIOS settings for your system board.
- BIOS memory is not holding the BIOS information.
- BIOS time and settings resets automatically. This is caused by either a bad CMOS battery, or a faulty motherboard.
- System attempts to boot to incorrect device. This is typically a sign that the BIOS has been set up improperly.
- The CMOS battery is not functioning to keep the system clock information.
- Excessive heat or electrical damage to the CPU. Use a temperature sensor along with cooling systems to combat overheating, and utilize standard electrostatic discharge (ESD) prevention methods.
- Electrical shorts on the system board due to improperly seated components or power surges. This is the most common cause of system board problems.
- Physical damage to the system board. Physical damage can lead to many issues. If the bus circuits on the board are affected, for example, the result could be slower information transfers by the system bus, and ultimately slower overall system performance.
- Damage to memory and expansion slots when replacing memory and adapter cards.
- Damage to the processor socket when installing a new CPU. This is common when the pins inside the socket get bent or broken when inserting the processor chip in the socket.

System Board Jumper Settings

System board jumper blocks are used to change the system board's function settings. For example, you can use the jumper block to clear CMOS information or to reset the advanced system BIOS configuration settings. This technique can be helpful when the system will not boot up from a recent configuration change or if the CMOS password is lost.

Preventing System Board Problems

When you have to touch the system board, you can prevent damage by handling it with care. When you install components into the system board, be sure not to bend or break any of the pins. This includes the pins on the cards as well as the system board. Also, the system board can crack if you push down too hard on the board itself or the expansion cards. When you secure the system board to the case, be sure not to overtighten the screws as this could also crack or damage the system board. ESD damage from handling or from electrical surges such as lightening strikes can ruin the system board electronics. Be sure to use proper surge protection as well as ESD-prevention techniques to help prevent such problems.

Repair vs. Replace

Today's system boards are highly integrated and generally not repairable. When you examine a system board, you will find that there are very few components on the board that are individually repairable. For example, if a built-in input/output (I/O) port fails, you will have to install an expansion card that provides that port's functionality. If the chipset or another integrated circuit fails, you will have to replace the entire system board. Even if you are highly skilled in the use of a soldering iron, in most cases, when a system board fails, you will replace it. Other than replacing the battery, there is virtually nothing on it you can repair it.

 Access the Checklist tile on your LogicalCHOICE course screen for reference information and job aids on How to Troubleshoot Motherboard Problems

ACTIVITY 14-4
Troubleshooting Motherboards

Scenario

Several trouble tickets related to motherboards have been assigned to you.

1. **Problem #1** When the user turns on the computer, he sees a message stating that the computer's date and time are incorrect. He must reset this information in the computer's BIOS each time he starts the computer.

   What should you do to resolve this issue?

2. **Problem #2** When the user turns on the PC, it does not always come on and sometimes it just shuts itself down abruptly, with no warning. When she turns on the system again, there is no fan noise. Her data is becoming corrupted from the frequent reboots.

   What should you do to resolve this issue?

3. **Problem #3** One of the other hardware technicians has been trying to troubleshoot a power problem. The computer periodically and randomly reboots. The other technician has determined that the user has an ATX motherboard and power supply. You have been assigned to take over this trouble ticket.

   What should you do to resolve this issue?

Common RAM Issues

RAM problems typically show themselves as memory-specific errors, erratic system behavior, or frequent crashes.

Symptom	Possible Causes
Computer crashes, system lockups, and unexpected shutdowns.	• ESD, overheating, or other power-related problems that can affect memory. • Registry writing to bad memory, General Protection Faults (GPFs), and exception errors caused by software and operating system.
Memory errors appear on screen.	• Memory address errors at boot time. • Applications that require large amounts of memory or that do not properly release memory.

Randomly
Blow up
Blue Screen
of death

Symptom	Possible Causes
Blank screen on bootup	• Memory is not correct for the system. For instance, the computer is expecting memory that uses error checking and you installed non-parity memory. • Memory module is not fully inserted into the slot.
Computer does not boot. POST beep codes sound.	• CPU cannot communicate with memory due to the memory being improperly installed or the BIOS not recognizing the memory. Beep codes are specific to the BIOS manufacturer and the ones for memory can be found in the manufacturer's beep codes list. • For additional information on specific beep codes visit **www.computerhope.com/beep.htm**.
Some or all newly installed RAM is not recognized.	• You exceeded the maximum amount of RAM that can be addressed by the system. Even though the slots can accept Dual In-line Memory Modules (DIMMs) containing more memory, the system can only recognize a certain amount of memory on most systems. • The wrong memory type was installed. • The memory was not installed in the proper sequence. • You might need to leave empty slots between multiple modules, or you might need to install modules containing more memory in lower-numbered slots than smaller modules.

 Access the Checklist tile on your LogicalCHOICE course screen for reference information and job aids on How to Troubleshoot RAM Problems

ACTIVITY 14-5
Troubleshooting RAM Issues

Scenario
You have been assigned some trouble tickets that deal with memory issues.

1. **Problem #1** The user is experiencing corrupted data in his database application. The hard drive has been checked and no problems were found with it. The application was reinstalled and the database was re-indexed and all data problems have been corrected. No other users are experiencing this problem when they enter data. He has been successfully entering data until just recently.

    After troubleshooting this trouble ticket, you have discovered symptoms of a memory problem. What factors could cause sudden memory problems in this situation?

    ☐ New virus

    ☐ Power loss

    ☐ New memory not compatible

    ☐ Power surge

2. **Problem #2** Additional memory was installed in a user's system, and now it will not boot.

    What steps would you take to resolve this trouble ticket?

3. **Problem #3** The user is complaining of application crashes. He is fine if he is running only his email and word processing programs. If he also opens his graphics program at the same time, then the applications are crashing.

    Why is the user experiencing the problem only when additional applications are opened?

    ○ There is not enough memory in the system.

    ○ Memory errors are occurring in one of the higher memory modules.

    ○ The memory modules are incompatible with one another.

Common External Power Source Problems

Problems with external power sources can result in data loss, erratic behavior, system crashes, and hardware damage.

Power Problem	Possible Causes
Line noise	
	Line noise occurs when there is a fluctuation in the electrical current. Causes include: • Electromagnetic interference (EMI) • Radio frequency interference (RFI) • Lightning

Power Problem	Possible Causes
	• Defective power supply.
Power sag	A *power sag* is when the power level drops suddenly below expected power levels. Causes include;
	• Many electrical systems starting up at once.
	• Switching loads at the electric company utility.
	• Electric company equipment failure.
	• Inadequate power source.
Power undervoltage or brownout	This symptom can last from several minutes to several days and can be caused by any of the following:
	• Decreased line voltage.
	• Demand exceeds power company supply.
	• Utility company reduced voltage to conserve energy.
	A variation on this is switching transient or instantaneous undervoltage that lasts only a matter of nanoseconds.
Frequency variation	Usually occurs when using a small power generator. As loads increase or decrease, the power frequency varies. Generators are not recommended for supplying direct power to computers and other sensitive equipment. The variance in frequency (square wave instead of sinusoidal wave) and the instability of the voltage will cause severe instability in computers, leading to crashes, data loss, and possible equipment damage. Using a power conditioner or an inverter with a generator will prevent these issues by stabilizing the voltage and frequency.
Overvoltage	*Overvoltage* occurs when power levels exceed acceptable levels.
	• Suddenly reduced loads.
	• Equipment with heavy power consumption is turned off.
	• Power company switches loads between equipment.
	• Lightning strikes.
Power failure	• Lightning strikes.
	• Electrical power lines down.
	• Overload of electrical power needs.

Common Power Supply Problems

Power supply damage from overheating, lightning strikes, or short circuits can produce a number of symptoms.

 Note:
POST error codes from 020 and 029 are related to the power supply.

Symptom	Possible Causes and Solutions
Fan will not work	The fan and openings around the power supply bring in air to cool system components, but they also allow dirt and dust to gather around the power supply. This can cause the fan bearings to wear and the fan to turn more slowly. You can use compressed air to remove this debris from the system. If the fan becomes damaged due to dust, replace the power supply or have qualified personnel replace the fan.

Symptom	Possible Causes and Solutions
No power	If the computer will not boot, then the first thing to check is that the power supply cable is securely connected at the supply and at the power source. Check to make sure there is power coming from the outlet or power strip. If the connection is secure, then you will need to open the computer case and verify that the motherboard status indicator light is on. The status indicator light is shown when the power is sufficiently supplied to the board. If the light is not on, then you should check the physical power connection from the board to the power supply.
Fans spin but no power to other devices	This symptom is a sure sign of a power connection issue. Check all connections from the power supply to the internal components. Verify that the motherboard is properly connected to the power supply. Look for the indicator light on the motherboard to confirm the connection is successful and there is power supplied to the board.
Computer will not start or reboots after startup	• If the computer does not start at all, make sure that there is power to the outlet. You can check by plugging in a lamp or other device that you know works. If that does not turn on, you know that you have a bad outlet and not necessarily a bad power supply. • Check that the connections from the power supply to the system board are secure, especially on ATX systems. Make sure the master switch to the power supply, at the rear of the system, is on before pressing the computer's power button. Also on ATX systems, check the voltage of the power being supplied using a multimeter. • A loose power supply drive connector landing on exposed metal can short-circuit the power supply. The power supply can detect this problem and disable itself. If you fix the short (by putting the power cable onto the drive correctly), the power supply should start working again. Unused drive connectors should be either covered (some technicians bring rubber end caps) or tie-wrapped to a safe location (not too tight to avoid damaging the wire). Also check for loose screws or foreign metallic objects that can cause shorts. • Check power supply output voltages with a digital multimeter to verify that the necessary voltages are being provided to the board. This will not measure voltage under load, but will allow you to determine whether the output is within the correct range. Most motherboards also provide a voltage reading within the BIOS. If the system boots, access this BIOS option to obtain readings as detected by the motherboard.
An odor or burning smell is coming from the power supply.	An odor coming from the power supply can be the first sign that there is something wrong. Start by visually inspecting the system and looking for any damaged parts or cables. To verify the smell is in fact coming from the power supply, you may need to remove some of the system components. This may include hard drives, the CD-ROM drive, or a DVD burner. Reboot the system from an external drive, and check for the smell once again. Once you confirm that the odor is indeed coming from the power supply, contact the manufacturer first. Some newer systems may have a smell initially, but will eventually fade away. However, in other cases, an odor can be a sign that the power supply is failing, the fan is damaged, or there is a problem with the electricity source going to the system.
Smoke coming from computer.	Smoke coming from the computer can be a sign that there is something seriously wrong with the power supply. Typically, the only component

Symptom	Possible Causes and Solutions
	that can generate smoke is a failing power supply. When the wrong power supply is installed in a computer, it can cause issues with not only the supply itself, but it can literally fry the motherboard and connected components. If you see smoke, in most cases you will need to replace the power supply, and possibly the motherboard if there are any other damaged components.
Loud noise is coming from the power supply.	Other components, especially drives, also can sometimes make a lot of noise. Make sure this is not where the noise is coming from.
	A loud whine or squeal from the power supply area is usually from the fan. A damaged fan with worn bearings will cause a grinding whine that worsens with time. Sometimes, when the bearings begin to fail, the fan blade assembly will shift, rubbing against the fan grill or the case, and produce a high-pitched noise. Also possible, after cleaning with compressed air, a wire inside the power supply unit could be shifted by the forced air and end up touching the fan, causing the very loud grinding noise, possibly stopping the fan altogether. With the power supply off, you can attempt to carefully shift the wire away from the fan by using a plastic tool (metal is not recommended so as to avoid damaging any components).
	If the noise is not from the fan, but from another power supply component, replace the power supply or take it out and send it for service.

Power Supply Troubleshooting Considerations

When troubleshooting power supplies, there are a few things you must consider in order to properly identify the issues.

Consideration	Additional Information
Wattages and capacity	You should always verify how much power each system component requires, before installing or replacing a power supply. If you are having issues with a power supply, then verify that the system component usage does not exceed the power supply's capacity. Ideally, you want a power supply that provides more, but not much more, power than the components require. Use proper power calculations to determine the power requirements of the system.
Connector types	Consider the power supply's connection type when replacing the unit. You must verify that the connection type on the system board matches the connection interface on the power supply unit. Also, verify that there are enough of each type of drive connector for the type and number of drives the system will be using.
Output voltage	The output voltage in a power supply is controlled by a feedback circuit inside the unit. Verify that the output voltages are within the range of what is expected.

rail with 5% (handwritten annotation)

 Access the Checklist tile on your LogicalCHOICE course screen for reference information and job aids on How to Troubleshoot Power Supplies

ACTIVITY 14-6
Troubleshooting Power Supplies

Scenario
You have been assigned a number of power problems to solve.

1. **Problem #1** When the user turns on the PC, it does not always come on and sometimes it just shuts itself down abruptly, with no warning. When she turns on the system again, there is no fan noise. She is using a legacy database application and the data is being corrupted during the improper shutdowns.

   What would you do to resolve this problem?

2. **Problem #2** A user is reporting an odor coming out of his computer. You have serviced this machine recently and replaced the computer's power supply unit.

   What would you do to resolve this problem?

3. **Problem #3** One of the other hardware technicians has been trying to troubleshoot a power problem. The system will not come on when the user turns on the power switch. He determined that the user has an ATX motherboard and power supply. You have been assigned to take over this trouble ticket.
   a) Set the multimeter for DC volts over 12 V.
   b) Locate an available internal power supply connector. If none are free, power off the system and unplug it, then remove one from a CD drive, and then power on the system again.
   c) Insert the black probe from the multimeter into one of the two center holes on the internal power supply connector.
   d) Insert the red probe from the multimeter into the hole for the red wire.
   e) Verify that the multimeter reading is +5 V DC.
   f) Move the red probe into the hole for the yellow wire.
   g) Verify that the multimeter reading is +12 V DC.
   h) Check the documentation for the ATX motherboard to see if there is a logic circuit switch that signals power to be turned on or off, that it is properly connected, and how it should be set.
   i) Verify that the motherboard, processor, memory, and video card are all correctly installed and working.

4. **Problem #4** The user turns on the power switch, but the system does not come on. He does not hear the fan, there is no power light on, and he hears no beeps or other sounds coming from the system. His system is plugged into a surge protector.

   What would you do to resolve this problem?

TOPIC E

Troubleshoot Laptops

In the previous topics, you focused on troubleshooting issues that may arise with a typical personal computer environment. While the PC is still often deployed in many organizations, more often than not, users are now working on laptops or other mobile devices. In this topic, you will troubleshoot laptops.

Installing and configuring portable devices is only the first step in your responsibilities as a computer support technician. You will also need to provide the ongoing maintenance for these devices, as well as to diagnose and resolve any problems that might occur with them during use. The information and skills in this topic should prepare you to assist users in proper maintenance of portable systems, as well as to efficiently and correctly resolve problems with these systems.

This topic covers all or part of the following CompTIA® A+® (2012) certification objectives:

- Exam 220–802: Objective 4.8: Given a scenario, troubleshoot and repair common laptop issues while adhering to the appropriate procedures.

Maintenance and Handling Techniques

There are many general maintenance and handling techniques that should be considered when supporting laptops.

Issue	Techniques
Cooling systems	Because laptops do not have the air circulation that desktop PCs do, it is important to keep the device air ducts clean. Dust trapped in cooling passages acts as an insulator and can prevent proper cooling, possibly resulting in overheating. Excessive heat should be avoided in such devices as it can shorten the life of components. In servicing laptops, it is a good practice to regularly blow dust from the cooling passages using compressed air or vacuum it with an electronics vacuum. When using the compressed air to clean the inside of the laptop, you must be extremely cautious of the internal components. It is easy to damage other components inside the laptop while cleaning.
	The bottom surface of the laptop gets quite hot when improperly ventilated. This can easily happen when laptops are put on soft surfaces (i.e., tables with coverings such as table cloths), on people's laps, or in places where there is not enough room between the vents and a wall. Sometimes people will get careless and unwittingly cover the vents with books, mouse pads, etc.
Batteries	Properly caring for the battery in a laptop not only prolongs battery life, but also diminishes health and safety concerns. Using an incorrect battery charging cable or exposing a battery to harsh environmental conditions, such as extreme heat, can result in an explosion. Some simple guidelines for acceptable battery maintenance include: <ul><li>Follow manufacturer instructions on the proper charging and discharging of the battery.</li><li>Use the battery charger provided by the manufacturer or an approved replacement charger.</li><li>Never expose the battery to fire or water.</li><li>Do not drop, throw, or jolt the battery.</li><li>Only use the recommended battery for your device.</li></ul>

Issue	Techniques
	• Make use of power management features included with your device/OS to prolong battery life.
Transportation and handling	Because laptops are carried from place to place, they are exposed to hazardous environments far more frequently than desktop computers. Careless handling can substantially reduce the life expectancy of such devices.
	Whether storing, shipping, or just transporting a laptop, it is important to choose an appropriate enclosure for the device. Such enclosures should protect the device from moisture, heat and cold, and dust and debris. The enclosure should shield the device from objects that could scratch or scrape, and also withstand the impact of a drop.
	When carrying a laptop, be careful not to hold on to it by a corner. This can cause the laptop to bend slightly and short out the system board.

Operating Environment Best Practices

If you can properly control environmental factors, such as temperature, humidity, RFI, and ESD, you can help ensure optimal performance and extend the life of your device.

Environmental Factor	Description
High temperature	Exposure to high temperatures can cause expansion within portable computing devices and compromise circuitry. High temperature can also lead to the failure of cooling systems to maintain adequate operating temperatures, leading to the overheating and failure of internal components such as the processor, video processor, and hard drive.
Rapid change in temperature	Rapid changes in temperature, such as those seen when transporting a device from one climate to another, could result in condensation within the device. Devices should be allowed to come to room temperature before being powered on after a temperature change.
High humidity	Avoid operating in high humidity as condensation within the device may occur and promote corrosion. All manufacturers specify operating humidity levels. It is important to follow manufacturer operating procedures/guidelines at all times. Most systems can operate at high humidity without a problem, as long as there is no condensation (5 to 95 percent relative humidity, non-condensing).
Low humidity	Be extra cautious as ESD is more likely to occur in low-humidity environments ranging anywhere from 10% - 35%.
RFI	Erratic errors may occur with laptops when exposed to *radio-frequency interference (RFI)*. Radio towers, two-way radios, and even cordless telephones and microwaves have been linked to RFI.
	Moving the device further from such sources will help in resolving interference issues. Properly shielded cables for peripherals will also minimize the effects of RFI.

General Laptop Issues

As an A+ certified technician, you will be responsible for interpreting a laptop's symptoms and determining what the specific issues are and how they can be resolved.

Symptom	Description
Display issues	Some common display device issues include: • Cannot display to external monitor, video device, or projector. Often this feature requires the user to toggle between display modes. Check the device documentation for more information on toggle modes for your specific device. • No display. In some cases, the LCD cutoff switch remains stuck down even after the laptop lid is opened. You may need connect the laptop to an external monitor to verify that the graphics card is still working properly. • Backlight/brightness functionality and pixelation have been changed. In some cases, the intensity of the backlight and the amount of pixelation can conserve power if configured correctly. Verify that the backlight and resolution settings are configured to suit the user's needs. Often, the laptop's display is optimized for certain dots per inch (DPI) and resolution settings. Changing these is not always recommended. In some laptops, the backlight/brightness settings are configured automatically, so check to see if you can enable or disable this setting. • Dim display. The screen goes dark and cannot be adjusted or the hues in the display are changing. This can be one of two issues: the screen has gone bad or the LCD inverter is bad. You may need to replace the screen or the inverter. Check the manufacturer's documentation to verify replacement options. • Flickering display. This can be a symptom of a number of different issues. First, verify that your video card drivers are up to date. Next, check the screen refresh rate within the display settings for the laptop. If the flickering continues, then it is most likely a loose wire connection from the motherboard to the display. In this case, the only way to fix the issue is to disassemble the laptop and secure the wires.
Battery issues	There are usually two main issues with laptop batteries. The first being that the battery does not stay charged long enough. Battery life can be maximized using the power management features of your device. Many devices also offer extended life batteries. To extend battery life, disable devices not being used, such as wireless (Wi-Fi, Bluetooth®, and infrared [IR]). If not on a network, you can also disable the network interface card (NIC). These devices have their own power management options that need to be set. The second is that the battery is not charging. This could be because of a bad AC adapter or cable. Nickel cadmium (Ni-Cad) batteries have battery memory, which means that they can lose most of their rechargeability if you repeatedly recharge them without draining the batteries first. The only solution to this problem is to use a conditioning charger, which is designed to first drain the Ni-Cd batteries before recharging them. Battery memory can sometimes affect nickel-metal hydride (NiMH) batteries, too. Try replacing the cable and see if that fixes the issue. If it does not, then you will most likely have to replace the battery. Replacing batteries is not uncommon and will need to be done periodically.
Device gets hot	Because laptops have very little space in between their internal components, you can have problems with laptops overheating, which leads to system lockups and even hardware failures. Strategies you can use to help reduce the heat within laptops include: • Use the power management features even when the laptop is connected to a power outlet, especially if you are using the laptop in a warm room.

Symptom	Description
	• Try to keep the bottom of the laptop ventilated. (For example, do not rest a laptop on a pillow in your lap.) • Be aware of the fan in the laptop. If you hear it running very fast on a regular basis, take steps to minimize heat in the laptop.
Laptop is not working properly when on battery power	This can be an indication that the battery contacts are dirty. You can clean them by using alcohol preps or even just a dry cloth.
No power when connected to AC power	The power cord or AC adapter might have failed, the outlet to which you are attempting to connect the laptop is bad, or the power supply in the laptop has failed. Start by checking the power outlet and plugging in a known good electrical device and verifying whether you can turn it on. If the problem persists, then try using a known good power cord and then an AC adapter to determine if either is the source of the problem. You might also test both AC and DC power by using a multimeter.
Ghost cursor	Laptops commonly have touch pads or pointing sticks. Touch pads can suffer from dirt and hand grease contamination that can make the touch pad behave erratically; make sure to clean with alcohol preps. Pointing stick heads can wear out and become slippery, making them very difficult to use; order replacements from the manufacturer or vendor. In some laptop models, you can actually recalibrate the touch pad to try and fix the issue. A *ghost cursor* is a cursor that jumps around on the screen randomly, or moves too slow, or opens windows and menus on its own. Causes of this problem include a corrupt driver, driver incompatibilities after an upgrade to a newer operating system, and a hardware failure. Steps to take to resolve this problem include reinstalling or upgrading the driver. If this does not resolve the problem, many portable devices allow users to connect an external mouse as a substitute for the touch pad or other integrated pointing devices.

Common Laptop Keypad Issues

Laptop keypads are the source of many user complaints due to their varied key arrangements.

Issue	Description
Nonstandard key placement	Due to size constraints, laptop manufacturers often rearrange function keys to make them all fit.
Function keys	Some keys on a standard desktop keyboard would not fit on a laptop and have instead been added as function keys. Several keys on a laptop keypad are shared. For an explanation of key functions, consult the device manual.
Numeric keypad	Laptop computers do not have the numeric keypad like desktop keyboards. Instead, many manufacturers place numbers on letter keys to be used when **NumLock** is on. **NumLock** indicator lights are displayed on the laptop to indicate that the **NumLock** function has been turned on.
Sticking keys	On occasion, a key will remain in the depressed position due to debris buildup or a malfunction in the mechanism. These issues can often be resolved by removing the key, cleaning it, and replacing the key. Methods for removing keys vary from model to model. Removing a key on a laptop keyboard can be a risky proposition. They are typically not the type of key where the key cap is in a peg, which you find on full-sized keyboards. Laptop

Issue	Description
	keys are usually floating on a dual-hinge mechanism, usually plastic, that will easily break if you attempt to remove it forcefully. Refer to the manufacturer's instructions when attempting to fix a key on the keyboard.
Keyboard too small	The strain of typing on a small or non-ergonomic keyboard may bother some users.

Common Wireless Connectivity Issues

There are several portable device issues that can cause wireless signal reception and connectivity problems.

Issue	Description
Intermittent wireless connectivity	Several factors could play a part in poor or intermittent wireless reception, including low battery, radio interference, and signal barriers such as masonry walls or floors. Anything metal can also block signal, such as large metal file cabinets and metal-clad fire doors, things many people forget to consider when determining the best location of wireless access points in an office. If there is an external antenna, check to be sure the antenna is fully extended, properly connected, and is not damaged. In some cases, if the wireless card is installed independently from the system board, then you can upgrade the wireless card to improve connectivity.
No Bluetooth connectivity	There are a number of issues that can cause Bluetooth connectivity problems: • The drivers might need to be updated. • The devices have not been set to "discoverable" mode. For security purposes, only enable discovery mode on your laptop when want a Bluetooth device to find your laptop; otherwise, keep that setting disabled. • The Bluetooth settings must be configured to allow devices to connect to the laptop. This is also referred to as pairing.
No wireless connectivity	Some portable computing devices allow the user to turn off the wireless receiver switch, which would result in no reception. Or, the user might simply be out of range of the wireless access point. You may also need to enter the appropriate security key for the wireless access point. This issue might also be the result of damage or a failure in the wireless device or the embedded antenna on the wireless network card. Some cards might have a flip-up antenna that might be damaged through improper handling. If the card or antenna is damaged, you would typically replace the wireless card.

Laptop Disassembly Best Practices

When disassembling a laptop, it's important to follow the proper disassembling process to ensure that the laptop can be reassembled correctly:

• Document and label all cable and screw locations as you go.
• Organize the parts as you remove them from the laptop.
• Refer to the manufacturer's documentation to help with locating components.
• Use the appropriate hand tools, such as a small screw driver to remove the screws.

Servicing laptop components can be difficult depending on where the component is located within the case. Many times, the components are not serviceable and replacing the entire laptop is required.

It's also important to check a manufacturer's warranty restrictions before you service a laptop and its components. In some cases, you can actually break the warranty if you crack open the case.

 Access the Checklist tile on your LogicalCHOICE course screen for reference information and job aids on How to Troubleshoot Laptops

ACTIVITY 14–7
Troubleshooting Laptop Issues

Scenario

In this activity, you will troubleshoot common laptop issues and provide a solution to fix the issues.

1. You received a user complaint about a laptop being extremely hot to the touch. What actions should you take in response to this issue?

2. Which components are typically soldered to a laptop motherboard and cannot be replaced without replacing the entire board?

3. What internal components can be independently replaced within a laptop?

TOPIC F

Troubleshoot Printers

In the previous topics, you employed troubleshooting tools and techniques for hardware components within the computer system itself. There are other peripheral devices that users may frequently use with their computer systems, like printers, that will experience problems or malfunctions that require your assistance. In this topic, you will troubleshoot printers.

As a support professional, you are well aware that one of the most unpleasant problems for users is being unable to print. If users need hard copies of documents and the systems do not work, it can be very frustrating. Users will look to you to identify and resolve their problems quickly, so you will need to perform proper maintenance to prevent problems, to recognize common issues, and to correct them efficiently when they occur.

This topic covers all or part of the following CompTIA® A+® (2012) certification objectives:

- Exam 220–802: Objective 4.9: Given a scenario, troubleshoot printers with appropriate tools.

Common Printer Troubleshooting Tools

Printing troubleshooting tools can be used to fix common printing issues and can also help you in diagnosing printer problems.

Tool	Description
Maintenance kit	Printer maintenance kits for laser printers are made up of printer components that get worn out with regular everyday use. Most printers are designed to notify users when they have reached their predetermined page count and maintenance schedule. Usually, the printer will display a message such as "Perform Printer Maintenance." This means that the printer manufacturer recommends installing a printer maintenance kit at this time. Once the kit is installed, you must reset the page count on the printer to keep an accurate schedule for maintenance. Common components included in the kit are: • Transfer rollers and pickup rollers • Corona assembly • Fan assembly • Fuser assembly • Cloths and gloves for handling printer components
Toner vacuum	When you suspect that the printer needs to be cleaned due to toner build up within the printer, then make sure to use a toner vacuum. Toner vacuums are specifically designed to clean up toner within a printer. The vacuum is able to reserve the particles within the tool so that it is not dispersed back into the air. Never use a conventional vacuum to clean up toner because the particles are so small that there is risk of them getting blown back into the air surrounding the printer. This can be harmful to your health.
Compressed air	Compressed air is sometimes used to clean out the dust and debris from inside the printer. Refer to your manufacturer's documentation for any guidelines on using compressed air to clean the printer. Some manufacturers advise against using the air, because it can actually cause moisture build up within the printer.

Tool	Description
Extension magnet	A telescoping wand with a magnet attached to the end is used to pick up screws or other metal pieces that may fall into the printer or scanner. For inkjet printers and dot matrix printers, it can come in handy to retrieve paper clips people have dropped into the paper-feed mechanism. But for laser printers, reaching inside the printer can be hazardous. If you need to reach inside a laser printer, take *extreme* caution as there are fragile components and high-voltage electronics inside laser printers.

Printer Software Tools

In addition to the standard toolkit, there are several specialized resources you can employ when you research and troubleshoot printing problems.

Troubleshooting Resource	Description
Test patterns	Depending upon your printer, you might be able to run test patterns to check the clarity and print quality of your printer. It allows you to determine what settings need to be adjusted or what ink colors need to be refilled. Test patterns are either built in or external to the printer and are used to test for calibration and alignment of the printhead and to check the color/grayscale tone.
Printer spooler	The printer spooler can be a useful tool when determining where a print job is faulting. If the job is getting through the spooler then it may indicate a hardware issue, but if its not, then it could be a issue with the application that the job was sent from or a connection issue.
Power cycling	Power cycling a device refers to turning the device off and letting it rest for 10 to 30 seconds before powering it back up. This can give the printer some time to clear the memory and start up again.
General diagnostic utilities	Many printers come with other self-diagnostic programs that can resolve basic hardware issues. Refer to the printer's manual on the specific steps required to perform the diagnostics.
	Windows and other operating systems often provide help for troubleshooting general problems as well as for problems specific to that system. In particular, Windows 7, Windows® Vista, and Windows XP® all provide troubleshooters that can walk you through the diagnosis and resolution of common printer problems or problems with other devices.
	In Windows 7, common printer problems can be resolved by displaying the pop-up menu from the **Printer** icon and selecting **Troubleshoot.**
	There are other generic utilities you can use, such as capturing a printer with the net use command, or redirecting output to a printer with the prn command.
Device documentation	For device-specific problems, consult the documentation that came with your printer or scanner.
Manufacturers' websites	Most device manufacturers will maintain technical information on their websites that can help with printer troubleshooting and ongoing maintenance. You can also download updated printer or scanner drivers or diagnostic software tools from the manufacturer, or use web-based utilities to help you diagnose the problem.

Troubleshooting Resource	Description
Software vendors' websites	Microsoft and other operating system vendors maintain libraries of technical information on their websites that can help with troubleshooting known problems with specific devices, or general issues related to the printing function in the specific operating system.
Error codes and reports	Review any error messages at the printer and at the computer. This might involve checking computer event logs. Some printers may have an out of memory error displayed when the printer memory is beyond capacity.
Service logs and reports	Check prior service records for the system to try to identify recurring problems. Check for previous user reports of similar issues to see how the issues were resolved.
Troubleshooting principles	As with all troubleshooting, follow a structured process: • Gather information and identify the symptoms. • Review the data and establish a possible cause. • Identify and test a solution.

Common Printer Symptoms

When troubleshooting various printers and print job issues, keep in mind that some of the simplest tasks such as pausing, restarting, or canceling a print job from the queue can easily fix some common printing problems. User education and awareness of these common problems and solutions will enable you to better support users. There are a number of common issues related to all types of printers.

Symptom	Possible Problems and Solutions
Backed up print queue or printer will not print	There are a number of issues that can a print queue to printer transfer problem: • If you suspect that the printer is out of toner, ink, or paper, then add what is necessary. Verify the printer's status and press the **Test** button on the printer. • If you suspect that there is a paper jam, or the printer is displaying an error code indicating a paper jam, then clear the jam. If the paper jams are frequent, then the printer may need to be serviced to clean or replace old or worn components such as rollers. • In Windows, there are a number of settings that will cause issues. The printer may be paused. In this case right-click on the printer and disable the pause printing option. The print spooler service may be stalled, so stop and start the service. Or, the **Use Printer Offline** option has been enabled. • If the printer has been configured to be available on a specified schedule, then you may need to verify and adjust the availability schedule. • An incompatible print driver will prevent sending print jobs to the printer. You may need to delete the driver and reinstall the updated one using the manufacturer's installation instructions, if available.
Printer does not print the way the user expects it to	If the print out is not showing the output you expect, then this could be a page setup, printer property, or settings issue. You should verify that the page setup options and the printer properties are configured correctly. If you have confirmed the settings for the printer and the application you are printing from, then you may need to use a maintenance kit or a driver software update to fix the issues.

Symptom	Possible Problems and Solutions
	If the printout is streaking, this could be a sign that the printhead needs to be cleaned.
Print quality issues	There are a number of different print quality issues that indicate the printer problems:
	• Streaks may indicate that the printer head needs to be cleaned due to clogged head openings.
	• Faded prints can be an indication of a bad toner cartridge. If you are using the re-manufactured cartridges, then you may need to try a new one. If that does not fix the issue, then there may be an issue with the fuser.
	• Vertical lines are a symptom of inkjet printheads being out of alignment. This can also be a sign that the printing ribbon needs to be replaced.
	• Color prints in the wrong color. Use the advanced printer settings to verify that the color settings are correct. You may need to select a different output option, such as the print quality.
Access denied	When users cannot access a network printer, then there is a possibility that there is no connectivity. Either the printer or the user has lost a connection to the network. In this case, you can verify which device needs to be reconnected and make necessary changes. If the connections are functional, then check the printer or print server status and restart, if necessary. Also verify that the IP address assigned to the printer is correct. Finally, you can check the printer's power cycle to make sure it is coming online once it has been powered up.
Garbled characters on paper, or is showing ghosted images	When a printer outputs garbled or ghosted images, there is something wrong with the printer. These symptoms can mean a number of different things:
	• The printer is low on memory. Check to see if you can install additional memory.
	• The resolution needs to be adjusted in the printer settings.
	• The driver is incompatible, so update or replace the driver.
	• The cabling may be damaged or not fully connected so check all cables to make sure they are secure and in tact.
	• In laser printers, this can be a sign that the drum is not being completely erased. You should contact the manufacturer or check the website for additional information and troubleshooting steps.
Print jobs never appear in print queue	General network problems. Check the network status of the client, printer, and print server.
	Insufficient user print permissions. The user probably got an error message. Update the permissions.
	Insufficient space on the drive containing the spool folder. Move the spool folder or add disk space.
Other sporadic print problems	Unfavorable environmental conditions can lead to unexplained problems with printers. Check for and correct these situations, if possible.
	• If the printer is installed in an environment with a large quantity of dust and dirt, such as a factory floor or a pet shop, debris can accumulate in the printer case. Keep the printer clean in an enclosure in these environments if possible, but be mindful of heat accumulation in the enclosure.
	• High humidity can lead to moisture problems; low humidity can lead to static problems. Try to maintain a relative humidity of 50 to 60 percent.
	• Low memory errors can indicate that the print driver memory settings need to be changed. Most print drivers will install a low memory default setting

Symptom	Possible Problems and Solutions
	that can be changed, if needed. You can update the driver setting to match the printer memory capabilities to resolve this issue.

 Note: In Windows 7, you can troubleshoot a printer by right-clicking the printer and choosing **Troubleshoot**. In Windows XP, the **Printing Troubleshooter** in **Help and Support Center** can be useful in stepping through and resolving common printing problems.

Laser Printer Problems

Laser printers contain chemicals, high voltages, and high-temperature areas that can hurt you. Make sure the printer is off and the parts are cool before you attempt to work on the machine. Some of the exposed wires are very thin and can be damaged easily, so treat the printer gently.

Symptom	Possible Problems	Solutions
Smeared output, or output rubs off the paper	Fuser temperature is too low: if the fuser is not hot enough, the toner not fused to the paper ; fuser roller is uneven; problem in paper path; paper not smooth enough.	Follow the manufacturer's instructions to set fuser mode for the paper; adjust the fuser roller; clear the paper path; use good-quality paper.
Low-quality image	Poor-quality paper does not accept charge and transfer toner; transfer corona is dirty or faulty; there's a transfer corona power supply problem; a faulty primary corona or power supply does not charge print drum.	Use good-quality paper; follow the manufacturer's instructions to clean the transfer corona; follow the manufacturer's instructions to troubleshoot other faulty components.
Repeating horizontal lines or white spaces	Dirty fuser roller; warped or worn fuser roller; scratched print drum due to debris between wipe blade and drum.	Clean all fuser rollers; compare the distance between the repetitions of the lines to the circumferences of the rollers, and consult manufacturer's documentation to find which may have the problem. Follow the manufacturer's instructions to adjust or replace rollers and fuser. Follow the manufacturer's instructions to replace the scratched print drum.
Repeating vertical lines or white spaces	Scratched print drum; dirty primary corona or transfer corona produces uneven charge; refilled toner cartridge produced substandard output.	Follow the manufacturer's instructions to replace scratched print drum or clean corona wires; or, replace with a new cartridge.
Pickup and path wheels	The paper slips or begins to pick up 2–3 pages or more at once, and then jams; paper is not feeding; paper is creased.	After a long period of use, these wheels lose their grip. Wheels either need to be cleaned with alcohol or replaced.

Inkjet Printer Problems

Most issues related to inkjet printers can be resolved by cleaning the printer, cleaning the paper feed rollers, replacing the print cartridge, and using good-quality paper. There are, however, occasions when a component will need to be replaced. In this case, it may be more cost effective to just replace the printer instead of trying to repair it. The following are common symptoms and potential solutions you can use when supporting users.

Symptom	Possible Problems	Solutions
Poor print quality	Clogged nozzles, incorrect paper; empty or defective cartridge.	Clean the interior of the printer; perform one or more print cartridge cleaning cycles; switch to a paper specifically designed for inkjet printers. Replace the cartridge. If you are using a refilled cartridge, replace with a new cartridge.
No output; paper passes through printer but is blank	Empty ink cartridges; clogged nozzles; tape sealing ink cartridge; incorrect cartridge or cartridge improperly seated.	Replace empty or incorrect ink cartridges; clean the printer and print cartridge; remove the tape seal from ink cartridge; align the cartridge; check the manufacturer's website for other troubleshooting procedures.
Feathering/ink bleed	Clogged nozzles; low ink in cartridge; faulty printhead; low-quality refilled cartridge.	Perform several cleaning cycles; replace ink cartridge with a new one (not refilled); replace the printhead; switch to a paper specifically designed for inkjet printers.
Pickup and path wheels	The paper slips or begins to pick up 2–3 pages or more at once, and then jams.	After a long period of use, these wheels lose their grip. Wheels either need to be cleaned with alcohol or replaced.

Common Impact Printer Problems

Dot-matrix printers and other impact printers are not as commonly used as the others but they are known to rugged and dependable. Most issues related to these printers are due to printhead problems. The following are common symptoms and potential solutions you can use when troubleshooting.

Symptom	Possible Problems	Solutions
Horizontal lines appear in the print so parts of characters are missing	Printhead is damaged or needs to be cleaned.	Attempts to repair a printhead can damage it beyond hope. You can clean the printhead with a lubricant like WD-40 or alcohol. Remove any visible grime.
Flecks and smudges on the paper	The ribbon is not aligned correctly, not feeding correctly, or is over-inked.	Reposition the ribbon. Replace the ribbon cartridge; cartridges are not economical to repair. Clean and lubricate the gears that advance the printhead.
Poor print quality	The printer adjustment for paper thickness is set to an incorrect value; poor-quality paper; bad ribbon; dirty printhead.	Set the thickness to match the paper you are using. Use good-quality paper. Replace the ribbon. Clean the printhead.

Symptom	Possible Problems	Solutions
Continuous-feed paper jams	Tractor feed problems.	Clean paper from gears. Align tractor feed. Replace worn gears.

 Access the Checklist tile on your LogicalCHOICE course screen for reference information and job aids on How to Troubleshoot Printers

ACTIVITY 14-8
Troubleshooting Common Printer Issues

Scenario

In this activity, you will respond to common printing issues and provide a suggested solution to fix the issues.

1. A user reports that they cannot print from Microsoft® Excel® to a network printer. After determining that other users are printing from that printer with no issues, what steps should you take next to troubleshoot the problem?

2. A user reports that he is attempting to print to his local printer, but none of the print jobs are printing. When you arrive at his desk, you check out the printer hardware and consumables and everything seems to be fine. When you double-click the printer in the Printers folder, you see the job is listed in the queue. What should you try next?

3. Another user says all his printouts look garbled. You check the properties of the print object in the Printers And Faxes window and find that the printer model listed in the Properties dialog box is not the same as the printer model on the printer itself. What should you do?

4. A user reports that inkjet printers in the corporate training area have various problems, including no output, fuzzy output, and generally poor print quality. List some of the steps you should take to resolve these problems.

Summary

In this lesson, you applied troubleshooting techniques to resolve issues related to many different computing hardware components. It is likely that most of your time as an A+ certified technician will be supporting users with hardware issues, so it is important to understand the theory and best practices used by professionals on a daily basis.

In your current job role, have you had to troubleshoot computer hardware problems? If so, what did you do and how did you resolve the issues?

What hardware components do you expect to have to troubleshoot most often at your workplace?

 Note: Check your LogicalCHOICE Course screen for opportunities to interact with your classmates, peers, and the larger LogicalCHOICE online community about the topics covered in this course or other topics you are interested in. From the Course screen you can also access available resources for a more continuous learning experience.

15 | Troubleshooting System–Wide Issues

Lesson Time: 2 hours

Lesson Objectives

In this lesson, you will troubleshoot system-wide issues.

- Troubleshoot operating systems.
- Troubleshoot wired and wireless networks.
- Troubleshoot common security issues.

Lesson Introduction

In the previous lesson, you focused on troubleshooting the hardware components that physically make up the computer system. You are well aware that there are other essential components needed for the entire computer system to work properly; the operating system, the network, and security are all integral parts of the computer environment. In this lesson, you will troubleshoot system-wide issues.

You can have all of the components of a PC properly installed and configured, and still not be able to perform the tasks that you need to perform. Software, network, and security issues can present their own sets of problems for you to troubleshoot and resolve.

This lesson covers all or part of the following CompTIA® A+® (2012) certification objectives:

- Topic A:
  - Exam 220–802: Objective 4.6
- Topic B:
  - Exam 220–802: Objective 4.5
- Topic C:
  - Exam 220–802: Objective 4.7

TOPIC A

Troubleshoot Operating Systems

In this lesson, you will troubleshoot system issues. The operating system is an essential component in the computer environment, managing all the resources that make up the system and providing the interface for users to interact with these resources. If the operating system is not functioning properly, the computer system will not be able to perform as needed. In this topic, you will troubleshoot operating systems.

As a computer support professional, you will be the first line of response to help users when problems arise with their systems. You will need the knowledge to recognize and diagnose problem conditions, and you will need to respond to those problems with the appropriate corrective action. The information, utilities, and skills in this topic should provide you with the diagnostic and troubleshooting toolkit you will need to identify and correct a range of possible system problems.

This topic covers all or part of the following CompTIA® A+® (2012) certification objectives:

* Exam 220–802: Objective 4.6: Given a scenario, troubleshoot operating system problems with appropriate tools.

Operating System Troubleshooting Tools

There are numerous tools and utilities available to help you troubleshoot operating system issues:

Tool	Description
Recovery Console	Use Recovery Console in Windows® XP and 2000 troubleshoot and manage the system. The console can be installed as a boot option or you can launch it from the Windows XP CD-ROM.
	The console allows you to enable and disable services, manage files and disks, and to fix any system boot problems.
WinRE	Use Windows Recovery Environment (WinRE) in Windows Vista® and Windows® 7 to troubleshoot and manage system errors that occur within the operating system.
Bootrec.exe	The *bootrec* tool is available within WinRE for Windows Vista or 7. It can be used to troubleshoot and resolve *master boot record (MBR)* issues, boot sector problems, and Boot Configuration Data (BCD) issues. Two bootrec options commonly used to troubleshoot and fix issues are:
	• The *fixmbr* option is used to fix MBR corruption issues by writing new files to the system partition.
	• The *fixboot* option is used to write a new boot sector to the system. It can be useful when you suspect that the boot sector is damaged or incompatible with the operating system.
	For more information on the bootrec tool capabilities, visit **http://support.microsoft.com/kb/927392**.
Sfc	*System File Checker (sfc)* is a Windows utility that scans systems for file corruptions on startup. The tool is available in Windows XP and Windows Server® 2003. In Windows 7, this tool can be found within the Windows Resource Protection center. There are a number of sfc commands that you can use to manage file corruptions:
	• scannow will scan all protected files

Tool	Description
	• `scanonce` scans all protected files one time
	• `scanboot` scans all protected files every time the system boots up
	• `revert` will revert the scan back to the default.
	• `purgecache` will purge all files in the Windows File Protection cache and scan protected files.
	For more information and full tool parameters, visit **www.microsoft.com/ resources/documentation/windows/xp/all/proddocs/en-us/ system_file_checker.mspx?mfr=true.**
Repair disks	Windows 7 allows for the creation of a system repair disk. This disk can be used to access system recovery options if you do not happen to have a Windows 7 installation disk handy. To use this option, you must create the disk from the Backup and Restore menu, and you will need to set the Basic Input/Output System (BIOS) to boot from a CD/DVD when you insert your repair disk into the drive. The System Repair Disk allows you to access:
	• Startup Repair
	• System Restore
	• System Image Recovery
	• Windows Memory Diagnostic
	• Command prompt
	In Windows XP, you can replace system files with the files on the XP CD used for the Repair Install. Your applications and settings will be left intact, but any Windows updates will need to be reinstalled.
Pre-installation environments	Windows *pre-installation environments (Windows PE or WinPE)* are lighter versions of Windows and Server that can be installed in either 32- or 64-bit versions to replace MSDOS. It is available for Windows XP, Server 2003, Vista, Windows 7, and Server 2008 R2. Windows PE is commonly used by large manufacturing companies to load a pre-installed version of Windows to provide to end users. It can also be used for troubleshooting and file system recovery by allowing administrators to run forensic and disk imaging tools. The pre-installation environments are available for free in the Windows Automated Installation kit (WAIK).
MSCONFIG	The *MSCONFIG* utility is a system configuration tool available in the **Tools** group from the **Help and Support Center**. This tool is frequently used to test various configurations for diagnostic purposes, rather than to permanently make configuration changes. Following diagnostic testing, permanent changes would typically be made with more appropriate tools, such as **Services** to change the startup settings of various system services. When troubleshooting system issues, you can use this tool to:
	• Determine what files are initiated on startup.
	• Manage services that launch on startup.
	• In Windows XP, you can disable any legacy configuration files such as System.ini and Win.ini.
DEFRAG	When systems are running slow and performance is suffering, then you may want to run the DEFRAG utility. This utility is used to reduce fragmentation on the hard disk by reorganizing stored data. This can affect disk performance. The tool can be launched from **Computer Management**.
REGSVR32	The *REGSVR32* utility is used to register Object Linking and Embedding (OLE) controls that are self-registerable. If you are having issues with Windows or Internet Explorer®, then you can launch this tool and unregister

Tool	Description
	these controls, then re-register them. Common controls managed with this tool are Dynamic Link Library (DLL) and ActiveX files.
REGEDIT	Use the REGEDIT utility to make changes to infected or corrupted files within the Registry. Use caution when viewing or modifying these files in the Registry.
Event Viewer	Use the Event Viewer to look at a system's event logs, which may contain specific information about system errors or significant events on the computer. This can be helpful in troubleshooting various system issues.
Safe Mode	*Safe Mode* is a Windows system startup method that loads only a minimal set of drivers and services. If a non-critical driver or service on your system is causing a severe error, you can use Safe Mode to omit all non-critical drivers and services from the boot sequence; start the system; load additional drivers, services, and applications as needed; and correct the problem.
Command prompt	Command prompt can be used when troubleshooting a number of different issues. Windows provides several different command interpreters. The typical command prompt interface is the standard Windows command interpreter, available in Windows XP and Windows 7. To access the command prompt interface, you can either run cmd.exe or select **Command Prompt** from the **Accessories** menu.
Remote Desktop	Remote Desktop can be used to access a user's computer to provide assistance with various types of issues. The problem with Remote Desktop for troubleshooting an end user's computer is that it must be enabled and a user must be granted privileges to log in with network access. If a user does not have a password set up to log in to his or her computer, Remote Desktop will not allow that user name to be used to log in. If no other user name exists, there is no opportunity for Remote Desktop to work.
Emergency repair disk	When you install Windows XP, the system stores information about the configuration of the operating system in a hidden folder called \Windows \Repair. If your installation is damaged, you may be able to repair it by using this information and the Windows Setup program. In Windows XP, you can create a copy of the repair information on a CD called *emergency repair disk (ERD)*. When you create an ERD, the system also updates the contents of the \Repair folder.
Automated System Recovery	*Automated System Recovery (ASR)* is a Windows XP process that uses backup data and the Windows installation source files to rebuild a failed computer system. To perform ASR, you will need: • The Windows XP installation disk. • An *ASR disk*, which provides the information Windows Setup needs to run ASR recovery. • An *ASR backup* set that contains a complete copy of the Windows system files and all configuration information.

Safe Mode Options

There are a few different options to choose from when running Safe Mode:

- Safe Mode: Starts the computer with a minimal set of drivers and services, including the mouse, keyboard, Video Graphics Array (VGA) display, and a hard disk. It is used when the system problem might be with the networking components.

- Safe Mode with Networking: Starts the computer with Safe Mode drivers and services, plus networking drivers and services. It is used when you need to use files on a network location to repair the system.
- Safe Mode with Command Prompt: Starts the computer with Safe Mode drivers and services, but with a command prompt interface. It is used when a system problem prevents the system from creating the Windows graphical user interface (GUI) desktop.

BSOD

Blue screen of death (BSOD) errors, or system stop errors, can be a symptom of file system errors, viruses, hard disk corruption, or controller driver problems. Stop errors are rare in Windows XP and Windows 7, but when they occur, they are normally preceded by a blue error screen containing a summary statement about the error condition and also hexadecimal memory data.

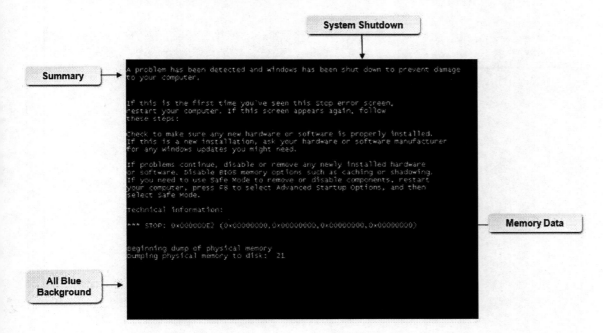

Figure 15-1: A BSOD error.

Responding to Stop Errors

If you experience a BSOD error, you should try to capture as much information as possible from the error summary information at the top of the screen. You can sometimes use this information to diagnose the problem. You can record the error codes and then search for the meaning of the error codes either on the Internet or from Microsoft's website.

You can also configure **Startup and Recovery** settings to perform a *memory dump*, which means that the system writes the contents of memory at the time of the error to a *dump file* on the hard disk for diagnostic purposes. You would need special tools and support from Microsoft technical engineers to interpret a dump file. To configure **Startup and Recovery** settings, go to the **Advanced** page of the **System Properties** dialog box, and under **Startup And Recovery,** select **Settings.**

If you want to prevent the system from restarting automatically after the stop error, reboot and press **F8** during the boot sequence to bring up the **Windows Advanced Options** menu. Select **Disable Automatic Restart On System Failure** and allow the system to restart. Another way of preventing the system from restarting automatically is to change the settings for the computer. To do this:

- In Windows 7, display the pop-up menu for **Computer,** and select **Properties.** Select the **Advanced system settings,** select **Continue** if prompted by the **User Account Control**, select the **Advanced** tab, and in the **Startup and Recovery** area, select **Settings.** Uncheck **Automatically restart** and select **OK.**

- In Windows XP, display the pop-up menu for **My Computer,** and select **Properties.** Select the **Advanced** tab, and in **Startup and Recovery,** select **Settings.** Uncheck **Automatically restart** and select **OK.**

System Lockup Errors

A *lockup error* is an error condition that causes the system or an application to stop responding to user input. The system display "hangs" or "freezes" in a particular state, or sometimes the contents of a window go blank. The system might return to normal after a brief delay for other processes to execute, or it might be necessary to terminate an unresponsive process. Application lockup errors are more common than complete system lockups.

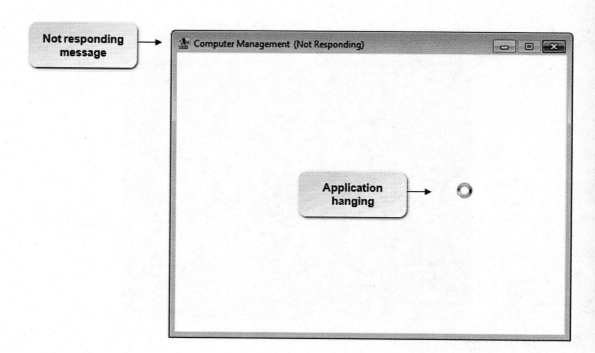

Figure 15–2: A lockup error

Responding to Lockup Errors

If your system or an application locks up, sometimes waiting a few minutes is sufficient for the system to recover resources and begin responding. If not, you can sometimes identify the particular offending process by running the **Task Manager.** On the **Applications** tab, look for applications with a **Not Responding** status. You can then select the **End Task** button to shut them down. On the **Processes** tab, look for processes that are monopolizing the central processing unit (CPU), and use the **End Process** button to shut them down. Sometimes it is necessary to restart the system.

Although applications might occasionally hang without indicating any serious problem, repeated system lockups or stop errors are a sign of trouble, and you should investigate them to see if there is an underlying hardware problem or if they could be caused by malicious software, such as a computer virus. In addition to hardware or malicious software, they could also be caused by unstable/incompatible drivers, applications conflicting with each other, resource allocation issues (multiple video-intensive applications trying to access the same resource), memory limitations (not enough memory or too many applications running at the same time), and so on.

I/O Device Issues

Some of the input/output (I/O) device issues that can affect Windows operation include:

- A missing or loose mouse or keyboard connection.
- Blocked signals for wireless devices.
- A missing or incorrect driver for a specialty input or output device.
- Misconfigured monitor settings resulting in display anomalies.

Display Configuration Issues

You can usually configure some settings for the monitor using controls on the device itself. For example, you can set the contrast and brightness, screen size, and screen rotation. If any of these are set to incorrect or extreme values, the display might not appear as desired.

You can also configure output settings from within Windows. Open the **Display Properties** dialog box from within the **Control Panel**, or by right-clicking the desktop and choosing **Display.** For example, the screen resolution might make items too small for some users to view comfortably. In this case, you can decrease the screen resolution, which will solve the problem, but a better solution is to increase the font dots per inch (DPI) setting. Also, the monitor might not display properly if advanced settings, such as the color quality or screen refresh rate, are set to a value that is not appropriate for the display device. You can reconfigure settings manually or use the Video Display Troubleshooter in the Windows **Help and Support Center** to walk through common problem scenarios.

Application Errors

There are some common error messages that indicate problems with applications.

Symptom	Suspected Problem
Application will not install	You are trying to install an application that needs to overwrite a file that is currently in use on the computer.
Application will not start or load	The application was installed incorrectly, a version conflict between the application and other applications on the computer exists, or your computer is experiencing memory access errors.
Application not found	One or more of the application files has been deleted, moved, or become corrupt.
General Protection Fault (GPF)	An application is accessing Random Access Memory (RAM) that another application is using, or the application is attempting to access a memory address that does not exist.
Illegal operation	An application is attempting to perform an action that Windows does not permit. Windows forces the application to close.
Invalid working directory	The application cannot find the directory for storing its temporary files (typically \Temp). This can happen if you delete the folder that an application needs for storing its temporary files.

Boot Issues

There are several errors that can occur during the boot process or Windows startup.

Issue	Description
POST errors	If there are errors during the Power On Self-Test (POST), the system might display a numeric error message. Typically, you can press **F1** to acknowledge the error and continue booting.
	For other POST errors, a series of audible beeps will tell you if a problem has been detected. The sequence of beeps is a code that indicates the type of problem.
Invalid boot disk	The most common cause of this is a non-bootable disk in a drive. If your system has floppy-disk drives, or bootable CD-ROM or thumb drives, check to see if you need to remove a disk from the drive. However, there could be a hardware problem with the hard disk. Also verify that the complementary metal oxide semiconductor (CMOS) is set to boot from the hard drive. Most BIOSes allow for the configuration of four or more boot devices as first, second, third, etc. If one fails, it will automatically try the next in line. The only way this process will fail is if the boot devices are set to "None" or all the same (which many do not allow). Also, it cannot be assumed that the user will want the CMOS to be set to "boot from the hard drive," since many times there is a need to boot from CD, or even boot through the network.
Failure to boot	There might be a hardware problem with the hard disk or hard disk controller. Check hard drive and hard drive controller connections. You may also have a missing Boot.ini file. In this case, you need to use the Bootcfg.exe to rebuild the file.
Missing operating system	If you receive an error message on boot up that states the operating system is missing, then this could be a sign that the hard disk is damaged. You should try connecting the disk to another machine to see if it boots up; if not, then you will need to replace the hard drive.
Missing NTLDR	In Windows XP, the NT loader (NTLDR) file might be missing or corrupt, in which case you might need to copy it from the Windows CD-ROM. However, the most common problem is that there is a non-bootable disk in the drive.
Missing dll message	On startup, if the device displays a "missing dll" message, then this can indicate an issue with one of the system files. A file may be disabled, damaged, or deleted completely. You should first boot to Safe Mode and run a virus scan on the computer to find any viruses that may have infected the system and remove them. The next step is to determine what files are missing. This can be a tedious task and in most cases a third party dll finder utility can be used. Once you determine the specific files needed, you can download them from the appropriate website or manufacturer and install them on the system.
System files fail to open or are missing	If NTOSKRNL.EXE is missing, you can copy it from the Windows installation CD-ROM. This error can also indicate a problem in the Advanced RISC Computing (ARC) path specifications in the Boot.ini file.
	If Bootsect.dos is missing on a dual-boot system, you will have to restore it from a backup file, as its contents are specific to a particular system.
	System files should not be deleted or become corrupt during normal system operation, so these errors are rare. They might indicate an underlying hardware problem, a disk error, or the presence of a computer virus.

Issue	Description
Device or service fails to start	There might be a problem with a missing or corrupted device driver, or there could be hardware resource conflicts (although this is rare on a Plug and Play [PnP] system).
Boots to safe mode	There may be a drive problem, if the computer continues to only boot into Safe Mode. Use the system BIOS utility to check drives and verify the boot order.
Device or program in Registry not found	A device driver or related file might be missing or damaged. You might need to reinstall the device.

POST Beep Error Codes

POST beep codes vary from one BIOS manufacturer to another. The following table lists some typical POST beep error codes and their meanings.

Beep Error Code	Video Output	Problem	Solution
One short beep	Command prompt	None (normal startup beep)	None.
None	None	Power	Check power cords, wall voltage, PC's power supply.
None	Cursor	Power	Check the PC's power supply; check for sufficient wall voltage.
None	Command prompt	None	May be a defective speaker.
One short, one long beep	None	Display	Check for monitor power; check video cable; check display adapter.
Two short beeps	None or incorrect display (garbage)	Display	Check for monitor power; check video cable; check display adapter.
Two short beeps	None	Memory	Check to see that all RAM chips are seated firmly, swap out RAM chips to determine which is defective, and replace the defective chip.
Repeating short beeps	Probably none	Power	Check the PC's power supply; check for sufficient wall voltage.
Continuous tone	Probably none	Power	Check the PC's power supply; check for sufficient wall voltage.
One long, one short beep	Probably none	System board	Check to see that all adapters, memory, and chips are seated firmly; check for proper power connections to the system board; use diagnostics software or hardware to further troubleshoot the system board.
One long, two short beeps	Probably none	Display	Check for monitor power; check video cable; check display adapter.
One long, three short beeps	Probably none	Display	Check for monitor power; check video cable; check display adapter.

Beep Error Code	Video Output	Problem	Solution
Two short beeps	Numeric error code		Varies depending upon the source of the problem as indicated by the numeric error code.

POST Numeric Error Codes

The following table lists common POST numeric error codes and their meanings.

POST Error Code	Problem
02#	Power
01##	System board
0104	Interrupt controller
0106	System board
0151	Real-time clock or CMOS RAM
0162	CMOS checksum error
0163	Time and date (clock not updating)
164 or 0164	System memory configuration incorrect
199 or 0199	User-indicated device list incorrect
02##	Memory
201 or 0201	Memory error (may give memory address)
0202	Memory address error
03##	Keyboard
0301	Stuck key (scan code of the key may be indicated)
0302	Keyboard locked
06##	Floppy disk driver or controller
0601	Floppy disk adapter failure
0602	Disk failure
17##	Hard disk or adapter
1701	Drive not ready or fails tests
1704	Hard drive controller failure
1707	Track 0 failure
1714	Drive not ready
1730–1732	Drive adapter failure

CMOS Error Codes

In addition to the POST error codes, you might also see a CMOS error code. The following are examples of CMOS error codes that you might see displayed after the POST.

- The error `Display Type Mismatch` is displayed if the video settings do not match the monitor attached to the system.
- The error `Memory Size Mismatch` is displayed if the amount of RAM detected and the amount specified in CMOS do not match. This error is usually self-correcting, although you might need

to reboot to fix it. Other devices such as hard drives can also generate mismatch errors. This generally happens when the physical device is different than what is specified in CMOS.

Common Operating System Symptoms

Operating systems can be difficult to troubleshoot because of their complex nature and file system. It is always helpful to first try to identify the cause of the problem, then categorize it, and finally document and take the appropriate actions.

Category of Problem	Possible Causes and Actions to Take
General issues	<ul><li>For boot process issues, use standard Safe Mode and boot-process troubleshooting techniques.</li><li>Viruses can cause a variety of general system problems. Install or update the user's virus software and perform a complete virus scan to try to identify what is causing issues.</li><li>If you suspect that the issue is stemming from a specific application, then use *Task Manager* to terminate the application and then troubleshoot its installation and configuration.</li><li>Graphical interface fails to load. This can be an indication of a video card problem, or that a virus has infected the operating system files.</li><li>Compatibility errors will display if an application or device software is not fully supported by the operating system.</li></ul>
Memory issues	An application or service might be leaking memory, which means that it is not releasing previously allocated memory back to the system after use.<ul><li>Use **Task Manager** to see which applications are using memory. Have the user reboot and run for a period of time, then check again to confirm.</li><li>Use **System Configuration** to see which applications are using memory. Have the user reboot and run for a period of time, then check again to confirm.</li><li>Use system monitoring techniques to check the overall memory performance.</li></ul>
Low system performance and disk issues	Low disk space can slow system performance. If there is less than 500 MB of free disk space:<ul><li>Delete temporary Internet files in the Internet Explorer cache and other browsers. *Windows/*</li><li>Empty the C:\Temp and C:\Tmp directories.</li><li>Search for and delete .chk files.</li><li>Run the **Disk Defragmenter**, **Disk Cleanup**, and **Check Disk** utilities.</li><li>Reduce the size of the **Recycle Bin**.</li><li>Reduce the amount of space allocated for virtual memory.</li><li>Upgrade the hard disk, if possible.</li></ul>It is actually preferable to keep at least 20 percent of the hard drive available, when possible.
CPU issues	Use **Task Manager** to identify processes that dominate the available CPU usage. Use **Services** to disable any unnecessary processes at startup.
Shutdown issues	Common issues include:

Category of Problem	Possible Causes and Actions to Take
	• Improper shutdown of system, which can lead to system file corruption and possible data loss. • Spontaneous shutdown or restart can indicate a hardware incompatibility issue or an incompatible application. If you receive an error code, then that may help you determine where the issue lies within the system.
RAID not detected	If Redundant Array of Independent Disks (RAID) is not detected during operating system installation, then there could be an issue with an older RAID that may have been used with the system so there are residual firmware files that are blocking the new RAID from being visible to the system. You will need to verify that you have the latest firmware for the RAID being used.

Note: For more troubleshooting and support information for Windows 7 visit **http://support.microsoft.com/ph/14019**

Note: The ultimate solution to some performance problems might be upgrading the system hardware by adding more memory or a larger hard disk. As a support technician, you might or might not be able to request this type of upgrade.

Error and Warning Messages in Event Viewer

Warning and error messages in the system or application event logs do not necessarily indicate a major problem on your system. Many warning and error messages are usually benign and do not indicate a problem. If you review the contents of your own system's logs regularly, you will be familiar with the events logged by normal system operations and be able to distinguish these from true problem conditions that require action.

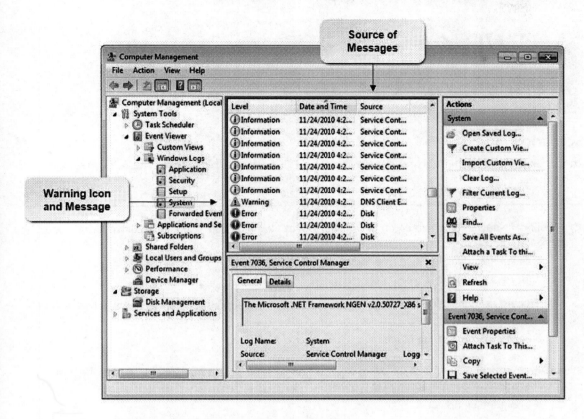

Figure 15-3: Error and warning messages in Event Viewer

The Structure of Event Log Entries

The structure of event log entries differs by operating system, but they generally share some common information, such as the type of log, the time the event occurred, the user name of who was logged on at the time of the event (or who caused the event), keywords, any identification numbers, and what category (or categories) that the event belongs to.

WER

The Windows Error Reporting (WER) node in the software environment category in **System Information** contains data about the faults generated by **Event Viewer.** When there is a severe error, Windows will also display an **Error Reporting** dialog box and generate report data. The **Error Reporting** dialog box gives you the option to send the report data to Microsoft for analysis.

Registry Error Messages

In extremely rare cases, you may receive a stop error or another error message that reports a problem with Registry access, Registry value entries, or the Registry files. For example, a hard disk problem or power failure may have corrupted the Registry hive files. To protect the Registry, always maintain proper system backups. The best solution to a specific Registry problem is to search for the text of the specific error message at **http://support.microsoft.com** and follow the instructions in any resulting Knowledge Base article.

ACTIVITY 15-1
Identifying System Errors

Scenario

In this activity, you will interpret system errors and discuss possible appropriate responses to error conditions.

1. A user calls saying that her screen occasionally goes blue and the system shuts down. What should you advise her to do?
   ○ Call the help desk the next time the shutdown is in progress.
   ○ Reboot manually after the automatic restart.
   ○ Record as much information from the top of the blue screen as she can so that you can research the particular error.
   ○ Run the system in Safe Mode.

2. A user reports that his Microsoft® Word window has gone blank and he cannot type text. What are possible approaches to resolving his problem?
   ☐ Reboot the computer.
   ☐ Run another copy of Microsoft Word.
   ☐ Wait a few minutes to see if the application returns to normal.
   ☐ Use Task Manager to shut down the application if it has a status of "Not Responding."

3. A user reports that her monitor display is "fuzzy" and hard to look at. What is a possible cause of this problem?
   ○ Display settings for the monitor are incorrectly configured.
   ○ The power cord is unplugged.
   ○ The monitor cable is not properly seated.
   ○ The monitor device is disabled in Windows.

4. A user reports that while she is editing a document, she receives an "invalid working directory" message from her application. What is the best diagnostic question to ask in response to this error?
   ○ Did the application work yesterday?
   ○ Is anyone else having this problem?
   ○ Who installed the application?
   ○ Have you deleted any files or folders lately?

Access the Checklist tile on your LogicalCHOICE course screen for reference information and job aids on How to Troubleshoot Microsoft Windows

ACTIVITY 15-2
Troubleshooting a Remote Computer with Remote Desktop

Scenario

You have been assigned to support a user whose office is several floors away from yours. You would like to be able to troubleshoot this computer without having to go to the user's office.

 Note: You are going to work with a partner to complete this activity. You will take turns playing the role of the helper and the user needing assistance. First, the user needing assistance will enable Remote Desktop. Then, the helper will connect to that computer using Remote Desktop Connection and the administrator user account.

1. Configure the first computer to support Remote Desktop connections.
    a) Open the **Control Panel** and select **System and Security.**
    b) Select the **System** link
    c) In the left pane, select **Remote settings.**
    d) In the **Remote Desktop** section, select **Allow connections from computers running any version of Remote Desktop (less secure).**
    e) Select **OK** twice and close the **System** window.

2. At the second computer, connect to the other computer using Remote Desktop Connection.
    a) On the second computer, select **Start→All Programs→Accessories→Remote Desktop Connection.**
    b) In the **Computer** text box, type the name of your partner's computer.
    c) Select **Connect.**
    d) Log on as *Admin##* (where the ## is your partner's number) with a password of *!Pass1234* and select **Enter.**
    e) If necessary, select **Yes** at the security prompt.
    f) If necessary, press the arrow button.

3. From the second computer, change the desktop theme of your partner's computer, and then log off of the remote session.
    a) Display the pop-up menu for the **Desktop** and select **Personalize.**
    b) Select a theme from the available options.
    c) In the **Client##** bar at the top of the screen, select the **Close** button, and select **OK** to exit the Remote Desktop session.

4. Log back in to the first computer and verify the changes.
    a) At the first computer, log back in as *Admin##*
    b) Examine the desktop, and confirm that the theme has changed.

TOPIC B

Troubleshoot Wired and Wireless Networks

In the previous topic, you examined troubleshooting for operating systems. In most organizations, that operating system will be running on a machine that is also running on a network to access the Internet and other important databases or servers. Just as the operating system is essential for the system to function, the network is essential for most organizations to function on a daily basis. In this topic, you will troubleshoot networks.

Every network will run into problems at some point. However, there is a lot you can do to minimize the problems you encounter. Regular, preventative maintenance will not only keep your network working at its peak, it will also reduce the risk of network corruption. Difficulties will arise, though, and good troubleshooting skills will enable you to identify, assess, and repair any network issues quickly and efficiently.

This topic covers all or part of the following CompTIA® A+® (2012) certification objectives:

- Exam 220–802: Objective 4.5: Given a scenario, troubleshoot wired and wireless networks with appropriate tools.

Common Network Issues

There are several common network issues you might be called upon to diagnose and resolve.

Network Issue	Possible Problems and Solutions
No connectivity or connection lost	No connectivity or a connection loss can be an indication that there is a physical problem with a loose cable or a defective network adapter. Check cables and connections and check for link or light emitting diode (LED) lights on the network adapter. Reseat connections, replace cables, or reinstall/replace the adapter, as necessary. On IP networks, check for a missing or incorrect IP address. If the address is manually configured, this could be a data entry error; reconfigure the connection. If automatically configured, the Dynamic Host Configuration Protocol (DHCP) server might be unavailable or unreachable. Make sure the DHCP server is up and that the client is physically connected to the network.
Slow transfer speeds	The network might be experiencing high traffic and many collisions. Check the activity status indicator light for the collision frequency. This should be a temporary condition that will pass; if not, network engineers might need to upgrade the network bandwidth or data rate to increase throughput.
Local connectivity but no Internet connection	The default gateway address might be configured incorrectly, the gateway might be down, or there might be a problem with the Internet Service Provider (ISP). Check the default gateway address, verify that the default gateway is functioning, and contact the ISP to find out if there are any problem conditions. The proxy settings may also be incorrect. Check the proxy configuration of your network connection.
Limited connectivity	Limited connections to a resource or network location can be due to insufficient permissions or an unavailable target network resource. Check to make sure the printer or server is running and connected to the network, and check to make sure the user has appropriate permissions.

Network Issue	Possible Problems and Solutions
IP conflict	Connections by IP address but not by name can be an indication that the Domain Name System (DNS) configuration is incorrect or the DNS server is down. Or, the hosts file might be configured incorrectly. Check the IP configuration settings and verify that the DNS server is running. Check the hosts file to make sure it does not contain incorrect entries.
Intermittent connectivity	Electrical noise, or *electrical interference*, is a general term for unwanted signals on the network media that can interfere with network transmissions. Interference or noise can come from natural sources, such as solar radiation or electrical storms, or from man-made sources, such as electronic interference from nearby motors or transformers. Electrical noise can also cause transient power problems. Some of the common sources of noise include: • Ambient noise can come from many sources, including solar disturbances that affect the earth's magnetosphere, or nearby radio broadcasting towers. • Nearby high-tension power lines or a building's own electrical wiring can create electrical noise. • Electric motors, such as those used in elevators, refrigerators, water fountains, and heating, ventilating, and air conditioning (HVAC) equipment, create noise while running, but it is worse when they start up. Motors require a huge amount of electricity to start up, causing a burst of noise. These bursts can create short temporary outages that resolve themselves when the motor reaches full speed or stops. • Like electric motors, electric heating elements use a lot of electricity and cause a significant amount of noise while running. • Fluorescent, neon, and high-intensity discharge (HID) lights produce a large amount of electrical noise, generally due to the transformers and ballasts required to make these lights work.
Low RF signals	If radio frequency (RF) signals are low, then it could mean that there is an issue with the access point. The access point may have failed, lost power, or been misconfigured. For example, if Media Access Control (MAC) filtering is enabled at the access point, then the PC may not be able to connect. If the issue is isolated to one PC, there it could be a configuration issue at the access point or the PC, so you will need to verify the configuration settings on both devices.
APIPA address issues	Automatic Private IP Addressing (APIPA) is automatically enabled on Windows computers unless it has been disabled in the Registry. It is commonly used as a backup IP addressing service to DHCP, so when DHCP is unavailable, local computers can still get an IP address. The issue with this configuration is that APIPA can only connect to local computers that also have APIPA addresses assigned, so connecting to the Internet is not allowed.

Network Troubleshooting Utilities

Microsoft includes a variety of tools in its Windows operating systems that you can use to troubleshoot networks.

Command line utilities include:

- IPCONFIG view
- PING See If server is Alive

- NSLOOKUP
- TRACERT —TRACE
- NETSTAT—
- NBSTAT - Names Cached in Bios
- NET

Software-based utilities include:

- Network troubleshooters can be used to walk you through the resolutions to various common network problems. There are several network-related troubleshooters in the **Help and Support Center** that can help.
- *Wi-Fi locators* are utilities that can be installed on computing devices to locate wireless networks within range of the device. Most locating utilities will not only locate networks, but will monitor them for anomalies. They will usually display the Service Set Identifier (SSID), signal quality, MAC address, and other network identifiers.

Network Troubleshooting Tools

Network tools can be used when troubleshooting or managing network connections. Useful tools include:

- Cable tester
- Loopback plug
- Punch down tools
- Toner probe
- Crimper
- Wire stripper

 Access the Checklist tile on your LogicalCHOICE course screen for reference information and job aids on How to Troubleshoot Wired and Wireless Networks

ACTIVITY 15–3
Troubleshooting Network Issues

Scenario

You have been assigned to assist users who are having network connectivity issues.

1. You receive a call from a client who reports that she is unable to access any websites in Internet Explorer. While talking with this user, you verify that she can ping the server's IP address on her network segment, the IP address of the default gateway, and the IP address of a computer on another network segment. You also determine that none of the other users on her network can connect to websites in Internet Explorer. What might be the problem?

2. One of your clients reports that he is unable to see computers when he opens the Network window. Which step should you take first?

   ○ Determine if any of the other users on the network are experiencing problems.

   ○ Ask the client to ping another computer on his network.

   ○ Ask the client to verify that the DHCP server is running.

   ○ Ask the client to run ipconfig /release and ipconfig /renew.

3. A user is trying to reach a website and is experiencing problems. How can you examine the path of the transmissions?

4. A client reports that he is unable to connect to any computers on the network or the Internet. You have him run the ipconfig command, and all his TCP/IP addressing parameters are correct. When you have him ping other computers on the network, his computer is unable to reach them. This computer is the only one that is experiencing a problem. What should you check next?

   ○ That the DHCP server is on and functioning properly

   ○ That the default gateway is on and functioning properly

   ○ That the DNS server is on and functioning properly

   ○ That his computer's network cable is plugged into both the network card and the wall jack

TOPIC C

Troubleshoot Common Security Issues

In the previous topics, you have examined troubleshooting for the hardware, software, and network components of a computer system. As important as it is to maintain these more concrete components of a system, it is equally important to make sure that the computer system is secure and that all security measures are functioning properly; if problems arise with security, you must be ready to address them. In this topic, you will troubleshoot common security issues.

As with many areas of computer support, your responsibility for computer security does not end as soon as the security measures are implemented. As with printing, networking, hardware, and software, it is your responsibility to your users and clients to ensure proper security functions on an ongoing basis as well as to correct security problems that might compromise your systems or prevent users from accessing the resources that they need. The information and skills in this topic should help you troubleshoot any security issues that arise and restore your organization's security functions.

This topic covers all or part of the following CompTIA® A+® (2012) certification objectives:

- Exam 220–802: Objective 4.7: Given a scenario, troubleshoot common security issues with appropriate tools and best practices.

Common Security Issues

Most common computer security problems stem from security that is too strict or too lenient, but there are some specific issues you should be aware of as well.

Symptom	Description
Pop-ups	*Pop-ups* are windows or frames that load and appear automatically when a user connects to a particular web page. They can sometimes contain buttons or links that include infected files.
Browser redirection	If users are complaining that browser links are taking them to an unwanted web page, then it probably means that the computer has been infected by a browser redirect virus. To remediate the issue, you need to remove the virus and verify that the browser functions properly.
Security alerts	In some cases, security alerts can be a sign that the computer has been infected with malware. Malware created today is complex and can be designed to look just like an actual security warning generated by the operating system so that you click on the rogue link and install the needed update that actually contains malware.
Internet connectivity issues	Internet connectivity issues can be sign that a computer has been infected by malware. If a security breach has occurred, then an attacker gained access and changed IP configurations and reconfigured network interface cards (NICs) or DNS redirectors. Check any other network-connected devices for similar issues, and if none are found, then the issues are due to an infected device.
PC locks up	Slow performance can lead to a PC locking up. This can be an indication that there is a problem with the system files, malware services were installed, or too many programs have been loaded into memory. This can also be a symptom of a virus. Make sure to run antivirus software to identify and remove any infections.

Symptom	Description
Windows update failures	If Windows updates fail, it could be a sign that the state of the machine has changed. This can be due to a virus. Scan the computer for infections and remove them.
Rogue antivirus	Rogue antivirus is a very sneaky attack that can cause major damage to a system if the user carries out the actions expected by the attacker. The method involves designing a rogue antivirus application window that looks like a legitimate antivirus solution. If users follow the instructions, then they are at risk for downloading a slew of malware.
Email issues	If there are noticeable changes to an email account, such as an excess amount of spam or you find that there have been emails sent from the account that the email account owner was unaware of, then the computer's security has been jeopardized. Email-specific issues to be aware of include: • *Spam* is an email-based threat where the user's inbox is flooded with emails which act as vehicles that carry advertising material for products or promotions for get-rich-quick schemes and can sometimes deliver viruses or malware. Spam can harbor malicious code in addition to filling up your inbox. Spam can also be utilized within social networking sites such as Facebook and Twitter. • Hijacked email is an account that has been accessed by an attacker and is being used by the attacker to send and receive emails. This means that an attacker can read, edit, an send emails from an account. In a corporate environment, a hijacked email account can result in unauthorized data access.
Access denied	Access may be denied if systems are unavailable or corrupted. The most common cause is when a user forgets a password or credentials. Have systems in place to reset passwords for users, when appropriate. Repeated patterns of access denial can be a sign of attempted security breaches.
Malicious software	Once malicious software has penetrated your system, numerous security issues can arise. The best solution to these problems is to prevent infections in the first place, but if your systems are infected, they must be isolated from the network and cleaned using various antivirus and security scanning tools. If your antivirus, anti-spyware, and pop-up blocker's protections are configured to be too restrictive, it is possible that users might not be able to load and run legitimate software. However, it is best to keep security tight in this area and deal with exceptions on a case-by-case basis.
File system issues	Changes in system files can indicate that there has been breach in security. Common file system security symptoms include: • Renamed system files • Files disappearing • File permission changes If permissions are set too tightly, users will not be able to access data. If they are too loose, there will be inappropriate access. Also, because permissions are cumulative, users may obtain permissions from a number of different groups of which they are members. If a user cannot access a resource, you might need to check the permissions assigned to all the relevant groups.

Symptom	Description
Data access issues	Data access across the network depends upon share permissions which, like file system permissions, might be set too high or too low. Also, like file system permissions, the user's effective permissions might be derived from several group memberships that you might need to examine.
	A special issue for Windows is the interaction of share and file system permissions—since both sets are evaluated for network file access, the user will have only the most restrictive of the two permission sets.
	If you have used policies to restrict accounts from accessing systems locally or across the network, make sure the policies are not so strict that legitimate users cannot gain access.
Backup security	Set system policies so that only legitimate users can restore data. However, if policies are too restrictive, you might not have enough users available to do backup restorations in an emergency. Verify that all legitimate backup administrators have the necessary rights. Do not forget to verify that the appropriate users have physical access to the backup storage location, especially if the backup tapes are maintained by a third party who has responsibility for controlling access.

Malware Removal Process

To properly remove malware from an infected computer, follow the process steps to ensure that the computer is "clean."

Process Step	Description
Identify malware symptoms	Use adware and spyware detectors. If your antivirus software does not guard against adware and spyware, you can install separate tools to specifically protect against these types of threats.
Disable system restore	When malware is detected, it is wise to disable system restore to prevent infected restore points in the system.
Schedule scans and updates	Schedule scans and antivirus update schedules. By scheduling regular system scans and updating your antivirus software, you are taking a more proactive approach to vulnerability detection before a full system infection occurs. Scanning systems regularly allows you to discover potential malware threats and to develop useful removal techniques accordingly.
Remediate infected systems *Re image*	In some cases, you may need to employ additional scanning and removal techniques to ensure that systems are clear of infections. When viruses infect critical operating system files that are "in use" when the operating system is running, you may need to perform an alternate startup process in order to prevent the files from being locked against a clean and repair cycle. You may also need to boot into Safe Mode to clean the infected files, or it may be necessary to boot into a completely different pre-installation environment in order to clean viruses that are deep-rooted into the core operating system files. If you suspect that the boot blocks have been affected by a virus, you may need to repair infected boot blocks using the Windows Recovery Console in Windows XP, or System Recovery in Windows 7
Quarantine infected systems	Once an infected system is discovered, you can then quarantine it and fix it to prevent the further spread of the virus to other systems.

Process Step	Description
Enable system restore and create restore point	Once the system is clean of all malware infections, then you should enable system restore and make sure to create a fresh restore point of the clean system.
Educate end users	Provide user awareness and education, which is the best protection against malicious software or any security threat. Providing end user education will enable users to recognize and delete hoax email messages, avoid unauthorized software, and keep antivirus definitions updated.
	Many types of malicious software are introduced through email attachments. Users should not save or open attachments they do not recognize, are not expecting, or are from senders they do not recognize.

Malware Removal Best Practices

When identifying and removing malware, there are several techniques you can employ to fully protect systems attacks.

Best Practice	Description
Trusted installation sources	Always use trusted installation sources and websites. This may include various "mirror" websites that offer authorized software downloads. Even software you install deliberately can be infected with viruses. Do not install software just because a particular website or Internet page prompts you to do so.
Email protection	Always use email attachment protection.
Research	Research malware types. In order to protect systems from infections, you must research all the possible malware types and symptoms. For example, using various virus encyclopedias, you can recognize possible malware types and develop solutions to fix them.

Security Troubleshooting Tools

Security measures are usually implemented to conform with the security requirements in an organization's security policy. There are a number of different tools used depending on the systems and the desired level of security. In many corporate environments, you will be working closely with the security administrator to install and manage security tools and controls based on the organization's security policies.

Tool	Description
Anti-malware software	Some anti-malware programs will scan for unknown, harmful software already installed on the computer and attempt to remove them. In most corporate environments, you will work closely with the security administrator to make sure all computers are configured to meet the guidelines set forth in the security policy. It is strongly recommended to install anti-malware software on all computers, and keep it updated according to your organization's patch management policies.
Antivirus software	Antivirus updates must be managed as they are made available. Antivirus engine updates can include enhancements, bug-fixes, or new features being added to the software engine, improving the manner in which it operates. Updates can be implemented automatically or

Tool	Description
	manually, depending on the software. Automatic updating refers to software that periodically downloads and applies updates without any user intervention, whereas manual updating means that a user must be involved to either initiate the update, download the update, or at least approve installation of the update.
Anti-spyware software	Some antivirus software packages include protection against adware and spyware, but, in some cases, you may need to also include anti-spyware protection in addition to antivirus protection.
Pop-up blockers	*Pop-up blockers* are included in most Internet browsers and will prevent pop-ups from launching when a website is visited.
Spam blockers	*Spam blockers* will detect specific words that are known to be included in a spam message. The message may be rejected once the words are found. This can cause issues if the detection system rejects legitimate messages that may contain one of the keywords. Other spam detection methods are used to block IP addresses of known spammers or to pose an email address that is not in use or is too old to collect spam. You can use any of these techniques to reduce the number of spam messages in your inbox.
Recovery Console	Recovery Console can be used to help identify when a security incident has occurred.
System Restore	You can use a restore point to help identify when a security breach occurred and to recover the system to an earlier state before the incident affected the system files and data.
Event Viewer	You can use Event Viewer to review the stored event logs for unusual activity or any logged errors.
Pre-installation environments	If a system has been infected and cannot be fixed using other methods, then a pre-installation environment can be used to rebuild the system.

 Access the Checklist tile on your LogicalCHOICE course screen for reference information and job aids on How to Troubleshoot Common Security Issues

ACTIVITY 15-4
Troubleshooting Common Security Issues

Scenario
You have been assigned to resolve several security issues raised by users.

1. John has reported that a pop-up security alert keeps coming up when he switches application windows on his laptop. What do you suspect is going on with his computer?

2. You have been asked to provide a list of common malware symptoms for users to be aware of in order to prevent security breaches within your organization. What common symptoms would you provide?

3. True or False? The safest way to deal with unsolicited email is to delete it without opening it.
   ☐ True
   ☐ False

4. Alex reports that in the midst of composing an email at work, an unfamiliar pop-up appeared on his screen, indicating that his email connection has been dropped and that he should log on again by using the pop-up screen. What do you suggest he do in this situation?

Summary

In this lesson, you used many different troubleshooting methods to resolve common issues related to operating systems, network connectivity, and security. In your role as an A+ technician, you will be advising and supporting users in a number of areas surrounding computing devices, so using the guidelines and procedures provided in this lesson will enable you to provide the required level of support to users.

What system wide area do you think you will provide the most support to users?

Have you ever had to recover a severely compromised computer system? If so, then describe your experience.

Note: Check your LogicalCHOICE Course screen for opportunities to interact with your classmates, peers, and the larger LogicalCHOICE online community about the topics covered in this course or other topics you are interested in. From the Course screen you can also access available resources for a more continuous learning experience.

Course Follow-Up

Congratulations! You have completed the *CompTIA® A+® Certification: A Comprehensive Approach (Exams 220-801 and 220-802)* course. You have acquired the essential skills and information you will need to install, upgrade, repair, configure, troubleshoot, optimize, and perform preventative maintenance of basic PC hardware and operating systems. If you are getting ready for a career as an entry-level IT professional or PC service technician, and if your job duties will include any type of PC service tasks or technical support for computer users, this course has provided you with the background knowledge and skills you will require to be successful. Completing this course is also an important part of your preparation for the CompTIA A+ certification examinations (220-801 and 220-802) that you must pass in order to become a CompTIA A+ Certified Professional.

What's Next?

If you want to learn more about networking technologies and supporting network users, you might want to attend the Logical Operations *CompTIA® Network+® (Exam N10-005)* course. If you want to learn more about security and helping users use safe computing practices, you might want to attend the Logical Operations *CompTIA® Security+® (Exam SY0-301)* course.

You are encouraged to explore PC and network support further by actively participating in any of the social media forums set up by your instructor or training administrator through the **Social Media** tile on the LogicalCHOICE Course screen.

A | Mapping Course Content to CompTIA® A+® Exam 220-801

Obtaining CompTIA A+ certification requires candidates to pass two examinations. This table describes where the objectives for CompTIA exam 220-801 are covered in this course.

Domain and Objective	Covered In
1.0 PC Hardware	
1.1 Configure and apply BIOS settings.	
• Install firmware upgrades – flash BIOS	Lesson 1, Topic A

• BIOS component information
  • RAM
  • Hard drive
  • Optical drive
  • CPU
	Lesson 5, Topic F

• BIOS configurations
  • Boot sequence
  • Enabling and disabling devices
  • Date/time
  • Clock speeds
  • Virtualization support
	Lesson 5, Topic F

• BIOS security (passwords, drive encryption: TPM, lo-jack)	Lesson 5, Topic F
• Use built-in diagnostics	Lesson 5, Topic F

• Monitoring
  • Temperature monitoring
  • Fan speeds
  • Intrusion detection/notification
  • Voltage
  • Clock
  • Bus speed
	Lesson 5, Topic F

Domain and Objective	Covered In
1.2 Differentiate between motherboard components, their purposes, and properties.	

• Sizes
  • ATX
  • Micro-ATX
  • ITX
	Lesson 5, Topic A

• Expansion slots
  • PCI
  • PCI-X
  • PCIe
  • miniPCI
  • CNR
  • AGP2x, 4x, 8x
	Lesson 5, Topic A

• RAM slots	Lesson 5, Topic A
• CPU sockets	Lesson 5, Topic B

• Chipsets
  • North Bridge
  • South Bridge
  • CMOS battery
	Lesson 5, Topic A

• Jumpers	Lesson 5, Topic A
• Power connections and types	Lesson 5, Topic A
• Fan connectors	Lesson 5, Topic A

• Front panel connectors
  • USB
  • Audio
  • Power button
  • Power light
  • Drive activity lights
  • Reset button
	Lesson 5, Topic A

• Bus speeds	Lesson 5, Topic A
1.3 Compare and contrast RAM types and features.	

• Types
  • DDR
  • DDR2
  • DDR3
  • SDRAM
  • SODIMM
  • RAMBUS
  • DIMM
	Lesson 5, Topics A and D;
	Lesson 10, Topic A

Domain and Objective	Covered In
• Parity vs. non-parity • ECC vs. non-ECC • RAM configurations	
• Single channel vs. dual channel vs. triple channel • Single sided vs. double sided	Lesson 5, Topic D
• RAM compatibility and speed	Lesson 5, Topic D
1.4 Install and configure expansion cards.	
• Sound cards	Lesson 4, Topic C
• Video cards	Lesson 4, Topic C
• Network cards	Lesson 4, Topic C
• Serial and parallel cards	Lesson 4, Topic C
• USB cards	Lesson 4, Topic C
• Firewire cards	Lesson 4, Topic C
• Storage cards	Lesson 4, Topic C
• Modem cards	Lesson 4, Topic C
• Wireless/cellular cards	Lesson 4, Topic C
• TV tuner cards	Lesson 4, Topic C
• Video capture cards	Lesson 4, Topic C
• Riser cards	Lesson 4, Topic C
1.5 Install and configure storage devices and use appropriate media.	

• Optical drives
  • CD-ROM
  • DVD-ROM
  • Blu-Ray
	Lesson 1, Topic B; Lesson 5, Topic E

• Combo drives and burners
  • CD-RW
  • DVD-RW
  • Dual Layer DVD-RW
  • BD-R
  • BD-RE
	Lesson 1, Topic B

• Connection types • External (USB, FireWire, eSATA, Ethernet)	Lesson 1, Topic B; Lesson 5, Topic E

Domain and Objective	Covered In
• Internal SATA, IDE and SCSI [IDE configuration and setup (Master, Slave, Cable Select), SCSI IDs (0 – 15)] • Hot swappable drives	

• Hard drives
   • Magnetic
   • 5400 rpm
   • 7200 rpm
   • 10,000 rpm
   • 15,000 rpm
	Lesson 1, Topic B

• Solid state/flash drives
   • Compact flash
   • SD
   • Micro-SD
   • Mini-SD
   • xD
   • SSD
	Lesson 1, Topic B; Lesson 5, Topic E

• RAID types
   • 0
   • 1
   • 5
   • 10
	Lesson 5, Topic E

• Floppy drive	Lesson 1, Topic B; Lesson 5, Topic E
• Tape drive	Lesson 1, Topic B; Lesson 5, Topic E

• Media capacity
   • CD
   • CD-RW
   • DVD-RW
   • DVD
   • Blu-Ray
   • Tape
   • Floppy
   • DL DVD
	Lesson 5, Topic E

1.6 Differentiate among various CPU types and features and select the appropriate cooling method.	

• Socket types
   • Intel: LGA, 775, 1155, 1156, 1366
   • AMD: 940, AM2, AM2+, AM3, AM3+, FM1, F
	Lesson 5, Topic B

• Characteristics	Lesson 5, Topic B

Domain and Objective	Covered In
<ul><li>Speeds</li><li>Cores</li><li>Cache size/type</li><li>Hyperthreading</li><li>Virtualization support</li><li>Architecture (32-bit vs. 64-bit)</li><li>Integrated GPU</li></ul>	
<ul><li>Cooling<ul><li>Heat sink</li><li>Fans</li><li>Thermal paste</li><li>Liquid-based</li></ul></li></ul>	Lesson 5, Topic B
1.7 Compare and contrast various connection interfaces and explain their purpose.	
<ul><li>Physical connections<ul><li>USB 1.1 vs. 2.0 vs. 3.0 speed and distance characteristics (Connector types: A, B, mini, micro)</li><li>Firewire 400 vs. Firewire 800 speed and distance characteristics</li><li>SATA1 vs. SATA2 vs. SATA3, eSATA, IDE speeds</li><li>Other connector types (Serial, Parallel, VGA, HDMI, DVI, audio, RJ-45, RJ-11)</li><li>Analog vs. digital transmission (VGA vs. HDMI)</li></ul></li></ul>	Lesson 1, Topic B; Lesson 1, Topic C; Lesson 8, Topic A
<ul><li>Speeds, distances and frequencies of wireless device connections<ul><li>Bluetooth</li><li>IR</li><li>RF</li></ul></li></ul>	Lesson 1, Topic C
1.8 Install an appropriate power supply based on a given scenario.	
<ul><li>Connector types and their voltages<ul><li>SATA</li><li>Molex</li><li>4/8-pin 12v</li><li>PCIe 6/8-pin</li><li>20-pin</li><li>24-pin</li><li>Floppy</li></ul></li></ul>	Lesson 5, Topic C
<ul><li>Specifications<ul><li>Wattage</li><li>Size</li><li>Number of connectors</li></ul></li></ul>	Lesson 5, Topic C

Domain and Objective	Covered In
• ATX • Micro-ATX	
• Dual voltage options	Lesson 5, Topic C
1.9 Evaluate and select appropriate components for a custom configuration, to meet customer specifications or needs.	
• Graphic / CAD / CAM design workstation • Powerful processor • High-end video • Maximum RAM	Lesson 7, Topic B
• Audio/Video editing workstation • Specialized audio and video card • Large fast hard drive • Dual monitors	Lesson 7, Topic B
• Virtualization workstation • Maximum RAM and CPU cores	Lesson 7, Topic A
• Gaming PC • Powerful processor • High-end video/specialized GPU • Better sound card • High-end cooling	Lesson 7, Topic B
• Home Theater PC • Surround sound audio • HDMI output • HTPC compact form factor • TV tuner	Lesson 7, Topic B
• Standard thick client • Desktop applications • Meets recommended requirements for running Windows	Lesson 7, Topic A
• Thin client • Basic applications • Meets minimum requirements for running Windows	Lesson 7, Topic A
• Home Server PC • Media streaming • File sharing • Print sharing • Gigabit NIC • RAID array	Lesson 7, Topic B

Domain and Objective	Covered In
1.10 Given a scenario, evaluate types and features of display devices.	

• Types
   • CRT
   • LCD
   • LED
   • Plasma
   • Projector
   • OLED
	Lesson 4, Topic A

• Refresh rates	Lesson 4, Topic A
• Resolution	Lesson 4, Topic A
• Native resolution	Lesson 4, Topic A
• Brightness/lumens	Lesson 4, Topic A
• Analog vs. digital	Lesson 4, Topic A
• Privacy/antiglare filters	Lesson 4, Topic A
• Multiple displays	Lesson 4, Topic A
1.11 Identify connector types and associated cables.	

• Display connector types
   • DVI-D
   • DVI-I
   • DVI-A
   • Display Port
   • RCA
   • DB-15
   • BNC
   • mini-HDMI
   • RJ-45
   • Din-6
	Lesson 1, Topic C; Lesson 8, Topic A

• Display cable types
   • HDMI
   • DVI
   • VGA
   • Component
   • Composite
   • S-video
   • RGB
   • Coaxial
   • Ethernet
	Lesson 1, Topic C

• Device connectors and various connector pin-outs	Lesson 1, Topic C; Lesson 8, Topic A

Domain and Objective	Covered In
• SATA • eSATA • PATA (IDE and EIDE) • Floppy • USB • IEEE1394 • SCSI • PS/2 • Parallel • Serial • Audio • RJ-45	
• Device cable types • SATA • eSATA • IDE • EIDE • Floppy • USB • IEEE1394 • SCSI (68pin vs. 50pin vs. 25pin) • Parallel • Serial • Ethernet • Phone	Lesson 1, Topic C; Lesson 8, Topic A
1.12 Install and configure various peripheral devices.	
• Input devices • Mouse • Keyboard • Touch screen • Scanner • Barcode reader • KVM • Microphone • Biometric devices • Game pads • Joysticks • Digitizer	Lesson 4, Topic B
• Multimedia devices • Digital cameras • Microphone • Webcam • Camcorder • MIDI enabled devices	Lesson 4, Topic D

Domain and Objective	Covered In

• Output devices
   • Printers
   • Speakers
   • Display devices
	Lesson 1, Topic B; Lesson 4, Topics A and D

2.0 Networking	
2.1 Identify types of network cables and connectors.	
• Fiber • Connectors: SC, ST and LC	Lesson 8, Topic A

• Twisted Pair
   • Connectors: RJ-11, RJ-45
   • Wiring standards: T568A, T568B
	Lesson 8, Topic A

• Coaxial • Connectors: BNC, F-connector	Lesson 8, Topic A
2.2 Categorize characteristics of connectors and cabling.	

• Fiber
   • Types (single-mode vs. multi-mode)
   • Speed and transmission limitations
	Lesson 8, Topic A

• Twisted pair
   • Types: STP, UTP, CAT3, CAT5, CAT5e, CAT6, plenum, PVC
   • Speed and transmission limitations
	Lesson 8, Topic A

• Coaxial
   • Types: RG-6, RG-59
   • Speed and transmission limitations
	Lesson 8, Topic A

2.3 Explain properties and characteristics of TCP/IP.	

• IP class
   • Class A
   • Class B
   • Class C
	Lesson 8, Topic B

• IPv4 vs. IPv6	Lesson 8, Topic B
• Public vs. private vs. APIPA	Lesson 8, Topic B
• Static vs. dynamic	Lesson 8, Topic B
• Client-side DNS	Lesson 8, Topic B
• DHCP	Lesson 8, Topic B
• Subnet mask	Lesson 8, Topic B

Domain and Objective	Covered In
• Gateway	Lesson 8, Topic B
2.4 Explain common TCP and UDP ports, protocols, and their purpose.	

• Ports
   • 21 – FTP
   • 23 – TELNET
   • 25 – SMTP
   • 53 – DNS
   • 80 – HTTP
   • 110 – POP3
   • 143 – IMAP
   • 443 – HTTPS
   • 3389 – RDP
	Lesson 8, Topic D

• Protocols
   • DHCP
   • DNS
   • LDAP
   • SNMP
   • SMB
   • SSH
   • SFTP
	Lesson 8, Topic D

• TCP vs. UDP	Lesson 8, Topic D
2.5 Compare and contrast wireless networking standards and encryption types.	

• Standards
   • 802.11 a/b/g/n
   • Speeds, distances and frequencies
	Lesson 9, Topic A

• Encryption types • WEP, WPA, WPA2, TKIP, AES	Lesson 9, Topic A
2.6 Install, configure, and deploy a SOHO wireless/ wired router using appropriate settings.	
• MAC filtering	Lesson 9, Topic A
• Channels (1 – 11)	Lesson 9, Topic A
• Port forwarding, port triggering	Lesson 9, Topic A
• SSID broadcast (on/off)	Lesson 9, Topic A
• Wireless encryption	Lesson 9, Topic A
• Firewall	Lesson 9, Topic A
• DHCP (on/off)	Lesson 9, Topic A

Domain and Objective	Covered In
• DMZ	Lesson 9, Topic A
• NAT	Lesson 9, Topic A
• WPS	Lesson 9, Topic A
• Basic QoS	Lesson 9, Topic A
2.7 Compare and contrast Internet connection types and features.	
• Cable	Lesson 8, Topic C
• DSL	Lesson 8, Topic C
• Dial-up	Lesson 8, Topic C
• Fiber	Lesson 8, Topic C
• Satellite	Lesson 8, Topic C
• ISDN	Lesson 8, Topic C
• Cellular (mobile hotspot)	Lesson 8, Topic C
• Line of sight wireless internet service	Lesson 8, Topic C
• WiMAX	Lesson 8, Topic C
2.8 Identify various types of networks.	
• LAN	Lesson 8, Topic C
• WAN	Lesson 8, Topic C
• PAN	Lesson 8, Topic C
• MAN	Lesson 8, Topic C

• Topologies
  • Mesh
  • Ring
  • Bus
  • Star
  • Hybrid
	Lesson 8, Topic C

2.9 Compare and contrast network devices their functions and features.	
• Hub	Lesson 8, Topic C
• Switch	Lesson 8, Topic C
• Router	Lesson 8, Topic C
• Access point	Lesson 8, Topic C
• Bridge	Lesson 8, Topic C

Domain and Objective	Covered In
• Modem	Lesson 8, Topic C
• NAS	Lesson 8, Topic C
• Firewall	Lesson 8, Topic C
• VoIP phones	Lesson 8, Topic C
• Internet appliance	Lesson 8, Topic C
2.10 Given a scenario, use appropriate networking tools.	
• Crimper	Lesson 8, Topic F
• Multimeter	Lesson 8, Topic F
• Toner probe	Lesson 8, Topic F
• Cable tester	Lesson 8, Topic F
• Loopback plug	Lesson 8, Topic F
• Punchdown tool	Lesson 8, Topic F
3.0 Laptops	
3.1 Install and configure laptop hardware and components.	

• Expansion options
  • Express card /34
  • Express card /54
  • PCMCIA
  • SODIMM
  • Flash
	Lesson 10, Topic A

• Hardware/device replacement
  • Keyboard
  • Hard Drive (2.5 vs. 3.5)
  • Memory
  • Optical drive
  • Wireless card
  • Mini-PCIe
  • screen
  • DC jack
  • Battery
  • Touchpad
  • Plastics
  • Speaker
  • System board
  • CPU
	Lesson 10, Topic B

Domain and Objective	Covered In
3.2 Compare and contrast the components within the display of a laptop.	

• Types
  • LCD
  • LED
  • OLED
  • Plasma
	Lesson 10, Topic A

• Wi-Fi antenna connector/placement	Lesson 10, Topic A
• Inverter and its function	Lesson 10, Topic A
• Backlight	Lesson 10, Topic A
3.3 Compare and contrast laptop features.	

• Special function keys
  • Dual displays
  • Wireless (on/off)
  • Volume settings
  • Screen brightness
  • Bluetooth (on/off)
  • Keyboard backlight
	Lesson 10, Topic A

• Docking station vs. port replicator	Lesson 10, Topic A
• Physical laptop lock and cable lock	Lesson 10, Topic A
4.0 Printers	
4.1 Explain the differences between the various printer types and summarize the associated imaging process.	

• Laser
  • Imaging drum, fuser assembly, transfer belt, transfer roller, pickup rollers, separate pads, duplexing assembly
  • Imaging process: processing, charging, exposing, developing, transferring, fusing and cleaning
	Lesson 12, Topic A

• Inkjet
  • Ink cartridge, printhead, roller, feeder, duplexing assembly, carriage and belt
  • Calibration
	Lesson 12, Topic A

• Thermal
  • Feed assembly, heating element
  • Special thermal paper
	Lesson 12, Topic A

• Impact
  • Printhead, ribbon, tractor feed
  • Impact paper
	Lesson 12, Topic A

Domain and Objective	Covered In
4.2 Given a scenario, install, and configure printers.	
• Use appropriate printer drivers for a given operating system	Lesson 12, Topic B
• Print device sharing • Wired (USB, Parallel, Serial, Ethernet) • Wireless [Bluetooth, 802.11x, Infrared (IR)] • Printer hardware print server	Lesson 12, Topic B
• Printer sharing • Sharing local/networked printer via Operating System settings	Lesson 12, Topic B
4.3 Given a scenario, perform printer maintenance.	
• Laser • Replacing toner, applying maintenance kit, calibration, cleaning	Lesson 12, Topic B
• Thermal • Replace paper, clean heating element, remove debris	Lesson 12, Topic B
• Impact • Replace ribbon, replace printhead, replace paper	Lesson 12, Topic B
5.0 Operational Procedures	
5.1 Given a scenario, use appropriate safety procedures.	
• ESD straps	Lesson 3, Topic B
• ESD mats	Lesson 3, Topic B
• Self-grounding	Lesson 3, Topic B
• Equipment grounding	Lesson 3, Topic B
• Personal safety • Disconnect power before repairing PC • Remove jewelry • Lifting techniques • Weight limitations • Electrical fire safety • CRT safety – proper disposal • Cable management	Lesson 3, Topics B and C
• Compliance with local government regulations	Lesson 3, Topic A
5.2 Explain environmental impacts and the purpose of environmental controls.	
• MSDS documentation for handling and disposal	Lesson 3, Topic C

Domain and Objective	Covered In
• Temperature, humidity level awareness and proper ventilation	Lesson 3, Topic C

• Power surges, brownouts, blackouts
   • Battery backup
   • Surge suppressor
	Lesson 3, Topic C

• Protection from airborne particles
   • Enclosures
   • Air filters
	Lesson 3, Topic C

• Dust and debris
   • Compressed air
   • Vacuums
	Lesson 3, Topic C

• Component handling and protection • Antistatic bags	Lesson 3, Topic C
• Compliance to local government regulations	Lesson 3, Topic A
5.3 Given a scenario, demonstrate proper communication and professionalism.	
• Use proper language – avoid jargon, acronyms, slang when applicable	Lesson 3, Topic D
• Maintain a positive attitude	Lesson 3, Topic D
• Listen and do not interrupt the customer	Lesson 3, Topic D
• Be culturally sensitive	Lesson 3, Topic D
• Be on time (if late contact the customer)	Lesson 3, Topic D

• Avoid distractions
   • Personal calls
   • Talking to co-workers while interacting with customers
   • Personal interruptions
	Lesson 3, Topic D

• Dealing with difficult customer or situation
   • Avoid arguing with customers and/or being defensive
   • Do not minimize customer's problems
   • Avoid being judgmental
   • Clarify customer statements (ask open ended questions to narrow the scope of the problem, restate the issue or question to verify understanding)
	Lesson 3, Topic D

• Set and meet expectations/timeline and communicate status with the customer	Lesson 3, Topic D

Domain and Objective	Covered In
• Offer different repair/replacement options if applicable • Provide proper documentation on the services provided • Follow up with customer/user at a later date to verify satisfaction	
• Deal appropriately with customers confidential materials • Located on a computer, desktop, printer, etc	Lesson 3, Topic D
5.4 Explain the fundamentals of dealing with prohibited content/activity.	

• First response
  • Identify
  • Report through proper channels
  • Data/device preservation
	Lesson 3, Topic D

• Use of documentation/documentation changes	Lesson 3, Topic D
• Chain of custody • Tracking of evidence/documenting process	Lesson 3, Topic D
• Anti-spyware	Lesson 13, Topic C

B | Mapping Course Content to CompTIA® A+® Exam 220–802

Obtaining CompTIA A+ certification requires candidates to pass two examinations. This table describes where the objectives for CompTIA exam 220-802 are covered in this course.

Domain and Objective	Covered In
1.0 Operating Systems	
1.1 Compare and contrast the features and requirements of various Microsoft Operating Systems.	
• Windows XP Home, Windows XP Professional, Windows XP Media Center, Windows XP 64-bit Professional	Lesson 2, Topic A
• Windows Vista Home Basic, Windows Vista Home Premium, Windows Vista Business, Windows Vista Ultimate, Windows Vista Enterprise	Lesson 2, Topic A
• Windows 7 Starter, Windows 7 Home Premium, Windows 7 Professional, Windows 7 Ultimate, Windows 7 Enterprise	Lesson 2, Topic A

• Features:
  • 32-bit vs. 64-bit
  • Aero, gadgets, user account control, bit-locker, shadow copy, system restore, ready boost, sidebar, compatibility mode, XP mode, easy transfer, administrative tools, defender, Windows firewall, security center, event viewer, file structure and paths, category view vs. classic view
	Lesson 2, Topics A, B, C, and E

• Upgrade paths – differences between in place upgrades, compatibility tools, Windows upgrade OS advisor	Lesson 6, Topic C
1.2 Given a scenario, install and configure the operating system using the most appropriate method.	
• Boot methods	Lesson 6, Topic B

Domain and Objective	Covered In
• USB • CD-ROM • DVD • PXE	

• Type of installations
   • Creating image
   • Unattended installation
   • Upgrade
   • Clean install
   • Repair installation
   • Multiboot
   • Remote network installation
   • Image deployment
	Lesson 6, Topic B

• Partitioning
   • Dynamic
   • Basic
   • Primary
   • Extended
   • Logical
	Lesson 6, Topic B

• File system types/formatting
   • FAT
   • FAT32
   • NTFS
   • CDFS
   • Quick format vs. full format
	Lesson 2, Topic D; Lesson 6, Topic B

• Load alternate third party drivers when necessary	Lesson 6, Topic B
• Workgroup vs. Domain setup	Lesson 6, Topic B
• Time/date/region/language settings	Lesson 6, Topic B
• Driver installation, software and windows updates	Lesson 6, Topic B
• Factory recovery partition	Lesson 6, Topic B
1.3 Given a scenario, use appropriate command line tools.	

• Networking
   • PING
   • TRACERT
   • NETSTAT
   • IPCONFIG
   • NET
   • NSLOOKUP
   • NBTSTAT
	Lesson 2, Topic C

Domain and Objective	Covered In
• OS • TASKKILL • BOOTREC • SHUTDOWN • TASKLIST • MD • RD • CD • DEL • FDISK • FORMAT • COPY • XCOPY • ROBOCOPY • DISKPART • SFC • CHKDSK • [command name] /?	Lesson 2, Topic C
• Recovery console • Fixboot • Fixmbr	Lesson 2, Topic C
1.4 Given a scenario, use appropriate operating system features and tools.	
• Administrative • Computer management • Device manager • Users and groups • Local security policy • Performance monitor • Services • System configuration • Task scheduler • Component services • Data sources • Print management • Windows memory diagnostics • Windows firewall • Advanced security	Lesson 2, Topic E
• MSCONFIG • General • Boot • Services • Startup • Tools	Lesson 2, Topic E

Domain and Objective	Covered In

• Task Manager
  • Applications
  • Processes
  • Performance
  • Networking
  • Users
	Lesson 2, Topic E

• Disk management
  • Drive status
  • Mounting
  • Extending partitions
  • Splitting partitions
  • Assigning drive letters
  • Adding drives
  • Adding arrays
	Lesson 2, Topic E

• Other • User State Migration tool (USMT), File and Settings Transfer Wizard, Windows Easy Transfer	Lesson 2, Topic E

• Run line utilities
  • MSCONFIG
  • REGEDIT
  • CMD
  • SERVICES.MSC
  • MMC
  • MSTSC
  • NOTEPAD
  • EXPLORER
  • MSINFO32
  • DXDIAG
	Lesson 2, Topic E

1.5 Given a scenario, use Control Panel utilities (the items are organized by "classic view/large icons" in Windows).	

• Common to all Microsoft Operating Systems
  • Internet options (Connections, Security, General, Privacy, Programs, Advanced)
  • Display (Resolution)
  • User accounts
  • Folder options (Sharing, View hidden files, Hide extensions, Layout)
  • System [Performance (virtual memory), Hardware profiles, Remote settings, System protection]
  • Security center
  • Windows firewall
  • Power options (Hibernate, Power plans, Sleep/suspend, Standby)
	Lesson 2, Topic B

Domain and Objective	Covered In

• Unique to Windows XP
  • Add/remove programs
  • Network connections
  • Printers and faxes
  • Automatic updates
  • Network setup wizard
	Lesson 2, Topic B

• Unique to Vista
  • Tablet PC settings
  • Pen and input devices
  • Offline files
  • Problem reports and solutions
  • Printers
	Lesson 2, Topic B

• Unique to Windows 7
  • HomeGroup
  • Action Center
  • Remote Applications and Desktop Connections
  • Troubleshooting
	Lesson 2, Topic B

1.6 Setup and configure Windows networking on a client/desktop.	
• HomeGroup, file/print sharing	Lesson 6, Topic B; Lesson 8, Topic E
• WorkGroup vs. domain setup	Lesson 6, Topic B
• Network shares/mapping drives	Lesson 3, Topic A; Lesson 8, Topic E

• Establish networking connections
  • VPN
  • Dial ups
  • Wireless
  • Wired
  • WWAN (Cellular)
	Lesson 8, Topic E

• Proxy settings	Lesson 8, Topic E
• Remote desktop	Lesson 8, Topic E
• Home vs. Work vs. Public network settings	Lesson 8, Topic E

• Firewall settings
  • Exceptions
  • Configuration
  • Enabling/disabling Windows firewall
	Lesson 8, Topic E

• Configuring an alternative IP address in Windows • IP addressing	Lesson 8, Topic E

Domain and Objective	Covered In
• Subnet mask • DNS • Gateway	

• Network card properties
  • Half duplex/full duplex/auto
  • Speed
  • Wake-on-LAN
  • QoS
	Lesson 8, Topic E

1.7 Perform preventive maintenance procedures using appropriate tools.	

• Best practices
  • Scheduled backups
  • Scheduled check disks
  • Scheduled defragmentation
  • Windows updates
  • Patch management
  • Driver/firmware updates
  • Antivirus updates
	Lesson 6, Topic D

• Tools
  • Backup
  • System restore
  • Check disk
  • Recovery image
  • Defrag
	Lesson 6, Topic D

1.8 Explain the differences among basic OS security settings.	

• User and groups
  • Administrator
  • Power user
  • Guest
  • Standard user
	Lesson 2, Topic D

• NTFS vs. Share permissions
  • Allow vs. deny
  • Moving vs. copying folders and files
  • File attributes
	Lesson 2, Topic D

• Shared files and folders
  • Administrative shares vs. local shares
  • Permission propagation
  • Inheritance
	Lesson 2, Topic D

• System files and folders	Lesson 2, Topic D

Domain and Objective	Covered In
• User authentication • Single sign-on	Lesson 2, Topic D
1.9 Explain the basics of client-side virtualization.	
• Purpose of virtual machines	Lesson 6, Topic A
• Resource requirements	Lesson 6, Topic A
• Emulator requirements	Lesson 6, Topic A
• Security requirements	Lesson 6, Topic A
• Network requirements	Lesson 6, Topic A
• Hypervisor	Lesson 6, Topic A
2.0 Security	
2.1 Apply and use common prevention methods.	

• Physical security
   • Lock doors
   • Tailgating
   • Securing physical documents/passwords/shredding
   • Biometrics
   • Badges
   • Key fobs
   • RFID badge
   • RSA token
   • Privacy filters
   • Retinal
	Lesson 13, Topics A and C

• Digital security
   • Antivirus
   • Firewalls
   • Antispyware
   • User authentication/strong passwords
   • Directory permissions
	Lesson 13, Topics A and C

• User education	Lesson 13, Topic A
• Principle of least privilege	Lesson 13, Topic A
2.2 Compare and contrast common security threats.	
• Social engineering	Lesson 13, Topic B
• Malware	Lesson 13, Topic B
• Rootkits	Lesson 13, Topic B
• Phishing	Lesson 13, Topic B
• Shoulder surfing	Lesson 13, Topic B

Domain and Objective	Covered In
• Spyware	Lesson 13, Topic B

• Viruses
  • Worms
  • Trojans
	Lesson 13, Topic B

2.3 Implement security best practices to secure a workstation.	
• Setting strong passwords	Lesson 13, Topic A
• Requiring passwords	Lesson 13, Topic A
• Restricting user permissions	Lesson 13, Topic A
• Changing default user names	Lesson 9, Topics A and B
• Disabling guest account	Lesson 2, Topic D
• Screensaver required password	Lesson 13, Topic D
• Disable autorun	Lesson 13, Topic D
2.4 Given a scenario, use the appropriate data destruction/disposal method.	
• Low level format vs. standard format	Lesson 13, Topic C

• Hard drive sanitation and sanitation methods
  • Overwrite
  • Drive wipe
	Lesson 13, Topic C

• Physical destruction
  • Shredder
  • Drill
  • Electromagnetic
  • Degaussing tool
	Lesson 13, Topic C

2.5 Given a scenario, secure a SOHO wireless network.	
• Change default user-names and passwords	Lesson 9, Topic B
• Changing SSID	Lesson 9, Topic B
• Setting encryption	Lesson 9, Topic B
• Disabling SSID broadcast	Lesson 9, Topic B
• Enable MAC filtering	Lesson 9, Topic B
• Antenna and access point placement	Lesson 9, Topic B
• Radio power levels	Lesson 9, Topic B
• Assign static IP addresses	Lesson 9, Topic B

Domain and Objective	Covered In
2.6 Given a scenario, secure a SOHO wired network.	
• Change default user names and passwords	Lesson 9, Topic B
• Enable MAC filtering	Lesson 9, Topic B
• Assign static IP addresses	Lesson 9, Topic B
• Disabling ports	Lesson 9, Topic B
• Physical security	Lesson 9, Topic B
3.0 Mobile Devices	
3.1 Explain the basic features of mobile operating systems.	

• Android 4.0.x vs. iOS 5.x
 	
   • Open source vs. closed source/vendor specific
   • App source (app store and market)
   • Screen orientation (accelerometer/gyroscope)
   • Screen calibration
   • GPS and geotracking
	Lesson 11, Topic A

3.2 Establish basic network connectivity and configure email.	
• Wireless / cellular data network (enable/disable)	Lesson 11, Topic B

• Bluetooth
 	
   • Enable Bluetooth
   • Enable pairing
   • Find device for pairing
   • Enter appropriate pin code
   • Test connectivity
	Lesson 11, Topic B

• Email configuration • Server address	Lesson 11, Topic B
• POP3	Lesson 11, Topic B
• IMAP	Lesson 11, Topic B

• Port and SSL settings
   • Exchange
   • Gmail
	Lesson 11, Topic B

3.3 Compare and contrast methods for securing mobile devices.	
• Passcode locks	Lesson 11, Topic B
• Remote wipes	Lesson 11, Topic B
• Locator applications	Lesson 11, Topic B

Domain and Objective	Covered In
• Remote backup applications	Lesson 11, Topic B
• Failed login attempts restrictions	Lesson 11, Topic B
• Antivirus	Lesson 11, Topic B
• Patching/OS updates	Lesson 11, Topic B
3.4 Compare and contrast hardware differences in regards to tablets and laptops.	
• No field serviceable parts	Lesson 11, Topic A
• Typically not upgradeable	Lesson 11, Topic A

• Touch interface
  • Touch flow
  • Multitouch
	Lesson 11, Topic A

• Solid state drives	Lesson 11, Topic A
3.5 Execute and configure mobile device synchronization.	

• Types of data to synchronize
  • Contacts
  • Programs
  • Email
  • Pictures
  • Music
  • Videos
	Lesson 11, Topic B

• Software requirements to install the application on the PC	Lesson 11, Topic B
• Connection types to enable synchronization	Lesson 11, Topic B
4.0 Troubleshooting	
4.1 Given a scenario, explain the troubleshooting theory.	
• Identify the problem • Question the user and identify user changes to computer and perform backups before making changes	Lesson 14, Topic A
• Establish a theory of probable cause (question the obvious)	Lesson 14, Topic A

• Test the theory to determine cause
  • Once theory is confirmed determine next steps to resolve problem
  • If theory is not confirmed re-establish new theory or escalate
	Lesson 14, Topic A

Domain and Objective	Covered In
• Establish a plan of action to resolve the problem and implement the solution	Lesson 14, Topic A
• Verify full system functionality and if applicable implement preventive measures	Lesson 14, Topic A
• Document findings, actions and outcomes	Lesson 14, Topic A
4.2 Given a scenario, troubleshoot common problems related to motherboards, RAM, CPU and power with appropriate tools.	

• Common symptoms
  • Unexpected shutdowns
  • System lockups
  • POST code beeps
  • Blank screen on bootup
  • BIOS time and settings resets
  • Attempts to boot to incorrect device
  • Continuous reboots
  • No power
  • Overheating
  • Loud noise
  • Intermittent device failure
  • Fans spin – no power to other devices
  • Indicator lights
  • Smoke
  • Burning smell
  • BSOD
	Lesson 14, Topic D; Lesson 15, Topic A

• Tools
  • Multimeter
  • Power supply tester
  • Loopback plugs
  • POST card
	Lesson 14, Topic D

4.3 Given a scenario, troubleshoot hard drives and RAID arrays with appropriate tools.	

• Common symptoms
  • Read/write failure
  • Slow performance
  • Loud clicking noise
  • Failure to boot
  • Drive not recognized
  • OS not found
  • RAID not found
  • RAID stops working
  • BSOD
	Lesson 14, Topic C

Domain and Objective	Covered In

• Tools
   • Screwdriver
   • External enclosures
   • CHKDSK
   • FORMAT
   • FDISK
   • File recovery software
	Lesson 14, Topic C

4.4 Given a scenario, troubleshoot common video and display issues.	

• Common symptoms
   • VGA mode
   • No image on screen
   • Overheat shutdown
   • Dead pixels
   • Artifacts
   • Color patterns incorrect
   • Dim image
   • Flickering image
   • Distorted image
   • Discoloration (degaussing)
   • BSOD
	Lesson 14, Topic B

4.5 Given a scenario, troubleshoot wired and wireless networks with appropriate tools.	

• Common symptoms
   • No connectivity
   • APIPA address
   • Limited connectivity
   • Local connectivity
   • Intermittent connectivity
   • IP conflict
   • Slow transfer speeds
   • Low RF signal
	Lesson 15, Topic B

• Tools
   • Cable tester
   • Loopback plug
   • Punch down tools
   • Toner probes
   • Wire strippers
   • Crimper
   • PING
   • IPCONFIG
   • TRACERT
   • NETSTAT
	Lesson 15, Topic B

Domain and Objective	Covered In
• NBTSTAT • NET • Wireless locator	
4.6 Given a scenario, troubleshoot operating system problems with appropriate tools.	

• Common symptoms
  • BSOD
  • Failure to boot
  • Improper shutdown
  • Spontaneous shutdown/restart
  • RAID not detected during installation
  • Device fails to start
  • Missing dll message
  • Services fails to start
  • Compatibility error
  • Slow system performance
  • Boots to safe mode
  • File fails to open
  • Missing NTLDR
  • Missing Boot.ini
  • Missing operating system
  • Missing Graphical Interface
  • Graphical Interface fails to load
  • Invalid boot disk
	Lesson 15, Topic A

• Tools
  • Fixboot
  • Recovery console
  • Fixmbr
  • Sfc
  • Repair disks
  • Pre-installation environments
  • MSCONFIG
  • DEFRAG
  • REGSRV32
  • REGEDIT
  • Event viewer
  • Safe mode
  • Command prompt
  • Emergency repair disk
  • Automated system recovery
	Lesson 15, Topic A

4.7 Given a scenario, troubleshoot common security issues with appropriate tools and best practices.	
• Common symptoms • Pop-ups	Lesson 15, Topic C

Domain and Objective	Covered In
• Browser redirection • Security alerts • Slow performance • Internet connectivity issues • PC locks up • Windows updates failures • Rogue antivirus • Spam • Renamed system files • Files disappearing • File permission changes • Hijacked email • Access denied	

• Tools
   • Antivirus software
   • Anti-malware software
   • Anti-spyware software
   • Recovery console
   • System restore
   • Pre-installation environments
   • Event viewer
	Lesson 15, Topic C

• Best practices for malware removal
   • Identify malware symptoms
   • Quarantine infected system
   • Disable system restore
   • Remediate infected systems
	Lesson 15, Topic C

• Update antivirus software	Lesson 15, Topic C

• Scan and removal techniques (safe mode, pre-installation environment)
   • Schedule scans and updates
   • Enable system restore and create restore point
   • Educate end user
	Lesson 15, Topic C

4.8 Given a scenario, troubleshoot, and repair common laptop issues while adhering to the appropriate procedures.	

• Common symptoms
   • No display
   • Dim display
   • Flickering display
   • Sticking keys
   • Intermittent wireless
   • Battery not charging
   • Ghost cursor
	Lesson 14, Topic E

Domain and Objective	Covered In
<ul><li>No power</li><li>Num lock indicator lights</li><li>No wireless connectivity</li><li>No Bluetooth connectivity</li><li>Cannot display to external monitor</li></ul>	
<ul><li>Disassembling processes for proper re-assembly<ul><li>Document and label cable and screw locations</li><li>Organize parts</li><li>Refer to manufacturer documentation</li><li>Use appropriate hand tools</li></ul></li></ul>	Lesson 14, Topic E
4.9 Given a scenario, troubleshoot printers with appropriate tools	
<ul><li>Common symptoms<ul><li>Streaks</li><li>Faded prints</li><li>Ghost images</li><li>Toner not fused to the paper</li><li>Creased paper</li><li>Paper not feeding</li><li>Paper jam</li><li>No connectivity</li><li>Garbled characters on paper</li><li>Vertical lines on page</li><li>Backed up print queue</li><li>Low memory errors</li><li>Access denied</li><li>Printer will not print</li><li>Color prints in wrong print color</li><li>Unable to install printer</li><li>Error codes</li></ul></li></ul>	Lesson 14, Topic F
<ul><li>Tools<ul><li>Maintenance kit</li><li>Toner vacuum</li><li>Compressed air</li><li>Printer spooler</li></ul></li></ul>	Lesson 14, Topic F

C | CompTIA A+ Acronyms

The following table lists the acronyms that appear on the CompTIA A+ exams. Candidates are encouraged to review this list and have a working knowledge of the acronyms and their associated terms, as a part of a comprehensive exam preparation program.

Acronym	Associated Term
AC	alternating current
ACL	access control list
ACPI	Advanced Configuration Power Interface
ACT	activity
ADSL	Asymmetrical Digital Subscriber Line
AGP	Accelerated Graphics Port
AMD	Advanced Micro Devices
APIPA	Automatic Private Internet Protocol Addressing
APM	advanced power management
ARP	Address Resolution Protocol
ASR	automated system recovery
ATA	Advanced Technology Attachment
ATAPI	Advanced Technology Attachment Packet Interface
ATM	Asynchronous Transfer Mode
ATX	Advanced Technology eXtended
A/V	Audio Video
BIOS	basic input/output system
BNC	Bayonet-Neill-Concelman or British Naval Connector
BTX	Balanced Technology eXtended
CAPTCHA	Completely Automated Public Turing Test To Tell Computers and Humans Apart
CCFL	Cold Cathode Fluorescent Lamp
CD	compact disc
CD-ROM	compact disc-read-only memory
CD-RW	compact disc-rewritable
CDFS	compact disc file system

Acronym	Associated Term
CFS	Central File System, Common File System, or Command File System
CMOS	complementary metal-oxide semiconductor
CNR	Communications and Networking Riser
COMx	communication port (x=port number)
CPU	central processing unit
CRIMM	Continuity Rambus Inline Memory Mode
CRT	cathode-ray tube
DAC	discretionary access control
DB-25	serial communications D-shell connector, 25 pins
DB-9	9-pin D-shell connector
DC	direct current
DDOS	distributed denial of service
DDR	double data-rate
DDR RAM	double data-rate random access memory
DDR SDRAM	double data-rate synchronous dynamic random access memory
DFS	distributed file system
DHCP	Dynamic Host Configuration Protocol
DIMM	dual inline memory module
DIN	Deutsche Industrie Norm
DIP	dual inline package
DLT	digital linear tape
DLP	digital light processing
DMA	direct memory access
DMZ	demilitarized zone
DNS	Domain Name Service or domain name server
DOS	denial of service
DRAM	dynamic random access memory
DSL	digital subscriber line
DVD	digital video disc or digital versatile disc
DVD-RAM	digital video disc-random access memory
DVD-ROM	digital video disc-read only memory
DVD-R	digital video disc-recordable
DVD-RW	digital video disc-rewritable
DVI	digital visual interface
ECC	error correction code
ECP	extended capabilities port

Acronym	Associated Term
EEPROM	electrically erasable programmable read-only memory
EFS	encrypting file system
EIDE	enhanced integrated drive electronics
EMI	electromagnetic interference
EMP	electromagnetic pulse
EPROM	erasable programmable read-only memory
EPP	enhanced parallel port
ERD	emergency repair disk
ESD	electrostatic discharge
EVGA	extended video graphics adapter/array
EVDO	evolution data optimized or evolution data only
FAT	file allocation table
FAT12	12-bit file allocation table
FAT16	16-bit file allocation table
FAT32	32-bit file allocation table
FDD	floppy disk drive
Fn	Function (referring to the function key on a laptop)
FPM	fast page-mode
FRU	field replaceable unit
FSB	Front Side Bus
FTP	File Transfer Protocol
FQDN	fully qualified domain name
Gb	gigabit
GB	gigabyte
GDI	graphics device interface
GHz	gigahertz
GUI	graphical user interface
GPS	global positioning system
GSM	global system for mobile communications
HAL	hardware abstraction layer
HAV	Hardware Assisted Virtualization
HCL	hardware compatibility list
HDD	hard disk drive
HDMI	high definition media interface
HPFS	high performance file system
HTML	hypertext markup language

Acronym	Associated Term
HTPC	Home Theater PC
HTTP	hypertext transfer protocol
HTTPS	hypertext transfer protocol over secure sockets layer
I/O	input/output
ICMP	internet control message protocol
ICR	intelligent character recognition
IDE	integrated drive electronics
IDS	Intrusion Detection System
IEEE	Institute of Electrical and Electronics Engineers
IIS	Internet Information Services
IMAP	internet mail access protocol
IP	internet protocol
IPCONFIG	internet protocol configuration
IPP	internet printing protocol
IPSEC	internet protocol security
IR	infrared
IrDA	Infrared Data Association
IRQ	interrupt request
ISA	industry standard architecture
ISDN	integrated services digital network
ISO	Industry Standards Organization
ISP	internet service provider
JBOD	just a bunch of disks
Kb	kilobit
KB	Kilobyte or knowledge base
LAN	local area network
LBA	logical block addressing
LC	Lucent connector
LCD	liquid crystal display
LDAP	lightweight directory access protocol
LED	light emitting diode
Li-on	lithium-ion
LPD/LPR	line printer daemon / line printer remote
LPT	line printer terminal
LVD	low voltage differential
MAC	media access control / mandatory access control

Acronym	Associated Term
MAPI	messaging application programming interface
MAU	media access unit or media attachment unit
Mb	megabit
MB	megabyte
MBR	master boot record
MBSA	Microsoft Baseline Security Analyzer
MFD	multi-function device
MHz	megahertz
MicroDIMM	micro dual inline memory module
MIDI	musical instrument digital interface
MIME	multipurpose internet mail extension
MIMO	Multiple Input Multiple Output
MMC	Microsoft management console
MMX	multimedia extensions
MP3	Moving Picture Experts Group Layer 3 Audio
MP4	Moving Picture Experts Group Layer 4
MPEG	Moving Picture Experts Group
MSCONFIG	Microsoft configuration
MSDS	material safety data sheet
MUI	multilingual user interface
NAC	network access control
NAS	network-attached storage
NAT	network address translation
NetBIOS	networked basic input/output system
NetBEUI	networked basic input/output system extended user interface
NFS	network file system
NIC	network interface card
NiCd	nickel cadmium
NiMH	nickel metal hydride
NLX	new low-profile extended
NNTP	network news transfer protocol
NTFS	new technology file system
NTLDR	new technology loader
NTP	Network Time Protocol
OCR	optical character recognition
OEM	original equipment manufacturer

Acronym	Associated Term
OLED	Organic Light Emitting Diode
OS	operating system
PAN	personal area network
PATA	parallel advanced technology attachment
PC	personal computer
PCI	peripheral component interconnect
PCIe	peripheral component interconnect express
PCIX	peripheral component interconnect extended
PCL	printer control language
PCMCIA	Personal Computer Memory Card International Association
PDA	personal digital assistant
PGA	pin grid array
PGA2	pin grid array 2
PII	Personally Identifiable Information
PIN	personal identification number
PKI	public key infrastructure
PnP	plug and play
POP3	Post Office Protocol 3
PoS	Point of Sale
POST	power-on self test
POTS	plain old telephone service
PPP	point-to-point protocol
PPTP	point-to-point tunneling protocol
PRI	primary rate interface
PROM	programmable read-only memory
PS/2	personal system/2 connector
PSTN	public switched telephone network
PSU	power supply unit
PVC	permanent virtual circuit or polyvinyl chloride
PXE	preboot execution environment
QoS	quality of service
RAID	redundant array of independent (or inexpensive) disks
RAM	random access memory
RAS	remote access service
RDRAM	RAMBUS dynamic random access memory
RDP	Remote Desktop Protocol

Acronym	Associated Term
RF	radio frequency
RFI	radio frequency interference
RGB	red green blue
RIMM	RAMBUS inline memory module
RIP	routing information protocol
RIS	remote installation service
RISC	reduced instruction set computer
RJ	registered jack
RJ-11	registered jack function 11
RJ-45	registered jack function 45
RMA	returned materials authorization
ROM	read only memory
RS-232 or RS-232C	recommended standard 232
RTC	real-time clock
SAN	storage area network
SAS	Serial Attached SCSI
SATA	serial advanced technology attachment
SC	subscription channel
SCP	secure copy protection
SCSI	small computer system interface
SCSI ID	small computer system interface identifier
SD card	secure digital card
SDRAM	synchronous dynamic random access memory
SEC	single edge connector
SFC	system file checker
SFF	Small Form Factor
SGRAM	synchronous graphics random access memory
SIMM	single inline memory module
SLI	scalable link interface
S.M.A.R.T.	self-monitoring, analysis, and reporting technology
SMB	server message block or small to midsize business
SMTP	simple mail transfer protocol
SNMP	simple network management protocol
SoDIMM	small outline dual inline memory module
SOHO	small office/home office
SP	service pack

Acronym	Associated Term
SP1	service pack 1
SP2	service pack 2
SP3	service pack 3
SP4	service pack 4
SPDIF	Sony-Philips digital interface format
SPGA	staggered pin grid array
SRAM	static random access memory
SSH	secure shell
SSID	service set identifier
SSL	secure sockets layer
ST	straight tip
STP	shielded twisted pair
SVGA	super video graphics array
SXGA	super extended graphics array
TB	terabyte
TCP	transmission control protocol
TCP/IP	transmission control protocol/internet protocol
TDR	time domain reflectometer
TFTP	trivial file transfer protocol
TKIP	Temporal Key Integrity Protocol
TPM	trusted platform module
UAC	user account control
UART	universal asynchronous receiver transmitter
UDMA	ultra direct memory access
UDP	user datagram protocol
UNC	universal naming convention
UPS	uninterruptible power supply
URL	uniform resource locator
USB	universal serial bus
USMT	user state migration tool
UTP	unshielded twisted pair
UXGA	ultra extended graphics array
VESA	Video Electronics Standards Association
VFAT	virtual file allocation table
VGA	video graphics array
VM	Virtual Machine

Acronym	Associated Term
VoIP	voice over internet protocol
VPN	virtual private network
VRAM	video random access memory
WAN	wide area network
WAP	wireless application protocol
WEP	wired equivalent privacy
WIFI	wireless fidelity
WINS	Windows Internet Name Service
WLAN	wireless local area network
WPA	wireless protected access
WUXGA	wide ultra extended graphics array
XGA	extended graphics array
ZIF	zero-insertion-force
ZIP	zigzag inline package

D | A Brief History of Personal Computers

Mechanical Computing Devices

Knowing a little about the history of computers can help you appreciate the current industry situation and prepare you for future developments. And, understanding how computers have evolved can help you appreciate how they are built and help you better understand why they work the way they do, which makes troubleshooting and repair that much easier.

The Abacus

The *abacus* is usually listed as the first mechanical computation device. Developed 2,000 or more years ago in India or the Far East, an abacus consists of columns of beads that can slide up and down on rods that are held together in a frame. The position of the beads represents a number. Skilled users could perform calculations more quickly than early electronic computers could.

Mathematical Advancements and Computing

The written number for zero appeared around 650 A.D. in India and made written calculations much easier. A Persian scholar wrote the first textbook on algebra in 830 A.D. During the 1100s, Europeans learned the written form of math used by the Arabs and wrote down multiplication tables to help merchants. Five hundred years later, John Napier, a Scotsman, carved a set of multiplication tables on ivory sticks that could slide back and forth to indicate certain results. The use of logarithms on *Napier's Bones* in 1617 led to the development of the slide rule. Today's mature engineers can still remember using slide rules in their college days.

Calculating Machines

The Frenchman Blaise Pascal is usually given credit for the first calculating machine. In 1642, to help his father—a tax collector—with his work, Pascal invented a machine with eight metal dials that could be turned to add and subtract numbers. Leonardo da Vinci and Wilhelm Schickard, a German, designed calculating machines before Pascal, but Pascal receives the recognition because he produced 50 models of his *Pascaline machine,* not just a prototype or description. In 1673, Gottfried von Leibniz, a German mathematician, improved on Pascal's design to create a *Stepped Reckoner* that could do addition, subtraction, multiplication, and division. Only two prototypes were produced.

A Frenchman, Thomas de Colmar, created an Arithmometer in 1820 that was produced in large numbers over the ensuing 100 years. The Swedish inventor Willgodt T. Odhner improved on the Arithmometer, and his calculating mechanism was used by dozens of companies in the calculating machines they produced.

Punchcard Technologies

Punched cards first appeared in 1801. Joseph Marie Jacquard used the holes placed in the card to control the patterns woven into cloth by power looms. In 1832, Charles Babbage was working on a Difference Engine when he realized Jacquard's punched cards could be used in computations. The *Analytical Engine,* which is the machine Babbage designed but never manufactured, introduced the idea of using memory for storing results and the idea of printed output. His drawings described a general-purpose, fully program-controlled, automatic mechanical digital computer. Lady Ada Augusta Lovelace worked with Babbage on his machine. She became the first computer programmer when she wrote out a series of instructions for the Analytical Engine.

Note: Charles Babbage's Difference Engine No. 1 was the first successful automatic calculator. Although the 12,000 parts were never assembled into a finished engine, the parts that were completed functioned perfectly.

Punched cards were used in the United States census of 1890, and a data-processing machine created by Herman Hollerith tabulated the census results in only 2.5 years—much shorter than the predicted 10 years. Punched cards provided input, memory, and output on an unlimited scale for business calculating machines for the next 50 years. The company Hollerith founded to manufacture his card-operated data processors, which used electrical contacts to detect the pattern of holes in each card, eventually became IBM®.

Electronic Computers and the Military

With the beginning of World War II, electronic computers took on national importance. The accurate calculation of projectile trajectories became a life-and-death concern for the military. The calculations needed to develop the atomic bomb also required more calculating power than was available before the war, and the calculations involved in trying to decode and break enemy codes saw researchers around the world start developing huge room-sized computers that could work on such problems more efficiently than a man with pencil and paper. Between 1939 and 1944, Howard H. Aiken developed the Harvard *Mark I*—also known as the IBM Automatic Sequence-Controlled Calculator (ASCC). The Mark I was made out of mechanical switches, electrical relays, rotating shafts, and clutches totaling 750,000 components weighing 5 tons. Programming instructions were fed to the Mark I on paper tape, and data was fed in on paper punched cards. Grace Hopper worked at Harvard on the Mark I, II, and III, and discovered the first real-life computer "bug" when she removed a moth that had flown into a mechanical relay, causing it to malfunction. Also, during the war, Konrad Zuse was working secretly on his Z3 computer in Germany. Because so little was known about the Z3 for so long, most people describe the Mark I as the first modern (but not electronic) digital computer.

Perhaps the most important and influential figure from this time was Alan Turing, an English mathematician who is now generally credited with being the father of computer science. Spending his time working in mathematics, logic, and cryptanalysis, Turing was heavily involved in Britain's codebreaking effort during World War II before he moved on to the University of Manchester. While at the University, he began work on the Manchester Mark I, one of the earliest computers. He is also credited with inventing the Turing Test, which has had profound implications in the development of Artificial Intelligence. The Turing Test was a low-tech test for the presence of Artificial Intelligence: if a person were to remotely converse by text with a human and a machine, and could not tell the difference between the two, then the machine would be said to pass the Turing Test.

Vacuum Tube Systems

The advent of vacuum tube technologies changed the face of electronic computing.

Vacuum Tubes and Digital Computing

Dr. John Vincent Atanasoff was an associate professor at Iowa State College when he designed an electronic digital computer that would use base two (binary) numbers. In 1939, with his assistant Clifford Berry, he built the world's first electronic digital computer using *vacuum tubes*. After a lecture,

Dr. John W. Mauchly asked to see Atanasoff's computer and later used so many of Atanasoff's ideas in the ENIAC that it took a lawsuit to declare that Atanasoff was the first to use vacuum tubes in an electronic digital computer.

ENIAC to UNIVAC

Dr. Mauchly and J. Presper Eckert were at the University of Pennsylvania in 1942 when they built the *Electronic Numerical Integrator And Computer (ENIAC)* to aid the United States military during World War II. ENIAC used 18,000 vacuum tubes, had 500,000 hand-soldered connections, was 1,000 times faster than the Mark I, and had to be rewired to change its program. ENIAC was used from 1946 to 1955, and because of its reliability, it is commonly accepted as the first successful high-speed electronic digital computer. Eckert and Mauchly also designed the *Electronic Discrete Variable Automatic Computer (EDVAC)*, which contained 4,000 vacuum tubes and 10,000 crystal *diodes*. After their success with ENIAC, Eckert and Mauchly proposed to build a *Universal Automatic Computer (UNIVAC)* machine to help the Census Bureau handle all its data. After four years of delays and cost overruns, Remington Rand Inc. worked with the Eckert-Mauchly Computer Corporation to develop UNIVAC, the first commercially successful computer. The computer used magnetic tape to store data, a major change from IBM's punched cards, and introduced many other features that are common today. Starting in 1951, 46 UNIVAC I computers were made for the government and businesses, although some experts at the time thought that five computers would be enough to handle all the computational needs of the world.

John von Neumann

John von Neumann did not design the electronics in computers, but he is credited with the theoretical work that all modern computers are based on. Von Neumann recommended that a computer program should be able to stop under certain conditions and start again at another point. He also recommended storing both the data and instructions in memory so both could be changed as needed. He realized that physically rewiring a computer to change the program, or feeding in another paper tape to meet different conditions, was not practical for successful high-speed computing. The *Electronic Delay Storage Automatic Computer (EDSAC)* at Cambridge University, England, and Eckert and Mauchly's EDVAC were among the first to use von Neumann's ideas. Combining von Neumann's stored program concept with a 1,000-word main memory, magnetic tape for secondary memory, printer and typewriter output, and a 2.25 MHz clock rate, UNIVAC set the standard for computers in the 1950s.

Transistorized Systems and Other Technological Advances

In the 1950s, the progress of electronic computing was limited by technology. Vacuum tubes, which were used to control the flow of electricity in digital computer circuits, were large (several inches high), red-hot to touch, and unreliable. Transistor technologies were the next great technical step forward in the development of computing power.

Transistors

In the 1940s and early 1950s, Dr. William Shockley worked at Bell Telephone Laboratories as co-head of a solid-state research group that developed the *transistor*. Transistors performed the same function as vacuum tubes, but were the size of a pencil eraser, generated almost no heat, and were extremely reliable. The replacement of vacuum tubes with transistors opened up new possibilities.

Magnetic Core Memory

Another important innovation was *magnetic core memory,* which allowed information to be stored in the magnetic orientation of tiny magnetic rings strung together on fine wire. Using magnetic core memory, the huge mainframes increased their memory from 8,000 to 64,000 words. Combining the computational capability made available through transistors with expanded magnetic core memory gave computers so much power that they had to be used in new ways to justify the cost. Some mainframes used batch processing, where a series of programs and data was stored on magnetic drums and fed to the computer one after the other so no computing time was wasted. Other computers used time sharing, where the computing power was shifted among several different programs running at the same time so no power was wasted waiting for an individual program's results to print or for more input to arrive.

Miniaturization and the Space Race

At this time, the United States and the former Soviet Union were involved in a race to see who would be first in space. The complex rockets demanded sophisticated computers to control them. The Soviet Union concentrated on designing bigger rockets to carry larger computers into space, while the United States worked on making smaller, more powerful computers that fit into the smaller rockets they had. The millions spent on research to miniaturize computer components used in the space race produced the technology needed for current computers.

Integrated Circuit Technologies

The development of the integrated circuit paved the way for the computers we know today.

Integrated Circuits

Combining several transistors and the *resistors* needed to connect them on a single semiconductor chip in an *integrated circuit* was a tremendous technical advance. In 1958, Jack Kilby at Texas Instruments made several components on a single-piece semiconductor. By 1961, Fairchild and Texas Instruments were mass-producing integrated circuits on a single chip. In 1967, Fairchild introduced the Micromosaic, which contained a few hundred transistors. The transistors could be connected into specific circuits for an application using computer-aided design. The Micromosaic was an Application-Specific Integrated Circuit (ASIC).

 Note: Now usually called just a chip, the first integrated circuit was fabricated in 1958 by Texas Instruments inventor Jack Kilby.

Integrated Circuit

Early RAM and Processor Circuits

In 1970, Fairchild introduced the first 256-bit static *RAM chip,* while Intel® announced the first 1,024-bit dynamic RAM. Computers that could make use of this memory were still monsters to maintain. Handheld calculators, on the other hand, appealed to everyone from scientists to school kids. Marcian "Ted" Hoff at Intel designed a general-purpose integrated circuit that could be used in calculators, as well as other devices. Using ideas from this circuit, Intel introduced, in 1972, the *8008,* which contained approximately 3,300 transistors and was the first *microprocessor* to be supported by a high-level language compiler called PL/M.

General-Purpose Microprocessors

A major breakthrough occurred in 1974 when Intel presented the 8080, the first general-purpose microprocessor. The 8080 microprocessor had a single chip that contained an entire programmable computing device on it. The 8080 was an 8-bit device that contained around 4,500 transistors and could perform 200,000 operations per second. Other companies besides Intel designed and produced microprocessors in the mid-1970s, including Motorola (6800), Rockwell (6502), and Zilog (Z80). As more chips appeared and the prices dropped, personal desktop computers became a possibility.

Personal Computers

These developments led to the personal computer that is ubiquitous in homes and businesses today.

The First PCs

About a dozen computers claim to be the first *Personal Computer (PC).* Credit for the first popular personal computer often goes to Ed Roberts, whose company, MITS, designed a computer called the Altair 8800 and marketed a kit for about $400 in 1974. The Altair 8800 used Intel's 8080 microprocessor, contained 256 bytes of RAM, and was programmed by means of a panel of toggle switches. In 1975, Bill Gates and Paul Allen founded Microsoft® and wrote a BASIC interpreter for the Altair. More than 2,000 systems were sold in 1975.

In 1975, MOS Technology announced its 6502-based KIM-1 desktop computer, and Sphere Corporation introduced its Sphere 1 kit. Both kits were strictly for computer fanatics.

Early General-Purpose PCs

In 1976, Steve Wozniak and Steve Jobs formed Apple® Computer Inc., and began creating their first commercial product, the Apple I. Unique for the time, the Apple I was a relatively inexpensive hobbyist computer that required users to provide their own case, monitor, keyboard and power supply. The Apple I was later modified to create the Apple II (with a 6502 microprocessor). In 1977, the Apple II cost $1,300, came with 16 KB of ROM, 4 KB of RAM, a keyboard, and color output. The Apple II is usually listed as the first personal computer that was available for the general public. The Commodore PET (6502) and Radio Shack's TRS-80 (Z80) were also popular. In 1979, VisiCalc, a spreadsheet program for the Apple II, made desktop computers attractive to businesses. As more businesses bought Apples, demand appeared for word-processing applications, and the software development industry took off. In 1981, IBM joined the party with its first PC. Dozens of other models and companies followed IBM's lead, but in 1984, Apple broke from the pack and produced the Macintosh® computer with a mouse and graphical user interface that opened the computer world to artists and publishers. Of all the computers designed during this period, only the IBM PC and Apple Macintosh have withstood the test of time.

Today's PCs

Today there are several types of PCs, including desktop, minitower, laptop, netbook, tablet PC, and handheld PDA. Most mobile devices have many of the functions of a small computer and the distinction between computer and communications device is blurring.

The Development of the Graphical User Interface

With the near-ubiquity of personal and portable computers today, it is difficult to imagine a time when computers were large, expensive, took several days to process a request and, most importantly, could only understand instructions via a series of card punches. However, this accurately describes many computers well into the early 1970s. Therefore, alongside the development of the microprocessor, one of the most important technological developments encouraging the wide adoption of easy-to-use personal computers has been the development of the graphical user interface (GUI).

Douglas Engelbart, a researcher at the Stanford Research Institute (SRI), is widely credited with developing the first GUI. Engelbart's research borrowed heavily from ideas spelled out by Vannevar Bush's 1945 essay titled "As We May Think." In this essay, Bush proposed a machine called a memex, which was a hypothetical way of navigating through large amounts of information using hypertext. The memex was based on how adults actually learn, store, and process information, and had increased relevance in an age where information was rapidly changing. While the memex was never created, Engelbart borrowed heavily from Bush's ideas when it came time to work on his own hypertext-based visual computer called the On-Line System, or NLS. The NLS debuted in 1968, and featured the first uses of a GUI, hypertext, a mouse, windows for organizing and displaying information, the use of a computer to deliver a presentation, and many other now-common computer features.

Note: Vannevar Bush's 1945 essay "As We May Think" can be read online at **www.theatlantic.com/doc/194507/bush.**

Note: A full-length video of Doug Engelbart's demo of the NLS can be found online at **www. 1968demo.org/.**

After the SRI's introduction of the NLS, work continued on graphical user interface design at Xerox PARC (Palo Alto Research Center). Xerox PARC created what many now consider the first personal computer that used a GUI, along with the now-familiar desktop metaphor. Dubbed the Xerox Alto, it was the first small-scale computer where a graphical tool could be used to create, delete, and manage local files—the Alto was *not* merely a terminal.

Apple founder Steve Jobs visited Xerox PARC, and during his visit became very interested in the mouse. The Alto was not available commercially for home use, but Apple was targeting a larger market. He incorporated what he liked about the Alto into Apple's design, and so the first two GUI computers from Apple—the Lisa and the MacIntosh—featured both a GUI and a mouse. Apple's GUIs also continued the Alto's use of the desktop metaphor, with icons of documents and folders representing files and directories. This proved to be an enormously popular way to use a personal computer. Shortly after Apple debuted their GUI, Microsoft released their first operating system that had a graphical interface. Windows 1.0 was a GUI that ran on top of the existing MS-DOS operating system, which was purely text-based up until that point.

Windows greatly changed the look and feel of their GUI with the release of Windows® 95 (the first 32-bit version of Windows), and subsequent Windows operating systems have stayed fairly true to that design: this was the first use in Windows of the Start menu and taskbar, which have been mainstays for more than a decade. Most operating system GUIs since then have shared this basic layout, though the complexity of the graphics may have evolved.

Graphical interface design today has gotten both grander and smaller. With the exploding popularity of handheld multimedia devices, GUIs are no longer limited just to PCs. Thanks to cell phones and smartphones, MP3 players, mobile Internet devices, ebook readers, and more, interfaces have the added challenge of needing to operate on very small screens, drawing far less power, and using weaker processors. On top of this, interface development has had to straddle the line between graphical appeal (such as with 3D desktops) and usability (where the drive for a more user-friendly interface outweighs any flashier graphical features).

Computing Today and Tomorrow

Today, in the early 21st century, computers and computing have become ubiquitous in the daily lives of almost everyone in the developed world. Computers are present not only as home and office productivity tools, but also as enhancements to everything from home appliances to SUVs. There is more computing power in the average consumer's automobile today than there was on board the Apollo spacecraft that took human beings to the moon and back in the 1960s and 1970s.

The Internet is no less influential than the PC in today's interconnected world. Since physicist Tim Berners-Lee of the CERN laboratory invented the basic technologies of the World Wide Web and posted the first website in 1991, the growth of the Internet has exploded to the point where virtually all computers on the planet are interconnected. Ordinary users can now communicate sophisticated information with each other instantaneously around the globe. The ongoing vision of "Web 2.0" may soon create a global society in which all types of information and all means of communication will be created and maintained cooperatively by ordinary individuals throughout the world. There is even a drive toward turning computers into little more than bootable machines with web browsers on them. In this system of "cloud computing," all computing power is provided through remote computers that function, essentially, as application servers. Microsoft's Office 365™ is a prime example of cloud computing, and all reports indicate that cloud computing is here to stay.

The ubiquity of computing power and the omnipresence of the Internet: these two factors have changed our world to an unimaginable extent in an extraordinarily short period of time. Society as a whole can look forward eagerly to the equally unimaginable and extraordinary changes technology will bring us in the years and decades just ahead.

Lesson Labs

Lesson labs are provided for certain lessons as additional learning resources for this course. Lesson labs are developed for selected lessons within a course in cases when they seem most instructionally useful as well as technically feasible. In general, labs are supplemental, optional unguided practice and may or may not be performed as part of the classroom activities. Your instructor will consider setup requirements, classroom timing, and instructional needs to determine which labs are appropriate for you to perform, and at what point during the class. If you do not perform the labs in class, your instructor can tell you if you can perform them independently as self-study, and if there are any special setup requirements.

Lesson Lab 1–1
Identifying Hardware Components

Activity Time: 10 minutes

Scenario
In this lab, you will identify the hardware components for several PCs.

---

1. Examine as many of the PCs that are in your environment as you can.

2. For each system:
   a) Locate the primary components, and determine what types of input devices, output devices, and external devices are present.
   b) Determine the type and form factor. For instance, is the system a desktop PC, a tower PC, a laptop, or some other type of system?
   c) Identify the ports available on the computer. See if you can tell which ports are built-in and which are provided by adapter cards.
   d) Try to determine what types of internal storage devices the system provides.

Lesson Lab 2–1
Configuring Windows Operating System Components

Activity Time: 15 minutes

Scenario

As a new help desk technician, you have been issued a PC with a fresh installation of Windows 7 Professional. You want to start personalizing the behavior of your new computer and examining its system configuration.

 Note: You can find a suggested solution for this activity in the \Solution\Configuring Windows Operating System Components.txt file in the data file location.

---

1. Configure the **Start** menu and taskbar settings to suit your preferences and work habits.

2. Configure the **Computer** view and folder options to suit your preferences and work habits.

3. In the **Documents** library, create a data folder and a new text file within the data folder. Determine the default permissions and attributes associated with the new folder and file.

4. Examine the tools available in several of the **Control Panel** categories.

5. Access **Help and Support** to learn more about the tools available in **Computer Management.**

6. Examine the Registry entries for some of the settings that you might have changed in this lab.

 Caution: Do not change any settings in the Registry, or you could affect the outcome of all subsequent activities and labs.

For instance:

- In the **HKEY_CURRENT_USER\Control Panel\Mouse** key, determine the value of **SwapMouseButtons.** This will be set to 0 if the left mouse button is configured as the primary button.
- In the **HKEY_LOCAL_MACHINE\SOFTWARE\Classes\txtfile\shell\open\command** key, determine the value of the **(default)** value entry. This will tell you what application Windows will use by default to open files that have the .txt extension.
- In the **HKEY_LOCAL_MACHINE\SOFTWARE\Microsoft\Windows\CurrentVersion** key, determine the value of **ProgramFilesDir.** This will tell you in which folder Windows will install new software programs by default.

Lesson Lab 3–1
Identifying Operational Procedures

Activity Time: 10 minutes

Scenario
In this lab, you will identify operational procedures and best practices for PC technicians.

1. List the items that you would want to have in your hardware toolkit.

2. Select the items that can pose an electrical hazard.
   - ☐ Chassis
   - ☐ Monitor
   - ☐ Printer
   - ☐ Power supply
   - ☐ Battery
   - ☐ Capacitor

3. Consider this scenario: A novice technician arrives at a user's workspace to troubleshoot a sound card. The user assures the technician that the power to the PC is off. As the technician begins working, he finds that the anti-static wrist strap gets in the way, so he removes it. Once the PC cover is off, the technician pulls the sound card out of the expansion slot and places it on a nearby metal filing cabinet, replacing it with a network card that he knows works properly. Finding that the network card does not work when installed in that expansion slot, the technician determines that there is a resource conflict, corrects the conflict, and replaces the network card with the user's original sound card. After testing the sound card, the technician and user agree that the problem is resolved. As the technician is repacking his toolkit, the user mentions a funny ozone smell coming from her laser printer. The technician assures the user that an occasional whiff of ozone is normal, and ends the service call. What would you do differently?

4. What are some examples of active listening techniques?
   - ☐ Paraphrasing the user's comments.
   - ☐ Nodding your head, and maintaining eye contact.
   - ☐ Avoiding interrupting the user by writing down your questions.
   - ☐ Empathizing with the user.

☐   Using open-ended questions to gather information about the problem that the user is experiencing.

Lesson Lab 4–1
Installing and Configuring Peripheral Components

Activity Time: 30 minutes

Before You Begin

To complete this activity, you will need the following hardware components. If you do not have these available, you can remove and reinstall the existing hardware:

- An external monitor.
- A keyboard and mouse or other pointing device.
- An expansion card.
- A multimedia device.

Scenario

You have been asked to assist a user whose computer needs refurbishing. You have several new peripheral components to install, configure, and verify for the user.

 Note: You can find a suggested solution for this activity in the Solution\Installing and Configuring Peripheral Components.txt file in the data file location.

1. Install and configure the monitor.

2. Install and configure the input devices.

3. Install and configure the multimedia device.

Lesson Lab 5–1
Managing System Components

Activity Time: 15 minutes

Before You Begin
To complete this lab, you will need the following hardware components. If you do not have these available, you can remove and reinstall the existing hardware:
- An optical drive that is compatible with your system.
- Optionally, rails to allow smaller drives to fit into larger drive bays.

Scenario
You have been assigned the task of repairing a computer for a client. The computer has an optical drive that needs to be replaced, and a PATA optical drive has been allocated for the task.

---

1. Remove the old optical drive from the computer.

2. Install the new optical drive in the computer.

Lesson Lab 6-1
Installing and Configuring Operating Systems

Activity Time: 20 minutes

Scenario

You've created a virtual machine named **Win7test##** to have an environment to try out new procedures and to test configuration changes to Windows 7.

1. Increase the memory available to the virtual machine to **1,024 MB.**

2. Install the Virtual PC Integration Components.

3. Increase the minimum pagefile size by 100 MB.

4. Schedule Check Disk to run on the virtual machine every Tuesday at 4:30 p.m.

Lesson Lab 8–1
Selecting and Using Networking Technologies

Activity Time: 45 minutes

Before You Begin
You will need two Windows 7 computers. Both computers must be connected to the Internet. You will also need a headset with a microphone, or a microphone and speakers, attached to each computer. If you have a partner, you can work with a partner to complete the hands-on portion of the lab. If you have existing Skype account information, you can use that in lieu of creating a new account for each Skype system.

Scenario
You are a support technician for My Footprint Sports. My Footprint Sports is opening a new retail store in the Midwest, and you have been assigned to support the installation of the new site. Your first duty is to work on a team to help identify the various network technologies the new store will require to enable its employees to communicate electronically both with the network servers that control operations from the head office in Greene City, as well as with other My Footprint Sports employees, preferred customers, colleagues, and suppliers throughout the world. Store managers and assistant managers have been issued wireless laptops that will need to be integrated into the store's network structure.

---

1. List the various networking technologies you would recommend for the My Footprint Sports retail outlet, and explain how each technology would support the employees' connectivity needs. Are there any network components that you would not employ? Are there any optional components? What are the pros and cons of implementing each one? You might wish to sketch a possible network design for this store to show the various connectivity components.

2. The decision has been made by management to investigate VoIP communications to help reduce the cost of long-distance telephone calls. Management has also asked for some ideas on accessing and troubleshooting remote servers. You know a little about Skype for Internet-based voice communication and Telnet for remote communication, but you want to test the features of Skype and Telnet before suggesting them to management as potential solutions. Download the Skype software from the **www.skype.com** website.

3. Follow the on-screen installation instructions, and install the software on both systems.

4. Either create a new Skype account on each system by entering a user name and password, or sign in to an existing Skype account on each system.

5. Check your sound equipment and make a test call.

6. Add the Skype account to the contact list of the other PC.

7. Initiate a Skype session between the two computers.

8. Disconnect from the call, sign out of Skype, and close the Skype window.

9. Enable Telnet.

10. In your web browser, open the www.telnet.org website and click the link for **places to telnet** to obtain addresses of remote hosts that maintain open Telnet connections. Some of the addresses are followed by any public login information you may need.

11. In a command prompt, initiate a Telnet session with a remote host. If you are unsuccessful in connecting, try **www.scn.org** or **www.torfree.net.**

12. After you connect to the remote host, log in (using the suggested login information from the **places to telnet** link) and investigate the commands and features offered by the remote host.

13. Disconnect the Telnet connection, and close all open windows.

Lesson Lab 13–1
Comparing Workgroup Security and Domain Security

Activity Time: 15 minutes

Scenario

Elise works at a company that has a Windows Active Directory domain in its network infrastructure. She also volunteers at a local food bank where the computers are connected by a Windows workgroup. She wants to use the same password (mypassword) on both networks, and she has asked for your advice about the feasibility of her plan. Although you know that you want to discuss with her the merits of using a strong password, you decide to test her plan before responding to her question.

---

1. On the **Win7test##** virtual machine, try to change the password and password hint from *IPass1234* to *mypassword*

2. Is the new password accepted?

3. On the physical computer, try to change the password and password hint from *IPass1234* to *mypassword*

4. Is the new password accepted?

5. Use Windows **Help and Support** to research this issue.

6. How will you explain the results of the test you conducted?

7. Close all open windows.

Lesson Lab 14-1
Troubleshooting Hardware Components

Activity Time: 45 minutes

Before You Begin

To set up this activity, your instructor will introduce one or more problems into your computer system.

Scenario

You are a hardware support technician for a large company. Various users have called the help desk with problems with their computer hardware that the help desk support staff has been unable to resolve over the phone. You will need to visit the users' work locations to diagnose and resolve the problems.

---

1. Identify the symptoms of the problems.

2. Diagnose the causes of the problems.

3. Resolve the problems.

4. Verify that all components and peripheral devices are functioning properly.

Lesson Lab 15-1

Troubleshooting System-Wide Issues

Activity Time: 30 minutes

Before You Begin

To set up this activity, your instructor will introduce one or more problems into your computer environment.

Scenario

You are a support technician for a large company. Various users have called the help desk with problems with their computer systems that the help desk support staff has been unable to resolve over the phone. You will need to visit the users' work locations to diagnose and resolve the problems.

---

1. A user is having trouble connecting to the local network and the Internet. He needs to be able to access several websites to do some research for his current project. The network administrator has ruled out general network and server errors because all of the other users in the user's vicinity have been able to connect to the network. It is your responsibility as the desktop support administrator to correct the problem for the individual user.
   a) Examine the network connection settings to identify any problems.
   b) Examine the local system's network connection hardware and cabling to identify any problems.
   c) Use the **Help and Support Center** to troubleshoot the network access problem.
   d) Correct any problems you find during your investigation.
   e) Verify that all problems have been resolved.

2. One of the users in your office is having a severe problem with new video drivers. He has asked you to reset the computer to a last known good configuration. Once you have returned the system to a usable state, you agree with the user that it would be a good precaution to create a complete backup of the healthy system.
   a) Use the **Last known good (advanced)** option to restore the computer.
   b) Complete a complete backup of the computer and save it to the second hard drive (or to the *Win7test##* VM if you did not add a second hard drive to the system).

Solutions

ACTIVITY 1–1: Identifying Personal Computer Components

3. Which computer components are part of the system unit?
   - ☑ Chassis
   - ☑ Internal hard drive
   - ☐ Monitor
   - ☐ Portable USB drive
   - ☑ Memory

4. What are the main categories of personal computer components?
   - ☑ System unit
   - ☑ Display
   - ☑ Input devices
   - ☐ Network devices
   - ☑ Peripheral devices

6. How many fans would you expect to find in a computer? How many do you think are in the computer you are using for this course?

   A: Answers will vary, but should indicate at least one fan for the power supply. A case fan and a fan for the CPU might also be present, as well as fans on some expansion cards.

7. Where is the system BIOS stored?
   - ○ On the primary hard drive
   - ○ In BIOS memory
   - ◉ On ROM chips
   - ○ In RAM

8. Which hardware components are checked during the POST?
   - ☑ Power supply
   - ☑ CPU
   - ☐ Display
   - ☑ RAM

9. Which system unit components are connected by the system bus?
   - ☑ CPU
   - ☑ Memory
   - ☐ Power supply
   - ☐ System board
   - ☐ Cooling system

ACTIVITY 1–2: Identifying Storage Devices

2. Which storage device records data magnetically and is most often used for backups?
   - ○ FDD
   - ○ HDD
   - ○ Optical disk drive
   - ◉ Tape drive
   - ○ SSD

3. What is the primary benefit of using solid state storage?

   A: Answers will vary, but should include the portability of thumb drives and other small solid state devices, and the speed of data access when compared to traditional magnetic storage media.

4. Which two optical drive media types enable you to write to an optical disk only once?
   - ☐ CD-ROM
   - ☑ CD-R
   - ☐ CD+RW
   - ☑ DVD+R
   - ☐ DVD-RW

5. True or False? No optical disk can hold more than 50 GB of data.
   - ☐ True
   - ☑ False

ACTIVITY 1–3: Identifying Device Connections and Interfaces

2. Identify the ports shown in the graphic. Use labels such as audio port, parallel port, PS/2 port, serial port, and USB port.

   A:

3. Which connection type supports up to 127 peripherals for a single connection?
   - ○ IEEE 1394
   - ○ SATA
   - ○ Parallel
   - ◉ USB

4. Which type of connection features small, thin data and power cables?
   - ○ SCSI
   - ○ PATA
   - ◉ SATA
   - ○ Parallel

5. Which connection type transfers data eight or more bits at a time over eight or more wires?
   - ○ Serial connection
   - ◉ Parallel connection
   - ○ USB connection
   - ○ FireWire connection

6. Which connection type connects a series of internal hard drives in a master/slave configuration?
   - ○ Parallel connection
   - ○ USB connection
   - ○ SCSI
   - ◉ PATA

7. Which connection type is associated with the IEEE 1394 Standard?
   - ○ USB connection
   - ◉ FireWire connection
   - ○ SCSI connection
   - ○ Serial connection

ACTIVITY 2-1: Discussing Operating Systems

2. Which screen element indicates that the Aero interface is active?

A: The transparent effect of the taskbar.

3. **True or False? Windows XP includes the Windows Aero interface.**
   - ☐ True
   - ☑ False

4. **What is the Windows Sidebar?**
   - ◉ A designated area of the desktop where users can add gadgets of their choice to provide information and access to frequently used tools or programs.
   - ○ A performance enhancer, available in Windows Vista and Windows 7, that allows the user to supplement the computer's memory with an external storage device like a flash drive.
   - ○ A security feature that provides full disk encryption protection for your operating system as well as all the data stored on the operating system volume.
   - ○ An application that displays information such as local weather data.

   Participants may question why they are investigating only some of the features that were described in this topic. Reassure them that they will access many of the other features later in the course.

7. **True or False? Gadgets must be downloaded from the Microsoft Windows website, or they will not work properly.**
   - ☐ True
   - ☑ False

   Facilitate a short discussion of the pros and cons of the ReadyBoost feature.

8. **Do you think that you or your users might take advantage of this performance-enhancing feature? Why or why not?**

   A: Answers will vary depending on individual preferences and organizational standards.

10. **Which editions of Windows would be appropriate if you needed to add computers to a Windows domain?**
    - ☐ Windows Vista Home Basic
    - ☐ Windows 7 Home Premium
    - ☑ Windows 7 Professional
    - ☑ Windows 7 Ultimate

11. **Which statements about UNIX are true?**
    - ☑ There are many versions of UNIX from different developers and distributors.
    - ☐ All versions of UNIX use the same shell, or user interface.
    - ☑ UNIX versions are proprietary.
    - ☑ UNIX is a multi-user, multi-tasking system.
    - ☐ UNIX was developed using the open-source methodology.

12. **Which statements about Linux are true?**
    - ☑ Linux was developed as open-source software.
    - ☐ Developers must obtain permission to access and modify the source code.
    - ☑ Development was initiated and managed by Linus Torvalds.
    - ☐ Releases of Linux are unstable.
    - ☑ Linux distributions can provide tools, utilities, and system support.

13. **Which statements about Mac OS X are true?**

☐ Mac OS X can be downloaded and modified freely.

☑ Mac OS X can integrate browsing for files created in other operating systems.

☑ Mac OS X provides many security features.

☐ Mac OS X can run the Windows XP user interface.

ACTIVITY 2-3: Exploring Command Line Tools

4. What command line tool would you use to make a copy of a directory structure and all the files within that directory structure?

   ○ copy

   ○ chkdsk

   ◉ robocopy

   ○ md

5. What is the best command line tool to use if you want to test TCP/IP communication to a specific IP address?

   ○ net

   ○ ipconfig

   ○ nbstat

   ◉ ping

6. Which tool is used to create a new partition boot sector?

   ○ fdisk

   ◉ fixboot

   ○ bootrec

   ○ fixmbr

7. Which system recovery tool restores a system image created by the user?

   ○ System Restore

   ◉ System Image Recovery

   ○ Memory Diagnostic

   ○ Startup Repair

8. Which is the best description of the Startup Repair utility?

   ○ Restores a system image created by the user

   ○ Checks the system's memory for errors

   ○ Restores computer settings and system files to a user-defined time

   ◉ Repairs system files that are missing or corrupted

ACTIVITY 2-5: Exploring NTFS Permissions

3. What level of permissions did the administrators group have?

   ◉ Full Control

  ○ Modify

  ○ Write

  ○ Read & Execute

4. **What level of permissions did the Users group have?**

  ○ Full Control

  ○ Modify

  ○ Write

  ◉ Read & Execute

6. **How were the permissions in the LocalData folder different from the permissions on the C drive?**

  ○ Administrators did not have Full Control to the LocalData folder.

  ○ Users could not read files in the LocalData folder.

  ◉ The permissions on the C drive were set explicitly; the permissions on the LocalData folder were inherited from the C drive.

  ○ The available permissions were different.

8. **True or False? The permissions in the New Text Document file were inherited from the LocalData folder permissions.**

  ☑ True

  ☐ False

ACTIVITY 2-7: Using Computer Management and Device Manager

3. **Did any devices have problems?**

  A: Answers will vary depending upon the state of the systems.
  Poll the participants to determine if anyone detected problems on their systems. If problems were found, conduct a short discussion about their possible causes.

ACTIVITY 3-1: Examining Basic Maintenance Tools and Techniques

1. **You are asked to repair a motherboard in a customer's PC. Which set of tools would be best suited for the task?**

  ○ Phillips screwdriver (#0), torx driver (size T8, T10, and T15), tweezers, and a three-prong retriever

  ◉ 30-W ceramic solder iron, miniature pliers, wire cutters, and a soldering iron stand with sponge

  ○ Wire strippers, precision wire cutters, digital multimeter, and cable crimper with dies

  ○ Chip extractor, chip inserter, ratchet, and Allen wrench

  ○ Anti-static cleaning wipes, anti-static wrist band, flashlight, and cotton swabs

2. You are asked to correct a network cabling problem at a customer site. Which set of tools would be best suited for the task?
   - ○ Phillips screwdriver (#0), torx driver (size T8, T10, and T15), tweezers, and a three-prong retriever
   - ○ 30-W ceramic solder iron, miniature pliers, wire cutters, and a soldering iron stand with sponge
   - ◉ Wire strippers, precision wire cutters, digital cable tester, and cable crimper with dies
   - ○ Chip extractor, chip inserter, ratchet, and Allen wrench
   - ○ Anti-static cleaning wipes, anti-static wrist band, flashlight, and cotton swabs

3. You suspect that contaminants from the environment have prevented the fan on a PC from working optimally. Which set of tools would be best suited to fix the problem?
   - ○ Phillips screwdriver (#0), torx driver (size T8, T10, and T15), tweezers, and a three-prong retriever
   - ○ 30w ceramic solder iron, miniature pliers, wire cutters, and a soldering iron stand with sponge
   - ○ Wire strippers, precision wire cutters, digital multimeter, and cable crimper with dies
   - ○ Chip extractor, chip inserter, ratchet, and Allen wrench
   - ◉ Anti-static cleaning wipes, anti-static wrist band, flashlight, and cotton swabs

4. True or False? Windows includes software diagnostic tests that help you find and correct hardware problems.
   - ☑ True
   - ☐ False

ACTIVITY 3-2: Identifying Electrical Safety Issues

1. True or False? If you are using an anti-static ESD floor mat, you do not need any other ESD safety equipment.
   - ☐ True
   - ☑ False

2. Electrical injuries include electrocution, shock, and collateral injury. Would you be injured if you are not part of the electrical ground current?

   A: Yes, you could receive a thermal burn from the head of an electric arc or electric equipment. Your clothes can catch on fire, or your skin can be burned.

3. Which computer component presents the most danger from electrical shock?
   - ○ System boards
   - ○ Hard drives
   - ◉ Power supplies
   - ○ System unit

4. Have you had any personal experience with any of the electrical hazards covered in this topic? What safety precautions could have prevented the incident?

   A: Answers will vary depending on individual experiences. Common precautions include disconnecting a computer from the electrical outlet or power strip before servicing it, using anti-static equipment to protect computer components, and implementing smoke and flame detectors to alert you of electrical fires.

ACTIVITY 3-3: Identifying Environmental Safety Issues

1. You are on a service call, and you accidentally spill some liquid cleaner on the user's work surface. What actions should you take?

    ☑ Refer to the MSDS for procedures to follow when the material is spilled.

    ☐ Wipe it up with a paper towel and dispose of the paper towel in the user's trash container.

    ☑ Report the incident.

2. Ozone is classified as an environmental hazard. Which device produces ozone gas?

    ⦿ Laser printer

    ○ CPU

    ○ Laptop

    ○ Power supply

3. What item reacts with heat and ammonia-based cleaners to present a workplace hazard?

    ○ Capacitor

    ○ Laser

    ⦿ Toner

    ○ Battery

ACTIVITY 3-4: Examining Professionalism and Communication Techniques

1. What is an example of verbal communication skills? What is an example of non-verbal communication skills?

    A: Answers will vary, but might include: For verbal communication skills, use clear, concise, and direct statements. For non-verbal communication skills, maintain the proper amount of eye contact.

2. Which is a good example of listening skills?

    ○ Maintain a neat and clean appearance.

    ○ Keep sensitive customer information to yourself.

    ○ Interrupt the customer to ask for more details.

    ○ Let your eyes wander around the room as the customer is speaking.

    ⦿ Allow the customer to complete statements without interrupting.

3. While answering a service call on a computer that is located in a common area of the office, you come across information showing that some unauthorized websites have been viewed. The activity has been linked to a particular user account. What is the appropriate action to take?

    A: Answers will vary, but will most likely include referring to procedures and guidelines documented by your specific organization and following the best practices used when responding to an incident, such as first response procedures, chain of custody guidelines, and documenting the entire process.

4. When a service technician does not share sensitive customer information with others, which skill or behavior is being practiced?

- ◉ Confidentiality
- ○ Ethical behavior
- ○ Respect
- ○ Active listening

5. You have received an off-site service call to service a network printer at a customer location. When you arrive, the user is at the printer and starts talking about how the printer is not working properly, and he cannot get his reports handed in on time. As a result, you start asking more clarifying questions to gather more information, so you can identify the specific issue with the printer. What type of technique are you using to gather information?

- ○ Passive listening
- ○ Non-verbal communication
- ◉ Active listening

6. Which are examples of displaying respect during a service call?

- ☑ Asking permission before changing display settings
- ☐ Asking "What happened just before you noticed the problem?"
- ☐ Sitting in a user's chair without permission
- ☑ Silencing your pager or mobile phone

ACTIVITY –5: Identifying Operational Procedures

1. List the items that you would want to have in your hardware toolkit.

   A: Answers will vary, but should include at least a large and small flat-head screwdriver, a large and small Phillips screwdriver, a pen or pencil, a flashlight, a container for screws, and a nut driver.

2. Select the items that can pose an electrical hazard.

- ☑ Chassis
- ☑ Monitor
- ☐ Printer
- ☑ Power supply
- ☐ Battery
- ☑ Capacitor

3. Consider this scenario: A novice technician arrives at a user's workspace to troubleshoot a sound card. The user assures the technician that the power to the PC is off. As the technician begins working, he finds that the anti-static wrist strap gets in the way, so he removes it. Once the PC cover is off, the technician pulls the sound card out of the expansion slot and places it on a nearby metal filing cabinet, replacing it with a network card that he knows works properly. Finding that the network card does not work when installed in that expansion slot, the technician determines that there is a resource conflict, corrects the conflict, and replaces the network card with the user's original sound card. After testing the sound card, the technician and user agree that the problem is resolved. As the technician is repacking his toolkit, the user mentions a funny ozone smell coming from her laser printer. The technician assures the user that an occasional whiff of ozone is normal, and ends the service call. What would you do differently?

   A: Responses should include the following safe practices: Never assume anything; verify for yourself that the power is off and power cables are unplugged before starting the troubleshooting process. No matter how uncomfortable it seems, wear the anti-static wrist strap and connect it to ground unless you are working on power supplies or monitors. Always store electronic parts that you intend to reuse in anti-static bags or on a dissipative mat. Check the area surrounding the laser printer to ensure that the printer is properly ventilated; if the airflow seems adequate, the ozone filter in the printer might need to be replaced.

4. What are some examples of active listening techniques?

☑ Paraphrasing the user's comments.

☐ Nodding your head, and maintaining eye contact.

☐ Avoiding interrupting the user by writing down your questions.

☑ Empathizing with the user.

☑ Using open-ended questions to gather information about the problem that the user is experiencing.

ACTIVITY 4–1: Examining Display Devices

1. What step should you complete first when you are installing a monitor?

○ Secure the monitor to the port by tightening the screws on each side of the connector.

◉ Turn off the computer.

○ Plug in the monitor power cord.

○ Locate the monitor port on the computer.

○ Align the pins on the monitor cable with the holes in the adapter port and plug in the monitor.

2. What kind of video is component video?

☑ Analog

☐ Digital

☐ HD

☐ Brightness only

ACTIVITY 4–6: Examining Expansion Cards

1. Which expansion card provides interfaces necessary to connect Small Computer Systems Interface (SCSI) devices?

◉ Input/output card

○ Multimedia card

○ Video card

○ Modem card

2. True or False? Before attempting to install an expansion card, verify that the computer has an available slot that matches the expansion card's bus type.

☑ True

☐ False

3. What is the first step in installing an expansion card?

○ Turn off power to the system and unplug the power and peripheral cables.

○ Remove the system cover and access the slots on the system board.

○ Remove the slot cover from an empty slot.

◉ Read the quick start guide to see if drivers or other software should be installed before or after installing the card.

ACTIVITY 4-8: Examining Multimedia Devices

1. If you want to watch TV on your PC, but you do not need to record the transmission on your hard drive, which multimedia adapter should you use?

◉ TV tuner card

○ Capture card

○ Video card

○ NIC

2. True or False? When you are installing a sound card, you do not have to worry about the available slots on the motherboard.

☐ True

☑ False

ACTIVITY 5-1: Identifying Motherboards

1. What type of motherboard is displayed here, and what characteristics did you use to help you identify the board type?

   A: Based on its small size dimensions and compact component design, this motherboard is a mini-ITX.

2. What type of motherboard is displayed here, and what characteristics did you use to help you identify the board type?

   A: You can tell by the large size and vast number of available components and slots that this motherboard is an ATX.
   Assist participants in identifying their motherboards.

ACTIVITY 5-3: Identifying RAM Slots

2. How many RAM slots are on your motherboard? Are they all being used?

   A: Answers will vary depending on the individual computers.

ACTIVITY 5-6: Selecting Cooling Systems

1. When might you need more than one cooling system in a computer?

   A: Answers will vary, but should include instances such as high processing levels that generate excessive heat.

2. When would liquid cooling systems be more appropriate than adding a fan?

A: Answers will vary, but might include when there is not much room inside the computer case or when an externally mounted fan is not appropriate.

ACTIVITY 5-10: Comparing RAM Types and Features

1. **When selecting a new RAM module, how do you determine the maximum running speed of the RAM once it has been installed?**

   A: The RAM module can run only as fast as the motherboard's bus speed, so you must determine the maximum speed of the system bus.
   Discuss the fact that you can install RAM of different speeds into the same computer. The point to make here is that all the installed RAM will run at the speed of the slowest module. If you add RAM that runs at 12 ns, all the RAM in the system will run at 12 ns.

2. **On a typical system with RAM that runs at 10 ns, what RAM can you add? (Select all that apply.)**
   - ☑ RAM that runs at 10 ns
   - ☑ RAM that runs at 12 ns
   - ☑ RAM that runs at 6 ns
   - ☑ RAM that runs at 8 ns

3. **When selecting a RAM module, when would you choose RAM enabled with ECC as opposed to RAM with only parity?**

   A: The difference between ECC and parity is that ECC can detect errors and correct them, while parity can only detect errors. If you are adding or replacing RAM in a high-end system or a server where errors can have a critical impact on data integrity, you should consider choosing ECC RAM.

ACTIVITY 6-2: Examining Installation Methods

1. **A user has had Windows 7 for several months, but a virus attack has corrupted some files.**
   - ○ Unattended
   - ○ Upgrade
   - ◉ Repair
   - ○ Multiboot

2. **Several identical PCs need their operating systems upgraded.**
   - ☑ Unattended
   - ☐ Clean
   - ☐ Repair
   - ☑ Image deployment

3. **A user has Windows XP and needs both Windows XP and Windows 7.**
   - ○ Clean
   - ○ Repair
   - ○ Remote network
   - ◉ Multiboot

ACTIVITY 6-4: Discussing Windows Upgrades

1. **When is the best time to use an in-place upgrade?**
   ○ Upgrading from Windows XP Professional to Windows 7 Professional.
   ○ Upgrading from Windows Vista Home to Windows 7 Starter.
   ◉ Upgrading from Windows Vista Business to Windows 7 Professional
   Emphasize that in-place upgrades should be considered only when the operating systems are one version apart or are different editions of the same version.

2. **Where can you go to find out if your hardware and software will work properly if you upgrade to Windows 7?**
   A: The Windows Compatibility Center.

3. From Angie: An answer needs to be included for the question below. If using the generic "Answers will vary..." please be sure to include at least one possible answer. From Pam: Fixed.
   Have you had experience with upgrading operating systems, either at home or at work? Share your experiences with the rest of the participants.

   A: Answers will vary depending on individual experiences. Some participants might have upgraded their home computers, while others might never have performed an upgrade at home or at work.
   To facilitate this part of the discussion, you might want to share some of your own experiences with upgrading operating systems, including successes and failures.

ACTIVITY 7-1: Identifying Standard Client Components

1. **The manager of the Human Resources department needs to be able to access the central employee data repository to run reports, but will not need access to the data entry application used to create, edit, and manage the employee data. The employee data is managed on a server that can be accessed with a log in. What type of client is best in this case?**
   ◉ Thin client
   ○ Virtualization workstation
   ○ Thick client

2. **June has recently been put in charge of making updates to the Human Resource employee benefits website. She will be publishing a monthly newsletter and posting company wide announcements, among other small updates and changes on a regular basis. All changes to the website must be tested on a number of platforms and web browsers to verify that the changes are correct regardless of the operating system and browser. What type of client setup would you suggest for her?**

   A: Answers will vary, but will most likely include a virtualization workstation so that she can switch from different operating system and test any website changes quickly.

3. **In order to properly support the HR employee benefits website, a new server running client VMs has been installed so that the environment that the application requires can be strictly administered by IT staff. Current PCs will be used to access the Client VM environment that is configured on the VM Server. What needs to be present at all PCs that will be accessing this new server and application??**
   ☑ Appropriately configured VM Client.
   ☑ Fast network connection to server hosting the VM environment.
   ☐ Upgrade to video cards.

4. **True or False? The HR manager's client computer must meet the recommended requirements to run Windows 7 so that she can access and use all of the HR related applications used by the organization. In this case, the best client option is a thick client.**

☑ True
☐ False

ACTIVITY 7-2: Selecting a Custom Client Configuration

---

1. Customer 1 is using a desktop PC to play home movies and to set up slide shows to show his family their vacation photos and is having difficulty with the computer freezing during the movies. He is looking for a solution that will allow him to store and play his movies seamlessly through a computer. He also wants his wife to be able to access the pictures and movies from her laptop within the house. What type of computer setup would you suggest for this customer? What specific questions might you ask this customer about additional component needs?

   A: Answers may vary, but will most likely include setting up a home server PC for easy file sharing among the household computing devices and to provide more speed to play movies from the PC. You may ask if they are in need of additional storage space and if they are looking for redundancy through a RAID array in the PC.

2. Customer 2 is from a small real estate office who has recently hired a Graphic Designer to produce informational pamphlets and other marketing materials for the agency such as, property drop sheets and circular layout designs. The office manager has asked your company to determine the hardware and software needs for the designer's workstation so that it can be ordered and set up before their scheduled start date in two weeks. What hardware and software requirement you would suggest for the Graphic Designer's workstation?

   A: Answers may vary, but will most likely include a PC with a newer powerful processor such as an Intel Core i7, a high end video card, and the maximum RAM that the motherboard can handle. The applications will most likely include Adobe's Create Suite of products.

3. Customer 3 is looking to make the switch from a traditional cable box, DVD player to a home theater PC, so that she can stream Netflix and DVR shows and movies from her TV. She already purchased a HTPC from a local home entertainment store but cannot figure out how why she cannot connect the cable TV wire into the HTPC. What required component might be missing that would enable her to make the connection?

   A: The TV tuner card installed in the HTPC. The tuner card provides the port to connect the cable from the provider to the HTPC.

ACTIVITY 8-1: Identifying Network Cables and Connectors

---

2. What type of cable is used to connect your computer to the network?

   A: Answers will vary depending on the location of the participant and the type of network interface is in the computer, and could range from twisted pair to wireless to virtual.

3. Are there any LED lights on the cable ports indicating activity?

   A: Answers will vary depending on the location of the participant and the level of network activity. Some participants might see the LED lights lit or blinking, while others might not.

ACTIVITY 8–2: Identifying Your Computer's TCP/IP Information

4. **If DHCP is enabled on your computer, when does the lease expire?**

   A: Answers will vary depending on the last time the computer was restarted. Briefly describe the DHCP lease process.

6. **How many DNS servers are listed?**

   A: Answers will vary depending on the configuration of the network.

ACTIVITY 8–3: Discussing Network Connectivity

1. **The transmission method that allows multiple signals to be carried separately on the same media at the same time is called _____**
   - ○ Baseband.
   - ◉ Broadband.
   - ○ Modulated.
   - ○ Multicast.

2. **Which broadband communication method uses existing telephone lines to transmit digital signals?**
   - ○ Cable modem
   - ◉ DSL
   - ○ ISDN
   - ○ Fiber
   - ○ Satellite

3. **Which broadband communication method uses the same physical media to provide high-speed transmission of data and television signals?**
   - ◉ Cable modem
   - ○ DSL
   - ○ ISDN
   - ○ Fiber
   - ○ Satellite

4. **Which broadband communication method uses light to carry signals?**
   - ○ Cable modem
   - ○ DSL
   - ○ ISDN
   - ◉ Fiber
   - ○ Satellite

5. **Which are wired connection technologies?**
   - ☐ Bluetooth
   - ☑ ISDN
   - ☑ Dial-up connections
   - ☐ Wi-Fi

6. Which are wireless connection technologies?

- ☑ Bluetooth
- ☐ Fiber optic
- ☑ Cellular WAN
- ☐ Twisted-pair

7. Which wireless technology provides broadband Internet coverage in rural or remote areas?

- ○ Cellular WAN
- ◉ Satellite
- ○ Wi-Fi
- ○ Infrared
- ○ Bluetooth

8. Which wireless technology is a short-range connection method requiring direct line of sight?

- ○ Cellular WAN
- ○ Satellite
- ○ Wi-Fi
- ◉ Infrared
- ○ Bluetooth

9. When would some of the different Internet connection types be used and when do you think you might encounter them within the workplace?

A: Answers will vary depending on the physical location and the needs of the organization, but might include wireless connectivity for a workplace that has a lot of laptops deployed.

10. If you have remote employees that need to connect to the corporate network but they are located in a remote area with no access to broadband Internet service, what do you think is the best Internet connection method to use in this situation?

A: Answers will vary, but will most likely include using either dial-up or satellite. However, because this employee needs to access the corporate network through a VPN connection, satellite will probably provide the faster connection. In some cases, tethering to a cell phone or connecting to a wireless network device is an option, but this will all depend on how remote the employee's location is and whether they can get a strong cellular signal.

ACTIVITY 8–6: Identifying Networking Tools

1. You need to determine if a cable is carrying a signal. Which networking tools might help you?

- ☐ Crimpers
- ☑ Cable testers
- ☑ Multimeters
- ☐ Toner probe
- ☐ Punch down tool

2. You need to connect cable wires to a patch panel. Which networking tool might help you?

- ○ Crimpers
- ○ Loopback plug
- ◉ Punch down tool
- ○ Toner probe

ACTIVITY -7: Selecting and Using Networking Technologies

---

1. List the various networking technologies you would recommend for the My Footprint Sports retail outlet, and explain how each technology would support the employees' connectivity needs. Are there any network components that you would not employ? Are there any optional components? What are the pros and cons of implementing each one? You might wish to sketch a possible network design for this store to show the various connectivity components.

A: The new store will require a local Ethernet LAN installation, probably using a twisted-pair media with the appropriate cables and connectors. If the store is configured to use the client-server resources available at headquarters, rather than in a workgroup, you do not have to worry about configuring multiple user accounts on the individual computers. Because the store employees need to communicate globally, they will need Internet access. It is unlikely that My Footprint Sports has a direct Internet connection, so the company will need to contract with a business-oriented ISP. Because of their communications needs, employees will need a high-speed, continuous high-bandwidth Internet connection. Selecting the particular connection technology will be a matter of negotiating the best combination of price and service with the available local ISPs. For Internet access, the local computers will need to run the TCP/IP protocol. There is no indication from the scenario that the store will need to run any legacy network protocols other than TCP/IP. The ISP will probably provide addressing and name resolution services. Employees will need email access. Because they are part of a larger organization, My Footprint Sports, rather than the ISP, will probably provide the email infrastructure and email addresses within the **www.myfootprintsports.local domain.** My Footprint Sports probably has email servers already implemented to provide SMTP services as well as POP3 and/or IMAP4 client protocols, depending upon the email client software in use at the company. The store will need to install Wi-Fi-capable WAPs to support the integration of the wireless laptop users with the wired Ethernet in the rest of the store, as well as for other workers with laptops. Other types of wireless support might or might not be needed depending upon the requirements of individual users; for example, there might be some staff who use Bluetooth to synchronize mobile-device data with their personal computers, and there might be wireless infrared peripheral devices in use, such as wireless mice. Staff do need to communicate globally. If they need to make a lot of international phone calls, the team might consider implementing VoIP connections to make voice phone calls over the existing Internet connections and save the incremental phone charges. Any other specialized networking tools, such as FTP client software, will depend upon the corporation's and individual users' communications needs.

ACTIVITY 9-1: Discussing Wireless SOHO Security Methods

What security methods do you think a SOHO organization is most likely invest in and implement? What methods do you think they are less likely to implement?

A: Answers will vary, but the more likely methods may include implementing encryption, implementing a firewall, and changing the default user name and passwords. Methods less likely to be implemented may include changing the SSID of the router and properly placing the WAP, because these methods are not as common and can take more expertise to implement correctly.

ACTIVITY 11-2: Examining Mobile Security

---

1. **How can the use of mobile devices by employees affect the security of an organization as a whole?**

   A: Mobile devices can function much like a regular computer; therefore, when they are used to send and receive corporate emails, and to access systems and data within the corporate network, they are a vulnerability. If lost or stolen, the devices can be used to access sensitive data or launch attacks. Mobile devices should be secured just as any other system on the corporate network.

2. **Examine some of the features on a mobile device. Using the main menu, open the security settings for your device. What specific security settings are available?**

   A: Answers will vary, but may include a screen lock setting, device encryption options, and GPS tracking features.
   Some participants might be hesitant to share their mobile devices with others. If possible, demonstrate different security features on mobile devices that are available to you.

ACTIVITY 12-1: Identifying Printer Technologies

1. **What printer process is displayed here?**
   - ○ Laser
   - ○ Impact
   - ◉ Inkjet
   - ○ Thermal

2. **What printer is displayed here?**
   - ○ Inkjet
   - ○ Thermal
   - ○ Laser
   - ◉ MFD

3. **True or False? The fuser assembly is a component of a laser printer.**
   - ☑ True
   - ☐ False

ACTIVITY 13-1: Identifying Security Concepts

1. **Katie works in a high-security government facility. When she comes to work in the morning, she places her hand on a scanning device in her building's lobby, which reads her handprint and compares it to a master record of her handprint in a database to verify her identity. This is an example of:**
   - ◉ Biometric authentication
   - ○ Multi-factor authentication
   - ○ Data encryption
   - ○ Tokens

2. **How does multi-factor authentication enhance security?**

   A: Requiring two or more authentication factors to gain access to a resource or physical location enhances the security of the resource or location, because more than one password, token, or biometric attribute is needed to gain access. Multi-factor authentication can be particularly secure with biometric, or "who you are," authentication where at least one of the factors is a unique physical characteristic of an individual.

3. While assigning privileges to the accounting department in your organization, Cindy, a human resource administrative assistant, insists that she needs access to the employee records database in order to fulfill change of address requests from employees. After checking with her manager and referring to the organization's access control security policy, Cindy's job role does not fall into the authorized category for access to that database. What security concept is being practiced in this scenario?

- ○ The use of strong passwords.
- ○ User education.
- ◉ The principle of least privilege.
- ○ Common user security practices.

ACTIVITY 13-2: Identifying Common Security Threats and Vulnerabilities

1. Recently there has been a number of issues within your organization due to the reorganization of a few departments and the reassignment of job roles. As a result, a disgruntled employee removes the UPS on a critical server system and then cuts power to the system, causing costly downtime. This physical threat is what type of threat?

   A: Because the attacker is within the organization and has access to cause damage to the critical server systems area and it was launched by an employee, this is both man-made and internal.

2. John is given a laptop for official use and is on a business trip. When he arrives at his hotel, he turns on his laptop and finds a wireless access point with the name of the hotel, which he connects to for sending work-related communications. This leaves him open for which type of wireless threat?

   A: Depending on the way the access point is configured, an attack can be achieved through a rogue access point or an evil twin. This situation leaves John open to an unauthorized wireless access point that has no security on a corporate or private network, which can give attackers access to the network and possibly lead to other types of attacks.
   As you discuss the third question, ask participants what they think makes up an acceptable password policy. You might want to mention solutions such as password vault software that can store users' passwords securely, yet enable users to access resources if they forget a password that is stored in the vault.

3. Lucy wants to use "password1" as her system login password. This new password meets all strong password requirements. What do you think of the password she chose?

   A: There are two issues with this password. The first is that the organization should require not only letters and numbers, but at least one special character, too. The other issue is that Lucy's password is too common and easy to crack because its a common string of letters that make up a word.

ACTIVITY 13-3: Identifying Security Protection Measures

1. Your organization has issued a new security policy that states that any laptop, desktop, or mobile device that is replaced must be completely sanitized to ensure that all sensitive data is removed. What sanitation method would you suggest to ensure that the data cannot be recovered?

   A: A combination of data wiping, degaussing, overwriting, and then physically destroying the drive will be the best approach.

2. What is the difference between a host-based and network-based firewalls?

A: Host-based firewalls are used to protect a single computer, while network-based firewalls are installed to protect all the computers on a network.

3. **What physical security measures are familiar to you and how have they been implemented?**

    A: Answers will vary, but may include locked doors and identification systems. Most organizations will have some sort of main entrance identification system in place to allow entry to employees and restrict access to visitors.

ACTIVITY -5: Comparing Workgroup Security and Domain Security

2. **Is the new password accepted?**

    A: Yes, the new password is accepted.

4. **Is the new password accepted?**

    A: No, the new password is not accepted.

6. **How will you explain the results of the test you conducted?**

    A: In a workgroup environment, unless an administrator has implemented password strength restrictions, they are not enabled by default. However, in a Windows Active Directory domain, password strength and other restrictions are enabled by default in the default domain policy.

ACTIVITY 14-2: Troubleshooting Hard Drive Problems

1. **A user has reported that there are grinding noises coming from her computer case. Once you take a closer look, you suspect that it is the hard drive. What is the possible cause and solution to this type of issue?**

    ◉   The hard drive is physically damaged, probably due to a head crash, so the drive must be replaced.

    ○   A virus has attacked the hard drive, so use antivirus software to mitigate the issues.

    ○   Data is corrupt on the drive, and has not been shut down correctly.

    To create this issue in Step 2, you could replace the drive with a non-functioning one, loosen the cables on the drive, or change the master or Cable Select setting on multiple drives so that they are all set as slaves. If you introduce different causes to different systems, you can have participants observe as each symptom is resolved.

3. **You recently installed a second hard drive into a user's system. He is now reporting that the drive is not showing up or is not recognized. You know that one of the things you forgot to check when you first performed the installation is CMOS settings for the drive. What in particular do you need to check in CMOS for this problem?**

    A: You need to verify that drive is enabled in CMOS and that the correct device settings for the hard drive are listed.

4. **Another thing you should check when a second hard drive is not recognized is that the drive was installed correctly. What exactly should you be checking?**

    A: Verify that the power cable is connected to the drive, that the power cable voltages are correct, and that the data cable is connected correctly to the drive and to the controller or host bus adapter (HBA). For a PATA drive, verify that it is set to master, Cable Select, or slave, as appropriate to its place in the drive chain. For a SCSI drive, verify that the termination and SCSI ID are set properly for its place in the SCSI chain. For a SATA drive, restart the setup process and press **F6** when prompted to install the driver.

5. **A second hard drive was properly installed, but you cannot access it by its drive letter. What should be your next step?**

A: Use DOS or Windows disk utilities to verify that the drive has been properly partitioned and formatted.

6. **A user is encountering the following problem: Her computer boots fine and everything works until the user tries to access data on the second hard drive, the D drive. The message "Can't Access This Drive" is displayed when she tries to access the D drive. The user would also like an explanation about what the error message means. List some of the steps you might take to resolve this problem.**

A: You see the "Can't Access This Drive" message when you attempt to access a drive that is not readable, or if the drive does not exist. Troubleshooting steps you should take include: determine if the user actually has a D drive; attempt to copy a file from the D drive to C or from C to D; run the Windows 7 error-checking option. Open **Computer,** display the pop-up menu for the drive you want to check, and select **Properties.** On the **Tools** tab, in the **Error-checking** section, select **Check Now** and then select **Start** to determine if there are errors; if none of the earlier steps fixed the problem, verify that there is a recent backup and try reformatting the drive; and if the previous step does not fix the problem, replace the drive.

7. **When a user tries to access the hard drive containing his data, the system locks up and makes a clicking sound. From the command prompt, he can change to drive D, but when he tries to access a file or list the files on the drive, it locks up and begins clicking again. What steps might you take to attempt to resolve this problem? What is the most likely cause of the problem?**

A: You could try running the Windows 7 error-checking option in the **Tools** pane of the **Local Disk Properties** dialog box. You could also try an older version of Scandisk from a removable disk to try to identify and repair the errors it encounters. Definitely back up the data if you can get to any of it. You can try using other software utilities to recover the data or take the drive to a data recovery facility. You will probably need to replace the hard drive. The most likely cause of this problem is a bad hard drive—some of the sectors on the hard drive are probably damaged.

8. **A user reports that some of his folders have begun disappearing and some folder and file names are scrambled with strange characters in their names. What steps might you take to attempt to resolve this problem? What is the most likely cause of the problem?**

A: You could try running the Windows 7 error-checking option in the **Tools** pane of the **Local Disk Properties** dialog box. Definitely back up the data if you can get to any of it. You can try using other software utilities to recover the data or take the drive to a data recovery facility. You will probably need to replace the hard drive. You should also check the system for viruses because the result of some infections looks like this problem. If it is not caused by a virus, the most likely cause of this problem is a bad hard drive.

9. **A user is questioning the difference between the sizes in GB and bytes. Why is there such a big difference? The disk reports in some places as 9.33 GB and in others as 10,025,000,960 bytes. Why is it not 10 GB?**

A: Hard drive manufacturers usually round 1,024 bytes to 1,000 because it is easier to work with round numbers. By the time you get up to billions of bytes, those extra 24 bytes really add up.

ACTIVITY 14-3: Troubleshooting CPU Issues

1. **What initial steps should you take to identify and resolve a potential CPU problem?**
   ☐ Replace the CPU with a known-good processor.
   ☑ Verify that the CPU fan and other cooling systems are installed and functional.
   ☐ Replace the motherboard.
   ☑ If the CPU is overclocked, throttle it down to the manufacturer-rated clock speed.

2. All other diagnostic and corrective steps have failed. You need to verify that it is the CPU itself that is defective. What should you do?

- ◉ Replace the CPU with a known-good chip.
- ○ Remove all the adapter cards.
- ○ Reinstall the operating system.
- ○ Replace the motherboard.

ACTIVITY 14-4: Troubleshooting Motherboards

1. What should you do to resolve this issue?

   A: The user is experiencing a problem that indicates the CMOS memory on the motherboard has failed. Replace the CMOS memory.

2. What should you do to resolve this issue?

   A: The user is experiencing problems that indicate the cooling fan on either the computer's processor or the motherboard is bad. Open the case to verify which cooling fan has failed. If it is the cooling fan on the CPU, replace the CPU. If it is the power supply's cooling fan, replace the power supply.

3. What should you do to resolve this issue?

   A: The user is experiencing a problem that indicates either the computer's CPU or the motherboard has failed. First, verify that the CPU is seated properly and that its cooling fan is working. If you have an available replacement CPU, try replacing the computer's CPU to see if that resolves the problem. If it does not, perform tasks such as scanning for viruses, verifying that all motherboard components are seated properly, updating the computer's BIOS, making sure all cooling systems are functioning properly, and, finally, replacing the motherboard.

ACTIVITY 14-5: Troubleshooting RAM Issues

1. After troubleshooting this trouble ticket, you have discovered symptoms of a memory problem. What factors could cause sudden memory problems in this situation?

   - ☑ New virus
   - ☑ Power loss
   - ☐ New memory not compatible
   - ☑ Power surge

2. What steps would you take to resolve this trouble ticket?

   A: First, verify that the correct memory was installed on the system, then check to see if the BIOS manufacturer has released any upgrades that would resolve the problem and try swapping memory around in the memory banks, and finally, verify that memory was installed and configured correctly.

3. Why is the user experiencing the problem only when additional applications are opened?

   - ○ There is not enough memory in the system.
   - ◉ Memory errors are occurring in one of the higher memory modules.
   - ○ The memory modules are incompatible with one another.

ACTIVITY 14-6: Troubleshooting Power Supplies

1. **What would you do to resolve this problem?**

   A: Unplug the power cord. Remove the system cover. Using compressed air, remove the dust from around the fan spindle. Verify that there is no obvious reason the fan is not spinning. Replace the power cord and restart the computer. Verify that the computer starts properly. If these actions did not fix the problem, you would need to replace the power supply. Leaving the problem alone would allow heat to build up to dangerous levels, causing serious damage to the system.

2. **What would you do to resolve this problem?**

   A: An odor coming from the power supply could be a sign that there is something wrong. Because you have just replaced the unit, verify that all the connections are secure and that the fan is functioning. Restart the machine and verify that the power supply is running as it should. Once the functionality of the unit is verified, then odor is probably a result of installing a new power supply unit. If the odor does not go away in a few days, then contact the power supply manufacturer.
   If you have power supply testers available, you can have students use them instead of multimeters. You will need to lead them through the testing process.

4. **What would you do to resolve this problem?**

   A: Verify that the power cord is securely connected to the power supply and to the electrical outlet on the surge protector. Verify that the surge protector is turned on and plugged in. Verify that the surge protector is working by plugging in a known good electrical device and turning it on. If the device did not turn on, check to see whether any reset buttons need to be reset on the surge protector, or check the electric outlet's circuit breaker. Restart the computer. If these actions did not solve the problem, you would need to replace the power supply.

ACTIVITY 14-7: Troubleshooting Laptop Issues

1. **You received a user complaint about a laptop being extremely hot to the touch. What actions should you take in response to this issue?**

   A: Overheating can be a sign that dust and dirt is restricting the necessary airflow within the device, so start by cleaning the ventilation duct with compressed air and then make sure that the device is getting proper air circulation around the outside of the case.

2. **Which components are typically soldered to a laptop motherboard and cannot be replaced without replacing the entire board?**

   A: Typically, the processor, the AC port, and USB ports are attached directly on the board and cannot be replaced without replacing the whole laptop motherboard.

3. **What internal components can be independently replaced within a laptop?**

   A: Generally, you can replace the hard drive, RAM, the fan, the screen, the battery, and the keyboard.

ACTIVITY 14-8: Troubleshooting Common Printer Issues

1. **A user reports that they cannot print from Microsoft® Excel® to a network printer. After determining that other users are printing from that printer with no issues, what steps should you take next to troubleshoot the problem?**

   A: Check the network availability of the network printer, then make sure that the printer is not paused. If the user can print from other applications, then the problem might be with Excel, but not with the printer or print driver.

2. **A user reports that he is attempting to print to his local printer, but none of the print jobs are printing. When you arrive at his desk, you check out the printer hardware and consumables and everything seems to be fine. When you double-click the printer in the Printers folder, you see the job is listed in the queue. What should you try next?**

   A: You should check to make sure that the printer is not paused, then try stopping and starting the print spooler service. If resetting the print spooler service does not resolve the problem, try adjusting the spool settings on the printer until you can print from all Windows programs.

3. **Another user says all his printouts look garbled. You check the properties of the print object in the Printers And Faxes window and find that the printer model listed in the Properties dialog box is not the same as the printer model on the printer itself. What should you do?**

   A: Remove the printer and reinstall it using the correct printer driver.

4. **A user reports that inkjet printers in the corporate training area have various problems, including no output, fuzzy output, and generally poor print quality. List some of the steps you should take to resolve these problems.**

   A: If the print quality is poor, perform one or more cleaning cycles. Clean the printer to make sure that there is no lint or other debris dragging across the wet ink. Change to a paper specifically designed for inkjet printers. Next, If the cartridge was recently reinstalled, make sure that the user pulled the tape off before installing the ink cartridge. Verify that the cartridge is seated correctly in the printer. Verify that the correct cartridge is installed. You might need to try a brand-new (not refilled) ink cartridge. Perform an alignment after installing new cartridges as per the documentation for the printer. If the printhead is separate from the ink cartridge, you might also need to replace the printhead. In addition, if there is nothing printing, check the documentation or website for the printer to see if there are any troubleshooting tips or diagnostic tools.

ACTIVITY 15-1: Identifying System Errors

---

1. **A user calls saying that her screen occasionally goes blue and the system shuts down. What should you advise her to do?**

   ○ Call the help desk the next time the shutdown is in progress.

   ○ Reboot manually after the automatic restart.

   ◉ Record as much information from the top of the blue screen as she can so that you can research the particular error.

   ○ Run the system in Safe Mode.

2. **A user reports that his Microsoft® Word window has gone blank and he cannot type text. What are possible approaches to resolving his problem?**

   ☐ Reboot the computer.

   ☐ Run another copy of Microsoft Word.

   ☑ Wait a few minutes to see if the application returns to normal.

   ☑ Use Task Manager to shut down the application if it has a status of "Not Responding."

3. **A user reports that her monitor display is "fuzzy" and hard to look at. What is a possible cause of this problem?**

   ◉ Display settings for the monitor are incorrectly configured.

   ○ The power cord is unplugged.

   ○ The monitor cable is not properly seated.

○   The monitor device is disabled in Windows.

4. A user reports that while she is editing a document, she receives an "invalid working directory" message from her application. What is the best diagnostic question to ask in response to this error?

○   Did the application work yesterday?

○   Is anyone else having this problem?

○   Who installed the application?

◉   Have you deleted any files or folders lately?

ACTIVITY 15-3: Troubleshooting Network Issues

1. You receive a call from a client who reports that she is unable to access any websites in Internet Explorer. While talking with this user, you verify that she can ping the server's IP address on her network segment, the IP address of the default gateway, and the IP address of a computer on another network segment. You also determine that none of the other users on her network can connect to websites in Internet Explorer. What might be the problem?

   A: The problem is most likely that her network's DNS server is down.

2. One of your clients reports that he is unable to see computers when he opens the Network window. Which step should you take first?

   ◉   Determine if any of the other users on the network are experiencing problems.

   ○   Ask the client to ping another computer on his network.

   ○   Ask the client to verify that the DHCP server is running.

   ○   Ask the client to run ipconfig /release and ipconfig /renew.

3. A user is trying to reach a website and is experiencing problems. How can you examine the path of the transmissions?

   A: Use the tracert command to trace the routes of packets between various source and destination hosts. This can help you locate a packet looping between routers, or the point at which a route fails.

4. A client reports that he is unable to connect to any computers on the network or the Internet. You have him run the ipconfig command, and all his TCP/IP addressing parameters are correct. When you have him ping other computers on the network, his computer is unable to reach them. This computer is the only one that is experiencing a problem. What should you check next?

   ○   That the DHCP server is on and functioning properly

   ○   That the default gateway is on and functioning properly

   ○   That the DNS server is on and functioning properly

   ◉   That his computer's network cable is plugged into both the network card and the wall jack

ACTIVITY 15-4: Troubleshooting Common Security Issues

1. John has reported that a pop-up security alert keeps coming up when he switches application windows on his laptop. What do you suspect is going on with his computer?

   A: Often, malware is delivered through legitimate-looking methods, such as a Windows security alert. In this case, his laptop was likely infected with a virus.

2. You have been asked to provide a list of common malware symptoms for users to be aware of in order to prevent security breaches within your organization. What common symptoms would you provide?

A: Answers will vary, but should include: keeping an eye out for unusual email messages that may be a hoax or social engineering attempt. Do not open or forward unrecognized email attachments. Avoid downloading any software from the Internet that has not been approved by the IT department.

3. **True or False? The safest way to deal with unsolicited email is to delete it without opening it.**

   ☑ True

   ☐ False

4. **Alex reports that in the midst of composing an email at work, an unfamiliar pop-up appeared on his screen, indicating that his email connection has been dropped and that he should log on again by using the pop-up screen. What do you suggest he do in this situation?**

   A: First, you let him know that he was right to report the incident without entering the information in the pop-up window. Next, you should run an antivirus scan to identify if the computer is infected and remove any viruses until the system is "clean."

Glossary

8008
Introduced by Intel in 1972, the 8008 was the first microprocessor to be supported by a high-level language compiler.

802.11
A family of specifications for wireless LAN communication.

802.11a
A fast, secure, but relatively expensive protocol for wireless communication. The 802.11a protocol supports speeds up to 54 Mbps in the 5 GHz frequency.

802.11b
Also called Wi-Fi, short for "wireless fidelity," 802.11b is probably the most common and certainly the least expensive wireless network protocol used to transfer data among computers with wireless network cards or between a wireless computer or device and a wired LAN. The 802.11b protocol provides for an 11 Mbps transfer rate in the 2.4 GHz frequency.

802.11e
A wireless LAN communication standard for home and business implementations.

802.11g
A specification for wireless data throughput at the rate of up to 54 Mbps in the 2.4 GHz band that is a potential replacement for 802.11b.

802.11n
A recent specification for wireless data throughput at a rate up to 600 Mbps in the 2.4 GHz or 5 GHz range. Released in 2009.

abacus
An early calculating instrument that uses sliding beads in columns that are divided in two by a center bar.

accelerometer
Mobile technology that can determine the orientation of a device with a sensor that measures the acceleration of the device direction.

Action Center
A utility unique to the Windows 7 Control Panel in which notifications can be enabled or disabled, and alerts are consolidated into a single location.

activity light
An indicator on a network adapter that flickers when packets are received or sent.

administrative shares
Hidden shares created by default on every Windows system. If administrative shares are deleted, by default, the system re-creates them when it restarts.

adware
Unwanted software loaded onto a system for the purposes of presenting commercial advertisements to the user.

632 | CompTIA® A+® Certification: A Comprehensive Approach (Exams 220-801 and 220-802)

Aero
A color scheme available in Windows Vista and Windows 7 that provides a visually rich experience, with a glossy and transparent interface and dynamic visual effects.

AES
(Advanced Encryption Standard) A symmetric 128-, 192-, or 256-bit block cipher based on the Rijndael algorithm developed by Belgian cryptographers Joan Daemen and Vincent Rijmen and adopted by the U.S. government as its encryption standard to replace DES.

AGP
(Accelerated Graphics Port) A bus architecture based on PCI and designed specifically to speed up the rendering of 3D graphics.

AIO MFD
(all-in-one multi-function device) A small sized MFD for home users with basic printing, scanning, and copying functions.

allocation unit
Same as cluster.

analog signal
A signal that oscillates over time between minimum and maximum values and can take on any value between those limits.

analog transmission
The transfer of information in the form of a continuous wave.

Analytical Engine
Charles Babbage's vision of a mechanical calculator that would follow programmed instructions to perform any mathematical operations. The engine could store results for use later, and look up values in tables and call on standard subroutines.

Android
An operating system for mobile devices such as smartphones.

anti-spyware software
Software that is specifically designed to protect systems against spyware attacks.

antivirus software
An application that scans files for executable code that matches patterns known to be common to viruses, and monitors systems for activity associated with viruses.

AP
(access point) A device or software that facilitates communication and provides enhanced security to wireless devices.

APIPA
(Automatic Private IP Addressing) A feature of Windows that enables a DHCP client computer to configure itself automatically with a random IP address in the range of 169.254.0.1 to 169.254.255.254 if there is no DHCP server available.

ASR
(Automated System Recovery) A Windows XP troubleshooting tool that enables you to back up data and Windows installation source files for rebuilding a failed system.

ATA
(Advanced Technology Attachment) The official ANSI term for IDE drives.

ATX
An older motherboard that was introduced by Intel in 1995 to provide better I/O support, lower cost, easier use, and better processor support than even earlier form factors.

audio/video editing workstation
A powerful computer setup that supports the editing of audio and video recordings.

AUP
(acceptable use policy) A policy that includes the practices and guidelines that should be followed by employees when using and accessing company resources and computer equipment.

auto negotiation
Negotiates a speed that is compatible with the network router or switch.

backlight
The typical form of illumination used in a full-sized LCD display.

badges
Also called security cards, that can be used to swipe through an identification system or can be configured as a proximity card and activated automatically when the card is within a specified distance from the system

baseband
A transmission scheme where a single signal sends data using the entire bandwidth of the transmission media. Compare with broadband.

battery backup
See UPS.

biconic
A screw-on type connector with a tapered sleeve that is fixed against guided rings and screws onto the threaded sleeve to secure the connection.

biometrics
Authentication schemes based on individuals' physical characteristics.

BIOS
(Basic Input/Output System) A set of instructions that is stored in ROM and that is used to start the most basic services of a computer system.

BIOS memory
Special memory that keeps track of its data even when the power is turned off, and is stored in EEPROMs.

BitLocker
A security feature in Windows 7 and Windows Server 2008 that provides full disk encryption protection for your operating system as well as all the data stored on the operating system volume.

blackout
A complete loss of electrical power.

bluejacking
A method used by attackers to send out unwanted Bluetooth signals from PDAs, mobile phones, and laptops to other Bluetooth-enabled devices.

bluesnarfing
A process in which attackers gain access to unauthorized information on a wireless device using a Bluetooth connection.

Bluetooth
A wireless radio technology that facilitates short-range (usually less than 30 feet) wireless communication between devices such as personal computers, laptop, mobile phones, wireless headsets, and gaming consoles, thus creating a wireless personal area network.

BNC
(Bayonet Neill-Concelman) A twist lock connector that is used with coaxial cable to carry radio frequencies to and from devices.

bootrec
A command line tool used via the Command Prompt in the Windows Recovery Environment In Windows Vista and Windows 7 only to troubleshoot or repair startup issues.

bridge
A network device that divides a logical bus network into subnets.

brightness
The amount of light emitted from a display device, as measured in lumens.

broadband communications
A category of network transmission technologies that provide high throughput by splitting communications pathways into multiple channels transmitted simultaneously over the network media.

brownout
A temporary power reduction that is used by electrical power companies to deal with high power demands.

BSOD
The blue screen of death error that is severe enough to stop all processes and shut the system down without warning.

bus
In a computer system, a group of wires that connect components. They provide a pathway for data transfer.

bus topology
A network topology where all nodes receive transmitted data at the same time, no matter how the physical wiring is configured.

cable
Transmissions that use a cable television connection and a specialized interface device known as a cable modem to provide high-speed Internet access to homes and small businesses.

cable tester
An electrical instrument that verifies if a signal is present on a cable. Also called a media tester.

cache memory
A type of memory that services the CPU. Level 1 (L1) cache is built into the CPU chip. Level 2 cache (L2) feeds the L1 cache. L2 can be built into the CPU chip, reside on a separate chip, or be a separate bank of chips on the system board. If L2 is built into the CPU, then level 3 cache (L3) can be present on the system board.

CAN
(campus area network) A network that covers an area equivalent to an academic campus or business park.

carputers
Wireless computing devices that are specifically designed for cars. Many devices include features such as GPS, media players, USB, and Bluetooth communications.

CCFL
(cold cathode fluorescent lamp) A light source that uses electrodes and mercury vapor to create ultraviolet light.

cd
A command line tool used to view the drive letter and folder for your current location, and to change to another directory or folder.

CDFS
(Compact Disc File System) A file system standard for optical disc media that is supported by multiple operating system types.

cellular
Uses radio signals to transmit network data over the cellular telephone system.

chain of custody
The record of evidence history from collection, to presentation in court, to disposal.

chipset
The set of chips on the system board that support the CPU and other basic functions.

chkdsk
A command line tool used to identify hard drive errors and correct the error, if possible.

Class A addresses
An IP subnetting scheme that provides 16,777,214 nodes per network.

Class B addresses
An IP subnetting scheme that provides 65,534 nodes per network.

Class C addresses
An IP subnetting scheme that provides 254 nodes per network.

client
A computer that makes use of the services and resources of other computers.

client–side virtualization
Takes place at the endpoints and separates the elements of a user's logical desktop environment—the applications, operating system, programs, etc.—and divides them from each other and from the physical hardware or a physical machine.

client/server network
A network in which some computers act as servers to provide special services for other client computers.

closed source
Refers to any application code, programming code, or operating system code that is not published or shared with the community.

cluster
A group of sectors that is the smallest unit of storage allotted on a given drive.

CMOS
(Complementary Metal-Oxide-Semiconductor) An old style of static memory that was used to store information about the computer setup that the system BIOS refers to each time the computer is started.

coax
Pronounced "CO-ax." A common abbreviation for coaxial cable.

coaxial cable
A type of cable that features a central conductor surrounded by braided or foil shielding. A dialectric insulator separates the conductor and shield and the entire package is wrapped in an insulating layer called a jacket. The data signal is transmitted over the central conductor. The outer shielding serves to reduce electromagnetic interference.

Component Services
An administrative tool that is used to deploy component applications and configure the behaviors of components and applications on the system.

component/RGB
A type of analog video information that is transmitted or stored as two or more separate signals.

composite video
The format of an analog (picture only) signal before it is combined with a sound signal and modulated onto a radio frequency (RF) carrier.

computer case
The enclosure that holds all of the components of your computer.

computer connection
A hardware component that enables the computer to communicate with internal or external devices.

computer forensics
Collecting and analyzing data from storage devices, computer systems, networks, and wireless communications and presenting this information as a form of evidence in a court of law.

computer image
A replica of the reference computer's hard disk and contains the operating system software used in the imaging process.

Computer Management
The primary administrative tool used to manage and configure the system. It consolidates several administrative utilities into a single console to provide easy access to the most common system tools.

controller
See disk controller.

cooling system
A system unit component that prevents damage to computer parts by dissipating the heat generated inside a computer chassis.

corona
An assembly within a laser printer that contains a wire (the corona wire), which is responsible for charging the paper.

CPU
(central processing unit) The main chip on the system board, the CPU performs software instructions and mathematical and logical calculations. Also referred to as the microprocessor or processor.

CRT display
(cathode ray tube) A display device that uses three electron beams, one for each primary color (red, blue, and green), within a vacuum tube to create images on a fluorescent screen.

data backup
A system-maintenance task that enables you to store copies of critical files and folders on another medium for safekeeping.

data restoration
A system recovery task that enables you to access the backed-up data.

Data Sources
An administrative tool that uses Open Database Connectivity (ODBC) to move data between different types of databases on the system.

data synchronization
The process of automatically merging and updating common data that is stored on multiple devices.

data wiping
A method used to remove any sensitive data from a mobile device and permanently delete it.

daughter board
Any circuit board that plugs into another circuit board.

DB-15
See VGA.

dead pixels
Pixels that do not display light as expected and will show up as small black dots.

Defender
The anti-spyware software that is included with Windows XP, Vista, and 7 installations.

definition
A code pattern that identifies a virus. Also called a signature.

del
A command line tool used to delete a file.

device driver
Software that enables the operating system and a peripheral device to communicate with each other. Often referred to as driver software or driver.

Device Manager
An administrative tool that is used to manage and configure system devices in a hardware profile.

DHCP
(Dynamic Host Configuration Protocol) A network service that provides automatic assignment of IP addresses and other TCP/IP configuration information on network systems that are configured as DHCP clients.

dial-ups
Local-loop phone connections that use modems and standard telephone technology.

digital signal
An electrical signal that holds only two values: ones and zeros.

digital transmission
The transfer of information in a signal that is comprised only of ones and zeroes.

DIMM
(Dual In-line Memory Modules) A RAM form factor that is found in most systems and that has a 64-bit data path.

diode
An electronic component that acts like a one-way valve. Diodes are often used to change Alternating Current (AC) to Direct Current (DC), as temperature or light sensors, and as light emitters.

DIP switches
A switch that is connected to the motherboard that allows you to configure the electric circuits located on the board.

direct thermal printer
A thermal printer that uses heated pins to form images directly onto specially coated thermal paper.

directory
A component in a file system hierarchy that provides a container to organize files and other directories (folders). Also called a folder.

directory service
On a network, a centralized database that includes objects such as servers, clients, computers, user names, and passwords, and provides centralized administration and authentication.

discovery mode
A device mode that will transmit a friendly signal to another device in close proximity.

disk controller
Circuitry that manages the transfer of data to and from a disk drive, whether it is a floppy disk drive, a hard disk drive, or an optical disk drive. The disk controller provides the communication path between the CPU and the disk drive.

disk partition
An isolated section of a disk that functions like a separate physical drive.

diskpart
A command line tool used to create, delete, or generally manage any hard drive partitions on the system.

display device
A personal computer component that enables users to view the text and graphical data output from a computer.

DisplayPort
A digital display standard that aims to replace DVI and VGA standards.

dissipative material
A conductor, but with high resistance that loses its electrical charge slowly.

DMZ
(demilitarized zone) A small section of a private network that is located between two firewalls and made available for public access.

DNS
(Domain Name System) The primary name resolution service on the network that maps computer names to their associated IP addresses.

docking station
Desktop devices that connect portable computers to standard desktop peripherals without the need to connect and disconnect the peripherals themselves when the user switches from stationary to mobile use.

domain
A Microsoft network model that an administrator implements by grouping computers together for the purpose of sharing a centralized user account database. Sharing this user account database enables users to use these accounts to log on at any computer in the domain.

domain controller
A server that stores the user account database for the domain and is responsible for authenticating users when they log on to the domain.

dongle
A short adapter cable used to connect a PC Card to a full-sized connector, or a device that attaches to a computer port to control access to a particular application.

dot-matrix printer
An impact printer that forms images out of dots on paper by using a set of pins to strike an inked ribbon.

drive rails
Metal strips that can be screwed onto an internal drive before installation.

DSL
A broadband technology that transmits digital signals over existing phone lines.

dump file
The file that stores the contents of a memory dump.

duplex scanning
A feature that scans both sides of a document automatically.

duplexing
Disk mirroring in which the two drives in the mirror each have a dedicated disk controller.

duplexing
The process that enables automatic printing on both sides of printing media, such as paper and envelopes.

duplexing assembly
A component that moves printing media through a printer twice to allow for double-sided printing.

DVI
(Digital Video Interface) A cable that keeps data in digital form from the computer to the monitor.

dye sublimation printer
Same as thermal dye transfer printer.

dynamic addressing
A method used to assign addresses using the DHCP service.

EAS
(Exchange ActiveSync) Microsoft's synchronization protocol that enables mobile devices to connect to an Exchange Server to access mail, calendar and contacts.

Easy Transfer
A built-in data migration utility in Windows Vista and Windows 7 that helps transfer files, data, and settings from one personal computer to another.

ECC
(Error Correction Code) An error correction method that uses several bits for error-checking.

EDSAC
(Electronic Delay Storage Automatic Computer) A well-engineered machine built by Maurice Wilkes and colleagues at the University of Cambridge Mathematics Lab in 1949 that was a productive tool for mathematicians.

EDVAC
(Electronic Discrete Variable Automatic Computer) The first computer to use stored programs.

EEPROM
(electronically erasable programmable read-only memory) A ROM chip that can be reprogrammed by using software from the BIOS or chip manufacturer through the flashing process.

EIA
(Electronic Industries Alliance) A standards and trades organization that developed industry standards for technologies such as network cabling. The EIA ceased operations in February 2011.

electrical interference
A general term for unwanted signals on the network media that can interfere with network transmissions.

electrical noise
The same as electrical interference.

EMI
(electromagnetic interference) The degradation of signal that occurs when a magnetic field around one electrical circuit interferes with the signal being carried on an adjacent circuit.

emulator
The software installed that allows the computer to virtually run another operating system, or another instance of the same operating system.

encryption
The process of converting data into a form that is not easily recognized or understood by unauthorized entities.

ENIAC
(Electronic Numerical Integrator And Computer) Developed for the U.S. Army by J. Presper Eckert and John Mauchly at the University of Pennsylvania in Philadelphia. ENIAC was programmed by plugging in cords and setting thousands of switches to direct how 18,000 vacuum tubes would perform 5,000 calculations per second.

EP drum
(Electrostatic Photographic drum) The component in a laser printer that carries the

electrical charge to attract toner and then to transfer the toner to the paper.

ERD

(emergency repair disk) A Windows XP troubleshooting tool that stores the contents of the \Windows\Repair folder.

ESD

(electrostatic discharge) The phenomenon that occurs when electrons rush from one body with a static electrical charge to another with an unequal charge, following the path of least resistance.

Ethernet

A family of networking technologies that provide connectivity by using Ethernet network adapters, contention-based media access, and twisted pair, coax, or fiber media.

Event Viewer

An administrative tool that is used to view the contents of event logs, which contain information about significant events that occur on your computer.

evil twin

A rogue wireless access point that appears to be a legitimate one offered on the premises, but actually has been set up to eavesdrop on wireless communications among Internet surfers.

expansion card

A printed circuit board that is installed in a slot on a system board to provide special functions for customizing or extending a computer's capabilities. Also referred to as adapter card, I/O card, add-in, add-on, or board.

ExpressCard

A mobile expansion card designed by the PCMCIA to replace traditional PC Cards to provide PCI Express and USB 2.0 connectivity.

external device

Devices that provide alternative input or output methods or additional storage for personal computers.

external enclosure

A plastic barrier that protects the inner workings of a hard drive.

F-connector

A coaxial cable connector used to connect TV and FM antennas.

factory recovery partition

A hidden partition on the hard disk containing the files and settings needed to do a fresh install of the operating system and pre-installed applications in order to restore the computer to factory settings.

FC

(Face Contact) Connectors that use a heavy duty ferrule in the center for more mechanical stability than SMA or ST connectors.

FC-AL

(Fibre Channel-Arbitrated Loop) A Fibre Channel implementation that can connect up to 127 nodes without using a switch. All devices share the bandwidth, and only two can communicate with each other at the same time, with each node repeating the data to its adjacent node.

FDD

(floppy disk drive) A personal computer storage device that reads data from and writes data to removable disks made of flexible Mylar plastic covered with a magnetic coating, and enclosed in a stiff, protective, plastic case. It is a legacy technology.

FDDI

(Fiber Distributed Data Interface) A push/ pull type, two-channel snap-fit connector used for multimode fiber optic cable. Also called a MIC (Media Interface Connector).

fdisk

A command line tool used to partition or re-partition a hard drive.

fiber

A method used to connect devices the Internet using fiber optic cable.

fiber optic cable
A type of cable in which one or more glass or plastic strands, plus additional fiber strands or wraps, are surrounded by a protective outer jacket. Light pulses carry the signal through fiber optic cable.

file attribute
A characteristic that can be associated with a file or folder that provides the operating system with important information about the file or folder and how it is intended to be used by system users.

file recovery software
Software that can recover deleted files from your computer system.

file system
An inherent organizational structure that is used to organize and store data and information in a logical manner on a system's storage device.

Files and Settings Transfer Wizard
A system tool that is available in Windows XP and earlier versions of Windows that transfers files and settings from an old computer to a new computer.

firewall
A software program or hardware device that protects networks from unauthorized data by blocking unsolicited traffic.

FireWire connection
A high-speed serial bus developed by Apple and Texas Instruments that allows for the connection of up to 63 devices. Originally a trademarked term for IEEE 1394, but is now used interchangeably.

firmware
Software stored in memory chips that retains data whether or not power to the computer is on.

first response
Refers to the individual and the immediate actions that follow an incident.

fixboot
A command line tool used to create a new partition boot sector to a hard drive partition.

fixmbr
A command line tool used to repair the master boot recovery record of the boot partition.

flash drive
See SSD.

Flash memory
A type of non-volatile storage method that provides devices with quick access to data.

flashing
Updating firmware electronically.

folder
See directory.

form factor
The size and shape of a given component. Often used in terms of motherboard and drive characteristics.

formed–character printer
Any type of impact printer that functions like a typewriter, by pressing preformed characters against the ink ribbon to deposit the ink on the page.

frontlight
A form of lighting devices from the front of the display.

full duplex
Permits simultaneous two-way communication.

fuser assembly
A component in a laser printer that uses two rollers to heat toner particles, melting them onto the paper.

gadget
A mini application in Windows that can perform an information display task.

gaming PC
A computer that is equipped with powerful graphics capabilities, fast processing capabilities, and a large amount of memory, to

support the needs of gaming software applications.

GAN

(global area network) Any worldwide network.

gateway

A device, software, or system that converts data between incompatible systems.

generator

A power protection device that creates its own electricity through the use of motors.

geotracking

Uses the GPS mobile technology component to constantly track and update device's location with applications that share and use positioning information.

GPRS

(General Packet Radio Service) A standard for wireless communications that runs at speeds up to 115 kbps and that supports a wide range of bandwidths.

GPS

Technology that determines the location, weather, and time zone information of a device using the satellite navigation system.

GPU

(Graphics Processing Unit) An integrated circuit that is specially configured to accelerate the rendering of images that are intended for output to a display device.

gyroscope

Mobile technology that changes the orientation of the device by reading the x and y coordinates of device's position.

half duplex

Permits two-way communication, but only in one direction at a time.

hard drive sanitation

The method used to repeatedly delete and overwrite any traces or bits of sensitive data that may remain on a hard drive after data wiping has been done.

HDD

(hard disk drive) A personal computer storage device that uses fixed media and magnetic data storage.

HDMI

(High-Definition Multimedia Interface) The first industry-supported uncompressed, all-digital audio/video interface that uses a single cable to provide an interface between any audio/video source and an audio and/or video monitor.

heat sink

A cooling device that is directly attached to the CPU to provide direct cooling using metal fins to increase its surface area to aid in heat dissipation.

heavy–duty MFD

A large network-enabled MFD capable of handling the documentation needs of an entire office.

hertz

A measure of the number of cycles per second in an analog signal. One cycle per second equals one hertz.

Hibernate

A power option available in Windows environments in which the computer will store whatever is currently in memory on the hard disk and shut down, and then return to the state it was in upon hibernation when it is awakened.

high–level formatting

See standard formatting.

hoax

Any message containing incorrect or misleading information that is disseminated to multiple users through unofficial channels.

HomeGroup

A utility unique to the Windows 7 Control Panel through which users can set up a home network and add users or computers to the group in order to share resources such as files and printers.

host

In a centralized network, the computer that controls network functions. In a TCP/IP network, any computer.

host machine

In virtualization technology, the computer on which the virtual environment is installed and which manages the VMs.

host or personal firewall

A firewall installed on a single or home computer.

hot swapping

Replacing a device without needing to power down the PC during removal of the old device or installation of the new device. Also referred to as hot plug or hot insertion.

HTPC

(home theater PC) A computer system that is dedicated and configured to store and stream digital movies, either from a local hard drive or through an online subscription service.

hub

A device that connects multiple twisted pair segments together to form a single network segment.

HVD

(high-voltage differential) A SCSI signaling scheme that uses two wires, one for data and one for the inverse of data. HVD devices use high voltage and cannot be used on a single-ended SCSI chain.

hybrid topology

Any topology that exhibits the characteristics of more than one standard topology.

hypervisor

In virtualization technology, an application that is installed on the host machine and is used to configure and manage the VMs running on the host.

IEEE

(Institute of Electrical and Electronic Engineers) Pronounced "I-triple-E." An organization of scientists, engineers, and students of electronics and related fields whose technical and standards committees develop, publish, and revise computing and telecommunications standards.

IEEE 802.16

A series of wireless broadband standards wireless metropolitan area networks. See WiMAX.

imaging

The process of creating a computer image from one main computer, called the reference computer, and copying that image onto one or more other computers, called the target computers, as a method of installing an operating system and other programs.

IMAP4

(Internet Mail Access Protocol) A protocol used to retrieve email messages and folders from a mail server.

impact printer

Any type of printer that strikes a component directly against the paper or ink to create characters on the paper.

impersonation

An approach in which an attacker pretends to be someone they are not, typically an average user in distress, or a help-desk representative.

in-place upgrade

The process of installing a newer version of an operating system without first removing the existing operating system that is currently installed on the computer.

in-rush

A surge or spike that is caused when a device that uses a large amount of current is started.

incident report

A record of any instance where a person is injured or computer equipment is damaged due to environmental issues. Also, a record of accidents involving hazardous materials, such as chemical spills, that could have an impact on the environment itself.

inkjet printer

A printer that forms images by spraying ink on the paper.

input device

A personal computer component that enables users to enter data or instructions into a computer.

integrated circuit

An electronic component consisting of several transistors and resistors, connected together on a semiconductor chip.

integration components

Software available for Windows client virtualization solutions that enable you to share resources between the host operating system and the VM more efficiently.

interference

Within wireless networking, the phenomenon by which radio waves from other devices interfere with the 802.11 wireless signals.

Internet appliance

A device that allows quick easy access to the Internet.

inverter

A laptop component that converts DC power to AC power for the display.

iOS

The operating system designed for Apple devices. It is the base software that allows all other applications to run on an iPhone, iPod touch, or iPad.

IP

(Internet Protocol) A group of rules for sending data across a network. Communication on the Internet is based on the IP protocol.

IP version 6

An Internet standard that increases the available pool of IP addresses by implementing a 128-bit binary address space.

ipconfig

A command line tool used to verify the configuration of TCP/IP and to release or renew DHCP IP address leases.

IPv4 address

A 32-bit binary number assigned to a computer on a TCP/IP network.

IPv6 address

The unique 128 bit identification assigned to an interface on the IPv6 Internet.

IR

(infrared) A form of wireless transmission in which signals are sent via pulses of infrared light.

IR waves

(infrared waves) Electromagnetic waves with frequencies ranging from 300 GHz to 400 THz.

iSCSI

(Internet SCSI) A protocol that serializes SCSI commands so that they can be transferred over a TCP/IP network.

iSCSI Initiator

A Windows 7 Administrative Tool that enables you to configure advanced connections between network storage devices.

ISDN

A digital transmission technology that carries both voice and data over digital phone lines or PSTN wires.

ISP

(Internet Service Provider) A company that provides access to the Internet.

IV

(initialization vector) A technique used in cryptography to generate random numbers to be used along with a secret key to provide data encryption.

IV attack

An attack where the attacker is able to predict or control the IV of an encryption process, thus giving the attacker access to view the encrypted data that is supposed to be hidden from everyone else except the user or network.

jumper

A set of pins and connectors used to configure hardware settings. You physically connect or disconnect a circuit by adding or removing a jumper to the block.

jumper block
A small rectangular connector, from a pair of pins attached to the system board or add-on card.

key fobs
Security devices small enough to attach to a key chain that contain identification information used to gain access to a physical entryway.

kill
A command line tool used to stop or terminate a process that is running.

KVM switch
(keyboard, video, mouse) A device that allows a computer user to control multiple computers with a single keyboard and mouse, with the display sent to a single monitor.

LAN
(local area network) A self-contained network that spans a small area, such as a single building, floor, or room.

laptop computer
A complete computer system that is small, lightweight, and portable.

laser printer
A type of printer that forms high-quality images on one page of paper at a time, by using a laser beam, toner, and an electrophotographic drum.

LC
(Local Connector) A small form factor ceramic ferrule connector for both single-mode and multimode fiber.

LCD
(Liquid Crystal Display) A type of flat-panel display that uses Cold Cathode Fluorescent Lamps as the source of backlight and that comes in large-screen sizes of 17 inches and more, with high screen resolution and high color depth.

LDAP
(Lightweight Directory Access Protocol) A communications protocol that defines how a client can access information, perform operations, and share directory data on a directory server.

least privilege
The principle that establishes that users and software should only have the minimal level of access that is necessary for them to perform the duties required of them.

LED
(light emitting diode) An electrical component frequently used as an indicator light on network adapters and other types of network equipment.

LED display
A display device that uses either Dynamic RGB light emitting diodes or White Edge-light emitting diodes as the light source.

LED printer
A type of printer that uses LEDs to print.

line noise
A power problem that is caused by a fluctuation in electrical current.

link light
An indicator on a network adapter that lights up when a network signal is detected.

Linux
An open-standards UNIX derivative originally developed and released by a Finnish computer science student named Linus Torvalds.

Linux distribution
A complete Linux implementation, including kernel, shell, applications, and utilities, that is packaged, distributed, and supported by a software vendor.

liquid-based cooling
Cooling methods that circulate a liquid or liquefied gas, such as water or freon, past the CPU to keep it cool.

Local Area Connection
A Windows troubleshooting tool used to verify that the computer is connected to the network and able to send and receive data.

local printer
A logical printer that is managed by the local computer, where the print device is generally directly attached.

Local Security Policy
An administrative tool that is used to view and edit the security settings for group policies.

local shares
Folders that are created on the local network by individual users and then shared with other network users via shared folder permissions.

Local Users and Groups
An administrative tool that is used to manage user accounts on the local system.

lockup error
An error condition that causes the system or an application to stop responding to user input.

logic bomb
A piece of code that sits dormant on a user's computer until it is triggered by a specific event, such as a specific date. Once the code is triggered, the logic bomb "detonates," erasing and corrupting data on the user's computer.

loopback plug
A special connector used for diagnosing network transmission problems that redirects electrical signals back to the transmitting system.

LOS
(Line-of-Sight) Wireless signals that travel over a direct visual path from a transmitter to a receiver.

low–level formatting
The process of writing track sector markings on a hard disk.

LTFS
(Linear Tape File Systems) An IBM specification that enables data stored on magnetic tapes to be accessed in a file format.

lumens
The unit of measurement for visible light that is being emitted from a light source.

LVD
(low-voltage differential) A SCSI signaling technique that uses two wires, one for data and one for the inverse of data. LVD devices use a low voltage and can be used on a single-ended SCSI chain.

MAC address
(Media Access Control address) Same as the physical address.

magnetic core memory
Memory that stores binary data (0 or 1) in the orientation of magnetic charges in ferrite cores about one-sixteenth-inch in diameter.

malicious software
Any unwanted software that has the potential to damage a system or create a nuisance condition.

malware
Any unwanted software that has the potential to damage a system, impede performance, or create a nuisance condition.

MAN
(metropolitan area network) A network that covers an area equivalent to a city or other municipality.

Mark I
A programmable, electromechanical calculator that combined 78 adding machines to perform three calculations per second. It was designed by Howard Aiken, built by IBM, and installed at Harvard in 1944.

MBR
(Master Boot Record) The first sector of a partitioned storage device, used for booting the computer and often a target of malware.

md
A command line tool used to create a directory.

media tester
See cable tester.

memory
A personal computer component that provides temporary workspace for the processor.

memory dump
The process of writing the contents of system memory at the time of a stop error to a file on the hard disk prior to system shutdown.

memory module
A system unit component that holds a group of memory chips that act as a single memory chip.

mesh topology
A network topology in which each node has a direct, point-to-point connection to every other node.

MFD
(multi-function device) A piece of office equipment that performs the functions of a number of other specialized devices.

microATX
Introduced in late 1997, and is often referred to as μATX, and has a maximum size of 9.6 inches by 9.6 inches.

MicroDIMM
(Micro Dual Inline Memory Module) A memory module standard used in small, sub-compact notebooks.

microprocessor
A complete central processing unit on a single chip, the microprocessor controls the operation of all the other computer components.

Mini-ATX
A smaller version of the full ATX board with a maximum size of 11.2 inches by 8.2 inches.

Mini-BNC
A bayonet-style connector using the traditional BNC connection method.

Mini-HDMI
(Mini High-Definition Multimedia Interface) A smaller version of the full size HDMI connector, except that it is specified for use with portable devices.

mini-ITX
A small compact board that fit the same form factor as the ATX, and the micro-ATX boards.

They have a maximum size of 6.7 inches by 6.6 inches.

Mini-PCIe
(PCI Express Mini Card) An extremely small expansion card, often just a few centimeters in length used to increase communication abilities by providing network adapters or modems and supports various connections and buses.

mirroring
A disk fault-tolerance method in which data from an entire partition is copied onto a second drive.

modem
A device that modulates and demodulates data over an analog signal sent via a telephone line.

motherboard
The main circuit board in a computer that acts as the backbone for the entire computer system. Also referred to as the system board.

MSConfig
A system utility that is specifically used to troubleshoot any issues with the system startup process.

MSDS
(Material Safety Data Sheet) A technical bulletin designed to give users and emergency personnel information about the proper procedures of storage and handling of a hazardous substance.

MT-RJ
(Mechanical Transfer Registered Jack) Also called a Fiber Jack connector, is a compact snap-to-lock connector used with multimode fiber.

multi-factor authentication
Any authentication scheme that requires validation of at least two of the possible authentication factors.

multimedia device
A computer peripheral or internal component that transfers sound, images or both to or from a personal computer.

multimeter
An electronic instrument used to measure voltage, current, and resistance.

multitouch
The technology used on the surface of the touch screen on tablets and other mobile devices that can recognize more than one contact on the surface at once.

mutual authentication
A security mechanism that requires that each party in a communication verifies its identity.

Napier's Bones
A set of rectangular rods with numbers etched on them that let users do multiplication by adding the numbers on properly positioned rods. Precursor to the slide rule.

NAS
(network-attached storage) A data storage device that can be connected to a network to provide direct data access and file sharing to multiple computing devices attached to the network.

NAT
(Network Address Translation) A simple form of Internet connection and security that conceals internal addressing schemes from the public Internet.

native resolution
The fixed resolution for LCD or other flat panel display devices.

nbtstat
A command line tool used to display TCP/IP information and other information for a remote computer.

net
A command line tool used to manage Microsoft network resources from a command line.

netstat
A command line tool used to show the status of each active network connection.

network
A group of connected computers that are connected together to communicate and share resources.

network directory
A centralized database that includes objects such as servers, clients, computers, user names, and passwords. Also called directory service.

Network Interference
The disruption of normal data transmissions over a network.

network share
See share.

network topology
A specification that determines the network's overall layout and transmission and flow patterns.

network-based firewall
A hardware/software combination that protects all the computers on a network behind the firewall.

network-based printer
A shared print device managed by a network print server. It's represented as a logical printer object on the client computer that accesses the server.

network-connected printer
Any print device than can connect directly to the network with a network adapter rather than using a physical cable to connect to a local computer or print server device.

NIC
(network interface card) An expansion card that enables a PC to connect to a LAN. Also referred to as a network adapter.

NLOS
(Non-Line-of-Sight) Wireless signals that reach a receiver through reflections and obstructions within the visual path in the environment.

node
A generalized term for any network device with its own address.

Northbridge
A component of the chipset that controls the system memory and the AGP video ports, and sometimes the cache memory.

nslookup
A command line tool used to verify that the computer can connect to a DNS server and successfully find an IP address for a given computer name.

Offline Files
A utility unique to the Windows Vista Control Panel that is used to enable or disable offline files and configure the settings for offline files.

OLED display
(organic light emitting diode) A type of LED flat panel display device that uses organic compounds that emit light when subjected to an electric current.

Open Handset Alliance
An association of 84 firms for developing open standards for mobile devices.

open source
Refers to application code, operating systems, and programming languages that are developed, published and shared among the developer and professional community.

optical disk
A personal computer storage device that stores data optically, rather than magnetically.

optical drive
A computer drive that is either internal or external to a computer system that reads and writes data to an optical disk.

organizational policy
A document that convey the corporate guidelines and philosophy to employees.

OS X
The proprietary operating system developed by Apple® Computing, Inc. and deployed on all Apple computers.

packet sniffing
An attack on wireless networks where an attacker captures data and registers data flows in order to analyze what data is contained in a packet.

page
A section of memory addresses in which a unit of data can be stored.

page fault
An interrupt generated when an application requests data that is no longer present in its virtual memory location.

pagefile
In a virtual-memory system, the section of the hard disk used to store memory contents that have been swapped out of physical RAM. In Windows systems, the pagefile is called Pagefile.sys.

paging
See swapping.

pairing
The process two devices use to establish a wireless connection through Bluetooth.

PAN
(personal area network) A network of devices used by a single individual.

parallel connection
A personal computer connection type that transfers data, usually 8 bits at a time, over eight wires, and is often used for a printer.

parity
An error correction method for electronic communications.

partitioning
The process of dividing a single hard disk into isolated sections that function as separate physical hard drives, called partitions.

Pascaline machine
A calculating machine that could add and subtract, developed in 1642 by Blaise Pascal.

PATA
(Parallel Advanced Technology Attachment) A type of hard drive that requires a parallel data channel to connect a disk controller to the disk

drive. Also referred to as ATA, IDE, EIDE, or UDMA.

patch
Fixes or updates for a software program or application, designed to eliminate known bugs or vulnerabilities and improve performance.

patch management
The practice of monitoring for, evaluating, testing, and installing software patches and updates.

PC
(personal computer) Stand-alone, single-user, desktop-size or smaller computers that can function independently. PC used to refer to any personal computer, but now refers to personal computers that follow the original design by IBM, use Intel or compatible chips, and usually have some version of Windows as an operating system.

PC card
A credit-card-sized expansion card that is used in portable computers rather than the full-sized expansion cards used in desktop systems.

PCI
(Peripheral Component Interconnect) See PCI bus.

PCI bus
(Peripheral Component Interconnect bus) A peripheral bus commonly used in PCs that provides a high-speed data path between the CPU and peripheral devices.

PCI Express
(Peripheral Component Interconnect Express) A video adapter bus that is based on the PCI computer bus. PCIe supports significantly enhanced performance over that of AGP.

PCIe
(Peripheral Component Interconnect Express) See PCI Express.

PCMCIA
(Personal Computer Memory Card International Association) See PC card.

PDA
(Personal Digital Assistants) Mobile devices used to manage personal information, such as address books, calendars, and emails.

peer-to-peer network
A network in which resource sharing, processing, and communications control are completely decentralized.

Pen and Input Devices
A utility unique to the Windows Vista Control Panel which is used to customize the settings for the pen and input devices that are used to interact with a tablet.

Performance Monitor
An administrative tool that monitors the state of services or daemons, processes, and resources on a system.

permissions
In Windows, security settings that control access to individual objects, such as files.

phishing
A type of email-based social engineering attack in which the attacker sends email from a spoofed source, such as a bank, to try to elicit private information from the victim.

physical address
For network adapter cards, a globally unique hexadecimal number burned into every adapter by the manufacturer.

physical security
The implementation and practice of various control mechanisms that are intended to restrict physical access to facilities.

piconet
A network of two to eight Bluetooth-enabled devices.

PictBridge
A technology that allows images to be printed directly on a printer from digital cameras.

ping
A command line tool used to test communications between two TCP/IP-based hosts.

pixel
The smallest discrete element on a display. A single pixel is composed of a red, a blue, and a green dot.

plasma
A type of flat panel that uses a gas mixture placed between two sheets of glass that have electrodes attached to their surfaces.

plasma display
A display device that uses xenon and neon rays and a flat panel of glass to provide a light source and images on screen.

plastics
The hard surfaces that protect the internal components of a laptop.

plenum
An air handling space, including ducts and other parts of the HVAC system in a building.

plenum cable
A grade of cable that does not give off noxious or poisonous gases when burned. Unlike PVC cable, plenum cable can be run through the plenum and firebreak walls.

PoE
(Power-over-Ethernet) An emerging technology standard that enables both power and data to be transmitted over an Ethernet cable.

pop-up
Windows or frames that load and appear automatically when a user connects to a particular web page.

pop-up blocker
Software that prevents windows or frames from automatically loading when users connect to websites that employ pop-ups.

POP3
(Post Office Protocol version 3) A protocol used to retrieve email from a mailbox on the mail server.

port
A hardware connection interface on a personal computer that enables devices to be connected to the computer, or the endpoint of a logical connection that client computers use to connect to specific server programs.

port replicator
A scaled-down version of a docking station with only the standard ports available.

POST
(Power-On Self Test) A built-in diagnostic program that is run every time a personal computer starts up.

POST card
A card can be plugged directly into the motherboard in an available expansion card slot that can read and display any error codes that get generated during the POST process of a computer.

power sag
See sag.

power supply
An internal computer component that converts line voltage AC power from an electrical outlet to the low-voltage DC power needed by system components.

power supply tester
A tool that connects to the power supply's 24-pin connector that tests the functionality of the unit.

Print Management
An administrative tool that is used to view and manage all of the printers and print servers installed on a network.

print queue
A list of jobs waiting to print.

print server
A computer somewhere on the network that manages a printer that has been shared for network clients to use.

printer
An output device that produces text and images from electronic content onto physical media such as paper or transparency film.

Printers

A utility in name only that is unique to the Windows Vista Control Panel, it is used to add, remove, and manage any printers installed on the computer. The Printers utility in Vista replaced the Printers and Faxes utility in Windows XP and was replaced with the Devices and Printers utility in Windows 7.

private IP address

Addresses used by organizations for nodes that require IP connectivity within their enterprise network, but do not require external connections to the global Internet.

Problem Reports and Solutions

A utility unique to the Windows Vista Control Panel that displays any recent problems that Windows has encountered and provides links to troubleshooting resources.

proxy

A system that acts as an intermediary for requests for resources.

PSTN

(Public Switched Telephone Network) An international telephone system that carries analog voice data.

public IP addresses

Addresses that can be used by organizations that can also be shared with external networks.

punch down tool

A tool used in a wiring closet to connect cable wires directly to a patch panel.

PVC

(polyvinyl chloride) A flexible rubber-like plastic used to surround some twisted pair cabling. It is flexible and inexpensive, but gives off noxious or poisonous gases when burned.

QoS

(Quality of Service) A set of parameters that controls the level of quality provided to different types of network traffic.

radio networking

A form of wireless communication in which signals are sent via RF waves, in the 10 KHz to 1 GHz range, to wireless antennas.

RAID

(Redundant Array of Independent or Inexpensive Disks) A set of vendor-independent specifications for fault-tolerant configurations on multiple-disk systems.

RAM

(Random Access Memory) A computer storage method that functions as a computer's main memory.

RAM chip

An integrated circuit that acts as the computer's primary temporary storage place for data.

RAM module

See RAM chip.

RCA

(Radio Corporation of America) A cable and connector that is used to carry audio and video transmissions to and from a variety devices such as TVs, digital cameras, and gaming systems.

rd

A command line tool used to delete a directory.

ReadyBoost

A performance enhancer, available on Windows Vista and Windows 7, that allows the user to supplement the computer's memory with an external storage device like a flash drive.

Recovery Console

A minimal version of Windows XP Professional that provides a command-line interface (CLI) to a Windows XP Professional installation.

reference computer

The main computer in the imaging process.

refresh rate

The number of times per second that the monitor is "refreshed," or scanned to illuminate the pixels.

Registry
The central configuration database where Windows stores and retrieves startup settings, hardware and software configuration information, and information for local user accounts.

regsvr32
A troubleshooting utility that registers and unregisters OLE controls such as DLL and ActiveX files.

Remote Desktop
A software application that operates a Windows computer from a remote location.

RemoteApp and Desktop Connections
A utility unique to the Windows 7 Control Panel in which users can access programs, remote computers, and virtual computers remotely that are made available by the network administrator.

resistor
An electronic component that resists the flow of electric current in an electronic circuit.

resolution
The number of pixels that make up the dimension of a display, represented in a ratio value as the number of horizontal pixels by vertical pixels.

RF
(radio frequency) A frequency in which network or other communications that take place using radio waves in the 10 KHz to 1 GHz range.

RFID badges
Security cards that contain a tag that reacts with the radio frequency of the identification system to allow or deny access.

RIMM
(Rambus Inline Memory Modules) A RAM form factor that has a metal cover that acts as a heat sink. Although they have the same number of pins, RIMMs have different pin settings and are not interchangeable with DIMMs and SDRAM

ring topology
A network topology in which all network nodes are connected in a circle.

riser card
A board that is plugged into the system board and provides additional slots for adapter cards.

robocopy
A command line tool used to copy files and folders/directories from one location to another, but with more options than the simple copy command.

rogue access point
An unauthorized wireless access point on a corporate or private network, which allows unauthorized individuals to connect to the network.

ROM
(Read-Only Memory) Memory that saves and stores a system data without a constant power source.

rootkit
Malicious code that is designed to hide the existence of processes or programs from normal detection methods and to gain continuous privileged access to a computer system.

rotation method
The schedule that determines how many backup tapes or other media sets are needed, and the sequence in which they are used and reused.

router
A networking device that connects multiple networks that use the same protocol.

RSA tokens
Small devices that include cryptographic keys, a digital signature, or even biometric information that is verified against an identification system to allow or deny access to a physical location, system, or network location.

S-Video
An analog video signal that carries the video data as two separate signals (brightness and

color). S-Video works in 480i or 576i resolution.

sag
A momentary low-voltage power failure.

SAS
(Serial Attached SCSI) A serial version of the SCSI interface. SAS is a point-to-point architecture that uses a disk controller with four or more channels operating simultaneously. SAS also supports SATA drives, which can be mixed with SAS drives in a variety of configurations.

SATA
(Serial Advanced Technology Attachment) A type of hard drive that requires a serial data channel to connect the drive controller and the disk drives.

satellite
Provide extremely long-range wireless network transmissions to relay network signals from the network service provider to individual customers.

SC
(Subscriber Connector or Standard Connector) Box-shaped connectors that snap into a receptacle. SC connectors are often used in a duplex configuration where two fibers are terminated into two SC connectors that are molded together.

screen calibration
The method used to update the sensors on the device to respond quicker and more effectively to tapping, swiping, and pinching components on the screen.

SCSI
(Small Computer System Interface) An older personal computer connection standard that provides high-performance data transfer between the SCSI device and the other components of the computer. Pronounced "scuzzy."

SCSI ID
Identifiers assigned to each SCSI device connected to the bus. The ID numbers range from 1 to 15.

sector
An individual storage area on a formatted disk.

security policy
A formalized statement that defines how security will be implemented within a particular organization.

serial connection
A personal computer connection that transfers data one bit at a time over a single wire and is often used for an external modem.

server
A computer that provides services and resources on the network.

server–side virtualization
Takes place centrally on a server and utilizes one logical device, typically the server, to act as the host machine for the "guest" machines that virtually use the applications and programs provided by the host.

Service Packs
Comprehensive software updates that generally include all prior patches and updates, but which can also include important new features and functions.

Services
An administrative tool that is used to view all of the services that run in the background on the system.

sfc
(System File Checker) A command line tool used to verify system files and replace them, if needed.

SFTP
(Secure FTP) A secure replacement for FTP that uses the SSH protocol to provide secure data connections.

Shadow Copy
A feature available on Windows XP and newer operating systems that creates backup copies or snapshots of the system's data and stores them locally or to an external location, either manually or at regularly scheduled intervals.

share
A network resource, such as a disk, folder, or printer, that is available to other computer users on the network.

shoulder surfing
A human-based attack where the goal is to look over the shoulder of an individual as he or she enters password information or a PIN.

shutdown
A command line tool used to log off, restart, or shut down the system.

Sidebar
A designated area of the Windows 7 and Windows Vista desktop, displayed vertically along the side of the desktop, where users can add gadgets of their choice to provide information and access to frequently used tools or programs.

signature
A code pattern that identifies a virus. Also called a definition.

SIMM
(Single In-line Memory Modules) A RAM form factor with a 32-bit data path.

SLA
(Service Level Agreement) An agreement entered into by the transmitter, ISP and the receiver, subscriber.

Sleep
A power option available in Windows Vista, Windows 7, Windows Server 2008, and Apple OSs, in which the computer conserves as much energy as possible by cutting off power to the parts of the machine that are not necessary to function, excluding RAM.

SMA
(Sub Multi Assembly or Sub Miniature type A) Connectors that use a threaded ferrule on the outside to lock the connector in place.

smart card
A device similar to a credit card that can store authentication information, such as a user's private key, on an embedded microchip.

smartphones
High-end mobile devices that provide users with a wide range of functions such as, portable media players, video cameras, GPS, high-resolution touch screens, high-speed Wi-Fi, web browsers, and mobile broadband.

SMB
(Server Message Block) A protocol that works on the Application layer and is used to share files, serial ports, printers, and communications devices, including mail slots and named pipes, between computers.

SNMP
(Simple Network Management Protocol) An Application-layer protocol used to exchange information between network devices.

social engineering attack
A type of attack where the goal is to obtain sensitive data, including user names and passwords, from network users through deception and trickery.

SODIMM
(Small Outline Dual In-line Memory Module) Memory that is half the size of DIMMs, are available in 32- or 64-bit data paths, and are commonly found in laptops and iMac systems.

software diagnostic tool
A computer repair tool that contains programs that test hardware and software components. Also referred to as utility.

SOHO MFD
(small office/home office multi-function device) A medium-sized network-enabled MFD suitable for small and home offices with enhanced printing, scanning, copying, and faxing functions.

SOHO network
(small office/home office) A small network that provides connectivity and resource sharing for a small office or home office.

soldered
A means of securing electronic components to a circuit board by using a combination of lead, tin, and silver (solder) and a tool called a soldering iron.

solid ink printer
A type of printer that uses ink from melted solid-ink sticks.

Southbridge
A component of the chipset that controls input/output functions, the system clock, drives and buses, APM power management, and various other devices.

spam
Originally, frequent and repetitive postings in electronic bulletin boards; more commonly, unsolicited or distasteful commercial email from anonymous sources.

spam blocker
Software that detects specific words or phrases that are known to be included in spam messages and rejects the messages as unwanted.

speed light
An indicator on a network adapter that shows whether the adapter is operating at 10 Mbps, 100 Mbps, or 1,000 Mbps.

spike
A short-term, high-voltage power malfunction.

spim
An IM-based attack similar to spam that is propagated through instant messaging instead of through email.

spoofing
A human-based or software-based attack where the goal is to pretend to be someone else for the purpose of identity concealment. Spoofing can occur in IP addresses, MAC addresses, and email.

spyware
Unwanted software that collects personal user data from a system and transmits it to a third party.

SSA
(Serial Storage Architecture) A fault-tolerant peripheral interface that transfers data at 80 and 160 MBps. SSA uses SCSI commands, allowing existing software to drive SSA peripherals such as disk drives. SSA uses a ring architecture that supports up to 128 devices; if one fails, the remaining devices continue to run. SSA distances are 25 meters over copper and 2.4 kilometers over fiber. SSA was designed to provide an alternative to Fibre Channel, but has not been as widely used.

SSD
(solid state drive) A personal computer storage device that stores data in non-volatile special memory instead of on disks or tape.

SSH
(Secure Shell) A protocol that enables a user or application to log on to another computer over a network, execute commands, and manage files.

SSID
(Service Set Identifier) A 32-bit alphanumeric string that identifies a wireless access point and all devices that connect to it.

SSL
(Secure Sockets Layer) A security protocol that uses certificates for authentication and encryption to protect web communication.

ST
(Straight Tip) Connects multimode fiber, ST connectors look like BNC connectors.

standard formatting
An operating system function that builds file systems on drives and partitions.

Standby
A power option available in Windows 98, Windows Server 2003, and Windows XP, in which the computer conserves as much energy as possible by cutting off power to the parts of the machine that are not necessary to function, excluding RAM.

star topology
A network topology that uses a central connectivity device with separate point-to-point connections to each node.

static addressing
Configuring TCP/IP statically on a network and requires that an administrator visit each

node to manually enter IP address information for that node.

static electricity

The buildup up of stationary electrical charge on any object.

Stepped Reckoner

A mechanical calculator developed by Gottfried von Leibniz that improved Pascal's design to include multiplication and division.

stop error

A system error severe enough to stop all processes and shut the system down without warning. Often referred to as "blue-screen errors" in Windows because they generate an error message screen with a blue background.

storage device

A computer component that enables users to save data for reuse at a later time, even after the personal computer is shut down and restarted.

striping

A disk-performance-enhancement feature in which data is spread across multiple drives to improve read and write access speeds.

strong password

A password that meets the complexity requirements that are set by a system administrator and documented in a password policy.

stuck pixels

Pixels that only show one color of light, so they appear out of place when the display is on.

subnet mask

A 32-bit number that is assigned to each host to divide the 32-bit binary IP address into network and node portions.

surge suppressor

A power protection device that provides power protection circuits that can reduce or eliminate the impact of surges and spikes.

Suspend

A power option available in Windows 95 and Linux, in which the computer conserves as much energy as possible by cutting off power to the parts of the machine that are not necessary to function, excluding RAM.

swapping

In a virtual memory system, the process of moving data back and forth from physical RAM to the pagefile. Also called paging.

switch

A "smart" network hardware device that joins multiple network segments together.

system BIOS

The BIOS that sets the computer's configuration and environment when the system is powered on.

system board

The same as motherboard.

system bus

The primary communication pathway between a CPU and other parts of the chipset. The system bus enables data transfer between the CPU, BIOS, memory, and the other buses in the computer. Also referred to as frontside bus or local bus.

System Configuration

An administrative tool that is used to identify and manage issues that may be causing the system to run improperly at startup.

system files

The files necessary for the operating system to function properly.

System Restore

A utility available in Windows XP, Windows Vista, and Windows 7 that monitors the system for changes to core system files, drivers, and the Registry, and creates restore points to be used to help restore the system if a failure occurs.

system restore point

A snapshot of the system configuration at a given moment in time that contains information about any changes to these components and is stored on the computer's hard disk. Restore points can be used to restore system settings to an earlier state without affecting changes in user data since that time.

system unit
A personal computer component that includes other devices necessary for the computer to function, including the chassis, power supply, cooling system, system board, microprocessor, memory chips, disk drives, adapter cards, and ports for connecting external devices. Often referred to as a box, main unit, or base unit.

Tablet PC Settings
A utility unique to the Windows Vista Control Panel where the user can configure settings for a tablet PC running Windows Vista.

tablets
Mobile computers that function similarly to a full sized desktop computer come with an integrated touchscreen and virtual onscreen keyboard.

tape drive
A personal computer storage device that stores data magnetically on a removable tape.

target computer
The computer that has the image installed on it in the imaging process.

Task Manager
A basic system-diagnostic and performance-monitoring tool included with the Windows operating system.

Task Scheduler
An administrative tool that allows the user to create and manage certain system tasks that will be automatically carried out by the computer at predetermined times.

TCP
(Transmission Control Protocol) A connection-oriented, guaranteed-delivery protocol used to send data packets between computers over a network such as the Internet.

TCP/IP
(Transmission Control Protocol/Internet Protocol) A nonproprietary, routable network protocol suite that enables computers to communicate over a network, including the Internet.

terminal
A client node on a centralized network, with few or no local computing resources of its own.

termination
Adding a resistor to the end of a coax network segment to prevent reflections that would interfere with the proper reception of network signals.

thermal dye transfer printer
A sophisticated type of color printer that uses heat to diffuse dye from color ribbons onto special paper or transparency blanks to produce continuous-tone output similar in quality to a photographic print. Also called dye sublimation printer.

thermal paper
Paper that contains a chemical designed to react with the heating element of a thermal printer to create images on paper.

thermal paste
A paste that is used to connect a heat sink to a CPU to provide a liquid thermally conductive compound gel that fills any gaps between the CPU and the heat sink to permit a more efficient transference of heat from the processor to the heat sink.

thermal printer
Any printer that uses heat to create the image on the paper with dye or ink from ribbons or with heated pins.

thermal wax transfer printer
A printer that uses a thermal printhead to melt wax-based ink from a transfer ribbon onto the paper.

thick client
A computer that performs most or all of the processing it requires to complete a given task.

thin client
A computer that depends on another computer such as a server to run most of its programs, processes, and services.

TIA
(Telecommunication Industry Association) A standards and trades organization that develops industry standards for technologies such as network cabling.

TKIP
(Temporal Key Integrity Protocol) A security protocol created by the IEEE 802.11i task group to replace WEP.

tlist
A command line tool used to display all the processes currently running on the system.

TLS
(Transport Layer Security) A security protocol that protects sensitive communication from eavesdropping and tampering by using a secure, encrypted, and authenticated channel over a TCP/IP connection.

token
A physical or virtual object that stores authentication information.

toner
An electrostatic-sensitive dry ink substance used in laser printers.

tracert
A command line tool used to determine the route that the computer uses to send a packet to its destination. If tracert is unsuccessful, you can use the results generated to determine at what point communications are failing.

traces
Wires etched on to the motherboard to provide electrical pathways.

trackpoint
A small button found on some laptops that enables you to move the mouse pointer when no mouse is connected to the computer.

transistor
A device containing semiconductor material that can amplify a signal or open and close a circuit. In computers, transistors function as electronic switches.

transistors
Switches that are etched on one sliver of a semiconductor that can be opened or closed when conducting electricity.

triboelectric generation
Using friction to create a static charge.

Trojan horse
Malicious code that masquerades as a harmless file. When a user executes it, thinking it is a harmless application, it destroys and corrupts data on the user's hard drive.

Troubleshooting
A utility unique to the Windows 7 Control Panel that provides troubleshooting resources for common Windows problems.

tunneling
A data transport technique in which a data packet is transferred inside the frame or packet of another protocol, enabling the infrastructure of one network to be used to travel to another network.

twisted pair
A type of cable in which multiple insulated conductors are twisted together and clad in a protective and insulating outer jacket.

UAC
(User Account Control) An enhanced security feature of Vista and Windows 7 that aims to limit the privileges of a standard user unless a computer administrator decides otherwise.

UDP
(User Datagram Protocol) A connectionless, best-effort delivery protocol used to send data packets between computers over a network such as the Internet.

UNIVAC
The Universal Automatic Computer, completed in 1951 by Eckert and Mauchly for the U.S. Bureau of the Census. It was the first commercial computer in the United States and could handle both numerical and alphabetical information.

UNIX

A family of operating systems originally developed at Bell Laboratories and characterized by portability, multiuser support, and built-in multitasking and networking functions.

UPS

(uninterruptible power supply) A device that continues to provide power to connected circuits when the main source of power becomes unavailable. This can help save computer components from damage due to power problems such as power failures, spikes, and sags.

USB

(universal serial bus) A hardware interface standard designed to provide connections for numerous peripherals.

USB connection

A personal computer connection that enables you to connect multiple peripherals to a single port with high performance and minimal device configuration.

user account

A collection of credentials and important information about a person with access to the system, including the rights and privileges assigned to the user.

user authentication

A network security measure in which a computer user or some other network component proves its identity in order to gain access to network resources.

USMT

(User State Migration Tool) A command-line utility that copies files and settings from one Microsoft Windows computer to another.

vacuum tube

A sealed glass or metal container that controls a flow of electrons through a vacuum.

VDI

(Virtual Desktop Infrastructure) A computing environment where the personal computing component is separated from a physical machine using desktop virtualization.

VGA

(Video Graphics Array) A connector used for monitors.

virtual desktops

The virtual machines that run on a desktop operating system.

virtual memory

The allocation by the computer system of a portion of the hard disk as if it was physical RAM.

virtualization

The technological process of creating a virtual version of a computer environment by separating the elements of the computing environment from each other and from the physical hardware it runs on via an additional software layer.

virus

A piece of code that spreads from one computer to another by attaching itself to other files.

vishing

A human-based attack where the goal is to extract personal, financial, or confidential information from the victim by using services such as the telephone system and IP-based voice messaging services (VoIP) as the communication medium.

VM

(virtual machine) In virtualization, a software implementation or emulation of a host machine, which is created by the hypervisor and run independently from the host on which they are installed.

VMM

(Virtual Memory Manager) The Windows system component responsible for managing physical-to-virtual memory mappings and virtual memory assignments.

VoIP

(Voice over IP) A Voice over Data implementation in which voice signals are transmitted over IP networks.

volume
A single storage unit made up of free space that is located on a single file system, but which may reside on one or more disks or partitions.

VPN
(virtual private network) A private network that protects communications sent through a public network such as the Internet.

VPN protocol
A protocol that provides VPN functionality.

WAN
(wide area network) A network that spans multiple geographic locations, connecting multiple LANs using long-range transmission media.

WAP
(Wireless Access Point) A device that provides connection between wireless devices and can connect to wired networks.

war chalking
Using symbols to mark a sidewalk or wall to indicate that there is an open wireless network which may be offering Internet access.

war driving
The act of searching for instances of wireless LAN networks while in motion, using wireless tracking devices like PDAs, mobile phones, or laptops.

waveform
The shape of an analog signal when plotted on an oscilloscope or graph.

WEP
(Wired Equivalent Privacy) Provides 64-bit, 128-bit, and 256-bit encryption for wireless communication that uses the 802.11a and 802.11b protocols.

whaling
A form of phishing that targets individuals who are known or are believed to be wealthy.

Wi-Fi
The popular implementation of the 802.11b wireless standard.

WiMAX
(Worldwide Interoperability for Microwave Access) A packet-based wireless technology that provides wireless broadband access over long distances.

Windows Firewall with Advanced Security
An administrative tool that is used to manage advanced firewall settings for the computer and any remote computers connected to the network.

Windows Memory Diagnostic
An administrative tool that is used to check the RAM on the system and make sure that it is functioning appropriately and efficiently.

Windows security policies
Configuration settings within Windows operating systems that control the overall security behavior of the system.

WinPE
(Windows pre-installation environment) A lightweight version of Windows or Windows Server that can be used for deployment of the full version of the OS or for troubleshooting OS problems.

WinRE
(Windows Recovery Environment) A set of tools included in Windows Vista and Windows 7 that is used to help diagnose and repair errors on startup.

wire crimper
A tool that attaches media connectors to the ends of cables.

wire stripper
A tool that is often incorporated into a wire crimper and that enables the user to remove the protective coating from electrical wires.

wireless connection
A network connection that transmits signals without using physical network media.

wireless encryption
The process of concealing and protecting data during wireless transmissions.

Wireless Network Connection

A Windows troubleshooting tool used to verify that a computer or other wireless device is connected to the network and able to send and receive data.

wireless security

Any method of securing your wireless LAN network to prevent unauthorized network access and network data theft while ensuring that authorized users can connect to the network.

WOL

(Wake-on-LAN) A networking capability that is built into a device's NIC circuitry that allows a device to turn on, or power up when a network message is received by another computing device.

workgroup

A peer-to-peer Microsoft network model that groups computers together for organizational purposes, often deployed in homes and small offices.

worm

A piece of code that spreads from one computer to another on its own, not by attaching itself to another file.

WPA

(Wi-Fi Protected Access) A strong authentication security protocol that was introduced to address some of the shortcomings in the WEP protocol during the pending development of the 802.11i IEEE standard.

WPAN

(Wireless Personal Area Network) A network that connects devices in very close proximity but not through a wireless access point.

WWAN

(Wireless Wide Area Network) A computer network that enables users to wirelessly connect to their offices or the Internet via a cellular network. Sometimes referred to as wireless broadband.

xcopy

A command line tool used to copy files or directories from one location to another.

XP mode

A downloadable add-on for Windows 7 that allows users running Windows 7 to access and use Windows XP-compatible software and programs directly on their desktops.

Index

Wide Area Network, *See* WAN
Wi-Fi
    connectivity *316, 408*
      IEEE standard 802.11b *369*
    laptop antenna *387*
    triangulation *404*
Wi-Fi locators *530*
Wi-Fi Protected Access, *See* WPA
Wifi-Protected Setup, *See* WPS
WiMAX *337*
Windows, *See* Microsoft Windows
Windows 7
    Control Panel *73*
    editions *54*
Windows Aero *52*
Windows Automated Installation kit, *See* WAIK
Windows Backup Utility *284*
Windows Compatibility Center *277*
Windows Defender *53*
Windows Error Reporting *525*
Windows Explorer *85*
Windows Firewall
    configuration *457*
    features *355*
    overview *461*
Windows Firewall with Advanced Security *99*
Windows Genuine Advantage Notifications *271*
Windows Memory Diagnostic *99*
Windows PowerShell *77*
Windows pre-installation environment, *See* WinPE
Windows security policies *460*
Windows Server *51*
Windows Update *69, 271*
Windows Vista
    Control Panel *72*
Windows Vista editions *54*
Windows XP
    compatibility modes *277*
    Control Panel *72*
    editions *54*
Windows XP Media Center Edition *260*
WinPE *515*
WinRE *79, 514*
Wired Equivalent Privacy, *See* WEP
Wireless Access Point, *See* WAP
wireless carrier, *See* mobile carrier
wireless communication
    signal strength *316*

wireless connectivity issues *500*
wireless device connections *41*
wireless encryption types *372*
Wireless Interoperability for Microwave Access, *See* WiMAX
Wireless Network Connection status *362*
Wireless Personal Area Network, *See* WPAN
wireless security *376, 377*
wireless threats and vulnerabilities *451*
Wireless WAN, *See* WWAN
WOL *356*
workgroups *268, 348*
workstations
    audio/video editing *296, 297*
    media design *295*
    standard client *292*
worm *448*
WPA *372*
WPA2, *See* 802.11i
WPAN *327*
WPS *369*
WWAN *337*

X

XP mode *53, 256*

093001S rev 2.2
ISBN-13 978-1-4246-2036-4
ISBN-10 1-4246-2036-8

90000

9 781424 620364